ORDINARY LEVEL MATHEMATICS

METRIC EDITION

WITH ANSWERS

By the same author

A NOTE BOOK IN APPLIED MATHEMATICS
A NOTE BOOK IN PURE MATHEMATICS
A GENERAL CERTIFICATE CALCULUS
TRIGONOMETRY AT ORDINARY LEVEL
MATHEMATICS ONE
MATHEMATICS TWO
MATHEMATICS THREE
MATHEMATICS FOUR
FUN WITH FIGURES
HINTS FOR ORDINARY LEVEL MATHEMATICS
HINTS FOR ADVANCED LEVEL MATHEMATICS
MODERN MATHEMATICS AT ORDINARY LEVEL
PURE MATHEMATICS AT ADVANCED LEVEL
ADDITIONAL PURE MATHEMATICS
FOUR FIGURE MATHEMATICS TABLES
EXERCISES AND EXAMPLES IN ORDINARY LEVEL MATHEMATICS
DECIMAL CURRENCY AND YOU

Also by L. Harwood Clarke and F. G. J. Norton

OBJECTIVE TESTS IN ORDINARY LEVEL MATHEMATICS
OBJECTIVE TESTS IN C.S.E. MATHEMATICS

All published by Heinemann Educational Books Ltd

ORDINARY LEVEL MATHEMATICS

by

L. HARWOOD CLARKE, M.A.

METRIC EDITION

WITH ANSWERS

HEINEMANN EDUCATIONAL BOOKS
LONDON

Heinemann Educational Books Ltd
LONDON EDINBURGH MELBOURNE TORONTO AUCKLAND
KUALA LUMPUR SINGAPORE HONG KONG
IBADAN JOHANNESBURG NAIROBI
NEW DELHI

ISBN 0 435 50252 2 (text)
ISBN 0 435 50253 0 (with answers)

First published 1958
Second Edition 1959
Reprinted with corrections 1960
Reprinted 1961 (twice)
Reprinted 1963 (with tables)
Third Edition 1964 (reset)
Reprinted 1965, 1967
Fourth Edition 1969
Reprinted 1969
Fifth Edition 1971
Reprinted 1972

Published by
Heinemann Educational Books Ltd
48 Charles Street, London W1X 8AH
Printed in Great Britain by
Butler & Tanner Ltd, Frome and London

FOREWORD

THIS book is intended to be used in the last years of the course for Mathematics at Ordinary level in the General Certificate of Education. It assumes a knowledge of the fundamental processes of Arithmetic and Algebra and avoids long explanations which are best left to the teacher. Two parallel sets of exercises are provided on each topic and it is hoped that the teacher will find it helpful to do one set in class and to give the other set for homework.

As this is to some extent a revision book, the sequence differs in some ways from that normally adopted and I thought it best to group subject-matter as far as possible. For example, in Algebra, equations of all types have been considered in the same chapter; and ratios, in Trigonometry, have been taken together, rather than separately, which is the modern practice.

In spite of the trend towards unified mathematics, I have listed the subject-matter under four heads: Arithmetic, Algebra and Calculus, Geometry, Trigonometry. This has been done mainly for the sake of reference as it is important that the student should find his way about the book easily and I think the difficulty of doing this is one of the main objections to a mixed mathematics book. In spite of this grouping, however, the book does contain the subject-matter needed for the alternative syllabus and will satisfy, I hope, the demands of those offering either option. It may be especially useful in schools which enter some forms for formal mathematics and others for the alternative papers.

BEDFORD, January 1958 L. H. C.

NOTE TO SECOND EDITION

IN this edition ten specimen examination papers have been added at the end of the text (p. 411). An index has also been supplied.

I should like, belatedly, to thank Mr. Alan Hill of Heinemann's for his interest and encouragement and also Mr. D. E. Armit, of the William Ellis School, Mr. J. Pomfret, Headmaster of the Grammar School, Cannock, and Mr. A. L. Flight, of Westminster City School, who were kind enough to read the proofs.

1959 L. H. C.

NOTE TO 1963 REPRINT

IN this printing, in response to a number of requests, the basic, necessary mathematical tables have been included in the book. Thanks are due to the Cambridge University Press Ltd., and the authors, for permission to reproduce these from Messrs. Godfrey and Siddon's *Four Figure Tables*.

BEDFORD, November 1962 L. H. C.

NOTE TO THIRD EDITION

FOR this edition the book has been completely reset. Short sections have been added on the area of an ellipse and on radians. A proof of the quadratic equation formula has also been included.

BEDFORD, January 1964 L. H. C.

NOTE TO FOURTH EDITION

IN this edition the book has been rewritten for decimal currency.

BEDFORD, 1969 L. H. C.

NOTE TO FIFTH EDITION

IN this edition, metric units are used throughout except in a few conversion examples.

1970 L. H. C.

CONTENTS

ARITHMETIC

TRIGONOMETRY

ARITHMETIC

ARITHMETIC FORMULAE

Areas and Volumes

The area of a triangle $= \frac{1}{2}$ base $\times$ height.
The area of a triangle $= \sqrt{s(s-a)(s-b)(s-c)}$, where s is the semi perimeter.
The area of a parallelogram = base $\times$ height.
The area of a trapezium $= \frac{1}{2}$ (sum of parallel sides) $\times$ distance between them.
The area of a rectangle = length $\times$ breadth.
The volume of a rectangular box = length $\times$ breadth $\times$ height.
The area of the walls of a room = perimeter $\times$ height.
The volume of a solid of uniform cross section = area of cross section $\times$ length.
The volume of a prism = (area of triangular base) $\times$ length.
The volume of a tetrahedron $= \frac{1}{3}$ (base area) $\times$ height.
Density = mass/volume.
The circumference of a circle $= 2\pi r$.
The area of a circle $= \pi r^2$.
The area of a ring $= \pi(R^2 - r^2)$.
The curved surface area of a right circular cylinder $= 2\pi rh$.
The volume of a right circular cylinder $= \pi r^2 h$.
The volume of a right circular cone $= \frac{1}{3}\pi r^2 h$.
The surface area of a cone $= \pi rl$.
The volume of a sphere $= \frac{4}{3}\pi r^3$.
The surface area of a sphere $= 4\pi r^2$.
The volume of material in a pipe $= \pi(R^2 - r^2)l$.
The volume of material in a spherical shell $= \frac{4}{3}\pi(R^3 - r^3)$.

Percentage

$$\text{Percentage gain} = \frac{\text{actual gain}}{\text{cost price}} \times 100.$$

$$\text{Percentage loss} = \frac{\text{actual loss}}{\text{cost price}} \times 100.$$

$$\text{Percentage error} = \frac{\text{actual error}}{\text{true value}} \times 100.$$

Simple Interest

$$I = \frac{PRT}{100}.$$

Compound Interest

$$A = P\left(1 + \frac{r}{100}\right)^n.$$

1

LOGARITHMS

THE theory of logarithms is included in the Algebra section of this book and, in this chapter, no serious attempt is made to explain the reasons behind the operations. The rules for finding a logarithm and for multiplying and dividing are stated and, for the moment, logarithms are regarded merely as a useful device to shorten computation.

The standard position of the decimal point

A number is said to be in its standard form when there is one figure (not zero) before the decimal point.

(1) Any number between 1 and 10 is in its standard form. (Note that 1 is in its standard form but 10 is not.)

(2) Any number larger than 10 is equal to the product of the number in its standard form and a power of 10.

For example,

$$23{,}000 = 2{\cdot}3 \times 10^4.$$
$$18{\cdot}6 = 1{\cdot}86 \times 10^1.$$

(3) Any number less than 1 is equal to the number in its standard form divided by a power of 10.

For example, $0{\cdot}62 = \dfrac{6{\cdot}2}{10^1}$ which can be written $6{\cdot}2 \times 10^{-1}$;

$$0{\cdot}004 = \frac{4{\cdot}0}{10^3} = 4{\cdot}0 \times 10^{-3}.$$

The logarithm of a number

The logarithm of a number consists of a whole number, called the characteristic, and a decimal part, called the mantissa.

The mantissa

To find the logarithm of a number, look up in the logarithm tables the sequence of figures comprising the number. Do not bother, at this stage, about the position of the decimal point. For example, look up 4623 whether you are finding the logarithm of 4·623 or 0·4623 or 0·004623. The result (6649) is the decimal part of the logarithm.

The characteristic

(1) The characteristic of a number in its standard form is zero.

(2) If the number is larger than 10, the characteristic is equal to the number of figures between the decimal point and its position if the number were in its standard form.

Example. 372·4 expressed in standard form is 3·724. The decimal point is moved two places. The characteristic of the logarithm of 372·4 is 2.

Examples.

$$\begin{aligned} \log 7{\cdot}2 &= 0{\cdot}8573;\\ \log 600 &= 2{\cdot}7782;\\ \log 6210 &= 3{\cdot}7931. \end{aligned}$$

(3) If the number is less than 1, the characteristic is still equal to the number of figures between the position of the decimal point and its standard place. This time, however, the characteristic is negative.

Example. 0·0072 in standard form is 7·2. The decimal point is moved three places. The characteristic of the log of 0·0072 is − 3.

Negative characteristics

The logarithm of a number less than 1 consists of the characteristic which is negative and the decimal part which is positive. To emphasise the fact that the characteristic only is negative, the characteristic is written with a bar over it.

Examples.

$$\begin{aligned} \log 0{\cdot}0072 &= \bar{3}{\cdot}8573;\\ \log 0{\cdot}06 &= \bar{2}{\cdot}7782;\\ \log 0{\cdot}621 &= \bar{1}{\cdot}7931. \end{aligned}$$

You will be required to add and subtract numbers with negative characteristics. Remember that the bar means that the whole number is negative and apply your ordinary rules for the addition and subtraction of negative numbers.

Examples. (*a*)

$$\begin{array}{rrr} 1{\cdot}4235 & \bar{1}{\cdot}4235 & \bar{1}{\cdot}4235 \\ +\ \bar{2}{\cdot}6137 & +\ \bar{2}{\cdot}6137 & +\ 2{\cdot}6137 \\ \hline 0{\cdot}0372 & \bar{2}{\cdot}0372 & 2{\cdot}0372 \end{array}$$

(*b*)

$$\begin{array}{rrr} \bar{2}{\cdot}7831 & 2{\cdot}7831 & \bar{2}{\cdot}7831 \\ -\ \bar{1}{\cdot}9256 & -\ \bar{1}{\cdot}9256 & -\ 1{\cdot}9256 \\ \hline \bar{2}{\cdot}8575 & 2{\cdot}8575 & \bar{4}{\cdot}8575 \end{array}$$

Subtraction may be checked by the addition of the last two lines. The sum should equal the first number (e.g. $\bar{1}{\cdot}9256 + \bar{2}{\cdot}8575 = \bar{2}{\cdot}7831$).

The antilogarithm

Given the logarithm, to find the number of which it is the logarithm, apply the reverse process.

Example. Find the number whose logarithm is 2·3724.

Look up the decimal part in the antilog. tables. You will find 2357. This is the sequence of figures for the result and you must supply the position of the decimal point yourself. The result in standard form is 2·357 and since the given characteristic is 2, move the decimal point two places to the right. The number is 235·7.

If the log had been $\bar{2}$·3724, the decimal point must be moved two places to the left. The result is 0·02357.

Multiplication

To multiply two numbers, add their logarithms. The product is the antilog. of this sum.

Example 1. Evaluate 41·3 × 28·6.

No.	Log.
41·3	1·6160
28·6	1·4564
1181·0 ←	3·0724

41·3 × 28·6 = 1181·0.

It is a good plan to make a rough estimate of the result as a check (40 × 30 = 1200). Remember that logarithms will give three-figure accuracy only and so your result in this question should be given as 1180 (to 3 significant figures).

Example 2. Evaluate 42·3 × 0·00072.

(Approximation: 40 × 0·0007 = 0·028.)

No.	Log.
42·3	1·6263
0·00072	$\bar{4}$·8573
0·03045 ←	$\bar{2}$·4836

∴ 42·3 × 0·00072 = 0·0305 (to 3 sig. fig.).

Division

To divide one number by another, subtract their logarithms. This difference is the logarithm of the quotient.

Example. Evaluate 0·0741 ÷ 23·82.

$$\left(\text{Approximation: } \frac{0\cdot07}{20} = 0\cdot0035.\right)$$

No.	Log.
0·0741	$\bar{2}$·8698
23·82	1·3770
0·003111 ←	$\bar{3}$·4928

$$\therefore \frac{0\cdot0741}{23\cdot82} = 0\cdot00311 \text{ (to 3 sig. fig.).}$$

EXERCISES 1A

Evaluate correct to three significant figures:

1. 321 × 0·0724. **2.** 0·627 × 0·742. **3.** 34·1 × 0·81.

4. 0·0076 × 34,200. **5.** 5·28 × 84·21. **6.** 321 ÷ 0·0724.

7. 0·627 ÷ 0·742. **8.** 34·1 ÷ 0·81. **9.** 0·0076 ÷ 0·342.

10. 5·28 ÷ 84·21.

EXERCISES 1B

Evaluate correct to three significant figures:

1. 282·1 × 0·0324. **2.** 0·0072 × 24,321. **3.** 0·716 × 0·312.

4. 0·0718 × 0·0234. **5.** 21·2 × 0·0667. **6.** 0·0324 ÷ 282·1.

7. 0·0072 ÷ 0·02431. **8.** 0·716 ÷ 0·312. **9.** 0·0718 ÷ 0·0234.

10. 21·2 ÷ 0·0667.

Powers

To square a number, double its logarithm. This gives the logarithm of the square.

To cube a number, treble its logarithm. This gives the logarithm of the cube.

To raise a number to the power of *n*, multiply its logarithm by *n*. This gives the logarithm of the *n*th power.

Example 1. Evaluate $(0\cdot621)^3$.

No.	Log.	
0·621	$\bar{1}$·7931	
0·2395 ← $(0\cdot621)^3$	$\bar{1}$·3793	(3 × $\bar{1}$·7931).

$$\therefore (0\cdot621)^3 = 0\cdot240 \text{ (to 3 sig. fig.).}$$

Example 2. Evaluate $(0{\cdot}0275)^2$.

	No.	Log.	
	$0{\cdot}0275$	$\bar{2}{\cdot}4393$	
$0{\cdot}0007561 \leftarrow$	$(0{\cdot}0275)^2$	$\bar{4}{\cdot}8786$	$(2 \times \bar{2}{\cdot}4393)$.

$\therefore (0{\cdot}0275)^2 = 0{\cdot}000756$ (to 3 sig. fig.).

Roots

To find the square root of a number, divide its logarithm by 2. This gives the logarithm of the square root.

To find the cube root of a number, divide its logarithm by 3. This gives the logarithm of the cube root.

To find the *n*th root of a number, divide its logarithm by *n*. This gives the logarithm of the *n*th root.

When finding a root of a number less than 1 you will be asked to perform a division in which the dividend has a negative characteristic. The method needs careful study. You increase the number under the bar to the next integer exactly divisible by your divisor. Balance by adding the appropriate whole number to the decimal part.

For example,

$$\frac{\bar{1}{\cdot}7821}{3} = \frac{\bar{3} + 2{\cdot}7821}{3} = \bar{1}{\cdot}9274.$$

$$\frac{\bar{4}{\cdot}6812}{7} = \frac{\bar{7} + 3{\cdot}6812}{7} = \bar{1}{\cdot}5259.$$

$$\frac{\bar{7}{\cdot}2132}{3} = \frac{\bar{9} + 2{\cdot}2132}{3} = \bar{3}{\cdot}7377.$$

$$\frac{\bar{1}{\cdot}6425}{5} = \frac{\bar{5} + 4{\cdot}6425}{5} = \bar{1}{\cdot}9285.$$

Example 1. Evaluate $\sqrt[5]{28{\cdot}37}$.

	No.	Log.	
	$28{\cdot}37$	$1{\cdot}4529$	
$1{\cdot}953 \leftarrow$	$\sqrt[5]{28{\cdot}37}$	$0{\cdot}2906$	$(1{\cdot}4529 \div 5)$.

$\therefore \sqrt[5]{28{\cdot}37} = 1{\cdot}95$ (to 3 sig. fig.).

Example 2. Evaluate $\sqrt[3]{0{\cdot}6274}$.

	No.	Log.	
	$0{\cdot}6274$	$\bar{1}{\cdot}7976$	
$0{\cdot}8561 \leftarrow$	$\sqrt[3]{0{\cdot}6274}$	$\bar{1}{\cdot}9325$	$(\bar{1}{\cdot}7976 \div 3)$.

$\therefore \sqrt[3]{0{\cdot}6274} = 0{\cdot}856$ (to 3 sig. fig.).

EXERCISES 2A

Evaluate:

1. $\bar{1}\cdot3621 - \bar{3}\cdot9815$.
2. $\bar{1}\cdot3621 + \bar{3}\cdot9815$.
3. $\bar{2}\cdot7621 \times 3$.
4. $\bar{3}\cdot7612 \div 4$.
5. $\bar{7}\cdot1111 \div 3$.
6. $\sqrt{28\cdot61}$.
7. $\sqrt[3]{0\cdot0761}$.
8. $(0\cdot721)^3$.
9. $\sqrt[4]{0\cdot008}$.
10. $(0\cdot2562)^3$.

EXERCISES 2B

Evaluate:

1. $\bar{2}\cdot2711 - \bar{3}\cdot8826$.
2. $\bar{2}\cdot2711 + \bar{3}\cdot8826$.
3. $\bar{1}\cdot7111 \times 3$.
4. $\bar{5}\cdot6222 \div 2$.
5. $\bar{3}\cdot8888 \div 4$.
6. $\sqrt[3]{32\cdot2}$.
7. $\sqrt[4]{0\cdot7111}$.
8. $(0\cdot955)^4$.
9. $\sqrt[5]{0\cdot0621}$.
10. $(1\cdot111)^7$.

Worked Examples

You will often be asked to evaluate more complicated expressions when you will need to use two or more of the methods considered. Some examples are given showing how the work should be set out.

Example 1. Evaluate, to three significant figures,

$$2\pi\sqrt{\frac{98\cdot1}{32\cdot2}}, \quad \text{where } \pi = 3\cdot142.$$

(Approximation: $6\sqrt{3} = 6(1\cdot73) = 10\cdot3$.)

No.	Log.	
98·1	1·9917	
32·2	1·5079	
Quotient	0·4838	
$\sqrt{\frac{98\cdot1}{32\cdot2}}$	0·2419	(dividing by 2).
2	0·3010	
π	0·4972	
10·96 ←	1·0401	

$$\therefore 2\pi\sqrt{\frac{98\cdot1}{32\cdot2}} = 10\cdot96 = 11\cdot0 \text{ (to 3 sig. fig.)}.$$

Example 2. Evaluate, to three significant figures,

$$\frac{\sqrt[3]{0{\cdot}0072} \times (81{\cdot}3)^2}{\sqrt{23{,}140}}.$$

$$\left(\text{Approximation: } \frac{0{\cdot}2 \times 6400}{150} = \frac{128}{15} = 8{\cdot}5.\right)$$

No.	Log.
$\sqrt[3]{0{\cdot}0072}$	$\bar{3}{\cdot}8573 \div 3 = \bar{1}{\cdot}2858$
$(81{\cdot}3)^2$	$1{\cdot}9101 \times 2 = 3{\cdot}8202$
Product	$3{\cdot}1060$
$\sqrt{23{,}140}$	$4{\cdot}3643 \div 2 = 2{\cdot}1822$
8·39	← 0·9238

The value of the expression is 8·39 (to 3 sig. fig.).

Example 3. Evaluate, to three significant figures,

$$\frac{1 + \sqrt[3]{0{\cdot}0075}}{1 - \sqrt[3]{0{\cdot}0075}}.$$

Remember that logarithms cannot be used for addition or subtraction and, in an example such as this, the work cannot be done in one operation.

First calculate $\sqrt[3]{0{\cdot}0075}$.

No.	Log.
0·0075	$\bar{3}{\cdot}8751$
0·1957 ← $\sqrt[3]{0{\cdot}0075}$	$\bar{1}{\cdot}2917$ ($\bar{3}{\cdot}8751 \div 3$)

$$\text{The expression} = \frac{1 + 0{\cdot}1957}{1 - 0{\cdot}1957} = \frac{1{\cdot}1957}{0{\cdot}8043}$$

Now evaluate this fraction by logarithms.

No.	Log.
1·1957	0·0778
0·8043	$\bar{1}{\cdot}9055$
1·487 ←	0·1723

Therefore the given expression is equal to 1·487 or 1·49 (to 3 sig. fig.).

EXERCISES 3: MISCELLANEOUS

(*Give your answers correct to 3 significant figures: take π to be 3·142.*)

1. Find the value of $\dfrac{12{\cdot}82 - 6{\cdot}41}{12{\cdot}82 \times 6{\cdot}41}$.

2. Evaluate $\sqrt{\dfrac{s(s-b)}{(s-a)(s-c)}}$, where $a = 18{\cdot}4$, $b = 12{\cdot}6$, $c = 11{\cdot}4$ and $2s = a + b + c$.

3. The distance of the horizon from a point h metres above the earth's surface is $\sqrt{\dfrac{2rh}{1000}}$ km, where r is the radius of the earth in km. If $r = 6370$, calculate the distance in km when $h = 186$.

4. The volume of a sphere is $\frac{4}{3}\pi r^3$. Find the volume of a sphere of radius 10·6 cm.

5. Find the value of $(0{\cdot}0823)^{\frac{3}{5}}$.

6. Evaluate $\dfrac{0{\cdot}81 + \sqrt{0{\cdot}81}}{1{\cdot}81}$.

7. Evaluate $\dfrac{(1{\cdot}31)^5 + 1}{(1{\cdot}31)^5 - 1}$.

8. The amount to which a principal of P amounts at r% compound interest for n years is given by the formula $A = P\left(1 + \dfrac{r}{100}\right)^n$. Find A if $P = 126$, $r = 4$ and $n = 5$.

9. Evaluate $\dfrac{187\{(1{\cdot}3)^{12} - 1\}}{3426}$.

10. Evaluate $\sqrt{\dfrac{8{\cdot}621 \times 27{\cdot}34}{52{\cdot}18 \times 0{\cdot}0724}}$.

11. Evaluate $(0{\cdot}647)^{\frac{2}{5}}$.

12. The area of a triangle is given by $\sqrt{s(s-a)(s-b)(s-c)}$, where $2s = a + b + c$. Find the area of a triangle given that $a = 14{\cdot}2$, $b = 12{\cdot}6$ and $c = 8{\cdot}4$.

13. Evaluate $\dfrac{0{\cdot}2463 \times (0{\cdot}1721)^2}{\sqrt{0{\cdot}7621}}$.

14. If $\frac{4}{3}\pi r^3 = 128{\cdot}1$, calculate $4\pi r^2$.

15. Find x given that $12x = 13{\cdot}41 - \frac{1}{9}\log 4{\cdot}82$.

16. Find x given that $10x = 8{\cdot}76 - \frac{1}{9}\log 0{\cdot}6$.

17. Evaluate $\log\left(\dfrac{28{\cdot}3}{13{\cdot}4} + \dfrac{12{\cdot}6}{\sqrt{27{\cdot}1}}\right)$.

18. Evaluate $\left(\dfrac{2347}{641} - \dfrac{751}{864}\right)^3$.

19. Evaluate $\sqrt[3]{0{\cdot}777}$.

20. Find the value of $\pi(R^2 - r^2)h$, given that $R = 8{\cdot}36$, $r = 6{\cdot}24$ and $h = 12{\cdot}2$.

21. Find the value of $\sqrt[3]{\dfrac{3V}{4\pi}}$, given that $V = 2{\cdot}821$.

22. Evaluate $\sqrt[3]{\dfrac{46{\cdot}2 \times 47{\cdot}1}{0{\cdot}0834}}$.

23. Find x if $\dfrac{2}{x} = \dfrac{1}{12{\cdot}3} + \dfrac{1}{15{\cdot}4}$.

24. Find the value of $\sqrt{x^2 + y^2}$ if $x = 12{\cdot}24$ and $y = 7{\cdot}213$.

25. Find the value of $\sqrt[3]{\left(\dfrac{1}{2{\cdot}71}\right)^2 + \left(\dfrac{3}{4{\cdot}25}\right)^2}$.

26. Find the value of $\sqrt{\dfrac{S}{4\pi}}$, given that $S = 18{\cdot}61$.

27. Find the value of $\dfrac{(8{\cdot}91)^2 + (7{\cdot}23)^2 - (6{\cdot}41)^2}{2(8{\cdot}91)(7{\cdot}23)}$.

28. Evaluate $\dfrac{\sqrt[3]{0{\cdot}8} - \sqrt{0{\cdot}7}}{\sqrt[3]{0{\cdot}8} + \sqrt{0{\cdot}7}}$.

29. Evaluate $\dfrac{28{\cdot}3}{\pi(16{\cdot}1^2 - 14{\cdot}3^2)}$.

30. Evaluate $\dfrac{\sqrt[3]{28{\cdot}1} \times (0{\cdot}721)^2}{\sqrt{0{\cdot}064} \times (18{\cdot}31)^3}$.

2

AREAS AND VOLUMES

The triangle

THE area (Δ) of a triangle is equal to half the product of its base and height. In the figure, $\Delta = \frac{1}{2}ah$. If one of the angles of the triangle is a right angle, the area is equal to half the product of the sides containing the right angle.

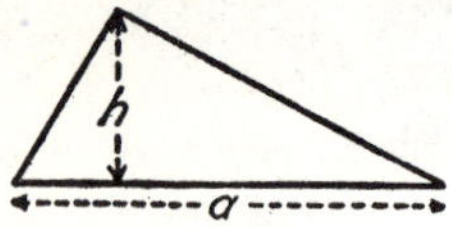

FIG. 1

It is worth noting that any one side may be taken as the base. There are thus three possible expressions for the area of the triangle. By equating two such expressions, the height of the triangle may be found as in the following example.

Example. A triangle ABC has $AB = 3$ cm, $AC = 4$ cm and the angle A a right angle. Find the length of the perpendicular from A to BC.

The area of the triangle $ABC = \frac{1}{2}(3)(4) = 6$ cm^2.

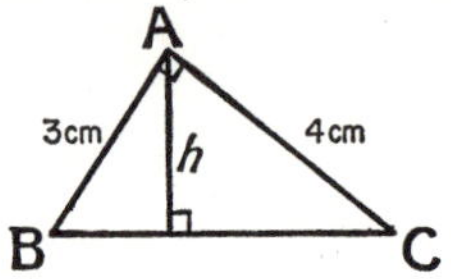

FIG. 2

By Pythagoras, $BC^2 = 3^2 + 4^2$. $\therefore$ $BC = 5$.

The area of the triangle is

$$\tfrac{1}{2}h(BC) = \frac{5h}{2}.$$

$$\therefore \frac{5h}{2} = 6$$

or $h = 2{\cdot}4$. $\therefore$ Height $= 2{\cdot}4$ cm.

The area of a triangle in terms of the sides

Another useful formula for the area of a triangle is

$$\sqrt{s(s-a)(s-b)(s-c)},$$

where a, b, c are the lengths of the sides and $s = \frac{1}{2}(a + b + c)$.

The parallelogram

A parallelogram is divided by a diagonal into two congruent triangles. The area of the parallelogram is therefore twice the area of one of these triangles.

The area of a parallelogram = base × height, where the base may be taken as any one of the sides.

Example. The parallelogram *ABCD* is such that $AB = 4$ cm, $AD = 3$ cm and the length of the perpendicular from *D* to *AB* is 1·5 cm. Find the length of the perpendicular from *D* to *BC*.

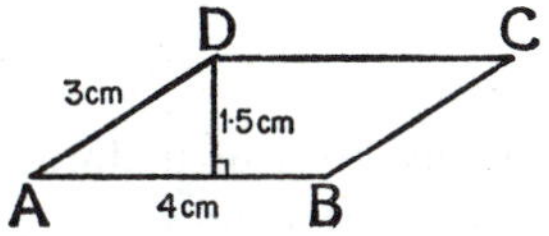

FIG. 3

If the length of the perpendicular required is h cm, the area of the parallelogram is equal to 4(1·5) or to $3h$ cm^2.

$$\therefore\ 3h = 6$$

or $h = 2$. ∴ Length of perpendicular = 2 cm.

The rectangle

The rectangle is a particular case of the parallelogram and the area of a rectangle = length × breadth.

From this it follows that the length of a rectangle is equal to its area divided by its breadth.

The box or cuboid

The volume of a box is equal to the product of the three edges of the box.

Volume = length × breadth × height.

Given the volume of a box and the dimensions of the base, to find the height, divide the volume by the area of the base.

The cube

The cube is a box with all its edges equal and so the volume of a cube is equal to the cube of an edge.

The area of the walls of a room

The perimeter of a room is twice the sum of length and breadth, i.e. $p = 2(l + b)$.

The total area of the walls of a room is equal to the product of perimeter and height, i.e. $A = p \times h = 2h(l + b)$.

Solid with uniform cross section

If, when a solid is cut by a plane perpendicular to its length, the area of the cross section is always exactly the same, the solid is said to be a body of uniform cross section. The volume of such a body is equal to the area of the cross section × length.

$$\text{Volume} = (\text{area of cross section}) \times \text{length}.$$

The prism

Generally, a prism is any body of uniform cross section, but in common usage the term refers to a body having a uniform triangular section.

$$\text{Volume} = (\text{area of triangular base}) \times \text{length}.$$

The tetrahedron

The tetrahedron is the solid figure obtained by joining the vertices of a triangle to another point not in the same plane. The volume of a tetrahedron is equal to one third the product of the area of the triangle and the perpendicular distance of the fourth point from the plane of the triangle. A similar formula holds for any solid formed by joining the points of a plane figure to another point not in its plane.

$$\text{Volume} = \tfrac{1}{3}(\text{base area})(\text{height}).$$

Units

An area is measured in square units and a volume in cubic units. A connection between units of length may be changed into connections between units of area and units of volume in the following way.

Example 1.

$$1\text{ m} = 100\text{ cm}$$
$$1\text{ m}^2 = 100^2\text{ cm}^2 = 10\,000\text{ cm}^2$$
$$1\text{ m}^3 = 100^3\text{ cm}^3 = 1\,000\,000\text{ cm}^3$$

Example 2.

$$1\text{ hectare} = 10\,000\text{ m}^2$$
$$1\text{ km} = 1000\text{ m}$$
$$1\text{ km}^2 = 1000^2\text{ m}^2$$
$$= 1\,000\,000\text{ m}^2$$
$$= 100\text{ hectares.}$$

Area between two rectangles

Example. A rectangular carpet measures 16 m by 12 m and it has a stained border of width 2 m surrounding it. What is the area of the border?

Always treat an area such as this as the difference between two rectangles.

The sides of the longer rectangle will each be 4 m longer than the parallel sides of the smaller rectangle.

$$\begin{aligned}\text{Therefore the area of stain} &= (20 \times 16) - (16 \times 12) \\ &= 16(20 - 12) \\ &= 128 \text{ m}^2.\end{aligned}$$

Volume between two boxes

Example. A closed box is made of wood everywhere $\frac{1}{2}$ cm thick and its external dimensions are 6 cm by 5 cm by 4 cm. Find the volume of wood used in making the box.

Always treat such a volume as the difference between two volumes. The edge of the internal box is 1 cm shorter than the parallel edge of the larger box.

$$\begin{aligned}\text{The external volume} &= 6 \times 5 \times 4 \text{ cm}^3 \\ \text{The internal volume} &= 5 \times 4 \times 3 \text{ cm}^3 \\ \text{The volume of wood} &= 6 \times 5 \times 4 - 5 \times 4 \times 3 \text{ cm}^3 \\ &= 60 \text{ cm}^3.\end{aligned}$$

If the box had no lid, the internal height would be $5\frac{1}{2}$ cm (assuming that the height is 6 cm).

The internal volume is $5\frac{1}{2} \times 4 \times 3$ cm³.

$$\begin{aligned}\text{The volume of wood} &= 6 \times 5 \times 4 - 5\tfrac{1}{2} \times 4 \times 3 \\ &= 54 \text{ cm}^3.\end{aligned}$$

Density

The density of a body is its mass per unit volume. It is measured in kg/m³ or g/cm³.

$$\text{Density} = \frac{\text{Mass}}{\text{Volume}}.$$

Specific Gravity

The specific gravity of a body is equal to the mass of the body divided by the mass of an equal volume of water. It is the number of times the body is heavier than water, volume for volume.

Since the mass of 1 cm³ of water is 1 gramme, the density of a body in g/cm³ is numerically equal to its specific gravity.

$$1 \text{ kg} = 1000 \text{ g};$$
$$1 \text{ tonne} = 1000 \text{ kg}.$$
$$1 \text{ litre} = 1000 \text{ cm}^3.$$

EXERCISES 4A

1. Find the area of a triangle whose sides are 4·2 cm, 5·8 cm and 6·0 cm.

2. A triangle has sides 5 cm, 12 cm and 13 cm. Find the length of the perpendicular from the opposite vertex to the side of length 13 cm.

3. The area of a rectangle is 33·12 cm². Given that one side is of length 4·6 cm, find the length of the other side.

4. A picture which measures 48 cm by 40 cm is surrounded by a frame which is 1 cm wide. Find the area of the frame.

5. A box of volume 90 cm³ has a base of area 20 cm². Find the height of the box.

6. The external dimensions of an open box are 8 cm by 5 cm by 4 cm high. Find the volume of wood used in making the box, if the wood is $\frac{1}{2}$ cm thick.

7. A tetrahedron has a base 3 m by 4 m by 5 m and a height of 10 m. Find its volume.

8. A solid wooden box of sides 10 cm, 8 cm and 7 cm is of mass 504 g. Find the specific gravity of the wood.

9. A tree trunk of uniform cross section of area 0·5 m² is made of wood of specific gravity 0·8. Find the mass of a length of 1 m of trunk.

10. Given that 1 m = 10 dm, find the number of dm² in 1 m².

EXERCISES 4B

1. Find the area of a triangle whose sides are 9 cm, 10 cm and 11 cm.

2. A parallelogram has sides of 12 cm and 8 cm. The distance between the 12 cm sides is 4 cm. Find the distance between the 8 cm sides.

3. A box with a square base and a height of 8 cm has a volume of 1352 cm³. Find the length of a side of the base.

4. The external dimensions of a closed box are 7 cm by 6 cm by 5 cm. If the wood used is $\frac{1}{4}$ cm thick, find the volume of wood in the box.

5. A square room has a square carpet symmetrically placed in it. This leaves an area uncovered of 9 m² and the area of the whole room is 25 m². Find the length of one side of the carpet.

6. A tetrahedron has a base of 5 m by 12 m by 13 m and a height of 10 m. Find its volume.

7. A right prism of length 10 cm has its cross section an equilateral triangle of side 6 cm. Find its volume.

8. A room 5 m by 4 m by 3 m high is to be papered with paper 50 cm wide. What length of paper is required?

9. A swimming pool is 30 m long and 10 m wide. The water at the deep end is 3 m deep and at the shallow end is 1 m deep. Find the volume of water in the pool.

10. Find the mass of 1 m^3 of water.

The circumference of a circle

The circumference of a circle is equal to $2\pi r$, where r is the radius.

$$\therefore\ C = 2\pi r \quad \text{or} \quad \pi d\ (d = \text{diameter}).$$

π is a constant which cannot be expressed accurately as a decimal or as a fraction. Its value correct to 4 significant figures is 3·142.

N.B. The value of π is not $\frac{22}{7}$. This is an approximation for π, but only use this value in your work when you are particularly instructed to do so.

The area of a circle

The area of a circle πr^2.

Example. The area of a circle of radius 4 cm is equal to

$$\pi(4)^2 = 16 \times 3{\cdot}142 = 50{\cdot}3\ \text{cm}^2.$$

The area of an ellipse

The area of an ellipse $= \pi ab$, where a and b are the lengths of the two semi-axes of the ellipse.

Example. The area of an ellipse whose axes are 10 cm and 8 cm in length is

$$\pi(5)(4) = 20\pi\ \text{cm}^2 \text{ or } 62{\cdot}8\ \text{cm}^2.$$

The surface area of a right circular cylinder

The surface area of a cylinder is equal to the product of the circumference of the base and the height.

$$\therefore\ S = 2\pi rh.$$

This gives the area of the curved surface only. If the cylinder has a base but no top, the total surface area is $2\pi rh + \pi r^2$; if the cylinder has both base and top, the total surface area is

$$2\pi rh + 2\pi r^2, \quad \text{or} \quad 2\pi r(h + r).$$

Example. Find the total surface area of a cylinder of height 6 cm and radius of base 4 cm.

The area of covered surface $= 2\pi rh = 2\pi(4)(6) = 48\pi \text{ cm}^2$.
The area of each end $= \pi(4)^2 = 16\pi \text{ cm}^2$.
The total surface area $= 48\pi + 2(16\pi) = 80\pi \text{ cm}^2$
$= 80(3{\cdot}142) \text{ cm}^2$
$= 251 \text{ cm}^2$ (to 3 sig. fig.).

N.B. Do not substitute the numerical value of π until the substitution can no longer be avoided.

The volume of a right circular cylinder

The volume of a right circular cylinder is equal to the product of the area of the base and the height.

$$\therefore\ V = \pi r^2 h.$$

This is a particular case of a solid of uniform cross section (see page 16).

Example. The volume of a cylinder whose height is 4 cm and whose base radius is 5 cm is equal to

$$\pi(5)^2(4) = 100\pi = 314 \text{ cm}^3 \text{ (to 3 sig. fig.)}.$$

The volume of a circular cone

This is a particular case of a solid obtained by joining the points of a plane figure to another point not in the same plane (see page 16).

The volume of a cone is equal to one third the product of its base area and height.

$$V = \tfrac{1}{3}\pi r^2 h.$$

Example. The volume of a cone of height 6 cm and base radius 5 cm is

$$\tfrac{1}{3}\pi(5)^2(6) = 50\pi = 157 \text{ cm}^3 \text{ (to 3 sig. fig.)}.$$

The surface area of a cone

The surface area of a cone (S) is given in terms of the radius of the base (r) and the slant height (l) by the formula

$$S = \pi rl.$$

This gives the area of the curved surface only.

If the cone has a base, the total surface area equals

$$\pi rl + \pi r^2 \quad \text{or} \quad \pi r(r + l).$$

Example. Find the area of the curved surface of a cone whose base radius is 3 cm and whose height is 4 cm.

First find the slant height.

From Fig. 4,

$$l^2 = h^2 + r^2.$$
$$\therefore\ l^2 = 4^2 + 3^2 = 25 \quad \text{and} \quad l = 5.$$
$$\therefore\ S = \pi rl = \pi(3)(5) = 15\pi = 47{\cdot}1 \text{ cm}^2 \text{ (to 3 sig. fig.)}.$$

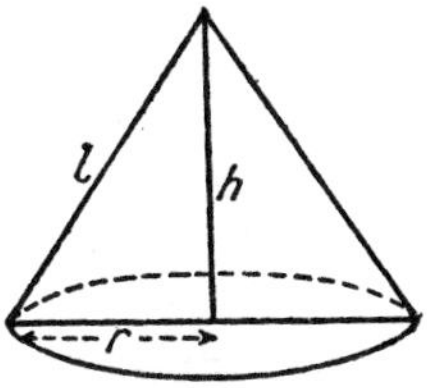

FIG. 4

The sphere

The formulae for the surface area and volume of a sphere are

$$S = 4\pi r^2;$$
$$V = \tfrac{4}{3}\pi r^3.$$

V is the volume, S the surface area and r the radius.

The area of a ring

Treat the area of a ring as the difference in area between two circles.

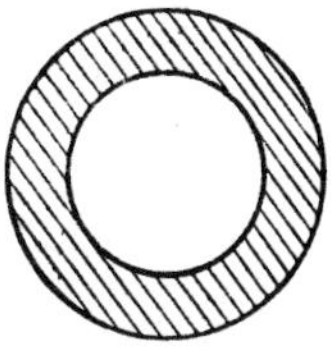

FIG. 5

If R is the radius of the larger circle and r the radius of the smaller, the area of the ring equals

$$\pi(R^2 - r^2), \quad \text{or} \quad \pi(R + r)(R - r).$$

The volume of material in a pipe

The hollow pipe has a uniform cross section. The cross section is a ring and if its outer and inner radii are R and r respectively, the area of the ring is $\pi(R^2 - r^2)$. The volume of the pipe is equal to the product of the area of the cross section and the length.

$$V = \pi(R^2 - r^2)l, \quad \text{or} \quad \pi(R + r)(R - r)l.$$

Example. A pipe, made of metal 1 cm thick, has an external radius of 11 cm. Find the volume of metal used in making 2·4 m of pipe.

$$\begin{aligned} \text{The external radius} &= 11 \text{ cm.} \\ \text{The internal radius} &= 10 \text{ cm.} \\ \text{The area of cross section} &= \pi(11^2 - 10^2) = 21\pi \text{ cm}^2 \\ \text{The volume of 240 cm of pipe} &= 21\pi(240) \text{ cm}^3 \\ &= 15\,800 \text{ cm}^3 \text{ (to 3 sig. fig.).} \end{aligned}$$

The volume of material in a spherical shell

To find the volume of a hollow sphere, subtract the volume of the inner sphere from the volume of the outer sphere.

$$\therefore \; V = \tfrac{4}{3}\pi R^3 - \tfrac{4}{3}\pi r^3 = \tfrac{4}{3}\pi(R^3 - r^3),$$

where R and r are the external and internal radii.

Discharge of water from a pipe

If water is flowing through a pipe at V m/sec, then in every second the water contained in a length of V metres of pipe will be discharged. If the pipe is always full and the area of cross section of the pipe is A m^2, the volume discharged per sec equals AV m^3.

Example. Water flows through a circular pipe of internal radius of 10 cm at 5 m/sec. If the pipe is always half full, find the number of m^3 discharged in half an hour.

$$\begin{aligned} \text{The area of the circular cross section} &= \pi(10)^2 = 100\pi \text{ cm}^2. \\ \text{The area of cross section of the water} &= 50\pi \text{ cm}^2 \\ &= \frac{50\pi}{100 \times 100} \text{ m}^2. \\ \text{The volume of water discharged per sec} &= \frac{250\pi}{100 \times 100} \text{ m}^3 \\ &= \frac{\pi}{40} \text{ m}^3. \end{aligned}$$

The number of m^3 discharged in half an hour

$$= \frac{(30)(60)\pi}{40}$$
$$= 45\pi$$
$$= 142 \text{ (to 3 sig. fig.).}$$

The areas of similar figures

You will find it useful to remember that the areas of similar figures are in the ratio of the squares on their corresponding linear dimensions. For example, if the radius of one circle is twice that of another, its area is four times as large; if a triangle is cut by a line parallel to its base so that each side of the smaller triangle is one third the corresponding size of the larger, its area is one ninth that of the larger; if the model of a sailing ship is made on a scale of 1 in 20, the deck area of the ship is 400 times as great as that of the model.

The volumes of similar solids

It is also useful to learn that the volumes of similar solids are in the ratio of the cubes on their corresponding linear dimensions. For example, if the radius of a sphere is doubled, its volume is increased eight-fold; if a cone is cut by a plane parallel to its base so that the height of the smaller cone is one third that of the larger, the volume of the smaller cone is one twenty-seventh part of the volume of the larger.

(N.B. If the top of a cone is cut off by a plane parallel to the base, the remainder is called *a frustum* of the cone.)

EXERCISES 5A

1. The circumference of a circle is 28 cm. Find its radius.

2. The area of a circle is 42 cm^2. Find its radius.

3. A cylinder of base radius 4 cm has a volume of 100 cm^3. Find its height.

4. A solid cone of base radius 3 cm and height 4 cm is made of metal of density 7 g/cm^3. Find its mass.

5. A pipe of thickness $\frac{1}{2}$ cm has an external diameter of 12 cm. Find the volume of 2·4 m of pipe.

6. Find the total surface area of a cylinder of base radius 5 cm and length 7 cm.

7. The volume of a sphere is 827 cm^3. Find its radius.

8. Find the total surface area of a cone of base radius 5 cm and height 12 cm.

9. Water flows through a circular pipe of radius 10 cm at 6 m/sec. How many m^3 does it discharge per minute?

10. A cone of height 6 cm and radius of base 4 cm has its top cut off by a plane parallel to its base and 4 cm from it. Find the volume of the remaining frustum.

11. The area of an ellipse is 132 cm^2. The length of its major axis is 14 cm. Find the length of its minor axis.

12. A right cone of height 6 cm has as its cross-section an ellipse of axes 10 cm and 7 cm. Find the volume of the cone.

EXERCISES 5B

1. A window in the form of a semicircle with diameter as base has a radius of 30 cm. Find its perimeter.

2. Find the area of a circular path 3 m wide surrounding a circular plot of radius 20 m.

3. Find the volume in cm^3 of 1 km of circular cable of radius 0·1 cm.

4. Find the volume of rubber used in making a hollow ball of radius 2 cm if the thickness of the rubber is 0·2 cm.

5. Find the total surface area of a cone radius of base 6 cm and height 8 cm.

6. Find the radius of a sphere whose surface area is 108 cm^2.

7. Find the radius of a sphere whose volume is 426 cm^3.

8. Water is flowing through a circular channel at 8 m/sec. Find the number of m^3 discharged per minute if the channel, always full, has a radius of 8 cm.

9. Find the volume of a frustum of a cone given that its height is 4 cm and that the radii of its ends are 3 cm and 6 cm.

10. Find the volume of a sphere whose surface area is 1000 cm^2.

11. The area of an ellipse is 308 cm^2. Find the length of its major axis given that it is twice as long as the minor axis.

12. A right cylinder has a volume of 66 cm^3. If the cross section of the cylinder is an ellipse whose axes are 4 cm and 3 cm long, find the length of the cylinder.

Worked Examples

Example 1. A test tube consists of a cylinder and a hemisphere of the same radius. 282 cm^3 of water are required to fill the whole tube and 262

cm^3 are required to fill it to a level which is 1 cm below the top of the tube. Find the radius of the tube and the length of the cylindrical part.

If r cm is the radius of the tube, the volume of a cylinder of length 1 cm is πr^2.

$$\therefore \pi r^2 = 282 - 262 = 20.$$

No.	Log.
20	1·3010
π	0·4972
r^2	0·8038
2·523 ← r	0·4019

The radius of the tube is 2·52 cm. (to 3 sig. fig.).

The volume of the hemisphere $= \frac{2}{3}\pi r^3$.

No.	Log.
2	0·3010
π	0·4972
r^3	1·2057
	2·0039
3	0·4771
33·63	1·5268

The volume of the hemisphere is 33·63 cm^3.

The volume of the cylinder $= 282 - 33{\cdot}63$
$= 248{\cdot}4$ cm^3.

If l cm is the length of the cylinder,

$$\pi r^2 l = 248{\cdot}4.$$

$$\therefore l = \frac{248{\cdot}4}{\pi(2{\cdot}523)^2}.$$

No.	Log.
248·4	2·3952
π	0·4972
r^2	0·8038
12·43 ←	1·0942

The length of the cylindrical part is 12·43 or 12·4 cm (to 3 sig. fig.).

Example 2. A bath containing 1 m^3 of water is filled in 10 min by a circular pipe of diameter 2 cm. Find the speed of water in the pipe.

The area of cross section of the pipe $= \pi$ cm^2

$$= \frac{\pi}{100 \times 100} \text{ m}^2.$$

If v m/sec is the speed of water in the pipe, the volume discharged per sec $= \frac{\pi v}{100 \times 100}$ m^3.

But 1 m^3 is discharged in 10 minutes.

$$\therefore \quad \frac{1}{10 \times 60} \text{ m}^3 \text{ are discharged per sec.}$$

$$\therefore \quad \frac{\pi v}{100 \times 100} = \frac{1}{10 \times 60} \quad \text{or} \quad v = \frac{100}{6\pi}$$

No	Log
100	2·0000
6	0·7782
π	0·4972
5·30 ←	0·7246

The speed of water in the pipe is 5·30 m/sec (to 3 sig. fig.).

EXERCISES 6: Miscellaneous

1. A sphere of radius 2 cm is dropped into water contained in a cylindrical vessel of radius 4 cm. If the sphere is completely immersed, find the rise in level of the water.

2. Four hundred metres of fencing are required to enclose a square field. What greater area can be enclosed by the same length of fencing if the enclosure is circular?

3. A swimming pool of length 30 m and width 12 m is 4 m deep at one end and 1 m deep at the shallow end. Find the number of m^3 of water in the pool.

4. Printing paper is wrapped round a wooden core of diameter 12 cm. If the diameter of the roll is 36 cm and the length of paper 600 m, find the thickness of the paper.

5. A solid cone of height 4 cm and radius of base 2 cm is lowered into a cylindrical jar of radius 6 cm which contains water sufficient to submerge the cone completely. Find the rise in water level.

6. A cube has an edge of 4 cm. A triangle is formed by joining the middle point of one face of the cube to the ends of a diagonal of the opposite face. Calculate the area of the triangle.

7. Construct a triangle having its sides 3 cm, 5 cm and 6 cm long. Construct the altitudes from the vertices to the opposite sides, measure them and calculate the area of the triangle from each of these measurements. Find the average of these three results and compare it with the calculated area of the triangle.

8. Given that 1 in = 2·54 cm, calculate the number of km^2 in a sq. mile.

9. Calculate the mass of water which falls on a hectare of ground in a rainfall of 1 cm. Give your answer in tonnes.

10. The external dimensions of a closed wooden box are 30 cm by 20 cm by 18 cm. The thickness of the wood is 1 cm. If the specific gravity of the wood is 0·7, calculate the mass of the box.

11. A tank of rectangular cross section 2 m by 1 m and of height 1 m is filled by a pipe of cross section 10 cm^2. If the pipe delivers 1 m^3 per minute, find (i) the rate of flow of water in the pipe, (ii) the time taken to fill the tank.

12. A tent has its base in the shape of a regular hexagon whose sides are 10 m. If the height of the tent is 12 m, find its volume.

13. A kite consists of an isosceles triangle with a semicircle on its base. If the isosceles triangle has sides 13 cm, 13 cm and 10 cm, find the area of the cardboard forming the kite.

14. Taking the radius of the earth to be 6370 km, find the velocity of a place on the equator in km/h.

15. The dimensions of a hut are shown in Fig. 6. Calculate the volume of the hut and its total surface area, omitting the floor.

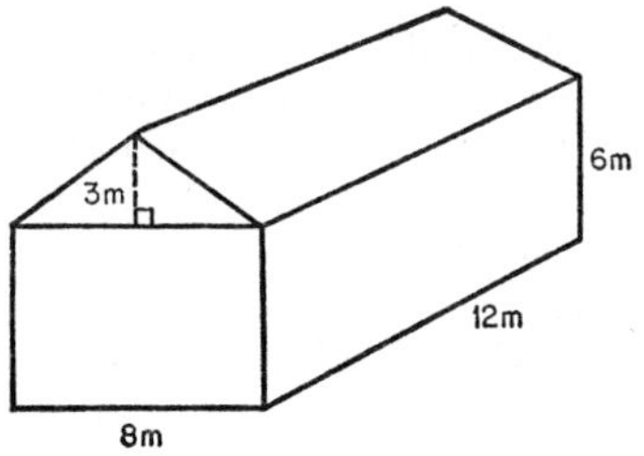

FIG. 6

C

16. The rainwater from a flat roof 15 m by 20 m drains into a tank 3 m deep on a base 4 m square. What depth of rainfall will fill the tank?

17. A hollow pipe is made of metal 0·5 cm thick. The volume of the metal in 30 m^3 of pipe is 1·03 m^3. Find the external diameter of the pipe.

18. A wire 2 m long is cut into two pieces which can be bent to make a square and the circle passing through the vertices of the square. Find the radius of the circle.

19. A wire encloses a circle of area 18 cm^2. The wire is now bent into the shape of a regular hexagon. Calculate the area of the hexagon.

20. A circular path has an external radius of 20 m and is 1 m wide. Find the total cost of gravelling the path at 25 new pence per m^2 and fencing both sides of the path at $37\frac{1}{2}$ new pence per m. Give your answer to the nearest pound.

21. A cylindrical tube when pushed vertically to the bottom of water contained in a cylindrical jar of radius 4 cm caused the water in the jar to rise from a height of 10·2 cm to a height of 10·32 cm. Assuming that some of the tube still projects from the water, calculate the diameter of the tube.

22. The distance round the Equator is 40 million metres. Calculate the radius of the earth in kilometres.

23. A wooden cube is of edge 6 cm. The corner *A* is cut off the cube by a plane which passes through the middle points of the edges through *A*. Find the volume of the wood removed.

24. 1000 lead shot each of diameter $\frac{1}{4}$ cm are melted down and recast into the form of a cube. Find the side of the cube.

25. A cylindrical vessel contains 250 g of a liquid whose density is 1·2 g/cm^3. If the height of liquid in the vessel is 8 cm, find the base radius of the cylinder.

26. The cross section of a prism is an equilateral triangle of side 3 m. The length of the prism is 5 m. Find (i) its volume, (ii) the area of its surface.

27. Find, in tonnes, the mass of water required to fill a rectangular tank 3·2 m long, 2·4 m wide and 1 metre high.

28. An equilateral triangle has the same area as a square. Express the perimeter of the triangle as a fraction of the perimeter of the square.

29. *ABCD* is a tetrahedron. *ABC* is an equilateral triangle of side 4 m and $DA = DB = DC = 6$ m. *DN* is the perpendicular from *D* to the face *ABC*. Find *DN* and the volume of the tetrahedron.

30. A pyramid is on a rectangular base of sides 6 m and 4 m. Each slant edge is 8 m long. Find the height and volume of the pyramid.

3

RATIO AND PERCENTAGE

RATIO

A COMMON scale for a detailed map is 2 cm to 1 km. This means that 2 cm on the map represents an actual horizontal distance of 1 km. This scale may also be given as 1 in 50 000 or 1 : 50 000, which compares the distance on the map with the actual horizontal distance.

Two different quantities of the same kind may always be compared in this way. If one of the quantities is expressed as a fraction of the other quantity, this fraction is said to be the ratio of their sizes. Care must be taken to make sure that the two quantities are in the same units.

Examples. 1. If I am 45 years old and my son is 11 years old, the ratio of my age to his is 45 : 11; the ratio of his age to mine is 11 : 45.

2. The speed of a cyclist is 10 km/h and of a car is 35 km/h. The ratio of the speed of the cyclist to that of the car is 2 : 7.

3. The price of tea is increased from 60 new pence per kg to 65 new pence per kg. The ratio of the old price to the new price is 60 : 65 or 12 : 13.

4. The price of an article is increased from £1·25 to £2. The ratio of the old price to the new price is 125 : 200 or 5 : 8.

EXERCISES 7A

Express each of the following ratios as simply as possible:

1. A length of 8 cm to a length of 3 m.

2. A speed of 12 km/h to a speed of 40 km/h.

3. A speed of 12 km/h to a speed of 10 m/sec.

4. A cost of 4 new pence per kg to a cost of 12 new pence per kg.

5. A cost of 2 new pence per g to a cost of £0·48 per g.

6. $62\frac{1}{2}$ new pence : £5.

7. 4 cm^2 : 10 mm^2.

8. 100 m : 1 km.

9. 7 g : 1 kg.

10. 1 hectare : 100 m^2.

EXERCISES 7B

Express each of the following ratios as simply as possible:

1. A length of 9 cm to a length of 24 cm.

2. A speed of 15 km/h to a speed of 35 km/h.

3. A speed of 15 km/h to a speed of 40 m/sec.

4. A cost of 80 new pence per kg to a cost of 72 new pence per kg.

5. A cost of 2 new pence per g to a cost of £1·68 per kg.

6. £3·12½ : £4·37½.

7. 1 km : 82 m.

8. 20 m : 1 km.

9. 140 g : 1 kg.

10. 15 new pence per g : £4 per kg.

Proportional parts

Three quantities A, B, C of the same kind may be expressed as ratios in the following way:

$$A:B:C = 3:4:5.$$

This means that the ratio of A to B is 3 to 4; that of A to C is 3 to 5 and that of B to C is 4 to 5.

The actual values of the quantities A, B, C must be $3k$, $4k$ and $5k$, where k is some number.

Example. A father leaves a legacy of £4500 to be divided between his three sons Arthur, Bernard and Charles in the ratios 3 : 5 : 7. What does each receive?

Method (i). If the money is divided so that Arthur receives 3 equal parts, Bernard 5 equal parts and Charles 7 equal parts, the total must be divided into (3 + 5 + 7) equal parts, or 15 equal parts.

$\frac{1}{15}$ of £4500 = £300.
Arthur receives 3 × £300 = £900.
Bernard receives 5 × £300 = £1500.
Charles receives 7 × £300 = £2100.

Method (ii). Suppose that Arthur receives £$3k$, Bernard £$5k$ and Charles £$7k$.

Then $3k + 5k + 7k = 4500.$

$\therefore\ 15k = 4500 \quad \text{or} \quad k = 300.$

Arthur receives £900, Bernard £1500 and Charles £2100.

EXERCISES 8A

1. The sides of a triangle are in the ratios 4 : 7 : 8 and its perimeter is 38 cm. Find the sides.

2. Divide a line of length 60 cm into three parts whose ratios are 3 : 7 : 10.

3. Divide £5 into two parts so that one is two thirds of the other.

4. Three men provided capitals of £1000, £1500 and £2500 for a business on the understanding that the shares of the profits were proportional to the capital provided. If the profits were £350, what should each receive?

5. If A is half as old again as B and B is half as old again as C and the sum of their three ages is 114 years, find their ages.

6. A sum of money worth £13 consists of an equal number of coins worth 50 new pence, 10 new pence and 5 new pence. How many coins of each kind are there?

7. Divide £140 between A, B and C so that A has twice as much as B and B has twice as much as C.

8. Archie does as much work in three hours as Bill does in four hours. Bill's son works half as fast as Bill. If the three working together are paid £8·50, how much should each receive?

9. If $p : q = 2 : 3$ and $q : r = 4 : 7$, find $p : q : r$.

10. If Alice deserves twice as many marks as Brenda and Brenda deserves half as many marks as Catharine, how many does each receive when their total marks are 125?

EXERCISES 8B

1. Divide 246 in the ratios $1\frac{1}{2} : 2 : 3\frac{1}{3}$.

2. A father leaves £1500 to be divided between his three sons in the ratios $\frac{1}{2} : \frac{1}{3} : \frac{1}{6}$. How much does each receive?

3. Three club servants agree to divide their Christmas fund in the ratios of their ages, which are 45 years, 48 years and 51 years. If the sum collected is £12, how much does each receive?

4. If the perimeter of a triangle is 36 cm and the ratios of the sides are 3 : 4 : 5, what is the length of each side?

5. Leonard is half as old as Martin and Martin is half as old again as Norman. The sum of their ages is 91 years. How old is Leonard?

6. A sum of money worth £13·65 consists of an equal number of coins worth 50 new pence, 10 new pence and 5 new pence. How many of each kind are there?

7. Divide £21 into two parts so that one is $\frac{3}{4}$ of the other.

8. Divide £15 between Jack, Jill, George and Georgina so that each boy has twice as much as each girl.

9. If Mark lends £400 for 9 months, Peter lends £300 for 8 months and the total interest paid is £25, how much should each receive?

10. If $x:y = 3\frac{1}{2}:2\frac{1}{3}$ and $y:z = 1\frac{1}{4}:2\frac{1}{7}$, find $x:y:z$.

PERCENTAGE

Suppose that, in a certain school, $\frac{2}{5}$ of the pupils are girls. The ratio of the number of girls in the school to the total number of pupils is 2 : 5 or 40 : 100. On the average, of every 100 pupils, 40 are girls and this fact may be more easily expressed by stating that 40 per cent (or 40%) of the pupils are girls. A percentage is simply a ratio in which the second number is arranged to be 100.

40% is equivalent to the ratio 40 : 100 or 2 : 5.
40% is equivalent to the fraction $\frac{40}{100}$ or $\frac{2}{5}$.
40% is equivalent to the decimal 0·4.

In the example we have considered, it is worth noting that 40% of the pupils in the school are girls and so the remaining 60% must be boys.

To express one quantity as a percentage of another quantity of the same kind, first express it as a fraction of the second quantity and then multiply by 100.

Some of the common percentages should be immediately associated with the fractions corresponding. For example,

75% is $\frac{3}{4}$;
$66\frac{2}{3}$% is $\frac{2}{3}$;
50% is $\frac{1}{2}$;
$33\frac{1}{3}$% is $\frac{1}{3}$;
25% is $\frac{1}{4}$;
$12\frac{1}{2}$% is $\frac{1}{8}$;
10% is $\frac{1}{10}$;
5% is $\frac{1}{20}$.

Example. In a town of 4280 inhabitants, there were 56 births during 1964. Find the percentage birth rate.

The percentage rate is $\frac{56}{4280} \times 100 = \frac{560}{428} = 1{\cdot}31\%$ (to 3 sig. fig.).

EXERCISES 9A

Express statements **1** to **6** in the form of a percentage.

1. 29 people out of 82 die before reaching the age of 45.

2. 5 eggs are bad in a box of 144.

3. Income tax is charged at £0·47½ in the pound.

4. The rates in a certain town are 74 new pence in the pound.

5. In a school of 960 pupils, 42 are absent.

6. The interest on £125 is £5·50.

7. 30% of the inhabitants of a town are men and 32% are women. What is the percentage of children?

8. A man spends 12% of his income on rent and 52% on food. What percentage of his income is left?

9. Express $\frac{3}{8}$ as a percentage.

10. What is 15% of £28·50?

EXERCISES 9B

Express statements **1** to **6** in the form of a percentage.

1. In a town of 42,500 there are 504 births in a year.

2. A man has a weekly income of £8·50 and spends £3·87$\frac{1}{2}$ on food.

3. A boy has 480 cigarette cards and gives 25 away.

4. A tax of 17$\frac{1}{2}$ new pence in the pound.

5. A rate of 91$\frac{1}{2}$ new pence in the pound.

6. In a room of area 216 m^2 there is a carpet of area 152 m^2.

7. At an election 42% vote Conservative, 37% vote Labour and the rest vote Liberal. What percentage vote Liberal?

8. Express 0·042 as a percentage.

9. What is 12$\frac{1}{2}$% of £17?

10. What percentage is £3·75 of £42·50?

Percentage gain and loss

If a man buys a watch for £10 and sells it for £7·50 he has lost £2·50. This loss is incurred on a capital outlay of £10 and his percentage loss is $\frac{£2{\cdot}50}{£10} \times 100 = 25\%$.

N.B. Percentage gain or loss is always expressed in terms of the cost price.

$$\text{Percentage gain} = \frac{\text{actual gain}}{\text{cost price}} \times 100.$$

$$\text{Percentage loss} = \frac{\text{actual loss}}{\text{cost price}} \times 100.$$

$$\text{Percentage error} = \frac{\text{actual error}}{\text{true value}} \times 100.$$

Percentage gain

A gain of 30% means that what was originally 100 is now 130.

The ratio of the new value to the old = 130 : 100.
The ratio of the new value to the gain = 130 : 30.
The ratio of the old value to the gain = 100 : 30.

Percentage loss

A loss of 30% means that what was originally 100 is now 70.

The ratio of the new value to the old = 70 : 100.
The ratio of the new value to the loss = 70 : 30.
The ratio of the old value to the loss = 100 : 30.

N.B. A gain of x% means that the new value is $\frac{100 + x}{100}$ of the old.

A loss of x% means that the new value is $\frac{100 - x}{100}$ of the old.

Examples are most easily worked by considering the ratio of the two quantities involved.

Example 1. A man sells a car for £420 at a gain of 5%. What did it cost him?

Cost price : selling price = 100 : 105.
Cost price = $\frac{100}{105}$ of selling price
= $\frac{100}{105} \times$ £420 = £400.

Example 2. A man receives 10% discount for cash and pays £63·45. What discount does he receive?

The ratio of the discount to the original price = 10 : 100.
The ratio of the discount to the cash price is 10 : 90.
Therefore the discount is $\frac{10}{90}$ of the cash price
= $\frac{10}{90} \times$ £63·45
= £7·05.

EXERCISES 10A

1. A man bought a car for £800 and sold it for £640. Find his loss per cent.

2. I buy eggs at 2 new pence each and sell for $2\frac{1}{2}$ new pence. Find my gain per cent.

3. A shopkeeper lost 30% by selling an article for £1·40. What did he lose?

4. An article costing £5 is sold at a gain of $12\frac{1}{2}$%. Find the selling price.

5. A dealer gains £4 when he sells an article to gain 8%. What is the selling price?

6. A line 8 cm long is measured as 8·04 cm. What is the percentage error?

7. A shopkeeper sells a carpet for £72 and gains 20%. What did it cost him?

8. A shopkeeper buys a desk for £25 and sells it for £28. What is his gain per cent?

9. A professional sells a golf bag for £5·50 and gains 10%. Find the cost to the professional.

10. I am 10% older than my wife. My wife is x% younger than I am. Find x.

EXERCISES 10B

1. I bought a car for £650 and sold it for £520. Find my loss per cent.

2. An increase in wages of 8% makes the weekly wage bill of a firm £432. What is the amount of the increase?

3. Coal has increased in price from £8·80 per tonne to £12·10 per tonne. Find the percentage increase.

4. A shopkeeper gains £1·75 by selling an article for £6·25. What is his percentage gain?

5. A shopkeeper gains 8% by selling a table for £27. What did it cost him?

6. A sells to B at a gain of 20%; B sells to C at the price A paid. What does B lose as a percentage?

7. At a sale, goods are marked down by 5 new pence in the pound. What was the original price of an article marked £2·85?

8. A television set is sold for £61·25 to gain $22\frac{1}{2}$%. What is the actual gain?

9. The price of a share rose 25% yesterday and fell 25% today. What is the total rise or fall per cent?

10. Soap before the war was $2\frac{1}{2}d.$ per tablet. It is now 3 new pence per tablet. Find the percentage increase in the price.

Worked Examples

Example 1. A shopkeeper marks his goods to gain 35%. He allows 10% discount for cash. Find his percentage profit on a cash transaction.

Method (i). Marked price : cost price $= 135 : 100$.
Cash price : marked price $= 90 : 100$.

Therefore the cash price $= \frac{90}{100}$ of the marked price
and the marked price $= \frac{135}{100}$ of the cost price.
So the cash price $= \frac{90}{100} \times \frac{135}{100}$ of the cost price

$$= \frac{121 \cdot 5}{100} \text{ of the cost price.}$$

The cash price : cost price $= 121\frac{1}{2} : 100$.

His gain per cent is $21\frac{1}{2}$.

Method (ii). Goods costing £100 are marked at £135.
Discount at 10% ($\frac{1}{10}$ of £135) is £13·50.
The cash price is £121·50.

His gain per cent is $21\frac{1}{2}$.

Example 2. A man buys eggs at $27\frac{1}{2}$ new pence a score. He finds that 10% of the eggs are unsaleable but sells the rest at 30 new pence a dozen. Find his percentage profit.

Method (i). Choose any convenient number of eggs and work with this number. Suppose he buys 440 eggs.
Cost of 440 eggs is

$$22 \times 27\tfrac{1}{2} \text{ new pence} = £6{\cdot}05.$$

He sells $440 - 44$ eggs $= 396$ or 33 dozen.

The selling price of the eggs is

$$33 \times 30 \text{ new pence} = £9{\cdot}90.$$

His gain is £3·85 on an outlay of £6·05.

$$\text{His percentage gain} = \frac{£3{\cdot}85}{£6{\cdot}05} \times 100$$

$$= \frac{385}{605} \times 100$$

$$= \frac{700}{11} = 63{\cdot}6 \text{ (to 3 sig. fig.).}$$

(440 was chosen because, after 10% reduction, it is divisible by 12.)

Method (*ii*). Suppose he buys x eggs.

The cost price is $\frac{27\frac{1}{2}x}{20}$ new pence.

He sells $\frac{9x}{10}$ eggs.

The selling price is $\frac{9x}{10} \times \frac{30}{12}$ new pence.

Therefore

$$\frac{\text{selling price}}{\text{cost price}} = \frac{9x \times 30 \times 20}{10 \times 12 \times 27\frac{1}{2}x} = \frac{9 \times 30 \times 20}{12 \times 275}$$

$$= \frac{18}{11} = 1{\cdot}636.$$

His gain per cent is 63·6 (to 3 sig. fig.).

Example 3. A motorist reduces his annual distance travelled by x% when the price of petrol is increased by y%. Find the increase per cent in his petrol bill.

Suppose his original distance was A km and the original price of petrol B new pence a litre. His original petrol bill was $\frac{AB}{M}$ new pence annually, where M is the number of km travelled on 1 litre of petrol.

His new distance is $\frac{100 - x}{100}A$ km and the new price of petrol $\frac{100 + y}{100}B$ new pence a litre.

His new annual bill in new pence is

$$\frac{(100 - x)(100 + y)}{100.100}\frac{AB}{M}.$$

Therefore

$$\frac{\text{New charge}}{\text{Old charge}} = \frac{(100 - x)(100 + y)}{100.100}$$

$$= \frac{10{,}000 - 100x + 100y - xy}{10{,}000}$$

$$= 1 + \frac{y - x}{100} - \frac{xy}{10{,}000}.$$

The new charge is $100\left(1 + \frac{y - x}{100} - \frac{xy}{10{,}000}\right)$% of the old charge.

The percentage increase is $y - x - \frac{xy}{100}$.

EXERCISES 11: MISCELLANEOUS

1. In making a television set, the costs for labour and materials are in the ratio of 3 : 2. The manufacturer sells for £75 to make a gain of 25% on his outlay. What is the cost of the materials for the set?

2. A legacy of £6000 is to be divided between Alfred, Arthur and Anne in the ratios 1 : 2 : 4, but first death duties of 12½% must be paid. What does each receive?

3. Of the total runs made by his side during the season, Harry made 6% and Bill 11%. If Bill scored 120 runs more than Harry, how many runs did Bill make during the season?

4. A bookseller makes a profit of 20% by selling a certain book for 30 new pence. When he has sold 90% of his stock, he finds he has to sell the rest at a sale price of 20 new pence each. What percentage profit does he make on the transaction?

5. A dealer buys 30 wireless sets, all at the same price. He sells 20 of them at a profit of 16%, and has to sell the remaining 10 at a loss of 4%. What is the percentage profit on the deal?

6. The radius of a circle is increased from 10·0 to 10·4 cm. Find the percentage increase in its area.

7. The radius of a sphere is increased from 10·0 to 10·4 cm. Find the percentage increase in its volume.

8. For an examination, 1200 of the candidates were boys. If 50% of the boys and 40% of the girls were successful, find the number of girl candidates, given that 46% of the total number of candidates were successful.

9. By selling an article for £5·35, a shopkeeper gains 7%. What should the selling price be for a profit of 15%?

10. A motorist's cost for petrol and oil is in the ratio 15 : 1. An increase of 6% in the price of petrol and 4% in the price of oil increases his annual bill for running costs by £4·70. Find his annual bill for petrol before the increase.

11. Salmon sells his goods at the prices marked in his window. Barker allows 10% reduction from the marked price, which means that he sells for £99 goods that Salmon sells for £100. What price does Barker mark an article which Salmon sells for £5?

12. I sell 12 eggs at the price for which I buy 20 eggs. What is my profit per cent?

13. When the price of petrol is increased by 5%, a driver reduces his annual distance travelled by 5%. As a consequence, he finds that he saves 20 new pence on his annual petrol bill. What was his annual petrol bill before the increase?

14. A greengrocer sells potatoes at 4 new pence a kg, which should give him a profit of 20%. To turn the scales he finds he actually gives 1·1 kg when he sells 1 kg. Find his real percentage profit.

15. Brown sold his house to Smith at a profit of 10%. Smith sold it to Robinson at a gain of 5%. Robinson paid £310 more for the house than Brown paid. What did Brown pay?

16. A circle is inscribed in a square. Express the area of the circle as a percentage of the area of the square.

17. A shopkeeper buys eggs at 15 new pence a score. He finds $\frac{1}{4}$ of them are unsaleable but sells the rest at 24 new pence a dozen. Find his profit per cent.

18. If a shopkeeper's weekly takings increase from £33 to £35·75 find the percentage increase. If he wishes to increase his profit by a further 5%, what must he aim to take?

19. A wholesaler sells goods to a retailer at a profit of $33\frac{1}{3}$%. The retailer sells to the customer at a profit of 50%. Express the price the customer paid as a percentage of the cost to the wholesaler.

20. A wholesaler sells goods to a retailer at a profit of 20%. The retailer sells to the customer, who pays 80% more than the cost to the wholesaler. Find the retailer's percentage profit.

21. The cost of manufacturing a car is made up of three items: cost of materials, labour and overheads. In 1967, the cost of these items were in the ratio 4 : 3 : 2. In 1968, the cost of materials rose by 10%, the cost of labour increased by 8% but the overheads reduced by 5%. Find the increase per cent in the price of a car.

22. An alloy is formed by mixing metal A with metal B so that the ratio of their volumes is 6 : 5. The specific gravity of A is 8·4 and that of B is 9·6. Find the percentage mass of metal A in the alloy.

23. The lorries belonging to a company are valued at £14,500. Each year 12% of the value is written off for depreciation. Find the value of the lorries at the end of 2 years.

24. A dealer sells a car for £770 at a profit of 40%. Find what he paid for the car and express his profit as a percentage of the selling price.

25. The purchase tax on a certain article sold for £6·30 is 50%. The retailer's profit is 40%. Find the cost to the retailer.

26. If $3\frac{1}{3}$% of a sum of money is £2·40, find $3\frac{3}{4}$% of the sum.

27. A shopkeeper marks his goods to gain 45% but allows 5% discount for cash. By selling a wireless set, he makes a profit of £18·87$\frac{1}{2}$ on a cash deal. Find what the shopkeeper paid for the set.

28. A man bought 12 hens at 75 new pence each. During a year he obtained from them 2400 eggs which he sold at 20 new pence a dozen. The cost of feeding them for the year was £15. At the end of the year he sold the 10 surviving hens at $62\frac{1}{2}$ new pence each. Find his percentage profit.

29. The cost of printing a book was £1250 for 4000 copies. The publisher sold to a bookshop at a profit of 15% and the bookseller sold the book at $52\frac{1}{2}$ new pence. Find the bookseller's profit per cent.

30. A dealer buys 100 oranges for £1. He is unable to sell 4 of the oranges but sells the rest at $22\frac{1}{2}$ new pence a dozen. Find his percentage profit and the price per dozen at which he should have sold them to have gained 8% more.

31. Death duties of 20% are paid on a legacy of £4500. The eldest son takes 50%, the second son 30%, and the youngest the remainder. What percentage of the original legacy does the youngest son receive?

32. Two blends of tea costing 35 new pence and 40 new pence per kg respectively are mixed in the proportion of 2 : 3 by mass. The mixture is sold at 60 new pence per kg. Find the gain per cent.

33. If a man runs a kilometre in 3 minutes dead, express his speed as a percentage of the speed of a train running at 80 km/h. If man and train both decrease their speeds by 5%, express the speed of the man now as a percentage of the new speed of the train.

34. Two partners Smith and Brown invest £3000 and £1800 respectively in a business. It is agreed that Brown should take 30% of the profits for running the business and that the remaining profit should be divided between them in the ratio of the capital investments. Find what percentage of the profits Smith receives.

35. A train is scheduled to go a certain distance in a certain time. Owing to stoppages, the train driver estimates that he must cover the distance in 75% of the scheduled time. By what percentage must he increase his speed?

4

SIMPLE AND COMPOUND INTEREST

Simple Interest

WHEN money is lent, the lender expects the borrower to pay for the use of the money. The amount of money lent is called the **Principal** and the charge made for lending it is called the **Interest.** Interest on money borrowed is paid at definite intervals (monthly, half-yearly or yearly) and the money is said to be lent at simple interest. Simple interest is obviously proportional to the amount lent and will be the same amount on a given principal during equal intervals of time.

Compound Interest

If the interest, when it falls due, is not paid direct to the lender but is added to the amount borrowed, then the principal will increase with the time. When money is lent at simple interest, assuming no repayment, the principal is constant. When the principal is increased each year (or at other intervals) by the addition of the interest, the money is said to be lent at **Compound Interest** and since the principal increases, the annual interest will also increase. The total sum owed after any interval of time (i.e. the new principal) is called the **Amount.**

The following abbreviations are traditional and will be used throughout the chapter:

P stands for principal;
I stands for interest;
A stands for amount;
R stands for rate per cent per annum;
T stands for the time in years.

SIMPLE INTEREST

Calculation of Simple Interest

Interest is usually expressed as a percentage of the principal. The interest is obviously proportional to the principal and to the rate of interest per annum. It is also proportional to the time. If money is lent at 4% per annum for 3 years, the total interest paid during that time will be 12% of the principal. Similarly if money is lent at $R\%$ per annum for T years, the interest is $RT\%$ of the principal.

$$\therefore I = RT\% \text{ of } P$$

$$= \frac{RT}{100} \text{ of } P;$$

and $$I = \frac{PRT}{100}.$$

This formula, by simple algebraic manipulation, may be used to express any one of I, P, R, T in terms of the other letters.

We get $$P = \frac{100I}{RT};$$

$$R = \frac{100I}{PT};$$

and $$T = \frac{100I}{PR}.$$

Example 1. Find the simple interest on £325 in 5 years at 3% per annum.

$$I = \frac{PRT}{100} = £\frac{325 \times 5 \times 3}{100} = £\frac{195}{4} = £48{\cdot}75$$

Example 2. Find at what rate per annum simple interest £525 will amount to £588 in 3 years.

$$I = A - P = £588 - £525 = £63.$$

$$R = \frac{100I}{PT} = \frac{100 \times 63}{525 \times 3} = \frac{4 \times 63}{21 \times 3} = 4\%.$$

To find the principal, given the amount

None of these formulae applies, if the amount and not the principal is given.

Example. A sum of money invested at 3% per annum simple interest amounts after 4 years to £280. Find the sum invested.

The interest in 4 years is 12% of the principal.
The amount is therefore 112% of the principal.

$$\therefore 112\% \text{ of the principal} = £280$$

and $$\text{the principal} = \tfrac{100}{112} \text{ of } £280 = £250.$$

EXERCISES 12A

1. Find the simple interest on £680 in 4 years at 5% per annum.

2. Find the simple interest on £121 in 5 years at 3% per annum.

3. If the simple interest on £280 in 4 years is £39·20, find the rate per cent per annum.

4. If the simple interest on £500 for 3 years is £37·50, find the rate per cent per annum.

5. If the simple interest on £220 at 4% per annum is £44, find the time.

6. If the simple interest on £720·50 at 4% per annum is £72·05, find the time.

7. If the simple interest on a sum of money invested at 3% per annum for $2\frac{1}{2}$ years is £123, find the principal.

8. Find the principal which amounts at simple interest to £218 in 2 years at $4\frac{1}{2}$% per annum.

9. Find the principal which amounts at simple interest to £530 in 3 years at 2% per annum.

10. Find the principal which amounts at simple interest to £585·80 in 4 years at 4% per annum.

EXERCISES 12B

1. Find the simple interest on £505 in 4 years at 4% per annum.

2. Find the simple interest on £220 in $2\frac{1}{2}$ years at 4% per annum.

3. If the simple interest on £192 in $2\frac{1}{2}$ years is £12, find the rate per cent per annum.

4. If the simple interest on £205 in 4 years is £28·70, find the rate per cent per annum.

5. If £210 amounts to £235·20 at 3% per annum, find the time.

6. If £168 amounts to £189 at 5% per annum, find the time.

7. If the simple interest on a sum of money invested at $2\frac{1}{2}$% per annum for 6 years is £127·20, find the sum.

8. Find the principal which amounts at simple interest to £840 in 3 years at 4% per annum.

9. Find the principal which amounts at simple interest to £103·70 in $2\frac{1}{2}$ years at $2\frac{1}{2}$% per annum.

10. Find the principal which amounts at simple interest to £597·50 in $3\frac{1}{4}$ years at 6% per annum.

COMPOUND INTEREST

Calculation of compound interest

In calculating the compound interest, the principal at the beginning of each year must be found. The work is best set out in tabular form. There is a useful device for finding 4% (for example) of a sum of money. Multiply the sum of money by 4, at the same time moving the decimal point two places to the left. This move of the decimal point is equivalent to division by 100.

Example 1. Find the compound interest on £450 in 3 years at 4% per annum.

Principal for first year	=	£450
Interest for first year	=	18
Principal for second year	=	468
Interest for second year	=	18·72
Principal for third year	=	486·72
Interest for third year	=	19·4688
Final amount	=	506·1888
Original amount	=	450
Interest	=	£56·1888

The interest to the nearest new penny is £56·19.

Example 2. Find the compound interest on £285·38 in 4 years at $2\frac{1}{2}$% per annum.

$2\frac{1}{2}$% is $\frac{1}{40}$ and so the amount at the beginning of any one year is divided by 40 to give the interest for that year.

To find the interest to the nearest new penny, you must get your final result correct to 2 decimal places of £1. To ensure this keep 4 decimal places in the working and then correct to 2.

Principal for the first year	=	£285·38
Interest for the first year	=	7·1345
Principal for the second year	=	292·5145
Interest for the second year	=	7·3129
Principal for the third year	=	299·8274
Interest for the third year	=	7·4957
		307·3231

Principal for the fourth year	=	£307·3231
Interest for the fourth year	=	7·6831
Final amount	=	315·0062
Original amount		285·38
Interest	=	29·6262
	=	£29·62 (to 2 decimal places)

The interest to the nearest new penny is £29·62.

Formula for compound interest

Supposing that the rate of interest is 4% per annum, the amount at the end of any particular year will be 104% of the amount at the beginning of that year. At the end of the first year, the amount is $1{\cdot}04P$ where P is the principal; at the end of the second year, the amount is $(1{\cdot}04)^2P$ and so on. Similarly if the rate of interest is r% per annum, the multiplying factor is $\left(1 + \frac{r}{100}\right)$. The amount after n years is $P\left(1 + \frac{r}{100}\right)^n$.

$$\therefore A = P\left(1 + \frac{r}{100}\right)^n.$$

This formula may be used in place of the tabular method. It is seldom permissible to use logarithms in the calculation, however, as accuracy to more than 3 significant figures is generally required.

EXERCISES 13A

(Give your answers to the nearest new penny)

1. Find the compound interest on £200 in 3 years at 4% per annum.

2. Find the compound interest on £360 in 4 years at 3% per annum.

3. Find the compound interest on £186·61 in 2 years at $2\frac{1}{2}$% per annum.

4. Find the compound interest on £370·50 in 3 years at 4% per annum.

5. Find the compound interest on £300 in 3 years at 3% per annum.

EXERCISES 13B

(Give your answers to the nearest new penny.)

1. Find the compound interest on £200 in 4 years at 5% per annum.

2. Find the compound interest on £280 in 2 years at 3% per annum.

3. Find the compound interest on £312·78 in 3 years at $2\frac{1}{2}\%$ per annum.

4. Find the compound interest on £181·31 in 2 years at 6% per annum.

5. Find the compound interest on £408·38 in 3 years at 3% per annum.

Periodical borrowing or repayment

If the principal varies due to fresh borrowing or repayment at the end of a year, the amount at the beginning of each year must be calculated separately and the interest for this amount worked out. The method is illustrated in the following examples.

Example 1. A man invests £100 on January 1st of each year at 4% per annum. Find the total amount of his investment at the end of 3 years.

He invests		£100
Interest for first year	=	4
Value at end of first year	=	104
He invests another £100		100
Value at beginning of second year	=	204
Interest for second year	=	8·16
Value at end of second year	=	212·16
He now invests		100
Value at beginning of third year	=	312·16
Interest for third year	=	12·4864
Value after three years	=	324·6464

The amount of his investment, to the nearest new penny, is £321·65.

Example 2. A man borrows £600 from a corporation at 3% per annum interest. He repays £200 at the end of each year. How much does he still owe after the third repayment?

He borrows		£600
Interest for the first year	=	18
Amount now owing is		618
He repays		200
Amount owing at the beginning of second year	=	418
Interest for the second year	=	12·54
Amount owing after this is		430·54
He repays		200
Amount owing at beginning of third year	=	230·54
Interest for the third year	=	6·9162
Amount now owing		237·4562
He repays		200
Amount owing after third repayment	=	£37·4562

The amount still owing is £37·46, to the nearest new penny.

EXERCISES 14: MISCELLANEOUS

1. A town borrows £20,000 at 5% per annum and repays £5000 at the end of each year. How much is still owing after the fourth repayment?

2. The value of a car depreciates by 12% each year. A man pays £800 for his car. What will be its value after 3 years? Give your answer to the nearest pound.

3. Find to the nearest pound the amount of £100 invested at 4% per annum compound interest after 20 years.

4. A man invests £1000 at 4% per annum. The interest is invested at the same rate. What is the value of his holding after 4 years?

5. A saving certificate costing 75 new pence is worth £1·02½ at the end of 10 years. To what rate per cent per annum compound interest is this equivalent?

6. How long would it take a sum of money to double itself at 5% per annum compound interest?

7. A bank lent £275 to a client at 4% per annum and £220 to another client at 5½% per annum. What is the bank's average percentage return on its capital?

8. A man borrows £700 at 4% per annum. He repays £200 each year. Find during which year the debt will be cleared.

9. A father leaves a legacy of £5000 to his son. After death duties of 10% have been paid, the money is invested for 4 years at 3% compound interest. What is now the value of the son's holding to the nearest pound?

10. A man borrowed £100 at $6\frac{1}{2}$% per annum and had to pay £2·14 interest when he repaid the loan. For how many days did he borrow the money?

11. Smith and Brown invest £165 and £192 respectively at the same rate of interest. When the value of Smith's holding is £184·80, what is the value of Brown's?

12. £100 invested at compound interest amounts to £130·50 after 5 years. What is its value after another 5 years?

13. In order to pay his son's school fees, a father invests £1000 at 4% per annum. Assuming that the money is invested at the beginning of the boy's school career and that £300 is withdrawn at the end of each year for the school fees, find how much is left after 3 years.

14. A man buys a house for £2500 and after allowing for annual repairs of £40, wishes to make a 5% per annum return on his money. What should be the annual rent of the house? The tenant pays rates which are $\frac{1}{5}$ of the rent. He spends £400 on furniture and sublets to get a clear return of 6% on his capital outlay. At what annual charge does he sublet?

15. How long will it take a sum of money invested at 5% per annum simple interest to increase in value by 40%?

16. Find the simple interest on £340·62½ in 3 years at $4\frac{1}{2}$% per annum.

17. Find the simple interest on £280 for $3\frac{1}{2}$ years at $3\frac{1}{2}$% per annum.

18. A sum of £312·50 is invested at 4% per annum simple interest. After how many years will this sum amount to £500?

19. The population of a town increases by 4% each year. If the population at one census is 42 500 what will it be at the next census, 4 years later?

20. Find the sum of money which yields £7·15 simple interest in 4 years at $2\frac{3}{4}$% per annum.

21. A man buys a house valued at £3600. He pays 30% of its value immediately, £1200 eighteen months later and the remainder after a further eighteen months. Simple interest is charged at $4\frac{1}{2}$% per annum. Find how much he pays altogether.

22. Find the sum of money which will amount to £826 at $4\frac{1}{2}$% per annum simple interest in 4 years.

23. If £400 invested for 5 years yields a simple interest of £38, what will be the interest on £240 invested at the same rate for $7\frac{1}{2}$ years?

24. Machinery worth £5200 was bought 3 years ago. What is its present value if depreciation is allowed for at 15% per annum?

25. Machinery valued at £4800 is revalued 3 years later at £2800. To what annual percentage depreciation is this equivalent?

26. Find the sum of money which invested at 4% per annum compound interest amounts after 5 years to £120.

27. A moneylender charges $1\frac{1}{2}$ new pence per week interest on every £1 borrowed. To what annual rate per cent is this equivalent and what would be the interest on £1000 in 4 years at this rate?

28. A sum of money at compound interest increases from £x to £y in t years. What will be the amount of the investment after a further period of $3t$ years?

29. A sum of £100 is invested at the rate of 4% per annum. Find the increase in interest during a year if the interest is calculated each month instead of at the end of the year.

30. A man earns £2400 and invests 15% of it each year at 5% per annum simple interest. What is his total interest in the first three years?

31. A man invests £100 each year at 3% per annum compound interest. What is the value of his investment just before he invests the fourth £100?

32. A sum of money invested at 4% per annum simple interest amounts after 5 years to £720. What would be the amount of the same sum invested at $3\frac{1}{2}$% per annum for 6 years?

33. Find the simple interest on £450 at 3% per annum for 2 years 8 months.

34. A sum of money invested at 4% per annum simple interest amounts after 5 years to £960. How long will it take the same sum to amount to £1080 at $3\frac{1}{2}$% per annum simple interest?

35. The simple interest on a sum of money invested for 4 years at $3\frac{1}{2}$% per annum exceeds the simple interest on the same sum invested at $4\frac{1}{2}$% per annum for 3 years by £1·34. What sum was invested?

5

RATES, TAXES AND STOCKS AND SHARES

RATES

EVERY flat, house and office in a town is given by the Inland Revenue Valuation Office what is called a 'rateable value'. This rateable value depends both upon the size of the building and on its position. The rates of a town, which are fixed each year to bring in the amount of money estimated to be necessary, are levied at so much in the pound of this rateable value. The money brought in by the rates is used for the administration of the town to cover all costs of such things as education, road sweeping, town parks, town sanitation, libraries and so on. A new penny rate means a charge of 1 new penny in the pound on the rateable value of the town. The income of a town is changed as necessary by altering the rate and not the rateable value, although this may be reviewed from time to time.

Example 1. Find the annual rates at $74\frac{1}{2}$ new pence in the £ on a house whose rateable value is £68.

Annual rates are $68 \times 74\frac{1}{2}$ new pence.

$$68 \times 74\tfrac{1}{2} = 5066.$$

The annual rates are therefore 5066 new pence or £50·66.

Example 2. The rateable value of a town is £43 840. The council has to estimate for an increase of £1560 in education costs. What increase in the rates (to the nearest half new penny) is necessary?

£43 840 is the equivalent of a rate of 100 new pence.

£1560 is the equivalent of a rate of $\dfrac{100 \times 1560}{43\,840}$ new pence

$$= \frac{975}{274} \text{ new pence} = 3{\cdot}56 \text{ new pence.}$$

To the nearest half new penny, the increase necessary is $3\frac{1}{2}$ new pence.

EXERCISES 15A

1. Find the rates at 86 new pence in the pound on a house of rateable value £54.

2. Find the rates of 92 new pence in the pound on a house of rateable value £78.

3. The rateable value of a town is £284 000 and its expenditure is £212 000. What are the rates, to the nearest new penny?

4. The expenditure of a town is £327 400 and its rates are 93 new pence in the pound. The cost of the library is £12 400. What rate is necessary for the library's upkeep?

5. The annual rates at 83 new pence in the pound on a house are £43·16. What is the rateable value of the house?

EXERCISES 15B

1. Find the rates at 94 new pence in the pound on a house of rateable value £94.

2. Find the rates at $89\frac{1}{2}$ new pence in the pound on a house of rateable value £66.

3. The rateable value of a town is £426 000 and its annual expenditure is £327 500. What rate must the town declare?

4. To raise an income of £417 600 a town declares a rate of 87 new pence in the pound. What is the rateable value of the town?

5. The annual rates at 73 new pence in the pound on a house are £52·56. What is the rateable value?

INCOME TAX

As distinct from each individual town or borough, the country as a whole must tax its subjects in order to produce income to pay for the fighting services, the civil service and many other major expenditures. Revenue is collected through many different taxes—customs and excise, purchase tax and entertainment tax, for example—but the largest revenue producer is income tax.

Each person in receipt of an income above a certain minimum has to pay part of it to the Government as a tax. Income tax is quoted as a percentage, e.g. $47\frac{1}{2}\%$, which means that of every pound of taxable income, $47\frac{1}{2}$ new pence must be paid as tax. The regulations for income tax vary from year to year and in any problem full details of how the tax is levied would be given. In one recent year, an allowance of two-ninths of the earned income was given. Certain tax-free allowances are usually made and, in that year, a personal allowance of £120 for a single person or £210 for a married person, with an extra £85 for each child was allowed. After these allowances have been deducted from the income, the residue is called the taxable income. The first £100 of this was taxable at the rate of $12\frac{1}{2}\%$, the next £150 at 25%, the next £150 at 35%, and the balance, if any, at 45%.

Let us work out on this basis the tax payable by a married man with two children and earning £945 a year.

Allowances.	$\frac{2}{9}$ of £945 =	£210
	For himself and wife	210
	For two children	170
		£590

Taxable income = £950 − £590 = £360.

Tax on £100 at $12\frac{1}{2}\%$	=	£12·50
Tax on £150 at 25%	=	£37·50
Tax on £110 at 35%	=	£38·50
Tax on £360	=	£88·50

EXERCISES 16A

1. Find the tax at 7% on a taxable income of £820.

2. When tax is at 11%, a man pays a tax of £92·40. What is his taxable income?

3. A single man was given allowances of $\frac{1}{5}$ of his earned income together with £110 personal allowance. Tax was levied at 25% on the first £150 of his taxable income and 50% on the remainder. What tax did he pay on an income of £1200?

4. A man is given £320 allowances on an income of £940. If the standard rate of tax is 40% and he is charged half the standard rate on the first £200 of his taxable income, find the tax payable.

5. A man is allowed $\frac{1}{5}$ of his income 'tax free' and pays 30% on the remainder. If he pays £240 tax, what is his income?

EXERCISES 16B

1. Find the tax at 6% on a taxable income of £780.

2. When income tax is at 8%, a man pays a tax of £40·56. What is his taxable income?

3. A man is given allowances of £280 on an income of £1000. If the standard rate of tax is $37\frac{1}{2}\%$ and he is charged half-rate on the first £250 of his taxable income, find the tax payable.

4. A man is allowed $\frac{1}{6}$ of his income 'tax free' and pays $37\frac{1}{2}\%$ on the remainder. If he pays £150 tax, what is his income?

5. A married man with two children was given personal allowances of £210 for himself and wife together with £85 for each child. He was also allowed $\frac{2}{9}$ of his income tax free. He pays tax at 20% on the first £200 of his income and 40% on the remainder. Find the tax payable if his income is £990.

STOCKS AND SHARES

A private individual often finds it impossible to produce sufficient capital for his business and may make it a public company. He issues shares in the company and invites the public to subscribe for these shares. These shares are issued generally in units of 5 new pence, 10 new pence, 25 new pence, 50 new pence or £1. This unit is called the **nominal value** of the share. At the end of the financial year, the company declares a dividend in the form of a percentage of the nominal value and the shareholder is paid the dividend due on his holding.

The buying and selling of shares is controlled by the Stock Exchange. If the company does well and declares a good dividend, the price of the shares will go up; if the company does not flourish, the quoted price of the shares will go down. The fluctuation in the price of the shares does not change the nominal value of the shares which always stays the same. The stock exchange prices for shares are quoted in most daily newspapers.

Preference and ordinary shares

There are several different types of shares of which the most usual are the preference and the ordinary. A preference share is issued at a fixed percentage—for example, Gaumont-British $5\frac{1}{2}\%$ Preference—and the payment of this dividend is the first charge on the profits of the company. The dividend on an ordinary share is not fixed and is declared by the directors of the company according to the profits made. If the preference dividend takes all or nearly all the profits of the company, the ordinary shareholders may get nothing. On the other hand, in a bumper year the ordinary shareholders may get a much larger dividend than the preference shareholders.

The preference share is therefore a safer holding but not so likely to appreciate (or depreciate) in capital value as is the ordinary share.

Difference between stock and share

If a company issues 25 new penny shares, for example, a subscriber has to buy an exact number of these shares. Government securities, on the other hand, are quoted in terms of £100 nominal value and it is possible to buy any amount of stock required. It is possible to buy, say, £77·60 stock of $3\frac{1}{2}\%$ War Loan.

Nominal value and market value

It is very important to appreciate the difference between nominal value and market value. The dividend of a company is always quoted on the nominal value, and the market value is the price which governs the buying and selling of the shares.

Example 1. David Whitehead 5 new penny shares are quoted at $7\frac{1}{2}$ new pence and declare a dividend of 15%. What does it cost me to buy 4000 shares and what dividend do I expect?

$$\begin{aligned} \text{The cost} &= 4000 \times 7\tfrac{1}{2} \text{ new pence} = £300. \\ \text{The dividend} &= 15\% \text{ of the nominal value} \\ &= \tfrac{15}{100} \text{ of } £200 \\ &= £30. \end{aligned}$$

Example 2. War Loan $3\frac{1}{2}\%$ stock is quoted at $37\frac{1}{2}$. What will be the cost of £400 stock and what dividend is due on that stock?

$$\begin{aligned} \text{Cost of } £400 \text{ stock} &= \tfrac{400}{100} \times £37{\cdot}50 = £150. \\ \text{Dividend} &= \tfrac{400}{100} \times £3\tfrac{1}{2} = £14. \end{aligned}$$

EXERCISES 17A

1. I buy 300 Courtauld shares at £1·80 and sell at £2·$12\frac{1}{2}$. What is my gain?

2. Standard Motor 25 new penny shares stand at $37\frac{1}{2}$ new pence and declare a dividend of 20%. What dividend shall I receive on an investment of £300 cash?

3. Lloyds Bank £1 shares stand at £3·50 and declare a dividend of 15%. What sum must I invest to get a dividend of £15?

4. Gaumont-British $5\frac{1}{2}\%$ Preference shares of £1 nominal value are quoted at £0·$72\frac{1}{2}$. What will be the cost of 200 shares and what dividend is payable on them?

5. $2\frac{1}{2}\%$ Consols are quoted at 65. How much cash must I invest in them to produce a dividend of £50?

6. Imperial Tobacco £1 shares stand at £3·$02\frac{1}{2}$ and declare an interim dividend of $8\frac{1}{2}\%$. What would it cost me to buy 176 shares and what would be my interim dividend?

7. Fairey Aviation £0·50 shares are quoted at £2·10 and pay a dividend of 25%. What dividend shall I get on an investment of £882?

8. A share of nominal value 10 new pence is quoted at 14 new pence and pays 10%. What would be my income on an investment of £280 cash?

9. 4% Victory Loan is quoted at 105. How much cash must I invest to produce a dividend of £40?

10. Cow and Gate 5 new penny shares are quoted at 11 new pence. How many shares can I buy for £550?

EXERCISES 17B

1. I bought enough $3\frac{1}{2}\%$ War Loan at 88 to give me an income of £63. I sell my holding at 93. What is my gain?

2. What income do I get from investing £250 in £0·25 copper shares standing at £0·62½ if they declare a dividend of 24%?

3. How much cash must I invest in a $6\frac{1}{2}\%$ Preference share, nominal value £1, standing at £0·92½ to produce an income of £39?

4. I buy £300 stock standing at 90. When I sell, I make a profit of £51. What do I sell at?

5. A share of nominal value 25 new pence stands at 30 new pence and declares a dividend of 8%. How much cash is needed for a dividend of £18?

6. Barclay's Bank shares are quoted at £2·42½. How many shares can I buy for £388?

7. Foster Clark's £0·50 shares are quoted at £0·42½. If I invest £170, how much shall I gain if I sell at £0·52½?

8. A $4\frac{1}{2}\%$ preference share, of nominal value £1, is quoted at £0·92½. What dividend do I receive from an investment of £370 cash?

9. If I sell £300 4% stock at 90 and reinvest the proceeds in $3\frac{1}{2}\%$ stock at 70, what is my gain in income?

10. I buy 400 shares of nominal value 25 new pence at $32\frac{1}{2}$ new pence. If the dividend declared is 4%, what is the income derived?

The yield

When an investor buys shares, one of the most important factors is the yield—that is the percentage return he gets on the cash invested. If he buys for example $5\frac{1}{2}\%$ preference shares, his yield will be $5\frac{1}{2}\%$ only if the shares stand at par, i.e. at their nominal value. If the shares are higher than their nominal value, his yield will be less than $5\frac{1}{2}\%$; if the shares are lower than the nominal value, his yield will be greater.

Example. Find the yield on $3\frac{1}{2}\%$ War Loan standing at 40.

£40 cash buys £100 stock and so gives $£3\frac{1}{2}$ interest.

$$\therefore \text{ £100 cash gives } \frac{£3\frac{1}{2} \times 100}{40} \text{ interest} = \frac{£35}{4} = £8\tfrac{3}{4}.$$

The yield is $8\frac{3}{4}\%$.

EXERCISES 18A

Find the yield on the following investments:

1. 4% stock at 90.

2. 25 new penny shares quoted at $32\frac{1}{2}$ new pence, when the dividend is 8%.

3. Shares of nominal value 30 new pence quoted at 40 new pence, when the dividend is 10%.

4. 6% stock at 110.

5. £0·50 shares quoted at $£0{\cdot}42\frac{1}{2}$, when the dividend declared is $4\frac{1}{2}\%$.

EXERCISES 18B

Find the yield on the following investments:

1. $3\frac{1}{2}\%$ stock at 75.

2. Shares of nominal value 10 new pence, quoted at $12\frac{1}{2}$ new pence, when the dividend declared is 8%.

3. $5\frac{1}{2}\%$ Preference shares of nominal value £1 quoted at £1·10.

4. 5% stock at 105.

5. £1 shares quoted at $£1{\cdot}12\frac{1}{2}$ when the dividend declared is 9%.

Worked Example

A worked example follows showing how to deal with the finance of a company.

Example. A company has issued 200 000 ordinary shares of £0·10 each and 50 000 4% preference shares of £1 each. In one year, after the company has paid the preference dividend and a dividend of 6% on the ordinary shares, its profits are just sufficient for it to put £2000 to reserve. What are the profits of the company for that year?

Nominal value of preference shares	= £50,000
4% dividend on this capital	= £2000.
Nominal value of ordinary shares	= 200 000 × £0·10
	= £20 000.
6% dividend on this capital	= £1200.
Total dividend	= £3200.
Reserve	= £2000.

∴ Total profits are £5200.

EXERCISES 19: MISCELLANEOUS

1. A man's income is assessed for tax as follows: One sixth of his total earnings and a personal allowance of £290 are deducted. On the next £250, tax is paid at half-rate and on the remainder at full rate. Find the tax paid by a man whose income is £900 when the full rate is 40%.

2. Find the net income of a man from an investment of £500 cash in $2\frac{1}{2}$% Consols at £75 after he has paid income tax at 45%.

3. A man bought 200 shares at £1·75 a share. He received a dividend of £0·$22\frac{1}{2}$ per share and a bonus of one share for every 5 held by him. He sold all his shares at £1·60 each. Find his gain (including his dividend).

4. In a certain year, the income of a married man with two children was £880 and he paid income tax as follows. One fifth of his income was free of tax and a further £170 was free of tax together with additional sums of £60 and £50 for his children. On the first £200 of the remainder, he paid $17\frac{1}{2}$% and on the rest 35%. What tax is payable?

5. A married man with 3 children earns £1200. He is allowed to deduct 20% as earned income and is also allowed a personal allowance of £180 for himself and his wife together with £60 for each child. He then pays 20% on the first £250 of his taxable income and 40% on the remainder. How much tax does he pay?

6. A man can either buy a house for £3500 which he has to borrow at 4% and then pay £45 per annum rates; or he can rent a flat at £3 per week inclusive of rates. Which is the cheaper proposition and by how much per year?

7. A company with a capital of £180 000 makes a profit during the year of £22 000. It places £10 000 to reserve and pays out the rest to shareholders. What is the percentage return on his money of a man who has bought 200 £1 shares at £0·90 each?

8. A man invested £100 in francs and sold them at a profit of 10% when they stood at 12 to the pound. At what price did he buy?

9. A man holds 200 shares in one company paying a dividend of $3\frac{1}{2}$%, the £ shares of the company standing at £0·80; he also holds 400 shares in another company paying a dividend of 6% whose £ shares stand at £1·25. He sells both holdings and reinvests all the money in 5% shares of nominal value £1 standing at £1·10. What is his decrease in annual income?

10. I require £330 cash and to realise it sell some of my holdings of $2\frac{1}{2}$% Consols at 66. How much stock must I sell and what is my loss of income?

11. The capital of a company is £40 000. Last year its income was

£200 000 and after paying all working expenses its net profits were 24% of the capital. This year the gross income increased by 5% but the working expenses increased by 10%. Find the net profits expressed as a percentage of the capital.

12. A man buys francs at the rate of 12 to the pound. He changes the francs into dollars at the rate of 3·75 to the dollar and finally changes the dollars into pounds at the rate of 2 dollars 40 cents to the pound. Find his gain or loss per cent.

13. A man buys 100 ordinary shares in a company at £1·60 each. The company issues one bonus share for every two shares held by him. The price of the shares fell to £1·37½ and he sells his holding. Find his percentage gain.

14. On the first £320 of his income, a man is charged no tax. On the next £280 he pays 22½%, and on the remainder of his income 45%. Find the tax paid by a man with an income of £954.

15. Smith and Brown are partners in a firm. Smith provides £8000 capital and Brown provides £3500. Brown manages the business and receives for doing so 20% of the profits each year. In addition each receives from the profits 4% on the capital provided. Any further profit is divided equally between them. Find the total profits made in a year when Brown receives £100 more than Smith.

16. A man invested £4000 in 3% stock at 80. He sold his holding at 86 and invested the proceeds in £1 shares standing at £1·07½. If the dividend declared on his new holding was 6%, find the change in his annual income.

17. A man holds 5000 shares in a company of nominal value £0·25. They pay a yearly dividend of 16% on which the man pays income tax at 45%. Find his net income from this source.

18. A man lives in a house of rateable value £65. He pays a rent of £1·35 a week and rates at 72½ new pence in the pound. What is the annual cost of the house in rent and rates?

19. A man invests £900 in £0·25 shares standing at £0·22½. The company declares an interim dividend of 3½% and a final dividend for the year of 4½%. What is the net income of the man from this holding if he pays tax at 45%?

20. A man invests £1000 in 3% stock at 75 and another £1000 in 4% stock at 80. What is the average yield on the two holdings?

21. A man invests £1000 in 3½% stock at 80 and another £800 in 5% stock at 120. What is his average yield on the two holdings?

22. A man is allowed £320 of his income tax free. On the rest he pays tax at 45%. If he pays £81 tax, find his gross income.

23. A man is allowed £350 of his income tax free. He pays $22\frac{1}{2}\%$ on the first £200 of his taxable income and 45% on the remainder. If he pays £135 tax, what is his gross income?

24. A man is allowed $\frac{2}{9}$ of his income free of tax together with £250 personal allowance. He pays tax at $22\frac{1}{2}\%$ on the first £250 of his taxable income and 45% on the rest. Find his gross income if the tax payable is £240·75.

25. £1200 is invested partly at 5% per annum and partly at 6% per annum. The interest in one year is £64. How much is invested at 5%?

26. £1800 is invested partly at 5% per annum and partly at $3\frac{1}{2}\%$ per annum. The interest in one year is £75. How much is invested at 5%?

27. At what price would $3\frac{1}{2}\%$ War Loan give a yield of $4\frac{1}{2}\%$?

28. A holder of 250 £1 shares in the Imperial Tobacco Company receives a dividend of $8\frac{1}{2}\%$ together with a bonus of $7\frac{1}{2}$ new pence per share. Tax is deducted on the dividend and bonus at 45 new pence in the pound. What does he receive?

29. A man buys 200 7% preference shares, nominal value £1, at £1·$22\frac{1}{2}$ each. What does he pay for them and what is his net annual income if he pays tax at $32\frac{1}{2}\%$?

30. What net income after deduction of tax at 45% is derived from investing £900 in $3\frac{1}{2}\%$ stock at 54?

ALGEBRA AND CALCULUS

ALGEBRA AND CALCULUS FORMULAE

Factors

$a^2 + 2ab + b^2 = (a + b)^2.$

$a^2 - 2ab + b^2 = (a - b)^2.$

$a^2 - b^2 = (a + b)(a - b).$

$a^2 + b^2$ has no factors.

$a^3 + b^3 = (a + b)(a^2 - ab + b^2).$

$a^3 - b^3 = (a - b)(a^2 + ab + b^2).$

Quadratic Equations

The solutions of $ax^2 + bx + c = 0$ are

$$x = \frac{-b \pm \sqrt{b^2 - 4ac}}{2a}.$$

Indices

$a^m \times a^n = a^{m+n}.$

$a^m \div a^n = a^{m-n}.$

$(a^m)^n = a^{mn}.$

$a^0 = 1.$

$a^{-n} = \frac{1}{a^n}.$

$a^{\frac{p}{q}} = (\sqrt[q]{a})^p.$

Logarithms

$\log x + \log y = \log xy.$

$\log x - \log y = \log \frac{x}{y}.$

$\log x^n = n \log x.$

$\log_b x = \frac{\log_a x}{\log_a b}.$

Arithmetic Progressions

nth term $= a + (n - 1)d.$

Sum to n terms $= \frac{n}{2}\{2a + (n - 1)d\}$ or $\frac{n}{2}(a + l).$

Geometric Progressions

nth term $= ar^{n-1}$.

Sum to n terms $= a\dfrac{1 - r^n}{1 - r}$ or $a\dfrac{r^n - 1}{r - 1}$.

Differentiation

$\dfrac{d}{dx}(\text{constant}) = 0.$

$\dfrac{d}{dx}(kx) = k.$

$\dfrac{d}{dx}(x^2) = 2x.$

$\dfrac{d}{dx}(x^3) = 3x^2.$

$\dfrac{d}{dx}\left(\dfrac{1}{x}\right) = -\dfrac{1}{x^2}.$

$\dfrac{d}{dx}\left(\dfrac{1}{x^2}\right) = -\dfrac{2}{x^3}.$

Velocity $= \dfrac{ds}{dt}.$

Acceleration $= \dfrac{dv}{dt}.$

Integration

$\int k\,dx = kx + C.$

$\int x\,dx = \frac{1}{2}x^2 + C.$

$\int x^2\,dx = \frac{1}{3}x^3 + C.$

The area under a curve $= \int y\,dx.$

Volume of rotation about x-axis $= \pi \int y^2\,dx.$

6

FACTORS

THE product of $(x + 4)$ and $(x + 5)$ is $x^2 + 9x + 20$.

Conversely, the factors of $(x^2 + 9x + 20)$ are $(x + 4)$ and $(x + 5)$.

To factorise an expression, we must find quantities which, when multiplied together, give the original expression.

When factorising, first look for an obvious factor.

Example.

$$ax^2 + 9ax + 20a = a(x^2 + 9x + 20) = a(x + 4)(x + 5).$$

When you have factorised an expression, make sure that none of your factors will factorise further.

Example. $9x^2 - 81 = 9(x^2 - 9) = 9(x + 3)(x - 3).$

There are various methods of factorisation, which are now considered one by one.

(1) Trinomials

A trinomial is a three-termed expression such as $x^2 + 9x + 20$. Other examples are $3x^2 - 2xy - y^2$, $x^4 + 2x^2y + y^2$ and $1 - 3x - 2x^2$. The method of factorisation is that of trial and error.

(a) When the coefficient of x^2 is unity

Example 1. Factorise $x^2 + 9x + 20$.

Look for two numbers whose product is 20 and whose sum is 9. These are obviously 5 and 4. The factors are therefore $(x + 4)(x + 5)$.

Example 2. Factorise $x^2 - 2x - 15$.

Look for two numbers whose product is -15 and whose sum is -2. These numbers are -5 and 3. The factors are $(x - 5)(x + 3)$.

(*b*) *When the coefficient of x^2 is not unity*

Example. Factorise $6x^2 + 11x - 10$.

Try pairs of factors of 6 and pairs of factors of -10, as shown in the following three cases:

6 5	3 5	3 −2
1 −2	2 −2	2 5
$-12 + 5$	$-6 + 10$	$15 - 4$
$= -7$	$= +4$	$= +11$

Cross multiply these numbers and add the two products. Look for an arrangement in which the sum of the products is equal to the co-efficient of x. i.e. $+ 11$. The third arrangement satisfies this condition and the factors are $(3x - 2)(2x + 5)$.

Similarly the factors of $6x^4 + 11x^2y - 10y^2$ are $(3x^2 - 2y)(2x^2 + 5y)$.

EXERCISES 20A

Factorise:

1. $x^2 + 5x + 6$.
2. $x^2 - 8x - 20$.
3. $x^2 - x - 6$.
4. $x^2 - 5x + 6$.
5. $x^2 - 8x + 15$.
6. $x^2 - 4x - 12$.
7. $x^2 + 11x + 18$.
8. $x^4 + 10x^2 + 24$.
9. $x^2 + 4xy + 3y^2$.
10. $x^4 - 4x^2y - 5y^2$.
11. $2x^2 - x - 3$.
12. $2x^2 - xy - 6y^2$.
13. $3x^2 - 7x - 6$.
14. $5x^2 + 17xy + 6y^2$.
15. $6x^2 - 19x + 10$.
16. $6 - x - x^2$.
17. $12 + x - 6x^2$.
18. $2x^2 + 11x + 15$.
19. $2x^2 - x - 15$.
20. $12x^2 + 7x - 10$.

EXERCISES 20B

Factorise:

1. $x^2 + 6x + 8$.
2. $t^2 - 7t - 18$.
3. $u^2 - 5u - 6$.
4. $v^2 + 7v + 10$.
5. $y^2 - 2y - 24$.
6. $x^2 - 10xy - 11y^2$.
7. $x^2 + 10xy + 16y^2$.
8. $x^4 + 5x^2 + 4$.
9. $x^2 + 6xy + 5y^2$.
10. $z^4 - 2z^2x - 8x^2$.
11. $2p^2 - 5p - 7$.
12. $6a^2 + 19ab + 10b^2$.
13. $6l^2 - 17lm + 12m^2$.
14. $7x^2 - 19x - 6$.
15. $12x^4 + 11x^2 + 2$.
16. $12 - x - x^2$.
17. $3 + x - 2x^2$.
18. $12y^2 + 11y + 2$.
19. $15 + x - 2x^2$.
20. $10 - 7x - 12x^2$.

(2) Difference of two squares

The fundamental identity is $A^2 - B^2 = (A + B)(A - B)$.
N.B. $A^2 + B^2$ has no rational factors.

Example 1. Factorise $9a^2 - 16x^2$.

The expression is the difference between the squares of $3a$ and $4x$.
The factors are $(3a + 4x)(3a - 4x)$.

Example 2. Factorise $(a - b)^2 - c^2$.

The expression is the difference between the squares of $(a - b)$ and c.
The factors are $(a - b + c)(a - b - c)$.

Example 3. Factorise $c^2 - (x - y)^2$.

The expression is the difference between the squares of c and $(x - y)$.
The factors are $[c + (x - y)][c - (x - y)]$ or $(c + x - y)(c - x + y)$.

Example 4. Factorise $16(a - b)^2 - 25(x - y)^2$.

The expression is the difference between the squares of $4(a - b)$ and $5(x - y)$.
The factors are $[4(a - b) + 5(x - y)][4(a - b) - 5(x - y)]$
or $(4a - 4b + 5x - 5y)(4a - 4b - 5x + 5y)$.

Example 5. Factorise $9 - 36x^2$.

There is an obvious factor, 9.
The factors are $9(1 - 4x^2)$ or $9(1 + 2x)(1 - 2x)$.

EXERCISES 21A

Factorise:

1. $x^2 - 16$. **2.** $p^2 - 9q^2$. **3.** $25x^2 - y^2$.
4. $25a^2 - 16b^2$. **5.** $a^2 - 4(b - c)^2$. **6.** $9a^2 - 4(b - c)^2$.
7. $25(a - b)^2 - c^2$. **8.** $(a - b)^2 - (c - d)^2$.
9. $4(a - b)^2 - (c - d)^2$.
10. $1 - 9x^2$. **11.** $4 - 25a^2$. **12.** $1 - (a - b)^2$.
13. $1 - 9(a - b)^2$. **14.** $16 - (a - b)^2$. **15.** $25 - 16(a - b)^2$.
16. $36 - z^2$. **17.** $108 - 3z^2$. **18.** $z^4 - 1$.
19. $x^4 - 16$. **20.** $4(a - b)^2 - 25(c - d)^2$.

EXERCISES 21B

Factorise:

1. $x^2 - 49$.
2. $a^2 - 64b^2$.
3. $25p^2 - 64q^2$.
4. $p^2 - 9q^4$.
5. $1 - 49x^2$.
6. $9(a - b)^2 - c^2$.
7. $(a - b)^2 - 9(c - d)^2$.
8. $49 - 4x^2$.
9. $p^2 - 49(r - s)^2$.
10. $9 - (a - b)^2$.
11. $1 - 16x^4$.
12. $7 - 63x^2$.
13. $16p^2 - 49q^2$.
14. $36 - 25z^2$.
15. $16 - 49(a - b)^2$.
16. $x^8 - 16$.
17. $25(a - b)^2 - 49(c - d)^2$.
18. $a^2 - 81b^4$.
19. $(2a - b)^2 - 9(3c - d)^2$.
20. $16(3a + 2b)^2 - 25(p + 2q)^2$.

(3) Grouping

To factorise an expression containing four terms, group in two pairs so that each pair has a common factor.

Find the other factor by division.

N.B. This method can be used only when there is a common factor.

Example 1. Factorise $ax + ay - bx - by$.

$$ax + ay - bx - by = (ax + ay) - (bx + by) = a(x + y) - b(x + y)$$
$$= (x + y)(a - b).$$

The common factor, $(x + y)$, should be written first and the second factor, $(a - b)$, is found by division.

Example 2. Factorise $x^2 - y^2 - 6x + 6y$.

$$x^2 - y^2 - 6x + 6y = (x - y)(x + y) - 6(x - y)$$
$$= (x - y)(x + y - 6).$$

Example 3. Factorise $ax - ay + 6y - 6x$.

$$ax - ay + 6y - 6x = a(x - y) + 6(y - x).$$

Here the common factor is not quite obvious, but remember that

$$(y - x) = -(x - y).$$

So $(x - y)$ is a factor. The other factor by division is $(a - 6)$.

$$\therefore ax - ay + 6y - 6x = (x - y)(a - 6).$$

EXERCISES 22A

Factorise:

1. $h(x + y) + (m + n)(x + y)$.
2. $px + pq - 6x - 6q$.
3. $x + y - ax - ay$.
4. $cx - dx + dq - cq$.
5. $ab + xy - ay - bx$.
6. $a^3 - a^2 - a + 1$.
7. $ah + bh + ch + ap + bp + cp$.
8. $x(2a - b) + 2a - b$.
9. $x(2a - b) - 2a + b$.
10. $ax^2 - ay^2 + bx^2 - by^2$.
11. $ab + ac - (b + c)^2$.
12. $ab - 2ac - 3b + 6c$.
13. $x^2 - y^2 - 6x - 6y$.
14. $x^2 - y^2 - 6x + 6y$.
15. $x^2 - y^2 - x - y$.
16. $x^2 - y^2 - x + y$.
17. $x^2 - (y + 4)x + 4y$.
18. $x^2 - (y - 5)x - 5y$.
19. $(a + b)(c + d) + a + b$.
20. $(a + b)(c + d) - a - b$.

EXERCISES 22B

Factorise:

1. $ap - 2aq + bp - 2bq$.
2. $ap - 2aq + 2bq - bp$.
3. $(a + b)(x + y) - 2x - 2y$.
4. $(a + b)(x + y) - (x + y)^2$.
5. $a^3 + a^2 + a + 1$.
6. $3ab + 3abc + 2c + 2c^2$.
7. $p^2 - q^2 + 4(p - q)$.
8. $p^2 - q^2 - 5p + 5q$.
9. $h^2 - k^2 - 6h - 6k$.
10. $a^2 - 4b^2 - ac - 2bc$.
11. $a^2 - 9b^2 - ax + 3bx$.
12. $a^3 + a^2 + a + a^2b + ab + b$.
13. $x - 1 - (x - 1)^2$.
14. $a(h - k) - b(k - h)$.
15. $a(h^2 - k^2) - b(k - h)$.
16. $x(y - 1) - y + 1$.
17. $a^2 - ab + ca - cb$.
18. $a^2 - a(b + c) + bc$.
19. $x^2 - x(2b + c) + 2bc$.
20. $z^2 - z(2a - b) - 2ab$.

(4) Sum and difference of two cubes

The fundamental identities are

$$A^3 + B^3 = (A + B)(A^2 - AB + B^2)$$

and

$$A^3 - B^3 = (A - B)(A^2 + AB + B^2).$$

Example 1. Factorise $x^3 + 8y^3$.

$$x^3 + 8y^3 = (x)^3 + (2y)^3 = (x + 2y)(x^2 - 2xy + 4y^2).$$

Example 2. Factorise $8z^6 - 27x^3y^3$.

$$8z^6 - 27x^3y^3 = (2z^2)^3 - (3xy)^3 = (2z^2 - 3xy)(4z^4 + 6xyz^2 + 9x^2y^2).$$

EXERCISES 23A

Factorise:

1. $8a^3 + b^3$. **2.** $z^3 + 1$. **3.** $z^6 + 1$. **4.** $z^6 - 1$.
5. $a^3 - b^3c^3$. **6.** $a^3 - 27b^3c^3$. **7.** $64h^3 - k^3$. **8.** $64h^3 + 27$.
9. $a^3 - 8$. **10.** $8 - 27b^3$.

EXERCISES 23B

Factorise:

1. $27a^3 + b^3$. **2.** $z^3 + 8$. **3.** $z^6 + 8$. **4.** $z^6 - 8$.
5. $h^3 - 8m^3n^3$. **6.** $1 - 27b^3c^3$. **7.** $64 - h^3$. **8.** $64h^3 - 27$.
9. $125a^3 - 1$. **10.** $8 - 125x^3$.

(5) Expressions containing five terms

To factorise an expression containing five terms (or a four-termed expression which will not factorise by grouping), LOOK FOR THE TRINOMIAL.

Example 1. Factorise $a^2 + 2ab + b^2 + a + b$.

$$(a^2 + 2ab + b^2) + a + b = (a + b)^2 + (a + b) = (a + b)(a + b + 1).$$

Example 2. Factorise $a^2 - ab - 3a + 2 + 2b$.

The trinomial is $a^2 - 3a + 2$.

$$\begin{aligned} a^2 - ab - 3a + 2 + 2b &= (a^2 - 3a + 2) - b(a - 2) \\ &= (a - 1)(a - 2) - b(a - 2) \\ &= (a - 2)(a - 1 - b). \end{aligned}$$

Example 3. Factorise $a^2 - b^2 - 4a + 4$.

The trinomial is $a^2 - 4a + 4$.

$$\begin{aligned} a^2 - b^2 - 4a + 4 &= (a^2 - 4a + 4) - b^2 \\ &= (a - 2)^2 - b^2 \\ &= (a - 2 + b)(a - 2 - b). \end{aligned}$$

EXERCISES 24A

Factorise:

1. $a^2 + 2a + 1 - ax - x$. **2.** $x^2 + ax + 4x + 3a + 3$.
3. $x^2 - z^2 + 2xy + y^2$. **4.** $4z^2 - 4x^2 - 4x - 1$.
5. $z^2 + 3z + 2 + az + 2a$. **6.** $ax + a - x^2 - 4x - 3$.
7. $x^2 + 2px - y^2 + p^2$. **8.** $4x^2 - 4xy + 5x + 1 - y$.
9. $1 - a^2 + 2ab - b^2$. **10.** $x^2 + 7x + yx + 10 + 5y$.

EXERCISES 24B

Factorise:

1. $a^2 + 5a + 6 + ax + 2x.$
2. $x^2 + ax + 3x + a + 2.$
3. $x^2 - z^2 + 4x + 4.$
4. $z^2 - x^2 - 6x - 9.$
5. $p^2 + pq - 5p - 6q - 6.$
6. $ay + a - y^2 - 2y - 1.$
7. $x^2 + 6px - 9y^2 + 9p^2.$
8. $2x^2 + 2xy + 3x + 1 + y.$
9. $16 - a^2 - 2ab - b^2.$
10. $x^2 + 7x + xy + 12 + 4y.$

EXERCISES 25: MISCELLANEOUS

1. Factorise $y^2 - y - 42.$
2. Evaluate $100^2 - 99^2.$
3. Evaluate $96^2 - 36.$
4. Factorise $2a^2 - 15ab + 18b^2.$
5. What number must be added to $(x^2 + 6x)$ to make the result a perfect square?
6. What number must be added to $(x^2 - 18x)$ to make the result a perfect square?
7. What number must be added to $(4x^2 - 12x)$ to make the result a perfect square?
8. What number must be added to $(9x^2 + 12x)$ to make the result a perfect square?
9. Factorise $ax + 3a - xy - 3y.$
10. Factorise $ax^2 + 2ax + a + x + 1.$
11. Factorise $1 - 9p^2 - 6pq - q^2.$
12. What is the square root of $(x^2 + 2x + 1)(x^2 - 6x + 9)$?
13. Factorise $(x + y)^2 - (xy + 1)^2.$
14. Factorise $(x^2 + x + 1)^2 - (y^2 + y + 1)^2.$
15. Factorise $xy - 8x + 5y - 40.$
16. Simplify $\dfrac{(x^2 - x - 6)(x^2 + 4x + 3)}{(x^2 - 9)(x + 1)}.$
17. Simplify $\dfrac{(x^2 - 16)(x + 2)}{(x^2 - 2x - 8)(x^2 + 5x + 4)}.$
18. Factorise $9a^2 - 6 + \dfrac{1}{a^2}.$
19. Factorise $(R - 2r)^2 - r^2.$

20. Factorise $ab^3 - 8a$.

21. Factorise $xy^3 + 64x$.

22. Factorise $1 - 125a^3b^3$.

23. Factorise $27 + 8a^3b^3c^3$.

24. Factorise $(a - b)^2 - (x - y - z)^2$.

25. Factorise $16c^2 - (a - b - d)^2$.

26. Factorise $9(a - b)^2 - 49(c - d)^2$.

27. Factorise $a^2 - ax + 9a - 7x + 14$.

28. Factorise $(x^2 + 6x + 7)^2 - (3x + 7)^2$.

29. Factorise $(2a^2 + 5a + 6)^2 - (a^2 + a + 3)^2$.

30. Divide $ab^3 - a$ by $b - 1$.

31. Divide $x^3 - 9x$ by $x^2 + 3x$.

32. Factorise $a(a - 1) - x(x - 1)$.

33. Factorise $(ax - by)^2 + (bx + ay)^2$.

34. Factorise $(lx + my)^2 - 3lx - 3my$.

35. Factorise $4\pi(R + r)^3 - 4\pi R^3$.

36. Factorise $x^3 + 5x^2 + 4x + 20$.

37. Factorise $\frac{1}{2}m(v + 2u)^2 - \frac{1}{2}m(v + u)^2$.

38. Find k if $(x + 2)$ is a factor of $x^3 + kx^2 - 4x - 8$.

39. Factorise completely $x^3 - 6x^2 + 11x - 6$, given that $(x - 3)$ is one of the factors.

40. Factorise completely $x^3 + 4x^2 - x - 4$, given that $(x + 1)$ is one of the factors.

7

EQUATIONS

AN equation tells us that two expressions are equal to each other. The quantity which we are asked to find from the equation is called the unknown. We may be asked to find the unknown as a number. In this case, the unknown will be the only letter in the equation. Or we may be asked to find the unknown in terms of other letters. Then the equation will contain more than one letter and we must find one specific letter in terms of the others.

The degree of an equation is the highest power of the unknown. For example, the equation $3x^2 - 2x - 1 = 0$ is of degree two; the equation $x^3 - x^2 - 7x = 5$ is of degree three. An equation of the first degree will, in general, have one solution; of degree two, two solutions and so on.

The expression on the left-hand side of the equal sign is called the left-hand side of the equation (L.H.S.); that on the right-hand side, the R.H.S.

It is most important to understand the difference between an expression and an equation.

An expression is a quantity and, if we are asked to simplify it, we must not alter its value in any way. We may not multiply it, divide it, add to it or subtract from it. We may bring the expression to its common denominator but we must never omit the denominator. An equation tells us that two expressions are equal to each other. Provided we multiply both sides of the equation by the same number, the resulting expressions will still be equal to each other. So we may multiply both sides of an equation by any number we please; we may add the same number to both sides of an equation. We may divide or subtract. The two expressions will be altered but the equation will still be true.

Simple equations

A simple equation in x is one which contains no power of x higher than the first. There are, for example, no terms in x^3 or x^2. Another name for a simple equation is a linear equation, because the graph obtained from it is a straight line.

Example 1. Solve the equation: $\dfrac{x-2}{3} - \dfrac{3x-4}{4} = 1.$

Multiply through by 12 (the L.C.M.),

$$4(x-2) - 3(3x-4) = 12.$$

Remove brackets, $4x - 8 - 9x + 12 = 12.$

Collect terms, $4x - 9x = 12 + 8 - 12$

or $-5x = 8.$

Divide by -5 (the coefficient of x),

$$x = -\tfrac{8}{5} = -1\tfrac{3}{5}.$$

Check. When $x = -1\tfrac{3}{5}$, the L.H.S. of the equation

$$= \frac{-1\frac{3}{5} - 2}{3} - \frac{-4\frac{4}{5} - 4}{4}$$

$$= \frac{-3\frac{3}{5}}{3} + \frac{8\frac{4}{5}}{4} = -1\tfrac{1}{5} + 2\tfrac{1}{5} = 1.$$

There now follows an example of an equation which does contain terms in y^2. These terms cancel and the equation reduces to a simple equation.

Example 2. Solve the equation: $\dfrac{2}{y-1} + \dfrac{3}{y+1} = \dfrac{5}{y}.$

Multiply through by $y(y-1)(y+1)$, the L.C.M.:

$$2y(y+1) + 3y(y-1) = 5(y-1)(y+1).$$

Remove brackets: $2y^2 + 2y + 3y^2 - 3y = 5y^2 - 5.$

Cancel the terms in y^2: $2y - 3y = -5.$

$\therefore -y = -5.$

Divide by -1: $y = 5.$

Check. When $y = 5$,

$$\text{L.H.S.} = \tfrac{2}{4} + \tfrac{3}{6} = \tfrac{1}{2} + \tfrac{1}{2} = 1.$$

$$\text{R.H.S.} = \tfrac{5}{5} = 1.$$

EXERCISES 26A

Solve the following equations:

1. $\dfrac{5x}{3} = 2.$
2. $5x - 1 = 4.$
3. $3(x-2) = 6.$
4. $3x - 2 = 2x - 1.$
5. $3(x-2) = 2(x-1).$
6. $\dfrac{x}{3} - \dfrac{x}{4} = 1.$

7. $x + \frac{x}{2} = 3.$

8. $\frac{x}{2} + \frac{x}{3} + \frac{x}{4} = 1.$

9. $\frac{x - 1}{2} - \frac{x - 2}{3} = 1.$

10. $\frac{2(x - 1)}{3} - \frac{3(x - 2)}{4} = 1.$

11. $\frac{3y}{7} - \frac{2y}{5} = \frac{4}{35}.$

12. $\frac{p + 1}{5} - \frac{3(p - 1)}{10} = 2.$

13. $\frac{2(p - 1)}{5} - \frac{3(p + 1)}{10} = p.$

14. $\frac{2(z - 1)}{3} - \frac{3(2z + 1)}{4} = \frac{z - 2}{5}.$

15. $\frac{t + 1}{t - 1} = \frac{3}{4}.$

16. $\frac{2}{t} = \frac{3}{t + 1}.$

17. $\frac{1}{z} + \frac{1}{z + 1} = \frac{2}{z - 1}.$

18. $\frac{1}{y - 1} + \frac{2}{y + 1} = \frac{3}{y}.$

19. $\frac{z - 1}{z + 1} = \frac{2z - 3}{2z + 3}.$

20. $\frac{2z + 1}{z - 1} = \frac{6z + 1}{3z - 2}.$

EXERCISES 26B

Solve the following equations:

1. $\frac{3x}{4} = 2.$

2. $3x - 4 = 2.$

3. $4(x - 3) = 5.$

4. $4x - 2 = 3x - 1.$

5. $2(x - 3) = 3(x - 1).$

6. $\frac{x}{4} - \frac{x}{5} = 2.$

7. $x + \frac{x}{3} = 4.$

8. $\frac{x}{3} + \frac{x}{4} + \frac{x}{5} = 1.$

9. $\frac{2x - 1}{3} - \frac{3x - 1}{4} = 1.$

10. $\frac{3(x - 2)}{2} - \frac{x - 3}{4} = 2.$

11. $\frac{2y}{5} - \frac{3y}{4} = \frac{3}{10}.$

12. $\frac{p + 1}{7} - \frac{3(p - 2)}{14} = 1.$

13. $\frac{p + 2}{6} - \frac{p - 3}{3} = p.$

14. $\frac{3}{4}(z - 1) - \frac{2}{3}(3z + 1) = \frac{1}{5}(z + 1).$

15. $\frac{3t + 1}{3t - 1} = \frac{2}{3}.$

16. $\frac{3}{t - 1} = \frac{4}{t + 1}.$

17. $\frac{1}{z} + \frac{2}{z+1} = \frac{3}{z-1}$.
18. $\frac{3}{y-1} + \frac{1}{y+1} = \frac{4}{y}$.

19. $\frac{2z-1}{2z+1} = \frac{3z-1}{3z+2}$.
20. $\frac{2z+3}{z-2} = \frac{6z}{3z+2}$.

Simultaneous linear equations

One linear equation containing x and y is satisfied by as many pairs of numbers as we please to find. Two such equations have, in general, only one pair of numbers which will satisfy both. Graphically, from the equations we shall get two straight lines which will usually meet in one point and one point only.

Example 1. Solve the equations:

$$3x + 2y = 12, 4x - 3y = -1.$$

$$3x + 2y = 12 \quad . \quad . \quad . \quad . \quad . \quad \text{(i)}$$
$$4x - 3y = -1 \quad . \quad . \quad . \quad . \quad . \quad \text{(ii)}$$

Multiply (i) by 4 and (ii) by 3. This is in order to produce equations in which the coefficients of x are equal. Sometimes it is easier to choose multipliers so that the coefficients of y become equal.

$$12x + 8y = 48 \quad . \quad . \quad . \quad . \quad . \quad \text{(iii)}$$
and
$$12x - 9y = -3 \quad . \quad . \quad . \quad . \quad . \quad \text{(iv)}$$

Subtract (iv) from (iii), so that the term in x disappears.

$$17y = 51.$$
$$\therefore y = 3.$$

Substitute in (i):
$$3x + 6 = 12.$$
$$\therefore 3x = 6 \quad \text{and} \quad x = 2.$$

Check. L.H.S. of (i) $= 3(2) + 2(3) = 12.$
L.H.S. of (ii) $= 4(2) - 3(3) = -1.$

There follows an example of a type of problem which is common and which is solved by the same method.

Example 2. The expression $(ax + by)$ is equal to 8 when $x = 1$ and $y = 2$; it is equal to 13 when $x = 2$ and $y = 3$. Find its value when $x = 3$ and $y = 2$.

Put $x = 1$ and $y = 2$. $\quad a + 2b = 8 \quad . \quad . \quad . \quad . \quad . \quad . \quad$ (i)
Put $x = 2$ and $y = 3$. $\quad 2a + 3b = 13 \quad . \quad . \quad . \quad . \quad . \quad . \quad$ (ii)

Multiply (i) by 2: $\quad 2a + 4b = 16 \quad . \quad . \quad . \quad . \quad . \quad . \quad$ (iii)
Do not alter (ii): $\quad 2a + 3b = 13 \quad . \quad . \quad . \quad . \quad . \quad . \quad$ (iv)
Subtract (iv) from (iii) $\quad b = 3.$

Substitute in (i): $a + 6 = 8$

$$\therefore a = 2.$$

The expression is therefore $2x + 3y$.
When $x = 3$ and $y = 2$, its value is

$$2(3) + 3(2) = 12.$$

Simultaneous equations may be given in such a form as

$$\frac{3x - y + 1}{3} = \frac{2x + y + 2}{5} = \frac{3x + 2y + 1}{6}.$$

Here are three expressions which give two equations only. Take the easiest of the three and equate it, in turn, to each of the other two. Simplify these two equations and proceed in the usual way.

Example 3. Solve the equations:

$$\frac{3x - y + 1}{3} = \frac{2x + y + 2}{5} = \frac{3x + 2y + 1}{6}.$$

Consider first: $$\frac{3x - y + 1}{3} = \frac{2x + y + 2}{5}.$$

Multiply by 15 (the L.C.M.):

$$5(3x - y + 1) = 3(2x + y + 2).$$

Remove brackets:

$$15x - 5y + 5 = 6x + 3y + 6.$$

Collect terms: $9x - 8y = 1$ . . . . . . (i)

Next consider: $$\frac{3x - y + 1}{3} = \frac{3x + 2y + 1}{6}.$$

Multiply by 6 (the L.C.M.):

$$2(3x - y + 1) = 3x + 2y + 1.$$

Remove brackets: $6x - 2y + 2 = 3x + 2y + 1.$
Collect terms: $3x - 4y = -1$ . . . . . . (ii)

Do not alter (i): $9x - 8y = 1$ . . . . . . (i)
Multiply (ii) by 2: $6x - 8y = -2$ . . . . . . (iii)
Subtract (iii) from (i): $3x = 3.$
$\therefore x = 1.$

Substitute in (ii): $3 - 4y = -1.$
$\therefore -4y = -4. \quad \therefore y = 1.$

Check. When $x = 1$ and $y = 1$,

$$\frac{3x - y + 1}{3} = \frac{3 - 1 + 1}{3} = \frac{3}{3} = 1;$$

$$\frac{2x + y + 2}{5} = \frac{2 + 1 + 2}{5} = \frac{5}{5} = 1;$$

$$\frac{3x + 2y + 1}{6} = \frac{3 + 2 + 1}{6} = \frac{6}{6} = 1.$$

EXERCISES 27A

Solve the pairs of equations in questions **1** to **12**.

1. $x + y = 8, x - y = 4.$

2. $2x + y = 7, 2x - y = 3.$

3. $2x + 3y = 8, 2x - 3y = 2.$

4. $3y + z = 7, 2y - z = 3.$

5. $2p + 3q = 5, 3p + 4q = 7.$

6. $3p - 2q = 4, 2p + 3q = 7.$

7. $5p + 4q = 22, 3p + 5q = 21.$

8. $\frac{c + d}{c - d} = \frac{1}{2}, \frac{c + 1}{d + 1} = 2.$

9. $\frac{u + 1}{2} = \frac{v + 2}{3} = \frac{v + 3}{4}.$

10. $\frac{h + k + 1}{4} = \frac{h}{2} = k.$

11. $\frac{h + 2k}{4} = \frac{h + k + 1}{7} = \frac{2h + k}{10}.$

12. $\frac{x}{2} + \frac{y}{3} = 2, 2x + 3y = 13.$

13. If $y = ax + b$, find the values of a and b, given that $y = 5$ when $x = 1$ and that $y = 7$ when $x = 2$.

14. If $y = ax + b$, find the value of y when $x = 4$, given that $y = 4$ when $x = 1$ and that $y = 7$ when $x = 2$.

15. If $y = ax^2 + b$, find the values of a and b, given that $y = -3$ when $x = 1$ and that $y = 5$ when $x = 2$.

16. If $s = ut + \frac{1}{2}ft^2$, find the value of s when $t = 3$, given that $s = 8$ when $t = 1$ and that $s = 20$ when $t = 2$.

17. Find x and y from the equations: $\frac{1}{x} + \frac{1}{y} = 3, \frac{2}{x} + \frac{3}{y} = 7.$

18. If the solutions of the pair $x + y = a$, $3x + 4y = b$ are $x = 2$, $y = 3$, find a and b.

19. Find x and y from the equations: $2x^2 + y^2 = 18, 3x^2 + 2y^2 = 35.$

20. The value of the expression $(ax^2 + bx)$ is 6 when $x = 1$ and 10 when $x = 2$. Find its value when $x = 3$.

EXERCISES 27B

Solve the pairs of equations in questions **1** to **12**.

1. $x + y = 6,\ x - y = 2.$

2. $3x + y = 8,\ 3x - y = 2.$

3. $3x + 4y = 7,\ 3x - 4y = -1.$

4. $2y + z = 8,\ 5y - z = 6.$

5. $3p + 4q = 7,\ 5p + 6q = 11.$

6. $2p - 3q = 1,\ 3p + 2q = 8.$

7. $3p + 2q = 13,\ 2p + 3q = 12.$

8. $\dfrac{a+1}{b+1} = 2,\ \dfrac{2a+1}{2b+1} = \dfrac{1}{3}.$

9. $\dfrac{u+1}{2} = \dfrac{2u+1}{3} = \dfrac{v+3}{4}.$

10. $\dfrac{c+d+2}{7} = \dfrac{c}{3} = \dfrac{d}{2}.$

11. $\dfrac{y+2z+1}{4} = \dfrac{3y+z+1}{8} = \dfrac{2y+3z+2}{9}.$

12. $\dfrac{x}{3} + \dfrac{y}{4} = 2,\ 3x + 4y = 25.$

13. If $y = ax + b$, find the values of a and b, given that $y = 6$ when $x = 1$ and $y = 10$ when $x = 2$.

14. If $y = ax + b$, find the value of y when $x = 0$, given that $y = -1$ when $x = 1$ and that $y = 4$ when $x = 3$.

15. If $y = ax^2 + b$, find the values of a and b, given that $y = 7$ when $x = 1$ and that $y = 13$ when $x = 2$.

16. If $P = aW + b$, find the value of P when $W = 4$, given that $P = 8$ when $W = 2$ and that $P = 20$ when $W = 3$.

17. Solve the equations: $\dfrac{3}{x} + \dfrac{4}{y} = 2,\ \dfrac{4}{x} - \dfrac{1}{y} = 3.$

18. If the solutions of the pair $2x + 3y = a$, $3x - y = b$ are $x = -1$, $y = 2$, find a and b.

19. Solve the equations: $x^2 + y^2 = 13,\ 3x^2 - 2y^2 = -6.$

20. The value of the expression $(ax^2 + bx)$ is 8 when $x = 2$ and 27 when $x = 3$. Find its value when $x = -1$.

Quadratic equations by factors

A quadratic equation in x is one in which the highest power of x is 2. Such an equation should be solved by factorisation whenever possible. A quadratic equation is satisfied by two values of x, but these values may be equal to each other.

Example 1. Solve the equation: $6x^2 + 7x - 3 = 0$.

Factorise: $(3x - 1)(2x + 3) = 0.$

If the product of two expressions is zero, one of them must itself be zero.

Therefore, either $3x - 1 = 0$, which gives $x = \frac{1}{3}$;
or $2x + 3 = 0$, which gives $x = -\frac{3}{2}$.

Check. When $x = \frac{1}{3}$, $6x^2 + 7x - 3 = \frac{6}{9} + \frac{7}{3} - 3 = \frac{27}{9} - 3 = 0.$

When $x = -\frac{3}{2}$, $6x^2 + 7x - 3 = 6(\frac{9}{4}) - \frac{21}{2} - 3 = \frac{6}{2} - 3 = 0.$

Example 2. Solve the equation: $\dfrac{3}{2x+1} + \dfrac{4}{5x-1} = 2.$

Multiply by $(2x + 1)(5x - 1)$, the L.C.M.:

$$3(5x - 1) + 4(2x + 1) = 2(2x + 1)(5x - 1).$$

Remove brackets:

$$15x - 3 + 8x + 4 = 20x^2 + 6x - 2.$$

Rearrange: $0 = 20x^2 - 17x - 3.$

Factorise: $0 = (20x + 3)(x - 1).$

$$x = 1 \text{ or } -\tfrac{3}{20}.$$

EXERCISES 28A

Solve the following equations:

1. $x^2 - 4x + 3 = 0.$

2. $x^2 - 5x + 6 = 0.$

3. $x^2 - 5x - 6 = 0.$

4. $x^2 + 7x + 10 = 0.$

5. $x^2 - 3x - 10 = 0.$

6. $x^2 - 4x - 12 = 0.$

7. $x^2 - 2x - 8 = 0.$

8. $x^2 - 10x + 9 = 0.$

9. $x^2 - 7x - 18 = 0.$

10. $2x^2 - 5x + 2 = 0.$

11. $6x^2 - 5x + 1 = 0.$

12. $6x^2 - 7x + 2 = 0.$

13. $3x^2 + 14x + 8 = 0.$

14. $x(2x + 1) = 10.$

15. $x(x + 1) + (x + 2)(x + 3) = 42.$

16. $\dfrac{1}{x+1} + \dfrac{4}{3x+6} = \dfrac{2}{3}.$

17. $\dfrac{1}{x} + \dfrac{1}{x+1} = \dfrac{9}{20}.$

18. $\dfrac{x+2}{x+3} = \dfrac{2x-3}{3x-7}.$

19. $\dfrac{3}{x-2} + \dfrac{8}{x+3} = 2.$

20. $\dfrac{x+1}{x-2} + \dfrac{x+11}{x+3} = 4.$

EXERCISES 28B

Solve the following equations:

1. $x^2 - 6x - 7 = 0$.
2. $x^2 - 6x - 16 = 0$.
3. $t^2 - 14t + 24 = 0$.
4. $x^2 - 4x - 21 = 0$.
5. $u^2 - u - 20 = 0$.
6. $v^2 + 11v + 18 = 0$.
7. $y^2 + 9y + 18 = 0$.
8. $x^2 + 8x + 16 = 0$.
9. $2z^2 - 7z + 3 = 0$.
10. $6x^2 - x - 2 = 0$.
11. $6p^2 - 17p + 12 = 0$.
12. $3x^2 - 13x - 10 = 0$.
13. $2x^2 + 35 = 19x$.
14. $(k + 1)(2k + 1) = 15$.
15. $x(x + 2) + (x + 1)(2x - 1) = 17$.
16. $\dfrac{1}{x+2} + \dfrac{1}{x+3} = \dfrac{7}{12}$.
17. $\dfrac{3}{q} + \dfrac{4}{q+1} = 2$.
18. $\dfrac{x+3}{x+2} = \dfrac{x+4}{x+1}$.
19. $\dfrac{6}{z+1} + \dfrac{5}{2z+1} = 3$.
20. $\dfrac{x+7}{x+1} + \dfrac{2x+6}{2x+1} = 5$.

Quadratic equations by completing the square and by formula

If a quadratic equation cannot be solved by factorisation, one of the following methods should be used.

(1) *Completing the square*

Example. Solve the equation: $3x^2 - 4x - 5 = 0$.

Arrange with terms containing x^2 and x on L.H.S.:

$$3x^2 - 4x = 5.$$

Divide through by 3 (the coefficient of x^2):

$$x^2 - \tfrac{4}{3}x = \tfrac{5}{3}.$$

Add to each side ($\tfrac{1}{2}$ coefficient of $x)^2$:

$$x^2 - \tfrac{4}{3}x + (\tfrac{2}{3})^2 = \tfrac{5}{3} + \tfrac{4}{9}.$$

$$\therefore (x - \tfrac{2}{3})^2 = \tfrac{19}{9}.$$

Take the square root of each side:

$$x - \tfrac{2}{3} = \pm\sqrt{\frac{19}{9}} = \pm\frac{4{\cdot}359}{3}.$$

Solve for x, $$x = \frac{2 \pm 4{\cdot}359}{3}.$$

$$x = \frac{6{\cdot}359}{3} \quad \text{or} \quad -\frac{2{\cdot}359}{3}.$$

$$x = 2{\cdot}12 \quad \text{or} \quad -0{\cdot}79,$$

each correct to two places of decimals.

(2) *Formula*

The solutions of the equation $ax^2 + bx + c = 0$ are

$$x = \frac{-b \pm \sqrt{b^2 - 4ac}}{2a}.$$

This formula should be memorised. The expression $(ax^2 + bx + c)$ may be made equal to any given quadratic expression, by giving a, b and c suitable values. To make $(ax^2 + bx + c)$ equal to $(5x^2 - 2x - 6)$, for example, put $a = 5$, $b = -2$ and $c = -6$.

The formula may be proved by the method of completing the square, applied to the equation $ax^2 + bx + c = 0$.

Rearrange: $$ax^2 + bx = -c.$$

Divide throughout by a: $$x^2 + \frac{b}{a} = -\frac{c}{a}.$$

Add to each side ($\frac{1}{2}$ coefficient of $x)^2$:

$$x^2 + \frac{b}{a}x + \left(\frac{b}{2a}\right)^2 = -\frac{c}{a} + \frac{b^2}{4a^2}$$

or $$\left(x + \frac{b}{2a}\right)^2 = \frac{b^2 - 4ac}{4a^2}.$$

Take the square root of both sides:

$$x + \frac{b}{2a} = \pm\frac{\sqrt{b^2 - 4ac}}{2a}.$$

Subtract $\frac{b}{2a}$ from each side:

$$x = -\frac{b}{2a} \pm \frac{\sqrt{b^2 - 4ac}}{2a}$$

or $$x = \frac{-b \pm \sqrt{b^2 - 4ac}}{2a}.$$

Example. Solve the equation: $3x^2 - 4x - 5 = 0$.

For this equation $a = 3$, $b = -4$, $c = -5$.

Substitute in $x = \dfrac{-b \pm \sqrt{b^2 - 4ac}}{2a}$:

$$x = \frac{4 \pm \sqrt{(-4)^2 - 4(3)(-5)}}{6}$$

$$x = \frac{4 \pm \sqrt{76}}{6}$$

$$= \frac{4 \pm 8{\cdot}718}{6}$$

$$= \frac{12{\cdot}718}{6} \quad \text{or} \quad \frac{-4{\cdot}718}{6}$$

$$= 2{\cdot}12 \quad \text{or} \quad -0{\cdot}79,$$

each correct to two places of decimals.

EXERCISES 29A

Solve the following equations, giving your answers correct to two places of decimals:

1. $2x^2 - 3x - 7 = 0$.

2. $3x^2 - x - 1 = 0$.

3. $u^2 - 3u = 8$.

4. $5x^2 - 8x + 2 = 0$.

5. $7z^2 - 2z - 3 = 0$.

6. $3x^2 + 5x + 1 = 0$.

7. $4y^2 + y - 3 = 0$.

8. $6x^2 + 10x + 3 = 0$.

9. $z^2 + z - 8 = 0$.

10. $u + \dfrac{1}{u} = 3$.

11. $v + \dfrac{1}{2v} = 4$.

12. $\dfrac{1}{x+1} + \dfrac{1}{x+2} = \dfrac{2}{3}$.

13. $(p - 1)(2p + 4) = 9$.

14. $\dfrac{c+1}{c-1} = \dfrac{2c-4}{3c-2}$.

15. $\dfrac{1}{x} + \dfrac{2}{x+1} = \dfrac{4}{x-1}$.

16. $(z - 1)(z + 1) + (2z - 1)(z + 2) = 6$.

17. $z + 1 + \dfrac{1}{z+1} = 3$.

18. $y(y + 1) + (y + 2)(y + 3) = 4$.

19. $\dfrac{1}{2x+1} + \dfrac{1}{3x-1} = 1.$

20. $p(p-1)(p+2) = p(p+2)(p-4).$

EXERCISES 29B

Solve the following equations, giving your answers correct to two decimal places:

1. $x^2 - 2x - 7 = 0.$
2. $3x^2 - 5x - 1 = 0.$
3. $u^2 - u - 3 = 0.$
4. $5v^2 + 2v - 1 = 0.$
5. $3z^2 - z - 1 = 0.$
6. $7z^2 - 3z - 8 = 0.$
7. $2x^2 + 5x + 1 = 0.$
8. $4y^2 + 2y - 5 = 0.$
9. $z^2 + z = 5.$
10. $u + \dfrac{1}{u} = 5.$
11. $v + \dfrac{1}{2v} = 6.$
12. $\dfrac{1}{x+2} + \dfrac{1}{x+3} = \dfrac{2}{3}.$
13. $(2p-1)(p+3) = 8.$
14. $\dfrac{x+1}{x-2} = \dfrac{3x+1}{2x-1}.$
15. $\dfrac{1}{x+1} + \dfrac{2}{x+3} = \dfrac{2}{3}.$
16. $(q-2)(2q+6) = 7.$
17. $(z-1)(z+3) + (2z+1)(z+4) = 6.$
18. $z + 1 + \dfrac{1}{z+1} = 5.$
19. $(y+1)(y+2) + (y+3)(y+4) = 4.$
20. $p(p+2)(p+3) = (p-1)(p+4)(p+5).$

Literal equations: change of subject

A literal equation in x contains x and other letters. We are usually asked to find x in terms of the other letters. This may also be called making x the subject of the equation. The procedure for solving is exactly the same as in a simple equation.

Example 1. Find x from the equation $\dfrac{x}{x-a} = \dfrac{x-b}{x-c}.$

Multiply through by $(x-a)(x-c)$, the L.C.M.:

$$x(x-c) = (x-a)(x-b).$$

Remove brackets:

$$x^2 - xc = x^2 - ax - bx + ab.$$

Arrange with terms containing x on L.H.S.:

$$ax + bx - cx = ab.$$

or $$x(a + b - c) = ab.$$

Divide by $(a + b - c)$, the coefficient of x:

$$x = \frac{ab}{a + b - c}$$

Example 2. Make g the subject of the formula $T = 2\pi\sqrt{\frac{l}{g}}$.

First remove the square root by squaring both sides of the equation.

$$T^2 = 4\pi^2\frac{l}{g}.$$

Multiply through by g: $$gT^2 = 4\pi^2 l.$$

Divide by T^2: $$g = \frac{4\pi^2 l}{T^2}.$$

EXERCISES 30A

Find x in questions **1** to **10**.

1. $ax + b = cx + d.$

2. $\frac{x}{a} - \frac{x}{b} = 1.$

3. $\frac{a}{x} + \frac{b}{x} = 1.$

4. $x(x - a) = (x - b)(x - c).$

5. $\frac{1}{x} + \frac{1}{x - a} = \frac{2}{x - b}.$

6. $\frac{x + a}{x + b} = \frac{l}{m}.$

7. $a(x + a) = b(x + b).$

8. $\frac{x}{x + a} = \frac{p}{q}.$

9. $\frac{x}{a} + \frac{x}{b} = \frac{1}{c}.$

10. $\sqrt{x^2 - a^2} = b.$

11. Make h the subject of the formula $A = 2\pi r(r + h)$.

12. Make r the subject of the formula $A = \pi\{(r + t)^2 - r^2\}$.

13. Make u the subject of the formula $\frac{1}{u} + \frac{1}{v} = \frac{1}{f}$.

14. Make l the subject of the formula $T = 2\pi\sqrt{\frac{l}{g}}$.

15. Make l the subject of the formula $A = \pi rl + \pi r^2$.

16. Make f the subject of the formula $s = ut + \frac{1}{2}ft^2$.

17. Make u the subject of the formula $v^2 = u^2 + 2fs$.

18. Make x the subject of the formula $(x - a)^2 + (y - b)^2 = r^2$.

19. Make s the subject of the formula $x = \sqrt{\frac{s - a}{s - b}}$.

20. Make d the subject of the formula $S = \frac{n}{2}\{2a + (n - 1)d\}$.

EXERCISES 30B

Find x in questions **1** to **10**.

1. $a(x + 1) = b(x + 2)$.

2. $x - \frac{x}{a} = 1$.

3. $\frac{a}{x} + b = 1$.

4. $x^2 = (x - c)(x - d)$.

5. $\frac{1}{x - a} + \frac{1}{x - b} = \frac{2}{x - c}$.

6. $\frac{ax + 1}{bx + 1} = \frac{c}{d}$.

7. $a(x - a) = b(x - b)$.

8. $\frac{x + a}{x + b} = \frac{p}{q}$.

9. $\frac{x - a}{b} + \frac{x - b}{c} = 1$.

10. $x^2 + y^2 = b^2$.

11. Make a the subject of the formula $S = \frac{n}{2}\{2a + (n - 1)d\}$.

12. Make b the subject of the formula $ax^2 + bx + c = 0$.

13. Make R the subject of the formula $I = \frac{PRT}{100}$.

14. Make r the subject of the formula $A = P\left(1 + \frac{r}{100}\right)$.

15. Make R the subject of the formula $H = \frac{v(P - R)}{550}$.

16. Make f the subject of the formula $v^2 = u^2 + 2fs$.

17. Make f the subject of the formula $\frac{1}{u} + \frac{1}{v} = \frac{1}{f}$.

18. Make x the subject of the formula $\frac{x^2}{a^2} + \frac{y^2}{b^2} = 1$.

19. Make u the subject of the formula $s = ut + \frac{1}{2}ft^2$.

20. Make s the subject of the formula $v^2 = u^2 + 2fs$.

Simultaneous equations—one linear and one quadratic

Two simultaneous equations, one linear and one quadratic, have in general two pairs of solutions. Graphically, the equations give a straight line and a curve as shown in Fig. 7. The values of x and y at the points of intersection are the solutions of the equations.

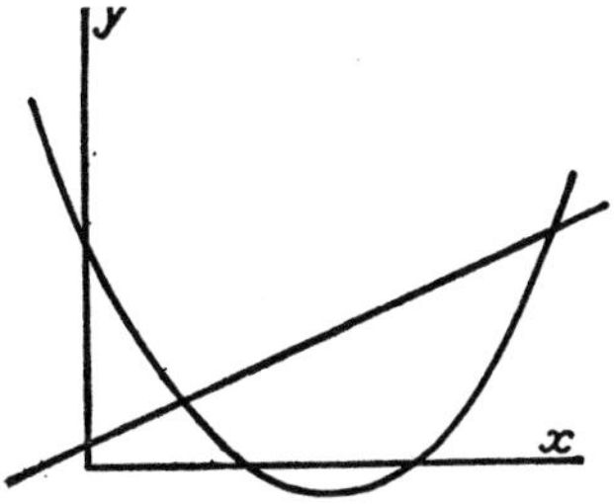

FIG. 7

Example 1. Solve the equations: $x + y = 2,\ 2x^2 + y^2 = 3$.

Find either x or y in terms of the other from the linear equation. Do whichever you think will make your working easier.

From $x + y = 2$,

$$y = 2 - x.$$

Substitute in the quadratic,

$$2x^2 + (2 - x)^2 = 3,$$

or $$2x^2 + 4 - 4x + x^2 = 3.$$

$$\therefore 3x^2 - 4x + 1 = 0 \quad \text{or} \quad (x - 1)(3x - 1) = 0.$$

$$\therefore x = 1 \quad \text{or} \quad \tfrac{1}{3}.$$

When $x = 1$,

$$y = 2 - 1 = 1.$$

When $x = \tfrac{1}{3}$,

$$y = 2 - \tfrac{1}{3} = 1\tfrac{2}{3}.$$

The solutions are $x = 1, y = 1$ or $x = \tfrac{1}{3}, y = 1\tfrac{2}{3}$.

N.B. Make it clear in your answer that $x = 1$ must pair with $y = 1$.

Do not write $x = 1$ or $\tfrac{1}{3}$, $y = 1$ or $1\tfrac{2}{3}$.

Example 2. Solve the equations: $2x + 3y = 8;$

$$x^2 - xy + y^2 = 3.$$

Find x in terms of y:

$$x = \frac{8 - 3y}{2}.$$

Substitute: $$\left(\frac{8-3y}{2}\right)^2 - \left(\frac{8-3y}{2}\right)y + y^2 = 3.$$

Remove brackets:
$$\frac{64 - 48y + 9y^2}{4} - \frac{8y - 3y^2}{2} + y^2 = 3.$$

Simplify:
$$64 - 48y + 9y^2 - 16y + 6y^2 + 4y^2 = 12,$$
or
$$19y^2 - 64y + 52 = 0.$$
$$\therefore (y-2)(19y-26) = 0,$$
and
$$y = 2 \quad \text{or} \quad \tfrac{26}{19}.$$
When $y = 2$,
$$x = \frac{8-6}{2} = 1.$$
When $y = \frac{26}{19}$,
$$x = \frac{8 - \frac{78}{19}}{2} = 4 - \tfrac{39}{19} = \tfrac{37}{19}.$$

EXERCISES 31 A

Solve the equations:

1. $x + y = 5, xy = 6.$
2. $2x + y = 7, x^2 - xy = 6.$
3. $2x + 3y = 2, 4x^2 + 9y^2 = 2.$
4. $x + y = 2, x^2 - xy + y^2 = 1.$
5. $3x - 5y = 1, x^2 - 3xy + 2y^2 = 0.$

EXERCISES 31 B

Solve the equations:

1. $x + y = 7, xy = 12.$
2. $3x + y = 5, x^2 + xy = 3.$
3. $x + 2y = 2, x^2 + 4y^2 = 2.$
4. $3x = 2y, x^2 + xy + y^2 = 19.$
5. $x + y = 3, x^2 + xy = 4.$

EXERCISES 32: MISCELLANEOUS

1. Solve the simultaneous equations:
$$0{\cdot}5x - 0{\cdot}3y = 1{\cdot}65.$$
$$0{\cdot}7x + 0{\cdot}2y = 0{\cdot}14.$$

2. The volume V and the surface area S of a cylinder, radius r and height h, are given by the formulae $V = \pi r^2 h$ and $S = 2\pi rh + 2\pi r^2$. Write down formulae which give h in terms of (i) V and r, (ii) S and r. Hence find a formula for V in terms of S and r, which does not include h.

3. Solve for x, the equation $x^2 - 2ax = b^2 - a^2$.

4. Factorise $x^3 + 3x^2 + 4x + 12$ and hence solve the equation $x^3 + 3x^2 + 4x + 12 = 0$.

5. Solve the equation $\frac{2}{x} - \frac{1}{6} = \frac{9}{2x} - 1$.

6. If $q = \frac{W}{\pi(R^2 - r^2)}$, express r in terms of π, R, q and W.

7. Solve the equations $\frac{x + y + 4}{4} = \frac{2x - y}{3} = \frac{3x - y - 2}{3}$.

8. Rearrange the formula $z = \sqrt{P^2 - Q^2} - H$, to express Q in terms of the other letters.

9. Solve the equations $\frac{x}{y} = \frac{4}{5}$, $x + y = 13{\cdot}5$.

10. The graph of the equation $y = A + \frac{B}{x}$ passes through the points (1,9) and (10,0). Find the values of A and B.

11. Find x in terms of y, given that

$$(3x + 5y)^2 - (3x + 5y)(2x - 3y) = 0.$$

12. Solve the equations $12x + 3y = 1{\cdot}8$, $4x + 4y = 1{\cdot}9$.

13. The graph of the equation $y - 3 = Ax + Bx^2$ cuts the x-axis at the points $(-1,0)$ and $(4,0)$. Find the values of A and B.

14. Solve the equation $x^2 - 2 + \frac{1}{x^2} = 0$.

15. Solve the equation $\frac{x + 2}{x - 2} = \frac{x + 3}{x - 9}$.

16. Solve the equation $9x^2 - 2x = 10$, giving your answers correct to two places of decimals.

17. Solve for x, the equation $x^2 - 2x = a^2 - 2a$.

18. Solve the equation $\frac{3x - 2}{6} - \frac{2x + 3}{8} = \frac{x - 5}{24}$.

19. From the formula $d = \frac{gvt^2}{v + gt}$, express v in terms of the other letters.

20. If $Z = \frac{2P - 3Q}{3Q + 2P}$, express P in terms of Z and Q.

21. If $9R^2 = 4(R - 3r)^2$, express R in terms of r.

22. Solve the equation $\dfrac{1-x}{x} + \dfrac{x}{1-x} = \dfrac{5}{2}$.

23. Solve for x and y the equations $px + qy = 2pq$,
$qx - py = q^2 - p^2$.

24. Solve the equations $3(x + y) - (x - y) = 10$,
$7(x + y) + (x - y) = 16$.

25. Find, correct to two decimal places, the roots of the equation

$$3x - 1 + \frac{1}{3x - 1} = 5.$$

26. If $x = c\dfrac{1 + 2y}{1 - 3y}$, express y in terms of the other letters.

27. Solve the equation $4(2x - 5)^2 - 3(2x - 5) - 1 = 0$.

28. If $x = 2 + 3t$, and $y = \dfrac{1 + t + t^2}{1 - t}$, find y in terms of x.

29. If $a^2 + 4ab + 4b^2 - 9c^2 = 0$, express a in terms of b and c.

30. Solve the equation $\dfrac{5}{(2x-1)^2} - \dfrac{30}{2x-1} = 18$, giving your answers correct to two places of decimals.

31. Solve for x and y, the equations $ax + by = c$,
$lx + my = n$.

32. Solve the equations $\dfrac{3}{x} - \dfrac{2}{y} = 7$, $\dfrac{12}{x} + \dfrac{1}{y} = 1$.

33. Solve the equations $\dfrac{x}{2} = \dfrac{y}{3}$, $x^2 + y^2 = 52$.

34. Solve the equations $\dfrac{x}{3} + \dfrac{y}{2} = 2$, $xy = 6$.

35. Solve the equations $3x - 2y = 2$, $x^2 - xy - y^2 = \frac{1}{4}$.

36. If $x + y = a + b$ and $x^2 + xy = a^2 + ab$, find x and y.

8

EXPRESSIONS AND IDENTITIES

EXPRESSIONS

IF you are asked to simplify an expression, you must not alter it by changing its sign, by multiplying it or by adding to it. If you bring fractions to their lowest common denominator, you must never omit the denominator.

Lowest common multiple

To find the lowest common multiple of a number of algebraic expressions, factorise each of the expressions. Each factor must be a factor of the L.C.M. The power of the factor in the L.C.M. is the highest power of the factor in the given expressions.

Example

$2(x^2 - 6x + 9) = 2(x - 3)^2.$

$3(x^2 - 4x + 3) = 3(x - 3)(x - 1).$ L.C.M.

$6x^2 - 6 = 2.3(x + 1)(x - 1).$ $= 6(x - 3)^2(x - 1)(x + 1).$

Example

$(a - b)(a - c)$

$(b - c)(b - a)$ L.C.M. $= (a - b)(a - c)(b - c).$

$(c - a)(c - b)$

The sign of the L.C.M. is of no great importance. $(b - a)$ divides into $(a - b)$, the quotient being $- 1$. So you do not need both these factors in the L.C.M. You could have chosen $(b - a)$ instead of $(a - b)$. In fact, the L.C.M. could equally well have been $(b - a)(c - a)(c - b)$ or $(a - b)(c - a)(b - c)$.

EXERCISES 33A

Find the L.C.M. of:

1. $(x^2 - 1), (x^2 - 3x + 2).$

2. $6(x - 1), 3(x + 1).$

3. $x^2 - a^2, x^2 - ax - bx + ab.$

4. $(x - a)^2, (x^2 - a^2).$

5. $x^2 + a^2, x + a, x - a.$

6. $y^2 - 2y, y^2 - 3y + 2.$

7. $z^2 - z, z^2 - 2z + 1.$

8. $z^2 - z, z^2 - 1, z^2 + z.$

9. $t^2 - 1, t - 1, 3(t + 1).$

10. $p^2 - 3p + 2, p^2 - 4p + 3, p^2 - 5p + 6.$

EXERCISES 33B

Find the L.C.M. of:

1. $x^2 - 4$, $x^2 - 3x + 2$.
2. $3(x + 1)$, $6(x + 1)^2$.
3. $x^2 - a^2$, $x^2 - ax - x + a$.
4. $x^2 - 2ax + a^2$, $x^2 - ax$.
5. $x^2 + 1$, $(x + 1)^2$, $x + 1$.
6. $y^2 - y$, $y^2 - 1$.
7. $y^3 - y$, $3(y + 1)$.
8. $z^3 - z$, $z + 1$, $z(z - 1)$.
9. $a^2 - b^2$, $3(a - b)$, $2(a + b)$.
10. $x^2 - 1$, $x^2 - 3x + 2$, $x^2 + x - 2$.

Simplification of fractions

To add or subtract fractions, find the L.C.M. of the denominators. Express each fraction as a fraction with this common denominator and simplify the numerator. Factorise the numerator and cancel if possible.

Example 1. Simplify $\frac{1}{x} - \frac{2}{x+1} + \frac{1}{x+2}$.

$$\frac{1}{x} - \frac{2}{x+1} + \frac{1}{x+2} = \frac{(x+1)(x+2) - 2x(x+2) + x(x+1)}{x(x+1)(x+2)}$$

$$= \frac{x^2 + 3x + 2 - 2x^2 - 4x + x^2 + x}{x(x+1)(x+2)}$$

$$= \frac{2}{x(x+1)(x+2)}.$$

Example 2. Simplify $\frac{x}{x^2 - 3x + 2} - \frac{x+3}{x^2 - 1}$.

$$\frac{x}{x^2 - 3x + 2} - \frac{x+3}{x^2 - 1} = \frac{x}{(x-1)(x-2)} - \frac{x+3}{(x-1)(x+1)}$$

$$= \frac{x(x+1) - (x+3)(x-2)}{(x-1)(x-2)(x+1)}$$

$$= \frac{x^2 + x - (x^2 + x - 6)}{(x-1)(x-2)(x+1)}$$

$$= \frac{6}{(x-1)(x-2)(x+1)}.$$

Example 3. Simplify $\dfrac{1}{x^2+3x+2}+\dfrac{1}{x^2+5x+6}$

$$\begin{aligned}\frac{1}{x^2+3x+2}+\frac{1}{x^2+5x+6} &= \frac{1}{(x+1)(x+2)}+\frac{1}{(x+2)(x+3)}\\ &= \frac{(x+3)+(x+1)}{(x+1)(x+2)(x+3)}\\ &= \frac{2x+4}{(x+1)(x+2)(x+3)}\\ &= \frac{2(x+2)}{(x+1)(x+2)(x+3)}\\ &= \frac{2}{(x+1)(x+3)}.\end{aligned}$$

EXERCISES 34A

Simplify:

1. $\dfrac{2}{3x}+\dfrac{3}{4x}$.
2. $\dfrac{1}{x+1}+\dfrac{1}{x-1}$.
3. $\dfrac{2}{2-x}-\dfrac{4}{4-x}$.
4. $\dfrac{x-2}{4}-\dfrac{x-3}{6}$.
5. $1+\dfrac{1}{x(x+2)}$.
6. $\dfrac{x}{4x+8}\times\dfrac{x^2+5x+6}{3x^2}$.
7. $\dfrac{x+3}{x^2-1}-\dfrac{3}{2(x-1)}$.
8. $\dfrac{1}{(a-b)(a-c)}+\dfrac{1}{(b-c)(b-a)}$.
9. $\dfrac{2}{x^2+x}-\dfrac{1}{x^2+3x+2}$.
10. $\dfrac{1}{x^2+x}+\dfrac{1}{x^2+3x+2}+\dfrac{1}{x^2+2x}$.

EXERCISES 34B

Simplify:

1. $\dfrac{3}{2x}-\dfrac{4}{3x}$.
2. $\dfrac{1}{4}+\dfrac{1}{x+2}$.
3. $\dfrac{3}{3-x}-\dfrac{2}{1-x}$.
4. $\dfrac{5(2x-1)}{6}-\dfrac{3(x+1)}{4}$.
5. $\dfrac{1}{x(x+3)}+\dfrac{1}{x^2+5x+6}$.
6. $\dfrac{2x}{3x+9}\times\dfrac{x^2+4x+3}{x^2}$.

7. $\dfrac{x + 1}{x^2 - 4} - \dfrac{5}{x + 2}$.

8. $\dfrac{1}{(a - b)(a - c)} + \dfrac{1}{(b - c)(b - a)} + \dfrac{1}{(c - a)(c - b)}$.

9. $\dfrac{3}{x^2 - x} - \dfrac{4}{x^2 - 1}$.

10. $\dfrac{1}{x^2 - x} + \dfrac{1}{x^2 - 3x + 2} + \dfrac{1}{x^2 - 2x}$.

Constructing formulae

A number of arithmetic results often follow the same law. All these results are particular cases of a more general result, which can be expressed in terms of symbols.

Example 1. A workman is paid n new pence for each day he works and is fined q new pence for each day he is absent. If he works for x days of a six-day week, find how much he earns.

He works for x days. For this he is paid nx new pence.
He is absent for $(6 - x)$ days. He is fined $q(6 - x)$ new pence.
His earnings are

$$nx - q(6 - x) = (nx + qx - 6q) \text{ new pence.}$$

Example 2. An author receives in royalties 10% of the selling price on the first 4000 copies of his book and $12\frac{1}{2}$% on any further copies sold. If the book sells at s new pence a copy, find how much the author receives if x copies of the book are sold, x being greater than 4000.

On the first 4000 copies, he receives 10% of $4000s$ new pence or $400s$ new pence.

On the remaining $(x - 4000)$ copies, he receives $12\frac{1}{2}$% of $(x - 4000)s$ new pence or $\frac{1}{8}(x - 4000)s$ new pence.

The author therefore receives $400s + \frac{1}{8}(x - 4000)s$ new pence or $(\frac{1}{8}x - 100)s$ new pence.

Example 3. The postage required for an inland letter of mass 250 g is 2p. For every additional 250 g, 1p is charged.

What is the postage required for a letter of mass $250n$ grammes, where n is greater than 1?

For 250 g, the charge is 2p.
The additional mass is $250(n - 1)$ grammes.
The additional charge is $(n - 1)$p.
The charge for $250n$ grammes is therefore $2 + (n - 1) = (n + 1)$p.

EXERCISES 35A

1. If I buy p books at P new pence each and q other books at Q new pence each, how many new pence change shall I have from a £5 note?

2. The cost of a hotel for an adult is $2p$ new pence a day. A child is taken at half-price. Find the total bill for a week for a party of 2 adults and 3 children.

3. The volume of a right circular cylinder is V cm and its length is h cm. Find the radius of its base.

4. A circular flower bed of radius x metres is surrounded by a path y metres wide. Find the area of the path in m^2.

5. Find a formula for the total surface area of a right circular cylinder closed at both ends, given that its radius is r and its length h.

6. A man buys eggs at x new pence per dozen. Find the cost in £ of y dozen eggs.

7. Find the area of the walls of a room x metres long, y metres wide and z metres high.

8. Local time is 4 min ahead of Greenwich time for each degree of longitude east of Greenwich. What is the time at a place of longitude (*a*) $x°$ E., (*b*) $y°$ W., when it is midday at Greenwich?

9. The average age of x boys in a class is m months. What is the average age in months after a boy of age y years joins the class?

10. A man buys a car for £P and sells it for £Q. What is his loss per cent?

11. A greengrocer buys p tonnes of potatoes at £P per tonne and a further q tonnes at £Q per tonne. He mixes the potatoes and sells them to make a profit of $z\%$. At what price per kg must he sell them?

12. A rectangle on a map has sides h and k cm. If the scale of the map is x cm to 1 km, find in km^2 the area represented by the rectangle.

13. A car is driven x km at u km/h and a further y km at v km/h. How long does the journey take and what is the average speed?

14. The boundary of an enclosure consists of two parallel sides each of length p metres and two semicircles, each of radius r metres. Find a formula for the area of the enclosure.

15. A car is driven x km a week and does g km per litre of petrol. Find the cost of petrol for the week in pounds, if petrol costs s new pence a litre.

EXERCISES 35B

1. A rectangular sheet of metal, x cm by y cm has a square of side z cm cut from each corner. The sheet is then bent to form a tray of depth z cm. Find the volume of the tray.

2. A classroom is x metres long, y metres wide and z metres high. If it is designed to accommodate n boys, find how many m^3 of air are allowed per boy.

3. If x cm^3 of a substance whose density is g g/cm^3 are mixed with y cm^3 of another substance of density h g/cm^3, write down a formula for the total mass of the mixture.

4. How many castings each weighing x kg y grammes can be made from c kg of metal? (Assume there is an exact number.)

5. A man travels a distance of $2x$ km. He walks for half the distance at v km/h and runs the rest of the way at $2v$ km/h. How long does he take and what is his average speed?

6. A room has dimensions p metres by q metres by r metres high. It has a door x metres by y metres and two windows each c metres by d metres. How many m^2 of paper are needed for the room?

7. A man is paid x new pence per hour for normal work and double rate for overtime. If he does a 50-hour week which includes w hours of overtime, find an expression for his weekly earnings.

8. During one week, a man posted x letters with 3 new penny stamps and y letters with 2 new penny stamps. Find his postage bill for the week.

9. An exam is taken by x boys and y girls. The boys score an average mark of p, the girls an average mark of q. Find the average mark of all the candidates.

10. In a school are p pupils of average age x years. At the end of the year, q pupils of average age y years leave and z new pupils of average age r years join the school. What is the average age of the school now?

11. A man walks x km at V km/h and finishes his journey by car at $6V$ km/h. If the ratio of the distance walked to that travelled by car is 2 : 7, find an expression for the total time taken for the journey.

12. A party of A adults and C children go to a boarding house for a week's holiday. The cost of a return train ticket is a new pence for an adult and the cost per day at the boarding house for an adult is b new pence. The charges for a child on the train and at the boarding house are half those for an adult. Find the total cost of the week's holiday.

13. A try at football scores three points and a goal five points. By how many points does a team which scores x tries and y goals beat a team which scores p tries and q goals?

14. A man can dig a trench y metres long in x days working z hours a day. How many hours a day must p men work to finish digging a trench q metres long in s days?

15. A rectangular sheet of metal x metres long and y metres wide has a circular hole cut from it. What is the radius of the hole if the area of the remaining metal is A m^2?

IDENTITIES

An equation in x is satisfied by only some values of x. A simple equation, e.g. $x = 4$, is satisfied by only one value of x. A quadratic equation, e.g. $x^2 = 9$, is satisfied by two values of x. A cubic equation is satisfied by three values of x and so on. An *identity*, on the other hand, is satisfied by **all** values of x. The equation $x^2 - 1 = (x + 1)(x - 1)$ is an identity because, whatever value you give x, the equation is true. In an identity, the two sides of the equation are different forms of the same expression. An identity is distinguished from an equation by replacing the $=$ sign by the symbol $\equiv$.

Example. Prove $(x - 1)^3 + (x + 1)^3 \equiv 2x(x^2 + 3)$.

Always work the two sides of the equation separately.

$$\begin{aligned} \text{L.H.S.} = (x-1)^3+(x+1)^3 &= (x^3-3x^2+3x-1)+(x^3+3x^2+3x+1) \\ &= 2x^3 + 6x \\ &= 2x(x^2 + 3) = \text{R.H.S.} \end{aligned}$$

Alternative method.

If $x = 0$,	L.H.S. $= -1 + 1 = 0$;	R.H.S. $= 0$.
If $x = 1$,	L.H.S. $= 0 + 8 = 8$;	R.H.S. $= 2(4) = 8$.
If $x = -1$,	L.H.S. $= -8 + 0 = -8$;	R.H.S. $= -2(4) = -8$.
If $x = 2$,	L.H.S. $= 1 + 27 = 28$;	R.H.S. $= 4(7) = 28$.

So there are four values of x which satisfy the equation. But the equation is of the third degree and so should be satisfied by three values of x only. Therefore the equation is an identity and is satisfied by all values of x.

EXERCISES 36A

1. Prove that the values 0, 1 and -1 for x all satisfy the equation $(x - 1)^2 + (x + 1)^2 = 2(x^2 + 1)$. What do you deduce?

2. Is $a^2 - b^2 = (a - b)^2$ an equation or an identity?

3. Prove $\left(x + \dfrac{1}{x}\right)^2 - \left(x - \dfrac{1}{x}\right)^2 \equiv 4$.

4. Prove $(a - b)(c - b) + (b - c)(a - c) \equiv (b - c)^2$.

5. Prove $a(b - c) + b(c - a) + c(a - b) \equiv 0$.

6. Prove $(x - y)^2 \equiv (x + y)^2 - 4xy$.

7. Prove $(a + b + c)^2 - (a - b - c)^2 \equiv 4a(b + c)$.

8. Prove $(px + qy)^2 + (qx - py)^2 \equiv (p^2 + q^2)(x^2 + y^2)$.

9. Prove $(a-b)(a+b)+(b-c)(b+c) \equiv a^2-c^2$.

10 Prove $(x+y+z)^2-(x^2+y^2+z^2) \equiv 2(xy+yz+zx)$.

EXERCISES 36B

1. Prove that the values 0, 2, -2 for x all satisfy the equation $(x-2)^2+(x+2)^2=2(x^2+4)$. What do you deduce?

2. Is $x^3+1=(x+1)(x^2-x+1)$ an equation or an identity?

3. Prove $(a-2b)^3 \equiv a^3-6a^2b+12ab^2-8b^3$.

4. Prove

$$a^2(b-c)+b^2(c-a)+c^2(a-b) \equiv -(a-b)(b-c)(c-a).$$

5. Prove $(a^2+b^2+c^2)^2-(a^2+b^2-c^2)^2 \equiv 4c^2(a^2+b^2)$.

6. Prove

$$a^3+b^3+c^3-3abc \equiv (a+b+c)(a^2+b^2+c^2-ab-bc-ca).$$

7. Prove

$$(a+b+c)(b+c-a)(a+b-c)(c+a-b) \equiv 2b^2c^2+2c^2a^2+2a^2b^2-a^4-b^4-c^4.$$

8. Prove $x^2-y^2-z^2+2yz \equiv (x-y+z)(x+y-z)$.

9. Prove $(x^2+12x+35)(x^2-3x-10) \equiv (x^2-25)(x^2+9x+14)$.

10. Prove $\dfrac{1}{2x-1}-\dfrac{1}{3x-1} \equiv \dfrac{x}{(2x-1)(3x-1)}$.

The remainder theorem

To find the remainder when an expression such as x^3-3x^2+2x-4 is divided by $(x-2)$, put $x=2$ in the expression. The value given to x is the value which makes the divisor, i.e. $(x-2)$, zero. To prove this, suppose that the quotient is Q and that the remainder is R. The quotient Q will contain x but the remainder R will not, because otherwise you could continue your division.

So $$x^3-3x^2+2x-4 \equiv Q(x-2)+R.$$

Since this is an identity, it is satisfied for all values of x.

Put $x=2$. $\quad 8-12+4-4=Q(0)+R. \quad \therefore R=-4.$

This theorem is called the remainder theorem and is specially useful when the remainder is zero. You may factorise an expression by using the theorem.

Example 1. Find the factors of $x^3-6x^2+11x-6$.

Put $x=1$, $x^3-6x^2+11x-6=1-6+11-6=0$.

Therefore $(x-1)$ is a factor.

By long division:

$$\begin{array}{r} x^2 - 5x + 6 \\ x - 1\,\big)\, x^3 - 6x^2 + 11x - 6 \\ \underline{x^3 - x^2 \qquad\qquad} \\ -5x^2 + 11x \quad \\ \underline{-5x^2 + 5x \quad} \\ 6x - 6 \\ \underline{6x - 6} \end{array}$$

$$\therefore x^3 - 6x^2 + 11x - 6 = (x - 1)(x^2 - 5x + 6)$$
$$= (x - 1)(x - 2)(x - 3).$$

Example 2. When divided by $(x + 1)$, the expression $ax^2 + bx + c$ leaves remainder 1. When divided by $(x + 2)$, the same expression leaves remainder -1. Given that $(x - 1)$ is a factor of the expression, find a, b and c.

Put $x = -1$: $\quad a - b + c = 1 \quad . \quad . \quad . \quad .$ (i)
Put $x = -2$: $\quad 4a - 2b + c = -1 \quad . \quad . \quad . \quad .$ (ii)
Put $x = 1$: $\quad a + b + c = 0 \quad . \quad . \quad . \quad .$ (iii)

Subtract (ii) from (i): $\quad -3a + b = 2.$
Subtract (iii) from (i): $\quad -2b = 1. \qquad \therefore b = -\frac{1}{2}.$
Substitute: $\quad -3a - \frac{1}{2} = 2$
$\therefore 3a = -2\frac{1}{2}$ and $a = -\frac{5}{6}.$
Substitute in (iii): $\quad -\frac{5}{6} - \frac{1}{2} + c = 0. \qquad \therefore c = \frac{4}{3}.$

Example 3. Find the value of k if $(x + 1)$ is a factor of

$$x^3 + kx^2 + 3x - 2.$$

Put $x = -1$, $\quad -1 + k - 3 - 2 = 0.$
$$k = 6.$$

EXERCISES 37A

1. Find the remainder when $x^3 - 6x + 1$ is divided by $x - 3$.

2. Find the remainder when $x^3 + x^2 + x + 1$ is divided by $x + 3$.

3. Find the factors of $x^3 - 4x^2 - x + 4$.

4. Find the values of a and b if $(x - 1)$ and $(x - 2)$ are both factors of $x^3 + ax^2 + bx - 6$.

5. Find the value of k if $(x + 1)$ is a factor of $x^3 + kx^2 + 6x + 4$.

6. The expression $x^2 + bx + c$ leaves remainder 1 when divided by $(x - 1)$. When the expression is divided by $(x + 1)$, the remainder is 3. Find b and c.

7. Given that $(x + 2y)$ is a factor of $x^3 - 7xy^2 - 6y^3$, factorise the expression completely.

8. Factorise $x^3 - 7x + 6$.

9. Given that $x = 1$ and $x = -1$ are solutions of the equation $x^4 - 3x^3 + x^2 + 3x - 2 = 0$, find the other solutions.

10. Find the value of k if $(x + 1)$ is a factor of $x^3 + 5x^2 + kx + 3$. Then find the other factors of the expression.

EXERCISES 37B

1. Find the remainder when $x^4 - 6x^2 + 1$ is divided by $x - 3$.

2. Find the remainder when $x^3 + 5x^2 + x + 1$ is divided by $x + 3$.

3. Find the factors of $x^3 + 4x^2 + x - 6$.

4. Find the value of k if $(x + 2)$ is a factor of $x^3 + kx^2 - 2x + 4$.

5. The expression $ax^2 + bx + 1$ has remainder 2 when divided by $(x - 1)$. When it is divided by $(x + 1)$, the remainder is 4. Find a and b.

6. Find the values of a and b if $(x + 1)$ and $(x + 2)$ are both factors of $x^3 + ax^2 + bx + 8$.

7. Given that $(x + 3y)$ is a factor of $x^3 + 6x^2y + 11xy^2 + 6y^3$, factorise the expression completely.

8. Factorise $x^3 + 6x^2 + 5x - 12$.

9. Given that $x = 2$ and $x = -2$ are solutions of the equation $x^4 + 3x^3 - 2x^2 - 12x - 8 = 0$, find the other solutions.

10. Find the value of k if $(x - 1)$ is a factor of $x^3 + 4x^2 + kx - 6$. Find also the other factors of the expression.

EXERCISES 38: MISCELLANEOUS

1. If the area of a rectangle is $(2pa + qa - 2pb - qb)$ m^2, and the length of one side is $(a - b)$ m, find the length of the other side.

2. Simplify $\dfrac{1}{x-1} - \dfrac{1}{x+1} - \dfrac{3}{2(x^2-1)}$.

3. Prove $(a + 2b)^3 \equiv a^3 + 8b^3 + 6ab(a + 2b)$.

4. Find the remainder when $x^5 - 40$ is divided by $x - 2$.

5. Find the values of a and b if the expression $x^3 + ax^2 + bx - 4$ is exactly divisible by $(x^2 - 4)$.

6. Find the remainder when $x^3 + 5x^2 - 2x + 4$ is divided by $x + 4$.

7. A cylindrical tank has a radius of x cm and a depth of y cm. Find an expression for the number of litres the tank will hold.

8. What must be added to $\frac{x}{y}$ to make $\frac{2y}{x}$?

9. Find, in new pence, the average cost of an egg if x eggs are bought for n new pence and a further y eggs for n pounds.

10. Find k if $(x + 3)$ is a factor of $x^3 + kx^2 - 3x - 18$.

11. Simplify $\dfrac{1}{2ax + x^2} - \dfrac{1}{2ax - x^2} - \dfrac{2}{x^2 - 4a^2}$.

12. A blanket is a cm long and b cm wide. When washed it loses $12\frac{1}{2}\%$ of its length and 10% of its width. Find its percentage loss in area.

13. The average speed of a car from Bedford to Cambridge, x km apart, is p km/h. Its average speed from Cambridge to Newmarket, y km apart, is q km/h. Find its average speed from Bedford to Newmarket.

14. A line x cm long is divided into two parts in the ratio $m : n$. Find the length of each part in centimetres.

15. What values of a and b will make $x^2 + 3x + 2$ a factor of $x^3 + ax^2 + bx + 4$?

16. Show that $x - a$ is a factor of $(x - b)^5 + (b - a)^5$.

17. Find the L.C.M. of $a^4 - x^4$, $a^2 - x^2$, $ax - x^2$.

18. Simplify $\dfrac{1}{a(a - b)(a - c)} + \dfrac{1}{b(b - a)(b - c)} + \dfrac{1}{c(c - a)(c - b)}$.

19. Simplify $1 + \dfrac{x}{2} + \dfrac{2}{x}$.

20. Simplify $\dfrac{3}{4(1 + x)} - \dfrac{2}{3(1 - x)} + \dfrac{1}{x^2 - 1}$.

21. Prove

$$a^3b^3 + b^3c^3 + c^3a^3 - 3a^2b^2c^2 \equiv (ab + bc + ca)\{a^2b^2 + b^2c^2 + c^2a^2 - abc(a + b + c)\}.$$

22. The expression $ax^2 + bx + c$ leaves remainder 4 when divided by $(x + 1)$, remainder 9 when divided by $(x + 2)$ and remainder 20 when divided by $(x + 3)$. Find a, b and c.

23. Prove that $x - 1$ is a factor of $x^n - 1$. Prove also that $(x + 1)$ is a factor provided that n is even.

24. A wire in the shape of an equilateral triangle encloses an area of A cm². If the same wire is bent to form a circle, find an expression for the area of the circle in cm².

25. Prove that $(x + y + z)^2 - (x + 2y)(x + 2z) \equiv (y - z)^2$.

26. What value of k will make $x^3 + 2x^2 + kx - 6$ vanish when $x = -1$? For what other values of x does the expression vanish?

27. A man bought E eggs at x new pence a dozen and M more eggs at y new pence a hundred. What was the average price of an egg in new pence?

28. A stationer buys $(x + y)$ copies of a certain book all at the same price. He sells x of them at a profit of $p\%$ but has to sell the remainder at a loss of $q\%$. Find his percentage profit on the whole transaction.

29. Prove

$$(2x+5)(2x+3)(2x+1)(2x-1)+10(2x+3)(2x+1)+1 \equiv 16(x+1)^4.$$

30. Simplify $\dfrac{1}{x(x-y)} + \dfrac{1}{y(x+y)} - \dfrac{2}{x^2-y^2}$.

31. Simplify $\dfrac{3}{(x+2)(x+5)} - \dfrac{2}{(x+6)(x+2)} + \dfrac{1}{(x+5)(x+6)}$.

32. Prove $(x-y)^3 + (y-z)^3 + (z-x)^3 = 3(x-y)(y-z)(z-x)$.

33. Simplify $\dfrac{1}{1-4x+3x^2} - \dfrac{2}{1-2x-3x^2} + \dfrac{3}{1-x^2}$.

34. If $y = \dfrac{1+2x}{x-2}$, express $2x + y$ (i) in terms of x only; (ii) in terms of y only.

35. In the expression $\dfrac{x+\frac{2}{x}}{x-\frac{1}{x}} - 1$, put $x = y + \frac{1}{y}$ and simplify your result.

36. Simplify $\dfrac{t^2}{1-t} - \dfrac{t^2}{1+t} + \dfrac{2t^2}{1-t^2}$.

37. Simplify $\dfrac{a+b}{2a-5b} - \dfrac{a-b}{2a+5b} - \dfrac{13ab}{4a^2-25b^2}$.

38. If $x : y = 3 : 5$, find the value of $\dfrac{3x^2+5xy-y^2}{2x^3+3xy+y^2}$.

39. The expression $ax^2 + 7x + b$ leaves remainder 8 when divided by $(x + 1)$ and remainder 10 when divided by $(x + 2)$. Find a and b.

40. Factorise $6x^3 - 11x^2 + 6x - 1$.

41. Factorise $6x^3 + 17x^2 + 11x + 2$.

9

PROBLEMS

REMEMBER that a letter is used to represent a *number* and not a quantity, such as an age or an area.

Your first statement should ensure that the letter chosen does represent a number.

Do not say, 'Let the height of the tree be x.'

Your statement should read, 'Let the height of the tree be x metres.'

Do not say, 'Let the boy's age be x.'

This should read, 'Let the boy's age be x years.'

The method of solving a problem by algebra may be divided into the following steps.

(1) Choose a letter (or letters) to represent the number (or numbers) required.

(2) Translate each statement given in the question to a statement containing your letter (or letters).

(3) By linking up the parts of the question, form an equation (or equations).

The resulting equation may be a simple equation or a quadratic equation. If two unknowns are used, you should arrive at simultaneous equations.

Problems leading to simple equations

Example 1. A man drives from Bedford to Cambridge, a distance of 48 km, in 45 minutes. Where the surface is good, he drives at 72 km/h; where it is bad, at 48 km/h. Find the number of km of good surface.

Suppose there are x km of good surface.
Then there are $(48 - x)$ km of bad surface.
Over the good surface he drives at 72 km/h.
Therefore he drives x km at 72 km/h.
The time taken is $x/72$ hours.
Over the bad surface, he drives at 48 km/h.
Therefore he drives $(48 - x)$ km at 48 km/h.
The time taken is $(48 - x)/48$ hours.
The total time taken is 45 minutes or $\frac{3}{4}$ hour.

$$\therefore \frac{x}{72} + \frac{48 - x}{48} = \frac{3}{4}.$$

Multiply by 144:

$$2x + 3(48 - x) = 108$$
$$2x + 144 - 3x = 108$$
$$-x = -36$$
$$\therefore x = 36$$

There are 36 km of good surface.

Check. Always check from the question and not from your equations.

He drives 36 km at 72 km/h. Time taken = 30 min.
" " 12 km " 48 km/h. " " = 15 min.
Total time taken = 45 min.

Example 2. A certain sum of money consists of 30 coins some of which are ten new penny pieces and the rest of which are 5 new penny pieces. If the total value of the coins is £2, find the number of 10 new penny pieces.

Let the number of ten new penny pieces be x.
The number of five new penny pieces must be $(30 - x)$.
The value of x ten new penny pieces is $10x$ new pence.
The value of $(30 - x)$ five new penny pieces is $5(30 - x)$ new pence.
The total value is 200 new pence.

N.B. Always make sure that both sides of your equation are expressed in the same units.

$$\therefore 10x + 5(30 - x) = 200$$
$$10x - 5x = 200 - 150$$
$$x = 10.$$

The number of ten new penny pieces is 10.

Check. The value of 10 ten new penny pieces is £1.
The value of 20 five new penny pieces is £1.
The total value is £2.

EXERCISES 39A

1. A boy is paid 50 new pence for each day he works and is fined 25 new pence for each day he fails to work. After 20 days, he is paid £7. For how many days has he worked?

2. A sum of money is made up of an equal number of ten new penny pieces and five new penny pieces. If the number of ten new penny pieces were doubled and the number of five new penny pieces halved, the sum would be increased by £1·80. Find the number of five new penny pieces originally.

3. A man has to go 10 km to catch a bus. He walks part of the way at 7 km/h and runs the rest of the way at 12 km/h. If he takes 1 hour 15 minutes to complete his journey, find how far he walks.

4. A shopkeeper bought tea at 55 new pence per kg and mixed it with twice as much tea at 50 new pence per kg. He sold the mixture at 60 new pence per kg and gained £10 on the transaction. Find how many kg of each kind of tea he bought.

5. A fraction not in its lowest terms is equal to $\frac{3}{4}$. If the numerator of the fraction were doubled, it would be 34 greater than the denominator. Find the fraction.

6. A father is three times as old as his son. In 12 years' time, he will be twice as old. How old is the father now?

7. Write down the value of the number having x as its unit digit and y as its ten digit.

A number is such that its ten digit is twice its unit digit. Prove that the number itself must be seven times the sum of its digits.

8. From London to Coventry is 144 km. A cyclist starts from London towards Coventry at a steady speed of 16 km/h. An hour later, a motorist starts from Coventry for London and travels at an average speed of 48 km/h. How far from London do they meet?

9. A concert is attended by 300 people. Some paid 15 new pence each and the rest $12\frac{1}{2}$ new pence each. The total receipts were £39·50. Find how many dearer tickets were sold.

10. A sum of £2800 is invested, partly at 5% and partly at 4%. If the total income is £128 per annum, find the amount invested at 5%.

EXERCISES 39B

1. A man averages 32 km/h between Bournemouth and London and 48 km/h between London and Cambridge. If the whole journey of 240 km takes 6 hours 40 min, find how far it is from London to Bournemouth.

2. A sum of money in 50 new penny pieces and 10 new penny pieces amounts to £60. If there are, in all, 440 coins, how many of them are 50 new penny pieces?

3. A sum of £3000 is invested partly at $3\frac{1}{2}$% and partly at 4%. If the annual income from the two investments is £112, find how much is invested at 4%.

4. A number of two digits is such that the sum of its digits is 10. When the digits are reversed, the number is increased by 36. Find the number.

5. A man who leaves home at 08.30h arrives at the station, 5 km away at 09.08h. He walked part of the way at 6 km/h and ran the rest of the way at 10 km/h. How far did he walk?

6. Tickets for a concert cost either $12\frac{1}{2}$ new pence each or $17\frac{1}{2}$ new pence each. If the number of cheaper tickets sold was twice the number of dearer tickets and the total receipts were £85, find the number of cheaper tickets sold.

7. In a factory, the men are paid £1·25 a day and the women £1 a day. If there are 400 people employed and the daily wage bill is £475, find the number of men employed.

8. A train leaves Edinburgh for London at 64 km/h and an express to Edinburgh leaves London an hour later at 96 km/h. If the distance between London and Edinburgh is 624 km, how far are the trains from London when they meet?

9. The same number is added to both numerator and denominator of the fraction $\frac{7}{17}$. If the fraction is then equal to $\frac{3}{5}$, find the number added.

10. Find two consecutive numbers such that the difference of their squares is 53.

Problems leading to simultaneous equations

Most problems which can be solved by using two unknowns and simultaneous equations may also be solved by using one unknown and a simple equation. In the following worked examples, the method of simultaneous equations is chosen.

Example 1. A tobacconist bought a certain number of pipes at $37\frac{1}{2}$ new pence each and others at $42\frac{1}{2}$ new pence each. Had he bought half as many at $37\frac{1}{2}$ new pence and twice as many at $42\frac{1}{2}$ new pence, his bill would have been £49 instead of the £47 which he actually paid. How many pipes did he buy altogether?

Suppose he bought x pipes at $37\frac{1}{2}$ new pence and y pipes at $42\frac{1}{2}$ new pence.

The cost of x pipes at $37\frac{1}{2}$ new pence each is $37\frac{1}{2}x$ new pence.

The cost of y pipes at $42\frac{1}{2}$ new pence each is $42\frac{1}{2}y$ new pence.

$$\therefore\ 37\tfrac{1}{2}x + 42\tfrac{1}{2}y = 4700$$

or
$$15x + 17y = 1880 \quad . \quad . \quad . \quad . \quad \text{(i)}$$

The cost of $\frac{1}{2}x$ pipes at $37\frac{1}{2}$ new pence is

$$\tfrac{1}{2}x(37\tfrac{1}{2}) = \frac{75x}{4} \text{ new pence.}$$

The cost of $2y$ pipes at $42\frac{1}{2}$ new pence is

$$2y\left(\frac{85}{2}\right) = 85y \text{ new pence}$$

$$\therefore\ \frac{75x}{4} + 85y = 4900$$

or
$$3\tfrac{3}{4}x + 17y = 980 \quad . \quad . \quad . \quad . \quad \text{(ii)}$$

Subtract (ii) from (i), $\quad 11\frac{1}{4}x = 900.$

Multiply by 4, $\quad 45x = 3600.$

$$x = 80.$$

Substitute in (i), $1200 + 17y = 1880.$

$$17y = 680.$$

or $y = 40.$

He bought 80 pipes at $37\frac{1}{2}$ new pence and 40 at $42\frac{1}{2}$ new pence, or 120 in all.

Check. 80 pipes at $37\frac{1}{2}$ new pence each cost £30.
40 pipes at $42\frac{1}{2}$ new pence each cost £17.
Total cost is £47.
40 pipes at $37\frac{1}{2}$ new pence each cost £15.
80 pipes at $42\frac{1}{2}$ new pence each cost £34.
Total cost is £49.

Example 2. A motorist travels 15 km to the litre of petrol and 600 km to the litre of oil. He estimates that an annual distance of 6000 km will cost him £34 in petrol and oil. In fact he used twice as much oil as he estimated and the cost was £36. Find the cost of a litre of petrol.

Suppose the cost of a litre of petrol is x new pence and the cost of a litre of oil is y new pence.

In travelling 6000 km, he estimates to use 400 litres of petrol and 10 litres of oil.

The cost of these is $(400x + 10y)$ new pence.

$$\therefore\ 400x + 10y = 3400 \quad . \quad . \quad . \quad . \quad \text{(i)}$$

He actually used 20 litres of oil.

$$\therefore\ 400x + 20y = 3600 \quad . \quad . \quad . \quad . \quad \text{(ii)}$$

Subtract(i) from (ii), $10y = 200$

$$y = 20$$

Substitute in (i), $400x + 200 = 3400$

$$400x = 3200$$

$$\therefore\ x = 8$$

The cost of a litre of petrol is 8 new pence.

Check. 400 litres of petrol at 8p cost £32.
10 litres of oil at 20p cost £2.
20 litres of oil at 20p cost £4.
The estimated cost is £34.
The actual cost is £36.

EXERCISES 40A

1. When petrol costs 10 new pence a litre and oil 25 new pence a litre, a motorist finds that his cost in petrol and oil is £10·50 for each 1000 km. When petrol is increased to $10\frac{1}{2}$ new pence a litre and oil to 26p a litre, the cost is £11·02. Find how many litres of petrol and oil he uses to travel 1000 km.

2. At a concert, tickets were $17\frac{1}{2}$ new pence or $12\frac{1}{2}$ new pence each. Three-quarters of those who paid $17\frac{1}{2}$ new pence bought programmes and half the $12\frac{1}{2}$ new penny seat-holders bought programmes. The receipts from the tickets were £145 and from the programmes £15. If programmes cost $2\frac{1}{2}$ new pence each, how many paid $17\frac{1}{2}$ new pence for the concert?

3. I invest £x at 4% and £y at 5%. My annual income is £230. Had I invested £x at 5% and £y at 4%, my annual income would have been £220. Find x and y.

4. The total cost of 12 kg of apples and 24 kg of plums is £4·32. The cost of 24 kg of apples and 12 kg of plums is £3·60. Find the cost of apples per kg.

5. A number of two digits is increased by 54 when the digits are reversed. The sum of the digits is 12. Find the number.

6. A bottle and a cork together cost 8 new pence. The bottle costs 6 new pence more than the cork. Find the cost of the cork.

7. A gramophone with 12 records cost £10. The same gramophone with 18 similar records costs £11·50. What is the cost of the gramophone?

8. 100 cigarettes and 4 cigars cost £2·45; 50 cigarettes and 8 cigars cost £3·02$\frac{1}{2}$. What is the price of a cigar?

9. A man walks at 8 km/h and runs at 12 km/h. To get to the station takes him 20 min. Had he run twice as far, it would have taken him $17\frac{1}{2}$ min. How far is the station?

10. A man travels x km at 8 km/h and y km at 20 km/h. His total time is $3\frac{1}{2}$ hours. The total time taken to travel $(2x + 4)$ km at 8 km/h and $y/3$ km at 20 km/h is 5 hours. Find x and y.

EXERCISES 40B

1. To travel 1000 km a motorist estimates that he will need 100 litres of petrol and 2 litres of oil, and that the cost will be £8·40. He actually uses 95 litres of petrol and 3 litres of oil and the cost is £8·20. Find the cost of a litre of petrol.

2. At an entertainment, the price of the first three rows of chairs was 25 new pence each and the other seats cost 15 new pence each. The takings were £51. On the second night of the entertainment, the price of the fourth row of chairs was increased to 25 new pence and the takings were £53. How many chairs were there in the hall, assuming it was full on each occasion and that there were the same number of chairs in each row?

3. If I invest £2000 at x% and £2500 at y%, my annual income is £160. Had I invested £2500 at x% and £2000 at y%, my income would have been £155. Find x and y.

4. 10 kg of apples and 20 kg of plums cost, in all, £3·80; 20 kg of apples and 10 kg of plums cost £2·80. What is the cost of plums per kg?

5. A number of two digits is such that twice the ten digit is 6 greater than the unit digit. When the digits are reversed, the number is increased by 9. What is the number?

6. The sum of the ages of a father and a son is 52 years. Eight years ago, the father was eight times as old as his son. How old is the father now?

7. The charge for electricity is 3 new pence per unit for lighting and $\frac{1}{2}$ new penny per unit for heating. A man's bill for a quarter should have been £8. By mistake, his lighting was charged at $\frac{1}{2}$ new penny per unit and his heating at 3 new pence per unit. The amount of the bill was £13. How many units of electricity did he use altogether?

8. 20 cigars and 200 cigarettes cost £4·25: 16 cigars and 100 cigarettes cost £2·87$\frac{1}{2}$. Find the cost of a cigar.

9. To go to the station in the morning, I first walk to the garage at 8 km/h and motor the rest of the way at 40 km/h. It normally takes me 21 min in all. One morning when I am late, I run to the garage at 16 km/h and motor at 60 km/h. I complete the journey in 11$\frac{1}{2}$ min. How far is the garage from the station?

10. The total time taken to travel x km at 30 km/h and y km at 60 km/h is 2$\frac{1}{2}$ hours. The time taken to travel x km at 15 km/h and y km at 45 km/h is 4 hours 20 minutes. Find x and y.

Problems leading to quadratic equations

The method for finding the equation is the same.

Factorise the resulting quadratic if possible.

Otherwise, solve by formula or by completing the square.

You will find two answers for your unknown. They may both be possible but often one will not be permissible owing to the physical conditions of the problem. For example, if you are finding a time and one of your answers is negative, it may be discarded.

Example 1. The distance from London to Bournemouth is 160 km. If the Bournemouth Belle were 16 km/h slower, it would take 20 minutes longer on the journey. Find the speed of the Belle.

The time taken to travel 160 km at x km/h is $\dfrac{160}{x}$ hours.

The time taken to travel 160 km at $(x - 16)$ km/h is $\dfrac{160}{x-16}$ hours.

20 minutes is $\frac{1}{3}$ of an hour.

$$\therefore \quad \frac{160}{x-16} - \frac{160}{x} = \frac{1}{3}.$$

Multiply by $3x(x - 16)$:

$$480x - 480(x - 16) = x^2 - 16x$$

i.e.

$$480x - 480x + 480(16) = x^2 - 16x$$

$$x^2 - 16x - 480(16) = 0$$

$$\therefore\ (x - 96)(x + 80) = 0$$

and

$$x = 96 \quad \text{or} \quad -80.$$

The negative speed may be discarded and so the speed of the Belle is 96 km/h.

Check. Time taken to travel 160 km at 96 km/h is 1 h 40 min.
Time taken to travel 160 km at 80 km/h is 2 h.
Time saved would be 20 min.

Example 2. I spend £45 a year on cigars. If the price of a cigar rises by $2\frac{1}{2}$ new pence, I should have to buy 20 cigars less a year. How many cigars do I smoke in a year?

Suppose I smoke x cigars a year.

The price of 1 cigar must be $\dfrac{4500}{x}$ new pence.

If I smoked 20 cigars less, I should smoke $(x - 20)$ cigars.

The price of 1 cigar would then be $\dfrac{4500}{x - 20}$ new pence.

$$\therefore\ \frac{4500}{x - 20} = \frac{4500}{x} + 2\tfrac{1}{2}.$$

Multiply by $2x(x - 20)$.

$$9000x = 9000(x - 20) + 5x(x - 20).$$

i.e.

$$5x(x - 20) = 9000 \times 20$$

or

$$x^2 - 20x - 36\,000 = 0$$

$$\therefore\ (x - 200)(x + 180) = 0$$

and

$$x = 200 \quad \text{or} \quad -180.$$

The negative answer is impossible and I smoke 200 cigars a year.

EXERCISES 41A

1. The sides of a right-angled triangle are $(2x + 1)$ cm, $2x$ cm and $(x - 1)$ cm. Find x.

2. The length of a rectangle is 3 m greater than its width and the area of the rectangle is 108 m^2. Find its length.

3. The product of two numbers, differing by 7, is 60. Find them.

4. A motorist has to travel 160 km. His average speed is 8 km/h slower than he estimated and he takes 1 hour longer on the journey. Find his actual average speed.

5. The average age of x boys in a form is 14 years 2 months. A boy of age 15 years 2 months joins the class and the average age is increased by 1 month. Find x.

6. A man spends £5 on cigars. Had they been $2\frac{1}{2}$ new pence cheaper each, he could have bought 10 more. How many did he buy?

7. A man can row at 5 km/h in still water. He rows 3 km up stream and back to his starting point. If the total time taken is 1 hour 15 minutes, find the speed of the current.

8. A room has an area of 288 m^2. If the length were increased by 6 m and the breadth decreased by 4 m, the area would be unaltered. Find the length of the room.

9. The perimeter of a right-angled triangle is 30 cm and one of the sides is 5 cm. Find the other sides.

10. x articles cost $(3x + 20)$ new pence; $(x + 4)$ similar articles cost $(5x - 4)$ new pence. Find x.

EXERCISES 41B

1. The sides of a right-angled triangle are $(4x + 1)$ cm, $(4x - 1)$ cm and $2x$ cm. Find x.

2. The length of a rectangle is 6 m greater than its width and the area of the rectangle is 520 m^2. Find the length.

3. The product of two numbers whose sum is 70 is 1200. Find them.

4. On a journey of 300 km, the driver of a train calculates that if he reduced his average speed by 5 km/h, he would take 40 minutes longer. Find his average speed.

5. The average of a cricketer is 32 runs per innings. In his last innings of the season he is bowled for 95 and thereby increases his average by 3. Find how many completed innings he played during the season.

6. A greengrocer buys a number of kg of apples for £2. Had the apples been 2p per kg cheaper, he could have bought 5 kg more for his money. How much did he pay for the apples per kg?

7. The speed of a stream is 2 km/h. A man rows 4 km up stream and back again in $1\frac{1}{2}$ hours. At what speed can he row in still water?

8. The area of a room is 300 m^2. If the length were decreased by 5 m and the breadth increased by 5 m, the area would be unaltered. Find the length of the room.

9. The sum of the squares of two numbers which differ by 6 is 596. Find the numbers.

10. $3x$ articles cost $(7x + 2)$ new pence; $4(x + 1)$ similar articles cost $(12x + 2)$ new pence. Find x.

EXERCISES 42: MISCELLANEOUS PROBLEMS

1. There are two turnstiles which admit spectators to a fair. The spectators take, on the average, $\frac{1}{8}$ sec less to pass through the first than through the second and 40 more spectators can pass through it per min. How many spectators can pass through the two turnstiles in 1 minute?

2. A sum of £1200 is invested partly at $3\frac{1}{2}\%$ and partly at 4%. The total annual income derived is £44. Find the amount invested at $3\frac{1}{2}\%$.

3. A cyclist leaves home at 10.00h to cycle to a church 7 km away. He cycles at 10 km/h until he has a puncture and has to push his bicycle the rest of the way at 3 km/h. He arrives at the church at 11.10h. Find how far he walked.

4. When the price of an orange is reduced by $\frac{1}{2}$ new penny, I find that by paying 3 new pence more, I can buy 3 dozen instead of $2\frac{1}{2}$ dozen. What was the price of an orange before the reduction?

5. A housewife walks to the shopping centre at 5 km/h, spends 20 min shopping and takes the bus, which averages 30 km/h, home. She is 55 min away from home. How far is the shopping centre?

6. A train is scheduled to do a certain stretch of line at a certain speed. If the train averages 48 km/h, it runs 3 min behind schedule; if it averages 60 km/h, it is 12 min ahead of schedule. Find the scheduled time for the stretch.

7. Sweets are divided equally between 20 children at a party. If there were 1 more sweet and 1 more child, each child would get 1 sweet less. How many sweets are divided?

8. A mother is three times as old as her daughter. Six years ago, she was five times as old. How old is the daughter now?

9. A motor-boat travelling at an average speed of v km/h is timed over a distance of 4 km. When its speed is increased to $(v + 3)$ km/h, it takes 4 min less for the journey. Find v.

10. The sum of the ages of x boys in a form is 84 years. When a new boy, aged 8 years 1 month, joins the form, the average age is increased by 1 month. Find x.

11. A batsman scores 450 runs in x completed innings. In his next innings, he is out for 63 and thereby increases his average by 2. Find x.

12. A man leaves Southampton at 11.20h and travels by train to Bournemouth at an average speed of 72 km/h. He spends 2 hours in Bournemouth and returns to Southampton by bus at an average speed of 40 km/h. If the bus route is 2 km longer than the train journey and if he arrives in Southampton at 15.15h, find the distance from Southampton to Bournemouth by train.

13. A train travelling between two stations arrives $\frac{1}{2}$ min early if its average speed is 60 km/h and $2\frac{1}{2}$ min late if its average speed is 40 km/h. Find the distance between the stations.

14. A man cycles from one town to another at 20 km/h and motors the return journey at 60 km/h. The double journey takes 1 hour longer than if he had travelled both ways by train at 40 km/h. Find the distance between the towns.

15. Two substances A and B are mixed in the ratio 3 : 4 by volume. If the density of A is 5 g/cm^3 and that of B 7 g/cm^3, find the volume of A used if the total weight is 258 g.

16. The cost of a journey, C new pence, is expressed by the equation $C = a + bx$, where x is the number of km travelled and a and b are constants. A journey of 50 km costs 50 new pence and a journey of 70 km costs $62\frac{1}{2}$ new pence. Find the cost of a journey of 90 km.

17. When the weekly wage of agricultural workers is increased by 15 new pence, a farmer found that by employing one less his weekly wage bill was reduced from £120 to £116·85. Find the original weekly wage of a worker.

18. A man sets out by bicycle at 10.00h to keep an appointment at 12 noon in a town 36 km away. After cycling at 20 km/h for some time, one of his tyres is punctured, and he waits 20 min before finishing his journey by bus at 40 km/h. If he is 16 min early for his appointment, find how far he cycled.

19. Half the sum of two numbers is 51; one quarter of their difference is 13. Find the numbers.

20. A number of three digits has the hundred digit 3 times the unit digit and the sum of the three digits is 19. If the three digits are written in reverse order, the value of the number is decreased by 594. Find the number.

21. When a bus makes an extra stop on a journey of 64 km, its average speed is reduced by 2 km/h and the bus takes 8 min longer for the journey. Find the new average speed.

22. I can buy y articles for £2 or $(y + 2)$ similar articles for £2·20. Find y.

23. I invest two sums of money which are in the ratio 3 : 5. The smaller amount I invest at 4%, the larger at 5%. My annual income from the two investments is £74. Find how much I invest at 4%.

24. When the price of an article is increased by $\frac{1}{2}$ new penny, I can buy 40 less for £2·40. Find the original price of the article.

25. $(5x - 10)$ articles cost x new pence; $3x$ similar articles cost $(10x - 10)$ new pence. Find x.

26. The perimeter of a rectangle is 72 m. If its length were decreased by 2 m and its breadth increased by 2 m, its area would be increased by 4 m^2. Find the length of the rectangle.

27. A greengrocer bought a certain number of kg of strawberries for £72. He was unable to sell 10% of them but made a profit of £14·40 by selling the rest at a profit of 8 new pence per kg. How many kg did he buy?

28. A buys a car for £300 and sells it to B at a profit of x%. B sells it to C at a profit of x%. C paid £$(6x + \frac{3}{4})$ more for the car than A paid. Find x.

29. A man allowed £30 for his holiday. He afterwards calculated that if he had spent 25 new pence less a day, he could have extended his holiday by 4 days on the same money. How long a holiday did he have?

30. A certain sum of money is made up of a number of ten new penny pieces and twice as many five new penny pieces. If the number of ten new penny pieces were doubled and the number of five new penny pieces decreased by 10, the sum of money would be increased by £1·10. Find the original number of five new penny pieces.

31. A square lawn is surrounded by a path 0·5 m wide. The area of the lawn is 23 m^2 bigger than the area of the path. Find the length of a side of the lawn.

32. A train must complete its journey of 200 km in a certain time. At the end of the first 70 km, it is 15 min behind its schedule, but by increasing its speed by $3\frac{1}{3}$ km/h over the scheduled speed, the driver is able to finish his journey at the correct time. What is the scheduled time for the journey?

33. If 7 is added to both numerator and denominator of a fraction, the fraction becomes equal to $\frac{5}{6}$. If 5 is added to the numerator and 7 to the denominator, the fraction becomes equal to $\frac{3}{4}$. Find the original fraction.

34. Two men, 66 km apart, are walking towards each other at uniform speeds. They meet in 6 hours and one takes 2 min longer than the other to walk a km. Find their walking speeds.

35. I am thinking of a number. I double the number, add 6 and multiply the result by 10. I now divide by 20 and subtract the number I first thought of. What is the result?

10

GRAPHS

Linear functions

THE function $ax + b$, where a and b are constants, is called a linear function of x. It contains no power of x above the first. If you plot such a function against x, you will always get a straight line. You can, of course, draw the line from two pairs of values only. However, it is much safer to consider three pairs of values. The third point will serve as a check for your arithmetic.

Example 1. Draw the graph of $y = 3x - 2$.
Consider the values 1, 2, 3 for x.

x	1	2	3
y	1	4	7

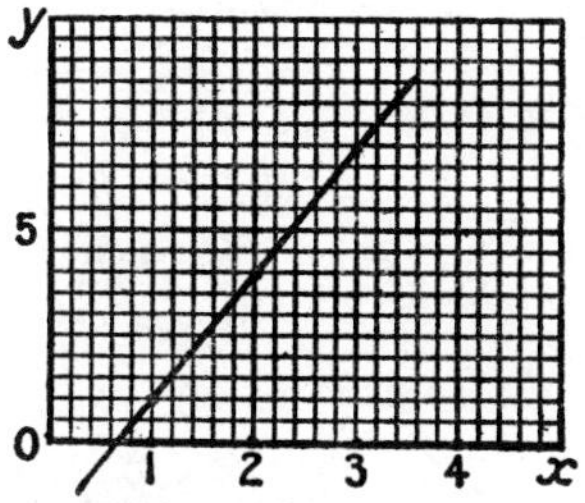

FIG. 8

Example 2. Draw the graphs of $3y = 5x + 1$ and $y = 3x - 1$, using the same scales and axes. Write down the point of intersection of the two graphs.

x	0	2	3
$\frac{5x+1}{3}$	$\frac{1}{3}$	$3\frac{2}{3}$	$5\frac{1}{3}$
$3x - 1$	-1	5	8

The graphs intersect at the point (1, 2). This gives the solutions $x = 1$, $y = 2$ for the pair of simultaneous equations $3y = 5x + 1$ and $y = 3x - 1$.

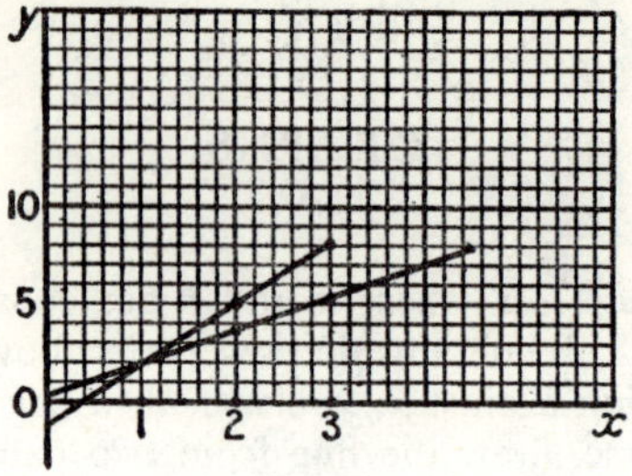

FIG. 9

EXERCISES 43A

Draw the graphs of:

1. $y = x + 1$.
2. $y = 3x - 2$.
3. $3y = 4x + 1$.
4. $x/2 + y/3 = 1$.
5. $2x + 3y = 6$.
6. $x = y + 2$ and $2y = x + 1$, using the same scales and axes.

Write down the point of intersection of the graphs.

EXERCISES 43B

Draw the graphs of:

1. $y + x = 2$.
2. $y = 2x - 1$.
3. $2y = 3x + 5$.
4. $x/3 + y/4 = 1$.
5. $3x + 4y = 12$.
6. $2x = y - 1$ and $x + y = 4$, using the same scales and axes.

Write down the point of intersection of the graphs.

Quadratic functions

The expression $ax^2 + bx + c$, where a, b and c are constants, is called a quadratic function of x. The highest power of the variable is the second. If such an expression is plotted against x, the resulting curve will have one of the shapes shown.

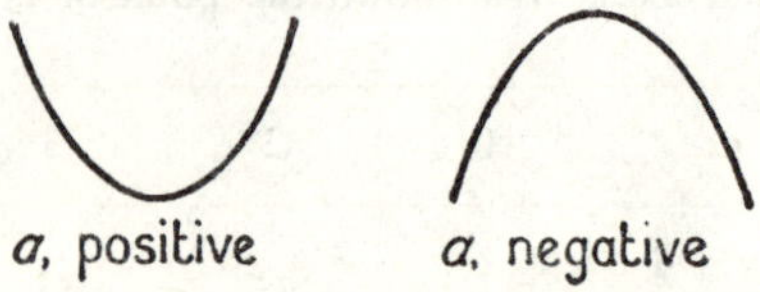

FIG. 10

The sign of a determines which way up the curve is.

Example 1. Draw the graph of $y = x^2 - 3x + 2$, taking values of x between 0 and 4.

x	0	1	2	3	4
x^2 $-3x$ 2	0 0 2	1 −3 2	4 −6 2	9 −9 2	16 −12 2
y	2	0	0	2	6

Since both $x = 1$ and $x = 2$ give $y = 0$, it is advisable to consider a value of x between 1 and 2.

When $x = 1\frac{1}{2}$, $y = 2\frac{1}{4} - 4\frac{1}{2} + 2 = -\frac{1}{4}$.

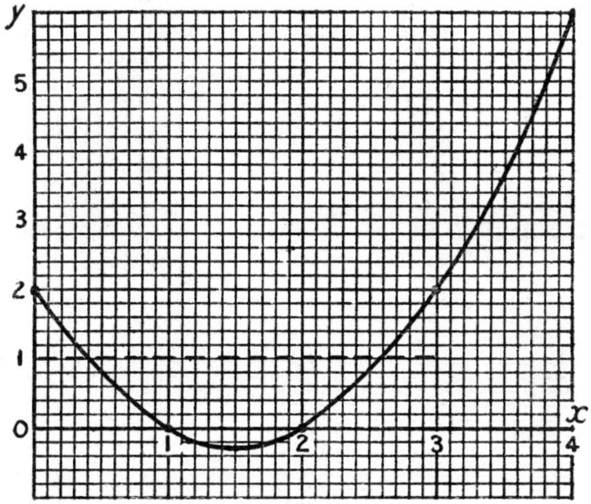

FIG. 11

N.B. The points where the curve crosses the x-axis are the points where $x = 1$ and $x = 2$. These are the points on the curve for which $y = 0$, or $x^2 - 3x + 2 = 0$. Therefore $x = 1$ and $x = 2$ are the solutions of the quadratic equation $x^2 - 3x + 2 = 0$.

Similarly, you can solve from the graph any equation of the type $x^2 - 3x = k$, where k is a constant. Suppose you are asked to solve $x^2 - 3x + 1 = 0$.

If $x^2 - 3x + 1 = 0$, by adding 1 to each side of the equation,

$$y = x^2 - 3x + 2 = 1.$$

You need the points on the curve for which $y = 1$. Draw the line $y = 1$ to meet the curve. The values of x at the points of intersection are the solutions of the equation.

From the graph, $x = 2{\cdot}6$ or $0{\cdot}4$.

Example 2. Draw the graph of $y = 1 - 2x - 3x^2$ between $x = -3$ and $x = +3$.

x	-3	-2	-1	0	$+1$	$+2$	$+3$
1	1	1	1	1	1	1	1
$-2x$	6	4	2	0	-2	-4	-6
$-3x^2$	-27	-12	-3	0	-3	-12	-27
y	-20	-7	0	1	-4	-15	-32

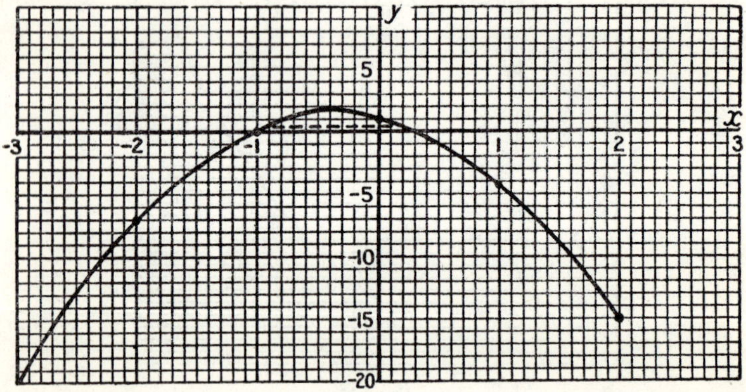

FIG. 12

N.B. The solutions of the equation $1 - 2x - 3x^2 = 0$ are given by the values of x at the points where the curve crosses the x-axis. They are $x = -1$ and $x = 0{\cdot}3$.

To solve from the graph the equation $6x^2 + 4x = 1$.

If $6x^2 + 4x = 1$,

$$3x^2 + 2x = \tfrac{1}{2} \quad \text{and} \quad y = 1 - 2x - 3x^2 = 1 - \tfrac{1}{2} = \tfrac{1}{2}.$$

Find the values of x at the points where the line $y = \frac{1}{2}$ cuts the curve. They are $0{\cdot}2$ and $-0{\cdot}85$.

EXERCISES 44A

1. Draw the graph of $y = x^2 - 1$, taking values of x between -2 and $+2$. Solve from your graph the equations (i) $x^2 - 1 = 0$, (ii) $x^2 - 4 = 0$.

2. Draw the graph of $y = x^2 + x - 2$, taking values of x between -3 and $+3$. Solve from your graph the equations (i) $x^2 + x - 2 = 0$, (ii) $x^2 + x - 5 = 0$.

3. Draw the graph of $y = x^2 + 4x + 3$, taking values of x between 0 and -5. Solve from your graph the equations (i) $x^2 + 4x + 3 = 0$, (ii) $x^2 + 4x + 2 = 0$.

4. Draw the graph of $y = x^2 + x + 1$, taking values of x from -3 to $+3$. Solve from your graph the equations (i) $x^2 + x - 2 = 0$, (ii) $x^2 + x - 1 = 0$. What can you say about the solutions of the equation $x^2 + x + 1 = 0$?

5. Draw the graph of $y = x^2 + x - 3$, taking values of x between -3 and $+3$. Solve from your graph the equations (i) $x^2 + x - 3 = 0$, (ii) $x^2 + x - 5 = 0$.

EXERCISES 44B

1. Draw the graph of $y = x^2 - 4$, taking values of x between -3 and $+3$. Solve from your graph the equations (i) $x^2 - 4 = 0$, (ii) $x^2 - 6 = 0$.

2. Draw the graph of $y = x^2 + 2x - 3$, taking values of x between -3 and $+3$. Solve from your graph the equations (i) $x^2 + 2x - 3 = 0$, (ii) $x^2 = -2x$.

3. Draw the graph of $y = x^2 - 4x + 3$, taking values of x between 0 and 5. From your graph, solve the equations (i) $x^2 - 4x + 3 = 0$, (ii) $x^2 - 4x + 1 = 0$.

4. Draw the graph of $y = 2x^2 + x + 1$, taking values of x between -3 and $+3$. Write down the coordinates of the lowest point of your graph. What is the least possible value of y? From your graph, solve the equation $2x^2 + x - 1 = 0$.

5. Draw the graph of $y = 1 + x - 2x^2$, taking values of x between -3 and $+3$. What is the greatest possible value of y? From your graph, solve the equations (i) $1 + x - 2x^2 = 0$, (ii) $4x^2 - 2x = 5$.

Intersecting graphs

Equations may also be solved graphically by the method of intersecting graphs. An example is given.

Example. Draw, using the same scales and axes, the graphs of $y = x^2 - 4x + 7$ and $y = x + 1$. Write down the x coordinates of the points of intersection of the graphs. Find the equation which has these values as roots.

Consider values of x from 0 to 5.

x	0	1	2	3	4	5
x^2 $-4x$ 7	0 0 7	1 −4 7	4 −8 7	9 −12 7	16 −16 7	25 −20 7
$x^2 - 4x + 7$	7	4	3	4	7	12
$x + 1$	1	2	3	4	5	6

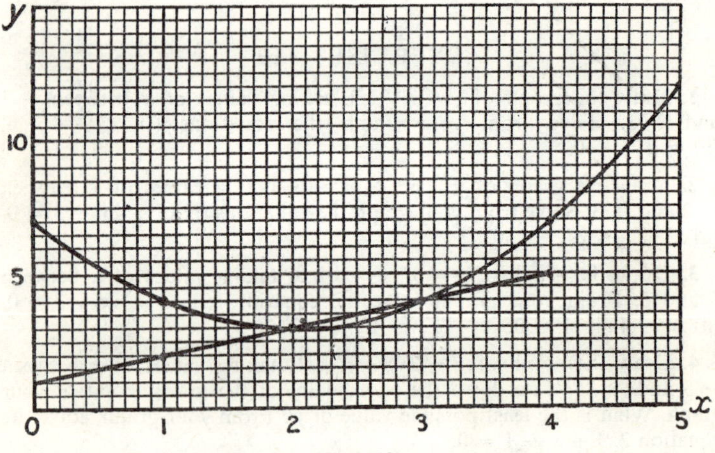

FIG. 13

The values of x at the points of intersection are 2 and 3. At these points, the value of y on one graph is equal to the value of y on the other graph.

Therefore $\qquad x^2 - 4x + 7 = x + 1$

or $\qquad x^2 - 5x + 6 = 0.$

The solutions of the equation $x^2 - 5x + 6 = 0$ are $x = 2$ and $x = 3$.

EXERCISES 45A

1. Draw, using the same scales and axes, the graphs of $y = x$ and $y = x^2 - 4$. Write down the values of x at the points of intersection of the graphs and find the equation which has these values as roots.

2. Draw, using the same scales and axes, the graphs of $y = 2x + 1$ and $y = x^2 + x + 1$. Write down the values of x at the points of intersection of the graphs and find the equation having these values as roots.

3. Draw, using the same scales and axes, the graphs of $y = x + 3$ and $y = x^2 - x + 1$. From your graphs, solve the equations

$$\text{(i) } x^2 - 2x - 2 = 0; \text{ (ii) } x^2 - x - 2 = 0.$$

4. Draw the graph of $y = \dfrac{3 - x^2}{5 + x}$ for values of x between -3 and $+3$. From your graph, solve the equation $2x^2 + x - 1 = 0$.

5. Draw, using the same scales and axes, the graphs of

$$y = (x - 1)(x + 2) \quad \text{and} \quad y = x.$$

From your graphs, write down an approximate value for the square root of 2.

EXERCISES 45B

1. Draw, using the same scales and axes, the graphs of $y = 2x$ and $y = x^2 + 1$. Explain why the line must be a tangent to the curve.

2. Draw, using the same scales and axes, the graphs of $y = 2x - 1$ and $y = x^2 - x + 1$. Write down the values of x at the points of intersection of the graphs and find the equation having these values as roots.

3. Draw, using the same scales and axes, the graphs of $y = x + 2$ and $y = 2x^2 - x - 1$. From your graphs solve the equations

$$\text{(i) } 2x^2 - 2x - 3 = 0; \text{ (ii) } 2x^2 - x = 0.$$

4. Draw the graph of $y = \dfrac{x^2}{x^2 + 2}$ for values of x between -4 and $+4$. On the same figure, draw the graph of $4y = x$. Write down the equation which has the values of x at the points of intersection as roots.

5. Draw the graph of $y = \dfrac{x^2 + 3}{x + 4}$ for values of x between -3 and $+3$. From your graph, solve the equation $x^2 - x - 1 = 0$.

Travel graphs

A completely different type of problem may often be solved by a graphical method. If the horizontal axis represents the time and the vertical axis the distance travelled, the position of a train or cyclist may be represented by a point.

Example. A man starts from Southampton at 09.00h walking to Winchester at 6 km/h. After an hour he meets the bus which runs from Winchester to Southampton. The bus waits a quarter of an hour at Southampton and then returns to Winchester. The bus travels at 24 km/h. Find when and where the man is overtaken by the returning bus.

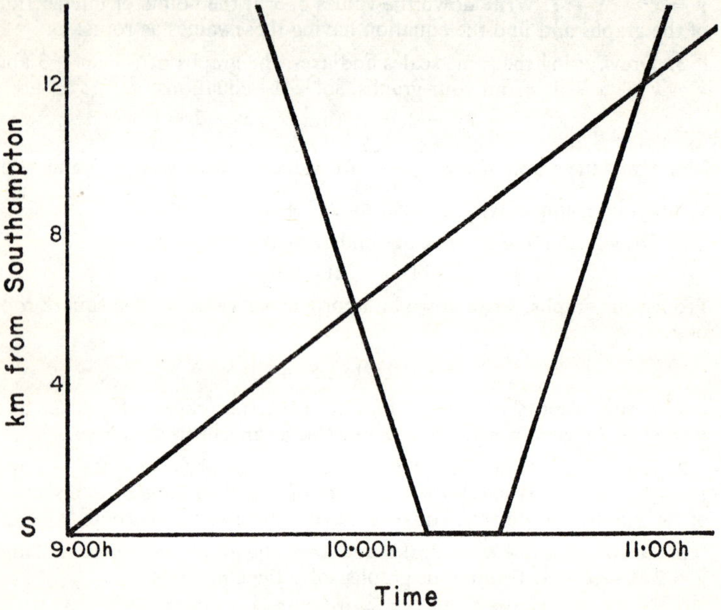

FIG. 14

Take suitable scales, time horizontally and distance from Southampton in km, vertically. The man will be 6 km from Southampton at 10.00h and the straight line joining the point represented by this to the origin represents the progress of the man. The progress of the bus is represented by the three straight lines shown in the diagram. The second point of intersection with the graph of the man shows where and when he is overtaken.

The bus overtakes the man at 11.00h, 12 km from Southampton.

EXERCISES 46A

1. A slow train starts from London for Carlisle at 10.00h travelling at 60 km/h. An hour later, a faster train leaves London for Carlisle at 96 km/h. Find graphically how far from London the faster train overtakes the slower.

2. A train leaves Waterloo for Bournemouth West at 10.12h travelling at 60 km/h. Another train leaves Bournemouth West for Waterloo at 10.32h travelling at 80 km/h. If the distance between stations is 160 km, find graphically when the trains pass each other.

3. A man starts from Bedford at noon to walk to Eaton Socon, 20 km away. A cyclist from Eaton Socon to Bedford passes him at 12.40h, goes on to Bedford where he waits 10 minutes before returning to Eaton Socon by the same route. Find graphically when the cyclist overtakes the man, assuming that he walks steadily at 6 km/h and that the cyclist travels at 16 km/h.

4. The tax on a bachelor's salary in a certain year is calculated as follows: two-ninths of his salary is free of tax and he is allowed a further £110 on which he does not pay tax; he pays $17\frac{1}{2}\%$ on the first £50 of the remainder, $27\frac{1}{2}\%$ on the next £200 and $47\frac{1}{2}\%$ on the rest. Calculate the tax paid on incomes of £90, £180, £270 and so on, and draw a graph to represent the tax paid on any income up to £900.

5. When I visit a friend's house, I can either go by car at an average speed of 60 km/h, or by train at an average speed of 90 km/h. It takes me 15 min to get from my house to the station and 20 min to get to my friend's house from the station. Assuming the distance is the same by train and by road, find this distance graphically, assuming the two journeys take exactly the same time.

EXERCISES 46B

1. A bus from London to Penzance leaves London at 13.00h and travels at 60 km/h. A car averaging 80 km/h leaves London by the same route an hour later. Find graphically when it overtakes the bus.

2. A train travels from X to Y at 80 km/h. Half an hour later another train leaves Y for X travelling at 90 km/h. If the distance from X to Y is 210 km, find how far from X the trains meet.

3. To travel by train costs me $2\frac{1}{2}$ new pence per km. To travel by car costs an annual outlay of £40 together with running costs of 1·25 new pence per km. Calculate the cost (i) by train, (ii) by car, of annual distances of 1200, 2400, 3600 and so on up to 12 000 km. Hence determine diagrammatically the least annual distance for which the car is the more economical.

4. A cyclist who averages 24 km/h leaves a town X at 07.00h. A car averaging 72 km/h leaves X by the same road half an hour later. He goes to Y, 90 km away, stays there 15 min and returns by the same road. How far from X does he meet the cyclist for the second time?

5. A train running between two stations arrives at its destination 50 min late when it averages 80 km/h and 20 min late when it averages 100 km/h. Find graphically the distance between the stations.

EXERCISES 47: MISCELLANEOUS GRAPHS

1. Plot, using the same scales and axes, the graphs of $y = \frac{1}{2}(3 - x)$ and $y = \frac{2}{3}\sqrt{9 - x^2}$. Write down the values of x at their points of intersection.

2. The volume of a cap of a sphere of radius 10 cm is given by $V = \pi h^2(10 - \frac{1}{3}h)$, where h is the height of the cap in cm and V is the volume in cm³. Taking values of h from 0 to 10, plot V/π against h. Find the height of the cap which gives a volume of $21{\cdot}4\pi$ cm³.

3. The distance from Oxford to Bournemouth is 144 km. Two cyclists start at 08·00h, one from Oxford and the other from Bournemouth, and ride towards each other. They pass 80 km from Oxford, and the faster reaches Bournemouth $2\frac{1}{4}$ hours before the slower reaches Oxford. Find their speeds, supposed uniform.

4. A cyclist leaves A for B at 09.00h and travels at 24 km/h. The distance between A and B is 72 km. After $\frac{3}{4}$ of an hour, he meets a car coming from B to A, where it waits 10 min and then returns to B. The car travels at 60 km/h. Find when the car overtakes the cyclist.

5. Draw the graph of $y = x^2 - 2x$ from $x = 0$ to $x = 4$. Use your graph to solve the equations (i) $x^2 - 2x + 1 = 0$, (ii) $x^2 - 2x - 1 = 0$.

6. Draw, using the same scales and axes, the graphs of $y = x^2$ and $y = x + 1$. From your graphs, solve the equation $x^2 - x - 1 = 0$.

7. Draw the graph of $y = x(x - 1)(x + 1)$ between $x = -2$ and $x = +2$.

8. The following table gives the height of the barometer in cm at various heights, measured in metres, above sea level.

Barometer reading .	76·2	63·5	52·1	43·2	36·8	30·5
Altitude	0	1500	3000	4500	6000	7500

Represent these readings graphically and from your graph estimate the barometric pressure at a height of 750 m above sea level, and the altitude at which the barometer reads 50 cm.

9. Draw the graph of $y = \dfrac{2(x - 1)(x + 3)}{x - 4}$ between $x = -3$ and $x = +3$. Using your graph, solve the equation $2x^2 + 3x - 2 = 0$.

10. A cyclist leaves home at 08.30h to meet the 09.35 train at a station

20 km away. He rides at a steady speed which would give him 5 min to spare at the station. His bicycle breaks down and he wastes 15 min before he continues his journey by bus at an average speed of 50 km/h. He arrives at the station 8 min before the train is due. Where did the breakdown occur?

11. Plot $y = x(3 - \frac{1}{2}x)$ for values of x between 0 and 6. For what value of x is y greatest?

12. The table gives the distance it is possible to see on a clear day in km from different heights in metres.

Distance	4·0	5·6	7·0	8·1	9·2	10·2
Height	1·5	3	4·5	6	7·5	9

Plot these values and from your graph estimate the distance to the horizon from a height of 4 m.

13. If a stone is thrown vertically upwards with a velocity of 49 m/s, the height above the ground after t sec is given in feet by the formula $s = 49t - 4{\cdot}9t^2$. Draw a graph showing the height for various times and from your graph find (i) the greatest height reached, (ii) the time taken for the stone to return to the ground.

14. The graph of the equation $y = 1 + Ax + Bx^2$ cuts the x-axis where $x = 1$ and $x = -1$. Find the values of A and B and plot the graph for values of x between $+3$ and -3. Find the gradients of the graph at the points where it crosses the x-axis.

15. A cyclist leaves home at 09.00h and cycles at a steady speed of 18 km/h. An hour later a motorist sets out along the same road at an average speed of 72 km/h. The motorist goes to a town 60 km away, stays there 10 min and returns by the same road. Find when he meets the cyclist on the return journey.

16. Draw the graph of $y = x^2 - 8x + 32$ for values of x between 0 and 8 and find, from your graph, the values of x for which $y = 18$.

17. The graph of $y = A + B/x$ passes through the points (1, 7) and (8, 0). Calculate the values of A and B. Plot y against x, taking values of x between 1 and 6.

18. Draw the graph of $3y = x(x^2 - 2)$ for values of x between $+3$ and -3. Using the same scales and axes, plot the graph of $3y + 3x = 1$ and from your graphs find a solution of the equation $x^3 + x = 1$.

19. A ball is thrown vertically upwards from a height of 16 m above the ground. If h is the height above this point after t sec, then $h = 24t - 4{\cdot}9t^2$, where h is in metres. Plot a graph showing the relationship between h

and t and from your graph find how long before the ball reaches ground level.

20. The extension in cm obtained by a load in newtons for a certain spring is given in the following table:

Load	2	4	6	8	10	12
Extension	1·4	2·7	4·3	5·5	7·0	8·3

Represent these points graphically and draw through them the straight line which most nearly fits. From your graph find the load required to give an extension of 5·0 cm.

21. A cyclist intends to ride from Southampton to Lyndhurst, 20 km away. He rides at 16 km/h until his bicycle breaks down and, after wasting 10 min, he walks the rest of the way at 8 km/h. If the whole journey takes 2 hours 10 min, find how far he walks.

22. Plot the graph of $y = x^2 - 3x + 1$ between $x = -1$ and $x = -4$. From your graph, solve the equation $x^2 - 3x + 1 = 0$.

23. The distance from Oxford to Bicester is 24 km. A man leaves Oxford at noon and walks to Bicester at 8 km/h. At 13.00h a cyclist leaves Bicester for Oxford at 16 km/h. Find when the two meet.

24. Draw the graph of $y = \dfrac{x^2 - 1}{x(x + 3)}$ for values of x between 1 and 6. From your graph find the value of x between 1 and 6 which satisfies the equation $2x^2 - 3x - 3 = 0$.

25. A right circular cone of height 4 cm and base radius 2 cm has an area of cross section A cm² at a distance x cm from the base where $A = \frac{\pi}{4}(4 - x)^2$. Draw the graph of $\frac{A}{\pi}$ against x for values of x between 0 and 4. Find the value of x which gives a cross section of π cm².

26. Draw the graph of $y = x^3 - 4x + 1$ for values of x between -3 and $+3$.

27. A ball is thrown from a window 14·7 m above the ground. The horizontal distance x m and the upward vertical distance y m travelled in t sec are given by $x = 12t$, $y = 9{\cdot}8t - 4{\cdot}9t^2$. Calculate the values of x and y for values of t between 0 and 3 and draw a graph to represent the relationship between x and y. Find how far the ball goes horizontally before it hits the ground.

28. Draw the graph of $y = x^2 + (6 - x)^2$ for values of x between 0 and 6. Find the least possible value of y.

11

INDICES AND LOGARITHMS

INDICES

THERE are three very important formulae connected with indices, which you should know.

$$a^m \times a^n = a^{m+n} \quad . \quad . \quad . \quad . \quad \text{(i)}$$

$$a^m \div a^n = a^{m-n} \quad . \quad . \quad . \quad . \quad \text{(ii)}$$

$$(a^m)^n = a^{mn} \quad . \quad . \quad . \quad . \quad \text{(iii)}$$

These formulae are true for all values of m and n, positive, negative and fractional.

Negative and fractional indices

These three formulae lead to meanings for negative and fractional indices.

(1) $$a^0 = \frac{a^n}{a^n} \text{ by (ii)}$$

$$= 1.$$

$$\therefore a^0 = 1.$$

Any number raised to zero power is equal to 1.

(2) $$a^{-n} = \frac{a^0}{a^n} \text{ by (ii)}$$

$$= \frac{1}{a^n}.$$

A number raised to a negative index is the reciprocal of the same number raised to the corresponding positive index.

(3) $$\left(a^{\frac{p}{q}}\right)^q = a^p \text{ by (iii)}$$

Take the qth root of each side.

$$a^{\frac{p}{q}} \text{ is a value of } \sqrt[q]{a^p} \text{ or of } (\sqrt[q]{a})^p.$$

Since a number may have more than one qth root, we say that $a^{\frac{p}{q}}$ is *a value of* the expression.

Examples.

$$3^{\circ} = 1.$$

$$3^{-2} = \frac{1}{3^2} = \frac{1}{9}.$$

$$27^{\frac{2}{3}} = (\sqrt[3]{27})^2 = 9.$$

$$27^{-\frac{2}{3}} = \frac{1}{27^{\frac{2}{3}}} = \frac{1}{9}.$$

EXERCISES 48A

Write down the values of the following:

1. 3^{-3}. **2.** $8^{\frac{2}{3}}$. **3.** $8^{-\frac{2}{3}}$. **4.** $16^{\frac{3}{4}}$. **5.** $16^{-\frac{3}{4}}$.

6. $4^{\frac{3}{2}}$. **7.** $27^{-\frac{1}{3}}$. **8.** $100^{-\frac{3}{2}}$. **9.** $(\sqrt[3]{2})^6$. **10.** $\left(\frac{144}{169}\right)^{-\frac{1}{2}}$.

EXERCISES 48B

Write down the values of the following:

1. 2^{-3}. **2.** $8^{\frac{1}{3}}$. **3.** $8^{-\frac{1}{3}}$. **4.** $25^{-\frac{1}{2}}$. **5.** $125^{-\frac{2}{3}}$.

6. $9^{-\frac{3}{2}}$. **7.** $64^{-\frac{2}{3}}$. **8.** $16^{-\frac{3}{2}}$. **9.** $(\frac{3}{8})^{-1}$. **10.** $(\frac{16}{25})^{-\frac{1}{2}}$.

LOGARITHMS

The logarithm of a number to the base 10 is the power to which 10 must be raised to give the number.

Examples.

$$\log_{10} 1000 = \log_{10} 10^3 = 3.$$
$$\log_{10} \tfrac{1}{100} = \log_{10} 10^{-2} = -2 \text{ or } \bar{2}.$$
$$\log_{10} \sqrt{10} = \log_{10} 10^{\frac{1}{2}} = \tfrac{1}{2}.$$

To every log. equation, there is a corresponding index equation.

Examples.

If $\log_{10} 1000 = 3$, then $1000 = 10^3$.
If $\log_{10} x = y$, then $x = 10^y$.

The base 10 is the most familiar because 10 is our accepted unit for counting and logarithms to this base are most helpful in arithmetic calculations. Logarithms, however, may be found to any base.

The logarithm of x to the base a is written $\log_a x$.

If the base is not given, it is understood to be 10.

The logarithm of a number to the base a is the power to which a must be raised to give the number.

For example, if $\log_a x = y$, then $a^y = x$.

When a number is expressed as a power of a, then its logarithm to the base a is equal to the index.

Examples.

$$\log_a a^3 = 3.$$
$$\log_a \sqrt{a} = \tfrac{1}{2}.$$
$$\log_2 8 = \log_2 2^3 = 3.$$
$$\log_5 5\sqrt{5} = \log_5 5^{\frac{3}{2}} = \tfrac{3}{2}.$$

EXERCISES 49A

Write down the values of the following:

1. $\log_a a^4$. **2.** $\log_2 16$. **3.** $\log_6 6\sqrt{6}$. **4.** $\log_2 8$.

5. $\log_4 2$. **6.** $\log_4 8$. **7.** $\log_{12} \sqrt{12}$. **8.** $\log_7 \sqrt[3]{7}$.

9. $\log_5 25\sqrt{5}$. **10.** $\log_5 \{(\sqrt[3]{5})(\sqrt{5})\}$. **11.** $\log_{10} 100$.

12. $\log_2 8$. **13.** $\log_5 5$. **14.** $\log_4 16$. **15.** $\log_8 1$.

Find x in questions 16 to 20.

16. $\log_{10} x = 2$. **17.** $\log_{10} x = -2$. **18.** $\log_3 x = 3$.

19. $\log_4 x = \tfrac{1}{2}$. **20.** $\log_2 x = 1$.

EXERCISES 49B

Write down the values of the following:

1. $\log_a \sqrt{a}$. **2.** $\log_3 27$. **3.** $\log_3 \tfrac{1}{3}$. **4.** $\log_3 \frac{1}{3^2}$.

5. $\log_3 9\sqrt{3}$. **6.** $\log_3 \sqrt{27}$. **7.** $\log_9 27$. **8.** $\log_{27} 3$.

9. $\log_{27} 9$. **10.** $\log_{10} \frac{10}{\sqrt{10}}$. **11.** $\log_{10} 1$. **12.** $\log_2 32$.

13. $\log_3 81$. **14.** $\log_3 \tfrac{1}{27}$. **15.** $\log_{16} \tfrac{1}{4}$.

Find x in questions 16 to 20.

16. $\log_{10} x = 4$. **17.** $\log_{10} x = -1$. **18.** $\log_4 x = 2$.

19. $\log_9 x = \tfrac{1}{2}$. **20.** $\log_8 x = 2$.

Formulae connecting logarithms

There are three formulae which hold for logarithms to any base and which correspond to the three index formulae already given. These are

$$\log_a x + \log_a y = \log_a xy \quad . \quad . \quad . \quad \text{(iv)}$$

$$\log_a x - \log_a y = \log_a \frac{x}{y} \quad . \quad . \quad . \quad \text{(v)}$$

$$\log_a x^n = n \log_a x \quad . \quad . \quad . \quad \text{(vi)}$$

They are proved from the corresponding index formulae in the following way.

Let $\log_a x = u$ and $\log_a y = v$.

Then $x = a^u$ and $y = a^v$.

$$\therefore xy = a^u \times a^v = a^{u+v}.$$

So $\log_a xy = u + v = \log_a x + \log_a y \quad . \quad \text{(iv)}$

Also $$\frac{x}{y} = \frac{a^u}{a^v} = a^{u-v}$$

and, therefore, $\log_a x = u - v = \log_a x - \log_a y \quad . \quad \text{(v)}$

Again $x^n = (a^u)^n = a^{un}$

and, therefore, $\log_a x^n = un = n \log_a x \quad . \quad . \quad . \quad \text{(vi)}$

The first of these formulae tells us how to add logarithms.

For example,

$$\log 2 + \log 5 = \log (2)(5) = \log 10 = 1,$$

and $\log_{12} 9 + \log_{12} 16 = \log_{12} (9)(16) = \log_{12} 144 = \log_{12} 12^2 = 2.$

The second tells us how to subtract logarithms.

For example,

$$\log 70 - \log 7 = \log \frac{70}{7} = \log 10 = 1,$$

and $\log_8 56 - \log_8 \left(\frac{7}{8}\right) = \log_8 \left(\frac{56}{7/8}\right) = \log_8 \frac{56 \times 8}{7} = \log_8 8^2 = 2.$

The third tells us how to find the logarithm of a power.

For example, $\log 8 = \log 2^3 = 3 \log 2. \therefore \frac{\log 8}{\log 2} = 3.$

Also $\log_7 \sqrt[3]{17} = \log_7 17^{\frac{1}{3}} = \frac{1}{3} \log_7 17.$

These formulae are, of course, equivalent to the laws we apply in numerical calculation.

(1) To multiply two numbers, add their logarithms and find the antilog. of the result.

(2) To divide two numbers, subtract their logarithms and find the antilog. of the result.

(3) To raise a number to a given power, multiply the logarithm of the number by the power and antilog. the result.

EXERCISES 50A

Simplify the following without using tables:

1. $\log 4 + \log 25$. **2.** $\log 20 - \log 2$. **3.** $\log_2 14 - \log_2 7$.

4. $\log_3 8{\cdot}1 + \log_3 10$. **5.** $\dfrac{\log 16}{\log 2}$. **6.** $\log 2^2 + \log 5^2$.

7. $\dfrac{\log 27}{\log 3}$. **8.** $\dfrac{\log a^3}{\log a}$. **9.** $\dfrac{\log \sqrt{5}}{\log 5}$.

10. $\log_a \sqrt{a} + \log_a a^2$.

EXERCISES 50B

Simplify the following without using tables:

1. $\log 2 + \log 50$. **2.** $\log_2 32 - \log_2 4$. **3.** $\log_3 21 - \log_3 7$.

4. $\log_4 3{\cdot}2 + \log_4 20$. **5.** $\dfrac{\log 25}{\log 5}$. **6.** $\log 3^2 + \log \frac{10}{9}$.

7. $\dfrac{\log 64}{\log 4}$. **8.** $\dfrac{\log \sqrt{a}}{\log a}$. **9.** $\dfrac{\log \sqrt[3]{5}}{\log \sqrt{5}}$.

10. $\dfrac{\log a}{\log \sqrt{a}}$.

Change of base

The formula which tells us how to change from one base to another is

$$\log_b x = \frac{\log_a x}{\log_a b}.$$

Suppose that $\log_b x = u$, so that

$$b^u = x.$$

Take logarithms to base a,

$$\log_a b^u = \log_a x.$$

or

$$u \log_a b = \log_a x.$$

$$\therefore u = \frac{\log_a x}{\log_a b}.$$

Therefore

$$\log_b x = \frac{\log_a x}{\log_a b}.$$

Worked Examples

There follow some worked examples illustrating how logarithm and index formulae are applied.

Example 1. Evaluate $\log_7 17$.

$$\log_7 17 = \frac{\log_{10} 17}{\log_{10} 7} = \frac{1{\cdot}2304}{0{\cdot}8451} = \frac{10^{0\cdot0899}}{10^{\bar{1}\cdot9270}} \quad \text{(using log. tables)}$$

$$= 10^{0\cdot1629}$$

$$= 1{\cdot}455 \quad \text{(antilog. tables).}$$

Example 2. Given that $x = a^2b$ and that $y = a^3\sqrt{b}$, express b in terms of x and y.

Eliminate a from the equations.

$$a^2 = \frac{x}{b} \quad \text{and} \quad a^3 = \frac{y}{\sqrt{b}}.$$

Therefore

$$a^6 = \frac{x^3}{b^3} \quad \text{or} \quad \frac{y^2}{b},$$

and so

$$\frac{x^3}{b^3} = \frac{y^2}{b}.$$

$$\therefore b^2 = \frac{x^3}{y^2} = x^3y^{-2} \quad \text{and} \quad b = x^{\frac{3}{2}}y^{-1}.$$

Example 3. Evaluate, without tables, $2 \log 5 + \log 36 - \log 9$.

$$2 \log 5 + \log 36 - \log 9 = \log 25 + \log 36 - \log 9$$

$$= \log \frac{25 \times 36}{9}$$

$$= \log 100$$

$$= 2.$$

Example 4. If $3^x = 8$, find x.

Whenever the unknown is an index, take logs.

$$3^x = 8.$$

$$\therefore \log 3^x = \log 8.$$

or

$$x \log 3 = \log 8.$$

$$x = \frac{\log 8}{\log 3} = \frac{0{\cdot}9031}{0{\cdot}4771}.$$

$$= \frac{10^{\bar{1}{\cdot}9557}}{10^{\bar{1}{\cdot}6786}}.$$

$$= 10^{0{\cdot}2771}$$

$$= 1{\cdot}892.$$

Example 5. If $\log y + 3 \log x = 2$, express y in terms of x.

$$\log y + 3 \log x = \log y + \log x^3 = \log yx^3.$$

$$\therefore \log yx^3 = \log 100$$

or

$$yx^3 = 100 \quad \text{and} \quad y = \frac{100}{x^3}.$$

EXERCISES 51: Miscellaneous

1. Find x from the formula $e^x = 10$, given that $e = 2{\cdot}718$.

2. Find y in terms of x from the equation $\log y + 2 \log x = 2$.

3. Find y in terms of x from the equation $\log_6 y + 2 \log_6 x = 3$.

4. Express $\sqrt[3]{(8x^{-3})^{-2}}$ as simply as you can.

5. Simplify the expression $\sqrt{\dfrac{25x^4}{16}} \times \left(\dfrac{x}{2}\right)^{-3}$.

6. Without using tables, write down the values of:

(i) $\sqrt[3]{\dfrac{x^9}{27}}$, (ii) $3^\circ \times 2^{-2}$, (iii) $(4x^{-8})^{\frac{3}{2}}$.

7. Given that $\log y - \frac{3}{4} \log x = 2$, find y in terms of x.

8. Without using tables, write down the values of:

(i) $27^{-\frac{2}{3}}$, (ii) $16^{\frac{1}{3}} \times 16^{\frac{1}{6}}$, (iii) $\dfrac{\log 27}{\log 9}$.

9. Calculate the value of $\log_3 8$.

10. Calculate the value of $\log_{\sqrt{2}} 1{\cdot}7$.

11. Calculate the value of $\log_{12} 14$.

12. Find the value of x if $2^x = \frac{1}{8}$.

13. Find the value of x^{-2y} if $x = 4{\cdot}2$ and $y = 0{\cdot}6$.

14. If $x = 5$ and $y = 6$, find the value of $(8x + 4y)^{\frac{x}{y}}$.

15. Evaluate, without tables, $4 \log 2 + \log 5 - \log 8$.

16. Given that $\log 12 = 1{\cdot}0792$ and that $\log 24 = 1{\cdot}3802$, deduce the values of $\log 2$ and $\log 6$, without using tables.

17. If $a^{-2} = b^3$ and $a^{\frac{1}{2}}b = c^{\frac{1}{3}}$, express c in terms of a.

18. If $2^{2x} - 4 . 2^x + 3 = 0$, find the possible values of x.

19. Evaluate, without tables, $3 \log 2 + \log 20 - \log 1{\cdot}6$.

20. Evaluate, without tables, $2 \log_6 3 + \log_6 12 + \log_6 8 - \log_6 24$.

21. If $a^{\frac{1}{2}} = b^{\frac{1}{3}}c^2$ and $a^{\frac{1}{3}} = b^{\frac{1}{2}}c^3$, find a.

22. If $3^x = 4^2$, find x.

23. If $4^{x+1} = 2^{x-1}$, find x.

24. If $3^{x+1} = 4^{x-1}$, find x.

25. If $(3^x - 1)(3^x - 2) = 0$, what are the possible values of x?

26. If $3^{2x} - 4 . 3^x + 3 = 0$, what are the possible values of x?

27. Simplify $2^x \times 4^{x-1} \times 8^{x+1}$.

28. Simplify $\dfrac{3^x \times 9^{x+1}}{27^{x-1}}$.

29. If $\log x + 2 \log y = 1$, find x in terms of y.

30. If $\log \sqrt{x} + \log y = 2 \log z$, express x in terms of y and z.

31. Write down the values of (i) $\log_2 8$, (ii) $\log_4 8$, (iii) $\log_{\sqrt{2}} 8$.

32. Simplify $2p^3 \times 3p^2 \times \frac{1}{4}p^{-1}$.

33. Simplify $2z^3y^2 \times 3z^2y \times (\frac{1}{4}zy)^{-1}$.

34. If $17^x = 35$, find x.

35. If $8^{x-1} = 16$, find x.

12

VARIATION

Direct proportion

If the ratio of y to x is always constant, then y is said to vary directly as x. The equation connecting the two quantities is $\frac{y}{x} = k$ or $y = kx$. The relationship may also be written, $y \propto x$, which reads 'y is proportional to x'. The graph of y plotted against x is a straight line through the origin. It is obvious that if x is doubled, y must also be doubled. If y is halved, x must be halved and so on.

Examples of direct proportion are common and a few are given.

1. The distance gone by a car moving at constant speed is directly proportional to the time taken.

2. The circumference of a circle is directly proportional to the radius.

3. The volume of a cylinder of given radius is directly proportional to the height.

Other cases of direct proportion

The volume of a cylinder is given by the equation $V = \pi r^2 h$. From this we see that the volume varies directly as the height but not as the radius. For a given height, $\frac{V}{r^2}$ is constant and V is said to vary directly as the square of the radius.

If y varies directly as the square of x, then $\frac{y}{x^2}$ is constant. This may be written $y \propto x^2$ and the algebraic relation is $y = kx^2$. If y varies directly as x^2 and x is trebled, y is 9 times greater than its previous value.

Again, the formula for the period of a simple pendulum is $T = 2\pi \sqrt{\frac{l}{g}}$. From this, we see that the periodic time varies directly as the square root of the length.

Example 1. The extension of a stretched string is directly proportional to its tension. If the extension produced by a tension of 8 newtons is 2 cm, find the extension produced by a tension of 12 newtons.

Method (*i*). $\dfrac{\text{Tension}}{\text{Extension}}$ is constant.

Let x cm be the extension produced. Then

$$\frac{8}{2} = \frac{12}{x}.$$

$$\therefore x = 3.$$

Method (ii). Let $T = kx$, where T is the tension in newtons and x the extension in centimetres. (A different choice of units will merely alter the value of k.)

When $T = 8$, $x = 2$.

$$\therefore 8 = 2k \quad \text{and} \quad k = 4.$$

So $T = 4x$ and when $T = 12$, $x = 3$.

Example 2. The cost of electroplating a square tray varies as the square of its length. The cost of a tray 8 cm square is £1·50. Find the cost for a tray 12 cm square.

Method (i). If C is the cost in new pence and x cm the side of the square, $\dfrac{C}{x^2}$ is constant.

$$\therefore \frac{150}{64} = \frac{C}{144} \quad \text{and} \quad C = \frac{144 \times 150}{64} = 337\tfrac{1}{2}.$$

The cost is £3·37½.

Method (*ii*). The equation connecting C and x is $C = kx^2$.

When $C = 150$, $x = 8$.

$$\therefore 150 = 64k \quad \text{and so} \quad k = \tfrac{75}{32}.$$

Therefore $C = \tfrac{75}{32}x^2$.

When $x = 12$, $C = \tfrac{75}{32} \times 144 = 337\tfrac{1}{2}$.

The cost is £3·37½.

EXERCISES 52A

1. Write down an equation connecting x and y, given that x metres of curtain material cost y new pence.

2. A disc of given thickness and radius r is of mass w kg. Write down a connection between r and w.

3. Watering cans are made of the same height but of varying diameter. If a can of diameter d cm holds g litres, write down a connection between d and g.

4. The resistance R newtons to the motion of a car varies directly as the square of the speed, v km/h. Write down a connection between R and v.

5. If y varies directly as x and $y = 8$ when $x = 3$, find y when $x = 18$.

6. If y varies directly as the square root of x and $y = 12$ when $x = 4$, find y when $x = 9$.

7. Complete the following statements:

(i) If $V \propto r^3$, then $r \propto$;
(ii) If $T \propto \sqrt{l}$, then $l \propto$;
(iii) If $S = kr^2$, then $r \propto$.

8. Models are made in different sizes of a ship. The mass of a model varies directly as the cube of its length. The mass of a model of length 3 cm is 1 kg. What is the mass of a model of length 12 cm?

9. The surface area of a sphere is proportional to the square of its radius. In order to treble the surface area of the sphere, in what ratio must the radius be altered?

10. The distance it is possible to see on a clear day varies directly as the square root of the height above sea level. At a height of 6 m above sea level, it is possible to see 10 km. What distance can be seen from a height of 54 m?

EXERCISES 52B

1. Squares of area A m² are cut from a piece of sheet metal. If the side of a square is x m, write down the equation connecting A and x.

2. If it takes t min to cut a circular lawn of radius r metres, write down the connection between t and r.

3. The radius of a sphere varies as V^n where V is its volume. What is the value of n?

4. The radius of a sphere varies as S^n where S is the surface area. What is the value of n?

5. If p varies directly as q and $q = 70$ when $p = 10$, find q when $p = 12$.

6. If y varies directly as the square root of x and y is 10 when $x = 1$, find y when $x = 4$.

7. Complete the following statements:

(i) If y varies as x^4, then x varies as ;
(ii) If A varies as $V^{\frac{3}{2}}$, then V varies as .

8. If $y - 3$ is directly proportional to x^2 and $y = 5$ when $x = 2$, find y when $x = 6$.

9. A solid sphere of radius 4 cm is of mass 16 kg. Find the mass of a sphere of the same material of radius 6 cm.

10. The time of revolution of a planet round the sun is proportional to $d^{\frac{3}{2}}$ where d is the distance of the planet from the sun. Compare the times of revolution of two planets, one of which is four times the distance of the other from the sun.

Inverse proportion

If $y \propto \frac{1}{x}$, y is said to be inversely proportional to x. The equation connecting x and y is $y = \frac{k}{x}$ or $xy = k$.

If y is plotted against $\frac{1}{x}$, the graph is a straight line through the origin.

If y varies inversely as x, y varies directly as $\frac{1}{x}$.

A few common examples of inverse proportion are given.

1. The time for a piece of work is inversely proportional to the number of men employed.
2. The volume of a gas at constant temperature is inversely proportional to the pressure.
3. The length of a rectangle of constant area is inversely proportional to the breadth.

Other cases of inverse proportion

One quantity may vary inversely as some power of another. Three examples are given.

(i) If $y \propto \frac{1}{x^2}$, y varies inversely as the square of x. The equation connecting x and y is $y = \frac{k}{x^2}$ or $yx^2 = k$.

(ii) If $y \propto \frac{1}{x^3}$, y varies inversely as the cube of x. The equation connecting x and y is $y = \frac{k}{x^3}$ or $yx^3 = k$.

(iii) If $y \propto \frac{1}{\sqrt{x}}$, y varies inversely as the square root of x. The equation connecting x and y is $y = \frac{k}{\sqrt{x}}$ or $y\sqrt{x} = k$.

Example. The electrical resistance of a wire varies inversely as the square of its radius. Given that the resistance is 0·4 ohms when the radius is 0·3 cm, find the resistance when the radius is 0·45 cm.

If R is the resistance in ohms and r the radius in cm, $R = \frac{k}{r^2}$.

When $R = 0{\cdot}4$, $r = 0{\cdot}3$.

$$\therefore\ 0{\cdot}4 = \frac{k}{(0{\cdot}3)^2} \quad \text{and} \quad k = 0{\cdot}036.$$

Therefore the connecting equation is

$$R = \frac{{\cdot}036}{r^2}.$$

When $r = 0{\cdot}45$, $R = \frac{{\cdot}036}{(0{\cdot}45)^2} = 0{\cdot}18$ ohm approximately.

Joint variation

The formula for the volume of a cone is $V = \frac{1}{3}\pi r^2 h$. Here the volume is a function of two variables, r and h, and the volume varies directly as the height and directly as the square of the radius. This is called joint variation, and V is said to vary jointly as the height and the square of the radius.

Example. The volume of a gas of given mass varies directly as the temperature and inversely as the pressure. Write down a formula for the volume.

Here $$V \propto T \quad \text{and} \quad V \propto \frac{1}{P}.$$

Therefore $$V = k\frac{T}{P}.$$

Given a set of corresponding values for V, T and P, you can find k.

Variation as the sum of two parts

The function $(ax + bx^2)$ obviously varies with x but it is neither directly proportional to x nor to x^2. The function is described as the sum of two quantities one of which (ax) varies directly as x and the other of which (bx^2) varies directly as the square of x. An alternative description is a function which varies partly as x and partly as the square of x.

N.B. Always read the question carefully to make sure whether you are dealing with joint variation or variation as the sum of two parts.

Example. The cost of printing a book varies partly as the number of pages and partly as the square of the number of diagrams. Write down a formula for the cost.

If C is the cost, x the number of pages and y the number of diagrams, then $C = ax + by^2$, where a and b are constants.

EXERCISES 53A

Write down formulae to express the following:

1. The volume of a cylinder varies directly as the square of the radius and directly as the height.

2. The height of a cone varies directly as its volume and inversely as the square of the radius.

3. The electrical resistance of a wire varies directly as the length and inversely as the square of the radius.

4. The resistance to motion of a car at high speeds is the sum of two parts, one of which varies as the velocity and the other as the square of the velocity.

5. The pressure of a given mass of gas varies directly as the temperature and inversely as the volume.

6. The cost of running a car is partly constant and partly varies as the number of miles travelled.

7. The time taken to dig a trench varies as the length of the trench and inversely as the number of men employed.

8. The volume of a tetrahedron varies jointly as the base area and the height.

9. The resistance to the motion of a train is partly constant and partly varies as the square of the velocity.

10. The distance travelled by a particle varies directly as the square of its speed and inversely as its acceleration.

EXERCISES 53B

1. The distance travelled by a particle varies jointly as the acceleration and the square of the time.

2. The time taken by a committee is partly constant and varies partly as the square of the number of members present.

3. The principal is proportional to the interest and inversely proportional to both the rate and the time.

4. The acceleration produced in a body is proportional to the force and inversely proportional to the mass.

5. The depth of water in a tank is proportional to the volume of water and inversely proportional to the area of cross section of the tank.

6. The distance gone by a particle varies partly as the time and partly as the square of the time.

7. The square of the time taken by a planet to go round the sun varies as the cube of its mean distance from the sun.

8. The time of a bus journey varies directly as the distance and inversely as the square root of the number of passengers who board the bus *en route*.

9. The time of swing of a pendulum varies directly as the square root of its length and inversely as the square root of the acceleration due to gravity.

10. The Kinetic Energy of a body is jointly proportional to its mass and the square of its velocity.

Worked Examples

Some worked examples on the different problems you are likely to meet in connection with variation are now given.

Example 1. The electrical resistance of a copper wire of circular cross section varies directly as the length and inversely as the square of the radius. Two wires have equal resistances and one is four times as long as the other. Find the ratio of their radii.

If R is the resistance, l the length and r the radius,

$$R = k\frac{l}{r^2}.$$

Suppose the first wire has resistance R', length l' and radius r'; and that the second wire has resistance R', length $4l'$ and radius x.

Then $$R' = k\frac{l'}{r'^2} \quad \text{and} \quad R' = k\frac{4l'}{x^2}.$$

$$\therefore \frac{l'}{r'^2} = \frac{4l'}{x^2} \quad \text{or} \quad x^2 = 4r'^2.$$

$$\therefore x = 2r'.$$

$\therefore$ The ratio of their radii is 1 : 2.

Example 2. The Kinetic Energy (E) of a body varies directly as its mass m and directly as the square of its velocity v. The momentum M varies jointly as the mass and the velocity. Show that if E is expressed in terms of M and m, then E varies as the square of M and inversely as m.

$$E = k_1mv^2 \quad \text{and} \quad M = k_2mv.$$

(Notice that the constants k_1 and k_2 must not be assumed equal.)

From the second equation,

$$v = \frac{M}{k_2 m}$$

Substitute, $$E = k_1 m . \frac{M^2}{k_2{}^2 m^2} = \frac{k_1}{k_2{}^2} \frac{M^2}{m}.$$

Since $\frac{k_1}{k_2{}^2}$ is a constant, E varies as the square of M and inversely as m.

Example 3. The cost of making a table is the sum of two parts. One is proportional to the area and the other to the square of the length. If the cost of a table 4 m by 6 m is £12·50 and the cost of a table 3 m by 8 m is £16, find the cost of a table 5 m square.

If l is the length of the table in metres, A the area in m² and C the cost in new pence,

$$C = aA + bl^2, \quad \text{where } a \text{ and } b \text{ are constants.}$$

When $l = 6$ and $A = 24$, $C = 1250$.

$$\therefore\ 1250 = 24a + 36b \quad . \quad . \quad . \quad . \quad . \quad . \quad \text{(i)}$$

When $l = 8$ and $A = 24$, $C = 1600$.

$$\therefore\ 1600 = 24a + 64b \quad . \quad . \quad . \quad . \quad . \quad . \quad \text{(ii)}$$

Subtract (i) from (ii), $350 = 28b$.

$$\therefore\ b = 12\tfrac{1}{2}.$$

Substitute: $$1250 = 24a + 450$$

$$\therefore\ a = 33\tfrac{1}{3}.$$

The equation connecting C, A and l is

$$C = \frac{100A}{3} + \frac{25l^2}{2}.$$

When $l = 5$ and $A = 25$,

$$C = \frac{2500}{3} + \frac{625}{2} = 833\tfrac{1}{3} + 312\tfrac{1}{2} = 1145\tfrac{5}{6}.$$

The cost is therefore £11·46.

EXERCISES 54: MISCELLANEOUS

1. If y is inversely proportional to x and $y = 2\tfrac{1}{2}$ when $x = 2$, find y when $x = 4$.

2. The greatest mass which can be supported by a beam of given thickness varies directly as the breadth and inversely as the length. If a beam of breadth 2 cm and length 15 m can support a mass of 200 kg, find the mass which can be supported by a beam 3 cm broad and 20 m long.

3. If Q varies inversely as the square of P and if $Q = 8$ when $P = 2$, find Q when $P = 4$.

4. A motorist estimates that his annual expenditure is partly constant and partly varies as the distance travelled. The cost for an annual distance of 5000 km is £50 and for an annual distance of 6000 km is £55. Find the cost for an annual distance of 8000 km.

5. The number of lead shot that can be made from a given weight of metal varies inversely as the cube of the radius of the shot. If 5000 shot of radius 1 mm can be made, find how many shot of radius $\frac{1}{2}$ mm can be made from an equal weight of metal.

6. The time taken to sink a well varies partly as the square of the depth and partly as the cube of the depth. If it takes 60 hours to sink a well 10 m deep and $146\frac{1}{4}$ hours to sink a well 15 m deep, find the time taken to sink a well 20 m deep.

7. The cost of catering per head is partly constant and partly inversely proportional to the number of people present. If the cost per head for 40 people is 15 new pence and 50 people $12\frac{1}{2}$ new pence, find the cost per head for 100 people.

8. If x varies directly as the cube of y and if the square of y varies inversely as the cube of z, prove that x^2z^9 is constant.

9. The safe speed for a train rounding a corner is proportional to the square root of the radius. If the safe speed for a curve of radius 50 m is 25 km/h, what is the safe speed for a curve of radius 98 m?

10. If x varies inversely as y and y varies inversely as z, how does x vary with z?

11. The square of the velocity of a particle varies as the cube root of its distance from a fixed point. When the distance of the particle from this point is 54 m, its velocity is 12 m/sec. What is its velocity when it is 16 m from the fixed point?

12. The illumination of a bulb varies inversely as the square of the distance. If the illumination is 4 candle-power at a distance of 4 m, what is the illumination at a distance of 3 m?

13. The attraction between two bodies is directly proportional to the product of their masses and inversely proportional to the square of the distance between them. If each mass is doubled, how must the distance between them be altered to give the same attraction?

14. The heat generated by a current in a wire varies directly as the time, directly as the square of the voltage and inversely as the resistance. If the voltage is 50 volts and the resistance 40 ohms, the heat generated is 75 calories per sec. Find the heat generated in $\frac{1}{2}$ min if the voltage is 40 volts and the resistance 50 ohms.

15. Electrical conductivity in a wire of circular cross section varies directly as the square of the radius and inversely as the length. The lengths of two wires are in the ratio 3 : 4 and their radii in the ratio 1 : 2. Find the ratio of their conductivities.

16. The cost of annealing a length of chain is the sum of two parts, one proportional to the length of chain and the other proportional to the square of the length. If the cost of annealing a chain of length l is £x and the cost of annealing a chain of length $2l$ is £y, find the cost of annealing a chain of length $3l$.

17. A solid sphere of radius 4 cm is of mass 64 kg. Find the mass of a shell of the same metal whose internal and external radii are 3 cm and 2 cm respectively.

18. A solid cone of height 8 cm is of mass 128 kg. A smaller cone of height 2 cm is cut away leaving a frustum. Find the mass of the frustum.

19. If V varies directly as the square of x and inversely as y, and if $V = 18$ when $x = 3$ and $y = 4$, find V when $x = 5$ and $y = 2$.

20. If $P \propto \dfrac{x^2}{z}$ and $z \propto xt$, find (i) how P varies with x and t, (ii) how P varies with z and t.

21. The resistance to the motion of a car is partly constant and partly proportional to the square of the velocity. When the velocity is 20 km/h, the resistance is 50 newtons; when the velocity is 30 km/h, the resistance is 100 newtons. Find for what speed the resistance is 170 newtons.

22. The effort required to raise a load is partly constant and partly proportional to the load. The effort necessary for a load of 8 newtons is 6 newtons and for a load of 12 newtons is 8 newtons. Find the effort necessary for a load of 20 newtons.

23. The braking force necessary to stop a train is directly proportional to the weight of the train and the square of its velocity and inversely proportional to the distance gone before stopping. If one train is twice as heavy as another and moving twice as fast, find the ratio of the stopping distances, assuming equal braking forces.

24. A model is made of a ship. If the ratio of the displacement of the ship to that of the model is 8000 : 1, find the ratio of the areas of deck space.

13

ARITHMETIC AND GEOMETRIC PROGRESSIONS

ARITHMETIC PROGRESSIONS

If a sequence of terms is such that the difference between any term and the one immediately preceding it is constant, the terms are said to form an arithmetic progression. This difference is called the common difference. Examples of arithmetic progressions are:

(i) $5, 8, 11, 14 \ldots.$; common difference $+ 3$.
(ii) $3, -1, -5, -9 \ldots.$; common difference $- 4$.
(iii) $-2, -\frac{3}{4}, +\frac{1}{2}, +1\frac{3}{4} \ldots.$; common difference $1\frac{1}{4}$.
(iv) $a, a + d, a + 2d, a + 3d \ldots.$; common difference d.

The *n*th term

Suppose the first term of an arithmetic progression (in future shortened to A.P.) is 7 and the common difference 3.

The second term is $7 + 1(3) = 10.$
The third term is $7 + 2(3) = 13.$
The fourth term is $7 + 3(3) = 16.$
The nth term is $7 + (n - 1)3 = 3n + 4.$

Similarly the nth term of an A.P. whose first term is a and whose common difference is d, is $a + (n - 1)d$.

Example. Find which term 383 is of the series $5 + 8 + 11 + \ldots.$

The difference between the first term and 383 is 378 and the common difference is 3. The common difference must therefore be added to the first term (378/3) times or 126 times. Therefore 383 is the 127th term.

The arithmetic mean

If a, b, c are three consecutive terms of an A.P., then the common difference equals $b - a$ or $c - b$.

Therefore $$b - a = c - b$$
or $$2b = a + c.$$

b is called the arithmetic mean of a and c and is what you usually call the average.

For example, the arithmetic mean of 3 and 15 is $\frac{1}{2}(3 + 15)$ or 9.

The sum of an A.P.

Suppose you wish to find the sum of 50 terms of the A.P.

$$3 + 5 + 7 + \ldots\ldots \qquad \text{(i)}$$

The 50th term is $3 + 49(2) = 101$.

Write the series backwards and it is:

$$101 + 99 + 97 + \ldots\ldots \qquad \text{(ii)}$$

Each term of series (i) added to the corresponding term of series (ii) is 104. There are 50 terms and so the sum of all terms is $50(104) = 5200$.

But you have added two equal series and so the sum of each series is 2600.

Now find in a similar way the sum of n terms of the A.P.

$$a + (a + d) + (a + 2d) + \ldots\ldots \qquad \text{(i)}$$

The nth term is $a + (n - 1)d$. Call this l.

Write the series backwards and it becomes

$$l + (l - d) + (l - 2d) + \ldots\ldots \qquad \text{(ii)}$$

Each term of series (i) added to the corresponding term of series (ii) gives $(a + l)$. There are n terms and so the total sum is $n(a + l)$. This is the sum of two equal series and so the sum of each is $\frac{1}{2}n(a + l)$.

But $l = a + (n - 1)d$ and so $a + l = 2a + (n - 1)d$.

$$\therefore S = \frac{n}{2}(a + l) = \frac{n}{2}\{2a + (n - 1)d\}.$$

Example. Find the sum of 28 terms of the **A.P.** $3 + 10 + 17 + \ldots\ldots$
Here $a = 3$, $d = 7$ and $n = 28$.

$$S = \frac{n}{2}\{2a + (n - 1)d\} = \frac{28}{2}\{6 + 27(7)\} = 14(195) = 2730.$$

EXERCISES 55A

1. Find the 23rd term of the A.P. $-7, -3, +1, \ldots\ldots$

2. Find the 40th term of the A.P. $8, 5, 2, \ldots\ldots$

3. Find the value of n given that 77 is the nth term of the A.P. $3\frac{1}{2}$, 7, $10\frac{1}{2}$, ...

4. Find the value of n given that -49 is the nth term of the A.P. 11, 8, 5, ...

5. If 3, x, y, 18 are in A.P., find x and y.

6. If $-5, p, q, 16$ are in A.P., find p and q.

7. Find the sum of 12 terms of the series $7 + 11 + 15 + \ldots.$

8. Find the sum of 18 terms of the series $2\frac{1}{2} + 3\frac{3}{4} + 5 + \ldots.$

9. What is the nth term of the A.P. 4, 9, 14, ...

10. What is the nth term of the A.P. 10, 7, 4, ...

EXERCISES 55B

1. Find the 50th term of the A.P. 100, 97, 94, ...

2. The first of the odd numbers is 1 and the second is 3. What is the 50th odd number?

3. Find n given that 697 is the nth term of the A.P. 4, 11, 18, ...

4. Is 280 a term of the A.P. $11 + 15 + 19 + \ldots$?

5. The 5th term of an A.P. is 9 and the 8th term is 27. Find the 6th term.

6. The 2nd term of an A.P. is 2 and the 6th term is -14. What is the first term?

7. Find the sum of the first 50 odd numbers.

8. Find the sum of n terms of the A.P. $3 + 6 + 9 + \ldots.$

9. What is the nth term of the A.P. 6, 5·9, 5·8, ...?

10. How many terms are there in the series 1, 4, 7, ... $(6n - 2)$?

GEOMETRIC PROGRESSIONS

If, in a sequence of terms, each term is a constant multiple of the preceding, the terms are said to be in geometric progression (G.P.). This multiple is called the common ratio.

Examples of terms in G.P. are:

(i) 3, 6, 12, 24,.... ; common ratio $+2$.
(ii) 8, 4, 2, 1, $\frac{1}{2}$,.... ; common ratio $\frac{1}{2}$.
(iii) $2, -10, +50$,.... ; common ratio -5.
(iv) a, ar, ar^2, ar^3,.... ; common ratio r.

The nth term

Suppose that 3 is the first term of a G.P. whose common ratio is 2.
The second term is 3(2).
The third term is $3(2^2)$.
The fourth term is $3(2^3)$.
The nth term is $3(2^{n-1})$.
Similarly the nth term of a G.P. whose first term is a and whose common ratio is r is ar^{n-1}.

The geometric mean

If x, y, z are three terms in G.P., the common ratio is equal to $\frac{y}{x}$ or to $\frac{z}{y}$.

$$\therefore \frac{y}{x} = \frac{z}{y} \quad \text{or} \quad y^2 = xz.$$

This is the condition for x, y, z to be three consecutive terms of a G.P.

y is said to be the geometric mean of x and z, so the geometric mean of two numbers is the square root of their product.

For example, the geometric mean of 4 and 9 is $\sqrt{4 \times 9}$ or 6.

The sum of a G.P.

Suppose S denotes the sum of n terms of the G.P. whose first term is a and whose common ratio is r.

Then $\quad S = a + ar + ar^2 + ar^3 + \ldots. + ar^{n-2} + ar^{n-1}.$ (i)

Multiply each side by r,

$$rS = ar + ar^2 + ar^3 + \ldots. + ar^{n-1} + ar^n \quad . \quad \text{(ii)}$$

Subtracting (ii) from (i).

$$S - rS = a - ar^n.$$

$$\therefore S(1 - r) = a(1 - r^n)$$

or $$S = \frac{a(1 - r^n)}{1 - r}.$$

If $r < 1$, both numerator and denominator of the fraction are positive and this is the most convenient form for S. If, however, $r > 1$, both top and bottom are negative and a more convenient form is

$$S = a\frac{r^n - 1}{r - 1}.$$

Example. Find the sum of eight terms of the G.P. 2, 6, 18, ...

Here $a = 2$, $r = 3$ and $n = 8$.

$$S = a\frac{r^n - 1}{r - 1} = 2\frac{3^8 - 1}{3 - 1} = 3^8 - 1 = 6560.$$

EXERCISES 56A

(Leave your answers in index form)

1. What is the 40th term of the G.P. 2, 14, 98, ... ?

2. What is the 17th term of the G.P. 16, − 8, 4, ... ?

3. Find n given that 1024 is the nth term of the G.P. 4, 8, 16, ...

4. Find n given that 3^{20} is the nth term of the G.P. 27, 81, 243, ...

5. Find the geometric mean of 18 and 72.

6. If 5, x, y, 40 are in G.P., find x and y.

7. Find the sum of 20 terms of the G.P. 4, 8, 16, ...

8. Find the sum of 17 terms of the G.P. 9, − 3, + 1, − ....

9. What is the nth term of the G.P. 6, 18, 54, ... ?

10. What is the nth term of the G.P. 5, $-\frac{5}{2}$, $\frac{5}{4}$, $-\frac{5}{8}$, ... ?

EXERCISES 56B

(Leave your answers in index form)

1. What is the 24th term of the G.P. 5, 15, 45, ... ?

2. What is the 18th term of the G.P. 3, − 1, $\frac{1}{3}$, ... ?

3. Find n given that $\dfrac{1}{2^{17}}$ is the nth term of the G.P. 16, 8, 4, ...

4. Is 2^n a term of the G.P. 81, 27, 9, ... ?

5. Find the geometric mean of 35 and 140.

6. If 7, x, y, 189 are in G.P., find x and y.

7. Find the sum of 18 terms of the G.P. 3, 6, 12, ...

8. Find the sum of $2n$ terms of the G.P. 2, − 6, 18, − 54 ....

9. What is the 18th term of the G.P. 8, 2, $\frac{1}{2}$, ... ?

10. What is the nth term of the G.P. x, $2xy$, $4xy^2$, ... ?

Worked Examples

Three typical examples of problems on progressions are now given.

Example 1. Find approximately how many grains of corn are needed to put one on the first square of a chess board, two on the second square, four on the third square, and so on.

There are 64 squares. So the required number is

$$1 + 2 + 2^2 + 2^3 \ldots\ldots \text{ to 64 terms.}$$

This sum equals

$$\frac{2^{64} - 1}{2 - 1} = 2^{64} - 1.$$

$$\log 2 = 0{\cdot}3010.$$
$$\log 2^{64} = 64 \times 0{\cdot}3010 = 19{\cdot}264.$$
$$\therefore\ 2^{64} = 1{\cdot}837 \times 10^{19}.$$

The subtraction of 1 from 2^{64} will not affect this answer, which is true to three significant figures only.

Example 2. Find a formula for the sum of the first n odd numbers. Prove that the sum of the odd numbers from 1 to 125 inclusive is equal to the sum of the odd numbers from 169 to 209 inclusive.

$$S = 1 + 3 + 5 + \ldots\ldots \text{ to } n \text{ terms.}$$

But $$S = \frac{n}{2}\{2a + (n-1)d\} = \frac{n}{2}\{2 + (n-1)2\} = n^2.$$

The number of terms from 1 to 125 is 63.

Therefore $$1 + 3 + 5 \ldots\ldots + 125 = 63^2.$$

Consider

$(169 + 171 + 173 \ldots\ldots + 209)$ as

$$(1 + 3 + \ldots\ldots + 209) - (1 + 3 + \ldots\ldots + 167).$$

There are 105 terms in the first bracket and 84 in the second bracket.

Therefore $1 + 3 + \ldots\ldots + 209 = 105^2$

and $1 + 3 + \ldots\ldots + 167 = 84^2$,

and so $169 + 171 + \ldots\ldots + 209 = 105^2 - 84^2 = (189)(21)$

by the difference of two squares.

But $$(189)(21) = 9.21.21 = 63^2.$$

Example 3. If x, y, z are in G.P., prove that $\log x$, $\log y$, $\log z$ are in A.P.

The condition that x, y, z are in G.P. is $y^2 = xz$.

Take logs: $$\log y^2 = \log (xz)$$

or $$2 \log y = \log x + \log z.$$

But this is the condition that $\log y$ should be the arithmetic mean of $\log x$ and $\log z$.

EXERCISES 57: Miscellaneous

1. Find the sum of n terms of the A.P. $1 + 2 + 3 + \ldots\ldots$ How many terms of this series are needed to give a sum greater than 500?

2. Find the sum of 20 terms of the A.P. $1 + 5 + 9 + \ldots$. Prove that the sum of n terms is equal to $n(2n - 1)$.

3. A man puts £10 in the bank for his son on each of his birthdays from the first to the twentieth inclusive. If the money accumulates at 3% compound interest, what is the total value on the son's twenty-first birthday?

4. In an A.P., the first term is 6 and the common difference is 3. How many terms are needed to make a sum greater than 600?

5. A man's salary in 1940 was £500 per annum and it increased by 10% each year. Find how much he earned in the years 1940 to 1949 inclusive.

6. A man is able to save £50 of his salary in a certain year and afterwards saves in any one year £20 more than he saved in the preceding year. How long does it take him to save £4370?

7. Insert 5 arithmetic means between 20 and 92.

8. Insert 3 geometric means between 15 and 1215.

9. Find how many terms of the G.P. $3 + 6 + 12 + \ldots$ are necessary to make the sum exceed 1000.

10. Find the values of x and y if x, 2, $4\frac{1}{2}$, y are (i) in A.P.; (ii) in G.P. Find the sum of twenty terms of the A.P.

11. One of these sets of numbers is in A.P. and the other in G.P.

$$\tfrac{1}{6}, \tfrac{1}{2}, \tfrac{5}{6}, \ldots ; \tfrac{1}{6}, \tfrac{1}{2}, \tfrac{3}{2}, \ldots$$

Find the sum of 18 terms of the A.P. and find the 7th term of the G.P.

12. The sum of n terms of a series for all values of n is $(n^2 + 3n)$. Find the first three terms of the series.

13. The third term of a G.P. is 18 and the sixth is 486. Find the first term and write down a formula for the sum to n terms.

14. If the first, second and fifth terms of an A.P. are three consecutive terms of a G.P., find the common ratio.

15. If the 16th term of an A.P. is 3 times the 4th term, prove the 23rd term is 5 times the 3rd term.

16. If the sum of the first $2n$ terms of an A.P. is equal to the sum of the next n terms, prove that the sum of the first $(n + 2)$ terms is $2a(n + 2)$, where a is the first term.

17. If the pth term of an A.P. is x and the qth term is y, find the rth term.

18. Find which is the first negative term of the A.P. 15, $13\frac{1}{2}$, 12, ... What is the sum of all the positive terms?

19. Find the sum of all numbers between 1 and 100 which are divisible by 3.

20. Find the sum of all numbers between 1 and 100 which are divisible by 3 but not by 5.

21. If the first term of a G.P. is a and the nth term b, find the sum of these n terms.

22. Find the sum of all integers between 50 and 100.

23. How many terms of the series $1 + 2 + 3 + \ldots.$ are necessary to give a sum greater than 450?

24. The series of positive integers is divided in the following way: $1 + (2 + 3) + (4 + 5 + 6) + (7 + 8 + 9 + 10) + \ldots.$ What is the first term of the nth group? What is the sum of the terms in the nth group?

25. The second term of an A.P. is $(x - y)$ and the 5th term is $(x + y)$. Find the third and fourth terms.

26. Find the sum of 20 terms of the series

$$\log 2 + \log 4 + \log 8 + \log 16 + \ldots.$$

27. Find the sum of all the numbers which can be made using all the digits 1, 2, 3 and 4.

28. The 3rd, 5th, and 8th terms of an A.P. are consecutive terms of a G.P. Find the common ratio.

29. The arithmetic mean of two numbers is 15 and their geometric mean is 9. Find the numbers.

30. How many terms of the G.P. $2 + 4 + 8 + \ldots.$ are necessary to give a sum greater than 10 000?

14

THE DERIVED FUNCTION

The gradient of a line

THE gradient of a line referred to axes of x and y is the ratio of the increase of y between any two points of the line to the increase of x between the same two points. If y decreases as x increases, the gradient is negative. Written as a fraction, the gradient equals

$$\frac{\text{increase of } y}{\text{increase of } x}.$$

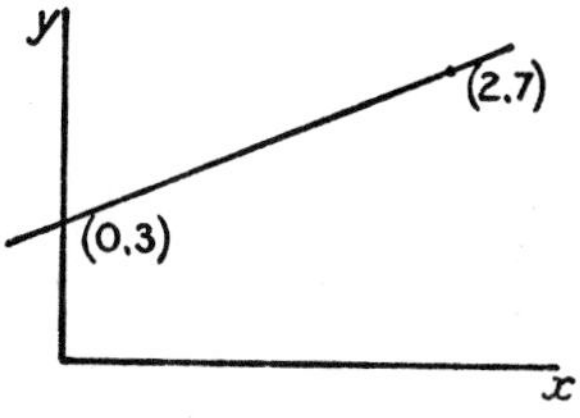

FIG. 15

Consider the line $y = 2x + 3$.

When $x = 0$, $y = 3$. So the point where $x = 0$ and $y = 3$ lies on the line. This point is written (0, 3).

(N.B. The x-coordinate is always written first.)

When $x = 2$, $y = 7$; so another point on the line is (2, 7). The increase of y between these points is $7 - 3 = 4$. The increase of x between these points is $2 - 0 = 2$. The gradient of the line is $\frac{4}{2}$ or 2.

(N.B. By similar triangles, the reader should prove that the gradient is the same whatever points are taken on the line.)

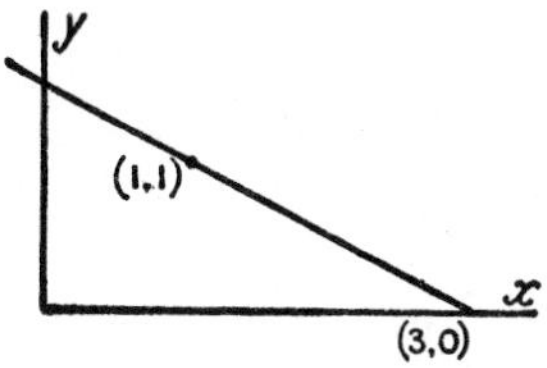

FIG. 16

Now consider the line $2y + x = 3$.

Two points on this line are (1, 1) and (3, 0). The increase of x between these points is $3 - 1 = 2$. The *decrease* of y between these points is $1 - 0 = 1$. The gradient of the line is therefore $\frac{-1}{2} = -\frac{1}{2}$.

In general, a line which makes an acute angle with the positive x direction has a positive gradient; a line which makes an obtuse angle with the positive x direction has a negative gradient.

The gradient of a curve

The gradient of a curve at a point is equal to the gradient of the tangent at that point. Consider the point (1,1) on the curve $y = x^2$.

Draw the tangent at this point and choose any two convenient points on this tangent. If you draw the curve accurately, you should find that the tangent passes through the two points (1, 1) and (2, 3).

The gradient of the tangent therefore equals $\frac{3-1}{2-1}$ or 2. This is also the gradient of the curve at the point (1, 1).

This is a drawing method of finding the gradient of a curve, but it is not very satisfactory because the tangent has to be drawn by guess-work. Suppose we take another point K on the curve and let it get nearer and nearer the point $H(1, 1)$. The gradient of the line HK will get nearer and nearer to the gradient of the tangent at H and we should be able to find a good approximation for the gradient of the tangent.

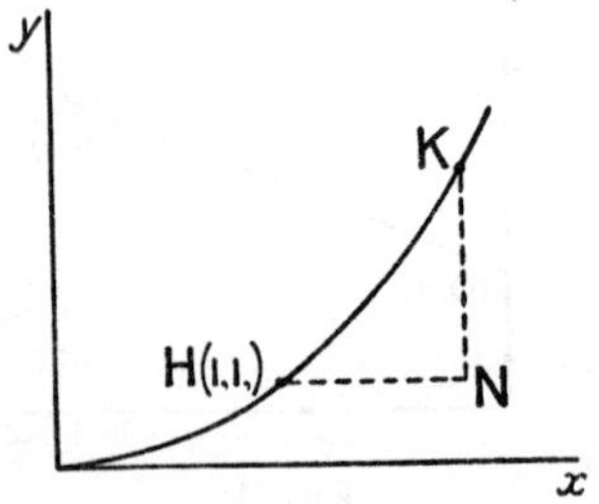

FIG. 17

Suppose we start with the point on the curve where $x = 2$. Since $y = x^2$, $y = 4$ at this point. In Fig. 17, the distance $KN = 4 - 1 = 3$ and the distance $HN = 2 - 1 = 1$. The gradient of HK is 3 which is not a good approximation because K is too far from H. We will now take several positions for K, getting nearer and nearer H, and tabulate the results.

The x coordinate of K	1·5	1·4	1·3	1·2	1·1	1·05	1·01	1·001
The y coordinate of K	2·25	1·96	1·69	1·44	1·21	1·1025	1·0201	1·002001
KN	1·25	0·96	0·69	0·44	0·21	0·1025	0·0201	0·002001
HN	0·5	0·4	0·3	0·2	0·1	0·05	0·01	0·001
The gradient of HK	2·5	2·4	2·3	2·2	2·1	2·05	2·01	2·001

The gradient of the line HK becomes very nearly equal to 2 but will never become exactly 2 as K cannot be made to coincide with H. Both quantities KN and HN would then become zero and the fraction $\frac{0}{0}$ cannot be evaluated.

Suppose now we have a further addition to the table and consider the point whose x coordinate is $(1 + h)$.

The x coordinate of $K = 1 + h$.
The y coordinate of $K = (1 + h)^2 = 1 + 2h + h^2$.

$$KN = 2h + h^2.$$
$$HN = h.$$

The gradient of $HK = \dfrac{2h + h^2}{h}$.

The point K cannot be made to coincide with H and therefore h is not zero. The fraction $\dfrac{2h + h^2}{h}$ equals $(2 + h)$, unless $h = 0$.

The gradient of the line HK is therefore $(2 + h)$, which is 1 greater than the x coordinate of the point $K(= 1 + h)$. Notice that the bottom line of the table is always one greater than the corresponding number of the top line.

The gradient $(2 + h)$ becomes very nearly equal to 2 as h becomes small. We say that the gradient of the line tends to 2 as h tends to 0. (Or, gradient $\rightarrow 2$ as $h \rightarrow 0$.)

We may also say that the limit of the gradient is 2 as h tends to 0. So the gradient of the curve $y = x^2$ at the point (1,1) is 2.

The gradient of $y = x^2$ at any point

Suppose that H is the point on $y = x^2$ whose x coordinate is x, and that K is another point on $y = x^2$ whose x coordinate is $(x + h)$.

The y coordinate of H is x^2.
The y coordinate of K is $(x + h)^2$.

$$KN = (x + h)^2 - x^2 = 2hx + h^2.$$
$$HN = (x + h) - x = h.$$

$$\text{The gradient of } HK = \frac{2hx + h^2}{h}$$
$$= 2x + h \text{ (if } h \text{ is not zero).}$$

As h tends to 0, the gradient tends to $2x$.

The gradient of the tangent is $2x$, or the gradient of the curve $y = x^2$ at the point (x, y) is $2x$.

It follows that the gradient of the curve at the point (1, 1) is 2; that the gradient at (2, 4) is 4; that the gradient at (3, 9) is 6 and so on.

Example. Find the gradient of the curve $y = 2x^2 - 3x - 4$ at the point (x, y).

Suppose that (x, y) and $(x + h, y + k)$ are two points on the curve.

Then $\quad y + k = 2(x + h)^2 - 3(x + h) - 4 \quad \text{(i)}$

and $\quad y = 2x^2 - 3x - 4 \quad \text{(ii)}$

Subtract (ii) from (i), $\quad k = 4xh + 2h^2 - 3h$

Therefore $\quad \dfrac{k}{h} = 4x + 2h - 3$ (if h is not zero).

$\dfrac{k}{h}$ is the gradient of the chord and tends to $(4x - 3)$ as h tends to 0.

The gradient of the curve at the point (x, y) is therefore $(4x - 3)$. For example, $(2, -2)$ is a point on the curve. The gradient of the curve at this point is $4(2) - 3 = 5$.

EXERCISES 58A

Find the gradients of the following curves at the points specified.

1. $y = 3x^2$ at (1, 3).
2. $y = x^2 + x$ at (1, 2).
3. $y = x^2 + x + 1$ at (1, 3).
4. $y = 2x^2 + x$ at (1, 3).
5. $y = 2x^2$ at (2, 8).
6. $y = x^2 - x$ at (2, 2).
7. $y = 7x$ at (x, y).
8. $y = 2x^2$ at (x, y).
9. $y = 3x^2 + x + 1$ at (x, y).
10. $y = 4x^2 - x - 2$ at (x, y).

EXERCISES 58B

Find the gradients of the following curves at the points specified.

1. $y = 4x^2$ at (1, 4).
2. $y = 3x^2 + x$ at (1, 4).
3. $y = x^2 - x + 1$ at (1, 1).
4. $y = 3x^2 - 1$ at (1, 2).
5. $y = 3x^2$ at (2, 12).
6. $y = 2x^2 - x$ at (2, 6).
7. $y = 4x$ at (x, y).
8. $y = 3x^2$ at (x, y).
9. $y = 2x^2 + x + 1$ at (x, y).
10. $y = 6x^2 - 2x$ at (x, y).

The derived function

The gradient of a curve at the point (x, y) on it is called its derived function. The derived function of x^2 is $2x$. The derived function of $(2x^2 - 3x - 4)$, as proved in the worked example, is $(4x - 3)$. The derived function of x^2 is written $D(x^2)$ and the derived function of $(2x^2 - 3x - 4)$ is written $D(2x^2 - 3x - 4)$.

$$\therefore D(x^2) = 2x,$$

and
$$D(2x^2 - 3x - 4) = 4x - 3.$$

The derived function of a constant

The graph of $y = c$ is a straight line parallel to the axis of x and its gradient is zero.

$$\therefore D(\text{any constant}) = 0.$$

The derived function of ax, where a is constant

Suppose (x, y) and $(x + h, y + k)$ are two points on the line $y = ax$.

Then $\qquad y + k = a(x + h) \quad . \quad . \quad . \quad . \quad$ (i)

and $\qquad y = ax \quad . \quad . \quad . \quad . \quad . \quad$ (ii)

Subtract (ii) from (i), $\qquad k = ah.$

$$\therefore \frac{k}{h} = a.$$

$$\therefore D(ax) = a.$$

The derived function of ax^2, where a is constant

Suppose (x, y) and $(x + h, y + k)$ are two points on the curve $y = ax^2$.

Then $\qquad y + k = a(x + h)^2 \quad . \quad . \quad . \quad$ (i)

and $\qquad y = ax^2 \quad . \quad . \quad . \quad . \quad . \quad$ (ii)

Subtract (ii) from (i), $\qquad k = 2axh + ah^2.$

$$\therefore \frac{k}{h} = 2ax + ah \text{ (if } h \text{ is not zero).}$$

The limit of the gradient as h tends to 0 is $2ax$.

$$\therefore D(ax^2) = 2ax.$$

Notice that $\qquad D(ax^2) = aD(x^2).$

The derived function of $ax^2 + bx + c$, where $a, b, c,$ are constants

Suppose that (x, y) and $(x + h, y + k)$ are two points on the curve $y = ax^2 + bx + c$.

Then $\qquad y + k = a(x + h)^2 + b(x + h) + c$

$\qquad\qquad = ax^2 + 2axh + ah^2 + bx + bh + c \quad$ (i)

and $\qquad y = ax^2 + bx + c \quad . \quad . \quad . \quad . \quad$ (ii)

Subtract (ii) from (i), $\quad k = 2axh + ah^2 + bh.$

$$\therefore \frac{k}{h} = 2ax + ah + b \text{ (if } h \text{ is not zero).}$$

The limit of the gradient as h tends to 0 is $(2ax + b)$.

$$\therefore D(ax^2 + bx + c) = 2ax + b.$$

Notice that $D(ax^2 + bx + c) = aD(x^2) + bD(x) + D(c)$.

Example 1. Find the derived function of $3x^2 - 7x - 1$.

$$\begin{aligned} D(3x^2 - 7x - 1) &= 3D(x^2) - 7D(x) - D(1) \\ &= 3(2x) - 7(1) - 0 \\ &= 6x - 7. \end{aligned}$$

Example 2. Find the derived function of $(3x + 2)(2x - 1)$.

$$\begin{aligned} (3x + 2)(2x - 1) &= 6x^2 + x - 2. \\ D(6x^2 + x - 2) &= 6D(x^2) + D(x) - D(2) \\ &= 6(2x) + 1 - 0 \\ &= 12x + 1. \end{aligned}$$

EXERCISES 59A

Find the derived functions of the following.

1. $4x^2 - 6x$. **2.** $\frac{3}{2}x^2 - 1$. **3.** $3x - x^2$.

4. $x^2 + \frac{3}{4}x + \frac{7}{8}$. **5.** $1 - 6x - 2x^2$. **6.** $4x^2 - 4x + 1$.

7. $(x - 1)(x - 2)$. **8.** $(x + 6)(2x - 1)$. **9.** $(2x - 1)(3x + 1)$.

10. $x(4x + 3)$.

EXERCISES 59B

Find the derived functions of the following.

1. $2x^2 - 8x$. **2.** $\frac{1}{2}x^2 - \frac{1}{4}$. **3.** $2x - x^2$.

4. $x^2 + \frac{2}{3}x + \frac{1}{6}$. **5.** $1 - 4x - 3x^2$. **6.** $3x^2 + 3x + 1$.

7. $(x + 1)(x - 1)$. **8.** $(2x - 3)(x - 4)$. **9.** $(2x + 1)(3x - 1)$.

10. $x\left(x + \frac{1}{x}\right)$.

The derived function of x^3

Suppose that (x, y) and $(x + h, y + k)$ are two points on the curve $y = x^3$.

Then
$$\begin{aligned} y + k &= (x + h)^3 = (x + h)(x^2 + 2xh + h^2) \\ &= x^3 + 3x^2h + 3xh^2 + h^3 \quad . \quad . \quad \text{(i)} \end{aligned}$$

and
$$y = x^3 \quad . \quad . \quad . \quad . \quad . \quad . \quad \text{(ii)}$$

Subtract (ii) from (i), $k = 3x^2h + 3xh^2 + h^3$.

$$\therefore \frac{k}{h} = 3x^2 + 3xh + h^2 \text{ (if } h \text{ is not zero).}$$

The limit of the gradient as h tends to 0 is $3x^2$.

$$\therefore D(x^3) = 3x^2.$$

The derived function of $\frac{1}{x}$

Suppose that (x, y) and $(x + h, y + k)$ are two points on the curve $y = \frac{1}{x}$.

Then $$y + k = \frac{1}{x + h} \quad . \quad . \quad . \quad . \quad . \quad \text{(i)}$$

and $$y = \frac{1}{x} \quad . \quad . \quad . \quad . \quad . \quad . \quad \text{(ii)}$$

Subtract (ii) from (i), $k = \frac{1}{x + h} - \frac{1}{x} = \frac{x - (x + h)}{x(x + h)}$

$$= -\frac{h}{x(x + h)}.$$

$$\therefore \frac{k}{h} = -\frac{1}{x(x + h)} \text{ (if } h \text{ is not zero).}$$

As h tends to 0, the gradient $\left(\frac{k}{h}\right)$ tends to $-\frac{1}{x^2}$.

$$\therefore D\left(\frac{1}{x}\right) = -\frac{1}{x^2}.$$

The derived function of $\frac{1}{x^2}$

Suppose that (x, y) and $(x + h, y + k)$ are two points on the curve $y = \frac{1}{x^2}$.

Then $$y + k = \frac{1}{(x + h)^2} \quad . \quad . \quad . \quad . \quad . \quad \text{(i)}$$

and $$y = \frac{1}{x^2} \quad . \quad . \quad . \quad . \quad . \quad . \quad \text{(ii)}$$

Subtract (ii) from (i), $k = \dfrac{1}{(x+h)^2} - \dfrac{1}{x^2} = \dfrac{x^2 - (x+h)^2}{x^2(x+h)^2}$

$$= \frac{-2xh - h^2}{x^2(x+h)^2}$$

$$\therefore \frac{k}{h} = \frac{-2x - h}{x^2(x+h)^2} \text{ (if } h \text{ is not zero).}$$

As h tends to 0, the gradient $\left(\dfrac{k}{h}\right)$ tends to $\dfrac{-2x}{x^4}$ or $-\dfrac{2}{x^3}$.

$$\therefore D\left(\frac{1}{x^2}\right) = -\frac{2}{x^3}.$$

General rule

Tabulating the results already proved, and remembering that $x^1 = x$ and that $x^0 = 1$;

$$D(x^3) = 3x^2.$$
$$D(x^2) = 2x.$$
$$D(x^1) = 1.$$
$$D(x^0) = 0.$$
$$D(x^{-1}) = -1x^{-2}.$$
$$D(x^{-2}) = -2x^{-3}.$$

The reader will guess from these results that $D(x^4) = 4x^3$ and that $D\left(\dfrac{1}{x^3}\right) = D(x^{-3}) = -3x^{-4}$.

In fact, it is true that $D(x^n) = nx^{n-1}$ and the reader may assume that this formula is true for all values of n, even fractional.

Notation

If $f(x)$ denotes any function of x, that is any expression containing x, we call its derived function $D\{(fx)\}$. The derived function of $f(x)$ may also be called $f'(x)$.

If $y = f(x)$, the most common way of expressing its derived function is $\dfrac{dy}{dx}$. This notation will be used in future. The reader must realise that $\dfrac{dy}{dx}$ is not an ordinary fraction which can be cancelled; that the d of dy is not a multiple (compare sin y) and that the dy cannot be separated from its denominator, dx. The expression $\dfrac{dy}{dx}$ actually compares the rate of change of y with that of x.

Finding the derived function of an expression is called differentiating the expression. The advantage of the notation $\dfrac{dy}{dx}$ is that it tells us what quantities are being compared; in fact, that we have differentiated y with respect to x. For example, if we know that $z = t^3 - t^2$, then $\dfrac{dz}{dt} = 3t^2 - 2t$, or we may write the result in the form $\dfrac{d}{dt}(t^3 - t^2) = 3t^2 - 2t$.

Worked Examples

Example 1. Find the derived function of $2x^3 - \dfrac{3}{x}$.

$$\begin{aligned} D\left(2x^3 - \frac{3}{x}\right) = D(2x^3) - D\left(\frac{3}{x}\right) &= 2D(x^3) - 3D(x^{-1}) \\ &= 2(3x^2) - 3(-1x^{-2}) \\ &= 6x^2 + \frac{3}{x^2}. \end{aligned}$$

Alternative method. Let $\qquad y = 2x^3 - \dfrac{3}{x}.$

Then $\qquad \dfrac{dy}{dx} = 6x^2 + \dfrac{3}{x^2};$

or simply, $\qquad \dfrac{d}{dx}\left(2x^3 - \dfrac{3}{x}\right) = 6x^2 + \dfrac{3}{x^2}.$

Example 2. Find the derived function of $2\sqrt{x} - \dfrac{3}{\sqrt{x}}$.

$$D\left(2\sqrt{x} - \frac{3}{\sqrt{x}}\right) = 2D(x^{\frac{1}{2}}) - 3D(x^{-\frac{1}{2}})$$

$$= 2(\tfrac{1}{2})(x^{-\frac{1}{2}}) - 3(-\tfrac{1}{2})x^{-\frac{3}{2}} = x^{-\frac{1}{2}} + \tfrac{3}{2}x^{-\frac{3}{2}} = \frac{1}{\sqrt{x}} + \frac{3}{2\sqrt{x^3}}$$

Alternative method. Let

$$y = 2\sqrt{x} - \frac{3}{\sqrt{x}} = 2x^{\frac{1}{2}} - 3x^{-\frac{1}{2}}.$$

$$\begin{aligned} \frac{dy}{dx} &= x^{-\frac{1}{2}} + \tfrac{3}{2}x^{-\frac{3}{2}}. \\ &= \frac{1}{\sqrt{x}} + \frac{3}{2\sqrt{x^3}}. \end{aligned}$$

Example 3. Find the derived function of $\dfrac{(1 + x)(1 + 2x^4)}{x}$.

Let

$$y = \frac{(1 + x)(1 + 2x^2)}{x} = \frac{1 + x + 2x^2 + 2x^3}{x} = \frac{1}{x} + 1 + 2x + 2x^2.$$

Then $$\frac{dy}{dx} = -\frac{1}{x^2} + 2 + 4x.$$

$$\left[\text{or,} \qquad \frac{d}{dx}\left\{\frac{1}{x} + 1 + 2x + 2x^2\right\} = -\frac{1}{x^2} + 2 + 4x.\right]$$

EXERCISES 60: MISCELLANEOUS

Find the derived functions of:

1. $3x^3 - 1$.
2. $1 - \dfrac{1}{x^2}$.
3. $\left(x + \dfrac{1}{x}\right)^2$.
4. $x + 2x^2 + 3x^3$.
5. $(x + 2)(x^2 + 1)$.
6. $\dfrac{x + 1}{\sqrt{x}}$.
7. $\sqrt{x} + x$.
8. $\dfrac{x^2 + 1}{x}$.
9. $1 - \dfrac{1}{x}$.
10. $1 + \dfrac{1}{x} + \dfrac{1}{x^2}$.

Find the following:

11. $\dfrac{d}{dx}(x^3 + x^2)$.
12. $\dfrac{d}{dx}(2 + 7x + 3x^2 - 4x^3)$.
13. $\dfrac{d}{dx}\left(\dfrac{1}{x} - \dfrac{1}{x^2}\right)$.
14. $\dfrac{d}{dx}\left(\dfrac{1}{\sqrt{x}} + x\right)$.
15. $\dfrac{d}{dx}\left(x + 2 + \dfrac{1}{x}\right)$.
16. $\dfrac{d}{dy}(y^3 - y)$.
17. $\dfrac{d}{dt}(3t^2 + t^3)$.
18. $\dfrac{d}{dz}(z^2 + 3z + 1)$.
19. $\dfrac{d}{dv}(3v - v^2 + 7v^3 + 1)$.
20. $\dfrac{d}{dt}(t^3 - 3t - 1)$.

Differentiate:

21. $1 + 6x + 2x^2 + 3x^3$.
22. $\dfrac{1}{x^2} + \dfrac{2}{x} + 3$.

23. $x - \dfrac{1}{\sqrt{x}}$.

24. $x^{\frac{5}{2}}$.

25. $x + 6x^2 + 7x^3$.

26. $(x + 1)(x^2 + 1)$.

27. $\dfrac{x^2 + x + 1}{x}$.

28. x^7.

29. $\dfrac{1}{x^7}$.

30. $x^7 + \dfrac{1}{x^7}$.

31. Find the gradient of the curve $y = 3x^2 - 2x - 1$ at the point (1, 0).

32. Find the gradient of the tangent to the curve $y = x^3 + x$ at the point (2, 10).

33. Find the coordinates of the point on the graph of $y = x^2 - x$ at which the tangent is parallel to $y = x$.

34. Find the gradient of the curve $xy = 1$ at the point (1, 1).

35. Given that $xy = 1$, find $\dfrac{dy}{dx}$ in terms of x.

36. Simplify $\dfrac{d}{dt}\{t^3 - 6t^2 + 4t - 1\}$.

37. Find the point on the curve $y = 1 - x^2$ at which the tangent is parallel to $y = 2x$.

38. If $x^2y = 4$, find $\dfrac{dy}{dx}$ in terms of y.

39. If $u + v = 5$, find $\dfrac{du}{dv}$.

40. If $y = x^2$, find $\dfrac{dy}{dx}$ (i) in terms of x; (ii) in terms of y.

41. Simplify $\dfrac{d}{dz}\left(z - \dfrac{1}{z}\right)$.

42. If $y = x^2$, prove that $x\dfrac{dy}{dx} = 2y$.

43. If $pv = 40$, find the value of $\dfrac{dp}{dv}$ when $p = 10$.

44. If $z = t + t^2$, find $\dfrac{dt}{dz}$.

45. Find the points on the curve $y = x^3 - x^2$ at which the tangent is parallel to the axis of x.

15

APPLICATIONS OF THE DERIVED FUNCTION

Maxima and minima

AT the point P to the curve shown in Fig. 18, the tangent is parallel to the axis of x. The gradient of this tangent is zero and therefore the value of the derived function at this point is zero. Such a point is called a **maximum point.** The value of y at such a point is called a maximum value of y. The value of y at a maximum point is larger than at points on either side of it; it is not necessarily the greatest value of all. For example, in the curve shown the value of y at P is less than that at R.

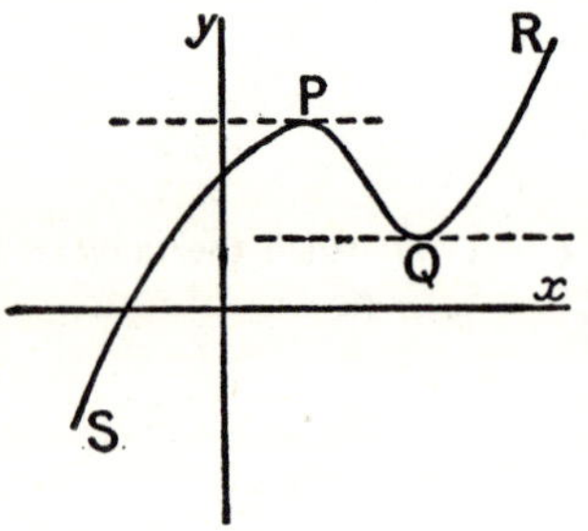

FIG. 18

The gradient at the point Q is also zero. At this point, the value of y is less than at points immediately on either side of it. It is not least of all possible values of y, because, for example, the value of y at S is smaller still. Such a point is called a **minimum point** and the value of y at such a point is called a minimum value of y.

Slightly before P, the gradient of the curve is positive; at P, it is zero; slightly after P, it is negative.

So at a maximum point, the gradient changes from positive to negative through the zero value.

Slightly before Q, the gradient is negative; at Q, it is zero; slightly after Q, it is positive.

So at a minimum point, the gradient changes from negative to positive through the zero value.

Maximum and minimum points are called **turning points**; the values of y at these points are called turning values.

At a maximum point, $\frac{dy}{dx}$ is zero; the value of $\frac{dy}{dx}$ changes from positive to negative as x increases through the point.

At a minimum point, $\frac{dy}{dx}$ is zero; the value of $\frac{dy}{dx}$ changes from negative to positive as x increases through the point.

There is one other type of point at which $\frac{dy}{dx} = 0$. This is shown in Fig. 19, and is not a turning point because the gradient does not change sign (or turn).

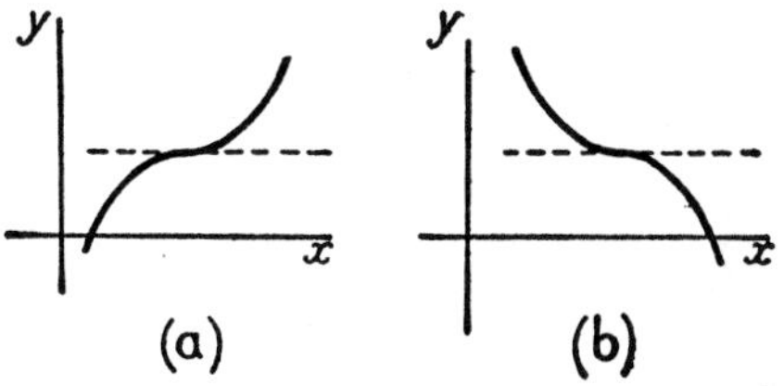

FIG. 19

In Fig. 19 (a), $\frac{dy}{dx}$ is positive both before and after its zero value.

In Fig. 19 (b), $\frac{dy}{dx}$ is negative both before and after its zero value.

A point where $\frac{dy}{dx} = 0$ but does not change sign is called a **point of inflexion.**

Example 1. Find the maximum or minimum value of $(x^2 - 4x - 6)$.

If
$$y = x^2 - 4x - 6,$$
$$\frac{dy}{dx} = 2x - 4.$$
$$\therefore \frac{dy}{dx} = 0, \text{ when } x = 2.$$

When x is slightly less than 2, $\frac{dy}{dx}$ is negative.

When $x = 2$, $\frac{dy}{dx} = 0$.

When x is slightly greater than 2, $\frac{dy}{dx}$ is positive.

Therefore the point where $x = 2$ is a minimum point.

The value of $(x^2 - 4x - 6)$ at this point is $4 - 8 - 6$ or -10.
$\therefore$ the minimum value of $(x^2 - 4x - 6)$ is -10 and occurs when $x = 2$.

Example 2. Find the maximum and minimum values of $x^2(x - 3)$.

If $$y = x^2(x - 3) \quad \text{or} \quad x^3 - 3x^2,$$

$$\frac{dy}{dx} = 3x^2 - 6x \quad \text{or} \quad 3x(x - 2).$$

$$\therefore \quad \frac{dy}{dx} = 0, \text{ when } x = 0 \text{ or when } x = 2.$$

(i) When x is slightly less than 0, x is negative and $(x - 2)$ is negative.

$\therefore$ $\frac{dy}{dx}$ is positive.

When $x = 0$, $\frac{dy}{dx} = 0$.

When x is slightly greater than 0, x is positive and $(x - 2)$ is negative.

$\therefore$ $\frac{dy}{dx}$ is negative.

So, at $x = 0$, $\frac{dy}{dx}$ changes from positive to negative. This is a maximum point and the corresponding value of y is 0.

(ii) When x is slightly less than 2, x is positive and $(x - 2)$ is negative.

$\therefore$ $\frac{dy}{dx}$ is negative.

When $x = 2$, $\frac{dy}{dx} = 0$.

When x is slightly greater than 2, x is positive and $(x - 2)$ is positive.

$\therefore$ $\frac{dy}{dx}$ is positive.

So, at $x = 2$, $\frac{dy}{dx}$ changes from negative to positive.

This is a minimum point and the corresponding value of y is $4(2 - 3)$ or -4.

Therefore the maximum value of $x^2(x - 3)$ is 0 and the minimum value is -4.

Example 3. Find the turning values of $x^3(x - 4)$.

If $$y = x^3(x - 4) \quad \text{or} \quad x^4 - 4x^3,$$

$$\frac{dy}{dx} = 4x^3 - 12x^2 \quad \text{or} \quad 4x^2(x - 3).$$

$$\therefore \quad \frac{dy}{dx} = 0, \text{ when } x = 0 \text{ or when } x = 3.$$

(i) When x is slightly less than 0, x^2 is positive and $(x - 3)$ is negative.

$\therefore \frac{dy}{dx}$ is negative.

When $x = 0$, $\frac{dy}{dx} = 0$.

When x is slightly greater than 0, x^2 is positive and $(x - 3)$ is negative.

$\therefore \frac{dy}{dx}$ is negative.

Since $\frac{dy}{dx}$ does not change sign, $x = 0$ is a point of inflexion.

(ii) When x is slightly less than 3, x^2 is positive and $(x - 3)$ is negative.

$\therefore \frac{dy}{dx}$ is negative.

When $x = 3$, $\frac{dy}{dx} = 0$.

When x is slightly greater than 3, x^2 is positive and $(x - 3)$ is positive.

$\therefore \frac{dy}{dx}$ is positive.

$\therefore \frac{dy}{dx}$ changes from negative to positive.

So $x = 3$ gives a minimum point and the minimum value of y is $3^3(3 - 4)$ or -27.

The curve has no maximum point.

Example 4. A farmer encloses sheep in a rectangular pen, using hurdles for three sides and a long wall for the fourth side. If he has 100 metres of hurdles, find the greatest area he can enclose.

Suppose the lengths of the sides of the rectangle are x metres (parallel to the wall) and y metres.

Then $$x + 2y = 100,$$
and so $$x = 100 - 2y.$$

If A m² is the area of the rectangle,

$$A = xy.$$
$$\therefore A = (100 - 2y)y = 100y - 2y^2.$$
$$\therefore \frac{dA}{dy} = 100 - 4y.$$
$$\therefore \frac{dA}{dy} = 0, \text{ when } y = 25.$$

When y is slightly less than 25, $\dfrac{dA}{dy}$ is positive.

When $y = 25$, $\dfrac{dA}{dy} = 0$.

When y is slightly greater than 25, $\dfrac{dA}{dy}$ is negative.

So $\dfrac{dA}{dy}$ changes from positive to negative and the point where $y = 25$ is a maximum point.

When $y = 25$, $x = 100 - 2y = 50$.
The value of A is 25×50 or $1250\ \text{m}^2$.
The greatest area the farmer can enclose is $1250\ \text{m}^2$.
(Note that when a curve has one turning point only, a maximum value is the greatest value; a minimum value is the least value.)

Example 5. A right circular cylinder is to be made so that the sum of its radius and its height is 6 m. Find the maximum volume of the cylinder.
Let r metres be the radius and h metres the height.

Then $$h + r = 6 \quad \text{or} \quad h = 6 - r.$$

Let V be the volume in m^3.

$$\therefore\ V = \pi r^2 h = \pi r^2(6 - r) = \pi(6r^2 - r^3).$$

We need to find the maximum value of V.

$$\frac{dV}{dr} = \pi(12r - 3r^2) = 3\pi r(4 - r).$$

$$\therefore\ \frac{dV}{dr} = 0, \text{ when } r = 0 \text{ or when } r = 4.$$

(i) When r is 0, the value of V is 0 and this is obviously not the greatest value.
(ii) When r is just less than 4, r is positive and $(4 - r)$ is positive.
$\therefore\ \dfrac{dV}{dr}$ is positive.

When $r = 4$, $\dfrac{dV}{dr} = 0$.

When r is just greater than 4, r is positive and $(4 - r)$ is negative.
$\therefore\ \dfrac{dV}{dr}$ is negative.

V is therefore a maximum when $r = 4$ and $h = 2$.
The maximum volume is $\pi r^2 h$ or $32\pi\ \text{m}^3$.

EXERCISES 61A

Find maximum and minimum values of the following (questions **1–6**).

1. $x^2 - 6x$. **2.** $1 - 2x - x^2$. **3.** $x^2 - 2x - 3$.

4. $3x - x^3$. **5.** $x - \sqrt{x}$. **6.** $x + \frac{1}{x}$.

7. The sum of two numbers is 24. What is their maximum product?

8. A rectangle has a perimeter of 12 m. Find its maximum area.

9. The volume of a right circular cylinder, open at one end, is to be 8π cm³. Find its minimum surface area.

10. The sum of two numbers is 20. Find the numbers so that the sum of their squares is a minimum.

EXERCISES 61B

Find maximum and minimum values of the following (questions **1–6**).

1. $x^2 - 8x$. **2.** $1 - 4x - x^2$. **3.** $x^2 - 4x - 1$.

4. $12x - x^3$. **5.** $x + \sqrt{x}$. **6.** $4x + \frac{1}{x}$.

7. The sum of two numbers is $2k$. What is their maximum product?

8. A rectangle has a perimeter of $4k$ metres. What is its maximum area?

9. The volume of a right circular cylinder, closed at both ends, is to be 16π cm³. Find its minimum surface area.

10. The sum of two numbers is $2k$. Find the numbers so that the sum of their squares may be a minimum.

Velocity

Fig. 20 shows a graph plotting the distance gone by a body, s metres (vertical axis) against the time taken, t seconds (horizontal axis). Such a graph is called a distance-time graph.

Suppose H, K are any two points on the graph and lines through H parallel to the t axis and through K parallel to the s axis meet at N. The length KN represents the distance gone between the two points and the length HN represents the time taken to cover this distance.

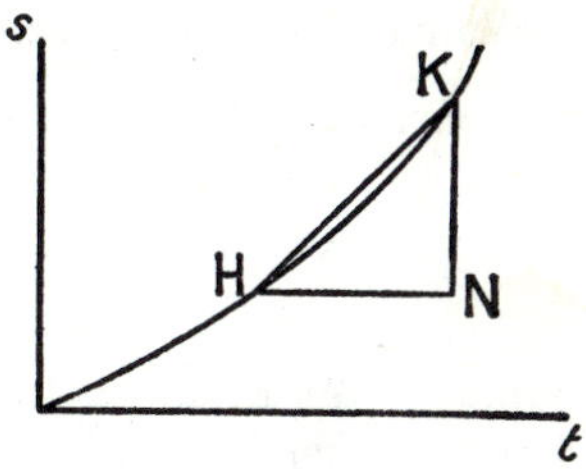

FIG. 20

The gradient of the line $\left(= \frac{KN}{HN}\right)$ therefore represents the average velocity of the body during this interval.

This is true however close K is to H. As the distance between H and K gets smaller, the average velocity becomes closer to the velocity at H. The actual velocity at H is, in fact, the limit of the average velocity as K moves along the graph towards H. The limit of the line HK as K moves towards H is the tangent at H.

Therefore the gradient of the tangent at H is equal to the velocity at that instant.

The gradient may be found by drawing and by measurement from the graph. It may also be found by differentiation if the relation between s and t is given.

The velocity v at time t is given by $v = \frac{ds}{dt}$.

Example 1. The distance moved by a point along a line in t sec is given in metres by $s = t^2 + 4t$. Find (i) the initial velocity; (ii) the velocity after 2 sec; (iii) the average velocity for the first 2 sec.

$$s = t^2 + 4t.$$

$$v = \frac{ds}{dt} = 2t + 4.$$

The velocity at time t is $(2t + 4)$ m/sec.

(i) The initial velocity is the velocity when $t = 0$ and is 4 m/sec.

(ii) The velocity after 2 sec is found by putting t equal to 2, and is 8 m/sec.

(iii) The distance gone in 2 sec is found by putting $t = 2$ in $s = t^2 + 4t$. The distance gone in 2 sec is therefore $4 + 8$ or 12 m. The average velocity is 6 m/sec.

Acceleration

We have seen that when a body moves along a straight line, the rate of change of distance is called the velocity $\left(v = \frac{ds}{dt}\right)$. The rate of change of velocity is called the **acceleration** $\left(a = \frac{dv}{dt}\right)$. If the rate of change of velocity is constant, then the acceleration is constant. Suppose, for example, that the velocity of a body after 1 sec is 4 m/sec, after 2 sec is 6 m/sec, after 3 sec is 8 m/sec. Then there is a steady increase in velocity of 2 m/sec in each second. The acceleration is said to be 2 m/sec per sec or 2 m/sec^2.

If a body is slowing down, it is said to have a negative acceleration or a **retardation**.

In the same way that the velocity is equal to the gradient of the distance-time graph, the acceleration is equal to the gradient of the velocity-time graph.

$$\therefore \text{ the acceleration, } a = \frac{dv}{dt}.$$

Example 1. The distance s metres gone by a body in t sec is given by $s = t^3 - 6t^2 + 4t$. Find (i) its initial velocity; (ii) its velocity after 2 sec; (iii) its acceleration after 2 sec.

$$s = t^3 - 6t^2 + 4t.$$

$$v = \frac{ds}{dt} = 3t^2 - 12t + 4.$$

(i) When $t = 0$, $v = 4$. The initial velocity is 4 m/sec.
(ii) When $t = 2$, $v = 12 - 24 + 4 = -8$.
The velocity after 2 sec is -8 m/sec (i.e. 8 m/sec reversed in direction).
(iii) $a = \dfrac{dv}{dt} = 6t - 12$.
When $t = 2$, $a = 0$.
The acceleration after 2 sec is zero.

Example 2. The velocity v m/sec of a point moving along a straight line, is given by $v = 4 - t^2$, where t is the time in seconds. Find the acceleration of the point when it is momentarily at rest.

The point is momentarily at rest when $v = 0$; i.e. when $4 - t^2 = 0$. The values of t are 2 and -2 and so the point is momentarily at rest after 2 sec. (The value -2 means that the point was at rest 2 sec ago.)

$$v = 4 - t^2.$$

$$a = \frac{dv}{dt} = -2t.$$

Putting $t = 2$, the acceleration after 2 sec is -4.
So when the body is at rest, it has a retardation of 4 m/sec^2.

EXERCISES 62A

1. A point moves in a straight line so that its distance from a fixed point O of that line is $27t - t^3$, after t sec. Show that it moves away from O for 3 sec.

2. The distance s metres moved by a point in t sec is given by

$$s = t^3 + 3t^2 + 4.$$

Find the velocity and acceleration after 3 sec.

3. The velocity v m/sec of a point moving in a straight line is given after t sec by $v = 3t^2 + 4t$. Find the acceleration after 2 sec.

4. The distance s metres moved by a particle along a line in t sec is given by $s = 3t + t^2$. Find its velocity and acceleration after n sec.

5. The velocity v m/sec of a point moving in a straight line after t sec is given by $v = t^2 - t$. Find the acceleration after 3 sec and also find when the acceleration is zero.

EXERCISES 62B

1. A point moves in a straight line so that its distance from a fixed point O in the line is $32t - 2t^2$ cm after t sec. Show that it moves away from O for 8 sec.

2. The distance s metres moved by a point in t sec is given by

$$s = t^3 + 3t^2 + 2t.$$

Find the velocity and acceleration after 2 sec.

3. After t sec, the velocity, v m/sec, of a point moving in a straight line is given by $v = 4t^2 + 5t$. Find the acceleration after 3 sec.

4. The distance s metres moved by a particle in t sec is given by $s = 4t + 2t^2$. Find the velocity and acceleration after n sec.

5. The velocity v m/sec of a point moving in a straight line is given in terms of the time, t sec, by $v = t^2 - 4t$. Find the acceleration after 3 sec and also find when the acceleration is zero.

Rate of change

$\frac{dy}{dx}$ compares the rate of change of y with that of x; if $\frac{dy}{dx} = 6$, y is increasing 6 times as fast as x, numerically; if x and y are distances and x is increasing at 4 m/sec, then y is increasing at 24 m/sec.

If $\frac{dy}{dx} = -6$, then y decreases 6 times as fast as x increases.

Example 1. The volume of a sphere of radius r is $\frac{4}{3}\pi r^3$. If the radius of a soap bubble is increasing at 0·1 cm/sec, find the rate of increase of its volume when the radius is 2 cm

$$V = \tfrac{4}{3}\pi r^3$$

$$\frac{dV}{dr} = 4\pi r^2.$$

When $r = 2$,
$$\frac{dV}{dr} = 16\pi.$$

The volume increases 16π times as fast as the radius.
The radius increases at 0·1 cm/sec.
Therefore the volume increases at $1{\cdot}6\pi$ cm^3/sec.

Example 2. Water is poured into an inverted cone of semi-vertical angle 45°, at a constant rate of 2 m^3 per min. At what rate is the depth of water increasing when it is 2 m deep?

When the depth is x metres, the radius of cross section is $x \tan 45°$ or x metres. The volume of water is $\frac{1}{3}\pi x^2(x)$ or $\frac{1}{3}\pi x^3$ m^3.

$$V = \tfrac{1}{3}\pi x^3.$$

$$\frac{dV}{dx} = \pi x^2.$$

When $x = 2$,
$$\frac{dV}{dx} = 4\pi.$$

The volume increases 4π times as fast as the depth.

The volume increases at 2 m^3 per min.

Therefore the depth increases at $\frac{2}{4\pi}$ metres per min $= \frac{1}{2\pi}$ metres per min.

EXERCISES 63A

1. Find the rate of increase of the area of a square when the length of side is 2 cm and is increasing at 0·3 cm/sec.

2. Find the rate of increase of the volume of a cube when the length of side is 3 cm and is increasing at 0·1 cm/sec.

3. Find the rate of increase of the volume of a cube when the length of side is 2 cm and the area of a face is increasing at 1 cm^2/sec.

4. Find the rate of increase of the surface area of a sphere when the radius is 4 cm and is increasing at 0·1 cm/sec.

5. Find the rate of increase of the volume of a sphere when the radius is 3 cm and is increasing at 0·2 cm/sec.

EXERCISES 63B

1. Find the rate of increase of the area of a square when the length of side is 3 cm and is increasing at 0·2 cm/sec.

2. Find the rate of increase of the volume of a cube when the length of side is 2 cm and is increasing at 0·2 cm/sec.

3. Find the rate of increase of the volume of a cube when the length of side is 3 cm and the area of a face is increasing at 0·5 cm^2/sec.

4. Find the rate of increase of the surface area of a sphere when the radius is 2 cm and is increasing at 0·4 cm/sec.

5. Find the rate of increase of the volume of a sphere when the radius is 2 cm and is increasing at 0·4 cm/sec.

Exercise 64: Miscellaneous

1. Find the gradient of the curve $y = x(x - 2)^2 + 1$, at the point (3, 4) and determine the points at which the tangent is parallel to the axis of x.

2. A cylindrical vessel with one end open is to have a volume of 100 m³. Find the least area of sheet metal needed.

3. A piece of wire of length 1 m is cut into two pieces and each is bent into the form of a square. Find the least possible sum of the two areas.

4. Find any maximum or minimum values of $x(x - 1)^2 + 1$, distinguishing between them.

5. A square sheet of metal has sides of length 8 cm. Equal square pieces are removed from each corner and the remaining piece is bent into the form of an open box. Find the maximum volume of the box.

6. Show that the gradient of $y = 1 + 4x + 4x^2$ at the point where $x = 4$ is three times the gradient at the point where $x = 1$.

7. Find the maximum and minimum values of $x^2(x^2 - 2)$, distinguishing between them.

8. A point starts from rest and moves in a straight line. Its velocity after t sec is $(6t - t^2)$ m/sec. Find the initial acceleration and the time when the acceleration is zero.

9. The length of a rectangular block is twice the width and its volume is 72 m³. Find the minimum surface area of the block.

10. Find the maximum and minimum values of $2x^2 - x^4$, distinguishing between them.

11. A cylinder is such that the sum of its height and circumference of base is 6 m. Find the greatest possible volume of the cylinder.

12. Two concentric circles are such that the radius of the larger is always twice the radius of the smaller. If the radius of the smaller is increasing at 0·1 cm/sec, find the rate at which the area between the circles is increasing when the radius of the smaller is 12 cm.

13. A sphere is expanding so that its volume is increasing at 2 cm³/sec. Find the rate of increase of its radius when the radius is 10 cm.

14. If $y^2 = 4x$, find $\dfrac{dy}{dx}$ when $x = 4$.

15. Find the turning values of $24x + 3x^2 - x^3$, distinguishing between them.

16. If the pressure and volume of a gas are connected by the relation $pv^{1 \cdot 4} = 20$, find $\dfrac{dp}{dv}$.

17. If $s = 6 + 4t - t^2$, find the velocity and acceleration after 2 sec.

18. Find the points on the graph of $y = 3x - x^2$ at which the tangent makes equal angles with the axes.

19. The graph of $y = Ax^2 + Bx + C$ passes through the origin and its gradient there is 2. The graph also passes through the point (1, 1). Find A, B and C.

20. If $\frac{d}{dx}(x^3 - x) = \frac{d}{dx}(x^2 - 1)$, find x.

16

INTEGRATION

The inverse of differentiation

WE know that the derived function of x is 1. Therefore, if we are asked to find an expression whose derived function is 1, one answer is x. But it is not the only answer, because $x + 2$, $x + 3$, and $x + 18\frac{1}{2}$ are all expressions whose derived functions equal 1. In fact, $(x + c)$ is the general solution, where c is called an **arbitrary constant** and may be equal to any number at all. Its precise value may only be found if we are given further information.

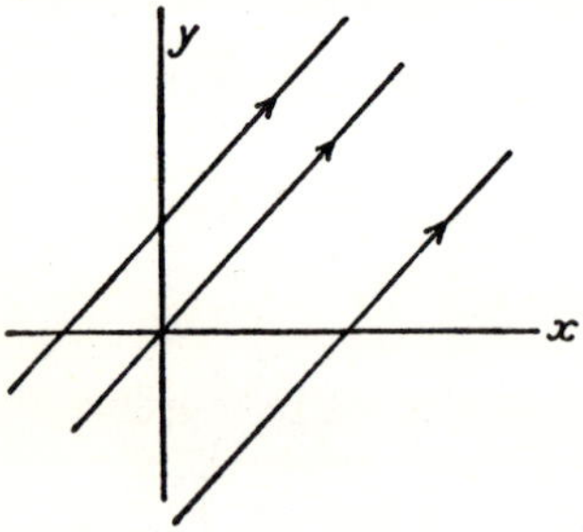

FIG. 21

Fig. 21 shows a number of straight lines, each of gradient 1. Any line parallel to these lines will also have gradient 1. The equation of any such line is $y = x + c$. Therefore if $\frac{dy}{dx} = 1$, $y = x + c$.

If we are also told that $y = 2$ when $x = 0$, by substituting in $y = x + c$, we see that $c = 2$, and therefore $y = x + 2$.

Again, the derived function of x^2 is $2x$. The general expression whose derived function equals $2x$ is therefore $x^2 + c$, where c is an arbitrary constant. The curves $y = x^2 + c$ are 'parallel' curves and are shown in Fig. 22. The curves are all exactly the same shape with the vertex moved along the axis of y. All the curves have the same gradient for any given value of x.

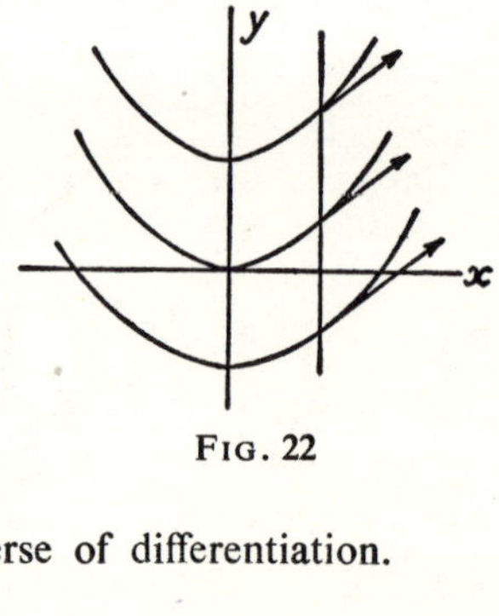

FIG. 22

The process of obtaining the function whose derived function is a given expression, is called integrating the expression. Integration is the inverse of differentiation.

If $\frac{dy}{dx} = 1,$ $\qquad y = x + c;$

if $\frac{dy}{dx} = x,$ $\qquad y = \frac{x^2}{2} + c;$

if $\frac{dy}{dx} = x^n,$ $\qquad y = \frac{x^{n+1}}{n+1} + c.$

(This applies for all values of n except -1.)

Notation

If y is a function of x, $\int y\,dx$ stands for the integral of y with respect to x. The integral sign $\int$ cannot be divorced from dx if the integral is with respect to x.

For example:

$$\int x\,dx = \frac{x^2}{2} + c;$$

$$\int t^2\,dt = \frac{t^3}{3} + c;$$

$$\int (v^2 + 3v + 1)\,dv = \frac{v^3}{3} + \frac{3v^2}{2} + v + c.$$

Example. Integrate $3x^3 - 4x - 5$.

Integrate each term separately.

The integral of x^3 is $\frac{x^4}{4}$.

The integral of x is $\frac{x^2}{2}$.

The integral of 5 is $5x$.

The integral of $(3x^3 - 4x - 5)$ is

$$\frac{3x^4}{4} - \frac{4x^2}{2} - 5x + c \quad \text{or} \quad \tfrac{3}{4}x^4 - 2x^2 - 5x + c.$$

EXERCISES 65A

Integrate:

1. x^3.
2. $x^3 + 2x^2$.
3. $x^2 + 6$.
4. $\frac{1}{x^2}$.

5. $ax^2 + bx + c$. **6.** $(x - 1)(x - 2)$. **7.** $\frac{1}{x^3}$. **8.** x^5.

9. The gradient of a curve which passes through the point (1, 1) is given by $2 + 2x - x^2$. Find the equation of the curve.

10. If $\frac{dy}{dx} = 6x - 2$, and $y = 2$ when $x = 0$, find y in terms of x.

EXERCISES 65B

Integrate:

1. $\sqrt{x}$. **2.** $x^2 + 3x + 4$. **3.** $x^2 - 4x$. **4.** $\frac{1 + x}{x^3}$.

5. $\frac{a}{x^2} + b$. **6.** $x(x + 1)$. **7.** $x^2(x + 2)$. **8.** $\frac{x^4 + 1}{x^2}$.

9. The gradient of a curve which passes through the point (2, 1) is given by $1 + 2x - 3x^2$. Find the equation of the curve.

10. If $\frac{dy}{dx} = x^2 + 1$, and $y = 1$ when $x = 0$, find y in terms of x.

Velocity and acceleration

If we are given the distance moved along a straight line by a point in time t, the velocity is found by differentiating the distance with respect to the time. Inversely, if we are given the velocity in terms of the time, the distance may be found by integration. Similarly, if we are given the acceleration in terms of the time, integration gives the velocity.

Example. The acceleration of a point moving in a straight line is given by $a = 3t + 4$. Find formulae for the velocity and distance, given that $s = 0$ and $v = 8$ when $t = 0$.

$$a = 3t + 4.$$

$$\therefore \frac{dv}{dt} = 3t + 4.$$

Integrating, $$v = \frac{3t^2}{2} + 4t + c.$$

When $t = 0$, $v = 8$. $\therefore c = 8$.

Since $$v = \frac{3t^2}{2} + 4t + 8,$$

$$\frac{ds}{dt} = \frac{3t^2}{2} + 4t + 8.$$

Integrating, $$s = \frac{t^3}{2} + 2t^2 + 8t + c.$$

Since $s = 0$ when $t = 0$, $c = 0$.

$$\therefore\ v = \frac{3t^2}{2} + 4t + 8 \quad \text{and} \quad s = \frac{t^2}{2} + 2t^2 + 8t.$$

EXERCISES 66A

(s, v, a, t, represent distance, velocity, acceleration and time in metre-second units.)

1. If $v = 3t + 1$ find s, given that $s = 0$ when $t = 0$.

2. If $a = t^2$, find v, given that $v = 2$ when $t = 0$.

3. If $a = t$, find s, given that when $t = 0$, $s = 0$ and $v = 4$.

4. If $v = t^2 + t + 1$, find s, given that $s = 0$ when $t = 0$.

5. If $a = t^2 + t$, find v, given that $v = 4$ when $t = 1$.

6. A stone falling under its own weight has a constant acceleration of 9·8 m/sec². If it starts from rest, find its velocity after 4 sec.

7. Find the velocity of a stone falling under gravity for 3 sec, if its initial velocity is 8 m/sec down.

8. Find the distance fallen by a stone in 4 sec starting from rest.

9. Find the distance fallen by a stone in 2 sec if its initial velocity is 8 m/sec down.

10. A stone is thrown vertically upwards with a velocity of 9·8 m/sec. Find how long it takes to reach its highest point.

EXERCISES 66B

1. If $v = t^2 + 1$, find s, given that $s = 0$ when $t = 0$.

2. If $a = t + 1$, find v, given that $v = 4$ when $t = 0$.

3. If $a = t^2$, find s, given that when $t = 0$, $s = 0$ and $v = 2$.

4. If $v = 2t^2 + 3t + 1$, find s, given that $s = 0$ when $t = 0$.

5. If $f = t^2 - t$, find v, given that $v = 3$ when $t = 2$.

6. A stone falls from rest. Find its velocity after 3 sec.

7. A stone has a velocity of 8 m/sec down. Find its velocity after 2 sec.

8. Find the distance fallen by a stone in 2 sec, if it starts from rest.

9. Find the distance fallen by a stone in 4 sec if its initial velocity is 6 m/sec down.

10. A stone is thrown vertically upwards with a velocity of 19·6 m/sec. Find how high it rises.

Area

Consider the area under the curve $y = x^2$ and enclosed by the lines $x = 1$ and $x = 2$. Suppose that HN, KM are the ordinates at $x = 1$ and $x = 2$ and let PQ be an ordinate somewhere between HN and KM. Suppose the distance of PQ from the axis of y is x, and let the area $NHPQ$ be A. This area A is obviously a function of x and is zero when $x = 1$. When $x = 2$, A is equal to the area required.

Suppose that PQ moves to another position $P'Q'$ whose distance from the axis of y is $(x + h)$.

Since P and P' are on the curve $y = x^2$,

$$PQ = x^2 \quad \text{and} \quad P'Q' = (x + h)^2.$$

The increase in A due to the movement from PQ to $P'Q'$ lies between the area of two rectangles, one of length x^2, the other of length $(x + h)^2$ and each of breadth h.

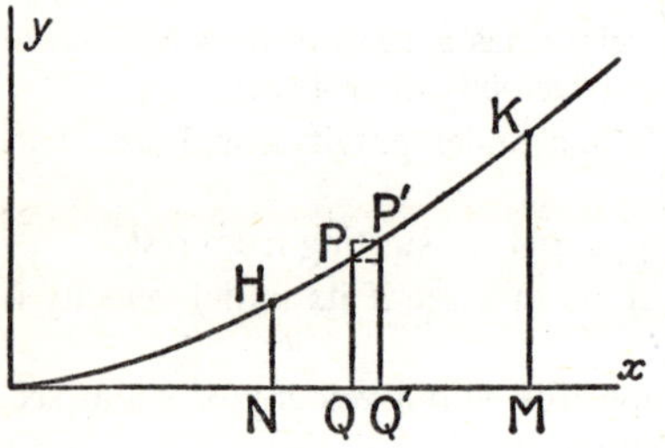

FIG. 23

$\therefore$ (the increase in A) $\div h$ lies between x^2 and $(x + h)^2$.

Now suppose that h tends to zero. (The increase in A) $\div h$ tends to x^2. But (the increase in A) $\div h$ tends to the derived function of A as h tends to 0.

$$\therefore \frac{dA}{dx} = x^2,$$

and $\qquad A = \frac{1}{3}x^3 + c.$

When $x = 1$, $A = 0$.

Substituting, $\qquad 0 = \frac{1}{3} + c \quad \text{and} \quad c = -\frac{1}{3}.$

$$\therefore A = \frac{1}{3}x^3 - \frac{1}{3}.$$

The area required is the value of A when $x = 2$, which is $(\frac{8}{3} - \frac{1}{3})$ or $\frac{7}{3}$. Therefore the area under the graph is $2\frac{1}{3}$ sq. units.

In general the problem of finding the area under a curve $y = f(x)$ between two given ordinates $x = h$ and $x = k$ is equivalent to the following problem.

Find the value of A when $x = k$, given that $\dfrac{dA}{dx} = f(x)$ and that $A = 0$ when $x = h$.

Area under a velocity–time graph

The area under a velocity–time graph represents the integral of the velocity with respect to the time. We have already seen that this is equal to the distance. If we are given a number of corresponding readings of velocity and time, the area under the graph may be found by addition of the small squares under the graph. A small square is included in the addition if more than half of it is in the required area, otherwise it is excluded. If we know the relation between velocity and time, the distance can be exactly calculated by integration.

Area under an acceleration–time graph

Similarly the area under an acceleration–time graph is equal to the integral of the acceleration with respect to the time. Therefore this area gives the velocity. The area between two times or ordinates equals the change of velocity between those two times. This may either be computed by adding squares or calculated by integration.

Example 1. Find the area between the curve $y = 2x - x^2$ and the x-axis.

Fig. 24 shows a sketch of the curve which cuts the axis of x at (0, 0) and (2, 0).

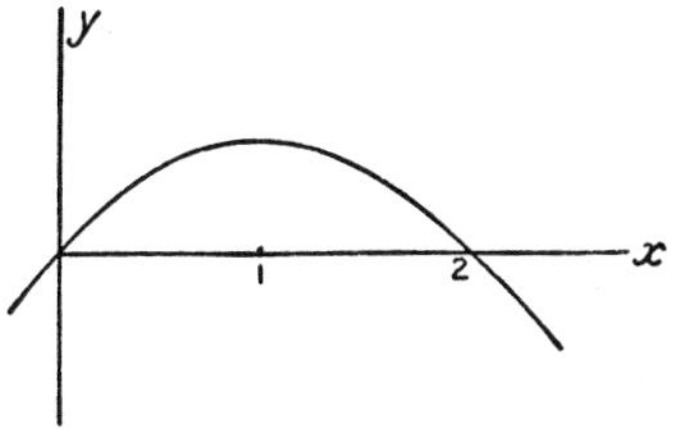

FIG. 24

We wish to find A when $x = 2$, given that $\dfrac{dA}{dx} = 2x - x^2$ and that $A = 0$ when $x = 0$.

$$\frac{dA}{dx} = 2x - x^2.$$

Integrating, $\quad A = x^2 - \tfrac{1}{3}x^3 + c.$

When $x = 0$, $A = 0$. $\quad \therefore\ c = 0.$

$$A = x^2 - \tfrac{1}{3}x^3.$$

When $x = 2$, $\quad A = 4 - \dfrac{8}{3} = \dfrac{4}{3}.$

Example 2. Find the area between the curve $y = x^2$ and the line $y = x$.

Fig. 25 shows a sketch of the curve and line. They meet where $x = x^2$, i.e. at the points (0, 0) and (1, 1).

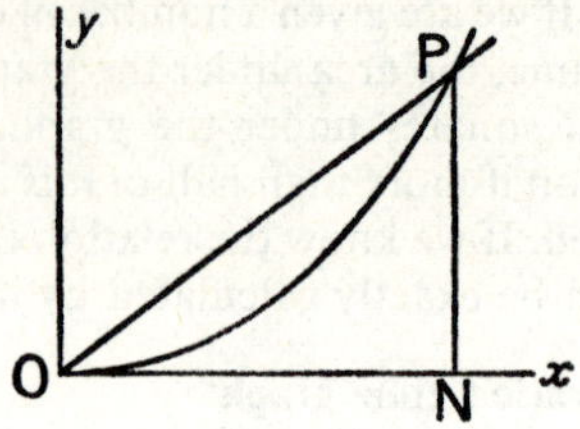

FIG. 25

To find the area under the curve between $x = 0$ and $x = 1$, we must find the value of A when $x = 1$, given that $\frac{dA}{dx} = x^2$ and that $A = 0$ when $x = 0$.

Integrating, $A = \frac{1}{3}x^3 + c.$

Since $A = 0$, when $x = 0$, $c = 0$. $\therefore A = \frac{1}{3}x^3$.

When $x = 1$, $A = \frac{1}{3}$.

The area of the triangle $OPN = \frac{1}{2}$.

The area between the curve and the line is

$$(\tfrac{1}{2} - \tfrac{1}{3}) = \tfrac{1}{6} \text{ sq. units.}$$

(This may be verified by counting squares. Be careful to draw as large a figure as possible on your graph paper.)

Example 3. A body moving in a straight line starts from rest and accelerates at 2 m/sec² for 4 sec. It then decelerates uniformly and comes to rest in another 6 sec. Find the distance gone.

The gradient of the velocity–time graph is the acceleration. When the acceleration is constant, the graph is a straight line.

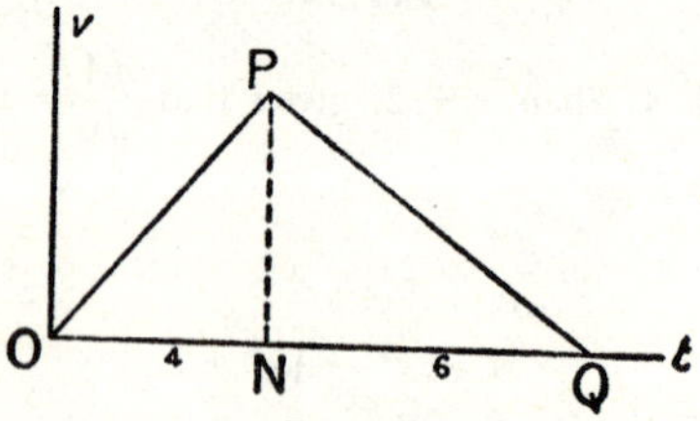

FIG. 26

The graph consists of two lines OP, of gradient 2, and PQ. The area under the graph equals the distance gone.

$$\frac{PN}{ON} = \text{the gradient of } OP = 2. \quad \therefore\ PN = 8.$$

The area of $OPQ = \frac{1}{2}(10)8 = 40$.
The distance gone is 40 m.

The definite integral

In example 1, we were asked to find the area between the curve $y = 2x - x^2$ and the x-axis.

$$\frac{dA}{dx} = 2x - x^2 \quad \text{and therefore} \quad A = \int (2x - x^2)\, dx.$$

From this equation, $A = x^2 - \dfrac{x^3}{3} + c$.

We know that $A = 0$ when $x = 0$ and we wish to find the value of A when $x = 2$.

Substituting, $$A = 2^2 - \frac{2^3}{3} + c$$

and $$0 = 0 + c.$$

Subtracting: $$A = \left(2^2 - \frac{2^3}{3}\right) - 0.$$

A therefore equals the value of $\left(x^2 - \dfrac{x^3}{3}\right)$ when $x = 0$ subtracted from the value of $\left(x^2 - \dfrac{x^3}{3}\right)$ when $x = 2$.

$A = \displaystyle\int (2x - x^2)\, dx$ is called an **indefinite integral** and must contain an arbitrary constant.

$A = \displaystyle\int_0^2 (2x - x^2)\, dx$ is called a **definite integral** and means that the integration is performed between the limiting values 0 and 2 for x.

To evaluate a definite integral, integrate the expression; from the value of the integral at the upper limit subtract the value at the lower limit. The work is set out as shown.

$$A = \int_0^2 (2x - x^2)\, dx = \left[x^2 - \frac{x^3}{3}\right]_0^2 = \left(4 - \frac{8}{3}\right) - 0 = \frac{4}{3}.$$

The area under the curve $y = f(x)$ between the ordinates $x = a$ and $x = b$ is given by

$$A = \int_a^b y\, dx \quad \text{or} \quad \int_a^b f(x)\, dx.$$

Example. Find the area under the curve $y = x^2 + 1$ between the ordinates $x = 1$ and $x = 2$.

$$\frac{dA}{dx} = x^2 + 1.$$

$$\therefore A = \int_1^2 (x^2 + 1)\,dx = \left[\frac{x^3}{3} + x\right]_1^2$$

$$= \left(\frac{8}{3} + 2\right) - \left(\frac{1}{3} + 1\right) = 3\tfrac{1}{3}.$$

EXERCISES 67A

1. Find the area under the curve $y = x + x^2$ between $x = 1$ and $x = 3$.
2. Find the area between the curve $y = x - x^2$ and the axis of x.
3. Find the area under the curve $y = \sqrt{x}$ between $x = 0$ and $x = 4$.
4. Find the area under the curve $y = \dfrac{1}{x^2}$ between $x = 1$ and $x = 4$.
5. Find the area under the curve $y = x^2 + 4$ between $x = 1$ and $x = 2$.
6. Find the area between the line $y = 2x$ and the curve $y = x^2$.
7. A body moving in a straight line starts with a velocity of 4 m/sec and moves with constant acceleration of 2 m/sec^2 for 8 sec. Find the distance gone.
8. A body starts from rest and accelerates at 4 m/sec for 5 sec. It then decelerates uniformly and stops in a further 10 sec. Find the distance gone.

EXERCISES 67B

1. Find the area under the curve $y = 2x + x^2$ between $x = 1$ and $x = 3$.
2. Find the area between the curve $y = (x - 1)(3 - x)$ and the axis of x.
3. Find the area under the curve $y = \sqrt{x}$ between $x = 1$ and $x = 9$.
4. Find the area under the curve $y = 1 + \dfrac{1}{x^2}$ between $x = 1$ and $x = 4$.
5. Find the area under the curve $y = 3x^2 + 1$ between $x = 1$ and $x = 3$.
6. Find the area between the line $y = 4x$ and the curve $y = 4x^2$.
7. A body moving in a straight line starts with a velocity of 10 m/sec and moves with constant acceleration of 3 m/sec^2 for 6 sec. Find the distance gone.

8. A body starts from rest and accelerates at 2 m/sec² for 6 sec. It moves with constant velocity for 2 sec and then decelerates uniformly to stop in another 4 sec. Find the distance gone.

Solid of revolution

If the area under a curve and included by two ordinates is rotated about the axis of x, the resulting solid is called a **solid of revolution.** A section of this solid by a plane perpendicular to the axis of x is a circle.

The area under a line parallel to the axis of x gives a right circular cylinder.

The area under a line through the origin gives a right circular cone.

We shall now find the volume of a solid of revolution, given the equation of the curve and the bounding ordinates.

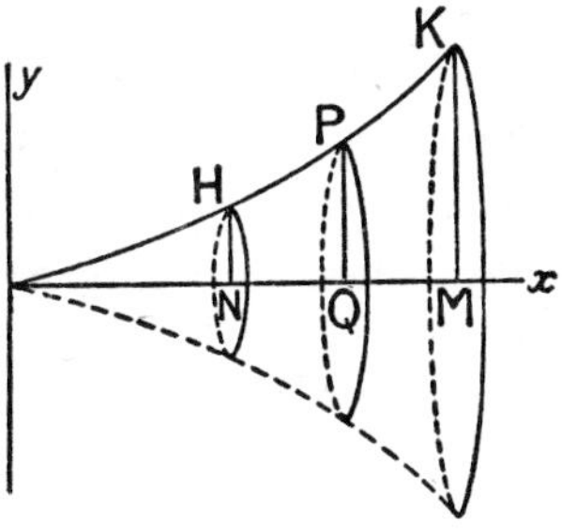

FIG. 27

As an example, consider the curve $y = x^2$ between the ordinates $x = 1$ and $x = 2$. Suppose the bounding ordinates are HN and KM and that PQ is any ordinate between them.

If we rotate PQ, we shall get a circle. If this circle moves from the position in which HN is a radius to the position when KM is a radius, it will trace out the volume required. Let V be equal to the volume between the starting position and the position when the distance of PQ from the y-axis is equal to x. Then V is a function of x which is zero when $x = 1$; we are asked to find V when $x = 2$. If PQ moves to a position $P'Q'$ whose distance from the axis of y is $(x + h)$, V is increased by a volume whose plane ends are circles of radii x^2 and $(x + h)^2$. This volume lies between that of a cylinder of radius x^2 and length h and that of a cylinder of radius $(x + h)^2$ and length h. The increase in V therefore lies between $\pi h x^4$ and $\pi h(x + h)^4$.

$\therefore$ (the increase in V) $\div h$ lies between πx^4 and $\pi(x + h)^4$.

$\therefore$ (the increase in V) $\div h$ tends to πx^4 as h tends to 0.

But (the increase in V) $\div h$ tends to the derived function of V as h tends to 0.

$$\therefore \frac{dV}{dx} = \pi x^4.$$

Integrating, $$V = \frac{\pi x^5}{5} + c.$$

But $V = 0$ when $x = 1$.

$$\therefore 0 = \frac{\pi}{5} + c.$$

$$\therefore V = \pi\left(\frac{x^5 - 1}{5}\right).$$

When $x = 2$, $$V = \pi\left(\frac{32 - 1}{5}\right) = \frac{31\pi}{5}.$$

The problem of finding the volume obtained by rotating about the axis of x the area under the curve $y = f(x)$ between $x = h$ and $x = k$ is equivalent to the following problem.

Find V when $x = k$, given that $\frac{dV}{dx} = \pi\{f(x)\}^2$ and that $V = 0$ when $x = h$.

The volume may also be expressed as a definite integral. The volume of rotation about the x-axis of the area under the curve $y = f(x)$ between $x = h$ and $x = k$ is given by

$$V = \pi \int_h^k y^2\,dx \quad \text{or} \quad \pi \int_h^k \{f(x)\}^2\,dx.$$

Example 1. Find the volume of a cone of height h and base radius r.

The cone is formed by the revolution about the axis of x of the area under a line which passes through the origin. The gradient of the line is $\frac{r}{h}$ and so its equation is $y = \frac{r}{h}x$.

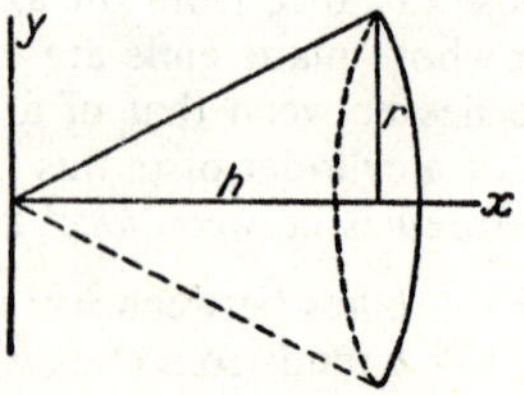

FIG. 28

We are asked to find V when $x = h$, given that $\frac{dV}{dx} = \pi\frac{r^2}{h^2}x^2$ and that $V = 0$ when $x = 0$.

Integrating, $$V = \pi\frac{r^2}{h^2}\frac{x^3}{3} + c.$$

Since $V = 0$ when $x = 0$, $c = 0$.

$$\therefore\ V = \frac{\pi r^2}{h^2}\frac{x^3}{3}.$$

When $x = h$ $$V = \frac{\pi r^2}{h^2}\frac{h^3}{3} = \tfrac{1}{3}\pi r^2 h.$$

Example 2. By rotating a quadrant of the circle $x^2 + y^2 = r^2$ about the axis of x, find a formula for the volume of a sphere.

By rotating a quadrant of a circle, we shall get a hemisphere.

We are asked to find V when $x = r$, given that $\frac{dV}{dx} = \pi y^2$ and that $V = 0$ when $x = 0$.

$$\frac{dV}{dx} = \pi y^2 = \pi(r^2 - x^2).$$

Integrating, $$V = \pi\left(r^2 x - \frac{x^2}{3}\right) + c.$$

(N.B. r^2 is a constant.)
When $x = 0$, $V = 0$ and therefore $c = 0$.

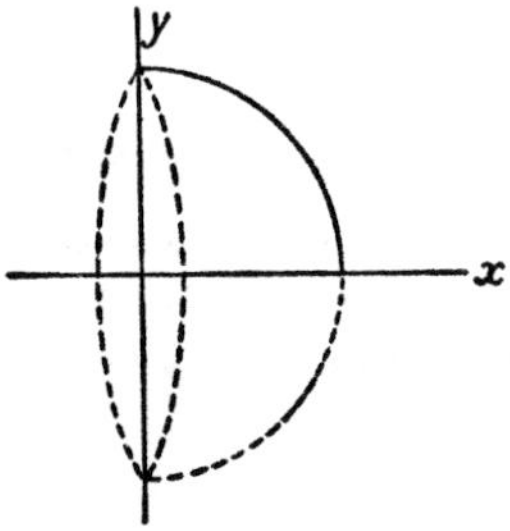

FIG. 29

When $x = r$, $$V = \pi\left(r^3 - \frac{r^3}{3}\right) = \tfrac{2}{3}\pi r^3.$$

This is the volume of a hemisphere and so the volume of a sphere of radius r is $\frac{4}{3}\pi r^3$.

Alternative method. Since

$$\frac{dV}{dx} = \pi y^2,$$

$$V = \pi \int_0^r y^2 \, dx.$$

But $y^2 = r^2 - x^2$, and therefore

$$V = \pi \int_0^r (r^2 - x^2) \, dx$$

$$= \pi \left[r^2 x - \frac{x^3}{3} \right]_0^r$$

$$= \pi \left[\left(r^3 - \frac{r^3}{3} \right) - 0 \right] = \tfrac{2}{3}\pi r^3.$$

The volume of the sphere is $\frac{4}{3}\pi r^3$.

EXERCISES 68A

Find the volume of rotation about the axis of x of the area under the following curves between the ordinates given.

1. $y = \sqrt{x}$ between $x = 1$ and $x = 4$.
2. $y = 4x^2$ between $x = 0$ and $x = 1$.
3. $y = \dfrac{1}{x}$ between $x = 1$ and $x = 2$.
4. $y = 4 - x^2$ between $x = 1$ and $x = 2$.
5. $y = 2 + x$ between $x = 2$ and $x = 6$.

EXERCISES 68B

Find the volume of rotation about the axis of x of the area under the following curves between the ordinates given.

1. $y = \sqrt{x}$ between $x = 1$ and $x = 9$.
2. $y = 2x^2$ between $x = 0$ and $x = 2$.
3. $y = \dfrac{1}{x}$ between $x = 1$ and $x = 3$.
4. $y^2 = r^2 - x^2$ between $x = \frac{1}{2}r$ and $x = r$.
5. $y = a + x$ between $x = 0$ and $x = a$.

EXERCISES 69: MISCELLANEOUS INTEGRATION

1. Find the area enclosed by the axis of x, the curve $y = x^2 + x + 1$ and the ordinates $x = 1$ and $x = 2$.

2. A point moves in a straight line so that after t sec its velocity is $(3t^2 + 4t)$ m/sec. Find the distance gone in the third second.

3. The area under the curve $y^2 = x^3$ between $x = 0$ and $x = 1$ is rotated about the axis of x. Find the volume of the solid of revolution so formed.

4. A point moves in a straight line and its acceleration in m/sec² is given by $a = t + 2$ where t is in seconds. If the point starts from rest, find the distance gone in 4 sec.

5. Show that the curves $y^2 = 4x$ and $x^2 = 4y$ meet at (4, 4). Draw a rough sketch and find the area enclosed by the curves.

6. Find the volume formed by the revolution between $x = 0$ and $x = 3$ of the ellipse $4y^2 = 9 - x^2$ about the x-axis.

7. Integrate $x^2(1 + x)^2$.

8. A point moves in a straight line so that its acceleration in m/sec² after t sec is given by $a = 3t + 2$. If its initial velocity is 4 m/sec, find its velocity after 2 sec.

9. Find the area between the curve $y = 2x - 3x^2$ and the line $y = x$.

10. Find the area bounded by the curve $y = 4 - x^2$ and the axis of x.

11. If $\frac{dy}{dx} = 2 - x^2$ and $y = 3$ when $x = 2$, find y in terms of x.

12. Find the area between the curve $y = x^2(5 - x)$ and the axis of x.

13. Calculate the volume of the solid formed by rotating the area between $y = x(2 - x)$ and the axis of x about that axis.

14. The following table gives the velocity at various times of a decelerating point:

t (sec) . . .	0	1	2	3	4	5	6
v (m/sec) . .	30	20	14	9	5	1·5	0

Find the distance gone in the six seconds.

15. The following table gives corresponding values of velocity and time:

t (sec) . . .	0	1	2	3	4	5	6
v (m/sec) . .	10	13	18	24	32	41	54

Find the distance gone in the six seconds.

16. The velocity of a point moving in a straight line is given by $v = 2t^2 + 3t$. Find the acceleration after 2 sec and the distance gone in the third second.

17. Find the volume formed by rotating the area enclosed by $y = 3x$, the axis of x and the line $x = 2$ about the axis of x.

18. Find the area bounded by the curve $y = 4x^2$ and the straight lines $x = 1$, $x = 2$, $y = 0$.

19. Find the area between the curve $y = 3x^2 - x^3$ and the axis of x.

20. Integrate $(3x + 1)^2$.

21. The acceleration of a particle moving in a straight line is given in m/sec^2 by $a = t + 3$ where t is in seconds. By drawing a graph and calculating the area under the graph, find the velocity of the particle after 3 sec given that the initial velocity is 2 m/sec.

22. The gradient of a certain curve is $x^2(3 - x)$ and the curve passes through the point (1, 1). Find the equation of the curve.

23. By rotating a quadrant of the ellipse $\dfrac{x^2}{a^2} + \dfrac{y^2}{b^2} = 1$ about the axis of x, find a formula for the volume of an ellipsoid.

24. The area under a certain curve cut off by the ordinates at 0 and x is equal to $4x - x^3$. Find the equation of the curve.

25. If $f_1(x) = 3x - x^2$ and $f(2) = 4$, find $f(x)$.

26. Evaluate $\displaystyle\int_2^3 (x^2 + x)\,dx$.

27. Evaluate $\displaystyle\int_{-1}^1 (1 - t^2)\,dt$.

28. Evaluate $\displaystyle\int_{-1}^2 (3u + u^2)\,du$.

GEOMETRY

LIST OF THEOREMS

The exterior angle of a triangle is equal to the sum of the two interior opposite angles. The sum of the angles of any triangle is 2 right angles.

In a convex polygon of n sides, the sum of the interior angles is $(2n - 4)$ right angles. The sum of the exterior angles is 4 right angles, whatever the value of n.

If two triangles have two sides of the one respectively equal to two sides of the other and the angles included between the equal sides are also equal, then the triangles are congruent.

If two triangles have two angles of the one respectively equal to two angles of the other and a side of one equal to the corresponding side of the other, then the triangles are congruent.

If two triangles have three sides of one respectively equal to the three sides of the other, then the triangles are congruent.

If two right-angled triangles have their hypotenuses equal and another side of one triangle equal to another side of the second triangle, then the triangles are congruent.

If two sides of a triangle are equal, then the angles opposite the equal sides are also equal.

If two angles of a triangle are equal, then the sides opposite these angles are also equal.

If, in a triangle, one side is greater than a second, then the angle opposite the greater side is greater than the angle opposite the smaller side.

If, in a triangle, one angle is greater than a second, the side opposite the greater angle is greater than the side opposite the smaller angle.

The shortest distance from a point to a straight line is the perpendicular distance.

Both pairs of opposite sides of a parallelogram are equal; both pairs of opposite angles are equal and a diagonal bisects the parallelogram.

The diagonals of a parallelogram bisect each other.

If the opposite sides of a quadrilateral are equal, then the quadrilateral must be a parallelogram.

If the opposite angles of a quadrilateral are equal, then the quadrilateral must be a parallelogram.

If the diagonals of a quadrilateral bisect each other, the quadrilateral must be a parallelogram.

The line drawn through the mid-point of one side of a triangle parallel to a second side bisects the third side.

The straight line joining the mid-points of two sides of a triangle is parallel to the third side and equal to half of it.

If there are three or more parallel straight lines and the intercepts made by them on any straight line that cuts them are equal, the corresponding intercepts on any other straight line that cuts them are also equal.

Parallelograms on the same base and between the same parallels are equal in area.

The area of a triangle is half that of a parallelogram drawn on the same base and between the same parallels.

If a straight line be drawn parallel to one side of a triangle, the other two sides are divided proportionally.

A straight line which cuts two sides of a triangle proportionally is parallel to the third side.

The internal bisector of an angle of a triangle divides the opposite side internally in the ratio of the sides containing the angle and, likewise, the external bisector externally.

If a line through the vertex of a triangle divides the base internally or externally in the ratio of the sides containing the vertex, then the line bisects the vertical angle internally or externally.

If two triangles are equiangular, their corresponding sides are proportional.

If two triangles have their corresponding sides proportional, they are equiangular.

If two triangles have one angle of the one equal to one angle of the other, and the sides about these equal angles proportional, the triangles are similar.

If a perpendicular be drawn from the right angle of a right-angled triangle to the hypotenuse, the triangles on each side of the perpendicular are similar to the whole triangle and to each other.

In a right-angled triangle, the square described on the hypotenuse is equal to the sum of the squares described on the sides containing the right angle. **(Pythagoras.)**

If the square on one side of a triangle is equal to the sum of the squares on the other two sides of the triangle, the angle included by these two sides is a right angle. **(Converse of Pythagoras.)**

The ratio of the areas of similar triangles is equal to the ratio of the squares on corresponding sides.

The locus of a point which is equidistant from two fixed points is the perpendicular bisector of the line joining the two fixed points.

The locus of a point which is equidistant from two intersecting straight lines consists of the pair of straight lines which bisect the angles between the two given lines.

The square on a side of a triangle opposite an acute angle is less than the sum of the squares on the other two sides. The difference is twice the rectangle contained by one of the sides and the projection on it of the other. **(First Extension of Pythagoras.)**

The square on a side of a triangle opposite an obtuse angle is greater than the sum of the squares on the other two sides. The difference is twice the rectangle contained by one of the two sides and the projection on it of the other. **(Second Extension of Pythagoras.)**

In any triangle, the sum of the squares on any two sides is equal to twice the square on half the third side together with twice the square on the median which bisects the third side. **(Apollonius.)**

A straight line drawn from the centre of a circle to bisect a chord which is not a diameter, is at right angles to the chord.

The perpendicular drawn from the centre of a circle to a chord bisects that chord.

There is one circle, and one only, which passes through three given points not in a straight line.

Equal chords of a circle are equidistant from the centre.

The angle which an arc of a circle subtends at the centre is double that which it subtends at the remaining part of the circumference.

Angles in the same segment of a circle are equal.

The opposite angles of any quadrilateral inscribed in a circle are supplementary.

The tangent at any point of a circle and the radius through the point are perpendicular to each other.

If a straight line touch a circle, and from the point of contact a chord be drawn, the angles which the chord makes with the tangent are equal to the angles in the alternate segments.

If two circles touch, the point of contact lies on the straight line through the centres.

If two tangents are drawn to a circle from a point outside the circle, then

(i) the tangents are equal in length;
(ii) the angle between these tangents is bisected by the line joining the point of intersection of the tangents to the centre;
(iii) this line also bisects the angle between the radii drawn to the points of contact.

If two chords of a circle intersect either inside or outside the circle, the rectangle contained by the parts of the one is equal to the rectangle contained by the parts of the other.

If, from a point outside a circle, a tangent and a secant are drawn to the circle, the square on the tangent is equal to the rectangle contained by the whole secant and that part of it outside the circle.

LIST OF CONSTRUCTIONS

(1) To construct an angle equal to a given angle.
(2) To bisect a given angle.
(3) To construct a perpendicular from a given point on a line to that line.
(4) To bisect a given straight line.
(5) To construct a perpendicular from a given point to a given line.
(6) To construct an angle of 60°.
(7) To construct through a given point a straight line parallel to a given straight line.
(8) To divide a given straight line into a given number of equal parts.
(9) To construct a triangle equal in area to a given quadrilateral.
(10) To construct a tangent to a circle at a given point of the circle.
(11) To construct the pair of tangents from a given point to a given circle.
(12) To construct the circumcircle of a given triangle.

(13) To construct the inscribed circle of a given triangle.
(14) To construct an escribed circle of a given triangle.
(15) To construct the direct common tangents to two given circles.
(16) To construct the transverse common tangents to two given circles.
(17) To construct the locus of a point at which a given straight line subtends a given angle.
(18) To construct a square equal in area to a given rectangle.
(19) To draw a regular polygon of n sides (i) in, (ii) about, a given circle.
(20) To construct a fourth proportional to three given lines.
(21) To construct a mean proportional to two given lines.

17

PARALLEL LINES; THE TRIANGLE AND POLYGON

Angle definitions

If the line OA turns from its original position OX to the new position OZ, where XOZ is a straight line, the line OA has turned through half a revolution or 180°. The angles AOX and AOZ are called adjacent; they are also supplementary.

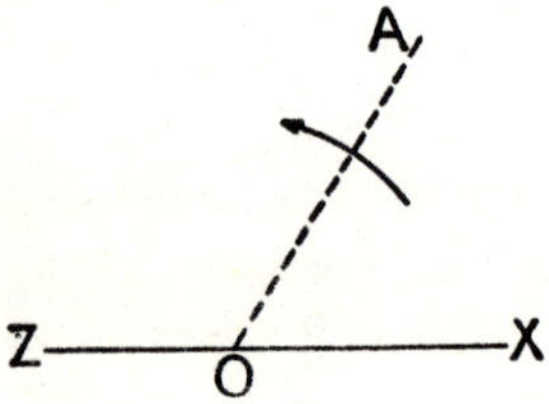

Fig. 30

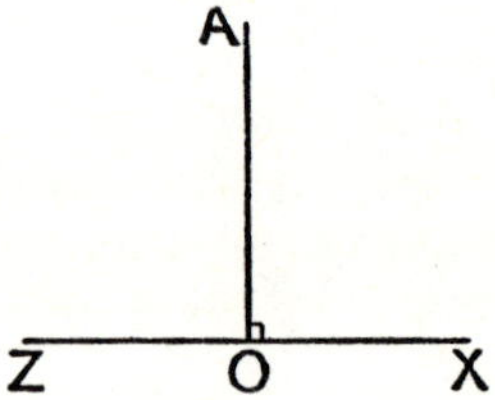

Fig. 31

In the position (Fig. 31) where OA makes equal angles with OX and OZ, the angles AOX, AOZ are equal and each is equal to 90°. AO is said to be perpendicular to XOZ.

An acute angle is an angle less than 90°.

An obtuse angle is an angle between 90° and 180°.

A reflex angle is an angle between 180° and 360°.

Complementary angles are angles whose sum is 90°.

Supplementary angles are angles whose sum is 180°.

When two straight lines XOY, AOB meet at O as shown in Fig. 32,

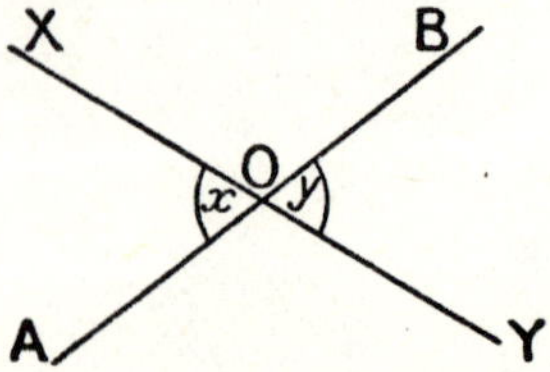

Fig. 32

the angles x and y are called vertically opposite angles. Similarly the angles XOB and AOY are vertically opposite angles.

Vertically opposite angles are equal; for example, $x = y$.

Corresponding, alternate and interior angles

In Fig. 33, AB and CD are straight lines cut by a transversal PQ.

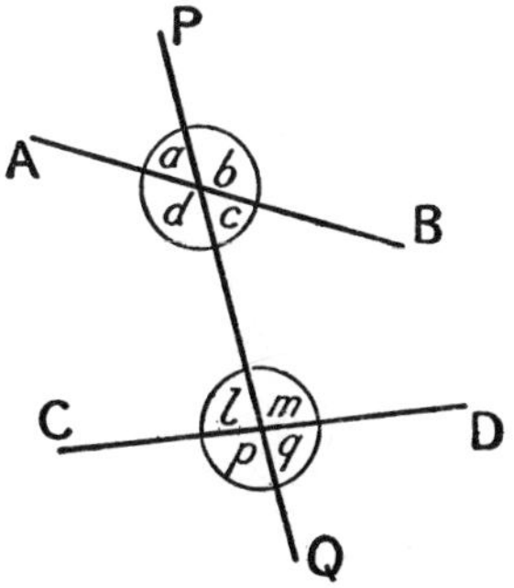

FIG. 33

Pairs of corresponding angles are a and l; d and p; b and m; c and q.

Pairs of alternate angles are d and m; c and l.

Pairs of interior angles are d and l; c and m.

PARALLEL LINES

Parallel lines are lines in the same plane which never meet however far they are produced in either direction.

If two straight lines are each parallel to a third, they are parallel to each other.

When two parallel lines are cut by a transversal as shown in Fig. 34;

(1) Corresponding angles are equal.

$a = l;\ b = m;\ c = n;\ d = p.$

(2) Alternate angles are equal.

$d = m;\ c = l.$

(3) Interior angles are supplementary.

$d + l = 180°;\ c + m = 180°.$

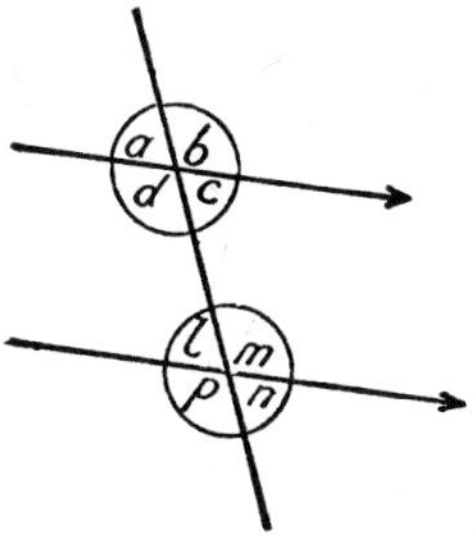

FIG. 34

Conversely, if two lines are cut by a transversal, the two lines are parallel if any one of the following is true.

(1) Two corresponding angles are equal.
(2) Two alternate angles are equal.
(3) Two interior angles are supplementary.

Example 1. In Fig. 35, given that AOB is a straight line, find x.

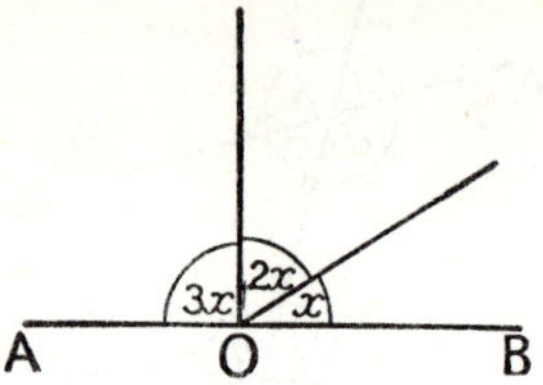

FIG. 35

The angle AOB is 180°.

$$3x + 2x + x = 180°$$

and

$$x = 30°.$$

Example 2. In Fig. 36, given that AB is parallel to DE, find x.

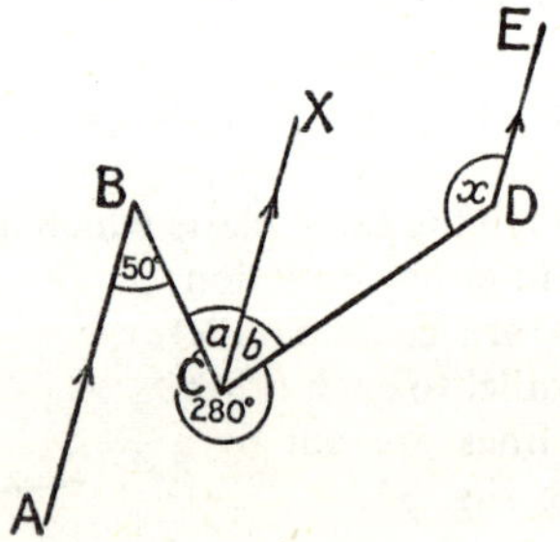

FIG. 36

Through C draw a line CX parallel to AB.
Then

$$a = 50° \text{ (alternate; } AB \parallel CX\text{)}.$$
$$b = 360° - 280° - 50° = 30°.$$
$$b + x = 180° \text{ (interior; } CX \parallel DE\text{)}.$$
$$\therefore x = 150°.$$

EXERCISES 70A

1. In Fig. 37, given that *AO* is perpendicular to *OB*, find x.

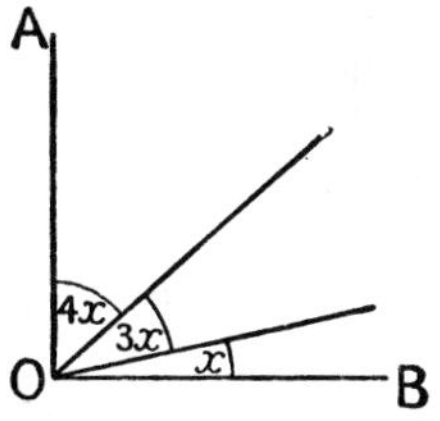

FIG. 37

2. Find a relationship between x and y from Fig. 38.

FIG. 38

3. Given that *AB* is parallel to *CD* in Fig. 39, find x, y and z.

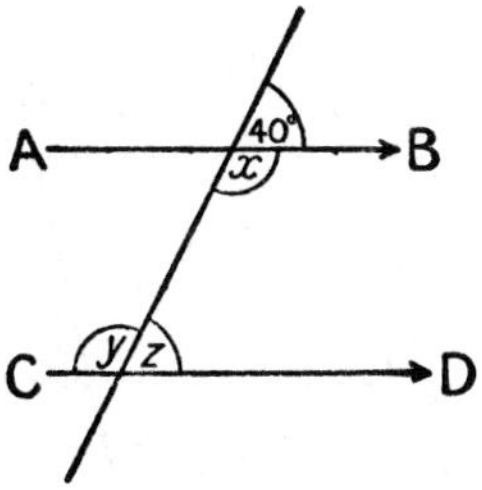

FIG. 39

4. In Fig. 40, given that AB is parallel to CD, find an equation connecting x, y and z.

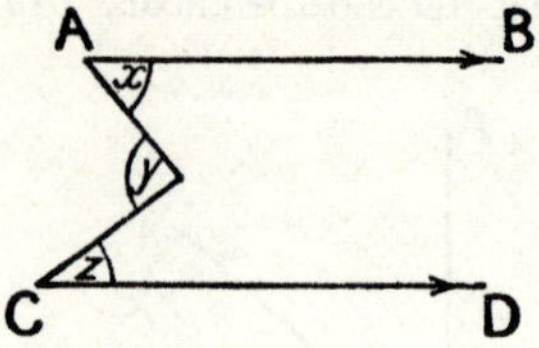

FIG. 40

5. If, in Fig. 41, $p = 110°$, $q = 120°$ and $r = 130°$, prove that BA is parallel to DE.

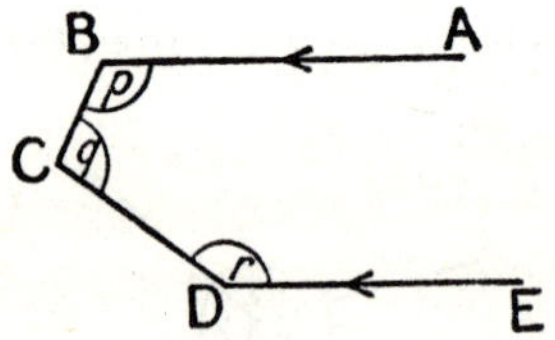

FIG. 41

6. In Fig. 41, if BA and DE are given parallel, find an equation connecting p, q and r.

7. In Fig. 41, if $p = 140°$ and $q = 110°$, prove that when BA is parallel to DE, $q = r$.

8. In Fig. 42, find the value of y when $x = 30°$. (Parallel lines are indicated by arrows in the figure.)

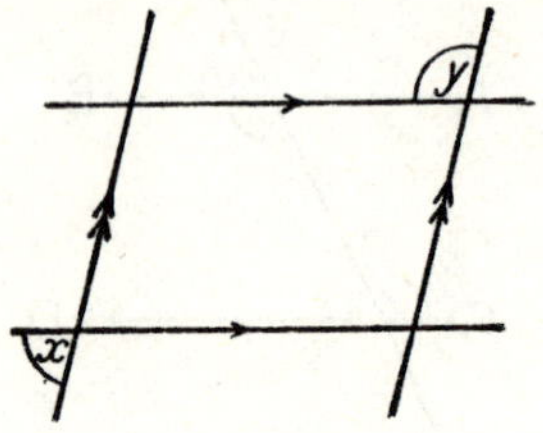

FIG. 42

9. Find a relationship between x and y from Fig. 43.

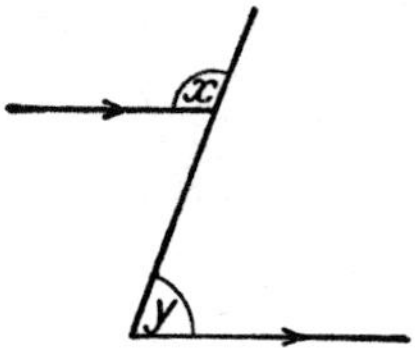

FIG. 43

10. In Fig. 44, prove that $p = q$.

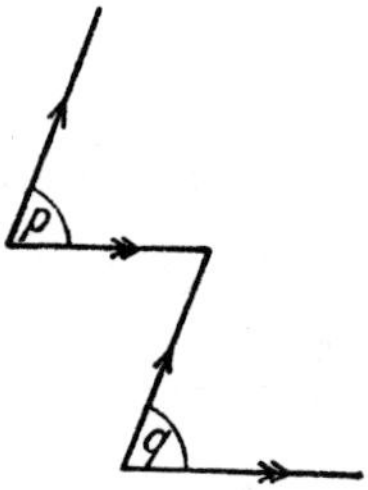

FIG 44

EXERCISES 70B

1. In Fig. 45, given that AO is perpendicular to OB, find x.

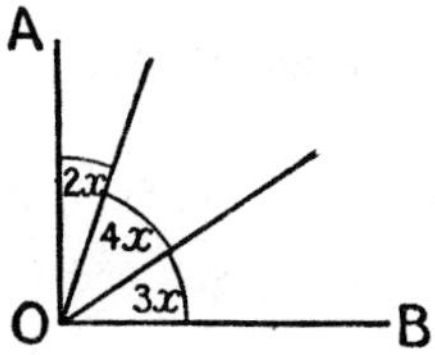

FIG. 45

2. Find a relationship between x and y from Fig. 46.

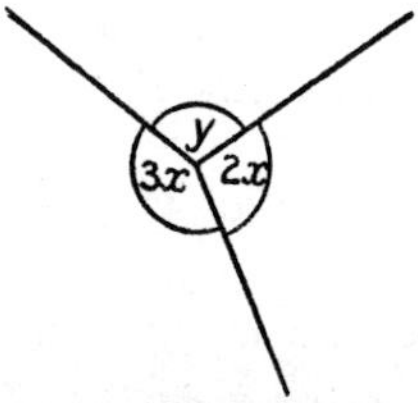

FIG. 46

3. Find x, y and z from Fig. 47.

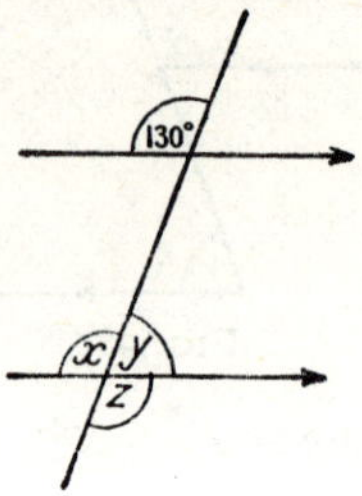

FIG. 47

4. Given in Fig. 48, that $x = 120°$, $y = 100°$, $z = 140°$, prove that AB is parallel to CD.

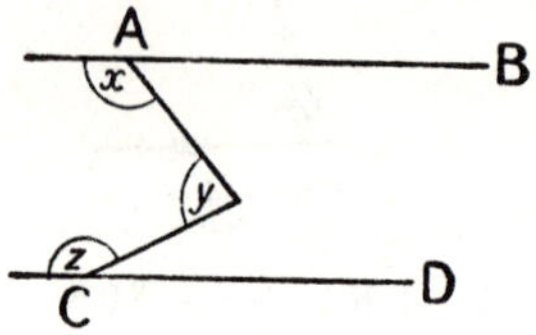

FIG. 48

5. If in Fig. 48, AB and CD are parallel, find an equation connecting x, y and z.

6. If in Fig. 48, $x = 100°$, $y = 140°$, find z if AB and CD are parallel.

7. In Fig. 49, if $y = 40°$ and $z = 80°$, find x.

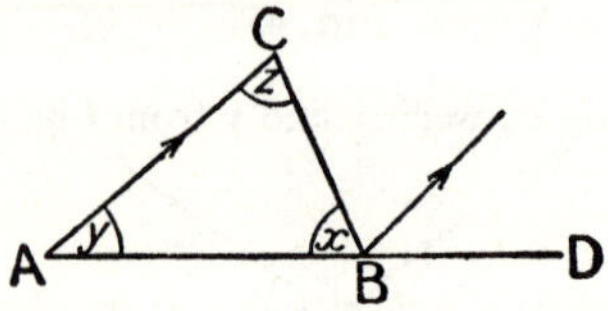

FIG. 49

8. Find a relationship between x, y and z from Fig. 49.

9. If, in Fig 49, $y = 50°$ and $z = 80°$, prove that $x = y$.

10. From Fig. 50, find an equation connecting *p*, *q* and *r*.

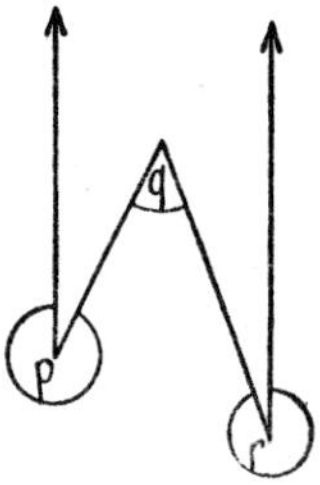

FIG. 50

THE TRIANGLE

A figure bounded by three straight lines is called a triangle.

A scalene triangle is one in which no two sides are equal in length.

An isosceles triangle is one in which two sides are equal in length.

An equilateral triangle is one in which all three sides are equal in length.

An obtuse-angled triangle is a triangle having one obtuse angle.

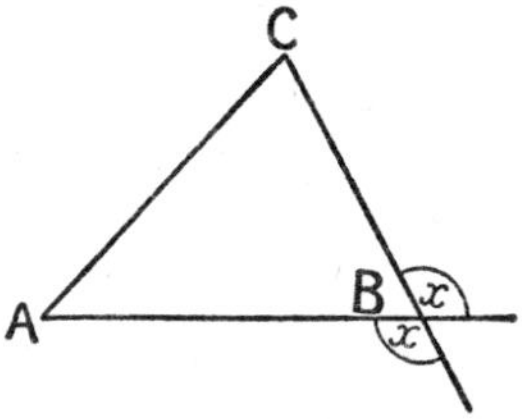

FIG. 51

Exterior angle

In Fig. 51 the angle *CBA* is called the interior angle *B*. Either of the angles marked *x* (they are equal; vertically opposite) is called the corresponding exterior angle.

Similarly, in the 6-sided figure (hexagon) shown in Fig. 52, *x* is the exterior angle corresponding to *a*; *y* is the exterior angle corresponding to *b*.

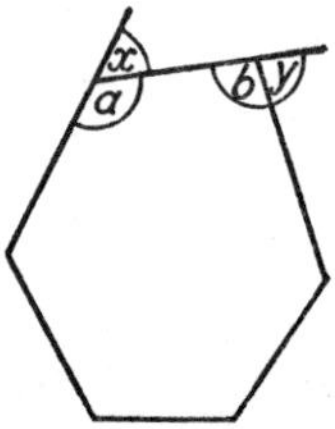

FIG. 52

THEOREM

The exterior angle of a triangle is equal to the sum of the two interior opposite angles. The sum of the angles of any triangle is 2 right angles.

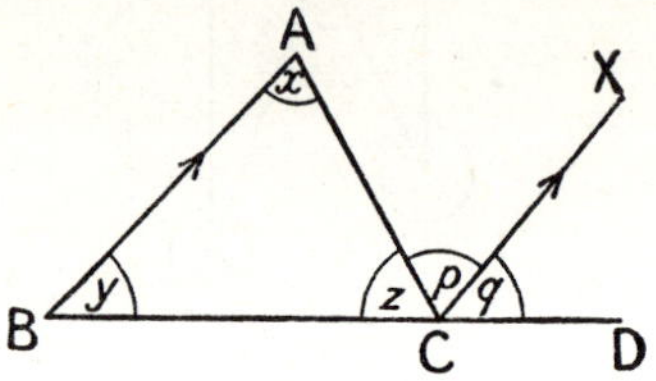

FIG. 53

Given the triangle ABC with BC produced to D.
To prove that the angle $ACD = x + y$, and that $x + y + z = 180°$.
Construction: Draw CX parallel to BA.

Proof:

$x = p$ (alternate; $BA \parallel CX$).
$y = q$ (corresponding; $BA \parallel CX$).

By addition, $p + q = x + y$,
or the angle $ACD = x + y$.
Also $x + y + z = p + q + z = 180°$ (straight line).

THE POLYGON

Any plane closed figure bounded by straight lines is called a polygon.

A convex polygon is one in which no interior angle is greater than 180°.

A re-entrant polygon is one in which at least one angle is greater than 180° (see Fig. 54).

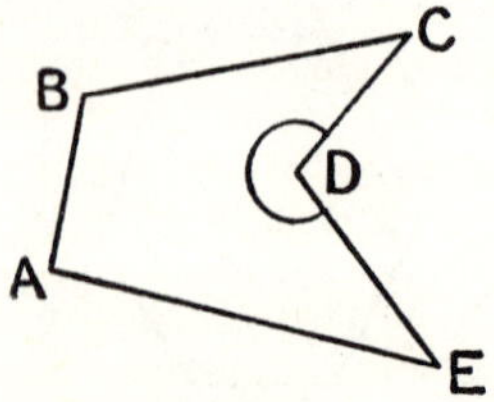

FIG. 54

A regular polygon has all its sides equal and all its angles equal.
A quadrilateral is a polygon of 4 sides.
A pentagon is a polygon of 5 sides.
A hexagon is a polygon of 6 sides.
An octagon is a polygon of 8 sides.

THEOREM

In a convex polygon of *n* sides, the sum of the interior angles is (2*n* − 4) right angles. The sum of the exterior angles is 4 right angles, whatever the value of *n*.

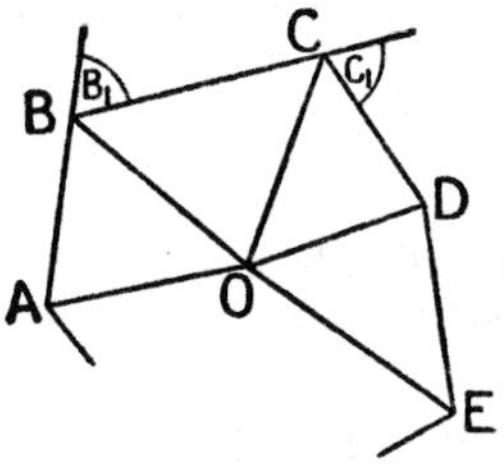

FIG. 55

Given a convex polygon *ABCDE*. . . . of *n* sides.

To prove that (i) $\widehat{ABC} + \widehat{BCD} + \ldots\ldots = (2n - 4)$ right angles;
(ii) the sum of the exterior angles is 4 right angles.

Construction: Join the vertices *A, B, C*. . . . to any point *O* inside the polygon.

Proof: (i) There are *n* triangles such as *AOB*, *BOC*, etc.
Therefore the sum of all the angles of all these triangles is 2*n* right angles.

These angles include $\widehat{AOB} + \widehat{BOC} + \widehat{COD} + \ldots\ldots$, i.e. 4 right angles (a complete revolution).

They also include $\widehat{ABC} + \widehat{BCD} + \widehat{CDE} + \ldots\ldots$, i.e. the sum of the interior angles of the polygon.

∴ the sum of the interior angles + 4 right angles = 2*n* right angles.
∴ the sum of the interior angles = (2*n* − 4) right angles.

(ii) Let B_1, C_1, etc. represent the exterior angles corresponding to *B, C*, etc.

Then $B + B_1 = 2$ right angles;
$C + C_1 = 2$ right angles; and so on.

There are n of these equations. By addition,

$$(B + C + \ldots.) + (B_1 + C_1 + \ldots.) = 2n \text{ right angles.}$$

But $(B + C + \ldots.) = (2n - 4)$ right angles (already proved).

$$(B_1 + C_1 + \ldots.) = 4 \text{ right angles.}$$

Particular cases

Putting $n = 4$, we see that the sum of the interior angles of a quadrilateral is 4 right angles.

Putting $n = 5$, we see that the sum of the interior angles of a pentagon is 6 right angles.

Putting $n = 6$, we see that the sum of the interior angles of a hexagon is 8 right angles.

Each angle of a regular pentagon is 108°; each angle of a regular hexagon is 120°.

N.B. In dealing with problems on the angles of a polygon, work if possible with the exterior angles rather than the interior.

Example 1. Each angle of a regular polygon is 170°. Find the number of sides of the polygon.

Each exterior angle = 180° − 170° = 10°.

The sum of the exterior angles is 360° and so there must be 36 exterior angles.

The number of sides is 36.

Example 2. One angle of a hexagon is 140°. The other five angles are equal to each other. Find them.

One exterior angle is 180° − 140° = 40°.

The sum of the other five equal exterior angles is 320°.

Each of these exterior angles must be 64°.

Each of the equal interior angles is (180° − 64°) = 116°.

EXERCISES 71A

1. Each angle of a regular polygon is 168°. How many sides has it?

2. One angle of a pentagon is 140°. Find each of the other angles, given that they are all equal to each other.

3. State for which of the following exterior angles a regular polygon is possible; (i) 20°; (ii) 25°; (iii) 30°.

4. State for which of the following interior angles a regular polygon is possible: (i) 165°; (ii) 160°; (iii) 155°.

5. Three of the angles of a hexagon are each $x°$. The other three are each $2x°$. Find x.

6. Write down the number of degrees in each angle of a regular 15-sided polygon.

7. In a 7-sided figure, three of the angles are equal and each of the other four angles is 15° greater than each of the first three. Find the angles.

8. If the angles of a pentagon are $y°$, $(y + 10)°$, $(y + 20)°$, $(y + 40)°$ and $(y + 50)°$, find y.

9. If the angles of a hexagon are $x°$, $(x + 10)°$, $(x + 20)°$, $(x + 30)°$, $(x + 40)°$ and $(x + 50)°$, find x.

10. Find the sixth angle of a hexagon when each of the others is 118°.

EXERCISES 71B

1. Each angle of a regular polygon is 162°. How many sides has it?

2. One angle of a pentagon is 160°. Find each of the other equal angles.

3. State for which of the following exterior angles a regular polygon is possible: (i) 24°; (ii) 28°; (iii) 36°.

4. State for which of the following interior angles a regular polygon is possible: (i) 170°; (ii) 168°; (iii) 164°.

5. Three of the angles of a hexagon are each $2x°$ and each of the others is $3x°$. Find x.

6. Write down the number of degrees in each angle of a regular 16-sided figure.

7. In an octagon (8-sided figure), four of the angles are equal and each of the others is 20° greater than each of the first four. Find the angles.

8. If the angles of a quadrilateral are $(p + 10)°$, $(2p - 30)°$, $(3p + 20)°$ and $4p°$, find p.

9. If four of the angles of a heptagon (7-sided figure) are equal and each of the other three is 20° greater than each of the first four, find the angles.

10. Find the fifth angle of a pentagon when each of the other angles is 120°.

EXERCISES 72: MISCELLANEOUS

1. If three angles of a quadrilateral are 40°, 100° and 150°, find the fourth angle.

2. If three angles of a quadrilateral are $x°$, $y°$ and $z°$, express the fourth angle in terms of x, y and z.

3. Find the third angle of a triangle when the other two are $(2x - 30)°$ and $(3x + 20)°$.

4. Find x when the three angles of a triangle are $(x + 20)°$, $(2x + 30)°$ and $(3x + 40)°$.

5. Find x when the four angles of a quadrilateral are $x°$, $2x°$, $(x + 10)°$ and $(x + 20)°$.

6. Find x from Fig. 56.

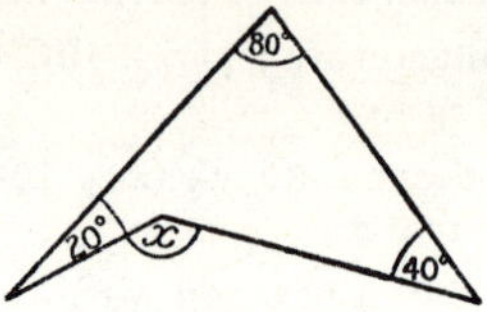

FIG. 56

7. Find x in terms of p, q, r from Fig. 57.

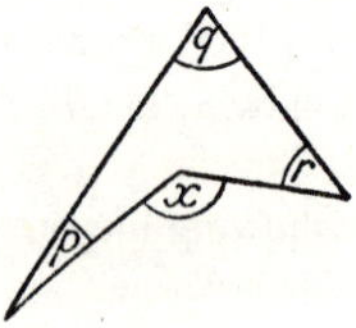

FIG. 57

8. From Fig. 58, prove that $z = 90°$.

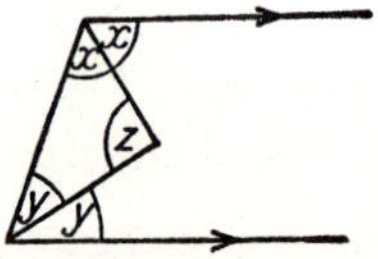

FIG. 58

9. Find x in Fig. 59.

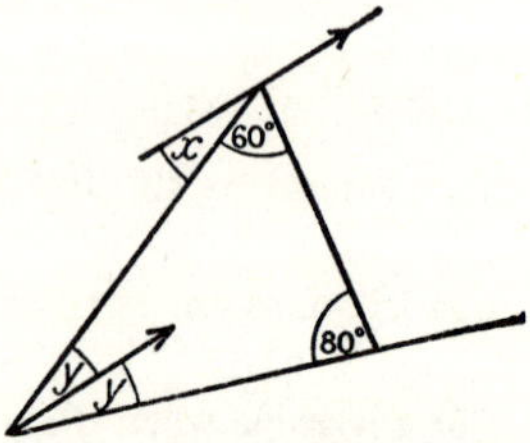

FIG. 59

10. Find y and z in Fig. 60.

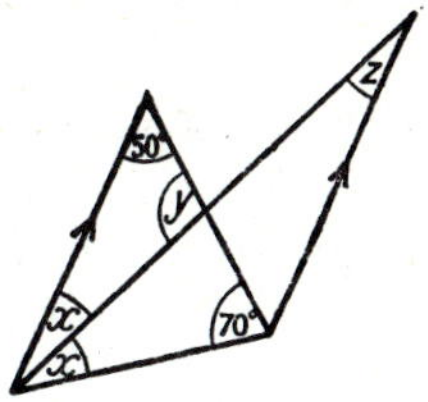

FIG. 60

11. Find z in Fig. 61.

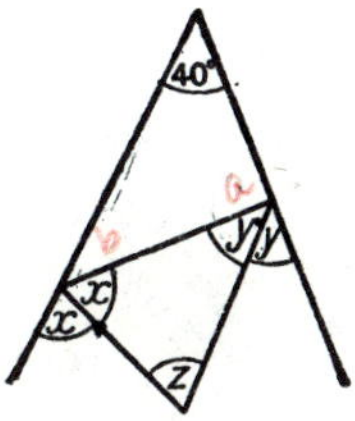

FIG. 61

12. Find x in Fig. 62.

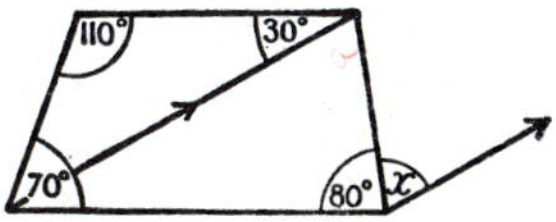

FIG. 62

13. Find x in terms of a, b and y from Fig. 63.

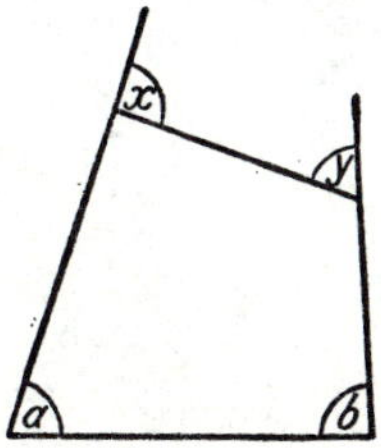

FIG. 63

14. In Fig. 63, given that $y = 20°$, $a = 40°$ and $b = 50°$, find x.

15. If the exterior angles of a quadrilateral are $x°$, $(x + 5)°$, $(x + 10)°$ and $(x + 25)°$, find x.

16. If three of the exterior angles of a hexagon are each $x°$ and each of the other three is $2x°$, find x.

18

CONGRUENT TRIANGLES; THE ISOSCELES TRIANGLE; INEQUALITIES

CONGRUENT TRIANGLES

Two triangles are said to be congruent if they are equal in all respects. The three sides of one must be respectively equal to the three sides of the other and the three angles of the first must be respectively equal to the three angles of the other.

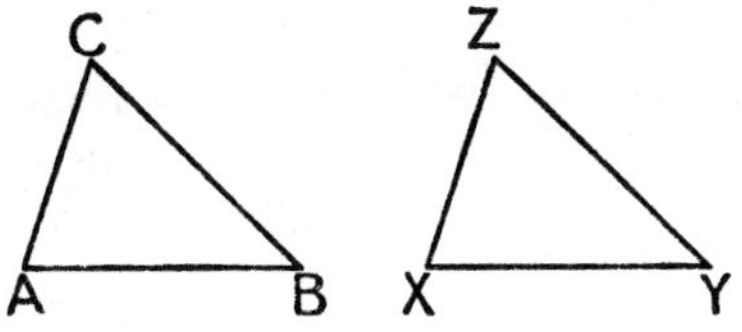

FIG. 64

If *ABC*, *XYZ* are congruent (in that order) then

$$AC = XZ \qquad \hat{A} = \hat{X}$$

$$AB = XY \quad \text{and} \quad \hat{B} = \hat{Y}$$

$$BC = YZ \qquad \hat{C} = \hat{Z}.$$

The triangles will of course be equal in area and any line in one figure (for example, the line joining *C* to the mid point of *AB*) will be equal to the corresponding line in the other figure.

$\triangle ABC \equiv \triangle XYZ$ is the usual notation for expressing the fact that the triangles *ABC* and *XYZ* are congruent.

If two triangles are congruent, the six elements of one (three sides and three angles) must be equal to the six elements of the other; but, in order to prove two triangles congruent, it is not necessary to prove all six equalities. There are four methods of proving triangles congruent which are listed in the following four theorems. The truth of these may be verified by drawing but no proofs are required.

THEOREM

If two triangles have two sides of the one respectively equal to two sides of the other and the angles included between the equal sides are also equal, then the triangles are congruent.

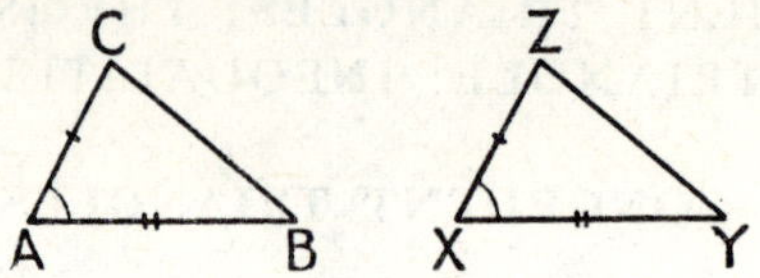

FIG. 65

The necessary equalities are shown in Fig. 65, and the reference when this theorem is used will be SAS.

THEOREM

If two triangles have two angles of the one respectively equal to two angles of the other, and a side of one equal to the corresponding side of the other, then the triangles are congruent.

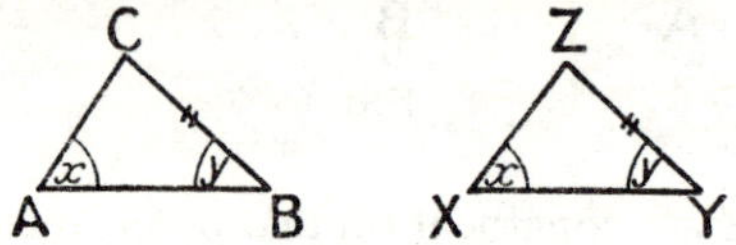

FIG. 66

For example, the triangles in Fig. 66 are congruent. The reference used for this theorem will be AAS.

Corresponding sides are opposite equal angles.

THEOREM

If two triangles have three sides of one respectively equal to the three sides of the other, then the triangles are congruent.

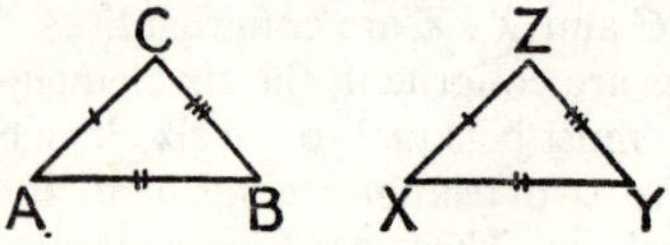

FIG. 67

The reference used for this theorem is SSS.

THEOREM

If two right-angled triangles have their hypotenuses equal and another side of one triangle equal to another side of the second triangle, then the triangles are congruent.

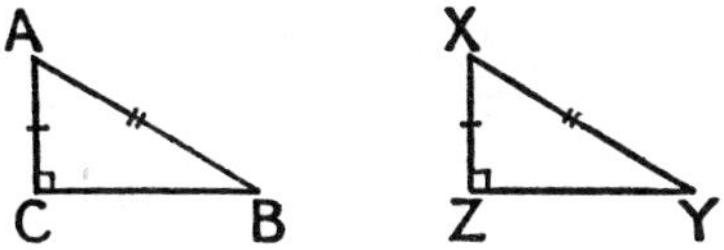

FIG. 68

This theorem will be referred to as R.H.S.

N.B. Notice that three equal angles are not sufficient to prove triangles congruent; neither are two sides and a non-included angle.

Example. In the quadrilateral *ABCD*, $BC = CD$ and the angles at *B* and *D* are right angles. Prove that *CA* bisects the angle *BAD*.

Construction. Join *AC*.

To prove $\widehat{DAC} = \widehat{CAB}$.

Proof. In the triangles *ABC* and *ADC*,

$$AC = AC \text{ (common)},$$
$$BC = CD \text{ (given)},$$
$$\widehat{CBA} = \widehat{CDA} \text{ (right angles)}.$$
$$\therefore \triangle ABC \equiv \triangle ADC \text{ (R.H.S.)}.$$

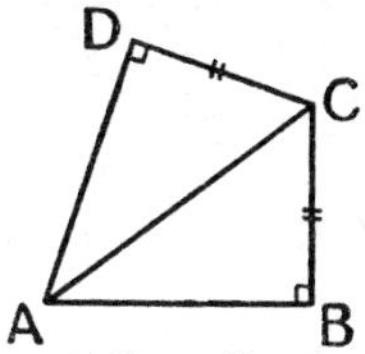

FIG. 69

DAC and *CAB* are corresponding angles in the two triangles and are therefore equal.

EXERCISES 73A

1. Given that two straight lines *AB*, *CD* bisect each other, prove that $AC = BD$.

2. In the isosceles triangle *ABC*, in which $AB = AC$, *AD* bisects the angle *BAC*. Prove that $BD = DC$.

3. In Fig. 70, prove that $\widehat{B} = \widehat{C}$.

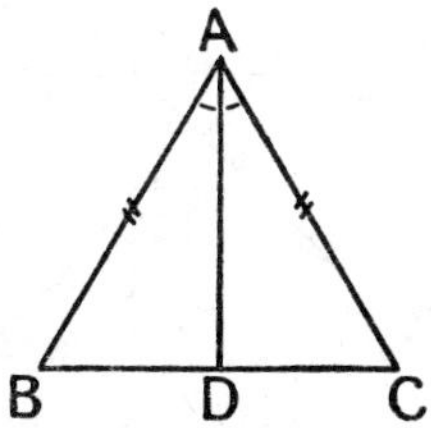

FIG. 70

4. In the triangle ABC, $AB = AC$ and X is the mid point of BC. Prove that $B\widehat{A}X = C\widehat{A}X$.

5. In the quadrilateral $ABCD$, $AB = CD$ and $BC = AD$. Prove that DC is parallel to AB.

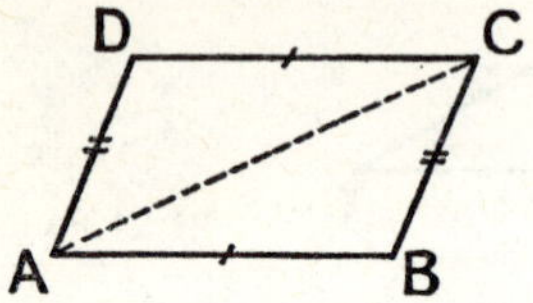

FIG. 71

6. In Fig. 71, prove that $\widehat{B} = \widehat{D}$.

7. Prove that the line drawn from the centre of a circle perpendicular to a chord bisects that chord.

8. Prove that the line joining the centre of a circle to the mid point of a chord is perpendicular to that chord.

9. X and Y are points on the sides AB, AC of a triangle ABC. Given that $AB = AC$ and that $AX = AY$, prove that $XC = YB$.

10. In the quadrilateral $ABCD$, $\widehat{B} = \widehat{D}$ and CA bisects the angle BCD. Prove that $AB = AD$.

EXERCISES 73B

1. In the quadrilateral $ABCD$, AB is parallel to DC and AD is parallel to BC (a parallelogram). Prove that a diagonal bisects the parallelogram.

2. Prove that the opposite angles of a parallelogram are equal.

3. Prove that the opposite sides of a parallelogram are equal.

4. Prove that the diagonals of a parallelogram bisect each other.

5. Prove that if one pair of opposite sides of a quadrilateral are equal and parallel, then the other pair of opposite sides are also equal and parallel.

6. In Fig. 72, $AD = BC$ and $AC = BD$. Prove that $A\widehat{B}D = B\widehat{A}C$.

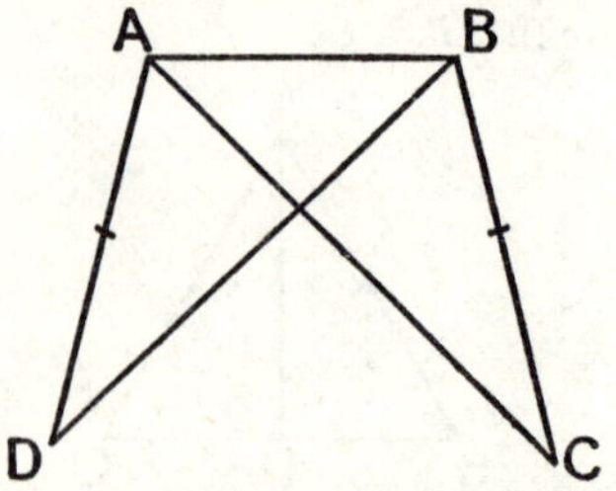

FIG. 72

7. Points D and E are taken on the side BC of a triangle ABC so that D is between B and E. Given that $AB = AC$ and that $B\widehat{A}D = C\widehat{A}E$, prove that $BD = EC$.

8. In Fig. 73, $D\widehat{A}B = A\widehat{B}C$ and $AD = CB$. Prove that $BD = AC$.

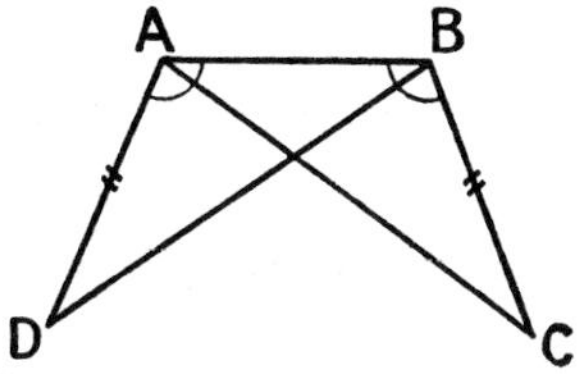

FIG. 73

9. $ABCD$ is a rectangle. Prove that its diagonals AC and BD are equal.

10. In the triangles ABC and XYZ, $AB = XY$ and the angles at A, B, X and Z are respectively 40°, 60°, 40° and 80°. Prove that the triangles are congruent.

THE ISOSCELES TRIANGLE

A triangle which has two sides equal in length is called isosceles. The next theorem states that, in such a triangle, the angles opposite the equal sides are equal. For example, given in an isosceles triangle that the third angle is 80°, the sum of the two equal angles is 100° and each of the equal angles is 50°. An equilateral triangle has all its sides equal and consequently all its angles equal. Each angle of an equilateral triangle is 60°.

THEOREM

If two sides of a triangle are equal, then the angles opposite the equal sides are also equal.

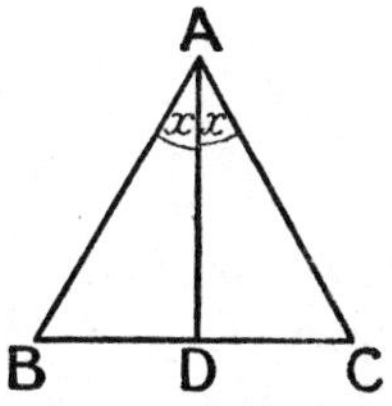

FIG. 74

Given $AB = AC$.

To prove that $\hat{B} = \hat{C}$.

Construction: Draw AD to bisect the angle BAC and to cut BC at D.

Proof: The proof is left as an exercise (see Exercises 73A, question 3).

The converse

The converse of this theorem is also true.

THEOREM

If two angles of a triangle are equal, then the sides opposite these angles are also equal.

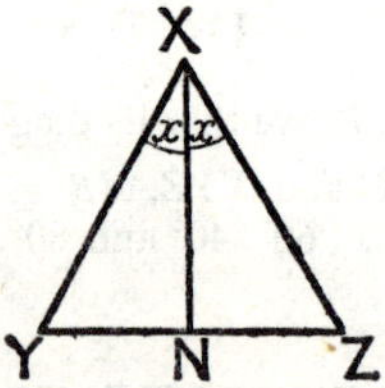

FIG. 75

Given $\hat{Y} = \hat{Z}$.

To prove that $XY = XZ$.

Construction: Draw XN to bisect the angle YXZ and to meet YZ at N.

Proof: The theorem is proved by congruent triangles and is left as an exercise.

EXERCISES 74A

1. Find the value of x from each of the given figures.

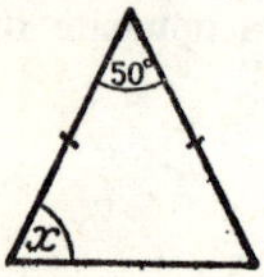

FIG. 76

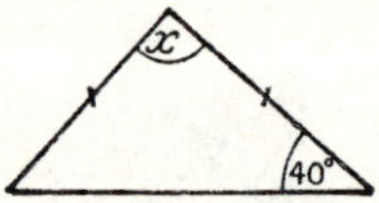

FIG. 77

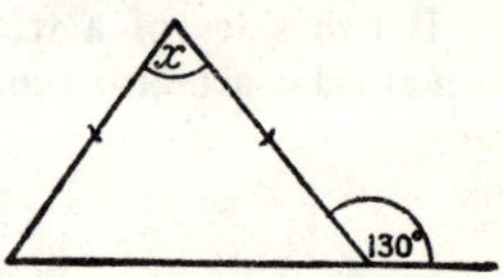

FIG. 78

2. $ABCDE$ is a regular pentagon. Calculate the angle BAC.

3. $ABCDE$ is a regular pentagon. Prove that AC is parallel to DE.

4. A chord AB subtends an angle of 80° at the centre O of a circle. Find the angle OAB.

5. The mid points of the equal sides AB, AC of an isosceles triangle are X, Y respectively. Prove that $BY = XC$.

6. In Fig. 79, $ABCD$ is a square and DEC is an equilateral triangle. Find the angle DAE.

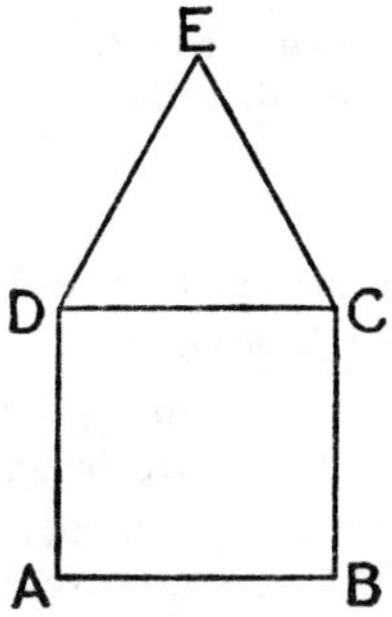

FIG. 79

7. In Fig. 79, prove that $EA = EB$.

8. In Fig. 79, calculate the angle AEB.

9. From Fig. 80, give y in terms of x.

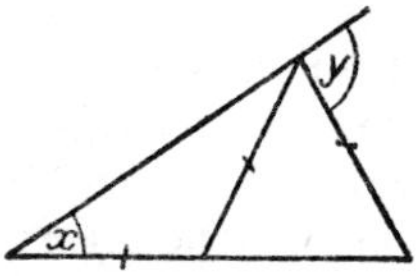

FIG. 80

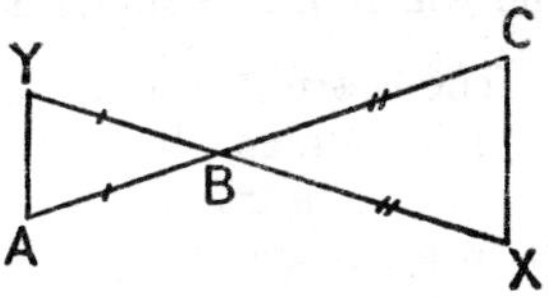

FIG. 81

10. In Fig. 81, given that $AB = BY$ and that $BX = BC$, prove that AY is parallel to XC.

EXERCISES 74B

1. Find the value of x from each of the given figures.

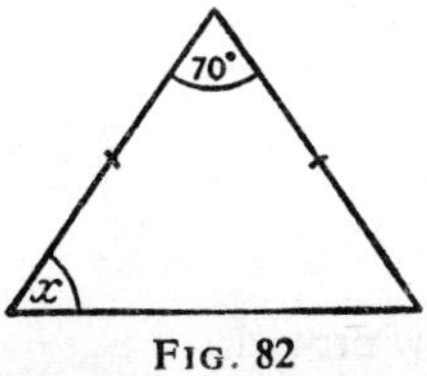

FIG. 82

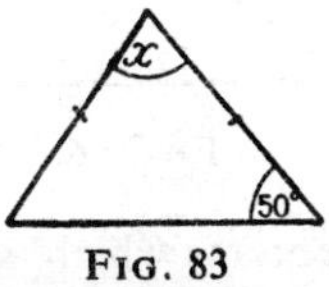

FIG. 83

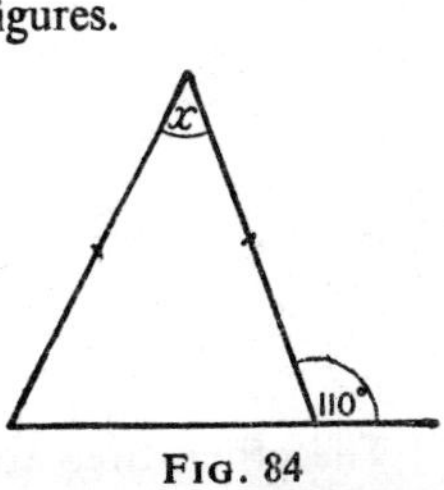

FIG. 84

2. *ABCDEF* is a regular hexagon. Find the angle *FAE*.

3. *ABCDEF* is a regular hexagon. Prove that *BD* is parallel to *AE*.

4. *ABCDEF* is a regular hexagon. Prove that *CF* is parallel to *AB*.

5. In the regular hexagon *ABCDEF*, calculate the angle *ADB*.

6. A chord *XY* subtends an angle of 100° at the centre *O* of a circle. Calculate the angle *OXY*.

7. Find x from Fig. 85.

8. *ABCD* is a parallelogram with $AB = AD$. Prove that *CA* bisects the angle *BAD*.

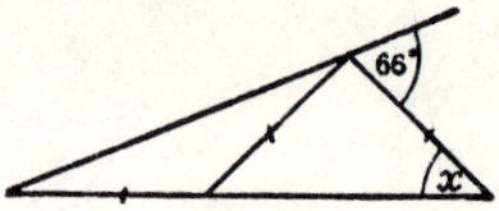

FIG. 85

9. *ABC* is a triangle. *X* is a point on *AB* such that $AX = XB = XC$. Prove that the angle *C* is a right angle.

10. The diagonals *AC*, *BD* of a quadrilateral meet at *X*. Given that *AB* is parallel to *DC* and that $AX = XB$, prove that $CX = XD$.

INEQUALITIES

There are four facts which may help when we are asked to prove that one line is greater in length than another or when we are asked to find which of two angles is the greater.

(1) The shortest distance between two points is the straight line joining them. In other words, the sum of the lengths of two sides of a triangle is greater than the length of the third side.
(2) In a triangle, the greatest angle is opposite the greatest side.
(3) In a triangle, the greatest side is opposite the greatest angle.
(4) The shortest distance from a point to a line is the perpendicular distance.

The first of these is taken as self-evident and in Fig. 86,

$$AC + CB > AB.$$

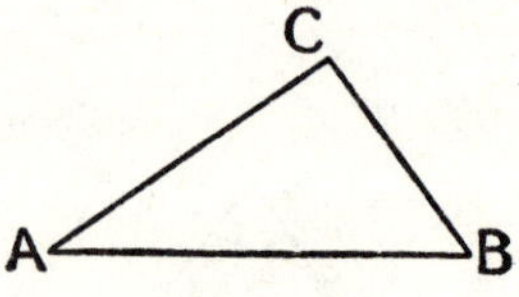

FIG. 86

The other three are theorems which are now proved.

THEOREM

If, in a triangle, one side is greater than a second, then the angle opposite the greater side is greater than the angle opposite the smaller side.

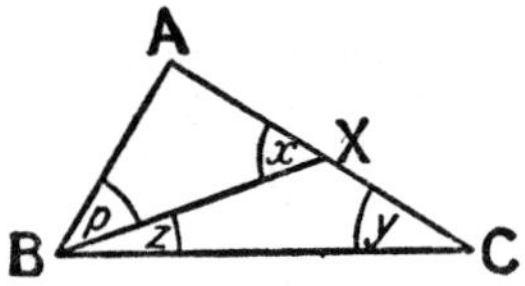

FIG. 87

Given $AC > AB$.

To prove $\widehat{ABC} > \widehat{ACB}$.

Construction: Take the point X on AC such that $AX = AB$. Join BX.

Proof: Since $AB < AC$, $AX < AC$.

Therefore X lies between A and C.

$x = y + z$ (exterior angle).

$\therefore x > y$.

But $x = p$ $(AB = AX)$

$\therefore p > y$

But $p < \widehat{ABC}$ and so $\widehat{ABC} > y$, i.e. $\widehat{ABC} > \widehat{ACB}$.

From this it follows that the greatest angle of a triangle is opposite the greatest side.

THEOREM

If, in a triangle, one angle is greater than a second, the side opposite the greater angle is greater than the side opposite the smaller angle.

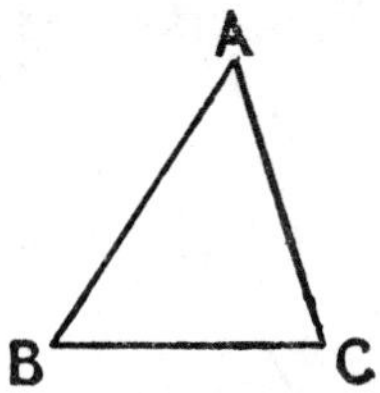

FIG. 88

Given $\widehat{C} > \widehat{B}$.

To prove $AB > AC$.

Proof: One of the following statements must be true.

(i) $AB < AC$; (ii) $AB = AC$; (iii) $AB > AC$.

(i) Suppose $AB < AC$. Then by the last theorem $\hat{C} < \hat{B}$. This is impossible as it is contrary to what is given.

(ii) Suppose $AB = AC$. Then $\hat{C} = \hat{B}$ (isosceles triangle). This is impossible as it is contrary to what is given. Therefore the third statement must be the correct one and $AB > AC$.

THEOREM

The shortest distance from a point to a straight line is the perpendicular distance.

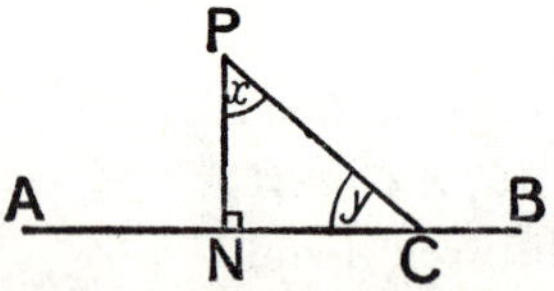

FIG. 89

Given a straight line AB and a point P not on the line. PN is the perpendicular from P to AB and C is any point on the line.

To prove $PN < PC$.

Proof: Since $P\hat{N}C = 90°$,

$$x + y = 90° \text{ (angle sum of triangle).}$$
$$\therefore y < 90°.$$
i.e. $$y < P\hat{N}C.$$
$$\therefore PN < PC \text{ (inequality theorem).}$$

EXERCISES 75A

1. In Fig. 90, is $AB > BC$?

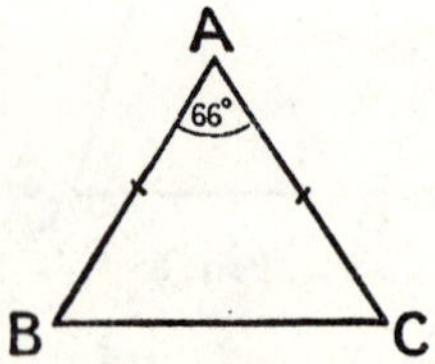

FIG. 90

2. In Fig. 91, place BC, CA, CD in order of magnitude.

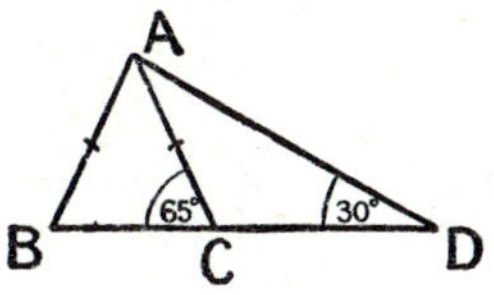

FIG. 91

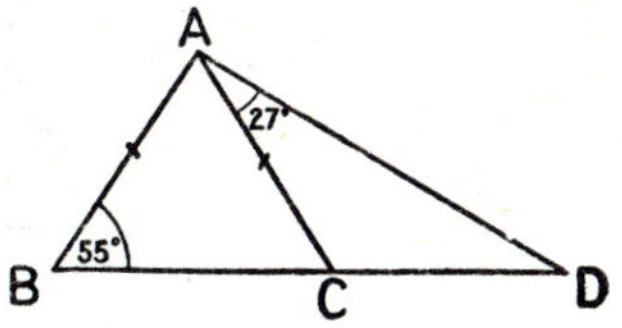

FIG. 92

3. In Fig. 92, place BC, CA, CD in order of magnitude.

4. In the triangle ABC, $AB > AC$. The internal bisectors of the angles B and C meet at X. Prove $XB > XC$.

5. X is any point on the side AB of an equilateral triangle ABC. Prove that $AC > CX > AX$.

6. X is a point on the side AB of an isosceles triangle ABC in which $CA = CB$. Prove that $CA > CX$.

7. A point P is taken on the side CA produced of an isosceles triangle in which $AB = AC$. Prove that $PB > AC$, given the angle A is acute.

8. In the quadrilateral $ABCD$, AB is the largest side and CD the shortest. Prove that $A\widehat{D}C > A\widehat{B}C$.

9. $ABCD$ is a parallelogram whose diagonals AC, BD meet at O. Prove that $AB + AD > 2AO$.

10. In the triangle ABC, the angle $A = 72°$ and the angle $B = 55°$. The internal bisectors of the angles B and C meet at X. Which is the greater, BX or CX?

EXERCISES 75B

1. In Fig. 93, is $AB > BC$?

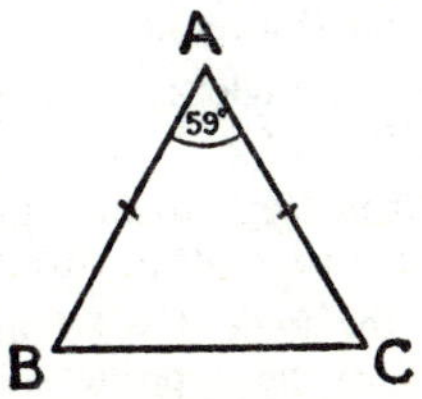

FIG. 93

2. In Fig. 94, place BC, CA, CD in order of magnitude.

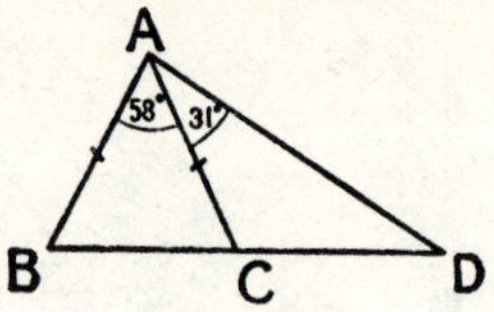

FIG. 94

3. In Fig. 95, place AB, CA, CD in order of magnitude.

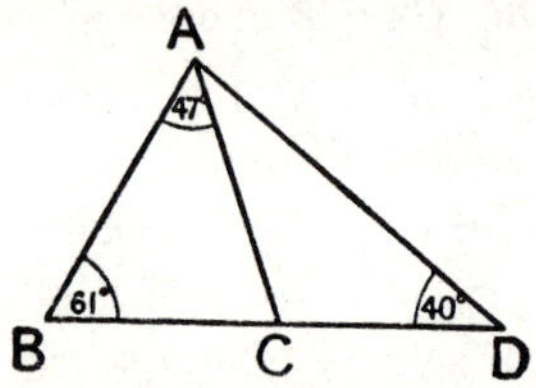

FIG. 95

4. In Fig. 96, given that $AB > AC$, prove that $CX > BX$.

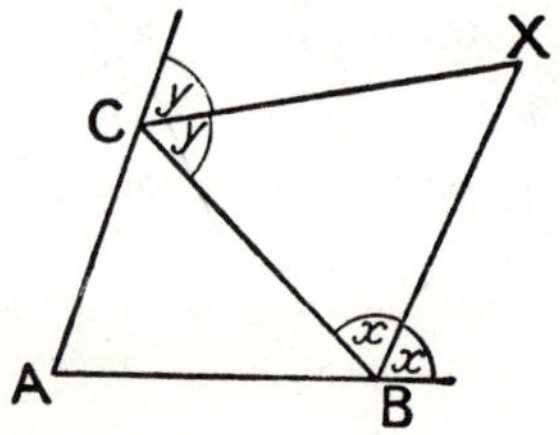

FIG. 96

5. P is any point inside a triangle ABC. Prove that $B\widehat{P}C > B\widehat{A}C$.

6. $ABCD$ is a parallelogram in which the angle A is 80°. The internal bisectors of the angles A and D meet at X. Prove $AX > DX$.

7. P is any point inside a triangle ABC. By producing BP to meet AC, prove that $AB + AC > PB + PC$.

8. The perpendiculars from B, C to the opposite sides of the triangle ABC meet at H. Given that $AB > AC$, prove that $HB > HC$.

9. In the triangle ABC, the angle $A = 80°$ and the angle $B = 40°$. The perpendiculars from B, C to the opposite sides meet at H. Prove that $HB > HC$.

10. In a circle, a chord *AB* subtends an angle of 50° at the centre. Prove that the radius of the circle is greater in length than *AB*.

EXERCISES 76: MISCELLANEOUS

1. In Fig. 97, *ABCD* is a square and *ABP* an equilateral triangle. Calculate the angle *DPC*.

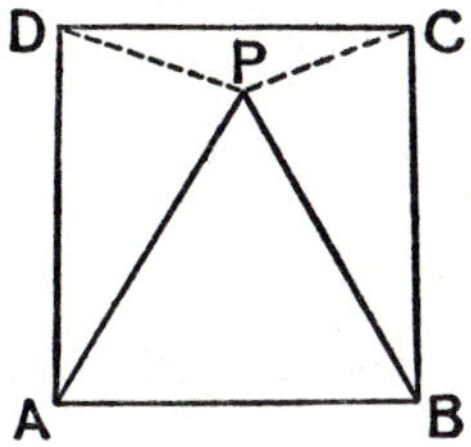

FIG. 97

2. *ABCD* is a parallelogram. If the bisectors of the angles *C* and *D* meet at *O*, prove that the angle *DOC* is a right angle.

3. *D* is the point on the side *BC* produced of a triangle *ABC* such that *CD* = *CA*. If the angle *ABC* = 58° and the angle *ACB* = 46°, calculate the angle *BAD*.

4. *ABCD* is a parallelogram. *DCXY* and *ADPQ* are squares drawn outside the parallelogram. Prove that *AY* = *CP*.

5. In the triangle *ABC*, the angle *B* = 66° and the angle *C* = 48°. If *AD* is the perpendicular from *A* to *BC* and *AX* is the internal bisector of the angle *A*, calculate the angle *DAX*.

6. *P* is any point on the bisector of the angle *A* of an isosceles triangle *ABC* in which *AB* = *AC*. Prove that *PB* = *PC*.

7. A quadrilateral *ABCD* is such that the bisectors of the four angles all meet at a point *O*. Prove that the angles *BOA* and *COD* are supplementary.

8. *ABCDEFGH* is a regular octagon. Calculate the angle *BDC*.

9. *BCD* are consecutive vertices of a regular polygon. If the angle *BDC* is 10°, how many sides has the polygon?

10. In the triangle *ABC*, the angles at *A* and *C* are 40° and 95° respectively. If *N* is the foot of the perpendicular from *C* to *AB*, prove that *CN* = *BN*.

11. Two straight lines *CB* and *DA* meet at *O*. Given that *CA* = *DB* and that *CB* = *DA*, prove that *CO* = *DO*.

12. In Fig. 98, AB is perpendicular to PX. If CXB is a straight line, and $AP = BP$, prove that $CB = CX + XA$. Hence prove that $CP + AP > CX + AX$.

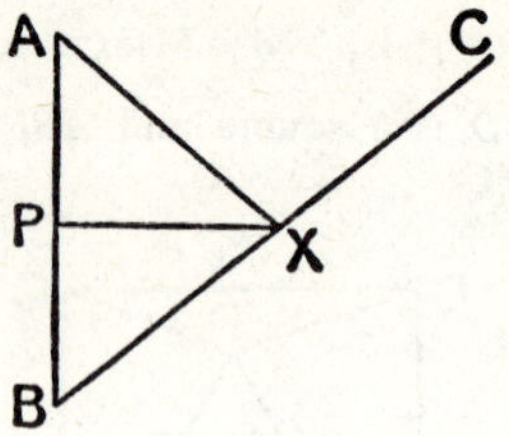

FIG. 98

13. ABC is an isosceles triangle in which $AB = BC$. X is any point on BA produced and Y is any point on the bisector of the angle ABC. Prove that $BX - CB < CY + XY$.

14. If the diagonals of a parallelogram are equal, prove that the parallelogram must be a rectangle.

15. ABC is a triangle and D is the mid point of BC. Prove that $AB + AC > 2AD$. (Hint: produce AD to X where $AD = DX$.)

16. The angles A, B, C of a triangle are respectively 50°, 60° and 70°. The internal bisectors of the three angles all meet at I. Place AI, BI, CI in order of magnitude.

17. $ABCD$ is a quadrilateral in which AD is equal to BC but not parallel to it. AB is parallel to DC. Prove that the angles ADC and BCD are equal.

18. The sum of the exterior angles of a convex polygon is two-sevenths of the sum of its interior angles. How many sides has the polygon?

19. Two points P, Q are on opposite sides of a straight line and equidistant from it. Prove that the line bisects PQ.

20. ABC is a triangle. D is the mid point of BC. If the perpendiculars from D to AB and AC are equal, prove that the triangle is isosceles.

19

THE PARALLELOGRAM; INTERCEPT THEOREMS; AREAS

THE PARALLELOGRAM

A PARALLELOGRAM is a quadrilateral with both pairs of opposite sides parallel.

The common properties of the parallelogram are:

(1) Both pairs of opposite sides are equal.
(2) A diagonal bisects the parallelogram.
(3) Both pairs of opposite angles are equal.
(4) The diagonals bisect each other.

The rhombus

A rhombus is a parallelogram with its adjacent sides equal. Its properties are those of the parallelogram, and in addition the following two properties are true:

(1) The diagonals bisect *at right angles.*
(2) A diagonal bisects the angles through which it passes.

The rectangle

A rectangle is a parallelogram in which one angle is a right angle. It follows that all the angles must be right angles. The rectangle has all the properties of the parallelogram and, in addition, its diagonals are equal.

The square

A square is a rectangle with its adjacent sides equal. A square has all the properties of the parallelogram, rhombus and rectangle.

THEOREM

The opposite sides of a parallelogram are equal; the opposite angles are equal and a diagonal bisects the parallelogram.

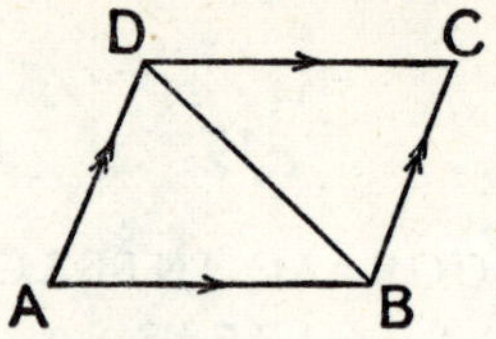

FIG. 99

Given a parallelogram *ABCD*.

To prove (i) $AD = CB$ and $DC = AB$.

(ii) $\hat{A} = \hat{C}$ and $A\widehat{D}C = C\widehat{B}A$.

(iii) $\triangle ADB \equiv \triangle CBD$.

The proof by congruent triangles is left as an exercise (see Exercises 73B, questions **1, 2** and **3**).

THEOREM

The diagonals of a parallelogram bisect each other.

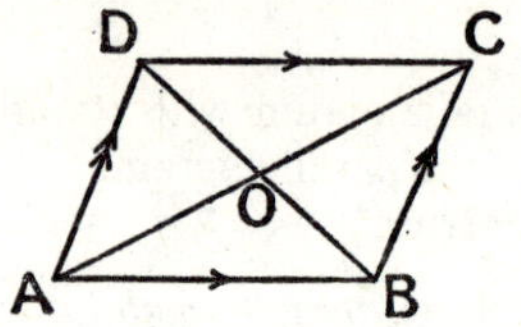

FIG. 100

Given a parallelogram *ABCD* whose diagonals meet at *O*.

To prove $OA = OC$ and $OB = OD$.

The proof is left as an exercise (see Exercises 73B, question **4**).

THEOREM

If one pair of opposite sides of a quadrilateral are equal and parallel, then the other sides must also be equal and parallel.

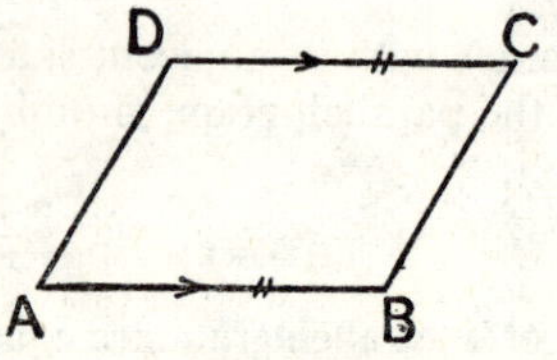

FIG. 101

Given $AB = DC$ and $AB \parallel DC$.
To prove (i) $AD = CB$; (ii) $AD \parallel BC$.
The proof is left as an exercise (see Exercises 73B, question **5**).

Necessary conditions for a parallelogram

A quadrilateral is a parallelogram if *any one* of the following is true.

(1) Its opposite sides are equal.
(2) Its opposite angles are equal.
(3) Its diagonals bisect each other.

THEOREM

If the opposite sides of a quadrilateral are equal, then the quadrilateral must be a parallelogram.

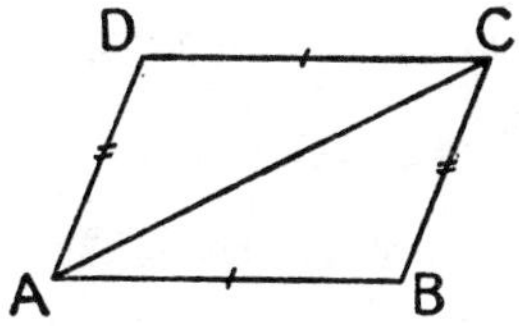

FIG. 102

Given a quadrilateral $ABCD$ in which $AB = CD$ and $AD = BC$.
To prove $ABCD$ is a parallelogram.
The proof is left as an exercise (see Exercises 73A, question **5**).

THEOREM

If the opposite angles of a quadrilateral are equal, then the quadrilateral must be a parallelogram.

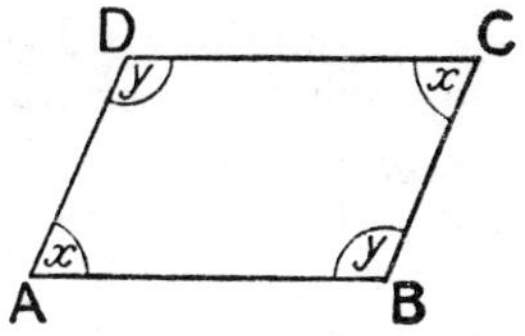

FIG. 103

Given a quadrilateral $ABCD$ with its opposite angles equal.
To prove that $ABCD$ is a parallelogram.
Proof: The sum of the angles of any quadilateral is 360°.

From the figure, $2x + 2y = 360°$.
$\therefore x + y = 180°$.
$\therefore AD \parallel BC$ (interior angles supplementary)
and $AB \parallel DC$ (interior angles supplementary).

THEOREM

If the diagonals of a quadrilateral bisect each other, the quadrilateral must be a parallelogram.

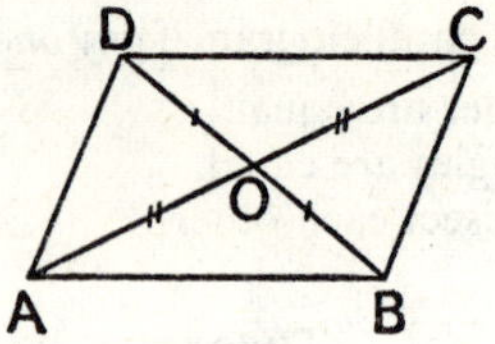

FIG. 104

Given a quadrilateral $ABCD$ with the diagonals meeting at O and bisecting each other.
To prove that $ABCD$ is a parallelogram.
The proof is left as an exercise.

EXERCISES 77A

1. One angle of a parallelogram is 62°. Find the other angles.

2. The angle between a diagonal of a rhombus and a side is 20°. Calculate the angles of the rhombus.

3. $ABCD$ is a parallelogram. DN and BM are perpendiculars from D and B to AC. Prove that $DN = BM$.

4. Prove that if, in a parallelogram, a diagonal bisects the angles through which it passes, the parallelogram must be a rhombus.

5. Prove that if the diagonals of a parallelogram are equal, it must be a rectangle.

6. The median AD of a triangle ABC is produced to X where $AD = DX$. Prove that $ABXC$ is a parallelogram.

7. $ABCD$, $CEFD$ and $ABXY$ are all parallelograms. Prove that FX and EY bisect each other.

8. The two parallelograms $ABCD$ and $ABXY$ are such that $CDXY$ is a straight line. Prove that $\triangle ADY \equiv \triangle BCX$.

9. $ABCD$ is a rhombus. BA is produced to X where $BA = AX$. Prove that the angle XDB is a right angle.

10. If the diagonals AC, BD of a parallelogram meet at O and a line through O meets AB at L and DC at M, prove that $LO = OM$.

EXERCISES 77B

1. One angle of a parallelogram is 57°. Find the other angles.

2. The angle between a diagonal and a side of a rhombus is 28°. Find the angles of the rhombus.

3. *ABCD* is a parallelogram. *BM* and *DN* are the perpendiculars from *B* and *D* to *AC*. Prove that $AM = CN$.

4. Prove that, if the diagonals of a parallelogram are perpendicular, it must be a rhombus.

5. The diagonals of a parallelogram *ABCD* meet at *O*. A line through *O* meets one pair of sides in *P*, *Q* and another line through *O* meets the other pair of sides in *R*, *S*. Prove that *PRQS* is a parallelogram.

6. If the angle *A* of a parallelogram *ABCD* is acute, prove that $AC > BD$.

7. The bisectors of the angles of a parallelogram are drawn. Prove these bisectors form another parallelogram.

8. *ABCD* is a parallelogram and *X* is the mid point of *CB*. If *AX* bisects the angle *A*, prove that $AD = 2AB$.

9. *ABCD* is a parallelogram. *L* is a point on *AB* and *M* another point on *CD*. Given that $AL = CM$, prove that *LM* and *BD* bisect each other.

10. Two circles are such that they have the same centre *O*. A line through *O* cuts one circle in *A*, *B*; another line through *O* cuts the other circle at *C*, *D*. Prove that $AC = BD$.

THE INTERCEPT THEOREMS

The line drawn through the mid point of one side of a triangle parallel to a second side bisects the third side.

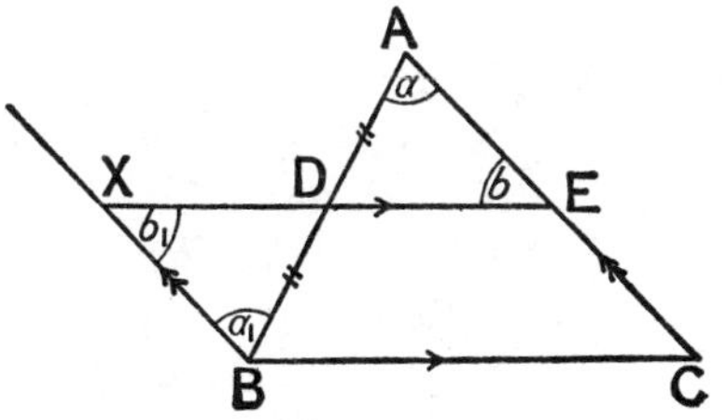

FIG. 105

Given $AD = DB$ and $DE \parallel BC$.
To prove $AE = EC$.
Construction: Draw through *B* a line $\parallel CA$ to meet *ED* produced at *X*.

Proof: In the triangles AED and BXD,

$$\begin{cases} AD = DB \text{ (given)}, \\ a = a_1 \text{ (alternate; } BX \parallel EA), \\ b = b_1 \text{ (alternate; } BX \parallel EA). \end{cases}$$

$$\therefore \triangle AED \equiv \triangle BXD \text{ (AAS)}.$$

In particular, $AE = BX$.

But $BCEX$ is a parallelogram ($BX \parallel CE$; $BC \parallel XE$).

$\therefore$ $BX = EC$ (opposite sides of parallelogram),

and $AE = EC$.

THEOREM

The straight line joining the middle points of two sides of a triangle is parallel to the third side and equal to half of it.

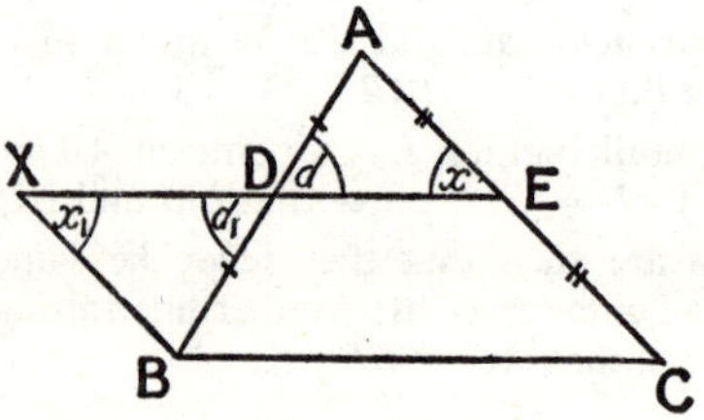

FIG. 106

Given $AD = DB$ and $AE = EC$.

To prove that $DE \parallel BC$ and that $DE = \frac{1}{2}BC$.

Construction: Through B draw a line $\parallel CE$ to meet ED produced at X.

Proof: In the triangles ADE, BDX,

$$\begin{cases} AD = DB \text{ (given)}, \\ d = d_1 \text{ (vert. opp.)}, \\ x = x_1 \text{ (alt.; } AE \parallel XB). \end{cases}$$

$$\therefore \triangle ADE \equiv \triangle BDX.$$

In particular, $XD = DE$ and $XB = AE$.

Since $XB = AE$ and $AE = EC$, $XB = EC$.

Therefore XB is equal and parallel to EC, and $XBCE$ is a parallelogram.

$$\therefore XE = BC \quad \text{and} \quad XE \parallel BC.$$

But $XD = DE$. $\therefore XE = 2DE$.

So $BC = 2DE$ and $DE \parallel BC$.

THEOREM

If there are three or more parallel straight lines and the intercepts made by them on any straight line that cuts them are equal, then the corresponding intercepts on any other straight line that cuts them are also equal.

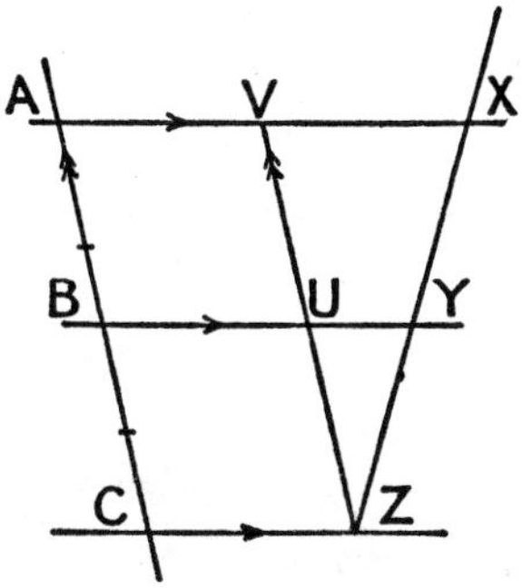

FIG. 107

Given three parallel straight lines AX, BY, CZ so that $AB = BC$.
To prove $XY = YZ$.
Construction: Through Z draw a line $\parallel CA$ to meet BY at U and AX at V.
Proof: By definition, $AVUB$ and $BUZC$ are parallelograms.

$\therefore AB = VU$ and $BC = UZ$ (opp. sides).

But $AB = BC$ (given) and therefore $VU = UZ$.

In the triangle VZX, U is the mid point of VZ and UY is parallel to the base VX.

$\therefore$ Y is the mid point of XZ (intercept theorem).

This proof may be extended to cover any number of parallel lines.

EXERCISES 78A

1. Calculate x in Fig. 108.

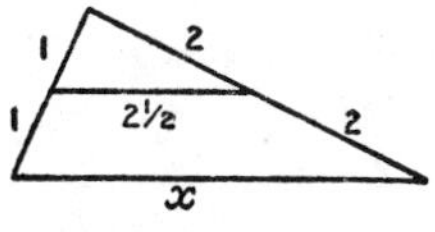

FIG. 108

2. Calculate x in Fig. 109.

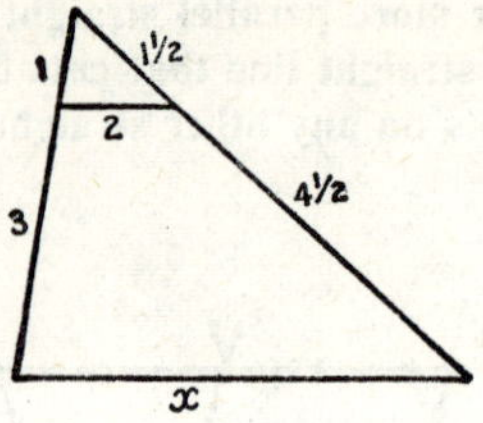

FIG. 109

3. If P is any point on the base BC of a triangle ABC, prove that the line joining the mid points of AB and AC also bisects AP.

4. Prove that the quadrilateral formed by joining the mid points of the sides of another quadrilateral is a parallelogram.

5. ABC is a triangle and D, E, F are the mid points of the sides. Prove that the triangles ABC and DEF are equiangular.

6. Calculate x in Fig. 110.

7. If ABC is a triangle right-angled at A and D is the mid point of BC, prove that $AD = \frac{1}{2}BC$.

8. BY and CZ are altitudes of the triangle ABC. Given that D is the mid point of BC, prove that $DY = DZ$.

9. $ABCD$ is a parallelogram. X is the mid point of DC and Y is the mid point of AB. Prove that DY and BX are parallel.

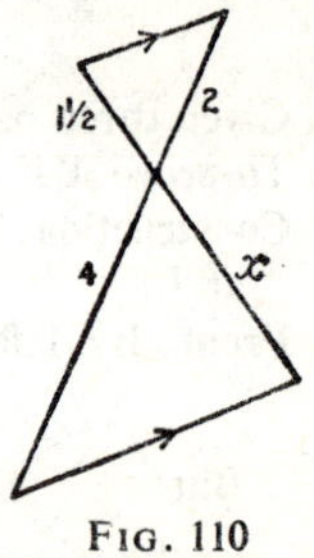

FIG. 110

10. Using the figure of question 9, prove that BX trisects AC.

EXERCISES 78B

1. Calculate x in Fig. 111.

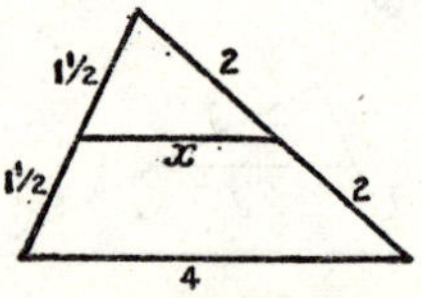

FIG. 111

2. Calculate y in Fig. 112.

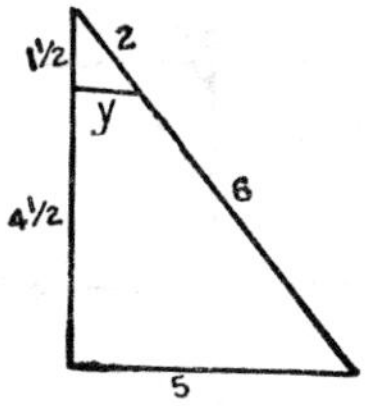

FIG. 112

3. If the diagonals of a quadrilateral are perpendicular, prove that the figure obtained by joining the mid points of its sides is a rectangle.

4. If the diagonals of a quadrilateral are equal, prove that the figure obtained by joining the mid points of its sides is a rhombus.

5. Calculate x in Fig. 113.

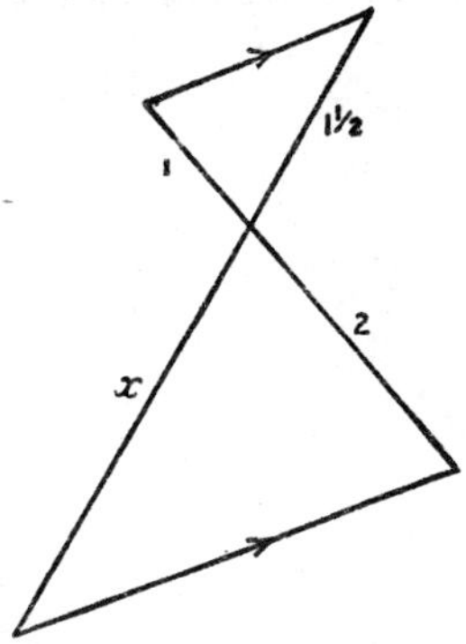

FIG. 113

6. If D, E, F are the mid points of the sides of the triangle ABC, prove that AD bisects EF.

7. Prove that the area of the triangle formed by joining the mid points of the sides of the triangle ABC is one-quarter of the area of the triangle ABC.

8. If E, F are the mid points of the sides AC, AB of a triangle ABC, prove that the area of AEF is one-quarter that of ABC.

9. In the parallelogram $ABCD$, X is the mid point of AD and Y the mid point of BC. Prove that XY bisects BD.

10. The diagonals of a parallelogram intersect at O. Prove that the line through O parallel to one pair of sides bisects each of the other sides.

AREAS

Distance between parallel lines

The distance between two parallel lines is their intercept on any line perpendicular to both.

AB is the distance between the parallel lines shown in Fig. 114.

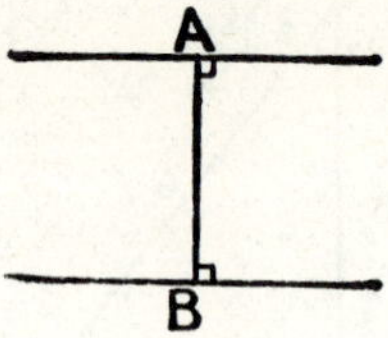

FIG. 114

Altitudes of a triangle

If *AX*, *BY*, *CZ* are the perpendiculars from the vertices of a triangle to the opposite sides, then *AX*, *BY*, *CZ* are called the altitudes of the triangle. *AX* is called the altitude corresponding to the base *BC*.

The three altitudes of a triangle all meet in a point.

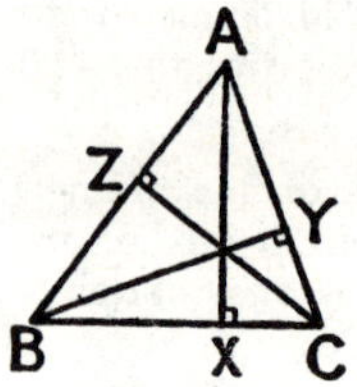

FIG. 115

THEOREM

Parallelograms on the same base and between the same parallels are equal in area.

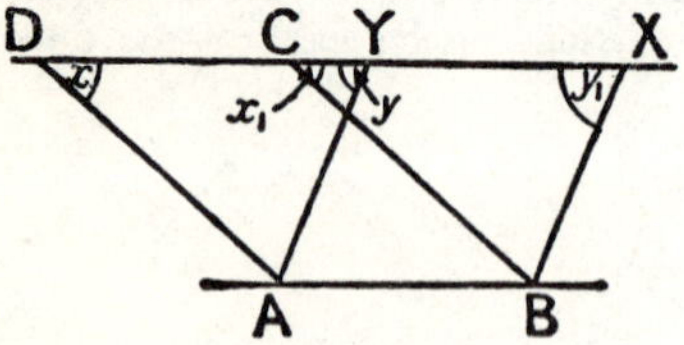

FIG. 116

(Parallelograms such as *ABCD*. *ABXY* are called parallelograms on the same base *AB* and between the same parallels, *AB* and *DCYX*.)

Given *DCYX* is a straight line, *ABCD* and *ABXY* are parallelograms.

To prove that *ABXY* and *ABCD* are equal in area.

Proof: In the triangles ADY and BCX,

$$\begin{cases} AD = BC \text{ (opp. sides of parallelogram),} \\ x = x_1 \text{ (corresponding; } AD \parallel BC\text{),} \\ y = y_1 \text{ (corresponding; } AY \parallel BX\text{).} \end{cases}$$

$$\therefore \triangle ADY \equiv \triangle BCX \text{ (AAS).}$$

Triangles which are congruent are equal in all respects and are therefore equal in area. Subtracting the area of each triangle in turn from the whole area $ABXD$, we see that the remainders $ABCD$ and $ABXY$ must be equal in area.

N.B. This method of proof applies also if C lies between Y and X. Other methods of proof apply to one figure or the other, but the proof given is the best as it covers all cases.

Area of a parallelogram

Referring to Fig. 117, all parallelograms on the base AB and between the same parallels are equal in area. Each of these parallelograms will therefore be equal in area to the one rectangle which can be drawn on the base AB between the given parallels.

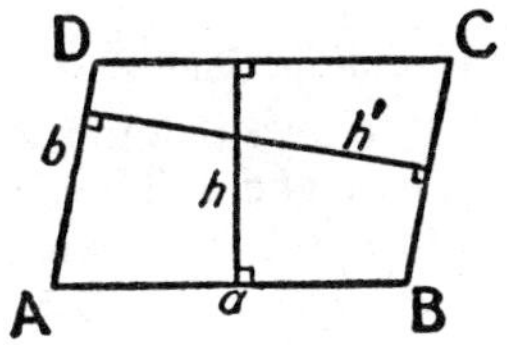

FIG. 117

The area of a rectangle = base × height.

The area of the parallelogram $ABCD$ therefore equals the product of the base AB and the distance between the parallel lines AB and DC.

The area of the parallelogram shown in Fig. 117 is equal to ah or to bh'.

Expressing the area of a parallelogram in two different ways often gives a useful method of finding the distance between two parallel lines.

The following properties follow:

(1) Parallelograms of equal bases and equal altitudes are equal in area.

(2) Parallelograms which are equal in area and have equal bases, have equal altitudes.

(3) Parallelograms which are equal in area and have equal altitudes, have equal bases.

THEOREM

The area of a triangle is half that of a parallelogram drawn on the same base and between the same parallels.

Given a triangle *ABC* with *XCY* ∥ *AB*.

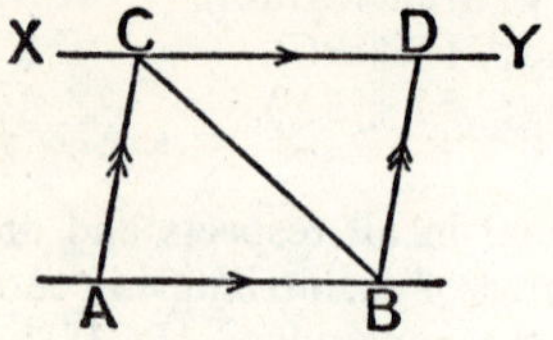

FIG. 118

To prove that *ABC* is half the area of any parallelogram drawn with *AB* as base between the parallels *AB* and *XY*.

Construction: Through *B* draw *BD* ∥ *AC* to meet *XY* at *D*.

Proof: The diagonal *BC* bisects the parallelogram *ABDC*.

∴ *ABC* and *BDC* are equal in area.

∴ *ABC* in area is half the parallelogram *ABDC*.

But all parallelograms on the base *AB* and between the same parallels are equal in area.

Therefore the triangle *ABC* is half the area of any parallelogram on the base *AB* and between the parallels *AB* and *XCY*.

Area of a triangle

It follows that the area of a triangle is equal to half the product of its base and altitude.

In Fig. 119, the area of the triangle *ABC* may be expressed as

(i) $\frac{1}{2}BC \times AD$; (ii) $\frac{1}{2}AC \times BE$; (iii) $\frac{1}{2}AB \times CF$.

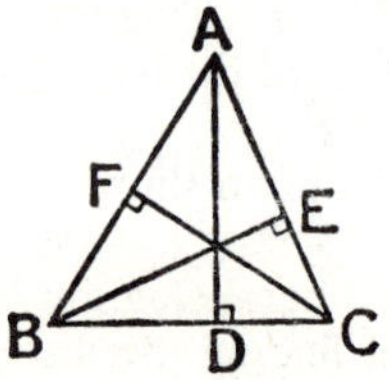

FIG. 119

Expressing the area of a triangle in two different ways gives a useful method of calculating the altitude of a triangle.

If, in Fig. 120, *ABC* is a triangle right angled at *B*, its area = $\frac{1}{2}AB \times BC$.

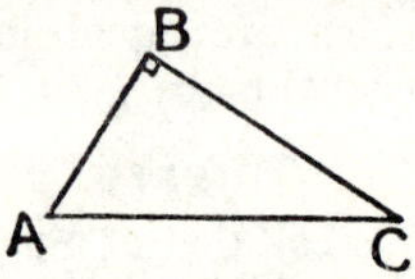

FIG. 120

The following properties follow:

(1) Triangles with equal bases and equal altitudes have equal areas.
(2) Triangles with equal areas and equal bases have equal altitudes.
(3) Triangles with equal areas and equal altitudes have equal bases.
(4) Triangles with equal bases have their areas proportional to their altitudes.
(5) Triangles with equal altitudes have their areas proportional to their bases.

Example. The triangle in which $AB = 3$ cm, $AC = 4$ cm and $BC = 5$ cm has the angle A a right angle. Calculate the length of the altitude through A.

The area of the triangle ABC is equal to $\frac{1}{2}AB \times AC$ (right-angled) or to $\frac{1}{2}BC \times AD$.

$$\therefore \tfrac{1}{2} \times 3 \times 4 = \tfrac{1}{2} \times 5 \times AD.$$

and $$AD = 2{\cdot}4 \text{ cm}.$$

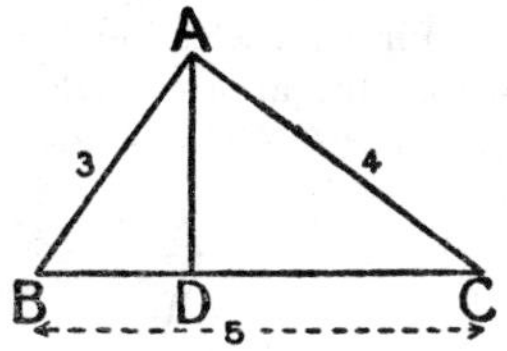

FIG. 121

Area of a trapezium

A quadrilateral with one pair of sides parallel is called a trapezium.

In Fig. 122, suppose that $AB = a$, and $DC = b$ and that the distance between AB and CD is h.

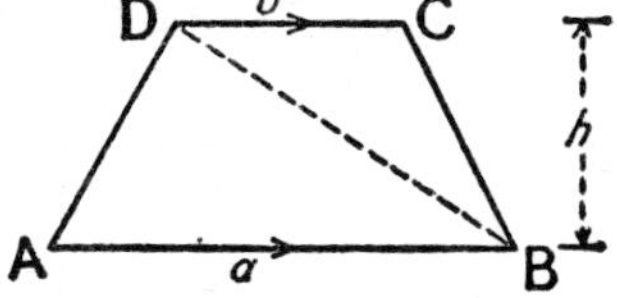

FIG. 122

The area of triangle ABD is $\frac{1}{2}ah$.
The area of triangle DCB is $\frac{1}{2}bh$.

The area of $ABCD$ is

$$\tfrac{1}{2}ah + \tfrac{1}{2}bh = \tfrac{1}{2}(a + b)h.$$

So the area of a trapezium is equal to one half the product of the sum of the parallel sides and the distance between them.

EXERCISES 79A

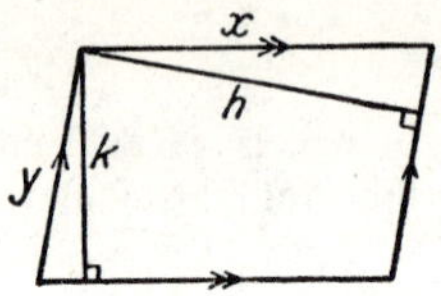

FIG. 123

1. From Fig. 123: (i) Find the area of the parallelogram when $x = 4$ cm, $k = 2$ cm. (ii) If the area is 10 cm², and $h = 2\frac{1}{2}$ cm, find y. (iii) If $x = 3$, $k = 2$ and $y = 4$, find h.

2. From Fig. 124: (i) Find an area of ABC given that $AD = 6$ cm, $BC = 4$ cm. (ii) Given that the area of ABC is 8 cm² and $CF = 4$ cm, find AB. (iii) Given that $AB = 6$, $CF = 4$ and $AC = 8$, find BE.

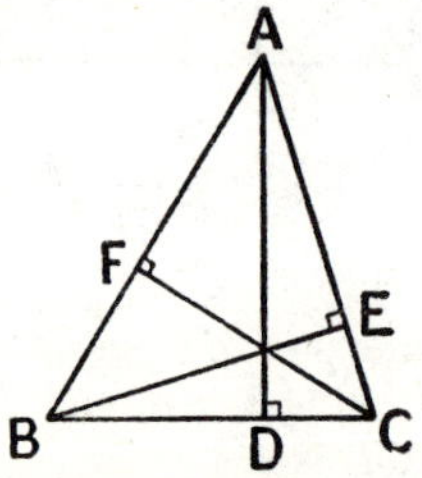

FIG. 124

3. What is the area of the trapezium shown in Fig. 125?

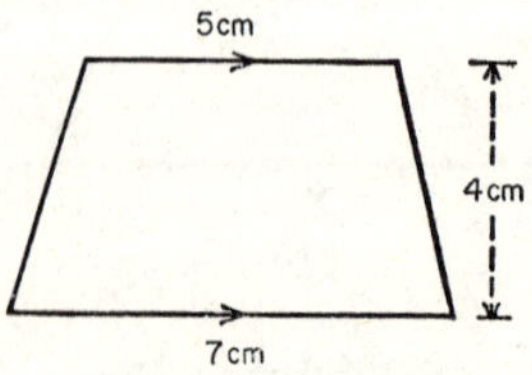

FIG. 125

4. The point D is taken on the side BC of a triangle ABC such that $BD = 2DC$. Prove that the area of the triangle ABD is twice that of the triangle ADC.

5. The diagonals of a trapezium $ABCD$, in which AB is parallel to DC, meet at O. Prove that the triangles AOD and BOC are equal in area.

6. $ABCD$ is a parallelogram and P is any point on DC. Prove that the area of the triangle APB is half that of the parallelogram.

7. $ABCD$ is a quadrilateral. The line through C parallel to DB meets AB produced at X. Prove that the area of the triangle ADX equals the area of the quadrilateral $ABCD$.

8. $ABCD$ is a parallelogram. Y is any point on AB produced. DY meets BC at X. Prove that the triangles ABX and CXY are equal in area.

9. $ABCD$ is a parallelogram and X is the mid point of BC. DX meets AC at Y. Prove that the area of ADY is twice that of DYC.

10. Prove that the area of a rhombus is equal to half the product of its diagonals.

EXERCISES 79B

1. In Fig. 126: (i) Find the area of the parallelogram if $y = 3$ cm, $h = 4$ cm. (ii) If the area of the parallelogram is 12 cm^2 and $x = 4$ cm, find k. (iii) If $x = 4$, $k = 3$, $h = 5$, find y.

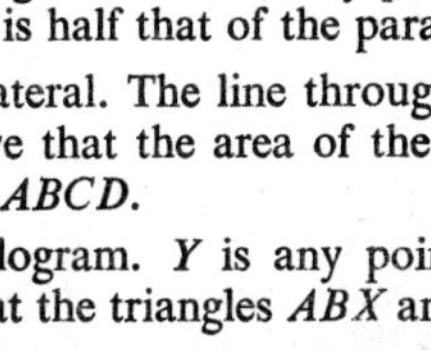

FIG. 126

2. In Fig. 127: (i) Find the area of the triangle ABC given that $AD = 5$ cm, $BC = 4$ cm. (ii) Given that the area of ABC is 12 cm^2 and $AC = 8$ cm, find BE. (iii) Given that $AB = 4$ cm, $CF = 6$ cm and $AD = 8$ cm, find BC.

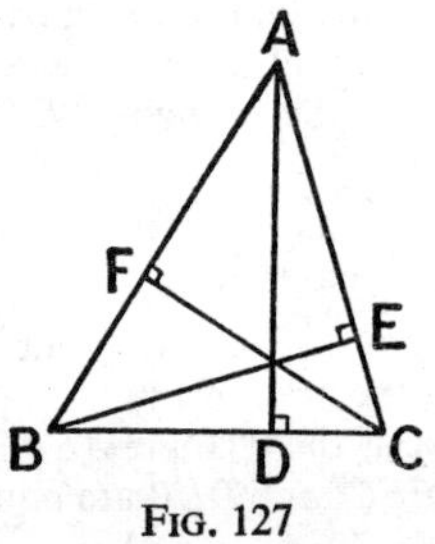

FIG. 127

3. Given that the area of the trapezium in Fig. 128 is 42 cm², find x.

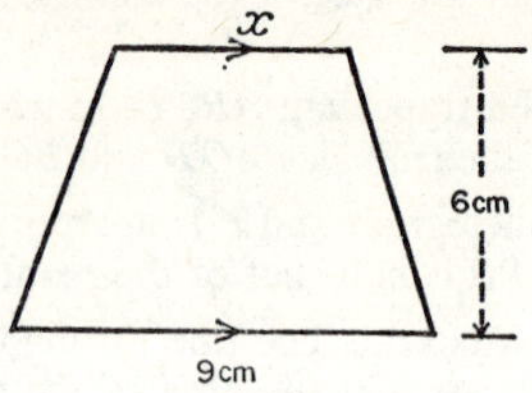

FIG. 128

4. A point X is taken on the diagonal AC of a parallelogram $ABCD$. Prove that the triangles AXB and AXD are equal in area.

5. E is the mid point of the side AB of a parallelogram $ABCD$. ED meets AC at X. Prove that the area of AEX is one-twelfth that of the parallelogram.

6. If L,M,N are respectively the mid points of the sides BC, CA, AB of the triangle ABC, prove that the area of ALN is one-quarter that of ABC.

7. $ABCD$ is a parallelogram. P is on BC and Q on DC, such that PQ is parallel to BD. Prove that the triangles PAB and DAQ are equal in area.

8. P is any point on the side AB of a parallelogram $ABCD$. Prove that provided P lies between A and B, the sum of the areas of ADP and PCB is constant.

9. If ABX and ABY are two triangles equal in area and X and Y are on the same side of AB, prove that XY is parallel to AB.

10. Any point P is taken inside the parallelogram $ABCD$. Prove that the sum of the areas of the triangles DPC and APB is half the area of the parallelogram.

EXERCISES 80: MISCELLANEOUS

1. The bisectors of the angles C and D of a parallelogram $ABCD$ meet at a point P which lies on AB. Prove that $AB = 2AD$.

2. If P is any point on the median AD of a triangle ABC, prove that the triangles APB and APC are equal in area. If the medians AD, BE of the triangle meet at G, prove that the triangles BGC, AGC, AGB are all equal in area.

3. Prove that if each diagonal of a quadrilateral bisects its area, the quadrilateral must be a parallelogram.

4. $ABCD$ is a parallelogram. E is any point on DC and AE, BC produced meet at P. Prove (i) the area of the triangle ADP is half that of the parallelogram; (ii) the area of the triangle AEB is half that of the parallelogram; (iii) the triangles BEC and DEP are equal in area.

5. $ABCD$ is a rectangle. P is the mid point of AB and Q is the mid point of BC. R is the point on CD such that $CR = 2RD$ and S the point on AD such that $DS = 2SA$. Prove that the area of the quadrilateral $PQRS$ is $\frac{37}{72}$ of the area of the rectangle.

6. The sides of a parallelogram are 3 cm and 2 cm and the distance between the two longer sides is $1\frac{1}{2}$ cm. Find the distance between the shorter sides.

7. Points P and Q are taken on the sides AB and DC respectively of a parallelogram $ABCD$ such that DP and BQ are parallel. Prove (i) $PBQD$ is a parallelogram; (ii) $AQ = CP$.

8. $ABCD$ is a parallelogram. X is a point on the side BC and Y is a point on the side DC, such that XY is parallel to BD. Prove that the triangles ABX and ADY are equal in area.

9. In the trapezium $ABCD$, AB is parallel to DC. The diagonals meet at O. Given that $DO = 2OB$, write down the ratios of the following areas: (i) $AOD : AOB$; (ii) $AOB : ACB$; (iii) $DOC : AOB$.

10. $ABCD$ is a parallelogram. Y is the mid point of CB and X any point on AB. XY and DC produced meet at Z. Prove that the quadrilateral $AXZD$ is equal in area to the parallelogram $ABCD$.

11. $ABCD$ is a parallelogram. The circle centre A, radius AD, cuts DC at a point P between D and C. Prove that the angles PAB and CBA are equal.

12. P is the mid point of the side BC of a triangle ABC. Through P are drawn two lines, one parallel to CA to meet BA at R, the other parallel to BA to meet CA at Q. Prove that RQ is parallel to BC and that the area of PQR is one-quarter that of ABC.

13. $ABCD$ is a parallelogram. E is the point on BA such that $BE = 2EA$; F is the point on DC such that $DF = 2FC$. Prove that $AECF$ is a parallelogram whose area is one-third that of $ABCD$.

14. The diagonals of a parallelogram $ABCD$ meet at O. Lines are drawn through A and B parallel to the diagonals to meet at X. Prove that the area of $AXBD$ is three-quarters that of the parallelogram.

15. $ABCD$ is a parallelogram whose diagonals meet at O. A line CY is drawn parallel to DB to meet AB produced at Y. Prove that the area of $OBYC$ is three-quarters that of the parallelogram.

16. XY is a line parallel to the base BC of a triangle ABC cutting AB at X and AC at Y. It is given that $AX : XB = 4 : 3$. Write down the ratios of the following areas:

(i) $AXY : BXY$; (ii) $AXY : XYC$.

Hence find the ratio of AY to YC.

17. *ABCD* is a trapezium with *AB* parallel to *DC*. A line parallel to *AC* cuts *AB* at *X* and *BC* at *Y*. Prove that the triangles *ADX* and *ACY* are equal in area.

18. *ABCD* is a parallelogram. *X* is the point on *AB* such that $AX = 2XB$. *Y* is the point on *BC* such that $BY = 2YC$. Find the ratio of the area of *AXYCD* to that of the parallelogram.

19. A quadrilateral *ABCD* is such that the diagonal *BD* bisects its area. Prove that *BD* also bisects *AC*.

20. *K* is any point inside the parallelogram *ABCD*. Prove that the area of *AKB* is less than half that of the parallelogram.

20

RATIO; SIMILAR TRIANGLES; PYTHAGORAS

RATIO

IF two lines are p cm and q cm long respectively, the ratio of their lengths is $p : q$ or p/q.

If two areas are z m^2 and y m^2, the ratio of their areas is $z : y$ or z/y.

The ratio of two quantities is possible only if the quantities are of the same kind—for example, it is not possible to express a length as a ratio of an area.

Proportion

The pairs of quantities a, b and x, y are said to be in proportion if $a : b = x : y$. y is called the fourth proportional of a, b and x.

Internal and external division

In Fig. 129, P divides AB internally in the ratio AP/PB.
In Fig. 130, P divides AB externally in the ratio AP/PB.

FIG. 129

FIG. 130

THEOREM

If a straight line be drawn parallel to one side of a triangle, the other two sides are divided porportionally.

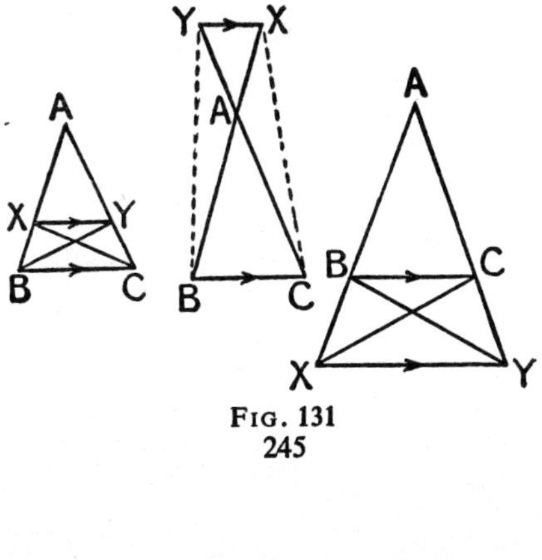

FIG. 131

Given XY parallel to BC, a side of the triangle ABC.
To prove $AX : XB = AY : YC$.
Construction: Join XC and YB.
Proof:

$$\frac{AX}{XB} = \frac{\triangle AXY}{\triangle BXY} \text{ (equal altitudes).}$$

But the triangles BXY and XYC are equal in area (base XY, parallels XY and BC).

$$\therefore \frac{AX}{XB} = \frac{\triangle AXY}{\triangle XYC}.$$

Since $$\frac{\triangle AXY}{\triangle XYC} = \frac{AY}{YC} \text{ (equal altitudes),}$$

$$\frac{AX}{XB} = \frac{AY}{YC}.$$

N.B. It follows that any ratio of the three quantities AX, XB, AB is equal to the corresponding ratio of the quantities AY, YC, AC. For example,

$$\frac{AX}{AB} = \frac{AY}{AC} \text{ and } \frac{XB}{AB} = \frac{YC}{AC}.$$

The converse theorem is also true and the proof is now given.

THEOREM

A straight line which cuts two sides of a triangle proportionally is parallel to the third side.

Given $\frac{AX}{XB} = \frac{AY}{YC}$.

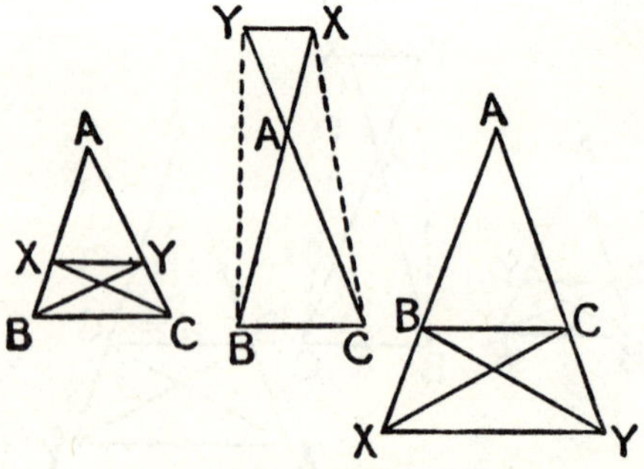

FIG. 132

To prove that XY is parallel to BC.
Construction: Join XC and YB.
Proof:

$$\frac{AX}{XB} = \frac{\triangle AXY}{\triangle BXY} \text{ (equal altitudes)}$$

and
$$\frac{AY}{YC} = \frac{\triangle AXY}{\triangle CXY} \text{ (equal altitudes).}$$

Therefore, since $\frac{AX}{XB} = \frac{AY}{YC}$ (given),

$$\frac{\triangle AXY}{\triangle BXY} = \frac{\triangle AXY}{\triangle CXY}.$$

$$\therefore \triangle BXY = \triangle CXY \text{ in area.}$$

Since these triangles have a common base XY and lie on the same side of XY, XY is parallel to BC.

EXERCISES 81A

1. Find x, y and z given that (i) $3:5 = 2:x$; (ii) $4:y = y:9$; (iii) £z : 40p = £3 : 20p.

2. A line AB, 6·4 cm long, is divided internally at P in the ratio $5:3$. Find AP.

3. A line AB is 6·4 cm long and P divides AB externally in the ratio $5:3$. Find BP.

4. A line AB, 14 cm long, is divided internally at P in the ratio $4:3$ and externally at Q in the ratio $9:2$. Find PQ.

5. The line HK is parallel to the base BC of a triangle ABC. If $AH:HB = 4:3$, find the ratio $KC:AC$.

6. AB, CD, EF are parallel straight lines which are cut by two transversals at P, Q, R and at X, Y, Z. Prove that $PQ:QR = XY:YZ$.

7. $ABCD$ is a trapezium with AB parallel to DC and O is the intersection of its diagonals. If $DO:OB = 2:3$, write down the ratios (i) $OC:OA$, (ii) $\triangle DOC : \triangle AOD$, (iii) $\triangle DOC : \triangle AOB$.

8. In the triangle ABC, X is on AB, Y is on AC and XY is parallel to BC. By drawing through Y a line parallel to AB, prove that $AX:AB = XY:BC$.

9. In Fig. 133, AC is parallel to BD and CX is parallel to DY. Prove that AX is parallel to BY.

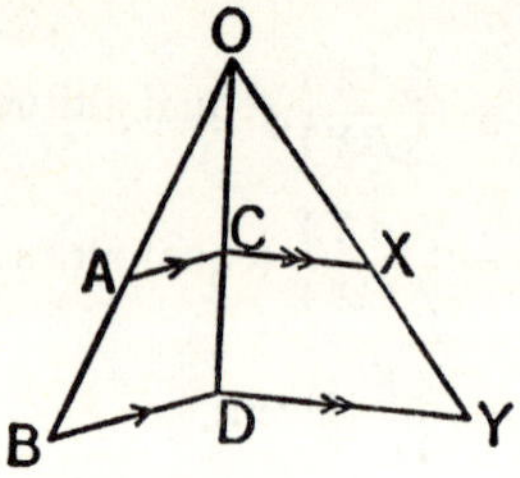

FIG. 133

10. The point X is taken on the diagonal AC of the parallelogram $ABCD$ such that $AX : XC = 2 : 3$. Prove that the area of the triangle ABX is one-fifth that of the parallelogram.

EXERCISES 81B

1. Find x, y, z given that (i) $4:7 = x:3$; (ii) $4:y = y:16$, (iii) z kg: 2 grammes = £1 : 4p.

2. A line AB is 6·6 cm long and P divides AB internally in the ratio 7 : 4. Find AP.

3. A line AB is 6·6 cm long and Q divides AB externally in the ratio 7 : 4. Find BQ.

4. A line AB, 7·7 cm long, is divided internally at P in the ratio 5 : 2 and externally at Q in the ratio 11 : 4. Find PQ.

5. The line HK is parallel to the base BC of a triangle ABC. If $AH : HB = 2 : 5$, find $KC : AC$.

6. The line through the corner A of the parallelogram $ABCD$ cuts BC at X and DC produced at Y. Prove that $AX : AY = AB : DY$.

7. $ABCD$ is a trapezium with AB parallel to DC and O is the intersection of its diagonals. If $DO : OB = 3 : 4$, write down the ratios (i) $OC : OA$, (ii) $\triangle DOC : \triangle AOD$, (iii) $\triangle DOC : \triangle AOB$.

8. In the triangle ABC, X is on AB, Y is on AC and XY is parallel to BC. If $AX : XB = 2 : 5$, find $XY : BC$.

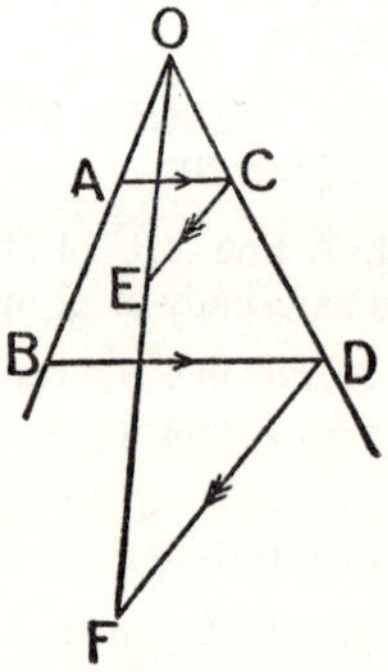

FIG. 134

9. In Fig. 134, AC is parallel to BD and CE is parallel to DF. Prove that AE is parallel to BF.

10. The point X is taken on the diagonal AC of a parallelogram $ABCD$ such that $AX : XC = 3 : 5$. Prove that the area of the triangle ABX is $\frac{3}{16}$ of the area of the parallelogram.

The angle bisector theorems

THEOREM

The internal bisector of an angle of a triangle divides the opposite side internally in the ratio of the sides containing the angle, and likewise the external bisector externally.

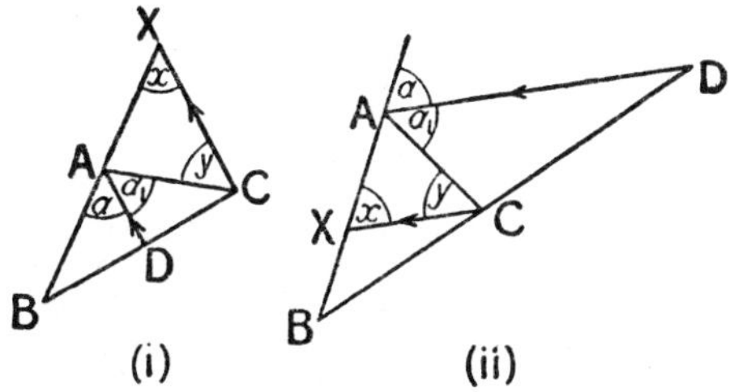

FIG. 135

Given ABC is a triangle. AD bisects the angle A internally in Fig. 135 (i), externally in Fig. 135 (ii).

To prove $\dfrac{BD}{DC} = \dfrac{BA}{AC}$.

Construction: Through C draw a line parallel to DA to meet BA or BA produced at X.

Proof:

$$a = x \text{ (corresponding; } AD \parallel XC\text{)},$$
$$a_1 = y \text{ (alt.; } AD \parallel XC\text{)}.$$

Since $a = a_1$ (given),

$$x = y.$$
$$\therefore AX = AC \text{ (isosceles triangle)}.$$

We know that $\dfrac{BD}{DC} = \dfrac{BA}{AX}$ $(AD \parallel XC)$.

$$\therefore \frac{BD}{DC} = \frac{BA}{AC}.$$

The converse of this theorem is also true.

THEOREM

If a line through a vertex of a triangle divides the base internally or externally in the ratio of the sides containing the vertex, then this line bisects the vertical angle internally or externally.

The proof is left as an exercise.

In Fig. 136, if $$\frac{BD}{DC} = \frac{BA}{AC},$$

then $$B\widehat{A}D = D\widehat{A}C.$$

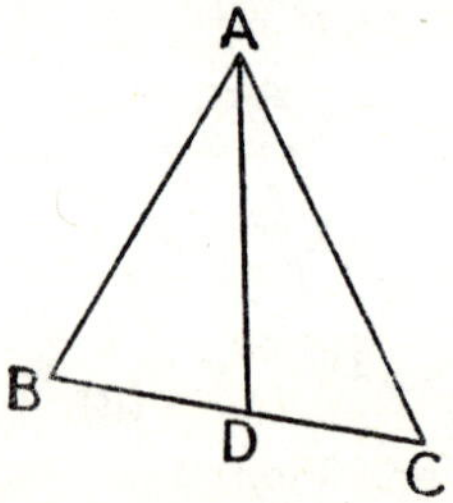

FIG. 136

In Fig. 137, if $$\frac{BD}{DC} = \frac{BA}{AC},$$

then $$C\widehat{A}D = D\widehat{A}X.$$

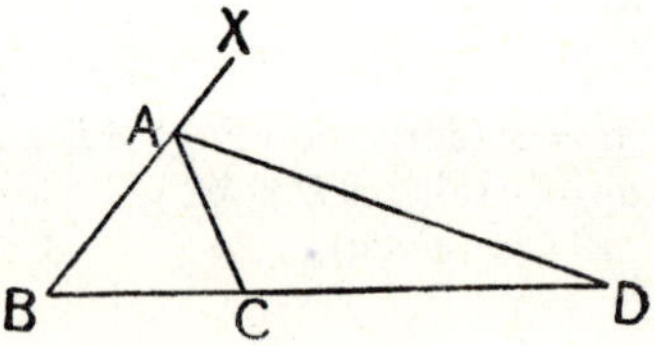

FIG. 137

EXERCISES 82A

1. The internal bisector of the angle A of a triangle ABC meets BC at D. If $AB = 7$ cm, $AC = 8$ cm and $BC = 9$ cm, calculate BD.

2. The external bisector of the angle A of a triangle ABC meets BC at X. If $AB = 5$ cm, $AC = 8$ cm, $BC = 6$ cm, calculate BX.

3. D is a point on the side BC of a triangle ABC. Given that $AB = 4$ cm, $AC = 6$ cm, $BD = 2$ cm, $BC = 5$ cm, prove that AD bisects the angle BAC.

4. The internal bisector of the angle A of a triangle meets BC at D; the external bisector meets CB produced at E. If $AB = 4$ cm, $AC = 6$ cm and $BC = 7$ cm, calculate DE.

5. The internal bisector of the angle A of a triangle ABC meets BC at D. Given that $AB : AC = 3 : 4$, find the ratio of the area of the triangle ABD to that of ABC.

6. If AX is a median of the triangle ABC and the internal bisectors of the angles AXB, AXC meet AB, AC respectively at P, Q, prove that PQ is parallel to BC.

7. ABC is an equilateral triangle. The internal bisector of the angle B meets the median AD at G. Prove that G is a point of trisection of AD.

8. In the quadrilateral $ABCD$, it is given that the internal bisectors of the angles B and D meet on AC. Prove that the internal bisectors of the angles A and C meet on DB.

9. D is a point on the side AB of the triangle ABC. It is given that $AB = 4$ cm, $BC = 4$ cm and $BD = 2$ cm. A line through D parallel to BC meets AC at E. Prove that BE bisects the angle B.

10. The bisectors of the angle A of the triangle ABC meet BC and BC produced at X and Y. If F is the mid point of XY, prove that $FA = FX$.

EXERCISES 82B

1. The internal bisector of the angle A of a triangle ABC meets BC at D. If $AB = 8$ cm, $AC = 6$ cm, $BC = 5$ cm, calculate BD.

2. The external bisector of the angle A of a triangle ABC meets BC produced at X. If $AB = 8$ cm, $AC = 6$ cm, $BC = 5$ cm, calculate CX.

3. D is a point on the side BC produced of a triangle ABC. If $AB = 6$ cm, $AC = 4$ cm, $BC = 3$ cm and $CD = 6$ cm, prove that AC is the external bisector of the angle A.

4. The internal bisector of the angle B of the triangle ABC meets AC at D and the external bisector meets AC produced at E. If $BA = 5$ cm, $BC = 3$ cm and $AC = 6$ cm, calculate DE.

5. The external bisector of the angle A of the triangle ABC meets BC produced at X. If $AB = 4$ cm, $AC = 3$ cm, find the ratio of the area of the triangle ACX to that of ABC.

6. ABC is a triangle in which $AB = 5$ cm, $BC = 3$ cm. D and E are points on the sides AB, AC such that DE is parallel to BC. If BE is the internal bisector of the angle B, calculate the length of BD.

7. In the triangle ABC, $AB : AC = 2 : 1$. The internal and external bisectors of the angle A meet BC and BC produced at D and E. Prove that $DE = \frac{4}{3}BC$.

8. $ABCD$ is a rectangle in which $AB = 2AD$. Prove that the bisectors of the angles A and C pass through the points of trisection of BD.

9. ABC is a triangle in which $AB > AC$. If the internal bisector of the angle A meets BC at D, prove that $BD > DC$.

10. If the diagonals of a quadrilateral bisect the angles of the quadrilateral, prove that the quadrilateral must be a rhombus.

SIMILAR TRIANGLES

Similar figures

Similar figures are figures which are the same shape. Photographically, one is an enlargement of the other.

Two polygons are similar if

(i) the angles of one are respectively equal to the angles of the other;

(ii) the ratio of any pair of sides of the first polygon is equal to the ratio of the corresponding sides of the other.

N.B. Note that the angles of one polygon being equal to the angles of the second polygon is not sufficient to prove the polygons similar. Consider a square and a rectangle which are obviously not similar.

Two triangles, however, must be similar if their angles are equal, each to each. This is one of three theorems dealing with similar triangles which are now quoted.

Theorem

If two triangles are equiangular, their corresponding sides are proportional.

Theorem

If two triangles have their corresponding sides proportional, they are equiangular.

Theorem

If two triangles have one angle of the one equal to one angle of the other, and the sides about these equal angles are proportional, the triangles are similar.

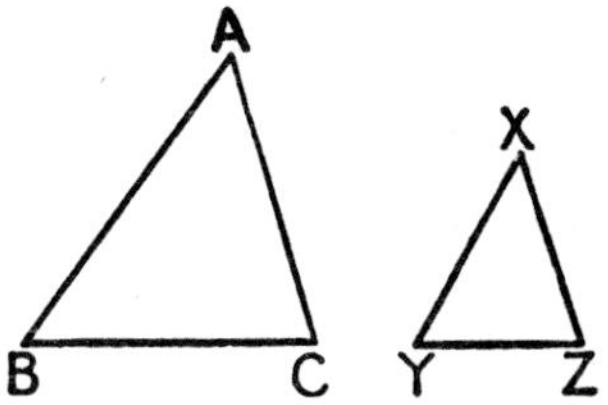

FIG. 138

To prove the triangles *ABC*, *XYZ* in Fig. 138 similar, it is necessary and sufficient to prove any one of the following:

(i) $\hat{A} = \hat{X}$ and $\hat{B} = \hat{Y}$ (it follows that $\hat{C} = \hat{Z}$).

(ii) $\dfrac{AB}{XY} = \dfrac{AC}{XZ} = \dfrac{BC}{YZ}$.

(iii) $\hat{A} = \hat{X}$ and $\dfrac{AB}{AC} = \dfrac{XY}{XZ}$.

Conversely, if the two triangles are given similar, write the two triangles with the equal angles under each other—$\left.\begin{matrix}ABC\\XYZ\end{matrix}\right\}$. Then the equations connecting the lengths of the sides may be obtained by writing down the sides of the first triangle and writing underneath the corresponding letters of the second triangle.

This gives $$\frac{AB}{XY} = \frac{BC}{YZ} = \frac{AC}{XZ}.$$

THEOREM

If a perpendicular be drawn from the right angle of a right-angled triangle to the hypotenuse, the triangles on each side of the perpendicular are similar to the whole triangle and to each other.

Given a triangle *ABC* with *B* a right angle. *BD* is perpendicular to *AC*.

To prove the triangles *ADB*, *ABC*, *BDC* similar.

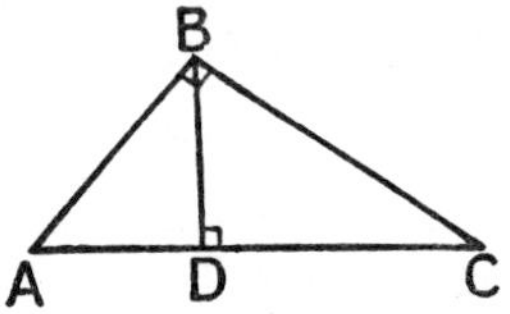

FIG. 139

Proof: In the triangles ADB and ABC,

$$\hat{A} \text{ is common.}$$

and $$A\hat{D}B = A\hat{B}C \text{ (right angles).}$$

$\therefore$ ADB and ABC are similar in that order.
In the triangles CDB and CBA,

$$\hat{C} \text{ is common,}$$

and $$C\hat{D}B = C\hat{B}A \text{ (right angles).}$$

$\therefore$ CDB and CBA are similar in that order.
Therefore ADB, ABC, BDC are all similar in that order.

Corollaries

Since ADB and ABC are similar,

$$\frac{AD}{AB} = \frac{AB}{AC}$$

$$\therefore AB^2 = AD.AC \quad . \quad . \quad . \quad . \quad \text{(i)}$$

Since ABC and BDC are similar,

$$\frac{BC}{DC} = \frac{AC}{BC}$$

$$\therefore BC^2 = AC.DC \quad . \quad . \quad . \quad . \quad \text{(ii)}$$

Since ADB and BDC are similar,

$$\frac{AD}{BD} = \frac{DB}{DC}$$

$$\therefore BD^2 = AD.DC \quad . \quad . \quad . \quad . \quad \text{(iii)}$$

These are three useful properties of a right-angled triangle, the first two of which are used in proving the theorem of Pythagoras.

PYTHAGORAS

Theorem of Pythagoras

In a right-angled triangle, the square described on the hypotenuse is equal to the sum of the squares described on the sides containing the right angle.

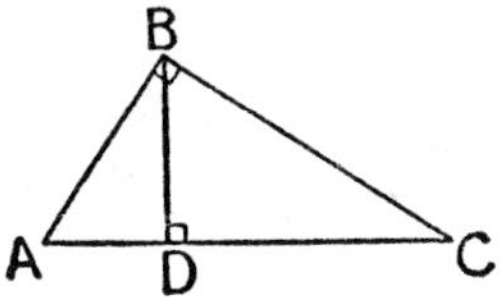

FIG. 140

Given a triangle ABC with B a right angle.
To prove $AC^2 = AB^2 + BC^2$.
Construction: Draw BD perpendicular to AC.
Proof: Since ADB, ABC, BDC are all similar,

$$AB^2 = AD.AC \text{ (already proved).}$$

and

$$BC^2 = AC.DC \text{ (already proved).}$$

By addition,

$$\begin{aligned} AB^2 + BC^2 &= AD.AC + AC.DC \\ &= AC(AD + DC) \\ &= AC(AC) \quad \text{or} \quad AC^2. \end{aligned}$$

The converse of Pythagoras' theorem is also true.

THEOREM

If the square on one side of a triangle is equal to the sum of the squares on the other two sides, the angle included by these two sides is a right angle.

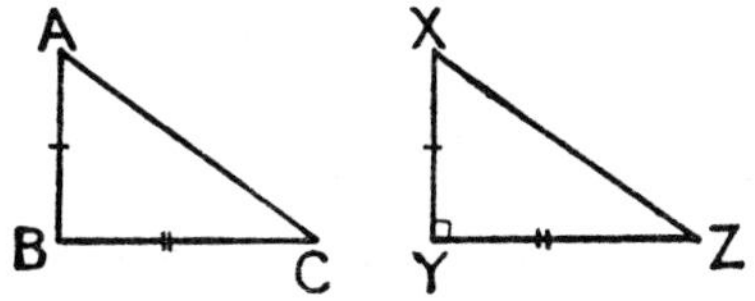

FIG. 141

Given a triangle ABC with $AC^2 = AB^2 + BC^2$.
To prove that the angle B is a right angle.
Construction: Draw another triangle XYZ in which $XY = AB$, $YZ = BC$ and the angle $Y = 90°$.
Proof: Since $AC^2 = AB^2 + BC^2$ (given)

and $AB = XY$, $BC = YZ$,

$$\begin{aligned} AC^2 &= XY^2 + YZ^2 \\ &= XZ^2 \text{ (Pythagoras).} \end{aligned}$$

$$\therefore AC = XZ.$$

In the triangles ABC, XYZ

$$\begin{cases} AB = XY \text{ (construction)}, \\ BC = YZ \text{ (,,)}, \\ AC = XZ \text{ (proved)}. \end{cases}$$

$$\therefore \triangle ABC \equiv \triangle XYZ.$$

In particular, $\hat{B} = \hat{Y}$.

There the angle B is a right angle.

EXERCISES 83A (Pythagoras)

1. What is the length of the hypotenuse of a right-angled triangle if the other two sides are 5 cm and 12 cm long?

2. The sides of a rectangle are 8 cm and 6 cm long. What is the length of the diagonal?

3. The diagonals of a rhombus are 8 cm and 6 cm long. What is the side of the rhombus?

4. Calculate the length of the altitude of an isosceles triangle whose base is 10 cm long and whose equal sides are 13 cm long.

5. Is the triangle whose sides are 17 cm, 15 cm and 8 cm long right-angled?

6. The altitude AD of a triangle ABC is 12 cm long. If $BD = 8$ cm, $DC = 18$ cm, prove that the angle BAC is a right angle.

7. AD is an altitude of the triangle ABC. Prove that $BA^2 - CA^2 = BD^2 - CD^2$.

8. The side of an equilateral triangle is a units. The length of an altitude is x units. Prove that $4x^2 = 3a^2$.

9. The angle B of a triangle ABC is a right angle. AD is a median of the triangle. Prove that $AD^2 = AC^2 - \frac{3}{4}BC^2$.

10. In the triangle ABC, the angle $B = 90°$. The internal bisector of the angle B meets AC at D. Given that $AB = 3$ cm, $BC = 4$ cm, find AD.

EXERCISES 83B

1. If the hypotenuse of a right-angled triangle is 37 cm long and a second side is 35 cm long, find the length of the third side.

2. The diagonals of a square $ABCD$ meet at O. Prove that $AB^2 = 2AO^2$.

3. The triangle ABC has a right angle at B and $AB = 5$ cm, $BC = 12$ cm. If BD is an altitude find AD and DC.

4. Is the triangle whose sides are 53 cm, 45 cm and 24 cm right-angled?

5. ABC is a triangle in which the angle B is 60° and the angle C is 30°. Prove that $BC = 2AB$.

6. ABC is an isosceles triangle in which $AB = AC = 2BC$. AD is an altitude. Prove that $4AD^2 = 15BC^2$.

7. Calculate the length of BC in Fig. 142.

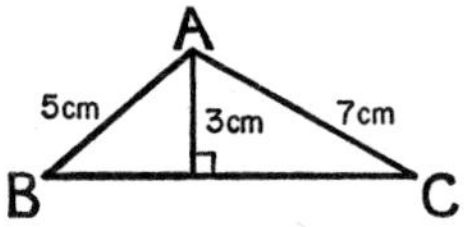

FIG. 142

8. If X is a point inside the rectangle $ABCD$, prove that $XA^2 + XC^2 = XB^2 + XD^2$.

9. ABC is a triangle in which $AB = BC$ and the angle $ABC = 120°$. Prove that $AC^2 = 3AB^2$.

10. Calculate the length of the diagonal of a rectangular box whose edges are 3 cm, 5 cm and 8 cm.

Areas of similar triangles

There is one theorem about the areas of similar triangles which is now proved.

THEOREM

The ratio of the areas of similar triangles is equal to the ratio of the squares on corresponding sides.

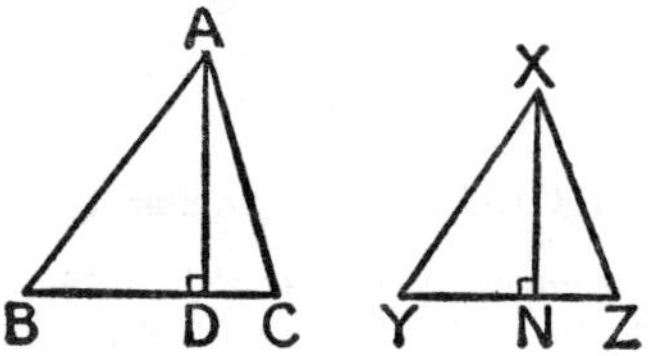

FIG. 143

Given two similar triangles ABC and XYZ.

To prove that $\dfrac{\triangle ABC}{\triangle XYZ} = \dfrac{BC^2}{YZ^2}$.

Construction: Draw the altitudes AD, XN of the two triangles.

Proof: The area of $ABC = \frac{1}{2}AD \cdot BC$.
The area of $XYZ = \frac{1}{2}XN \cdot YZ$.

In triangles ABD and XYN,

$$A\hat{B}D = X\hat{Y}N \text{ (given)},$$

$$A\hat{D}B = X\hat{N}Y \text{ (right angles)}.$$

Therefore the triangles ABD and XYN are similar, and

$$\frac{AD}{XN} = \frac{AB}{XY}$$

$$= \frac{BC}{YZ} \text{ (}ABC\text{ and }XYZ\text{ similar)}.$$

$$\therefore \frac{\triangle ABC}{\triangle XYZ} = \frac{\frac{1}{2}AD.BC}{\frac{1}{2}XN.YZ}$$

$$= \frac{AD}{XN}.\frac{BC}{YZ}$$

$$= \frac{BC}{YZ}.\frac{BC}{YZ} \text{ (already proved)},$$

$$= \frac{BC^2}{YZ^2}.$$

The areas of any similar figures are also in the ratio of the squares on corresponding linear dimensions; the volumes of similar solids are in the ratio of the cubes of the corresponding linear dimensions.

For example, if two bottles are such that any linear dimension of one is twice the corresponding length for the other, the surface area of one bottle is four times the surface area of the other and the capacity of the first bottle is eight times that of the second.

EXERCISES 84A (Similar Triangles)

1. $ABCD$ is a trapezium with AB parallel to DC. The diagonals meet at X. Prove that the triangles DXC and BXA are similar and that $\triangle DXC : \triangle AXB = DC^2 : AB^2$.

2. The sides of a triangle are 8 cm, 7 cm and 6 cm long. The shortest side of a similar triangle is 2 cm long. Find the other sides and the ratio of the two areas.

3. In the triangle ABC, D and E are points on AB, AC respectively such that DE is parallel to BC. Prove that (i) the triangles ADE and ABC are similar; (ii) $\frac{BC}{DE} = \frac{AB}{AD}$; (iii) $\frac{\triangle ABC}{\triangle ADE} = \frac{BC^2}{DE^2}$.

4. The triangles OAB and OCD are similar in that order. Prove that OAC and OBD are similar.

5. ABC is a triangle right-angled at A. AD is an altitude. Prove that $\frac{\triangle ABD}{\triangle ACD} = \frac{AB^2}{AC^2}$.

6. The medians BD, CE of a triangle ABC meet at G. Prove that the triangles EGD and CGB are similar. Hence prove that $CG = 2GE$.

7. Using the notation of question **6**, prove that $\triangle EGD : \triangle ABC = 1 : 12$.

8. Y is a point on the side BC produced of a parallelogram $ABCD$. AY meets DC at X. Prove that $AY : AX = BY : AD$.

9. The lines AOB, COD meet at O. DB is parallel to AC and $DO : OC = 3 : 2$. Write down the ratios (i) $\triangle DOB : \triangle AOC$; (ii) $\triangle DOA : \triangle BOC$.

10. The altitudes BN, CM of a triangle ABC meet at H. Prove that $CH.HM = BH.HN$.

EXERCISES 84B

1. D and E are points on the sides AB, AC respectively of a triangle ABC such that $AD : DB = 2 : 3$ and $AE : EC = 2 : 3$. Find the ratio of the area of the triangle ADE to that of the triangle ABC.

2. The sides of a triangle are 9 cm, 7 cm and 6 cm long. The longest side of a similar triangle is 6 cm. Find the lengths of the other sides and the ratio of the two areas.

3. In the trapezium $ABCD$, AB is parallel to DC and $AB = 2DC$. Given that $DA = 3$ cm and that BC = 4 cm and that AD, BC produced meet at E, find (i) the length of ED; (ii) $\triangle EDC$: the trapezium $ABCD$.

4. In Fig. 144, AB, NX and CD are parallel. If $AB = 3$ cm, $CD = 5$ cm, calculate NX.

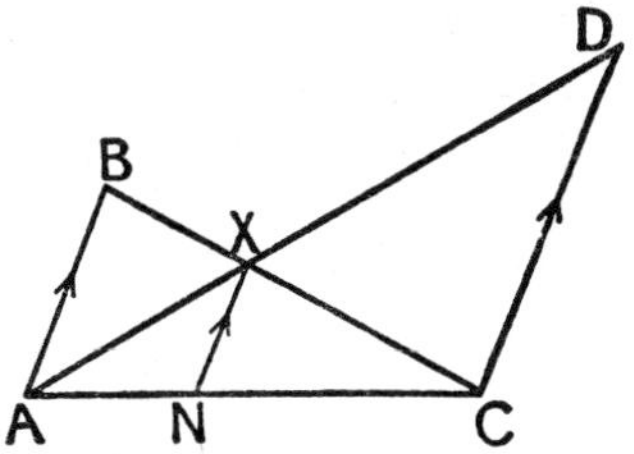

FIG. 144

5. A cone is of height 8 m and of base radius 4 m. Find the radius of the circular section cut from the cone by a plane parallel to the base and 2 m from it.

6. *ABC* is a triangle. *X* is the point of trisection of *BA* nearer *B* and *Y* is the point of trisection of *CA* nearer *C*. Given that *XC*, *YB* meet at *Z*, find $\triangle XYZ : \triangle ABC$.

7. The triangle *ABC* is right-angled at *A* and *AD* is an altitude. Prove that $AB.AD = BD.AC$.

8. The internal bisectors of the angles *B* and *C* of a triangle *ABC* meet the opposite sides at *D* and *E*. If *DE* is parallel to *CB*, prove that $AB = AC$.

9. In the parallelogram *ABCD*, *X* is the mid point of *AB* and *Q* is the mid point of *CD*. The point *P* divides the side *CB* in the ratio 1 : 2, the point *Y* divides the side *AD* in the ratio 1 : 2. Prove that the triangles *AXY*, *CQP* are similar. Find the ratio of the area of the hexagon *XBPQDY* to that of the parallelogram.

10. A line is drawn through *D*, the mid point of the side *BC* of a triangle *ABC*, to meet *BA* at *P*, *CA* produced at *Q* and the parallel to *AB* through *C* at *K*. If $AB = AC$, prove that $\frac{AP}{PB} = \frac{QP}{QK}$.

EXERCISES 85: Miscellaneous

1. *ABCD* is a quadrilateral and *X* is any point on the side *AD*. *P* is the point of trisection of *AX* nearer *A* and *Q* the point of trisection of *DX* nearer *D*. The line through *P* parallel to *AB* meets *BX* at *Y*; the line through *Q* parallel to *DC* meets *XC* at *Z*. Prove that *YZ* is parallel to *BC*.

2. The quadrilateral *ABCD* has the angles at *D* and *B* right angles, and the diagonals *AC*, *BD* are perpendicular. Prove that $DC = BC$.

3. In the triangle *ABC*, $AB = 6$ cm and $AC = 2$ cm. If the angle $A = 60°$, calculate the length of *BC*. If the internal bisector of the angle *A* meets *BC* at *D*, calculate the length of *BD*.

4. In the triangle *ABC*, $AB = x$, $AC = y$ and the angle $A = 60°$. Calculate the length of *BC* in terms of *x* and *y*.

5. *AD* is a median of the triangle *ABC*. The internal bisector of *ADB* meets *AB* at *X*; the internal bisector of *ADC* meets *AC* at *Y*. *XY* meets *AD* at *Z*. Prove that *Z* is the mid point of *XY*.

6. *ABC* is a triangle in which the angle $A = 90°$ and *AD* is perpendicular to *BC*. Prove that $\frac{BD}{BC} = \frac{AB^2}{BC^2}$.

7. *ABCD* is a rectangle. *DP* is the perpendicular from *D* to *AC*. Prove that $AD^2 = AP.AC$.

8. *AD*, *BE*, *CF* are the altitudes of a triangle *ABC*. Prove that $BD^2 + EC^2 + AF^2 = DC^2 + EA^2 + FB^2$. (You may assume that the altitudes meet in a point.)

9. P and Q are the points of trisection of the side BC of the triangle ABC. PX is drawn parallel to CA to meet AB at X; QY is drawn parallel to BA to meet AC at Y. Prove that XY is parallel to BC.

10. The internal bisector of the angle A of the triangle ABC meets BC at D. Through D are drawn lines parallel to CA, BA to meet BA, AC respectively at X and Y. Prove that the ratio of the parallelogram $DYAX$ to the triangle ABC is $2bc : (b + c)^2$, where b and c are the lengths of AC and AB.

11. The internal bisector of the angle A of the triangle ABC meets BC at D. The circle, centre C and radius CD, meets AD at X. Prove that $AB.AX = AC.AD$.

12. $ABCD$ is a trapezium with AB parallel to DC. It is given that the angles DAC and ABC are equal. Prove that $CA.BC = AB.AD$.

13. The bisector of the angle B of the triangle ABC, right-angled at A, meets the altitude AD at X and the side AC at Y. Prove that $AX.AY = XD.CY$.

14. L, M, N, P are respectively the points of trisection of the sides AB, BC, CD, DA of the quadrilateral $ABCD$. L and M are the points of trisection nearer B, N and P the points of trisection nearer D. Prove that $LMNP$ is a parallelogram whose area is four-ninths that of $ABCD$.

15. ABC, AXY are two similar triangles with a common vertex A. Prove that the angles ABX and ACY are equal.

16. The diagonals of a quadrilateral are perpendicular. Prove that the sum of the squares on two opposite sides is equal to the sum of the squares on the other two sides.

17. The bisector of the angle A of the triangle ABC meets the median BD at X. Prove that $BX.AC = 2BA.XD$.

18. BD is an altitude of the triangle ABC. Prove that $AC(AD - DC) = AB^2 - BC^2$.

19. $ABCD$ is a trapezium with AB parallel to DC. The diagonals AC, BD meet at X. Prove that the areas of the triangles AXB and DXC are in the ratio $AB^2 : DC^2$.

20. ABC is a triangle and AD an altitude. If $CD^2 - DB^2 = \frac{1}{2}CB^2$, prove that $CD : CB = 3 : 4$.

21

LOCUS; EXTENSIONS OF PYTHAGORAS; APOLLONIUS

LOCUS

A CURVE is said to be the *locus* of a moving point if, when the point satisfies certain given conditions, it lies on the curve and conversely, if when the point is on the curve, it satisfies those certain given conditions.

The locus here defined applies only to a point moving in a plane. If the point moves in space, the locus will, in general, be a surface.

Example 1. A point P moves in a plane so that it is always 3 cm from a fixed point O in the plane.

The locus of P is a circle centre O and radius 3 cm.

(i) Any point satisfying the conditions must lie on this circle.

(ii) Any point on this circle does satisfy the conditions.

Example 2. ABC is a triangle. Its base AB is fixed and is 2 cm long. Given that the area of the triangle ABC is 3 cm², find the locus of C.

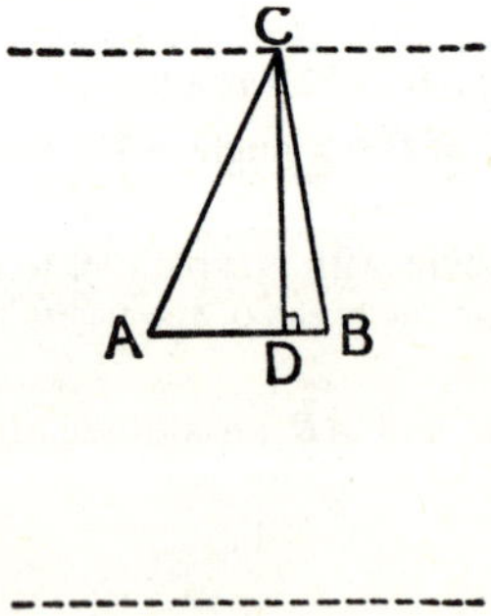

FIG. 145

(i) If ABC is a triangle of area 3 cm² and $AB = 2$ cm, the altitude CD must equal 3 cm.

The point C therefore moves so that it is always 3 cm from the fixed line AB.

C must lie on one or other of two parallel straight lines, each 3 cm from AB.

(ii) A point on either of these parallel lines is 3 cm from AB and the area of the triangle formed by joining the points to AB is 3 cm². The locus of C is two parallel straight lines.

Intersection of loci

The position or positions of a point may often be found as the intersection of two loci.

Example. A triangle ABC has a fixed base AB, 2 cm long, and its area is 3 cm². Given that $AC = 4$ cm, find the possible positions of the point C.

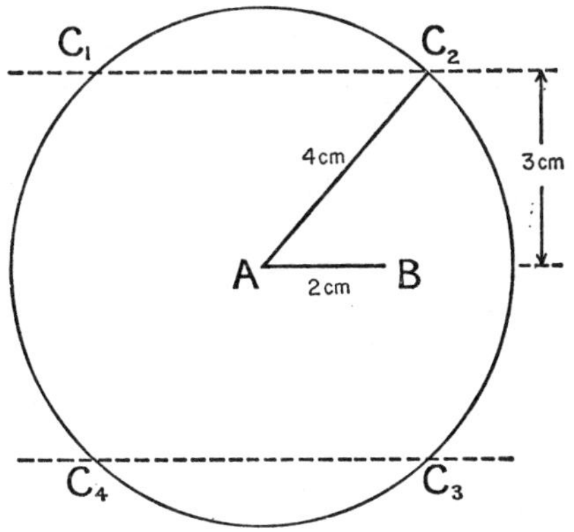

FIG. 146

The locus of the point which moves so that the area of triangle ABC is constant, is two parallel straight lines.

The locus of the point which moves so that $AC = 4$ cm is the circle, centre A, radius 4 cm.

There are, therefore, 4 possible positions of the point C. These are the points of intersection of the circle and the two parallel straight lines.

THEOREM

The locus of a point which is equidistant from two fixed points is the perpendicular bisector of the straight line joining the two fixed points.

The proof is divided into two parts.

(i) *A point equidistant from two given points lies on the perpendicular bisector of the line joining the two points.*

Given two points A and B and another point P such that $PA = PB$.
To prove that P lies on the perpendicular bisector of AB.
Construction: Join P to X, the mid point of AB.

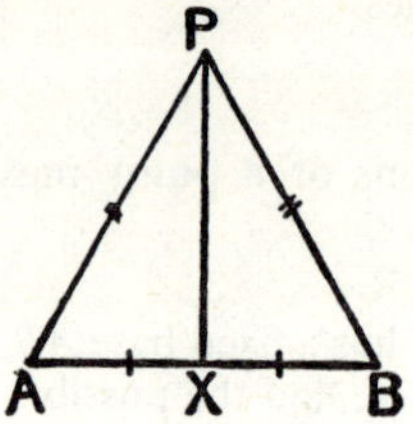

FIG. 147

Proof: In the triangles APX, BPX,

$$\begin{cases} PX = PX \text{ (common)}, \\ AP = PB \text{ (given)}, \\ AX = XB \text{ (construction)}. \end{cases}$$

$$\therefore \triangle APX \equiv \triangle BPX \text{ (SSS)}.$$

In particular, the angles PXA and PXB are equal.
Since the sum of these angles is 180°, each must be 90°.
Therefore PX is perpendicular to AB and P lies on the perpendicular bisector of AB.

(ii) *Any point on the perpendicular bisector of a straight line joining two given points is equidistant from these points.*

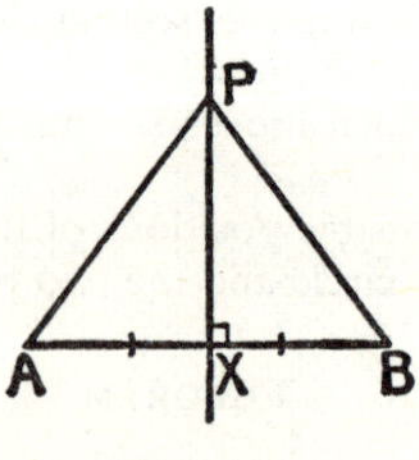

FIG. 148

Given two points A, B with X the mid point of AB and P any point on the perpendicular bisector of AB.
To prove $PA = PB$.

Proof: In the triangles APX, BPX,

$$\begin{cases} AX = BX \text{ (given)}, \\ \widehat{AXP} = \widehat{BXP} \text{ (right angles)}, \\ PX = PX \text{ (common)}. \end{cases}$$

$$\therefore \triangle APX \equiv \triangle BPX \text{ (SAS)}.$$

In particular, $AP = BP$.

THEOREM

The locus of a point which is equidistant from two intersecting straight lines consists of the pair of straight lines which bisect the angles between the two given lines.

The proof of this is divided into two parts.

(i) *A point which moves within an angle formed by two intersecting straight lines so that it is equidistant from the two lines must lie on the bisector of the angle.*

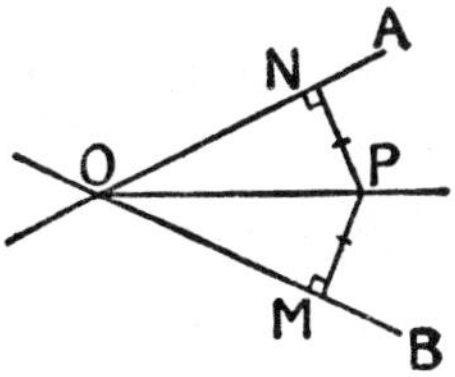

FIG. 149

Given two intersecting straight lines AO, BO. A point P moves within the angle AOB so that the perpendiculars PN, PM are equal.

To prove $\widehat{PON} = \widehat{POM}$.

Proof: In the triangles PON, POM,

$$\begin{cases} PO = PO \text{ (common)}, \\ PN = PM \text{ (given)}, \\ \widehat{PNO} = \widehat{PMO} \text{ (right angles)}. \end{cases}$$

$\therefore \triangle PON \equiv \triangle POM$ (right angle, hypotenuse and another side).

In particular $\widehat{PON} = \widehat{POM}$.

If the point P lies in the obtuse angle formed by the lines, it must lie on the other angle bisector.

(ii) *Any point on the bisector of an angle is equidistant from the arms forming the angle.*

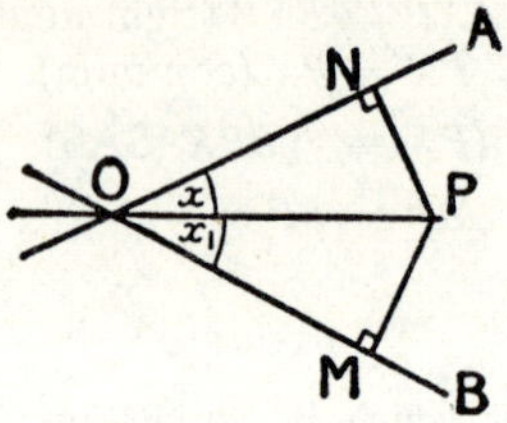

FIG. 150

Given two lines AO, BO and any point P on the bisector of the angle AOB; PN, PM are the perpendiculars to OA, OB respectively.
To prove $PN = PM$.
Proof: In the triangles PON, POM,

$$\begin{cases} x = x_1 \text{ (given)}, \\ PO = PO \text{ (common)}, \\ P\hat{N}O = P\hat{M}O \text{ (right angles)}. \end{cases}$$

$$\therefore \triangle PON \equiv \triangle POM \text{ (AAS)}.$$

In particular, $PN = PM$.

These results together prove that the locus of a point which moves so that it is equidistant from two given fixed lines is the pair of angle bisectors.

The locus is shown by the dotted lines in Fig. 151.

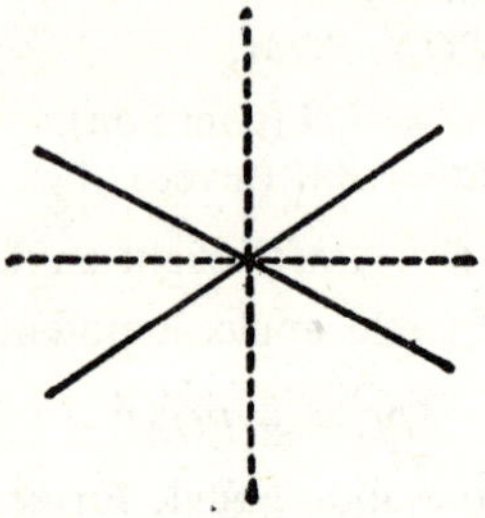

FIG. 151

EXERCISES 86A

1. What is the locus of a point P which moves in a plane so that it is always 3 cm distant from an infinitely long straight line?

2. What is the locus of a point P which moves in a plane so that it is equidistant from two given parallel straight lines?

3. What is the locus of the intersection of the diagonals of a parallelogram whose area is constant and one of whose sides is fixed?

4. A and B are fixed points. P moves so that $PA^2 - PB^2$ is constant. Find the locus of P.

5. Prove that the three perpendicular bisectors of the sides of a triangle meet in a point.

6. P moves on a circle. O is any point on the circle. Find the locus of the mid point of OP.

7. The base AB of a triangle ABC is fixed. The median CD is of constant length. Find the locus of C.

8. What is the locus in space of a point P which moves so that it is always at a constant distance from a fixed point?

9. OX, OY are two perpendicular straight lines. A lies on OX and B lies on OY. Given that AB is of constant length, find the locus of the mid point of AB.

10. Find the locus in space of a point which moves so that it is at constant distance from an infinitely long straight line.

EXERCISES 86B

1. A point P moves along a given straight line. Find its position when it is equidistant from two given fixed points A and B.

2. Two lines, AO, BO intersect at O. How many points are there distant 3 cm from AO and 4 cm from BO?

3. A is a fixed point and P moves on a given straight line which does not pass through A. Find the locus of the mid point of AP.

4. AB and CD are parallel straight lines. P is any point on AB, Q any point on CD. Find the locus of the mid point of PQ.

5. Prove that the three internal bisectors of the angles of a triangle meet in a point.

6. ABC is a triangle. The external bisectors of the angles B and C meet at P. Prove that PA bisects the angle BAC.

7. P lies on a given circle. O is a fixed point outside the circle. Find the locus of the mid point of OP.

8. On a given base AB construct a triangle of given area, given that the third vertex lies on a fixed straight line.

9. What is the locus in space of a point P which is equidistant from two given parallel straight lines?

10. What is the locus in space of a point which is equidistant from two given fixed points A and B?

Projection

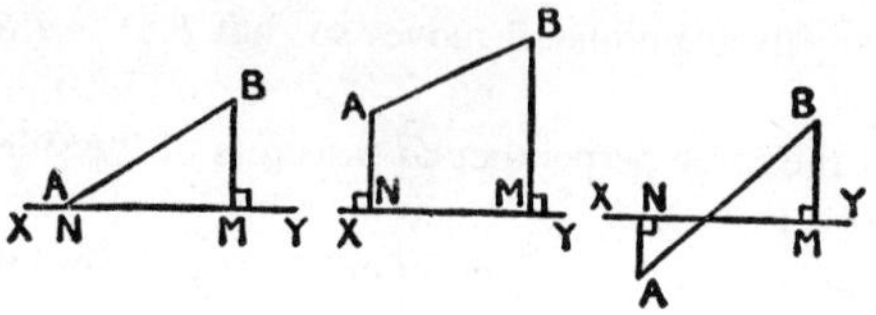

FIG. 152

If AN, BM are the perpendiculars from the points, A, B to a line XY, then NM is called the projection of AB on XY.

If θ is the angle between the lines AB and XY, the length of the projection of AB on XY is $AB \cos \theta$.

EXTENSIONS OF PYTHAGORAS

THEOREM (FIRST EXTENSION OF PYTHAGORAS)

The square on a side of a triangle opposite an acute angle is less than the sum of the squares on the other two sides. The difference is twice the rectangle contained by one of the two sides and the projection on it of the other.

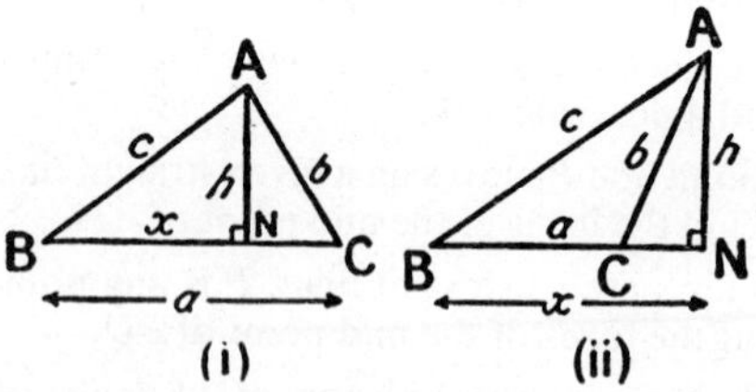

FIG. 153

Given the triangle ABC and AN the altitude through A. The angle B is acute.

Let $BC = a$, $AC = b$, $AB = c$, $AN = h$ and $BN = x$.

To prove that $b^2 = a^2 + c^2 - 2ax$.
Proof: In Fig. 153 (i)

$$h^2 = c^2 - x^2 \text{ (Pythagoras)}$$

and $$h^2 = b^2 - (a - x)^2 \text{ (Pythagoras).}$$

In Fig. 153, (ii)

$$h^2 = c^2 - x^2 \text{ (Pythagoras)}$$

and $$h^2 = b^2 - (x - a)^2.$$

Thus in both figures,

$$c^2 - x^2 = b^2 - (a^2 - 2ax + x^2)$$

or $$b^2 = a^2 + c^2 - 2ax.$$

THEOREM (SECOND EXTENSION OF PYTHAGORAS)

The square on a side of a triangle opposite an obtuse angle is greater than the sum of the squares on the other two sides. The difference is twice the rectangle contained by one of the two sides and the projection on it of the other.

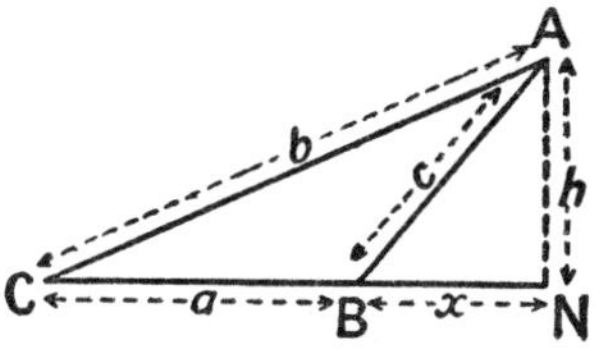

FIG. 154

Given a triangle ABC with angle B obtuse. Let $BN = x$.
To prove $b^2 = a^2 + c^2 + 2ax$.
Proof: $$h^2 = b^2 - (a + x)^2 \text{ (Pythagoras),}$$

and $$h^2 = c^2 - x^2 \text{ (Pythagoras).}$$

$$\therefore b^2 - (a + x)^2 = c^2 - x^2$$

or $$b^2 = c^2 + a^2 + 2ax.$$

Example 1. The sides of a triangle are 13 cm, 8 cm and 6 cm. Is the triangle obtuse angled?

The largest side is 13 cm. If the triangle has an obtuse angle, that angle must be opposite the longest side.

$$13^2 = 169;\ 8^2 + 6^2 = 100.$$

Since $13^2 > 8^2 + 6^2$, the triangle has an obtuse angle.

Example 2. In the triangle ABC, $AB = 13$ cm, $BC = 8$ cm and $CA = 6$ cm. Calculate the length of the projection of CA on BC.

Let AN be the perpendicular from A to BC produced.

$$13^2 = 8^2 + 6^2 + 2(8)CN.$$

$$\therefore\ 16CN = 69 \quad \text{and} \quad CN = 4\tfrac{5}{16} \text{ cm.}$$

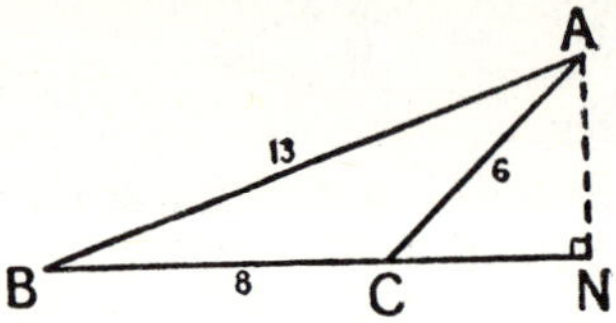

FIG. 155

THEOREM OF APOLLONIUS

In any triangle, the sum of the squares on any two sides is equal to twice the square on half the third side together with twice the square on the median which bisects the third side.

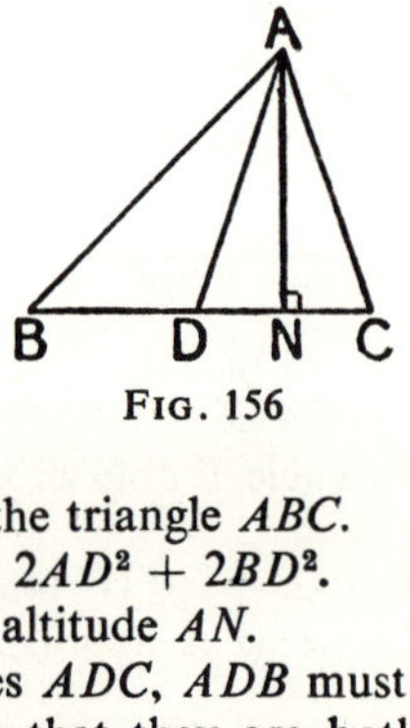

FIG. 156

Given AD a median of the triangle ABC.

To prove $AB^2 + AC^2 = 2AD^2 + 2BD^2$.

Construction: Draw the altitude AN.

Proof: One of the angles ADC, ADB must be acute and the other obtuse. (It is possible that they are both right angles; then the proof is an easy application of Pythagoras'.)

Suppose $A\hat{D}C$ is acute.

Then $\qquad AC^2 = AD^2 + DC^2 - 2DC.DN,$

and $\qquad AB^2 = AD^2 + BD^2 + 2BD.DN.$

By addition, remembering that $BD = DC$,

$$AC^2 + AB^2 = 2AD^2 + 2BD^2.$$

EXERCISES 87A

The triangle ABC has $AB = 7$ cm, $AC = 8$ cm and $BC = 12$ cm. AD, BE, CF are the altitudes.

1. Is the triangle ABC obtuse-angled?
2. Calculate the length of BD.
3. Calculate the length of AE.
4. Calculate the length of AF.
5. Calculate the length of the median through A.
6. Calculate the length of the median through B.
7. Calculate the length of the median through C.

EXERCISES 87B

The triangle ABC has $AB = 5$ cm, $AC = 8$ cm and $BC = 9$ cm. AD, BE, CF are the altitudes.

1. Is the triangle obtuse-angled?
2. Calculate the length of BD.
3. Calculate the length of AE.
4. Calculate the length of AF.
5. Calculate the length of the median through A.
6. Calculate the length of the median through B.
7. Calculate the length of the median through C.

EXERCISES 88: MISCELLANEOUS

1. Prove that the sum of the squares on the diagonals of a parallelogram is equal to the sum of the squares on the four sides.

2. AX, BY, CZ are the medians of the triangle ABC. Prove that $AX^2 + BY^2 + CZ^2 = \frac{3}{4}(AB^2 + BC^2 + CA^2)$.

3. ABC is a triangle in which AB is greater than AC. Given that AD is an altitude and AX a median, prove that $AB^2 - AC^2 = 4BX.XD$.

4. In the triangle ABC, $AB = 12$ cm, $AC = 8$ cm and $BC = 10$ cm. The angle bisector of the angle A meets BC at X and AN is an altitude. Calculate the length XN.

5. If A and B are fixed points, what is the locus of a point P which moves in space so that $PA = PB$?

6. If A and B are two fixed points, what is the locus of a point P which moves in space so that $PA^2 + PB^2$ is constant?

7. AX is a median of the triangle ABC. XN is the perpendicular from X to AB. Prove that $3AB^2 + AC^2 = BC^2 + 4AB.AN$.

8. X, Y are the mid points of the diagonals AC, BD of the quadrilateral $ABCD$. Prove that $AB^2 + BC^2 + CD^2 + DA^2 = 4XY^2 + DB^2 + AC^2$.

9. The diagonals AC, BD of a parallelogram meet at O, and X is the mid point of AB. Prove that $4CX^2 = 8AO^2 + 2AD^2 - AB^2$.

10. $ABCD$ is a quadrilateral of constant area. A, B, C are fixed points. What is the locus of D?

11. BD, CE are altitudes of the triangle ABC. Prove that $AD.AC = AB.AE$.

12. ABC is an isosceles triangle in which $AB = AC$. If CF is an altitude, prove that $BC^2 = 2AB.BF$.

13. Given that two medians of a triangle are equal, prove that the triangle is isosceles.

14. A, B, C, D are four points in line so that $AB = BC = CD$. Given that P is any point not on the line, prove that

$$PA^2 + PD^2 = PB^2 + PC^2 + AC^2.$$

15. In the triangle ABC, $AB = 2AC$ and the angle $A = 60°$. Prove that $BC^2 = 3AC^2$.

16. Two sides of a triangle are 5 cm and 3 cm and the angle included between them is 120°. Find the length of the third side.

17. The diagonals of a parallelogram are 8 cm and 10 cm long and one side is 5 cm long. Find the length of the other side.

18. If X, Y are the points of trisection of the side BC of the triangle ABC, prove that $AB^2 - AC^2 = 3(AX^2 - AY^2)$.

19. In the triangle ABC, the angle $A = 120°$. Prove that $BC^2 = AC^2 + AB^2 + AC.AB$.

20. ABC is a triangle in which the angle B is obtuse. AN is an altitude. Prove that $NC^2 = NB^2 + BC^2 + 2BC.BN$.

22

THE CIRCLE

Definitions

A POINT which moves in a plane so that its distance from a fixed point in that plane is constant lies on the circumference of a circle.

The fixed point is called the centre of the circle and the constant distance is called the radius.

A chord of a circle is a straight line joining two points on the circumference.

A chord through the centre is called a diameter.

Concentric circles are circles having the same centre.

THEOREM

A straight line drawn from the centre of a circle to bisect a chord which is not a diameter, is at right angles to the chord.

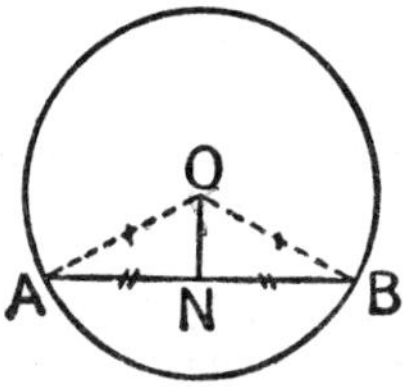

FIG. 157

Given AB is a chord of a circle centre O. N is the mid point of AB.
To prove that ON is perpendicular to AB.
Construction: Join OA, OB.

The proof is left as an exercise (see Exercises 73A, question **8**).

The converse theorem is also true.

THEOREM

The perpendicular drawn from the centre of a circle to a chord bisects that chord.

The proof is left as an exercise (see Exercises 73A, question **7**).

THEOREM

There is one circle and one only, which passes through three given points not in a straight line.

Given three points, A, B, C not in the same straight line.
To prove that one and only one circle can be drawn through A, B, C.
Construction: Draw the perpendicular bisectors of AB and BC.

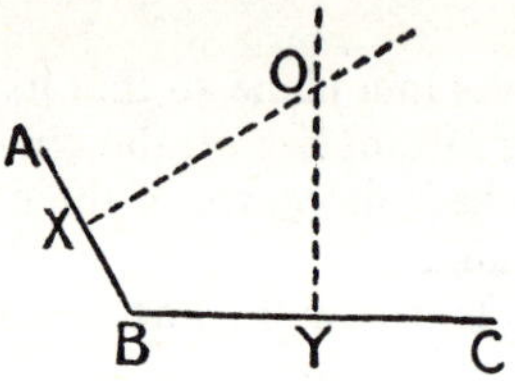

FIG. 158

Proof: Since A, B, C are not in the same straight line, the perpendicular bisectors of AB and BC cannot be parallel and must therefore meet. Suppose they meet at O.

Then $OA = OB$ (O on the perp. bisector of AB),
and $OB = OC$ (O on the perp. bisector of BC).
$\therefore OA = OB = OC$.

A circle can therefore be drawn with centre O and radius OA to pass through A, B and C.
Also, since AB is a chord of any circle which passes through A, B and C, the centre of the circle must lie on the perpendicular bisector of AB.
Similarly, the centre of any circle through A, B and C must lie on the perpendicular bisector of BC.
These perpendicular bisectors meet in one point only. Therefore the circle through A, B, C is unique.
N.B. Since AC is also a chord of the circle, the perpendicular bisector of AC must pass through O.
Therefore the three perpendicular bisectors of the sides of a triangle all meet in a point. This point is the centre of the circle which circumscribes the triangle.

THEOREM

Equal chords of a circle are equidistant from the centre.

Given AB, CD are two equal chords of the circle, centre O, and OM, ON are perpendiculars to these chords.

To prove that $OM = ON$.
Construction: Join AO, CO.
Proof: Since the perpendicular from the centre bisects the chord,

$$AM = MB \quad \text{and} \quad CN = ND.$$

But $\quad AB = CD$ and therefore $AM = CN$.

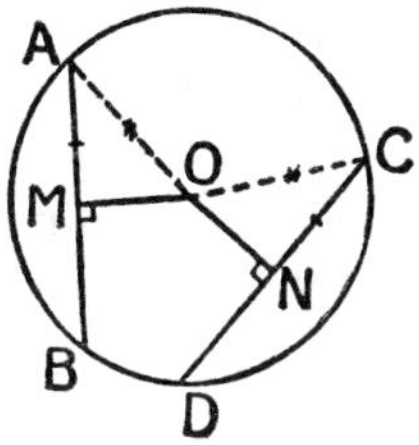

FIG. 159

In the triangles AOM, CON

$$\begin{cases} AO = CO \text{ (radii)}, \\ AM = CN \text{ (proved)}, \\ A\hat{M}O = C\hat{N}O \text{ (right angles)}. \end{cases}$$

$\therefore \triangle AOM \equiv \triangle CON$ (right angle, hypotenuse and another side).

In particular, $OM = ON$.

The converse theorem, enunciated below, is also true and the proof is left as an exercise.

THEOREM

Chords which are equidistant from the centre of a circle are equal.
The proof is left as an exercise.

EXERCISES 89A

1. In a circle of radius 5 cm, calculate the length of a chord which is 3 cm from the centre.

2. In a circle of radius 13 cm, calculate the distance from the centre of a chord which is 24 cm long.

3. An isosceles triangle whose sides are 13 cm, 13 cm and 10 cm is inscribed in a circle. Find the radius of the circle.

4. Two parallel chords of a circle are of lengths 6 cm and 8 cm and lie on the same side of the centre. If the radius of the circle is 5 cm, find the distance between the chords.

5. A chord of a circle of radius x cm is y cm distant from the centre. Find its length.

6. Show that in a circle the greater of two chords is nearer the centre.

7. A line cuts two concentric circles at points A, B, C, D. Prove that $AB = CD$.

8. An equilateral triangle is inscribed in a circle of radius r. Find the area of the triangle.

9. An equilateral triangle of side 4 cm is inscribed in a circle. Find the radius of the circle.

10. Prove that the line joining the mid points of two parallel chords of a circle passes through the centre.

EXERCISES 89B

1. In a circle of radius 13 cm, calculate the length of a chord which is 5 cm distant from the centre.

2. In a circle of radius 5 cm, calculate the distance from the centre of a chord which is 8 cm long.

3. An isosceles triangle whose sides are 5 cm, 5 cm and 6 cm is inscribed in a circle. Find the radius of the circle.

4. Two parallel chords of a circle are of lengths 10 cm and 24 cm and lie on opposite sides of the centre. If the radius of the circle is 13 cm, find the distance between the chords.

5. A chord of a circle is x cm long. If it is distant y cm from the centre, find the radius of the circle.

6. AB, CD are chords of a circle, meeting at O. If O is the mid point of each of the chords, prove that AB and CD must be diameters of the circle.

7. The triangle ABC has a right angle at B. Prove that the circle which passes through A, B and C must have the mid point of AC as centre.

8. A square of side x cm is inscribed in a circle. Find the radius of the circle.

9. An equilateral triangle of side x cm is inscribed in a circle. Find the radius of the circle.

10. What is the locus of the centre of the circle which passes through two fixed points A and B.

Angle in a segment

The chord AB divides the circumference of the circle into two arcs, APB, called the major arc, and AQB, the minor arc.

The area APB is called a segment of a circle. Any angle subtended by AB at a point on the arc APB is called the angle in the segment APB. Such an angle is also called the angle subtended by the arc AQB at the circumference.

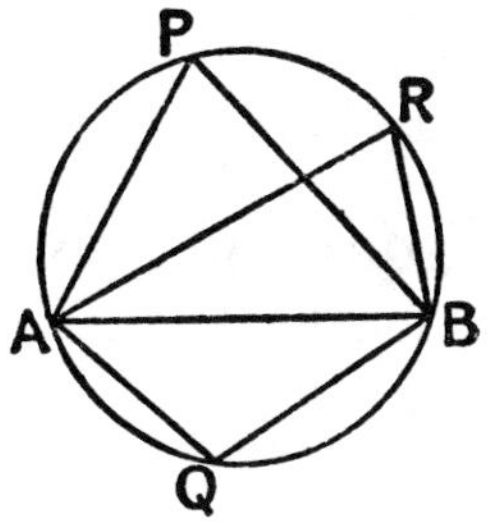

FIG. 160

$\widehat{APB}$ and $\widehat{ARB}$ are called angles in the same segment.

The angle AQB is the angle subtended by the major arc at the circumference.

THEOREM

The angle which an arc of a circle subtends at the centre is double that which it subtends at any other point on the remaining part of the circumference.

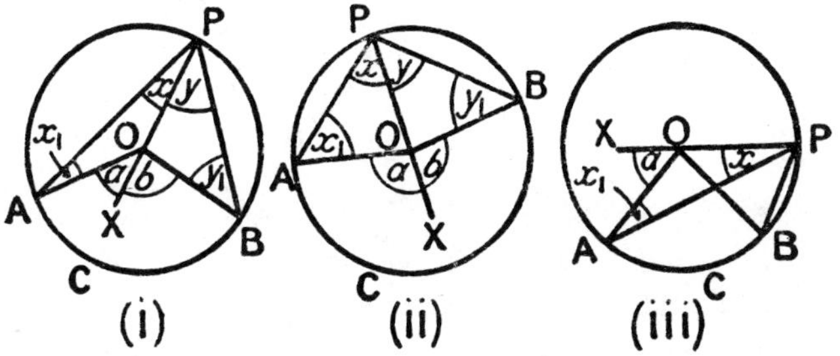

FIG. 161

Given ACB an arc of a circle centre O. P is any point on the remaining arc.

To prove $\widehat{AOB} = 2\widehat{APB}$.

Construction: Join PO and produce to X.

Proof: Since $AO = OP$ (radii),
$$x = x_1.$$
Also $a = x + x_1$ (exterior angle)
$$= 2x.$$
Similarly $b = 2y$.
(In Fig. 161 (iii),
$$b = X\widehat{O}B \quad \text{and} \quad y = X\widehat{P}B).$$
Adding in Figs. 161 (i) and (ii),
$$a + b = 2(x + y),$$
or $$A\widehat{O}B = 2A\widehat{P}B.$$
Subtracting in Fig. 161 (iii),
$$b - a = 2(y - x),$$
or $A\widehat{O}B = 2A\widehat{P}B$. (In Fig. 161 (ii), reflex $A\widehat{O}B = 2A\widehat{P}B$.)

THEOREM

Angles in the same segment of a circle are equal.

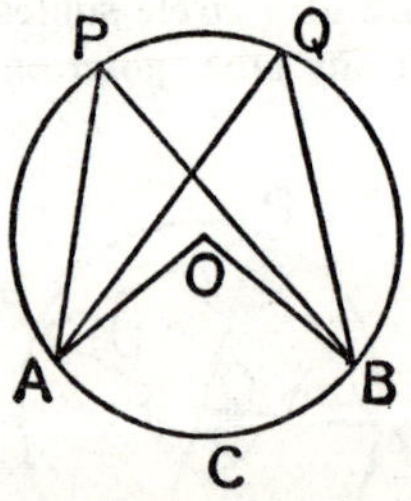

FIG. 162

Given an arc ACB of a circle centre O. Any two points P and Q are on the remaining arc.

To prove $A\widehat{P}B = A\widehat{Q}B$.

Proof: $A\widehat{P}B = \frac{1}{2}A\widehat{O}B$ (angle at centre).

$A\widehat{Q}B = \frac{1}{2}A\widehat{O}B$ (angle at centre).

$\therefore A\widehat{P}B = A\widehat{Q}B$.

THEOREM

The opposite angles of any quadrilateral inscribed in a circle are supplementary.

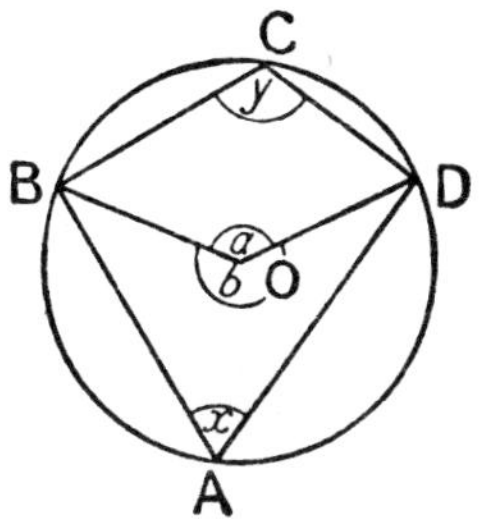

FIG. 163

Given a quadrilateral *ABCD* inscribed in a circle centre *O*.
To prove $x + y = 180°$.
Construction: Join *OB*, *OD*.
Proof: $a = 2x$ (angles on arc *BCD*),
$b = 2y$ (angles on arc *BAD*).
$\therefore a + b = 2(x + y)$.
Since $a + b = 360°$, $x + y = 180°$.

N.B. If *BOD* is a straight line, i.e. a diameter, $a = 180°$ and therefore $x = 90°$.

This is the important theorem, that **the angle in a semicircle is a right angle.**

Corollary. If the side *AB* of the cyclic quadrilateral *ABCD* is produced to *X*, $C\hat{B}X$ is supplementary to $C\hat{B}A$. Since $C\hat{D}A$ is also supplementary to $C\hat{B}A$ (opposite angles of cyclic quadrilateral),

$$C\hat{B}X = A\hat{D}C.$$

Therefore the exterior angle of a cyclic quadrilateral is equal to the interior opposite angle.

Two converse theorems give useful tests for proving that four points lie on a circle.

(1) A quadrilateral in which two opposite angles are supplementary is cyclic.

(2) If the line joining two points subtends equal angles at two other points on the same side of it, the four points lie on a circle.

Theorems Connecting Arcs and Chords

The following theorems may be assumed.
In the same circle or in equal circles,

(1) Equal chords stand on equal arcs.
(2) Equal arcs subtend equal angles at the circumference.
(3) Equal arcs are subtended by equal angles at the circumference.

EXERCISES 90A

1. Find the angle subtended at the circumference of a circle by the side of a regular 12-sided figure inscribed in the circle.

2. *ABCD* is a cyclic quadrilateral. The angle $DAB = 80°$, and the angle $ACB = 50°$. Prove that $AD = AB$.

3. Find the angles of the triangle formed by joining the points representing 03.00h, 08.00h and 11.00h.

4. *ABCDE* is a regular pentagon inscribed in a circle. Prove that *AE* is parallel to *BD*.

5. *ABCD* is a cyclic quadrilateral. The sides *AB*, *DC* produced meet at *E*; the sides *AD*, *BC* produced meet at *F*. Given that the angle $CEB = 20°$ and that the angle $AFB = 50°$, calculate the angles of the quadrilateral.

6. *ABCD* is a quadrilateral in which the angle $ADB = 51°$, the angle $ABC = 89°$ and the angle $BAC = 40°$. Prove that *ABCD* lie on a circle.

7. A circle passes through the points *A*, *B* and *O*. A second circle, centre *O*, also passes through the points *A* and *B*. Any line *AXY* through *A* meets the first circle at *X* and the second circle at *Y*. Prove that $BX = XY$.

8. Two chords of a circle *AB* and *CD* meet at a point *O* inside the circle. Prove that the triangles *AOC*, *DOB* are similar and hence prove that $AO.OB = CO.OD$.

9. *AB* is a diameter of a circle and *C* is a point on the circle so that $B\hat{A}C = 30°$. The internal bisector of the angle *ABC* meets the circle again at *X*. Prove that *CA* is the internal bisector of the angle *BAX*.

10. *BE*, *CF* are altitudes of a triangle *ABC*. Prove that the angles *AEF* and *ABC* are equal.

EXERCISES 90B

1. Find the angle subtended at the circumference of a circle by the side of a regular 10-sided figure inscribed in the circle.

2. *ABCD* is a cyclic quadrilateral. Given that the angle $DAB = x$ and that the angle $ACB = y$, find a relationship between x and y if $AB = AD$.

3. Find the angles of the triangle formed by joining the points representing 02.00h, 06.00h and 11.00h.

4. *ABCDEFG* is a regular 7-sided figure inscribed in a circle. If *FB* and *AE* meet at *X*, prove that $FE = FX$.

5. *ABCD* is a cyclic quadrilateral. The sides *AB*, *DC* produced meet at *E*; the sides *AD*, *BC* produced meet at *F*. Given that the angle $CEB = 40°$ and that the angle $AFB = 50°$, calculate the angles of the quadrilateral.

6. *ABCD* is a quadrilateral in which the angle $BAC = x$, the angle $ADB = y$ and the angle $ABC = z$. Find a relationship between x, y and z if *ABCD* is cyclic.

7. Two chords *AB*, *CD* of a circle centre *O* are perpendicular. Given that the angle $AOC = 110°$, calculate the angle *BOD*.

8. Two chords of a circle, *AB* and *CD*, meet when produced at a point *O* outside the circle. Prove that the triangles *AOC*, *DOB* are similar and hence prove that $OA.OB = OC.OD$.

9. Prove that the internal bisectors of the angles of a cyclic quadrilateral themselves form a cyclic quadrilateral.

10. The altitudes *BE*, *CF* of a triangle *ABC* meet at *H*. If *X* is the mid point of *AH*, prove that $XF = XE$.

EXERCISES 91: Miscellaneous

1. The point *P* inside a circle is such that the shortest chord through it is 8 cm long. The greatest distance from *P* to the circumference is 16 cm. Find the radius of the circle.

2. *XY* and *AB* are diameters of a circle. *P* is any point on the circumference of the circle such that the angle *APY* is acute. Prove that the angles *XPA* and *BPY* are equal or supplementary.

3. In the cyclic quadrilateral *ABCD*, $AB = AC$. Given that *X* is any point on *CD* produced, prove that *AD* bisects the angle *BDX*.

4. Two circles intersect at *A* and *B*. Lines *PAQ*, *RBS* are drawn to meet one circle at *P* and *R*, and other circle at *Q* and *S*. Prove that *PR* is parallel to *QS*.

5. *ABCDEF* is a regular hexagon. Prove that *BDF* is an equilateral triangle.

6. *ABCDEF* is a hexagon inscribed in a circle. Prove that the sum of the angles at *A*, *C* and *E* is equal to the sum of the angles at *B*, *D* and *F*.

7. *O* is the centre of a circle and *P* a point distant 2 cm from *O*. If the radius of the circle is 8 cm, calculate the length of the chord through *P* which makes an angle of 45° with *OP*.

8. *PQR* is a triangle inscribed in a circle of radius 4 cm. Given that the angle $PQR = 30°$, calculate the distance of the chord *PR* from the centre of the circle.

9. Two circles intersect at *A* and *B*. Lines *PAQ*, *RAS* are drawn to meet one circle at *P*,*R* and the other circle at *S* and *Q*. Prove that the angles *PBR* and *QBS* are equal.

10. In the figure, $XC = CD = DA = AB$. Prove that *XD* is parallel to *CA*.

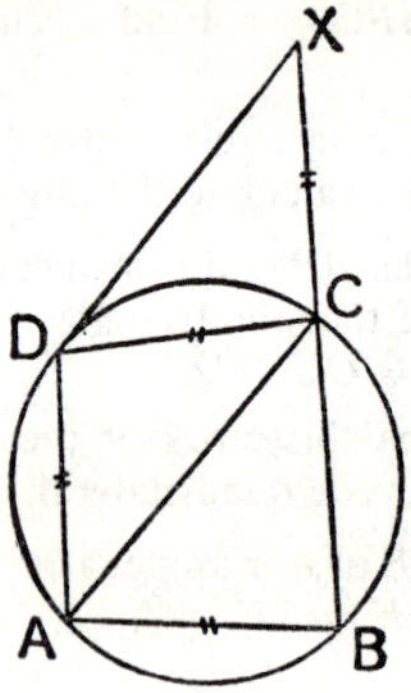

FIG. 164

11. *ABC* is an acute-angled triangle inscribed in a circle. Prove that the sum of the angles subtended by *AB*, *BC*, *CA* in their minor segments is 4 right angles.

12. *AB* is a fixed chord of a circle and *P* a variable point on the major arc *AB*. *AP* is produced to *Q* so that $BP = PQ$. Prove that the angle *AQB* is constant.

13. *ABC* is a triangle in which $AB = 2$ cm and the angle $ACB = 30°$. Calculate the radius of the circle passing through *A*, *B* and *C*.

14. Two equal circles intersect at *A* and *B*. Any line through *B* meets one circle at *P* and the other at *Q*. Prove that *PAQ* is an isosceles triangle.

15. *ABCD* is a trapezium with *AB* parallel to *DC*. Given that *AC* and *BD* meet at *X* and that $AX = XB$, prove that the points *A*, *B*, *C*, *D* are concyclic.

16. *ABC* is a triangle in which the angle *C* is 60°. The circle through the points *A*, *B*, *C* has centre *O*. The circle through the points *O*, *A*, *B* is cut again by *CA* produced at *X*. Prove that *CBX* is an equilateral triangle.

17. *ABCD* is a rectangle. The line through *C* perpendicular to *AC* meets *AB* produced at *X* and meets *AD* produced at *Y*. Prove that the points *D*, *B*, *X*, *Y* are concyclic.

18. P is a point on the circumcircle of the triangle ABC. The perpendicular from P to AB meets AB at N and the perpendicular from P to BC meets BC at L. Prove that the angles PLN and PCA are equal.

19. AB is a chord of a circle centre O. A point C on the minor arc AB is such that BC produced meets the perpendicular from O to AB at X. Prove that $AXCO$ is a cyclic quadrilateral.

20. $ABCD$ is a cyclic quadrilateral whose diagonals AC, BD meet at X. Given that $AD = DC$, prove that the triangles DAX and DBA are similar. Hence prove that $DA^2 = DB.DX$.

23

SECANT AND TANGENT

SECANT

A STRAIGHT line which cuts a circle in two distinct points is called a secant (see Fig. 165).

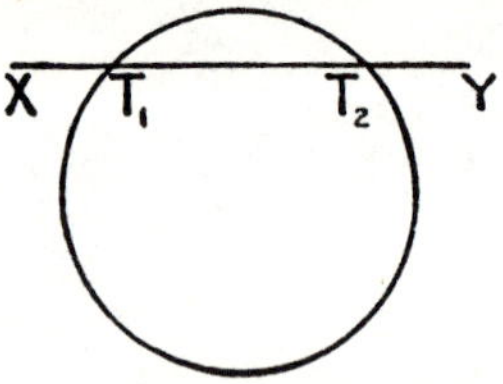

FIG. 165

TANGENT

A straight line which however far produced meets a circle at one point only is called a tangent to the circle. In Fig. 166, the line

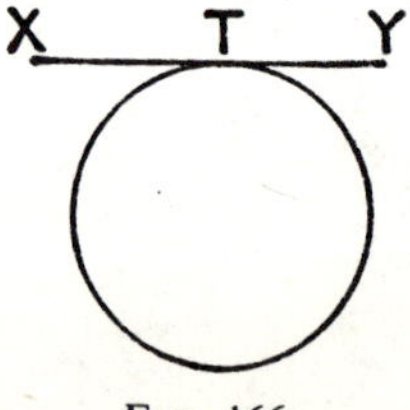

FIG. 166

XTY is a tangent to the circle and *T* is the point of contact of the tangent.

(A tangent may be regarded as the limiting case of a secant. If the two points T_1 and T_2 in Fig. 165 become closer and closer to each other until eventually they coincide at *T*, the secant becomes a tangent. A tangent may therefore be said to meet the circle at two coincident points.)

THEOREM

The tangent at any point of a circle and the radius through the point are perpendicular to each other.

Given *TP* is the tangent at *T* and *OT* is a radius.
To prove that the angle $OTP = 90°$.

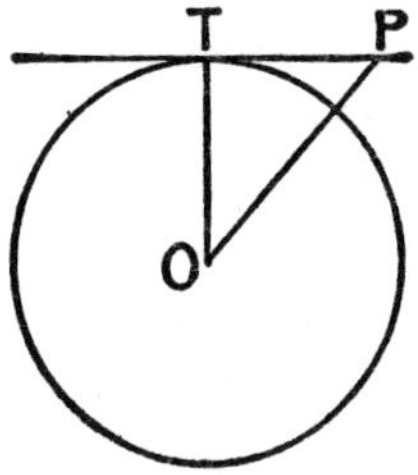

FIG. 167

Proof: Wherever *P* is on the tangent, *OP* is greater in length than the radius *OT*. Therefore *OT* is the shortest distance between the point *O* and the tangent. Therefore *OT* is perpendicular to the tangent.

Aliter. In Fig. 165, the line joining *O* to the mid point of T_1T_2 is perpendicular to the chord. When the two points T_1, T_2 coincide at *T*, the mid point of T_1T_2 also becomes *T*. Therefore *OT* is perpendicular to the tangent.

Corollary. There is one, and only one, tangent at a point *T* to a circle. This tangent is perpendicular to the radius through *T*.

Alternate segment

In Fig. 168, *PTQ* is the tangent to the circle at *T* and *TA* is any chord through *T*. If we consider the angle *ATQ*, the segment *TXA*

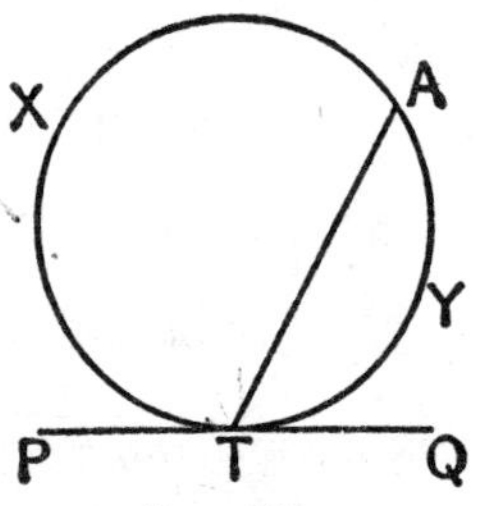

FIG. 168

is called the alternate segment; if we consider the angle *PTA*, the segment *AYT* is the alternate segment. We shall now prove that, in either case, the angle between the tangent and the chord is equal to the angle in the alternate segment.

THEOREM

If a straight line touch a circle, and from the point of contact a chord be drawn, the angles which the chord makes with the tangent are equal to the angles in the alternate segments.

Given *PTQ* is the tangent at *T* to a circle, centre *O*. *TA* is a chord of the circle. Denote the angle *ATQ* by x and the angle subtended at any point *C* in the alternate segment by y.

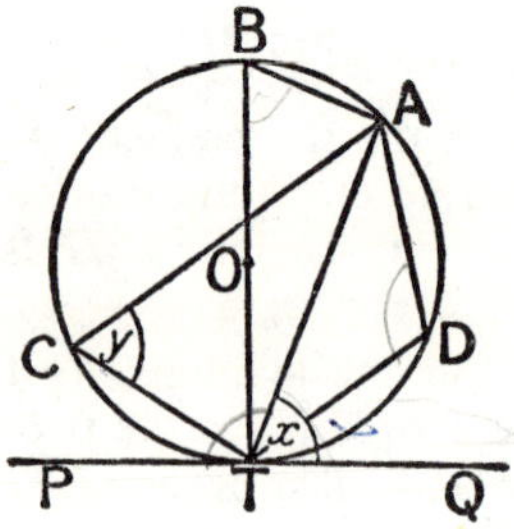

FIG. 169

To prove (i) $x = y$; (ii) $P\hat{T}A = T\hat{D}A$.

Construction: Draw the diameter *TO* to meet the circle again at *B*.

Proof: (i) Since $B\hat{T}Q = 90°$ (tangent and radius),

$$B\hat{T}A = 90° - x.$$

Now $B\hat{A}T = 90°$ (angle in semicircle) and therefore

$$A\hat{B}T + B\hat{T}A = 90°.$$

$$\therefore T\hat{B}A = x.$$

Now $T\hat{C}A = T\hat{B}A$ (on the same arc),

$$\therefore y = x.$$

(ii) $\widehat{ADT} + x = 180°$ (cyclic quadrilateral).

Also $\widehat{PTA} + x = 180°$ (straight line).

$$\therefore\ \widehat{ADT} = \widehat{PTA} \text{ (each angle equal to } 180° - x).$$

Conversely. If a straight line be drawn from the extremity of a chord of a circle making with the chord an angle equal to the angle in the alternate segment, then the line is a tangent to the circle.

EXERCISES 92A

1. Given that the tangents at two points *A*, *B* of a circle meet at *T*, prove that $TA = TB$.

2. Prove that equal chords of a given circle all touch another concentric circle.

3. The angles of a triangle whose sides touch a circle are 50°, 60° and 70°. Find the angles of the triangle formed by their points of contact.

4. *AT* is the tangent to a circle at the point *A* and *AB* is a chord of the circle. The bisector of the angle *TAB* meets the circle again at *X*. Prove that $AX = XB$.

5. The tangents at *A*, *C* to a circle meet the tangent at another point *B* at *P* and *Q* respectively. Given that the angle $APB = 50°$ and that the angle $CQB = 70°$, calculate the angle *ABC*.

6. *ABC* is a triangle inscribed in a circle. The tangent *PAT* to the circle at *A* meets the tangent at *C* in the point *T*. Given that the angle $BCT = 80°$ and that the angle $ATC = 42°$, calculate the angle *PAB*.

7. *A*, *B*, *C* are three points on a circle centre *O*. The tangent at *C* meets *AB* produced at *T*. Given that the angle $AOB = 80°$ and that the angle $CBT = 64°$, calculate the angle *TCB*.

8. *AB* is a diameter of a circle and *C* a point on the circle so that the angle $BAC = 24°$. If the tangent at *C* meets *AB* produced at *T*, calculate the angle *CTB*.

9. *AB* is a diameter of a circle. The tangent at a point *P* is such that the angle $APT = 112°$. Calculate the angle *BAP*.

10. *A*, *B*, *C* are three points on a circle. The tangent at *C* meets *BA* produced at *T*. Given that the angle $ATC = 36°$ and that the angle $ACT = 48°$, calculate the angle subtended by *AB* at the centre of the circle.

EXERCISES 92B

1. Given that the tangents at two points *A*, *B* of a circle, centre *O*, meet at *T*, prove that *OT* bisects the angle *ATB*.

2. Given that the tangents at two points A, B of a circle, centre O, meet at T, prove that OT bisects the angle AOB.

3. The angles of a triangle whose sides touch a circle are 48°, 54° and 78°. Find the angles of the triangle formed by their points of contact.

4. AB is a chord of a circle, centre O. The tangent at another point T meets AB produced at C. Given that the angle $BCT = 20°$ and that the angle $BTC = 65°$, prove that the triangle AOB is equilateral.

5. The tangents at A, C to a circle meet the tangent at another point B at P and Q respectively. Given that the angle $APB = x$ and that the angle $CQB = y$, calculate the angle ABC in terms of x and y.

6. ABC is a triangle inscribed in a circle. The tangent PAT to the circle at A meets the tangent at C in the point T. Given that the angle $BCT = x$ and that the angle $ATC = y$, calculate the angle PAB in terms of x and y.

7. A, B, C are three points on a circle centre O. The tangent at C meets AB produced at T. Given that the angle $AOB = x$ and that the angle $CBT = y$, calculate the angle TCB in terms of x and y.

8. AB is a diameter of a circle and C a point on the circle. If the tangent at C meets AB produced at T and the angle $BAC = x$, find the angle CTB in terms of x.

9. AB is a diameter of a circle. The tangent PT at a point P is such that the angle $APT = x$. Find, in terms of x, the angle BAP.

10. A, B, C are three points on a circle. The tangent at C meets BA produced at T. Given that the angle $ATC = x$ and that the angle $ACT = y$, find the angle subtended by AB at the centre of the circle in terms of x and y.

Internal and external contact

Two circles are said to touch at a point T if they have a common tangent at the point T.

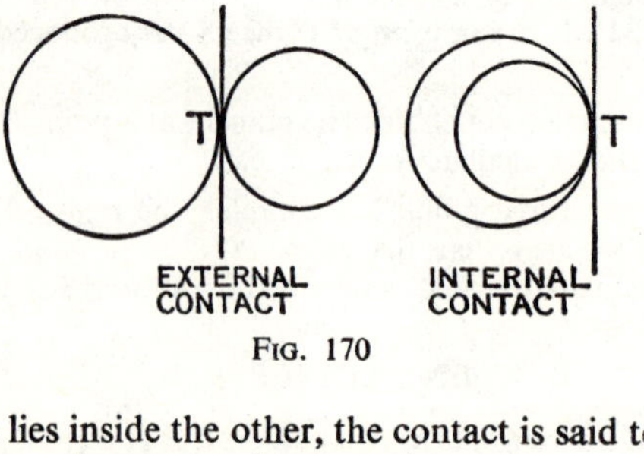

FIG. 170

If one circle lies inside the other, the contact is said to be internal; in all other cases, the contact is external.

THEOREM

If two circles touch, the point of contact lies on the straight line through the centres.

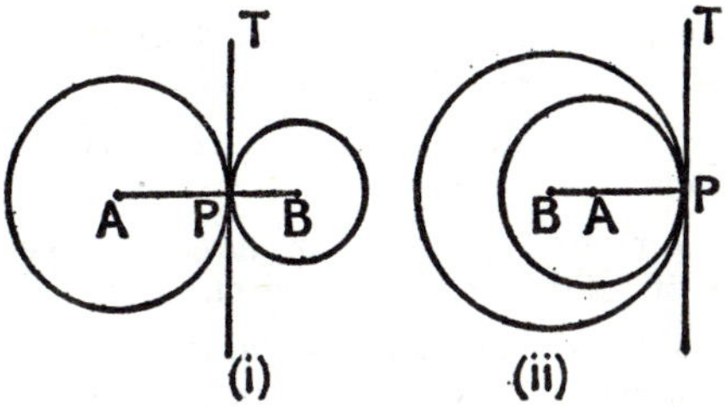

FIG. 171

Given two circles, centres A and B, touching at P.
To prove that P lies on the line AB.
Construction: Join AP, PB and draw the common tangent PT at P.

Proof: $\widehat{APT} = 90°$ (tangent and radius),

and $\widehat{BPT} = 90°$ (tangent and radius).

Therefore in Fig. 171 (i),

$\widehat{APT} + \widehat{BPT} = 180°$,

and so APB is a straight line.

In Fig. 171 (ii), the lines BP and AP must both be perpendicular to PT and so BAP is a straight line.

THEOREM

If two tangents are drawn to a circle from a point outside the circle, then

(i) the tangents are equal in length;

(ii) the angle between the tangents is bisected by the line joining the point of intersection of the tangents to the centre;

(iii) this line also bisects the angle between the radii drawn to the points of contact.

The proof is left as an exercise (see Exercises 92A, question **1** and Exercises 92B, questions **1** and **2**).

EXERCISES 93A

1. Find the length of the tangents drawn to a circle of radius 5 cm from a point 13 cm from the centre.

2. Find the length of the chord of contact in question **1**.

3. A quadrilateral is circumscribed to a circle. Prove that the sums of the opposite sides of the quadrilateral are equal.

4. Two circles, radii 9 cm and 4 cm, touch externally. Find the length of a common tangent.

5. Two circles, radii 7 cm and 2 cm, have their centres 13 cm apart. Find the length of a direct common tangent.

6. Two circles, radii 8 cm and 4 cm, have their centres 13 cm apart. Calculate the length of a transverse common tangent.

7. Two circles touch externally at P. Two lines, APB and CPD, are drawn so that A, C lie on one circle and B, D lie on the other. Prove that AC is parallel to DB.

8. P is a point so that the length of a tangent from P to a given circle is constant. What is the locus of P?

9. Three equal circles touch at A, B, C. Prove that the triangle ABC is equilateral and that its side is equal in length to the radius of a circle.

10. Two circles touch externally at P. A common tangent touches the circles at R, S. Prove that the angle RPS is a right angle.

EXERCISES 93B

1. The length of a tangent from a point distant 5 cm from the centre of a circle is 4 cm. Find the radius of the circle.

2. Find the length of the chord in question **1**.

3. A tangent to a circle centre O meets two parallel tangents at P and Q. Prove that the angle POQ is a right angle.

4. Two circles, radii R and r, touch externally. Find the length of a common tangent.

5. Two circles, radii R and r, have their centres a distance d apart. Find the length of a direct common tangent.

6. Two circles, radii R and r, have their centres a distance d apart. Find the length of a transverse common tangent.

7. What is the locus of the centre of a circle which touches two given equal circles?

8. What is the locus of a point from which tangents to a given circle are perpendicular?

9. The centres of three circles which touch externally form a triangle whose sides are 5 cm, 6 cm and 9 cm. Find the radii of the circles.

10. Two circles touch internally at P. T is any point on the tangent at P. Tangents TX, TY are drawn to the two circles. Prove that $TX = TY$.

THEOREM

If two chords of a circle intersect either inside or outside the circle, the rectangle contained by the parts of the one is equal to the rectangle contained by the parts of the other.

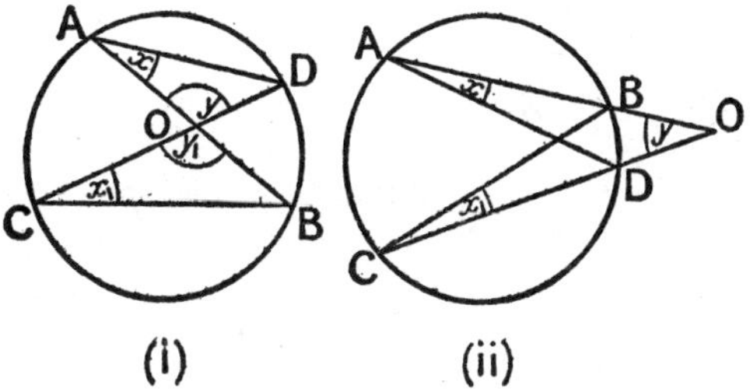

FIG. 172

Given AB and CD two chords of a circle meeting at O.
To prove that $AO.OB = CO.OD$.
Construction: Join AD and CB.
Proof: In the triangles AOD and COB,

$x = x_1$ (on arc BD),
$y = y_1$ (vert. opp. in Fig. 172 (i)),
or y is common (Fig. 172 (ii)).
Therefore in each figure the triangles AOD, COB are similar.

$$\therefore \frac{AO}{CO} = \frac{OD}{OB} \quad \text{or} \quad AO.OB = CO.OD.$$

(Note that each distance mentioned contains the point O.)

THEOREM

If from a point outside a circle a tangent and a secant are drawn to the circle, then the square on the tangent is equal to the rectangle contained by the whole secant and that part of it outside the circle.

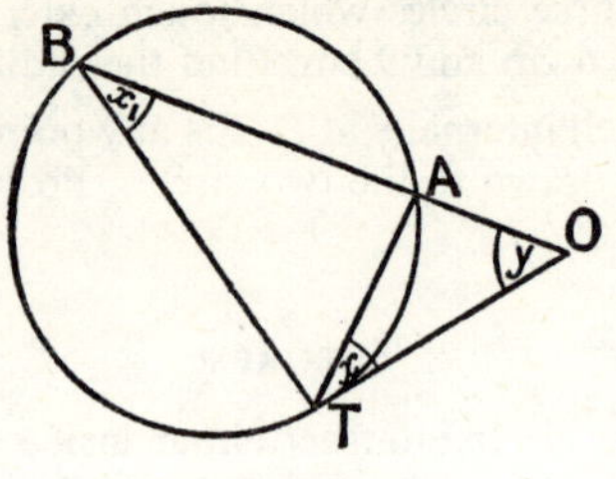

FIG. 173

Given a secant OAB and a tangent OT.
To prove that $OT^2 = OA.OB$.
Construction: Join TA and TB.
Proof: In the triangles OAT and OTB,

$$x = x_1 \text{ (alternate segment)},$$

and y is common.

Therefore the triangles are similar and

$$\frac{OA}{OT} = \frac{OT}{OB} \quad \text{or} \quad OT^2 = OA.OB.$$

(N.B. This theorem could have been deduced from the previous theorem. If, in Fig. 172 (ii), the secant ODC is chosen so that it becomes the tangent OT, C and D both coincide with T. The statement $OA.OB = OC.OD$ becomes $OA.OB = OT^2$.)

Converses

The converses of these two theorems are also true.

(1) If two straight lines AB, CD intersecting at O are such that $OA.OB = OC.OD$. then the points A, B, C, D are concyclic.

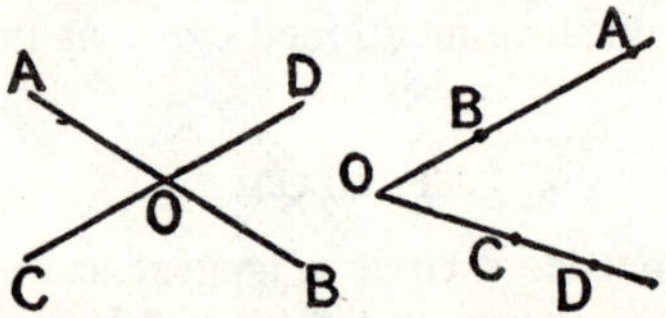

FIG. 174

(2) If two lines BAO and TO intersecting at O are such that $OA.OB = OT^2$ then OT is a tangent to the circle circumscribing the triangle ABT.

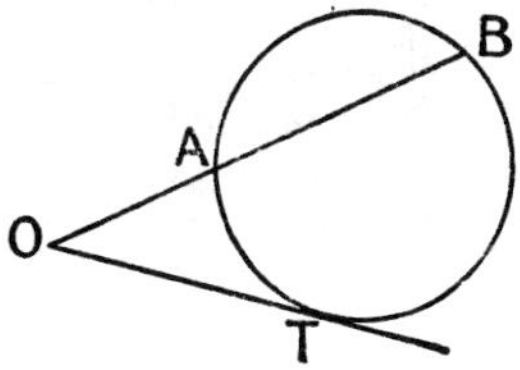

FIG. 175

EXERCISES 94A

1. The chords AB, CD of a circle meet at a point O outside the circle. Given that $OA = 7$ cm, $OB = 4$ cm and $OD = 2$ cm, find OC.

2. The chords AB, CD of a circle meet at a point O outside the circle. Given that $OA = 8$ cm, $AB = 3$ cm, $OD = 4$ cm, find CD.

3. The chords AB, CD of a circle meet at a point O outside the circle. Given that $OA = 8$ cm, $OB = 3$ cm and $CD = 10$ cm, find OD.

4. The chords AB, CD of a circle meet at a point O inside the circle. If $OA = 5$ cm, $OB = 10$ cm and $OD = 4$ cm, find OC.

5. The chords AB, CD of a circle meet at a point O inside the circle. If $OA = 4$ cm, $AB = 12$ cm and $CD = 18$ cm, find OD, given that it is larger than OC.

6. From a point O outside a circle, a secant OAB is drawn and a tangent OT. If $OT = 6$ cm and $AB = 5$ cm, find OA.

7. OAB and OCD are two straight lines. If $OA = 4$ cm, $AB = 5$ cm, $OC = 3$ cm and $CD = 9$ cm, prove that $ABDC$ is a cyclic quadrilateral.

8. OAB and OT are straight lines. If $OT = 8$ cm, $OA = 4$ cm and $AB = 12$ cm, prove that the angles OTA and OBT are equal.

9. The altitudes BE, CF of a triangle ABC meet at H. Prove that $CH.HF = BH.HE$.

10. Prove that the common chord of two intersecting circles when produced bisects their common tangents.

EXERCISES 94B

1. The chords AB, CD of a circle meet at a point O outside the circle. Given that $OA = 12$ cm, $OB = 4$ cm and $OD = 6$ cm, find OC.

2. The chords AB, CD of a circle meet at a point O outside the circle. Given that $OB = 4$ cm, $BA = 8$ cm and $OD = 6$ cm, find CD.

3. The chords AB, CD of a circle meet at a point O outside the circle. Given that $OA = 9$ cm, $OB = 4$ cm and $CD = 9$ cm, find OC.

4. The chords AB, CD of a circle meet at a point O inside the circle. If $OA = 7$ cm, $OB = 4$ cm and $OD = 3{\cdot}5$ cm, find OC.

5. The chords AB, CD of a circle meet at a point O inside the circle. If $OA = 6$ cm, $AB = 14$ cm and $CD = 16$ cm, find OD given that it is less than OC.

6. From a point O outside a circle a secant OAB and a tangent OT are drawn. If $OT = 8$ cm, $AB = 12$ cm, find OA.

7. AOB and COD are straight lines. If $OA = 4$ cm, $OB = 9$ cm, $OD = OC = 6$ cm, prove that $ABCD$ is a cyclic quadrilateral.

8. OAB and OT are straight lines. If $OT = 6$ cm, $OA = 4$ cm, $AB = 5$ cm, prove that the angles OTB and OAT are equal.

9. BE, CF are altitudes of a triangle ABC. Prove that $AF.AB = AE.AC$.

10. T is any point on the common chord (produced) of two circles. Prove that the tangents from T to the two circles are equal.

EXERCISES 95: MISCELLANEOUS

1. What is the locus of the centre of a circle which touches two given straight lines?

2. A circle is inscribed in a quadrilateral. Prove that the angles subtended at the centre of the circle by opposite sides are supplementary.

3. Two circles touch externally at P. Through P a straight line is drawn to cut the circles again at Q and R. Prove that the tangents at Q and R are parallel.

4. Two circles intersect at A and B. Through P, a point on the first circle, lines PAC and PBD are drawn to cut the second circle at C and D. Prove that CD is parallel to the tangent at P.

5. Show that the direct common tangents to two circles intersect on the line of centres produced.

6. The tangent at T to a circle cuts a chord AB produced at C. Prove that the triangles TBC and ATC are similar.

7. The tangent at T to a circle cuts a chord AB produced at C. Prove that $BC:AC = TB^2:TA^2$.

8. Two circles intersect at P and Q. A common tangent touches one circle at A and the other at B. Prove that the angles APB and AQB are supplementary.

9. Two circles touch internally at *T*. A tangent to the inner circle at *P* meets the larger circle at *X* and *Y*. Prove that *TP* bisects the angle *XTY*.

10. *X* is a point on the side *BC* of a triangle *ABC*. The tangents at *B* and *C* to the circles through *ABX* and *ACX* respectively meet at *T*. Prove that *ABTC* is a cyclic quadrilateral.

11. Two circles, centres *A* and *B*, touch externally at *P*. A common tangent of the circles touches them at *S* and *T* respectively. Prove that *AS* touches the circle through *S*, *T* and *P*.

12. Two circles, centres *A* and *B*, touch externally at *P*. A common tangent of the circles touches them at *S*, *T* respectively. Prove that the circle on *ST* as diameter touches *AB* at *P*.

13. Two circles, centres *A* and *B*, touch externally at *P*. A common tangent of the circles touches them at *S*, *T* respectively. Prove that the circle on *AB* as diameter touches *ST*.

14. Prove that, if it is possible to inscribe a circle in a parallelogram, the parallelogram must be a rhombus.

15. *AB* is a diameter of the circle *ACB*. The tangent at *C* meets the circle on *AC* as diameter at *X*. If *AX*, *BC* produced meet at *Y*, prove that *C* is the mid point of *BY*.

16. *ABC* is a triangle inscribed in a circle. The bisector of the angle *C* meets *AB* at *H* and the tangent at *A* to the circle in *X*. Given that $CH = HA = HX$, prove that *AHX* is an equilateral triangle.

17. *AD* and *BE* are altitudes of a triangle *ABC* intersecting at *H*. If *AH* produced meets the circle *ABC* again at *Q*, prove that the triangles *HBD*, *QBD* are congruent and hence prove that $BH.HE = \frac{1}{2}AH.HQ$.

18. The diagonal *AC* of the parallelogram *ABCD* is equal in length to *AB*. Prove that *BC* touches the circle through *A*, *C* and *D*.

19. Two circles intersect at *A* and *B*. Lines *PAC*, *PBD* are drawn through *P*, a point of one circle to meet the second circle at *C* and *D*. Prove that the tangents at *C* and *D* make equal angles with the tangent at *P*.

20. *ABC* is a triangle inscribed in a circle. *AD* is an altitude of the triangle. The tangent at *A* is drawn and *N* is the foot of the perpendicular from *C* to this tangent. Prove that *DN* is parallel to *AB*.

21. A diameter *BA* of a circle of radius 6 cm is produced to *T* where $AT = 4$ cm. *TX* is a tangent from *T* to the circle and *TX* produced meets the tangent at *B* in *Y*. Calculate the lengths of *TX* and *XY*.

22. *ABC* is an acute-angled triangle. A circle is drawn to pass through *B* and to touch *AC* at *A*; a second circle is drawn to touch *AC* at *C* and to pass through *B*. These circles meet again at *O*. Prove that the angles *AOC* and *ABC* are supplementary.

23. A diameter AB of a circle bisects a chord CD at X. If $AX = 9$ cm and $CX = 6$ cm, find the radius of the circle.

24. BE, CF are altitudes of the triangle ABC. If X and Y are the mid points of AC, AB respectively, prove that $XEYF$ is a cyclic quadrilateral.

25. Two circles, centres A and B, touch internally at P. Parallel radii AX and BY are drawn. Show that XYP is a straight line.

26. Two circles touch externally at P. Any point T on the tangent at P has two lines drawn through it. The first cuts one circle at A and B; the second cuts the other circle at C and D. Prove that $ABCD$ is a cyclic quadrilateral.

27. Two circles intersect at A and B. The tangent at A to the first circle meets the second circle at C; the tangent at A to the second circle meets the first circle at D. Prove that the angles ABC and ABD are equal.

28. If, in question **27**, CBD is a straight line, prove that the angle CAD is a right angle.

29. ABC is a triangle right-angled at B. The circle on AB as diameter cuts AC at D. Prove that the line joining D to the mid point of BC is a tangent to the circle.

30. C is the mid point of the minor arc AB of a circle. The tangent at A meets BC produced at X; the tangent at B meets AC produced at Y. Prove that $CY = CX$.

24

CONSTRUCTIONS

COMMON constructions which should be known are now listed. Proofs are not given fully and should be completed by the reader. Methods of proof are indicated.

CONSTRUCTION 1

To construct an angle equal to a given angle.

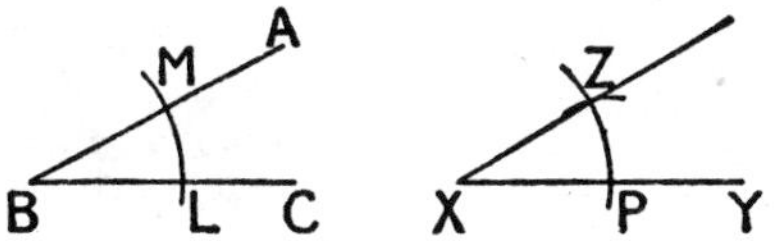

FIG. 176

Given an angle ABC and a straight line XY.

To construct a line through X making with XY an angle equal to ABC.

Construction: With centre B and any radius draw a circle to cut BC at L and BA at M.

With centre X and the same radius draw a circle (S) to cut XY at P.

With centre P and radius equal to LM draw a circle to cut S at Z.

Then XZ makes with XY the required angle.

Proof: The triangles LBM and PXZ are congruent. In particular the angles B and X are equal.

CONSTRUCTION 2

To bisect a given angle.

Given an angle ABC.

To construct the internal bisector of the angle ABC.

Construction: With centre B and any radius, draw an arc to cut BC at X and BA at Y. With centres X and Y and equal radii, greater than $\frac{1}{2}XY$, draw arcs to meet at P.

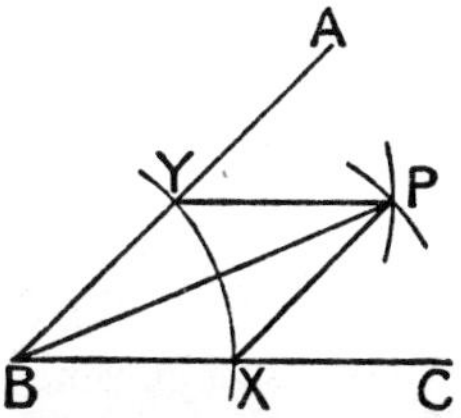

FIG. 177

Then BP is the required bisector.

Proof: The triangles PYB and PXB are congruent and in particular the angles PBX and PBY are equal.

CONSTRUCTION 3

To construct a perpendicular from a given point on a line to that line.

Given a straight line AB with a point P on it.

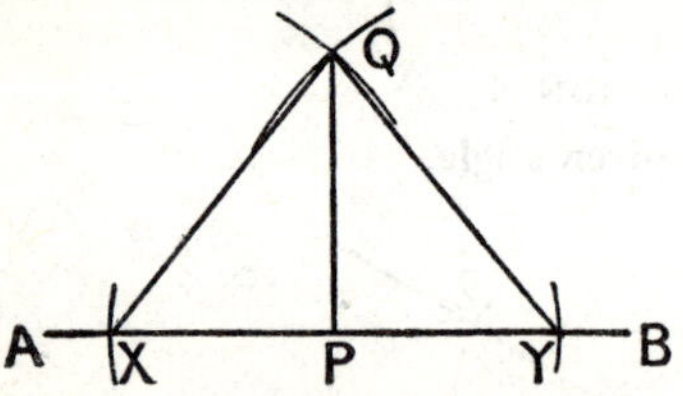

FIG. 178

To construct a line through P perpendicular to AB.

Construction: With centre P and any radius, draw a circle to cut AB at X and Y.

With centres X and Y and equal radii greater than XP, draw arcs to meet at Q.

Then PQ is the required perpendicular.

Proof: The triangles PXQ and PYQ are congruent. In particular, the angles QPX and QPY are equal.

CONSTRUCTION 4

To bisect a given straight line.

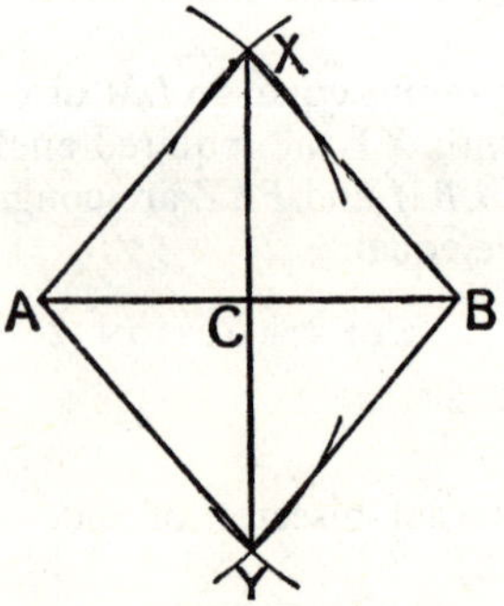

FIG. 179

Given a straight line AB.

To construct the mid point of AB.

Construction: With centres A and B and equal radii, greater than $\frac{1}{2}AB$, draw circles to cut at X and Y. Join X and Y to meet AB at C.

Then C is the mid point of AB and XY is the perpendicular bisector of AB.

Proof: The triangles AXY and BXY are congruent. In particular, the angles AXC and BXC are equal. Next, the triangles AXC and BXC may be proved congruent.

CONSTRUCTION 5

To construct a perpendicular from a given point to a given line.

Given a straight line AB and a point P not on the line.

To construct the perpendicular from P to AB.

Construction: Draw a circle with centre P to cut AB at X and Y. With equal radii, and centres X and Y, draw two circles to meet at Q (on the opposite side of AB from P).

Then PQ is the required perpendicular.

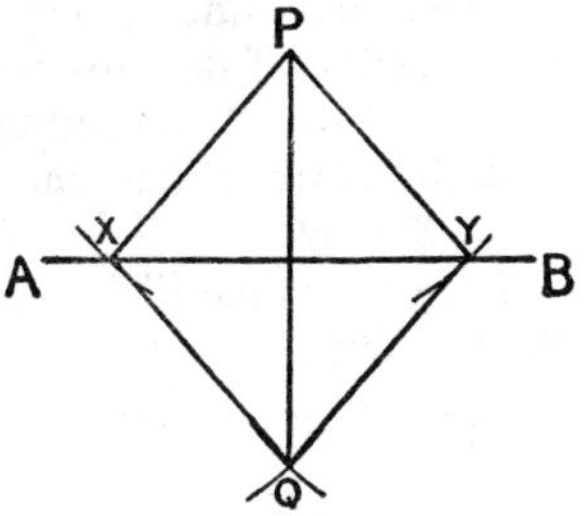

FIG. 180

Proof: The triangles PXQ and PYQ are congruent. In particular, the angles XPQ and YPQ are equal. Now the triangles XPZ and YPZ may be proved congruent, where Z is the foot of the perpendicular.

CONSTRUCTION 6

To construct an angle of 60°.

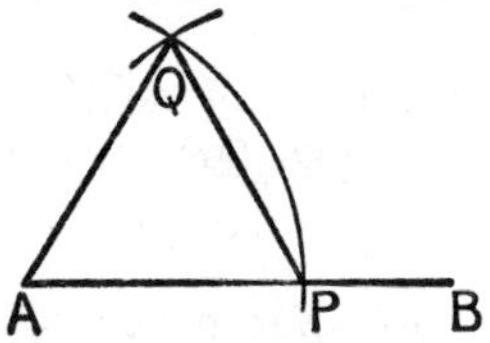

FIG. 181

Construction: Draw any line AB.

With centre A and any radius, draw a circle S to cut AB at P.

With centre P and the same radius, draw an arc to cut S at Q.

Then the angle $PAQ = 60°$.

Proof: The triangle AQP is equilateral.

(N.B. By bisecting an angle of 60°, an angle equal to 30° may be constructed. An angle of 45° is constructed by bisecting a constructed right angle.)

CONSTRUCTION 7

To construct through a given point a straight line parallel to a given straight line.

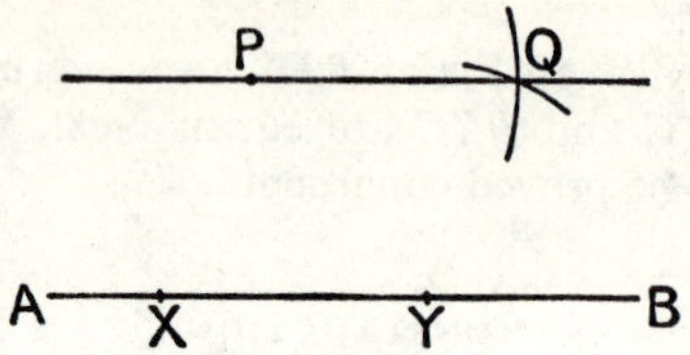

FIG. 182

Given a straight line *AB* and a point *P* not on the line.
To construct a line through *P* parallel to *AB*.
Construction: Take any two points *X* and *Y* on *AB*.
With centre *P* and radius equal to *XY*, draw a circle *S*.
With centre *Y* and radius equal to *XP*, draw another circle to cut *S* at *Q*.
Then *PQ* is parallel to *XY*.
Proof: *XPQY* is a quadrilateral with its opposite sides equal. It is therefore a parallelogram.

CONSTRUCTION 8

To divide a given straight line into a given number of equal parts.

Suppose the number of parts to be five. A similar construction holds for any other integral number of parts.

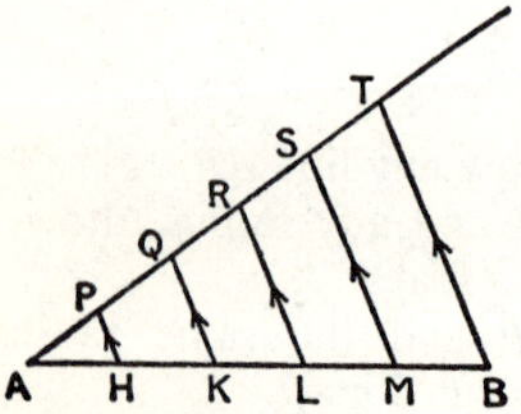

FIG. 183

Given a straight line *AB*.
To construct the points which divide *AB* into five equal parts.
Construction: Draw any other line through *A*.
With compasses, mark off any five equal distances *AP*, *PQ*, *QR*, *RS*, *ST* on this line.
Join *TB*.
Draw *PH*, *QK*, *RL*, *SM* parallel to *TB* to meet *AB* at *H*, *K*, *L*, *M*.
Then *H*, *K*, *L*, *M* divide *AB* into five equal parts.
Proof: By the intercept theorem.

CONSTRUCTION 9

To construct a triangle equal in area to a given quadrilateral.

Given a quadrilateral *ABCD*.

To construct a triangle equal in area to *ABCD*.

Construction: Join *DB*.

Through *C* draw a line parallel to *DB* to meet *AB* produced at *X*. Then *ADX* is a triangle equal in area to *ABCD*.

Proof: The triangles *DCB* and *DXB* are equal in area. Add to each the area of *ADB*.

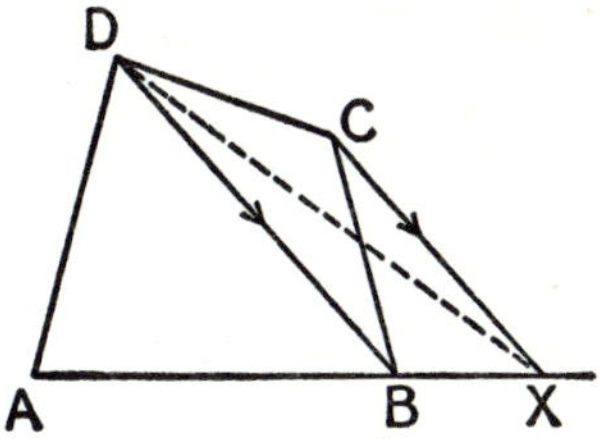

FIG. 184

(N.B. By a similar construction, a polygon of $(n - 1)$ sides may be constructed equal in area to a given polygon of n sides. By successive reduction, a triangle may be constructed equal in area to any given polygon.)

CONSTRUCTION 10

To construct a tangent to a circle at a given point of the circle.

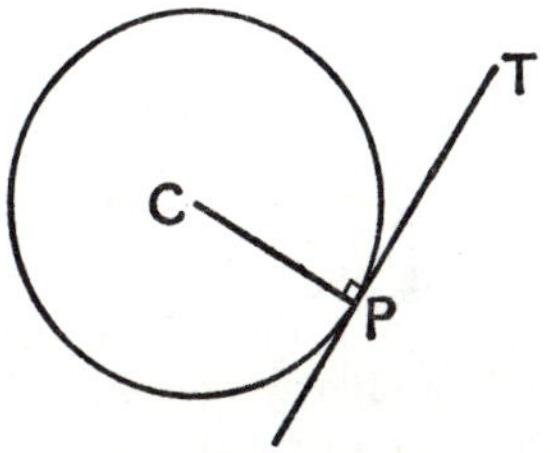

FIG. 185

Given a point *P* on a circle centre *C*.

To construct the tangent at *P* to the circle.

Construction: Draw through *P* a line *PT* so that the angle *CPT* is a right angle.

PT is the tangent at *P*.

Proof: The tangent is perpendicular to the radius at the point of contact.

CONSTRUCTION 11

To construct the pair of tangents from a given point to a given circle.

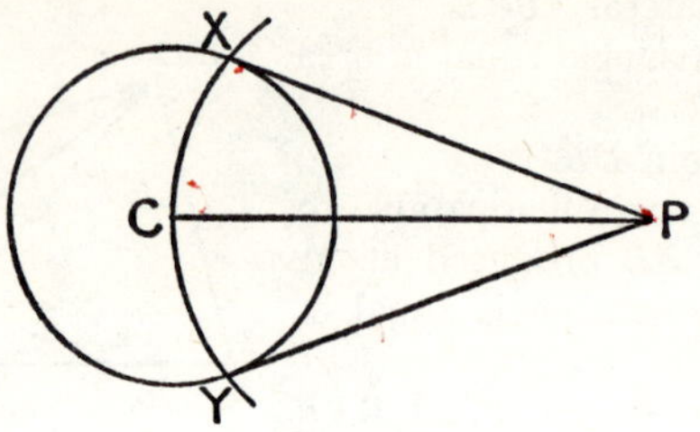

FIG. 186

Given a circle centre *C* and a point *P* outside the circle.
To construct the tangents from *P* to the circle.
Construction: Join *CP*.
Draw the circle on *CP* as diameter to meet the given circle at *X* and *Y*. Then *PX* and *PY* are the required tangents.
Proof: The angles *CXP* and *CYP* are angles in a semicircle.

CONSTRUCTION 12

To construct the circumcircle of a given triangle.

Given a triangle *ABC*.
To construct the circumcircle of *ABC*.
Construction: Construct the perpendicular bisectors of *CA* and *CB* to meet at *O*.
With centre *O* and radius equal to *OC*, draw a circle. This is the circumcircle of the triangle *ABC*.
Proof: *O* lies on the perpendicular bisector of *AC* and so is equidistant from *A* and *C*. Similarly *O* is equidistant from *B* and *C*.

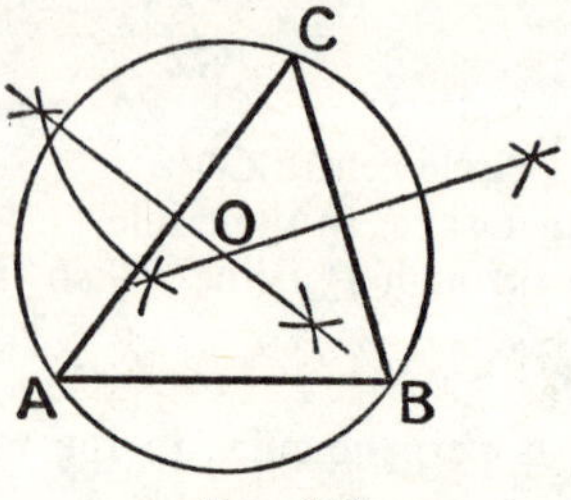

FIG. 187

CONSTRUCTION 13

To construct the inscribed circle of a given triangle.

Given a triangle ABC.

To construct its incircle.

Construction: Construct the internal bisectors of the angles A and B to meet at I.

Construct IX, the perpendicular from I to AB.

With centre I and radius IX, draw a circle.

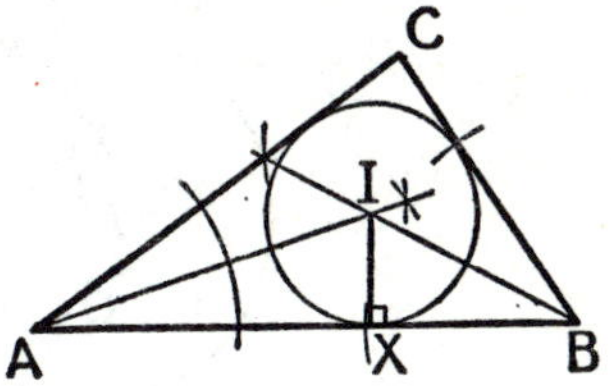

FIG. 188

This is the inscribed circle of the triangle ABC.

Proof: I lies on the internal bisector of the angle A and is therefore equidistant from AB and AC. Similarly I is equidistant from AB and BC.

CONSTRUCTION 14

To construct an escribed circle of a given triangle.

A triangle ABC has three escribed circles. These are called the escribed circles opposite A, B and C respectively. The escribed circle opposite A touches BC internally and touches AB and AC produced.

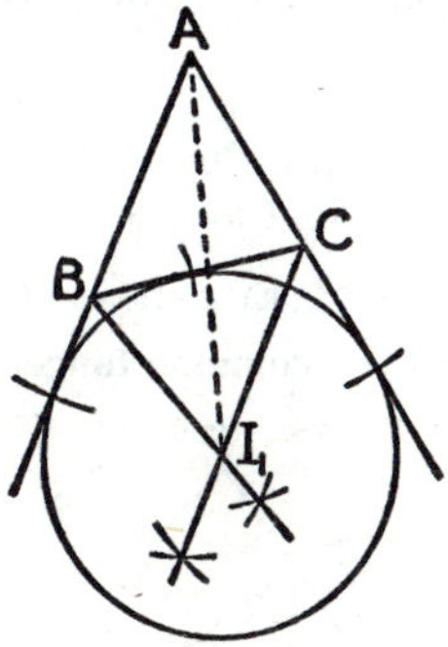

FIG. 189

The internal bisector of the angle A and the external bisectors of the angles B and C all meet in a point I_1, which is the centre of the escribed circle opposite A.

The centres of the escribed circles opposite B and C are conventionally called I_2 and I_3 respectively.

CONSTRUCTION 15

To construct the direct common tangents to two given circles.

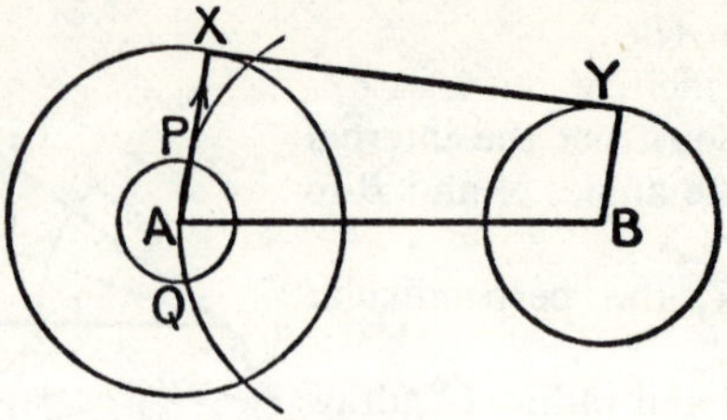

FIG. 190

Given two circles centres A and B, radii a and b, where a is greater than b.

To construct their direct common tangents.

Construction: Draw a circle centre A, radius $(a - b)$.

Draw a circle on AB as diameter to cut the first constructed circle at P and Q.

Produce AP to meet the given circle centre A at X.

Through B draw the line parallel to AX to meet the circle centre B at Y.

Then XY is a direct common tangent.

The second direct common tangent is constructed similarly by producing AQ.

Proof: $XP = XA - AP = a - (a - b) = b = BY$.

So $PXYB$ is a parallelogram. But APB is a right angle and therefore AXY and BYX are right angles.

CONSTRUCTION 16

To construct the transverse common tangents to two given circles.

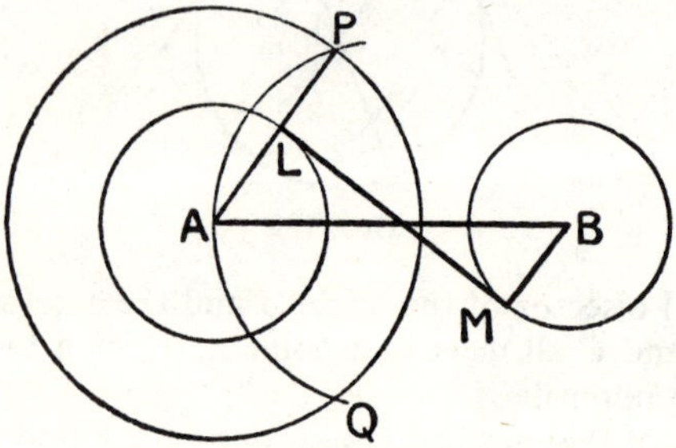

FIG. 191

Given two circles centres A and B, radii a and b.
To construct their transverse common tangents.
Construction: Draw a circle centre A, radius $(a + b)$.

Draw the circle on AB as diameter to cut the first constructed circle at P and Q.

Join AP to meet the given circle centre A at L.

Draw BM parallel to PL to meet the given circle centre B at M.

Then LM is a transverse common tangent.

The other transverse common tangent is constructed similarly by joining AQ.

Proof: $PL = AP - AL = (a + b) - a = b = BM$.

So $LPBM$ is a parallelogram.

But $\widehat{APB} = 90°$ and therefore $LPBM$ is a rectangle.

$$\therefore \widehat{ALM} = \widehat{BML} = 90°.$$

CONSTRUCTION 17

To construct the locus of a point at which a given straight line subtends a given angle.

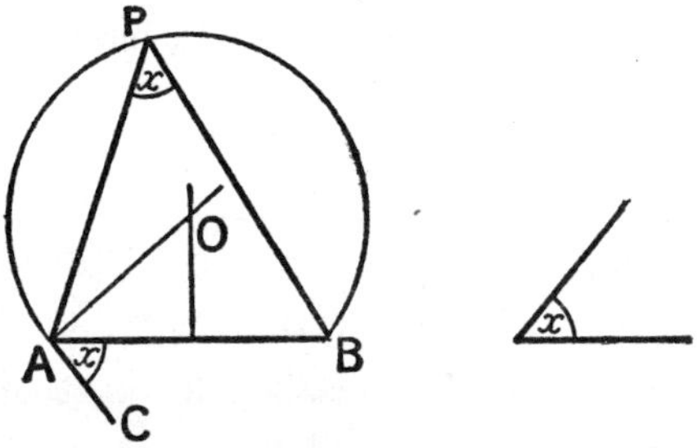

FIG. 192

Given a fixed straight line AB and an angle x.

To construct the locus of a point P which moves so that $\widehat{APB} = x$.

Construction: Draw AC so that $\widehat{BAC} = x$.

Through A draw the perpendicular to AC to cut the perpendicular bisector of AB at O.

With centre O and radius OA draw an arc of a circle terminated by A and B.

This arc is the required locus.

Proof: Since O is on the perpendicular bisector of AB, $OA = OB$.
The arc therefore passes through A and B.

AC is a tangent to the circle and $A\hat{P}B = x$.
(N.B. The complete locus consists of two equal arcs, one on each side of AB.)

Construction 18

To construct a square equal in area to a given rectangle.

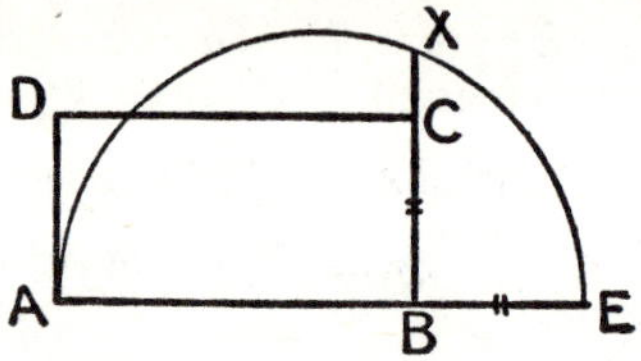

Fig. 193

Given a rectangle $ABCD$.
To construct a square equal in area to $ABCD$.
Construction: Produce AB to E so that $BE = BC$.
Draw the circle on AE as diameter to meet BC, produced if necessary, at X.
Then BX is a side of the required square.
Proof: AE bisects any chord of the circle perpendicular to it.

$$\therefore AB.BE = BX^2.$$

Construction 19

To draw a regular polygon of *n* sides (i) in, (ii) about a given circle.

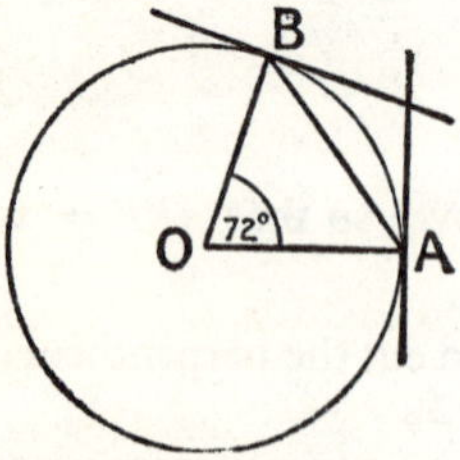

Fig. 194

We shall suppose the polygon has five sides. A similar construction holds for any other integral number of sides.
Given a circle centre O.
To draw a polygon of 5 sides (i) in, (ii) about the circle.
Construction: (i) Draw an angle at the centre equal to $\frac{360°}{5}$, i.e. 72°.

If the arms of this angle meet the circle at A and B, then AB is one side of the required pentagon.

(ii) The tangents at A and B are two sides of the regular pentagon drawn about the circle.

Proof: The symmetry of the figure.

CONSTRUCTION 20

To construct a fourth proportional to three given lines.

Given three distances a, b and c, the fourth proportional is x where $a : b = c : x$.

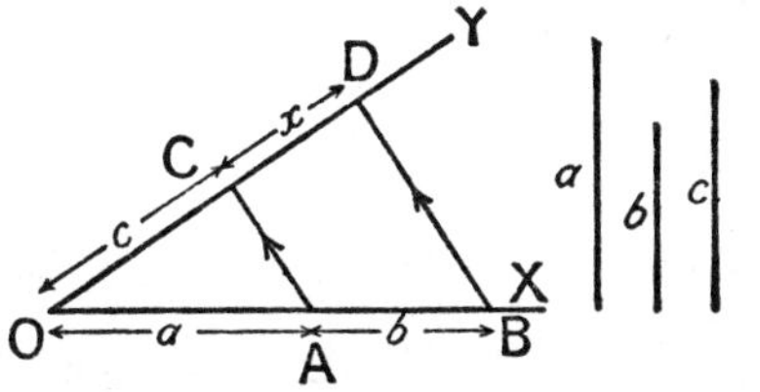

FIG. 195

Given three straight lines a, b and c.

To construct a line x such that $a : b = c : x$.

Construction: Draw any two lines OX and OY.

Along OX, mark off $OA = a$ and $AB = b$.

Along OY, mark off $OC = c$.

Join AC.

Through B draw BD parallel to AC to meet OY at D.

Then CD is the fourth proportional.

Proof: By parallels, $\dfrac{OA}{AB} = \dfrac{OC}{CD}$.

CONSTRUCTION 21

To construct a mean proportional to two given lines.

Given two distances a and b, their mean proportional is x where $a : x = x : b$.

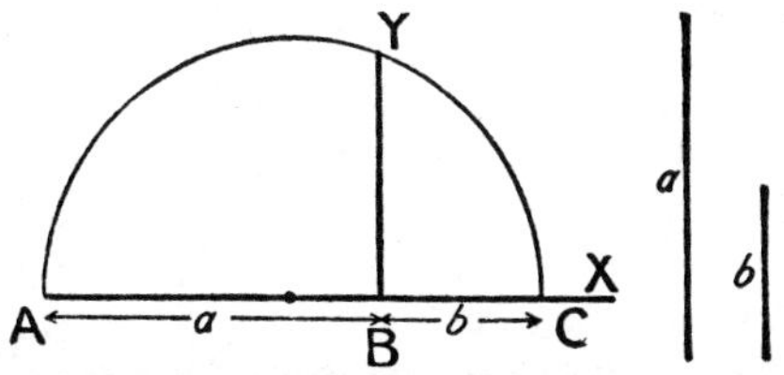

FIG. 196

L

Given two lines a and b.

To construct a mean proportional to a and b.

Construction: Draw any line AX.

Along AX, mark off $AB = a$ and $BC = b$.

Draw the circle on AC as diameter.

Through B draw the perpendicular to AC to cut the circle at Y.

Then BY is the mean proportional to a and b.

Proof: AC bisects any chord perpendicular to it.

$$\therefore\ AB.BC = BY^2.$$

Exercises 96: Miscellaneous Constructions

1. Draw the triangle ABC of sides 6·8 cm, 3 cm and 3·8 cm. Construct its circumcircle.

2. Draw a triangle ABC in which $AB = 5{\cdot}6$ cm, the angle $B = 80°$ and the angle $C = 50°$. Construct the inscribed circle of the triangle.

3. On a straight line 3·6 cm long describe a segment of a circle to contain an angle of 50°.

4. Construct a circle of radius 2 cm to touch both the circumference and a diameter of a circle of radius 4 cm.

5. Construct a triangle of sides 4 cm, 6 cm and 8 cm. Construct the altitudes of this triangle and verify that they are concurrent.

6. A triangle XYZ is such that $XY = 4$ cm, $YZ = 6$ cm and the angle $Y = 60°$. Construct the triangle and the escribed circle of the triangle opposite Y.

7. Two circles radii 6 cm and 4 cm have their centres 8 cm apart. Construct a direct common tangent and measure its length.

8. Two circles radii 4 cm and 5 cm have their centres 12 cm apart. Construct a transverse common tangent and measure its length.

9. Without using set square or protractor construct a triangle XYZ in which $XY = 2{\cdot}4$ cm, $YZ = 3$ cm and the angle $Y = 120°$. Find a point P such that $Y\hat{X}P = 90°$ and $YP = ZP$.

10. Construct a rhombus with sides 6 cm long with one diagonal 8 cm long. Construct also the circle which touches all the sides of the rhombus.

11. Draw two lines XY, YZ to include an angle of 50°. Construct a circle of radius 2·8 cm to touch both XY and YZ.

12. Draw a circle of radius 4 cm and inscribe in it a regular hexagon. By making suitable measurements, calculate the area of the hexagon.

13. Draw a triangle ABC given that $AB = 6$ cm, the angle $ACB = 52°$ and the area of the triangle is 15 cm².

14. A given rectangle has sides 6 cm and 8 cm long. By construction, find the other side of a rectangle of equal area given that one of its sides is 10 cm long.

15. A given rectangle has sides 6 cm and 8 cm. By construction, find and measure the side of a square of equal area.

16. Construct a parallelogram given that one side is 5 cm long and that the diagonals are 8 cm and 6 cm in length.

17. Draw a triangle ABC in which $BC = 5$ cm, $BA = 4$ cm and $AC = 3$ cm. Construct a rectangle $ABXY$ equal in area to the triangle. Hence construct a square equal in area to the triangle.

18. Using ruler and compasses only, construct a trapezium $ABCD$ in which the parallel sides AB and DC are 2 cm apart, given that $AB = 4{\cdot}8$ cm, the angle $A = 60°$ and $BC = 3{\cdot}2$ cm. Is it possible to draw more than one such trapezium?

19. Draw a circle centre O of radius 4 cm. P is a point distant 6 cm from O. Construct two chords of the circle, each distant 2 cm from the centre, which pass through P when produced.

20. Using ruler and compasses only, draw a quadrilateral $ABCD$ in which the angle $DAB = 60°$, $AB = 4$ cm, the angle $CDA =$ the angle $ABC = 90°$ and $BC = 3{\cdot}5$ cm. Construct a triangle on base AB equal in area to the quadrilateral.

21. Construct a triangle XYZ given that XY is greater than XZ and that $YZ = 4$ cm, the angle $X = 60°$ and the altitude through $X = 3$ cm.

22. Draw a triangle ABC in which $BC = 7$ cm, $CA = 5$ cm and $AB = 4$ cm. Find by construction a point P such that the angle $APB = 40°$ and the angle $APC = 90°$.

23. AB is a diameter of a circle of radius 2 cm. Construct a circle of radius 4 cm to touch the circle externally and also to touch AB produced.

24. Draw a quadrilateral $ABCD$ given that $AB = 4$ cm, $BC = 5$ cm, $CD = 3{\cdot}4$ cm, $DA = 3{\cdot}4$ cm and the angle $B = 70°$. Construct a triangle on base BC equal in area to the quadrilateral.

25. Construct a triangle ABC given that $AB = 4$ cm, $BC = 5$ cm and that the length of the median through A is $3\frac{1}{2}$ cm.

26. Draw a triangle of sides 5 cm, 6 cm and 7 cm and construct the side of a square equal in area to the triangle.

27. The area of an acute-angled triangle is $5{\cdot}6$ cm^2. Two of the sides are known to be $4{\cdot}8$ cm and 3 cm. Construct the triangle.

28. Draw a circle of radius 6 cm and mark a point P distant 4 cm from the centre. Construct a chord of length 8 cm to pass through P.

29. Draw a triangle ABC in which $BC = 4$ cm, the angle $B = 50°$ and the angle $C = 70°$. Construct a point P which is equidistant from the lines AB and AC and which is also equidistant from B and C.

30. Draw two lines OX and OY inclined at an angle of 60°. On OX, mark points P, Q such that $OP = 6$ cm and $OQ = 10$ cm. Construct a circle to pass through the points P and Q and to touch the line OY.

31. Using ruler and compasses only, construct a triangle PQR in which the angle $P = 45°$, $PQ = 5$ cm and $PR = 6$ cm. Construct a point X inside the triangle which is equidistant from Q and R so that $PX = 4$ cm.

32. Draw a circle of radius 4 cm and mark a point P distant 6 cm from its centre. Construct two circles each of radius 5 cm to touch the given circle externally and also to pass through P.

33. Draw a quadrilateral $ABCD$ given that $AB = 5$ cm, $AD = 6$ cm and the diagonal $BD = 8$ cm. You are also given that the areas of the two triangles BAD and BCD are equal and that the angle at C is a right angle. How many such quadrilaterals are possible?

34. Construct a parallelogram $ABCD$ such that its diagonals are 7·2 cm and 5·6 cm long and such that the angle between the diagonals is 60°. Find a point X on AB produced so that the angle $CXB = 45°$.

35. Draw a triangle ABC in which $BC = 8$ cm, $CA = 6$ cm and $AB = 4$ cm. Construct the circle which touches BC at B and which also passes through A. Find a point P on this circle and inside the triangle equidistant from CA and CB.

36. Draw a circle of radius 4 cm. Construct a regular hexagon to circumscribe the circle. Given that AB and BC are adjacent sides of the hexagon, construct a point O which is equidistant from A and B and also equidistant from A and C. What is the point O?

37. Draw a triangle ABC in which $AC = 5$ cm, $CB = 7$ cm and $AB = 6$ cm. Mark D, the mid point of AB. Draw the circle which touches BC at C and passes through D. Find a point P on this circle such that the angle APB is a right angle.

38. Two circles with centres P and Q intersect at A and B. The radii of the circles are 4 cm and 5 cm and the distance between their centres is 7 cm. Construct a common tangent to the circles and verify that AB produced bisects this common tangent.

39. Draw a parallelogram $ABCD$ in which $AB = 3·6$ cm, $AD = 2·7$ cm and the angle $A = 50°$. Construct an equiangular parallelogram of the same area with one side 3 cm long.

40. Show how to bisect the area of a triangle by a straight line drawn through a given point of one of its sides.

41. A point P is 4 cm from a given line AB. Draw two circles each of radius 3 cm to touch AB and to pass through P.

42. Two parallel lines are cut by a transversal. Show how to draw a circle to touch all three lines.

43. In a circle of radius 4 cm inscribe a rectangle one of whose sides is 6 cm long.

44. Draw a circle of radius 5 cm. Construct two tangents to the circle which include an angle of 80°.

45. Draw a triangle *ABC* with sides 6 cm, 7 cm and 8 cm long. Find a point *P* inside the triangle at which *AB*, *BC* and *CA* all subtend equal angles.

46. Draw a circle of radius 5 cm. From a point 8 cm from its centre, construct the two tangents to the circle. Construct a circle to touch these tangents and the given circle.

47. Draw a circle of radius 6 cm and two radii which include an angle of 80°. Construct a circle to touch these two radii and the given circle.

48. Construct a right-angled triangle given that the length of the hypotenuse is 10 cm and that the altitude to the hypotenuse is 4·8 cm long.

49. Draw a regular pentagon of side 4 cm and construct a square of equal area.

50. Draw a circle of radius 6 cm. Construct a chord *AB* which is 8 cm long. Find a point *P* on the minor arc *AB* such that $AP : PB = 4 : 3$.

TRIGONOMETRY

TRIGONOMETRY FORMULAE

The ratios

$$\sin \text{ is } \frac{\text{opp.}}{\text{hyp.}};$$

$$\cos \text{ is } \frac{\text{adj.}}{\text{hyp.}};$$

$$\tan \text{ is } \frac{\text{opp.}}{\text{adj.}};$$

$$\text{cosec is } \frac{\text{hyp.}}{\text{opp.}};$$

$$\sec \text{ is } \frac{\text{hyp.}}{\text{adj.}};$$

$$\cot \text{ is } \frac{\text{adj.}}{\text{opp.}}.$$

$\sin(90° - A) = \cos A.$

$\sec(90° - A) = \text{cosec } A.$

$\tan(90° - A) = \cot A.$

$\sin 0° = 0;$ $\quad \sin 30° = \frac{1}{2};$ $\quad \sin 45° = \frac{1}{\sqrt{2}};$

$\sin 60° = \frac{\sqrt{3}}{2};$ $\quad \sin 90° = 1.$

$\cos 0° = 1;$ $\quad \cos 30° = \frac{\sqrt{3}}{2};$ $\quad \cos 45° = \frac{1}{\sqrt{2}};$

$\cos 60° = \frac{1}{2};$ $\quad \cos 90° = 0.$

$\tan 0° = 0;$ $\quad \tan 30° = \frac{1}{\sqrt{3}};$ $\quad \tan 45° = 1;$

$\tan 60° = \sqrt{3};$ $\quad \tan 90° = \infty.$

$\sin(180° - A) = \sin A.$

$\cos(180° - A) = -\cos A.$

$\tan(180° - A) = -\tan A.$

Identities

$$\tan A = \frac{\sin A}{\cos A}.$$

$$\sin^2 A + \cos^2 A = 1.$$

$$\sec^2 A = 1 + \tan^2 A.$$

$$\operatorname{cosec}^2 A = 1 + \cot^2 A.$$

Sine formula

$$\frac{a}{\sin A} = \frac{b}{\sin B} = \frac{c}{\sin C}.$$

Cosine formula

$$c^2 = a^2 + b^2 - 2ab \cos C$$

$$\text{or } \cos C = \frac{a^2 + b^2 - c^2}{2ab}.$$

Area of a triangle

$$\triangle = \tfrac{1}{2}bc \sin A = \sqrt{s(s-a)(s-b)(s-c)}.$$

Arc and sector

$$\text{Length of arc} = \frac{x}{360}(2\pi r).$$

$$\text{Area of sector} = \frac{x}{360}(\pi r^2).$$

25

RATIOS OF AN ACUTE ANGLE

The tangent

DRAW a triangle ABC, right-angled at B and with the angle at A equal to 40°, say. Take points C' on AC and B' on AB so that $C'B'$ is parallel to CB. By similar triangles, the two ratios $\frac{CB}{AB}$ and $\frac{C'B'}{AB'}$ are equal to each other. Moreover the ratio $\frac{C'B'}{AB'}$ is the same wherever $C'B'$ is drawn, provided it remains parallel to CB. Therefore this ratio $\frac{CB}{AB}$ is one which is independent of the triangle ABC and which depends only on the angle A, or 40°. The ratio is called the **tangent** of 40° and, in a similar way, the tangent of any angle may be defined.

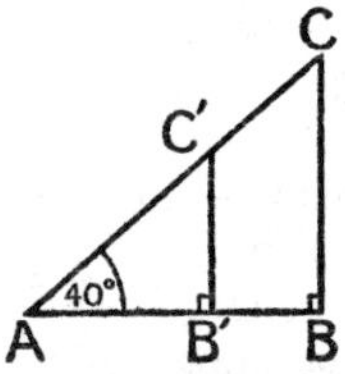

FIG. 197

When considering the angle A in the right-angled triangle ABC, the side BC is called the opposite side and AC, the side opposite the right angle, is called the hypotenuse. The remaining side AB is called the adjacent side.

The tangent of an angle is therefore the ratio of the opposite side to the adjacent, in a right-angled triangle. The equation is usually written $\tan A = \frac{CB}{AB}$.

The sine

In Fig. 197, the ratio $\frac{CB}{AC}$ is equal to the ratio $\frac{C'B'}{AC'}$. This ratio must depend on the angle A and not on the triangle ABC. This particular ratio is called the **sine** of the angle A.

The sine of an angle is therefore the ratio of the opposite side to the hypotenuse in a right-angled triangle.

The equation is usually written $\sin A = \frac{CB}{AC}$.

The cosine

In Fig. 197, the ratio $\frac{AB}{AC}$ is equal to the ratio $\frac{AB'}{AC'}$. This ratio, too, must depend on the angle A and not on the triangle ABC. This ratio is called the **cosine** of the angle A.

The cosine of an angle is therefore the ratio of the adjacent side to the hypotenuse in a right-angled triangle.

The equation is usually written $\cos A = \frac{AB}{AC}$.

The cotangent

The triangle ABC has three sides and from these three sides you can get six ratios. The six ratios are the three we have already considered $\frac{CB}{AB}, \frac{CB}{AC}, \frac{AB}{AC}$, and their reciprocals $\frac{AB}{CB}, \frac{AC}{CB}, \frac{AC}{AB}$. The ratio $\frac{AB}{BC}$ is, of course, equal to $\frac{1}{\tan A}$, but it is found more convenient to give it a separate name and this ratio is called the **cotangent** of the angle A.

The cotangent of an angle is the ratio of the adjacent side to the opposite in a right-angled triangle.

The equation is usually written $\cot A = \frac{AB}{BC}$.

You know from the definition that $\tan A = \frac{1}{\cot A}$ and that $\cot A = \frac{1}{\tan A}$.

The cosecant

Similarly there is a special name given to the reciprocal of sin A and this is called the cosecant of the angle A. The cosecant of an angle is the ratio of the hypotenuse to the opposite side in a right-angled triangle.

The equation is usually written $\operatorname{cosec} A = \frac{AC}{CB}$.

You know from the definition that $\sin A = \frac{1}{\operatorname{cosec} A}$ and that $\operatorname{cosec} A = \frac{1}{\sin A}$.

The secant

The name given to the reciprocal of the cosine of an angle is the **secant.**

The secant of an angle is the ratio of the hypotenuse to the adjacent side in a right-angled triangle.

The equation is usually written $\sec A = \frac{AC}{AB}$.

You know from the definition that $\cos A = \frac{1}{\sec A}$ and that $\sec A = \frac{1}{\cos A}$.

The six ratios

These six quantities sin, cos, tan, cosec, sec and cot are called the trigonometrical ratios and are usually remembered in the order given. For convenience, the values of the six ratios are listed together using the abbreviations O for opposite side, A for adjacent side and H for hypotenuse. Remember that each of the second set of three is merely the reciprocal of the corresponding member of the first set.

$$\sin A = \frac{O}{H}; \qquad \text{cosec A} = \frac{H}{O};$$

$$\cos A = \frac{A}{H}; \qquad \sec A = \frac{H}{A};$$

$$\tan A = \frac{O}{A}; \qquad \text{cotan } A = \frac{A}{O}.$$

N.B. Do not use these formulae unless the triangle is right-angled.

EXERCISES 97A

1. From Fig. 198, write down the values of sin A, cos C, tan A, cot C, sec A, cosec C.

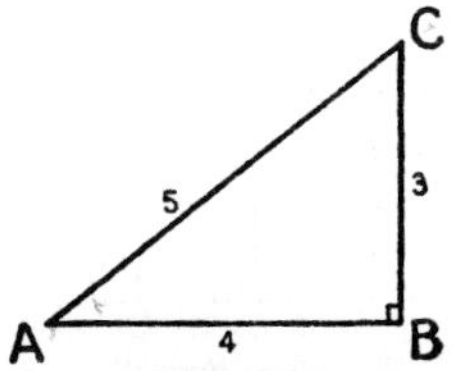

FIG. 198

2. From Fig. 199, write down the values of tan A, sin C, cot A, cosec C.

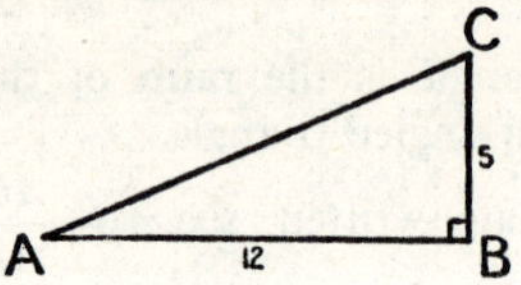

FIG. 199

3. From Fig. 200, write down the values of sin x and cot y.

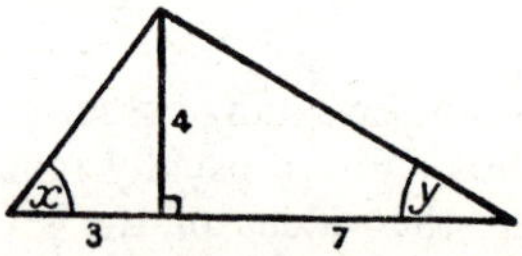

FIG. 200

4. From Fig. 201, write down the values of tan A and cot C.

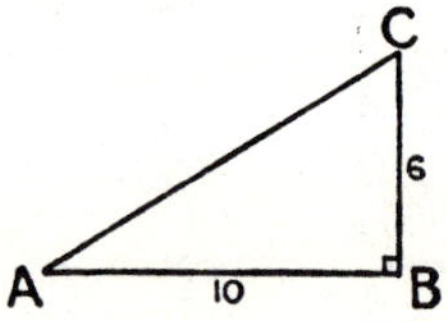

FIG. 201

5. From Fig. 202, write down the value of cos x and calculate the value of tan x.

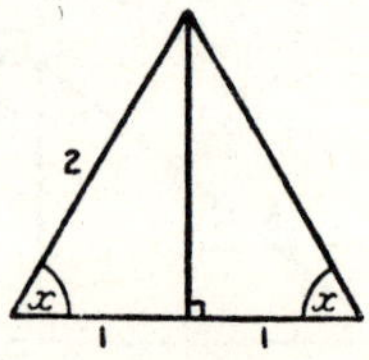

FIG. 202

EXERCISES 97B

1. From Fig. 203, write down the values of sin *A*, cos *C*, tan *A*, cot *C*.

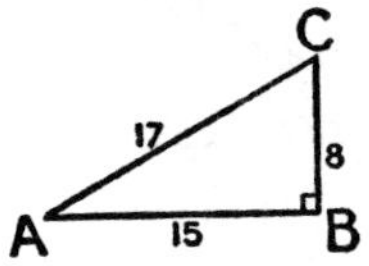

FIG. 203

2. From Fig. 204, write down the values of sin *A* and sin *C*.

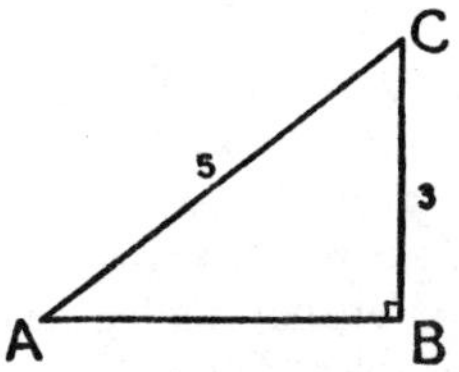

FIG. 204

3. From Fig. 205, write down the values of cos *x* and tan *y*.

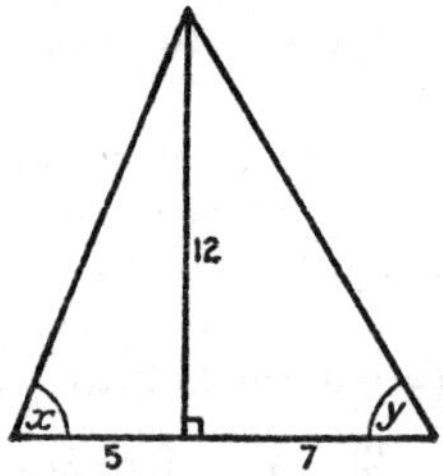

FIG. 205

4. From Fig. 206, write down the values of sec *A* and cosec *C*.

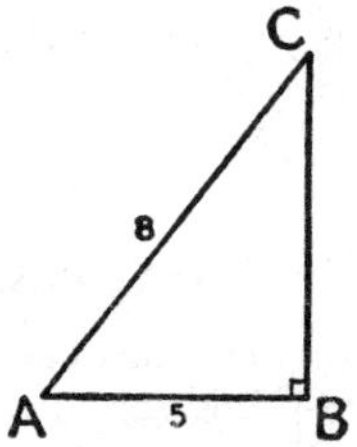

FIG. 206

5. From Fig. 207, write down the value of $\tan x$ and calculate the value of $\sin x$.

FIG. 207

Use of tables

You should have tables which give the values of the six ratios of any acute angle. When you need to know the value of a ratio of a certain angle, use these tables. You are not expected to find an approximate value by drawing a triangle.

Conversely, if you are given the value of a ratio of an unknown angle, you can find the angle, if you know that it is acute. Supposing that $\sin A = 0{\cdot}6721$. Look for the number nearest 0·6721 and below it in the body of the sin tables. This is 0·6717 which is 4 short of 0·6721. The difference 4 corresponds to 2′. The acute angle A is therefore 42° 14′.

N.B. Remember to **subtract** the difference in the tables for those ratios which begin with the prefix **co.** That is for cosine, cosecant and cotangent.

The angle whose sine is 0·6721 is sometimes written arc sin 0·6721, sometimes anti-sin 0·6721 but most commonly $\sin^{-1} 0{\cdot}6721$. This is read 'the angle whose sine is 0·6721', and it is true to say that $\sin^{-1} 0{\cdot}6721 = 42° \, 14'$.

This gives the same information as the equation

$$\sin 42° \, 14' = 0{\cdot}6721.$$

In your book of tables, you will also find tabulated values for log sin, log cos, etc. The log sin tables are given to save you the double operation of looking up firstly the sine of an angle and secondly its logarithm.

EXERCISES 98A

1. Write down the values of the following: sin 20°, cos 70°, cot 40°, tan 13° 12′, tan 63° 27′, cosec 14° 26′, sec 70° 33′, cot 14° 3′, sin 24° 15′, cos 32° 16′.

2. Find the acute angles equal to the following: $\sin^{-1} 0{\cdot}5$, $\cos^{-1} 0{\cdot}5$, $\tan^{-1} 0{\cdot}8341$, $\text{cosec}^{-1} 1{\cdot}6241$, $\sec^{-1} 1{\cdot}9999$, $\cot^{-1} 2$, $\sin^{-1} \frac{1}{3}$, $\cos^{-1} \frac{2}{3}$, $\tan^{-1} 1$, $\tan^{-1} 2$.

EXERCISES 98B

1. Write down the values of the following: sin 25°, cosec 42°, tan 18°, sin 68° 13′, cos 72° 11′, cot 11° 22′, sec 75° 32′, cosec 14° 28′, cosec 22° 3′, cosec 60°.

2. Find the acute angles equal to the following: $\sin^{-1} 0{\cdot}866$, $\cos^{-1} 0{\cdot}866$, $\tan^{-1} 3{\cdot}0$, $\text{cosec}^{-1} 2$, $\sec^{-1} 2$, $\text{cosec}^{-1} 2{\cdot}413$, $\sin^{-1} \frac{1}{5}$, $\tan^{-1} \frac{4}{3}$, $\cot^{-1} 3$, $\cot^{-1} 1$.

Given one ratio, to find the others

Supposing you are given the value of sin A and are asked to find the other ratios of the angle A without using tables. Sketch a right-angled triangle chosen so that the sine of one of its angles is equal to the given quantity. There is no need for a figure drawn to scale. Calculate the other side of the right-angled triangle by Pythagoras and then you will be able to write down the values of the other ratios.

Example 1. Given that A is an acute angle and that $\tan A = \frac{4}{3}$, find the value of cosec A.

Sketch a right-angled triangle so that the lengths of the sides containing

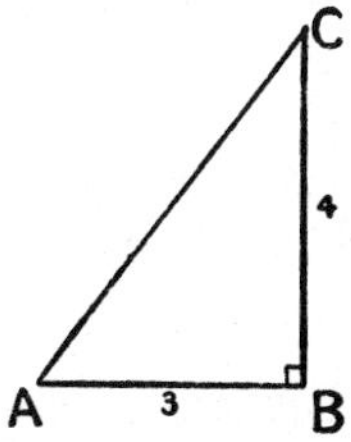

FIG. 208

the right angle are 4 cm. and 3 cm. The angle opposite the side of length 4 cm. is equal to A. The other side of the triangle is given by

$$AC^2 = 3^2 + 4^2, \quad \text{and therefore} \quad AC = 5 \text{ cm.}$$

$\therefore$ cosec $A = \frac{5}{4}$.

Example 2. Given that x is an acute angle and that $\sin x = \frac{m}{n}$, find $\cot x$.

The triangle shown has $\sin x = \frac{m}{n}$, By Pythagoras, the length of the third side is $\sqrt{n^2 - m^2}$.

$$\therefore \cot x = \frac{\sqrt{n^2 - m^2}}{m}.$$

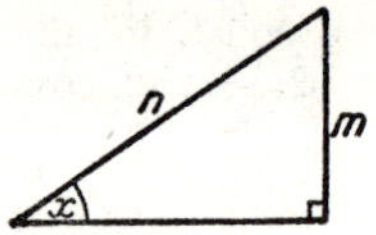

FIG. 209

N.B. It is well worth noting that, since the hypotenuse must be the longest side of a triangle, the sin and cosine of an angle are always less than 1; for the same reason, the sec and cosec of an angle are always greater than 1. There is no restriction on the value of the tangent or the cotangent of an angle.

EXERCISES 99A

1. Given that $\sin A = 0{\cdot}6$, find $\cos A$.
2. Given that $\tan A = \frac{5}{12}$, find $\operatorname{cosec} A$.
3. Given that $\sec X = \frac{17}{15}$, find $\sin X$.
4. Given that $\cos Y = \frac{21}{29}$, find $\tan Y$.
5. Given that $\tan B = \frac{m}{n}$, find $\operatorname{cosec} B$.

EXERCISES 99B

1. Given that $\tan A = 0{\cdot}75$, find $\sin A$.
2. Given that $\sin X = \frac{5}{13}$, find $\cot X$.
3. Given that $\operatorname{cosec} Y = \frac{17}{8}$, find $\tan Y$.
4. Given that $\sin A = \frac{20}{29}$, find $\sec A$.
5. Given that $\sec B = \frac{p}{q}$, find $\cot B$.

Complementary angles

Complementary angles are angles whose sum is 90° and so in a triangle ABC, right-angled at B, the angles A and C are complementary.

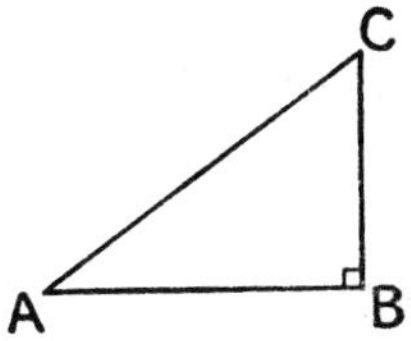

FIG. 210

From the definitions of the ratios,

$$\sin A = \frac{CB}{AC}; \qquad \cos C = \frac{CB}{AC};$$

$$\tan A = \frac{CB}{AB}; \qquad \cot C = \frac{CB}{AB};$$

$$\sec A = \frac{AC}{AB}; \qquad \operatorname{cosec} C = \frac{AC}{AB}.$$

So $\sin A = \cos C;$

$\tan A = \cot C;$

and $\sec A = \operatorname{cosec} C.$

Since $C = 90° - A$, these equations may be written

$$\sin A = \cos (90° - A);$$
$$\tan A = \cot (90° - A);$$
$$\sec A = \operatorname{cosec} (90° - A).$$

You may have noticed that three of the names (co-sine, co-tangent and co-secant) are formed by the addition of the prefix *co* to the other names. This prefix is short for 'complementary' and means that the ratio of any angle is equal to the co-ratio of the complementary angle.

To give a few examples:

$$\sin 20° = \cos 70°; \qquad \cos 20° = \sin 70°;$$
$$\sec 42° = \operatorname{cosec} 48°; \qquad \operatorname{cosec} 42° = \sec 48°;$$
$$\tan 37° = \cot 53°; \qquad \cot 37° = \tan 53°.$$

The isosceles triangle

Suppose that ABC is an isosceles triangle with AB equal to AC. Since the triangle is not right-angled, you cannot write down immediately an expression for sin B, for example. However, by drawing the perpendicular AD from A to BC, the ratios of the angle B may be easily calculated.

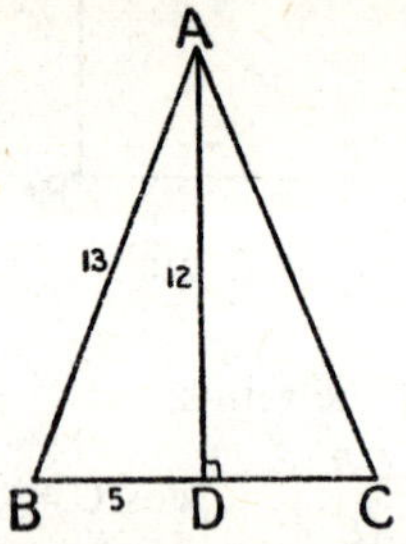

FIG. 211

Let $AB = AC = 13$ cm. and $BC = 10$ cm.

The triangles ABD and ACD are congruent and therefore $BD = 5$ cm.

By Pythagoras, $AD^2 = AB^2 - BD^2 = 13^2 - 5^2$.

$\therefore AD = 12$ cm.

From the right-angled triangle ABD,

$$\sin B = \tfrac{12}{13}, \quad \cos B = \tfrac{5}{13}, \quad \text{and } \tan B = \tfrac{12}{5}.$$

The ratios of 45°

Draw an isosceles right-angled triangle XYZ. Then angle X = angle $Z = 45°$. The size of the triangle will not affect the ratios of 45° so let $XY = YZ = 1$ cm and then by Pythagoras $XZ = \sqrt{2}$ cm.

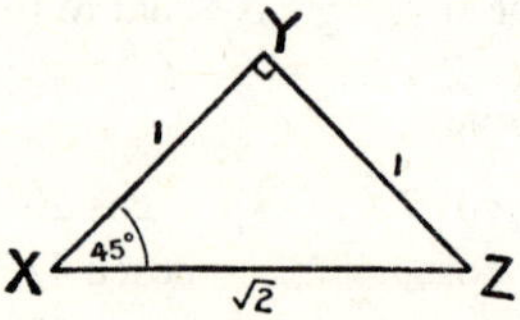

FIG. 212

From the definitions:

$$\sin 45^\circ = \frac{1}{\sqrt{2}}; \qquad \operatorname{cosec} 45^\circ = \sqrt{2};$$

$$\cos 45^\circ = \frac{1}{\sqrt{2}}; \qquad \sec 45^\circ = \sqrt{2};$$

$$\tan 45^\circ = 1; \qquad \cot 45^\circ = 1.$$

The ratios of 30° and 60°

Draw an equilateral triangle. For convenience, choose each side to be 2 cm. Draw the perpendicular *AD* from *A* to *BC*.

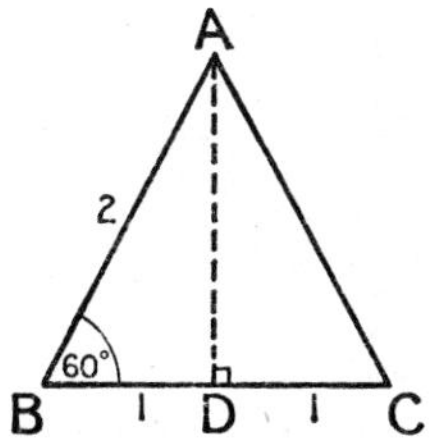

FIG. 213

Since *ABD* and *ACD* are congruent, $BD = 1$ cm.

$$\therefore\ AD^2 = 2^2 - 1^2 \quad \text{and} \quad AD = \sqrt{3}\ \text{cm}.$$

ABD is a right-angled triangle with *B* equal to 60° and angle *BAD* equal to 30°.

From the definitions:

$$\sin 60^\circ = \frac{\sqrt{3}}{2}; \qquad \operatorname{cosec} 60^\circ = \frac{2}{\sqrt{3}};$$

$$\cos 60^\circ = \tfrac{1}{2}; \qquad \sec 60^\circ = 2;$$

$$\tan 60^\circ = \sqrt{3}; \qquad \cot 60^\circ = \frac{1}{\sqrt{3}}.$$

Also

$$\sin 30^\circ = \tfrac{1}{2}; \qquad \operatorname{cosec} 30^\circ = 2;$$

$$\cos 30^\circ = \frac{\sqrt{3}}{2}; \qquad \sec 30^\circ = \frac{2}{\sqrt{3}};$$

$$\tan 30^\circ = \frac{1}{\sqrt{3}}; \qquad \cot 30^\circ = \sqrt{3}.$$

The ratios of 0° and 90°

Draw a triangle LMN in which M is a right angle and in which L is a very small angle. The angle N will consequently be very

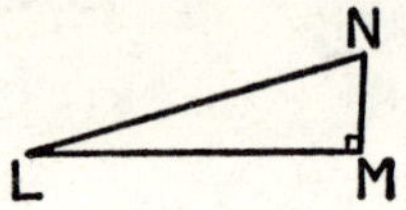

FIG. 214

nearly 90°. As the angle L gets smaller, LM will get more nearly equal to LN. The ratio $\frac{LM}{LN}$ will tend to become 1; the ratios $\frac{MN}{ML}$ and $\frac{MN}{NL}$ will tend to become zero.

The ratios $\frac{ML}{MN}$ and $\frac{NL}{MN}$, on the other hand, become infinitely large as the denominators become zero.

Hence we are able to write down the ratios of 0° and 90°.

$$\sin 90° = 1; \qquad \operatorname{cosec} 90° = 1;$$
$$\cos 90° = 0; \qquad \sec 90° = \infty;$$
$$\tan 90° = \infty; \qquad \cot 90° = 0.$$

Also

$$\sin 0° = 0; \qquad \operatorname{cosec} 0° = \infty;$$
$$\cos 0° = 1; \qquad \sec 0° = 1;$$
$$\tan 0° = 0; \qquad \cot 0° = \infty.$$

EXERCISES 100A

Without using tables, write down the values of the following:

1. $\frac{\sin 20°}{\cos 70°}$. **2.** $\frac{\sec 40°}{\operatorname{cosec} 50°}$. **3.** $\frac{\cot 25°}{\tan 65°}$.

4. $\tan^2 60° + \tan^2 45°$. **5.** $\cos^2 30° + \sin^2 30°$.

6. $\sec^2 60° - \tan^2 60°$. **7.** $\operatorname{cosec}^2 45° - \cot^2 45°$.

8. $1 + \tan^2 30°$. **9.** $1 - \sin^2 45°$.

10. $\operatorname{cosec}^2 60° - 1$.

EXERCISES 100B

Without using tables, write down the values of the following:

1. $\dfrac{\cos 10^\circ}{\sin 80^\circ}$. **2.** $\dfrac{\operatorname{cosec} 15^\circ}{\sec 75^\circ}$. **3.** $\dfrac{\tan 72^\circ}{\cot 18^\circ}$.

4. $\sin^2 60^\circ + \tan^2 45^\circ$. **5.** $\cos^2 60^\circ + \sin^2 60^\circ$.

6. $\sec^2 45^\circ - \tan^2 45^\circ$. **7.** $\operatorname{cosec}^2 30^\circ - \cot^2 30^\circ$.

8. $1 + \tan^2 60^\circ$. **9.** $1 - \sin^2 30^\circ$.

10. $1 - \cos^2 60^\circ$.

EXERCISES 101: MISCELLANEOUS

1. Find by drawing an approximate value for tan 37°.

2. Find by drawing and measurement the acute angle whose sine is 0·7.

3. In Fig. 215, B is a right angle and X is the middle point of BC. Calculate the ratio $\dfrac{\tan AXB}{\tan ACB}$.

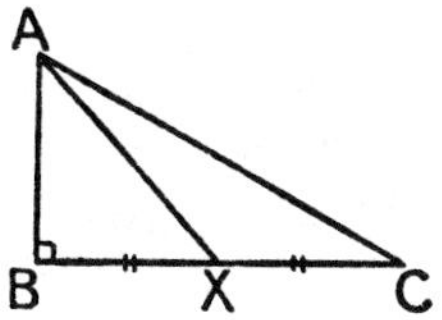

FIG. 215

4. PQR is an isosceles triangle in which $PQ = PR = 5$ cm. and $QR = 8$ cm. Calculate sin Q.

5. In Fig. 216, prove that $\theta + \phi = 90^\circ$. Prove also that there are two

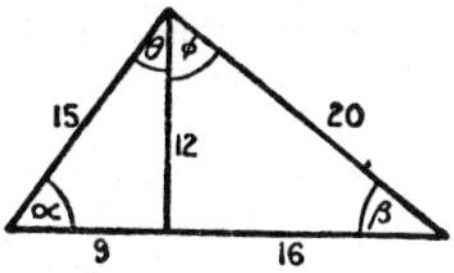

FIG. 216

other right angles in the figure. Write down the values of (i) $\sin \alpha$; (ii) $\cos \beta$; (iii) $\sec \phi$; (iv) $\operatorname{cosec} \theta$.

6. Evaluate without using tables:
(i) tan 20° cot 20°, (ii) cosec 25° cos 65°, (iii) $\sin^2 30^\circ + \cos^2 30^\circ$.

7. Given that x is an acute angle such that $\sin x = p/q$, find the value of $\tan x$.

8. Given that x is an acute angle and that $\cot x = 8/15$, find, without using tables, the values of (i) $\cos x$, (ii) $\sin x$, (iii) $\cos^2 x + \sin^2 x$.

9. Find values of x from the following:
(i) $\sin x^\circ = \cos 24^\circ$, (ii) $\tan x^\circ = \cot 18^\circ$, (iii) $\operatorname{cosec} x^\circ = \sec 51^\circ$.

10. In Fig. 217, D is a right angle. Write down, in terms of a and b, (i) $\sin B$, (ii) $\cot B\hat{A}D$.

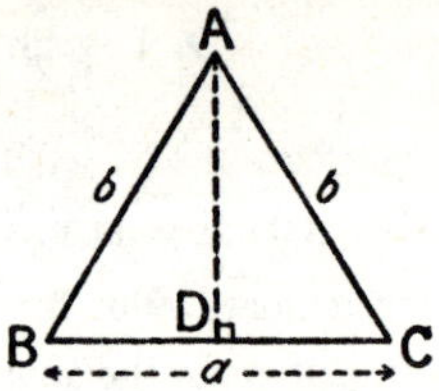

FIG. 217

11. In Fig. 218, BD is an altitude. Write down, in terms of a, c and h, (i) $\sin A$, (ii) $\tan A\hat{B}D$, (iii) $\sec C$.

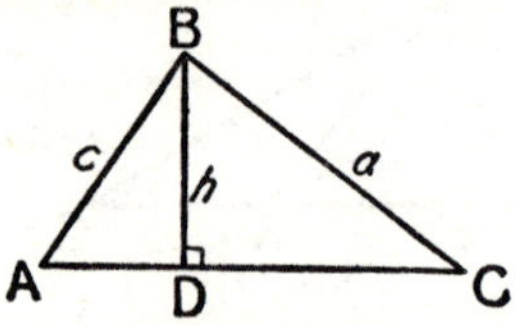

FIG. 218

12. Which of the following equations are impossible? (i) $\sin x^\circ = 1{\cdot}2$, (ii) $\cos y^\circ = 0{\cdot}8$, (iii) $\tan y^\circ = 2{\cdot}4$, (iv) $\operatorname{cosec} \alpha^\circ = 0{\cdot}7$, (v) $\sec \alpha^\circ = \frac{1}{2}$.

13. Given that x is acute, prove that $\tan x$ is always greater than $\sin x$.

14. If $\tan \theta = \frac{3}{4}$ evaluate, without using tables, $\dfrac{\cos \theta - \sin \theta}{\cos \theta + \sin \theta}$.

15. In Fig. 219, the angle B is a right angle and $AB = BC = 1$ cm.

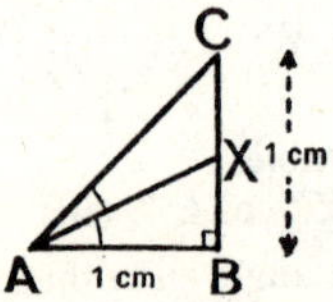

FIG. 219

The bisector of the angle A meets BC at X. Using the angle bisector theorem, calculate BX and hence write down the value of tan $22\frac{1}{2}°$.

16. In Fig. 220, the angle B is a right angle, $BC = 1$ cm and the angle

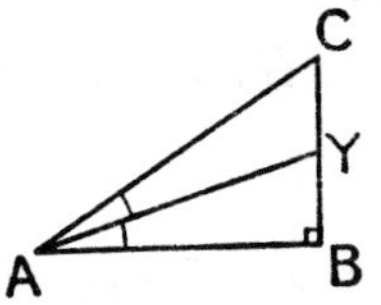

FIG. 220

$A = 30°$. The bisector of the angle A meets BC at Y. Calculate the length of BY and hence write down the value of tan 15°.

17. In Fig. 221, $B = 90°$. Prove that $AC = h(\cot x - \cot y)$.

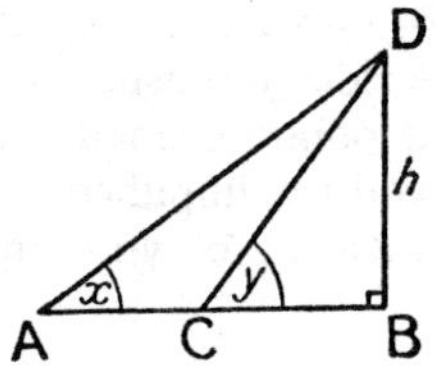

FIG. 221

18. In Fig. 222, write down the values of sin α and cot α.

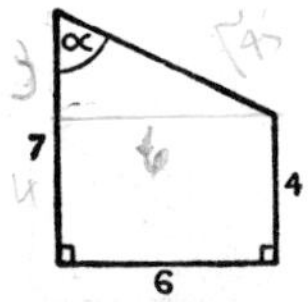

FIG. 222

19. If $\sin x° = a/b$, write down the value of $\sin (90 - x)°$.

20. If $\tan x° = l/m$, write down the value of $\tan (90 - x)°$.

21. Simplify the following:

(i) $\tan x° \tan (90 - x)°$; (ii) $\operatorname{cosec} x° \cos (90 - x)°$.

22. Find a value of θ if $\tan \theta = 3 \tan 15°$.

23. Find a value of x if $\sin 2x = \frac{1}{2}$.

24. Find a value of x if $\cos 2x = 2 \cos 80°$.

25. Evaluate, without using tables, $\dfrac{\sin^2 60° + \cos^2 60°}{\sin^2 60° - \cos^2 60°}$.

26

SOLUTION OF A RIGHT-ANGLED TRIANGLE

Given one angle and one side

IF you are given one angle and one side of a right-angled triangle, you can find the other sides by trigonometry. The remaining angle is, of course, the complement of the given angle. To find one of the unknown sides, write down the fraction $\frac{\text{unknown side}}{\text{known side}}$. Express this as a trigonometrical ratio of the given angle. You can then find the unknown side by solving the equation. It is conventional to call the lengths of the sides opposite the angles A, B, C in the triangle ABC by the corresponding small letters a, b, c.

N.B. Your arithmetic will be simplified if you make sure that the unknown side is the numerator of your fraction. This will avoid awkward division.

Example 1. The hypotenuse of a right-angled triangle is 18·1 cm. and one of the angles is 32°. Find the other sides.

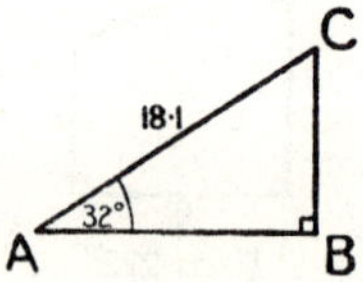

FIG. 223

From the figure,

$$\frac{BC}{18{\cdot}1} = \sin 32°.$$

$$\therefore\ BC = 18{\cdot}1 \sin 32° = 9{\cdot}59 \text{ cm.}$$

Also

$$\frac{AB}{18{\cdot}1} = \cos 32°.$$

$$\therefore\ AB = 18{\cdot}1 \cos 32° = 15{\cdot}3 \text{ cm.}$$

Example 2. In the triangle ABC, angle $A = 28°$ and $a = 8$ cm. Find b and c, given that the angle $B = 90°$.

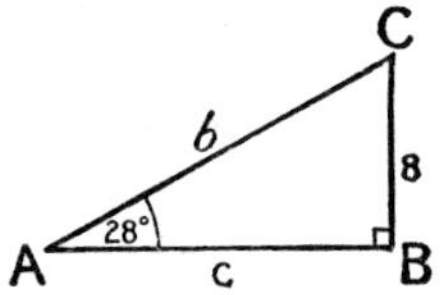

FIG. 224

From Fig. 224,

$$\frac{b}{8} = \text{cosec } 28°.$$

$$\therefore b = 8 \text{ cosec } 28° = 17{\cdot}0 \text{ cm}.$$

Also

$$\frac{c}{8} = \cot 28°.$$

$$\therefore c = 8 \cot 28° = 15{\cdot}0 \text{ cm}.$$

EXERCISES 102A

Find the other sides of the triangles given that angle $B = 90°$.

1. $a = 13{\cdot}6$ cm, $A = 72°$.
2. $b = 4{\cdot}7$ cm, $A = 62°$.
3. $c = 8{\cdot}3$ cm, $C = 20°\ 40'$.
4. $b = 12{\cdot}0$ m, $C = 28°\ 32'$.
5. $c = 22{\cdot}6$ cm, $A = 30°$.

EXERCISES 102B

Find the other sides of the triangles given that angle $B = 90°$.

1. $a = 16{\cdot}7$ cm, $A = 22°$.
2. $a = 23{\cdot}4$ cm, $C = 72°$
3. $b = 16{\cdot}4$ cm, $A = 21°\ 30'$.
4. $b = 6{\cdot}2$ m, $C = 40°\ 20'$.
5. $c = 7{\cdot}6$ cm, $A = 42°\ 10'$.

Given two sides

If you are given two sides of a right-angled triangle, you can find the third side by applying Pythagoras. To find one of the angles, express the ratio of the given sides as a fraction. You will find it helpful to put the simpler number in the denominator. Find the trigonometrical ratio this fraction is of the unknown angle. The angle may then be found from your tables.

Example 1. Given that $B = 90°$, $b = 18{\cdot}1$ cm and $c = 15{\cdot}0$ cm, find the angle A.

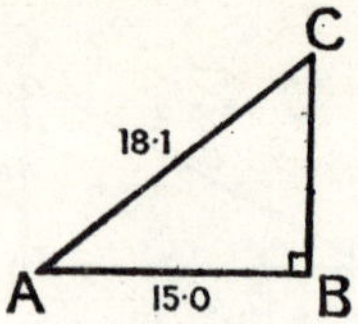

FIG. 225

$$\frac{18{\cdot}1}{15{\cdot}0} = \frac{\text{hypotenuse}}{\text{adjacent side}} = \sec A.$$

$\left(\text{It is easier to work out } \frac{18{\cdot}1}{15} \text{ than } \frac{15}{18{\cdot}1}.\right)$

$$\therefore \sec A = 1{\cdot}2067 \quad \text{and} \quad A = 34°\ 2'.$$

Example 2. Given that angle $B = 90°$, $a = 8{\cdot}1$ cm and $c = 7{\cdot}5$ cm, find the angle A.

$$\frac{8{\cdot}1}{7{\cdot}5} = \tan A.$$

$$\therefore \tan A = 1{\cdot}08 \quad \text{and} \quad A = 47°\ 12'.$$

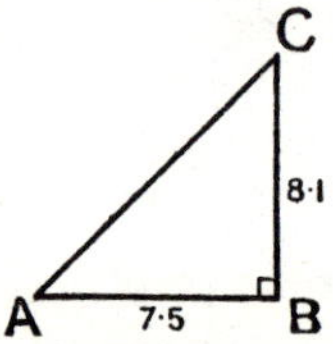

FIG. 226

EXERCISES 103A

Find the angles of the following triangles, given that angle $B = 90°$.

1. $a = 12{\cdot}6$ cm, $b = 18{\cdot}0$ cm.
2. $a = 2{\cdot}4$ cm, $c = 3{\cdot}2$ cm.
3. $b = 7{\cdot}2$ cm, $c = 2{\cdot}43$ cm.
4. $a = 8{\cdot}2$ cm, $b = 9{\cdot}1$ cm.
5. $c = 24{\cdot}6$ cm, $b = 28{\cdot}3$ cm.

EXERCISES 103B

Find the angles of the following triangles, given that angle $B = 90°$.

1. $a = 2$ cm, $b = 3$ cm.
2. $a = 7{\cdot}6$ cm, $c = 4{\cdot}0$ cm.

3. $b = 20{\cdot}4$ cm, $c = 7{\cdot}62$ cm. 4. $a = 3{\cdot}41$ cm, $b = 7{\cdot}16$ cm.

5. $c = 12{\cdot}2$ cm, $b = 73{\cdot}4$ cm.

The isosceles triangle

To solve an isosceles triangle of given sides, draw the perpendicular from the vertex to the opposite side.

Example. Find the angles of the triangle *ABC*, given that $a = 8{\cdot}2$ cm, $b = 8{\cdot}2$ cm and $c = 9{\cdot}6$ cm.

Draw *CD*, the perpendicular from *C* to *AB*. This divides the triangle *ABC* into two congruent triangles and therefore bisects the angle *C* and the side *AB*.

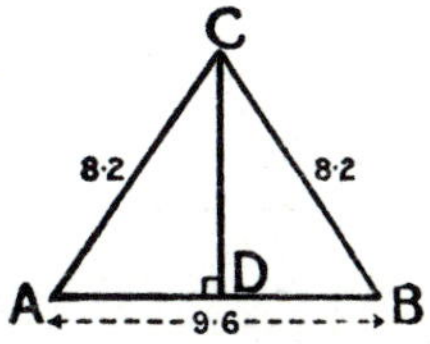

FIG. 227

$$\therefore\ AD = 4{\cdot}8 \text{ cm.}$$

and in the right-angled triangle *ADC*,

$$\frac{4{\cdot}8}{8{\cdot}2} = \cos A.$$

$$\therefore\ \cos A = \frac{24}{41} = 0{\cdot}5854$$

and $$A = 54°\ 10'.$$

Since the triangle *ABC* is isosceles,

$$B = 54°\ 10' \quad \text{and} \quad C = 180° - 2(54°\ 10') = 71°\ 40'.$$

Angles of elevation and depression

The angle of elevation of an object *B* from an observer at *A* who is below the level of *B* is the angle which the line *BA* makes with the horizontal.

If *C* is below *A*, **the angle of depression** of *C* from *A* is the angle which *AC* makes with the horizontal.

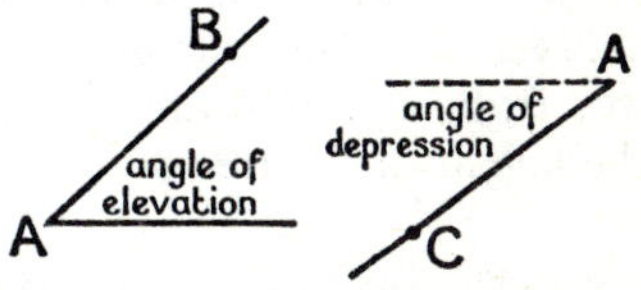

FIG. 228

N.B. Notice that both angles are measured with the horizontal and that the angle of elevation of B from A is equal to the angle of depression of A from B.

An instrument called the theodolite is used for measuring angles of elevation or depression. This gives a simple method of finding the height of a tree or building, illustrated in the next example.

Example. A man walks 12 m directly away from a tree and from this position, the angle of elevation of the top of the tree is 24°. If the measurement is taken from a point 1·5 m above ground level, find the height of the tree.

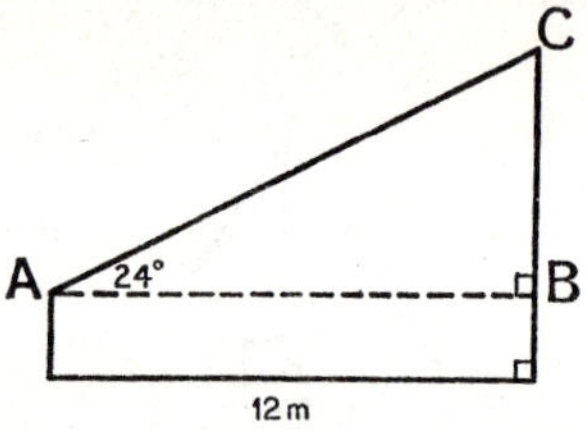

FIG. 229

From the figure, $\frac{BC}{12} = \tan 24°.$

$$\therefore \frac{BC}{12} = \tan 24° = 0{\cdot}4452,$$

and $BC = 5{\cdot}34$ m (to 3 sig. fig.).

The height of the tree is therefore 6·84 m (to 3 sig. fig.).

Height of an inaccessible object

You cannot use the method of finding the height of a tree just illustrated if you cannot get to the foot of the tree. The tree may, for example, be on the opposite bank of a river. Two convenient points A and B are taken in line with the tree and the distance between them measured. The angles of elevation of the top of the tree from A and B are also measured. From these measurements, the height of the tree may be calculated.

Example 1. From two points P and Q, 30 m apart, and in line with a tree, the angles of elevation of the top of the tree are 22° and 32° respectively. Find the height of the tree.

Call the distance QB x metres and the distance TB h metres.

From the right-angled triangle *TPB*,

$$\frac{PB}{TB} = \cot 22°.$$

$$\therefore \frac{x + 30}{h} = \cot 22°$$

or $$x + 30 = h \cot 22° = 2{\cdot}4751h \quad . \quad . \quad . \quad \text{(i)}$$

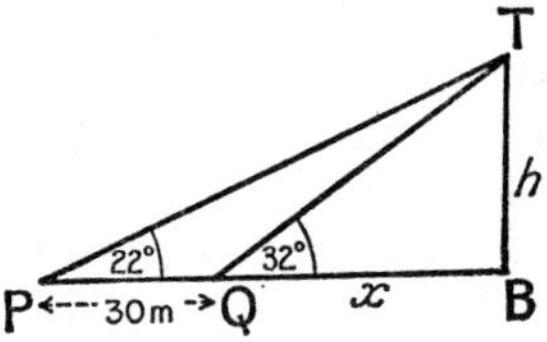

FIG. 230

From the right-angled triangle *TQB*,

$$\frac{QB}{h} = \cot 32° \quad \text{or} \quad x = h \cot 32° = 1{\cdot}6003h \quad . \quad . \quad \text{(ii)}$$

Subtracting (ii) from (i),

$$30 = 2{\cdot}4751h - 1{\cdot}6003h$$
$$= 0{\cdot}8748h.$$

$$\therefore h = \frac{30}{0{\cdot}8748} = 30(1{\cdot}143) = 34{\cdot}3 \text{ m (to 3 sig. fig.)}.$$

Example 2. Find a formula for the length *AD* of the perpendicular from *A* to *BC* in the triangle *ABC* in terms of *a*, *B* and *C*.

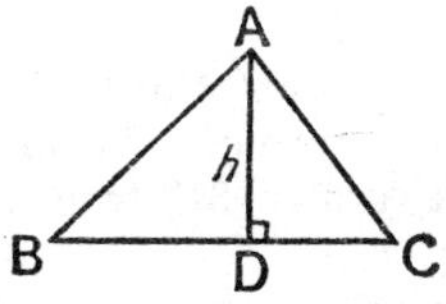

FIG. 231

Let $AD = h$. In the right-angled triangle *ABD*,

$$\frac{BD}{h} = \cot B. \quad \therefore BD = h \cot B.$$

In the right-angled triangle *ADC*,

$$\frac{DC}{h} = \cot C. \quad \therefore DC = h \cot C.$$

By addition, $$BD + DC = h(\cot B + \cot C).$$

$$\therefore\ a = h(\cot B + \cot C).$$

and $$h = \frac{a}{\cot B + \cot C}.$$

Gradient

It is unfortunate that the word **gradient** has two different meanings. It is used in graphical work to denote the ratio of the vertical distance moved to the horizontal distance. When used in connection with roads or railways, however, the gradient means the ratio of the vertical distance moved to the corresponding distance measured along the slope, i.e. the sine of the angle of inclination.

If you say that the gradient of a road is 1 in 16, you mean that for every 16 m along the slope, the road rises 1 m vertically.

Example. A mountain railway has a gradient of 1 in 5. What angle does the track make with the horizontal?

If θ is the required angle,

$$\sin\theta = \tfrac{1}{5} = 0{\cdot}2.$$

$$\therefore\ \theta = 11°\ 32'.$$

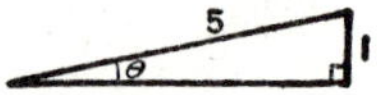

FIG. 232

Bearings

The four cardinal directions are North, South, East and West. A bearing of N. 27° E. means a turn of 27° from the North towards the East; S. 31° E. means a turn of 31° from the South towards the East.

When bearings are measured in this way, they are always measured from the North or South, never from the East or West. You should not write, for instance, E. 17° S. This particular bearing should be written S. 73° E.

There is an alternative method of giving bearings or directions commonly used in the army and in the air force. North is reckoned to be zero and angles are measured from the North in a clockwise direction. To lessen the chance of error, three figures are always given, e.g. 006° is written for 6°, 034° is written for 34°. In this system East is written 090°, South 180° and West 270°. The bearing considered first in this paragraph (N. 27° E.) may also be written 027° : N. 27° W. is the same bearing as 333°.

Example. A ship sails 3 km due E. and then 4 km due N. Find its bearing from the original position.

From the figure,

$$\tan\theta = \tfrac{4}{3} = 1{\cdot}3333.$$

$$\therefore\ \theta = 53°\ 8'$$

and the bearing to the nearest degree is 037°.

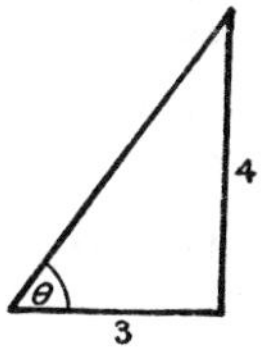

FIG. 233

Projections

If AA', BB' are perpendiculars drawn from two points A, B to a given line l, then $A'B'$ is said to be the projection of AB on the line l.

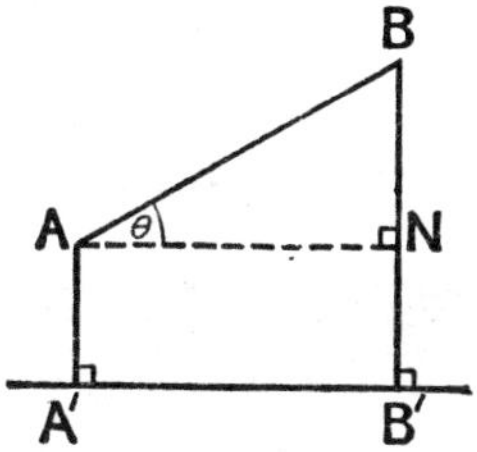

FIG. 234

If θ is the angle between AB and the line l, and AN is the perpendicular from A to BB',

$$\frac{AN}{AB} = \cos\theta.$$

$$\therefore\ AN = AB\cos\theta.$$

But $AN = A'B'$ and so the length of the projection of AB on l is $AB\cos\theta$. To project one line on to another, multiply its length by the cosine of the angle between the lines.

Projections are very useful when dealing with problems on courses and bearings and also in solving quadrilaterals. Examples of the method are given.

Example 1. A ship steams 3 km from a port P on a bearing of 080° and then 4 km on a bearing of 047°. Find its distance and bearing from P.

Suppose PQ and QR represent the two courses. Take the East and North directions as axes of reference.

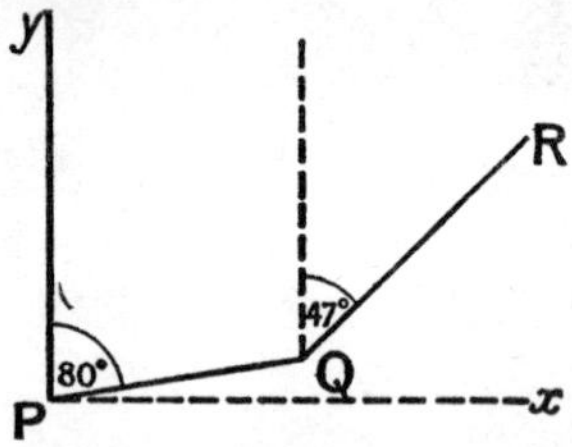

FIG. 235

PQ makes an angle of 10° with the East; QR makes an angle of 43° with the East.

The projection of PQ on the x-axis is 3 cos 10°.

The projection of QR on the x-axis is 4 cos 43°.

The distance the ship is East of P is

$$3 \cos 10° + 4 \cos 43° = 2{\cdot}954 + 2{\cdot}926 = 5{\cdot}880 \text{ km.}$$

PQ makes an angle of 80° with the North;
QR makes an angle of 47° with the North.
The distance the ship is North of P is

$$3 \cos 80° + 4 \cos 47° = 3{\cdot}249 \text{ km.}$$

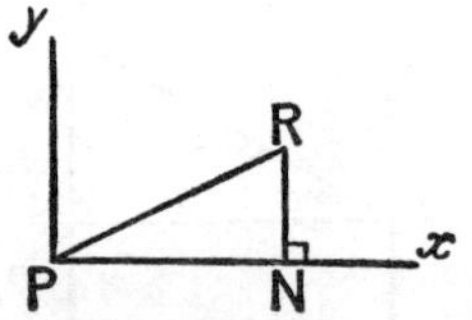

FIG. 236

$$\begin{aligned} PR^2 &= PN^2 + RN^2 \\ &= (5{\cdot}880)^2 + (3{\cdot}249)^2 \\ &= 34{\cdot}57 + 10{\cdot}56 \\ &= 45{\cdot}13. \\ \therefore PR &= 6{\cdot}72 \text{ km (to 3 sig. fig.).} \\ \tan N\hat{P}R &= \frac{RN}{PN} = \frac{3{\cdot}249}{5{\cdot}880} \end{aligned}$$

and $$N\hat{P}R = 28° \, 55'.$$

The distance and bearing of R from P are 6·72 km and 061° to the nearest degree.

Example 2. $ABCD$ is a quadrilateral such that $AB = 10$ cm, $BC = 8$ cm, $AD = 6$ cm, the angle $A = 72°$ and the angle $B = 60°$. Find the length of CD and the angles at C and D.

Take AB and the perpendicular to AB through A as axes of reference.
The projection of AD on the x-axis is 6 cos 72°.
The projection of BC on the x-axis is 8 cos 60°.
The projection of DC on the x-axis is therefore

$$10 - 1{\cdot}854 - 4 = 4{\cdot}146 \text{ cm.}$$

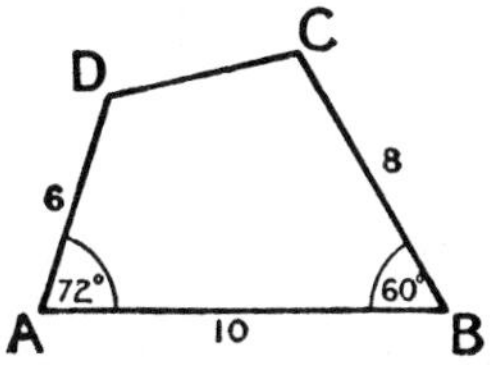

FIG. 237

The projection of AD on the y-axis = 6 cos 18° (or 6 sin 72°).
The projection of BC on the y-axis = 8 cos 30° (or 8 sin 60°).
The projection of DC on the y-axis = 8 cos 30° − 6 cos 18°.
= 6·928 − 5·707
= 1·221 cm.

If CN and DN are drawn parallel to the y-axis and the x-axis respectively:

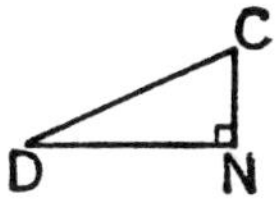

FIG. 238

$$CN = 1{\cdot}221 \quad \text{and} \quad DN = 4{\cdot}146 \text{ cm.}$$

$$\therefore CD^2 = CN^2 + DN^2$$
$$= (1{\cdot}221)^2 + (4{\cdot}146)^2$$
$$= 1{\cdot}49 + 17{\cdot}19$$
$$= 18{\cdot}68.$$
$$\therefore CD = 4{\cdot}32 \text{ cm. (to 3 sig. fig.).}$$

Also $\tan N\hat{D}C = \dfrac{CN}{DN} = \dfrac{1{\cdot}221}{4{\cdot}146}$ and $N\hat{D}C = 16°\ 24'$.

$$\text{Angle } D = 108° + N\hat{D}C = 124°\ 24'.$$

$$\text{Angle } C = 120° - N\hat{D}C = 103°\ 36'.$$

EXERCISES 104A

1. In the triangle *ABC*, $b = c = 12{\cdot}2$ cm and $a = 8{\cdot}4$ cm. Find the angle *B*.

2. In the triangle *ABC*, $b = c = 6{\cdot}4$ cm and angle $A = 80°$. Find *a*.

3. In the triangle *ABC*, $b = c$ and $a = 7{\cdot}2$ cm. Given also that $A = 72°$, find *b*.

4. A man 1·8 m tall is 12 m away from a tree 7·2 m high. What is the angle of elevation of the top of the tree from his eyes?

5. A man 1·8 m tall observes that the angle of elevation of the top of a tree 12 m distant is 32°. What is the height of the tree?

6. A man on the top of a cliff 80 m high observes that the angle of depression of a buoy at sea is 12°. How far is the buoy from the cliff?

7. A road has a gradient of 1 in 7·2. What angle does the road make with the horizontal?

8. A mountain railway track is inclined at 14° to the horizontal. Express its gradient in the form 1 : *n*.

9. A man on the top of a cliff 100 m high is in line with two buoys whose angles of depression are 17° and 19°. Find the distance between the buoys.

10. *A* and *B* are two points in line with a tree such that $AB = 20$ m. The angles of elevation of the top of a tree from *A* and *B* are 17° 30′ and 19° respectively. Find the height of the tree.

11. A man walks 1 km due E. and then 2 km due S. Find his bearing from his original position.

12. A ship steams 2 km due N. and then 3 km on a bearing of 060°. Find its distance and bearing from the original position.

EXERCISES 104B

1. In the triangle *ABC*, $b = c = 7{\cdot}6$ cm and $a = 4{\cdot}2$ cm. Find the angle *B*.

2. In the triangle *ABC*, $b = c = 8{\cdot}2$ cm and angle $A = 80°$. Calculate *a*.

3. In the triangle *ABC*, $b = c$ and $a = 4{\cdot}3$ cm. Given also that angle $A = 64°$, calculate *b*.

4. A man 1·5 m tall is 15 m away from a building, 24 m high. What is the angle of elevation of the top of the building?

5. A man 1·5 m tall observes that the angle of elevation of the top of a building 24 m away is 41°. What is the height of the building?

6. A man on the top of a cliff 100 m high observes that the angle of depression of a boat at sea is 18°. How far is the boat from the cliff?

7. A road has a gradient of 1 in 6·4. What angle does it make with the horizontal?

8. A funicular railway track is inclined at 17° to the horizontal. If its gradient is 1 in n, find n.

9. A man on the top of a cliff 80 m high is in line with two buoys whose angles of depression are 15° 20′ and 12° 30′. What is the distance between the buoys?

10. P and Q are two points in line with a tree. If PQ is 30 m and the angles of elevation of the top of the tree from P and Q are 12° and 15° respectively, find the height of the tree.

11. A boat sails 4 km due W. and then 8 km due S. Find its bearing from its original position to the nearest degree.

12. $AB = 2$ km and $BC = 3$ km. If the bearing of B from A is 024° and the bearing of C from B is 282°, find the bearing of C from A.

EXERCISES 105: MISCELLANEOUS

1. A ladder leaning against a vertical wall makes an angle of 24° with the wall. The foot of the ladder is 5 m from the wall. Find the length of the ladder.

2. The semi-vertical angle of a cone is 38° and the diameter of its base is 4 cm. Find its height.

3. A vertical stick is 8 m high and the length of its shadow is 6 m. What is the angle of elevation of the sun?

4. A bell tent has a radius of 8 m and its pole is 7 m high. What angle does a slant side make with the ground?

5. One angle of a rhombus is 72°. The shorter diagonal is 8 cm long. Find the length of the other.

6. A chord of a circle is 18 cm long and subtends an angle of 110° at the centre. Find the radius of the circle.

7. The greatest and least heights of a bicycle shed are 3 m and 2·5 m. The shed is 3·5 m wide. Find the angle of slope of the roof.

8. An equilateral triangle is inscribed in a circle of radius 5 cm. Find its side.

9. Two men are on opposite sides of a tower. They measure the angles of elevation of the top of the tower as 22° and 18° respectively. If the height of the tower is 100 m, find the distance between the men.

10. Find the angle between the diagonals of a rectangle whose sides are 3 cm and 4 cm.

11. A man standing 60 m away from a tower notices that the angles of elevation of the top and bottom of a flagstaff on top of the tower are 64° and 62° respectively. Find the length of the flagstaff.

12. From a man, the angle of elevation of the top of a tree is 28°. What is the angle of elevation from the man of a bird perched halfway up the tree?

13. A man walks 2 km up a hill whose slope is 1 in 12 and 3 km up a hill whose slope is 1 in 15. How much higher is he than when he started?

14. A stick 4 m long casts a shadow 3 m long when the sun is vertically overhead. What is the inclination of the stick?

15. The legs of a pair of compasses are each 6 cm long and they are used to draw a circle of radius 4 cm. Find the angle between the legs.

16. A cliff 1 km long is represented on a map of scale 2 cm to 1 km by a line of length 0·42 cm. What is the average inclination of the cliff to the horizontal?

17. A man walks 100 m up a slope of 14° and then 50 m up a slope of 12°. How much higher is he than when he started?

18. The bob of a pendulum 4 m long is 25 cm higher at the top of its swing that it is at the bottom. Find the angle of swing on each side of the vertical.

19. A man starts at *A* and walks 2 km on a bearing of 017°. He then walks 3 km on a bearing of 107° to *C*. What is the bearing of *C* from *A*?

20. A slab of stone 2 m by 5 m rests as shown in Fig. 239. What is the height of *D* above the ground?

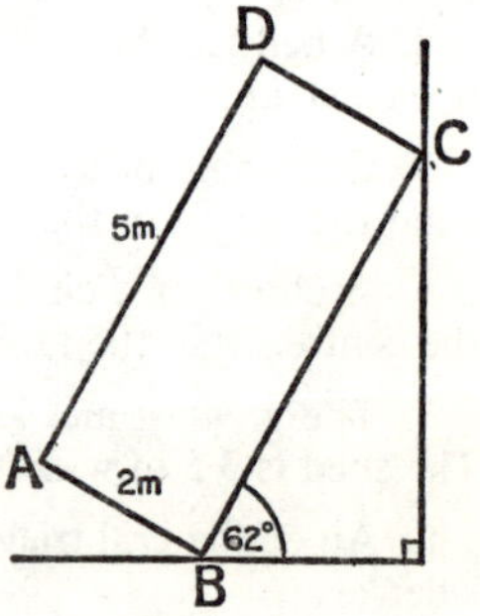

FIG. 239

21. A kite flying at a height of 67·2 m is attached to a string inclined at 55° to the horizontal. What is the length of string?

22. A boat 4 km South of the Needles is steaming on a course of 084° at 12 km/h. What is the bearing of the boat from the Needles after half an hour?

23. A man 1·8 m tall can just see the sun over a fence 3 m high, which is 4 m away from him. What is the angle of elevation of the sun.

24. In a circle of radius 6 cm, two radii are drawn making an angle of 40° with each other. Calculate the length of the chord joining the ends of the radii and the length of the perpendicular from the centre to the chord.

25. The vertical angle of a cone of height 6·2 cm is 44°. Find the area of the curved surface.

26. Three places X, Y, Z are in a straight line on a map and the horizontal distance between X and Y as shown on the map is 1500 m and between Y and Z 2000 m. The angle of elevation of Y from X is $4° 28'$ and the angle of depression of Z from Y is $2° 50'$. Find the vertical height of Z above X and the angle of elevation of Z from X.

27. AB is a side of regular 12-sided polygon having O as centre. If $AB = 10$ cm, calculate AO.

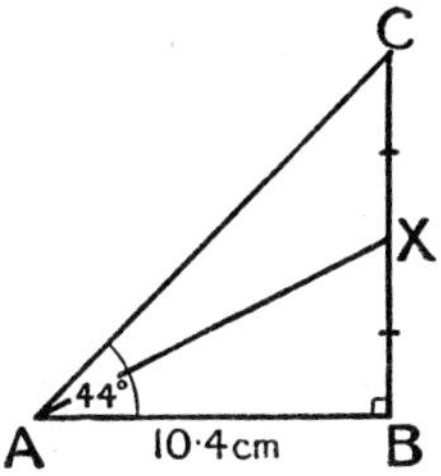

FIG. 240

28. In Fig. 240, $AB = 10{\cdot}4$ cm and the angle $BAC = 44°$. It is known that $CX = XB$. Calculate the angle XAB and the length of AX.

29. A rhombus has sides of length 6 cm and the length of one of the diagonals is 8 cm. Calculate the length of the other diagonal and the angles of the rhombus.

30. If $\cos A = \frac{12}{13}$ and A is an acute angle, calculate the value of $\dfrac{\sin A + \operatorname{cosec} A}{\sin A + \tan A}$.

31. The angle of elevation of the top of a tower of height 60 m from a point A on the same level as the foot of the tower is 25°. Calculate the angle of elevation of the top of the tower from another point B, 20 m nearer the foot of the tower.

32. A triangle XYZ is such that $XZ = 24$ cm, $YZ = 32$ cm and the perpendicular from X to YZ meets YZ at T where $TZ = 12$ cm. Calculate the angles XZY and XYZ.

33. AB is a vertical tower 50 m high whose foot B stands on level ground. X and Y are points on the ground, east and south of the tower respectively. The angles of elevation of A from X and Y are 30° and 38°. Calculate the distance XY.

34. The figure shows a rectangle standing on a plane inclined at 40° to the horizontal. If $OA = 6$ m, $AB = 3$ m, $BC = 4$ m, calculate the height of C above O.

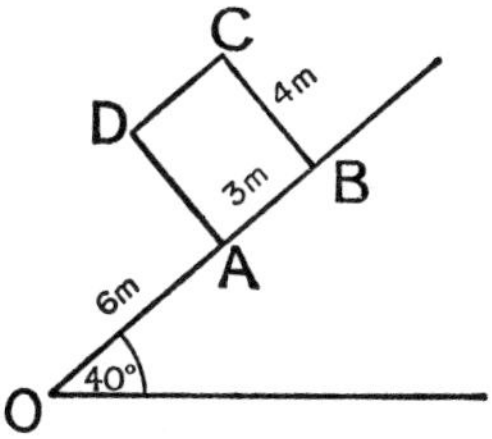

FIG. 241

35. From the measurements given in Fig. 242, calculate *AD* and *AB*,

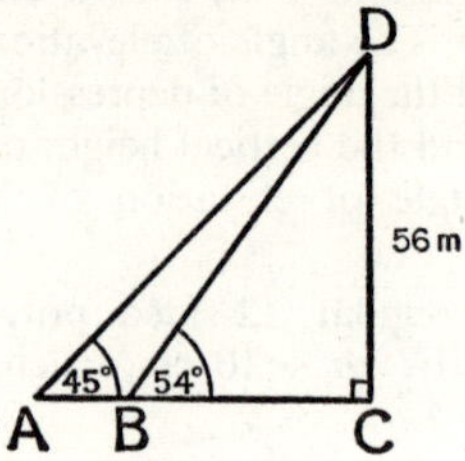

FIG. 242

36. A boat starting from a port *A* steams towards another port *P* which is 18 km away on a bearing 040°. When the boat reaches a point *C*, 10 km from *A*, it is allowed to drift 4 km in a direction 100° to a point *X*. Find the bearing of *X* from *A*.

37. A chord *PQ* of a circle is distant 4·8 cm from the centre *O*. If the angle *POQ* = 142°, calculate the length of the chord and the radius of the circle. If the tangents at *P* and *Q* meet in *T*, find *OT*.

38. *ABCD* is a trapezium in which *AB* is parallel to *DC*. If *AB* = 12 cm, *DC* = 6·5 cm, the angle *BAD* = 42° and the distance between the parallel sides is 2·8 cm, calculate the other sides and angles of the trapezium.

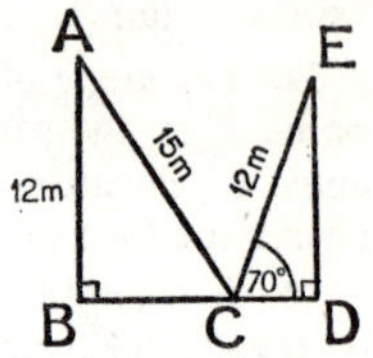

FIG. 243

39. From the measurements given in Fig. 243, calculate the angle *ACE* and the length of *BD*.

40. A flagstaff 6 m high stands on the top of a vertical tower. From a position on the level ground, the angles of elevation of the top of the tower and of the top of the flagstaff are 28° and 35°. Calculate the height of the tower.

27

THE GENERAL ANGLE

WE have considered so far the ratios of acute angles only. The definitions of the ratios apply to a right-angled triangle which cannot have an angle greater than 90°. Another definition, which must of course agree with the definition already given, is needed for angles larger than 90°.

Axes and coordinates

In drawing graphs, two perpendicular lines are taken as axes of coordinates. The horizontal one is usually called the x-axis and the vertical one the y-axis.

Any point P in the plane of the axes has two coordinates. Its distance from the y-axis, PN, is called the x coordinate and its distance from the x-axis, PM, is called the y coordinate. If $PN = 3$ and $PM = 4$, the point P is written (3, 4), the x coordinate being written first. Points to the left of the y-axis have a negative x coordinate and points below the x-axis have a negative y coordinate.

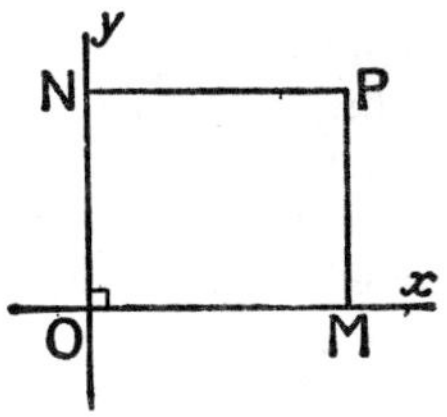

FIG. 244

Fig. 245 shows the signs of the coordinates of a point in each of the four quadrants.

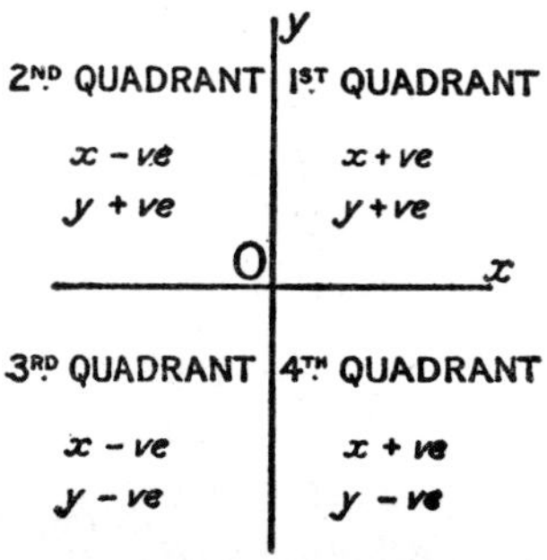

FIG. 245

Ratios of angles larger than 90°

Draw a circle centre O of unit radius. With O as origin, draw two perpendicular lines, the axes. Now, suppose you wish to find the ratios of 128°, for example. Take the point P on the circle so that the angle xOP is equal to 128°.

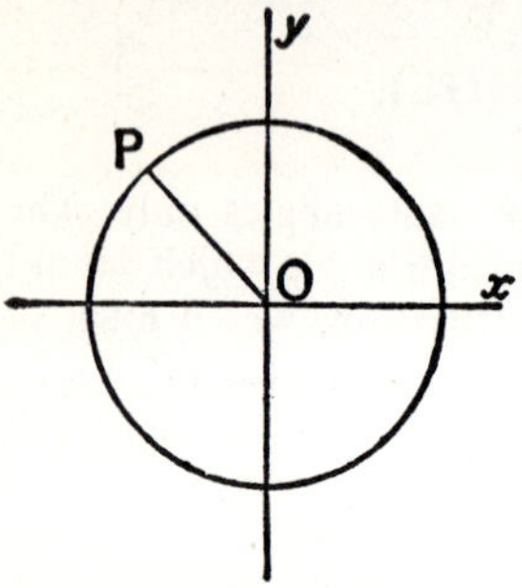

FIG. 246

(N.B. The angle, if positive, should always be measured counter-clockwise from Ox.)

Then we define the x coordinate of P as equal to cos 128°; the y coordinate of P as equal to sin 128°. The appropriate signs must be taken with the x and y coordinates, so that cos 128° is negative, sin 128° is positive.

Generally, if P is a point on the circumference of this circle of unit radius, so that $x\hat{O}P$ is equal to θ, then the x coordinate of P is equal to $\cos\theta$ and the y coordinate of P is equal to $\sin\theta$.

Definition of tangent

If ABC is a triangle in which B is a right angle,

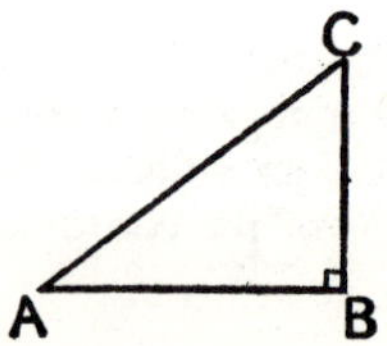

FIG. 247

$$\sin A = \frac{CB}{AC},$$

$$\cos A = \frac{AB}{AC}$$

$$\tan A = \frac{CB}{AB}.$$

$$\therefore \frac{\sin A}{\cos A} = \frac{CB/AC}{AB/AC} = \frac{CB}{AB} = \tan A.$$

So, for an acute angle, $\tan A = \dfrac{\sin A}{\cos A}$. This is taken as the definition of the tangent for an angle of any magnitude, i.e. it is equal to the sine of the angle divided by the cosine.

The cosec, sec and cotangent are defined as the reciprocals of sine, cos and tangent respectively.

Suppose you take an acute angle xOP and draw the perpendicular PN to the axis of x.

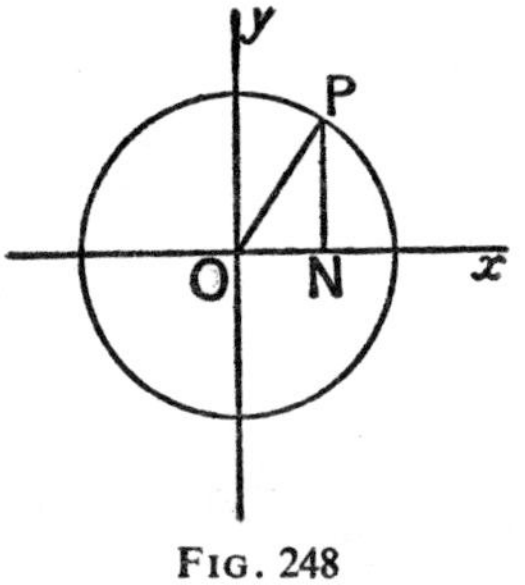

FIG. 248

By the definition of the cosine of an acute angle, $\cos xOP = \dfrac{ON}{OP}$. But since the radius is unity, $\cos xOP = ON$, which is the x coordinate of P. Similarly, $\sin xOP = \dfrac{PN}{OP} = PN$, which is the y coordinate of P. This shows that the definitions of the ratios for a general angle do fit with the definitions for an acute angle.

Negative angles

The angle xOP is called positive when it is measured counter-clockwise; so a negative angle is measured clockwise from Ox. The position of a radius OP may be given by many different angles. For example, 320°, 680°, − 40° all give the same position of the radius and a particular trigonometrical ratio of each of these angles has the same value.

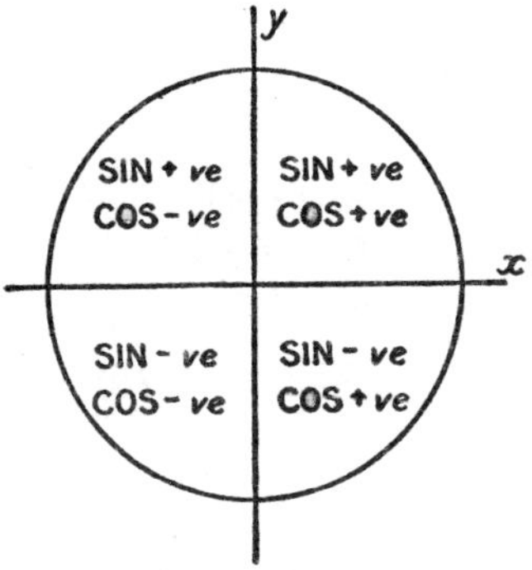

FIG. 249

Signs of the ratios

The sign of the cosine is the same as the sign of the x coordinate; that of the sine is the same as the sign of the y coordinate. It is simple to write down the signs of the sine and cosine in the four quadrants as in Fig. 249.

The tangent is defined as sine divided by cosine and so the sign of the tangent is easily found. In the third quadrant, for example, sin and cos are both negative; the tangent therefore is positive. The signs of the sine, cosine and tangent in the four quadrants may be remembered by the word CAST, placed as shown in Fig. 250.

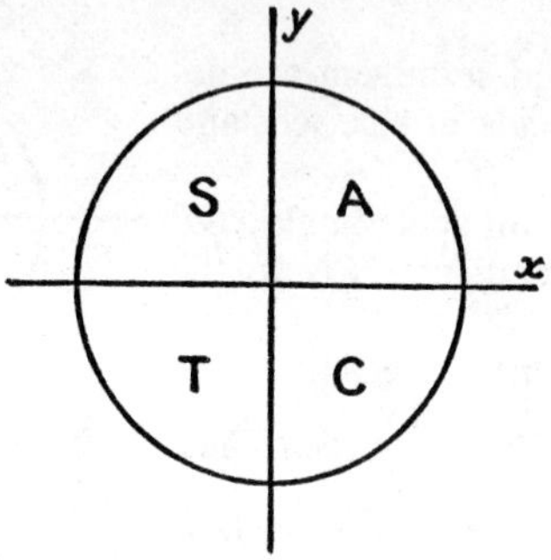

FIG. 250

C stands for cos +ve (sin and tan −ve);
A stands for all +ve;
S stands for sin +ve (cos and tan −ve);
T stands for tan +ve (cos and sin −ve).

The signs of cosec, sec and cot are the same as the signs of their reciprocals, sin, cos and tan.

EXERCISES 106A

Write down the signs of the following:

1. tan 170°. **2.** sec 320°. **3.** cos 160°.
4. sin 220°. **5.** cosec 320°. **6.** sin (− 40°).
7. cos (− 100°). **8.** cot 310°. **9.** sec 170°.
10. sec 190°.

EXERCISES 106B

Write down the signs of the following:

1. tan 210°. **2.** sec 195°. **3.** cos 125°.
4. sin 236°. **5.** cosec 400°. **6.** sin (− 20°).
7. cos (− 80°). **8.** cot 240°. **9.** sec 250°.
10. cosec 250°.

Magnitudes of the ratios

Suppose that P and P' are two points on the circle of unit radius so that OP, OP' make equal angles with the x-axis. Then since

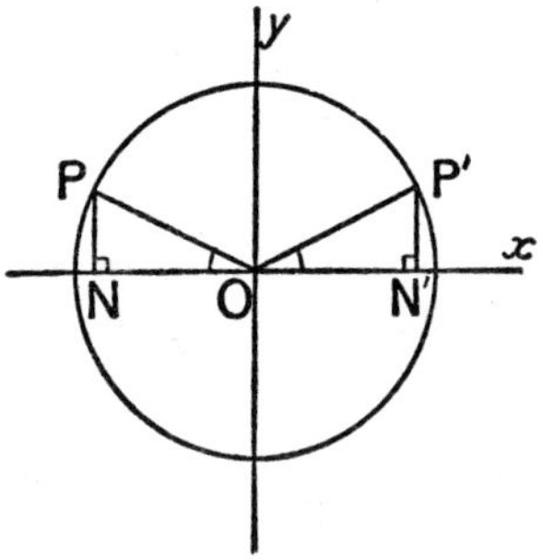

FIG. 251

triangles PNO, $P'N'O$ are congruent, the coordinates of P will be numerically equal to the coordinates of P'. The ratios of the angle xOP' are therefore numerically equal to the ratios of xOP.

The ratios of any angle are therefore equal numerically to the same ratios of the **acute** angle which the radius defining the angle makes with the **x-axis.**

Example 1. Find the value of tan 220°.

First, find its sign.

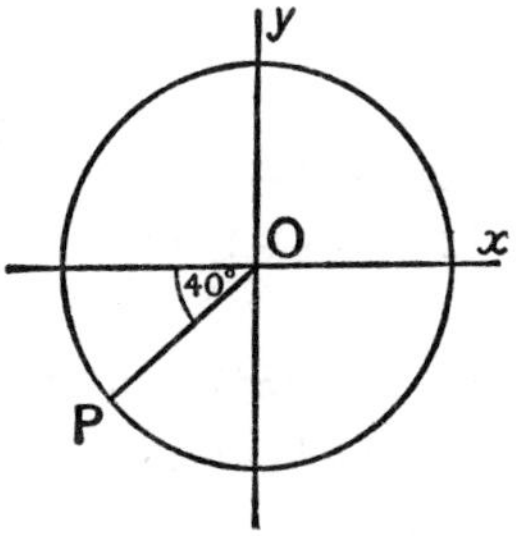

FIG. 252

220° is in the third quadrant; its tangent is positive.

The acute angle OP makes with the x-axis is 40°.

$$\therefore \tan 220° = +\tan 40° = 0{\cdot}8391.$$

Example 2. Find the value of cosec 340°.

340° is in the fourth quadrant; in this quadrant sin and cosec are both negative.

The acute angle *OP* makes with the *x*-axis is 20°.

$$\therefore \text{cosec } 340° = -\text{cosec } 20° = -2{\cdot}9238.$$

Example 3. Find the value of cos (− 120°).

− 120° is measured clockwise from *Ox* and so is in the third quadrant. Its cosine is therefore negative.

The acute angle *OP* makes with the *x*-axis is 60°.

$$\therefore \cos(-120°) = -\cos 60° = -0{\cdot}5.$$

Obtuse angles

The angle greater than 90° which occurs most frequently is the obtuse angle. It is worth remembering that

the sin of an obtuse angle is equal to the sin of its supplement;
the cosine of an obtuse angle is minus the cosine of its supplement;
the tangent of an obtuse angle is minus the tangent of its supplement.

EXERCISES 107A

Write down the values of the following using your tables:

1. cos 100°.	**2.** sin 110°.	**3.** tan 120°.
4. cos 190°.	**5.** sin 200°.	**6.** tan 210°.
7. tan 260°.	**8.** tan 280°.	**9.** sin 290°.
10. cos 300°.	**11.** sec 120°.	**12.** cosec 140°.
13. cot 150°.	**14.** cosec 200°.	**15.** sec 210°.
16. cot 220°.	**17.** cosec 280°.	**18.** sec 285°.
19. cot 295°.	**20.** sin (− 20°).	**21.** cos (− 130°).
22. cosec (− 210°).	**23.** sec (− 190°).	**24.** cot (− 185°).

EXERCISES 107B

Write down the values of the following using your tables:

1. cos 110°.	**2.** sin 120°.	**3.** tan 130°.
4. cos 200°.	**5.** sin 220°.	**6.** tan 220°.
7. tan 290°.	**8.** sin 180°.	**9.** sin 300°.
10. cos 310°.	**11.** sec 130°.	**12.** cosec 150°.
13. cot 160°.	**14.** cosec 210°.	**15.** sec 220°.

16. cot 230°. **17.** cosec 290°. **18.** sec 300°.
19. cot 310°. **20.** tan (− 80°). **21.** cos (− 170°).
22. sec (− 170°). **23.** cosec (− 80°). **24.** cot (− 160°).

General angle formulae

We have already mentioned that

$$\sin (180 - x)^\circ = \sin x^\circ; \quad \cos (180 - x)^\circ = -\cos x^\circ$$

and

$$\tan (180 - x)^\circ = -\tan x^\circ.$$

Other similar formulae may be deduced as follows:

Example 1. Simplify $\cos (270 + x)^\circ$.

For convenience consider x° to be acute and then $(270 + x)^\circ$ is in the fourth quadrant. The cosine of an angle in the fourth quadrant is positive. The arm making $(270 + x)^\circ$ will make an acute angle of $(90 - x)^\circ$ with the x-axis.

$$\therefore \cos (270 + x)^\circ = +\cos (90 - x)^\circ$$
$$= +\sin x^\circ.$$

Example 2. Simplify $\cos (360 - x)^\circ$.

If x is considered as acute, $(360 - x)^\circ$ is in the fourth quadrant. $\cos (360 - x)^\circ$ is therefore positive.

The arm making $(360 - x)^\circ$ makes an acute angle x° with the x-axis.

$$\therefore \cos (360 - x)^\circ = +\cos x^\circ.$$

(N.B. If x is not acute, the formulae proved in these two examples will still hold.)

EXERCISES 108A

Simplify:

1. $\sin (180 + x)^\circ$. **2.** $\cos (90 + x)^\circ$. **3.** $\tan (270 - x)^\circ$.
4. $\cot (360 - x)^\circ$. **5.** $\sec (-x)^\circ$. **6.** $\sec (x - 90)^\circ$.
7. $\operatorname{cosec} (x - 180)^\circ$. **8.** $\tan (270 + x)^\circ$. **9.** $\tan (360 - x)^\circ$.
10. $\sec (180 + 2x)^\circ$.

EXERCISES 108B

Simplify:

1. $\cos (180 + x)^\circ$. **2.** $\sin (90 + x)^\circ$. **3.** $\cos (270 - x)^\circ$.
4. $\tan (360 - x)^\circ$. **5.** $\sin (-x)^\circ$. **6.** $\operatorname{cosec} (x - 90)^\circ$.
7. $\sec (x - 180)^\circ$. **8.** $\cot (360 - x)^\circ$. **9.** $\sec (360 - x)^\circ$.
10. $\cot (180 + 2x)^\circ$.

Ratios of 0°, 90°, 180°, 270°

The coordinates of A are (1, 0).

$$\therefore \cos 0° = 1; \quad \sin 0° = 0.$$

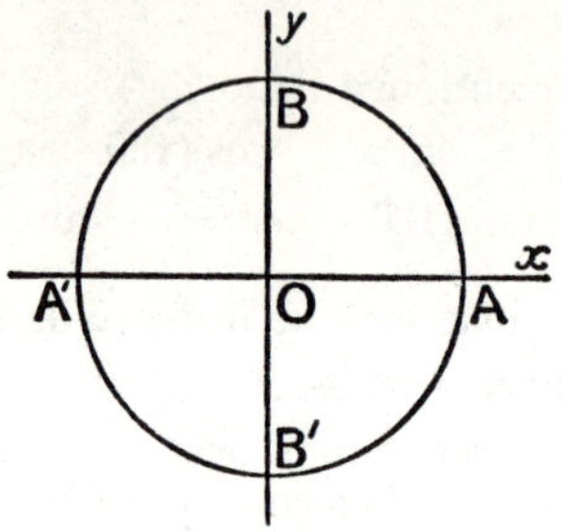

FIG. 253

The coordinates of B are (0, 1).

$$\therefore \cos 90° = 0; \quad \sin 90° = 1.$$

The coordinates of A' are (– 1, 0).

$$\therefore \cos 180° = -1; \quad \sin 180° = 0.$$

The coordinates of B' are (0, – 1).

$$\therefore \cos 270° = 0; \quad \sin 270° = -1.$$

Identities

There are four important identities which exist between the ratios. The first of these follows from the definition of tangent,

$$\tan x = \frac{\sin x}{\cos x} \quad . \quad . \quad . \quad . \quad \text{(i)}$$

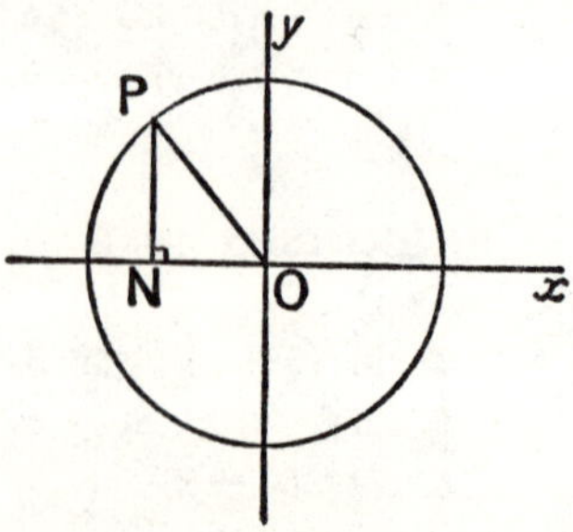

FIG. 254

If P is the point on the circle of unit radius such that $x\widehat{O}P = x$, then the coordinates of P are ($\cos x$, $\sin x$).

But $$NO^2 + PN^2 = PO^2,$$

or $$\cos^2 x + \sin^2 x = 1 \quad . \quad . \quad . \quad \text{(ii)}$$

Divide equation (ii) by $\cos^2 x$ and

$$1 + \tan^2 x = \sec^2 x \quad . \quad . \quad . \quad \text{(iii)}$$

Divide equation (ii) by $\sin^2 x$ and

$$\cot^2 x + 1 = \text{cosec}^2 x \quad . \quad . \quad . \quad \text{(iv)}$$

These formulae are all true for angles of any magnitude.

Example 1. Prove $(\cos x + \sin x)^2 + (\cos x - \sin x)^2 = 2$.

$$(\cos x + \sin x)^2 + (\cos x - \sin x)^2$$
$$= \cos^2 x + 2 \cos x \sin x + \sin^2 x + \cos^2 x - 2 \cos x \sin x + \sin^2 x$$
$$= 2(\cos^2 x + \sin^2 x) = 2.$$

Example 2. Prove that $\cot x + \tan x = \sec x \text{ cosec } x$.

(In proving identities, it is often a good plan to express all quantities in terms of cos and sin.)

$$\cot x + \tan x = \frac{\cos x}{\sin x} + \frac{\sin x}{\cos x} = \frac{\cos^2 x + \sin^2 x}{\cos x \sin x}$$
$$= \frac{1}{\cos x \sin x} = \sec x \text{ cosec } x.$$

Example 3. Find all values of x between 0° and 360° which satisfy the equation $$5 \cos x = 2 \sin x.$$

Divide both sides of the equation by $\cos x$

$$5 = 2 \tan x.$$
$$\therefore \tan x = 2{\cdot}5.$$

$x = 68° 12'$ is one solution. $\tan x$ is positive in the first and third quadrants and so the only other possible solution is the angle in the third quadrant which makes 68° 12′ with the x-axis, i.e.

$$180° + 68° 12' = 248° 12'.$$
$$x = 68° 12' \quad \text{or} \quad 248° 12'.$$

EXERCISES 109: MISCELLANEOUS

1. What can you say about x if $\sin x$ is positive and $\cos x$ negative?

2. By drawing and measurement, find values for cos 80°, sin 100°, cos 220°, sin 340°.

3. If $\cos x^\circ = -\cos 200^\circ$ and x is acute, find x.

4. If $\sin x^\circ = \sin 160^\circ$ and x is acute, find x.

5. What values between 0 and 360 satisfy the equation

$$\cos x^\circ = -0{\cdot}4?$$

6. What values between 0 and 360 satisfy the equation

$$\sin x^\circ = -0{\cdot}4?$$

7. If $\sin x^\circ > \frac{1}{2}$ and x lies between 0 and 360, what further limits can you impose on x?

8. If $\cos x^\circ < \frac{1}{2}$, what do you know about x?

Find two values of x between 0° and 360° to satisfy the following equations:

9. $\sin x = 0{\cdot}7$. **10.** $\cos x = -0{\cdot}6$. **11.** $\sin x = 2\cos x$.

12. $\cot x = -2{\cdot}1$. **13.** $\tan x = -0{\cdot}4$. **14.** $\sec x = -2$.

Simplify the following expressions:

15. $\operatorname{cosec}(90^\circ + x)$. **16.** $\sec(270^\circ - x)$. **17.** $\sec(-x)$.

18. $\cos(180^\circ + x)$. **19.** $\cot(270^\circ + x)$. **20.** $\tan(360^\circ - x)$.

21. Find x if $\sin x = \frac{4}{5}$ and $\cos x = -\frac{3}{5}$.

22. Find x if $\sin x = -\frac{4}{5}$ and $\cos x = -\frac{3}{5}$.

23. Find x if $\sin x = -\frac{4}{5}$ and $\cos x = \frac{3}{5}$.

24. Find x if $\sin x = \frac{4}{5}$ and $\tan x = -\frac{4}{3}$.

25. Find x if $\sin x = -\frac{4}{5}$ and $\tan x = -\frac{4}{3}$.

26. Find x if $\sin x = -\frac{4}{5}$ and $\tan x = +\frac{4}{3}$.

27. If A, B, C are the angles of a triangle, express in terms of A: (i) $\sin(B + C)$; (ii) $\cos(B + C)$; (iii) $\tan(B + C)$; (iv) $\sin\frac{1}{2}(B + C)$; (v) $\cos 2(B + C)$.

28. What do you know about θ if $\tan\theta$ is less than 1 and $\sin\theta$ is negative? ($0^\circ < \theta < 360^\circ$.)

29. Find the values of θ ($0^\circ < \theta < 360^\circ$) from the equations: (i) $\sin\theta = -0{\cdot}3$; (ii) $\cos\theta = -0{\cdot}2$; (iii) $\tan\theta = 1{\cdot}2$.

30. The sine of an obtuse angle is $\frac{3}{4}$. Find its cosine.

31. The cos of an angle between 270° and 360° is $\frac{p}{q}$. Find its sin.

32. Simplify (i) $\dfrac{\sin(90^\circ + \theta)}{\cos\theta}$; (ii) $\dfrac{\cos(90^\circ - \theta)}{\cos(90^\circ + \theta)}$; (iii) $\dfrac{\sin(180^\circ - \theta)}{\cos(270^\circ + \theta)}$.

33. If $\sin\theta = -0{\cdot}28$, find the possible values of $\cos\frac{1}{2}\theta$.

34. If $2\sec\alpha = \left(t + \dfrac{1}{t}\right)$, find $\tan\alpha$.

35. Simplify $\cos^2\theta + \cos^2(90° - \theta)$.

36. Simplify $\sin^2(180° - \theta) + \cos^2(360° - \theta)$.

37. Simplify $\operatorname{cosec}^2(90° - \theta) - \cot^2(90° - \theta)$.

38. Prove the identity $\dfrac{\tan^2\theta}{\sin^2\theta} = \dfrac{\sin^2\theta}{\cos^2\theta} + 1$.

39. Prove the identity $\dfrac{\sin^2\theta}{1 + \cos\theta} = 1 - \cos\theta$.

40. Prove the identity

$$\cot(90° - \theta) + \tan(90° - \theta) = \sec(90° - \theta)\sec\theta.$$

28

GRAPHS

Graphs of sine, cosine and tangent

THE graphs of the three ratios sine x, cosine x and tan x are very important. You should be able to sketch the general shape of any of these three curves.

The sine curve

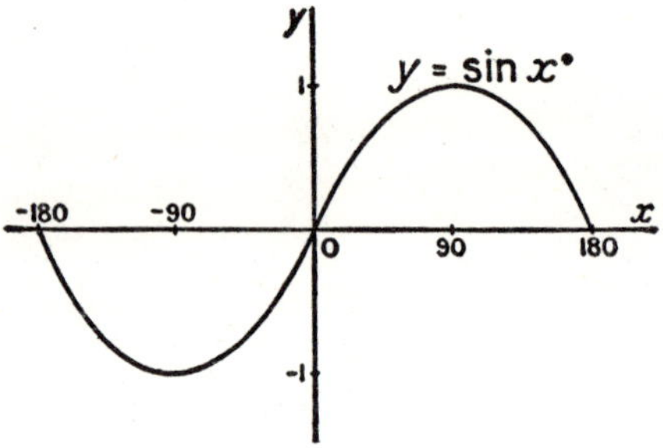

FIG. 255

The sine curve is a wave which lies between the values + 1 and − 1 of y. Its value is zero at multiples of 180°. If you remember the general shape, you can tell whether the sine of an angle is positive or negative from the graph.

The cosine curve

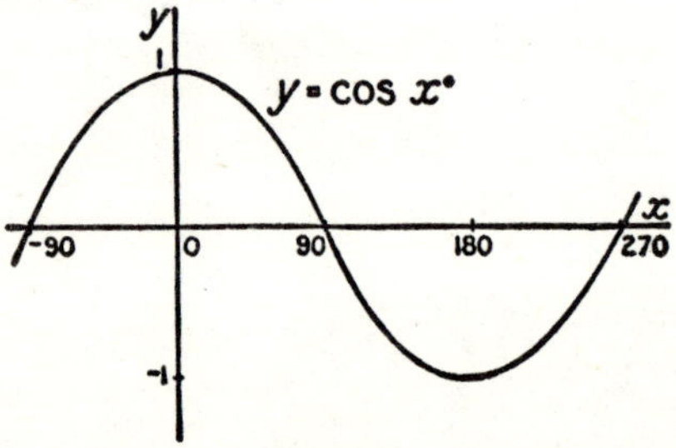

FIG. 256

The shape of the cosine curve is the same as the shape of the sine curve. The only difference between the two graphs is that they start at different places. The two curves can be made identical by a shift of the y-axis. The value of the cosine is zero at odd multiples of 90° (90°, 270°, etc.).

The tangent curve

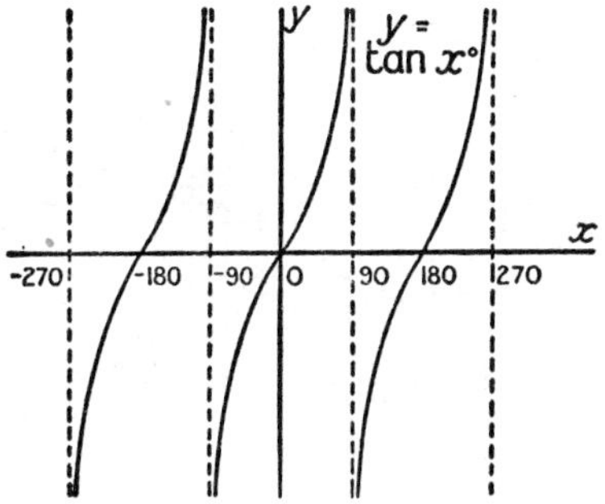

FIG. 257

The tangent curve is quite different. It consists of an infinite number of branches, all of the same shape. The tangent is zero at multiples of 180°.

Graphical applications

The drawing of trigonometrical graphs is a similar process to the drawing of algebraic graphs. The graphs, too, have the same applications which are chiefly the solutions of equations and the finding of maximum and minimum values. Two examples illustrating the methods used are given.

Example 1. Draw the graph of $2 \sin x° + 3 \cos x°$ between $x = 0$ and $x = 90$. Find from your graph (i) the maximum value of $2 \sin x° + 3 \cos x°$; (ii) a value of x for which $2 \sin x° + 3 \cos x° = 3{\cdot}2$; (iii) a value of x for which $2 \sin x° + 3 \cos x° = x/10$.

Let $y = 2 \sin x° + 3 \cos x°$ and find the values of y corresponding to values of x at 10° intervals.

x . .	0	10	20	30	40	50	60	70	80	90
$2 \sin x°$.	0	0·35	0·68	1·0	1·29	1·53	1·73	1·88	1·97	2·0
$3 \cos x°$.	3	2·95	2·82	2·60	2·30	1·94	1·50	1·03	0·52	0
y . .	3	3·3	3·5	3·6	3·59	3·47	3·23	2·91	2·49	2·0

(i) The maximum value of $2 \sin x° + 3 \cos x°$ is slightly larger than 3·6 and occurs when $x = 34$.

(ii) If $y = 3{\cdot}2$, from the graph $x = 8$ or 60·5.

(iii) Draw, using the same scales and axes, the graph of $y = x/10$. When $x = 20$, $y = 2$; when $x = 40$, $y = 4$. The graph is the straight line joining these two points.

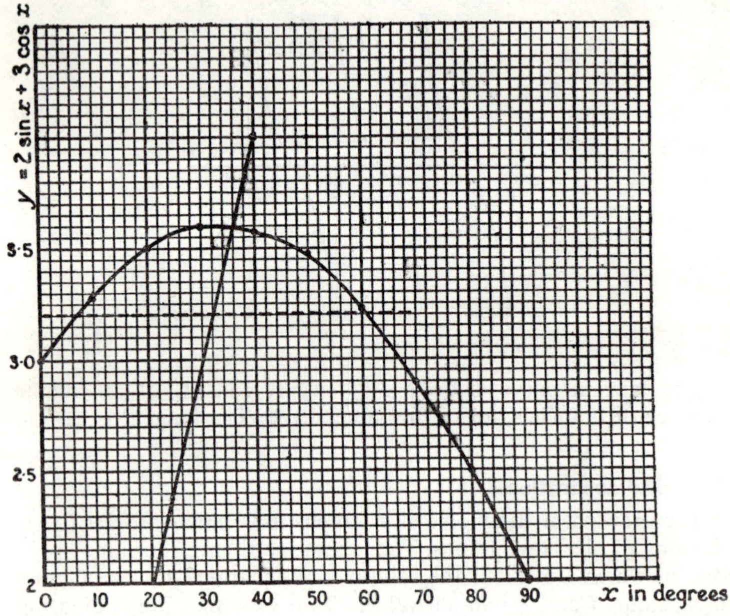

FIG. 258

The value of x at the point of intersection of the straight line with the curve (36) is a value of x for which $2 \sin x° + 3 \cos x° = x/10$.

Example 2. Draw, using the same scales and axes, the graphs of $y = \tan 2x°$ and $y = 4 \cos x° - 1$, for values of x from 10 to 35. Deduce a value of x for which $4 \cos x° - \tan 2x° = 1$.

First prepare two tables of values.

x	10	15	20	25	30	35
$\tan 2x°$ . . .	0·36	0·58	0·84	1·19	1·73	2·75

x	10	15	20	25	30	35
$4 \cos x°$	3·94	3·86	3·76	3·63	3·46	3·28
$4 \cos x° - 1$	2·94	2·86	2·76	2·63	2·46	2·28

The value of x where the two curves cross (33·5) is a solution of the equation

$$4 \cos x° - 1 = \tan 2x° \quad \text{or of} \quad 4 \cos x° - \tan 2x° = 1.$$

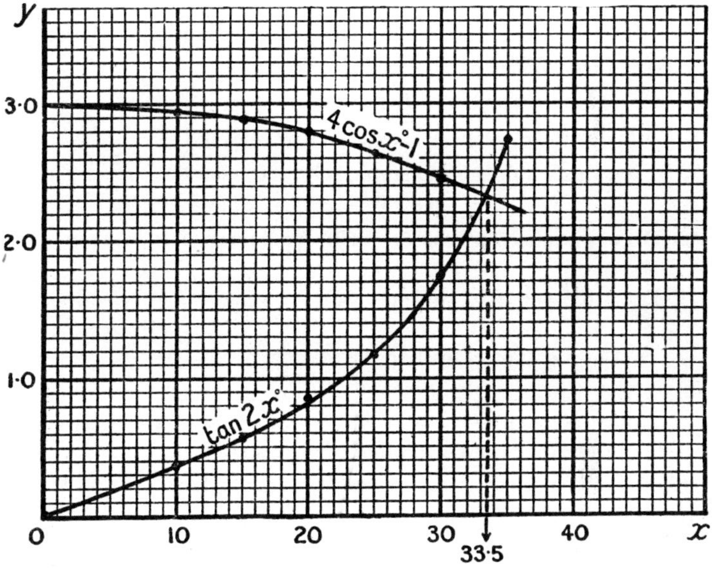

FIG. 259

Check. $\quad 4 \cos 33° 30' = 4(0·8339) = 3·3356.$

$\tan 2(33° 30') = \tan 67° = 2·356.$

The difference is 0·98.

EXERCISES 110: MISCELLANEOUS

Draw the graph of $y = 2 \sin x° + 3 \cos x°$ between $x = 0$ and $x = 90$.

1. Read off the values of $2 \sin x° + 3 \cos x°$ when $x = 8, 25, 72, 77$.

2. Find values of x to satisfy the equations: (i) $2 \sin x° + 3 \cos x° = 2·25$; (ii) $2 \sin x° + 3 \cos x° = 3·2$; (iii) $\sin x° + 1·5 \cos x° = 1·7$; (iv) $\frac{2}{3} \sin x° + \cos x° = 0·8$.

3. By drawing a straight-line graph, find a value of x which satisfies the equation $2 \sin x^\circ + 3 \cos x^\circ = x/20$.

Draw the graph of $y = 4 \cos x^\circ - 1$ between $x = 0$ and $x = 35$.

4. Read off the values of $4 \cos x^\circ - 1$ when $x = 8, 16, 24, 32$.

5. Find values of x to satisfy the equations: (i) $4 \cos x^\circ - 1 = 2{\cdot}6$; (ii) $\cos x^\circ = 0{\cdot}95$.

6. By drawing a straight-line graph, solve the equation

$$4 \cos x^\circ - 1 = \tfrac{3}{10}x.$$

Draw the graph of $\tan 2x^\circ$ between $x = 0$ and $x = 45$.

7. Write down values of x to satisfy the equations

$$\text{(i) } \tan 2x^\circ = 0{\cdot}4; \quad \text{(ii) } \tan 2x^\circ = 2{\cdot}3.$$

8. Write down the values of $\tan 16^\circ$, $\tan 24^\circ$ and $\tan 38^\circ$.

9. By drawing a straight-line graph, solve the equation

$$\tan 2x^\circ = x/15.$$

10. Draw the graph of $\cos (x + 60)^\circ$ for values of x between -60 and $+60$.

11. Draw the graph of $\sin 2(x + 30)^\circ$ for values of x between -30 and $+60$.

12. Find by a graphical method the maximum value of

$$5 \sin x^\circ + 12 \cos x^\circ.$$

13. Draw the graph of $\cos x^\circ + \cos 2x^\circ$ for values of x between 0 and 45. Using your graph, find a solution of the equation

$$\cos x^\circ + \cos 2x^\circ = 1.$$

14. Find graphically a solution of the equation $1 + \sec x^\circ = x/20$.

15. Draw on the same diagram rough sketches of the curves $y = \cos x^\circ$ and $y = \sin x^\circ$. Hence deduce the shape of the curve $y = \frac{1}{2}(\cos x^\circ + \sin x^\circ)$.

16. Draw on the same diagram the graphs of $\cos (x + 20)^\circ$ and $\sin (x - 20)^\circ$. Hence find a solution of the equation

$$\cos (x + 20)^\circ = \sin (x - 20)^\circ.$$

17. Draw on the same diagram the graphs of $\sec (x - 10)^\circ$ and $\operatorname{cosec} (x + 30)^\circ$. Hence find a solution of the equation

$$\operatorname{cosec} (x + 30)^\circ = \sec (x - 10)^\circ.$$

18. Draw the graph of $\sin \theta^\circ + \cos 2\theta^\circ$ between $\theta = 0$ and $\theta = 180$ and hence find a solution of the equation $\sin \theta^\circ + \cos 2\theta^\circ = 0{\cdot}4$.

19. Find all the angles between 0 and 360 which satisfy the equation $4 \cos \theta^\circ + 7 \sin \theta^\circ = 5$.

20. Draw the graph of $y = \sin x^\circ - \sin 2x^\circ + \sin 3x^\circ$ for values of x between 0 and 90. Hence find a value of x for which $\sin x^\circ + \sin 3x^\circ = \sin 2x^\circ$.

21. Draw on the same diagram the graphs of $y = \cos x^\circ + \cos^2 x^\circ$ and $y = 1 - \dfrac{x}{360}$, taking values of x from 0 to 180. From your graphs find a solution of the equation $\sin^2 x^\circ - \cos x^\circ = \dfrac{x}{360}$.

22. Draw on one diagram the graphs of $\sin x^\circ$ and of $1 - \left(\dfrac{x}{90}\right)^2$ taking values of x from 0 to 90. Hence find a solution of the equation $1 - \sin x^\circ = \dfrac{x^2}{8100}$.

23. Find all solutions of the equation $4 \cos x^\circ - \sin x^\circ = 1$ lying between 0 and 180.

24. Draw the graph of $\cos \theta^\circ - \cos 2\theta^\circ$ between $\theta = 0$ and $\theta = 90$.

25. Draw the graph of $2 \sin \theta^\circ - \sin 2\theta^\circ$ between $\theta = 0$ and $\theta = 90$ and find the maximum value of $2 \sin \theta^\circ - \sin 2\theta^\circ$.

26. Find all solutions of the equation $4 \sin \theta^\circ - 2 \cos 2\theta^\circ = 3$ between 0 and 360.

27. Solve graphically the equation $\cos \theta^\circ + \sin \theta^\circ = 0{\cdot}6$ for values of θ between 0 and 180.

29

SOLID TRIGONOMETRY

The plane

A PLANE is a surface such as the cover of this book in which the line joining any two points of the surface lies entirely in that surface.

A plane is determined by any one of the following:

1. Two intersecting straight lines.
2. Two parallel lines.
3. Three points not in the same straight line.
4. A line and a point not on the line.

Two planes which are not parallel intersect in a straight line. An example of this is the intersection of a wall and the floor of a room.

Three planes will in general intersect in a point. An example of this is two intersecting walls and the floor of a room.

Skew lines

Skew lines are lines which are not parallel and which do not meet. They cannot lie in the same plane. The angle between two skew lines is equal to the angle between lines which intersect and which are parallel to the skew lines.

Angle between a line and a plane

If a line PO intersects a given plane at O and PN is the perpendicular from P to the plane, the angle between the line and the plane is defined as the angle PON.

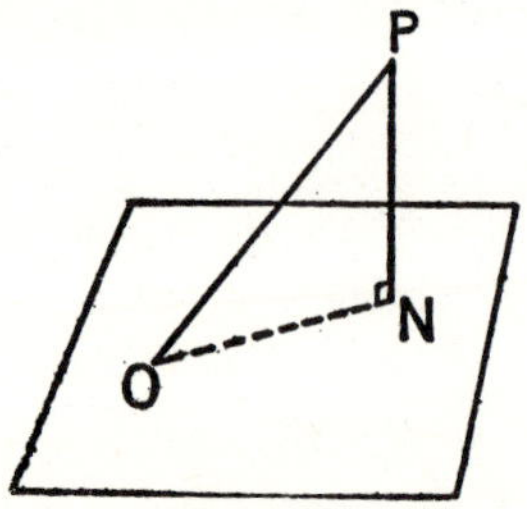

FIG. 260

It is the angle between the line and its projection on the plane.

Line of greatest slope

The line of greatest slope in a plane is a line perpendicular to any horizontal line in the plane.

Angle between two planes

Two planes which are not parallel intersect in a straight line. Draw two lines, one in each plane and each perpendicular to the common line of intersection. The angle between these two lines is defined as the angle between the planes.

Problems

When dealing with problems in three dimensions, choose and draw suitable triangles in different planes and find the sides and angles of these triangles as necessary.

Example 1. The figure shows a room in which $AB = 20$ m, $BC = 16$ m and $CC' = 12$ m. Calculate

(i) the length of the diagonal AC';

(ii) the angle AC' makes with the floor;

(iii) the angle which the plane $D'ABC'$ makes with the floor.

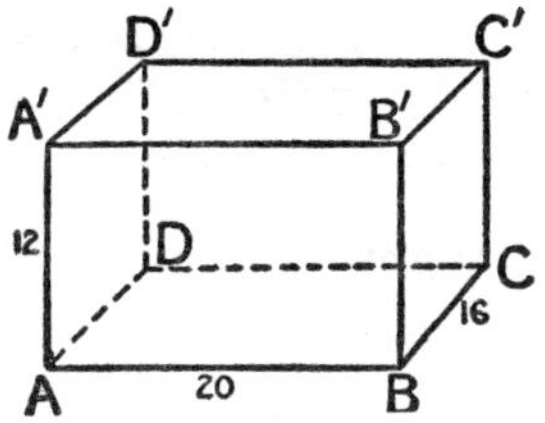

FIG. 261

(i) To find AC', consider the triangle ACC'.
From the triangle ACB, which is right-angled at B,

$$AC^2 = AB^2 + BC^2 = 20^2 + 16^2 = 656.$$

From the triangle ACC' in Fig. 262,

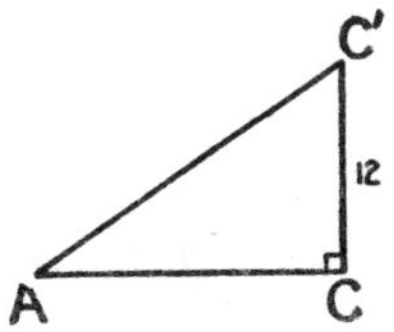

FIG. 262

$$AC'^2 = AC^2 + CC'^2$$
$$= 656 + 12^2$$
$$= 800.$$
$$\therefore AC' = 28{\cdot}3 \text{ m (to 3 sig. fig.).}$$

(ii) The projection of AC' on the floor is AC.
Therefore the angle between AC' and the floor is CAC'.

From Fig. 262, $\sin CAC' = \dfrac{12}{28{\cdot}3}$.

$$\therefore CAC' = 25° 6'.$$

(iii) The intersection of $D'ABC'$ with the floor is AB.
Lines perpendicular to AB, one in each plane, are AD and AD'.

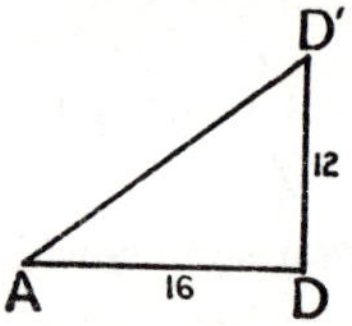

FIG. 263

$$\tan DAD' = \tfrac{12}{16} = 0{\cdot}75.$$
$$\therefore DAD' = 36° 52'.$$

Example 2. The figure represents a pyramid with a square base $ABCD$ of side 5 m. $OA = OB = OC = OD = 8$ m. Calculate

(i) the height, ON, of the pyramid;
(ii) the angle which OA makes with the base;
(iii) the angle which the plane OAD makes with the base.

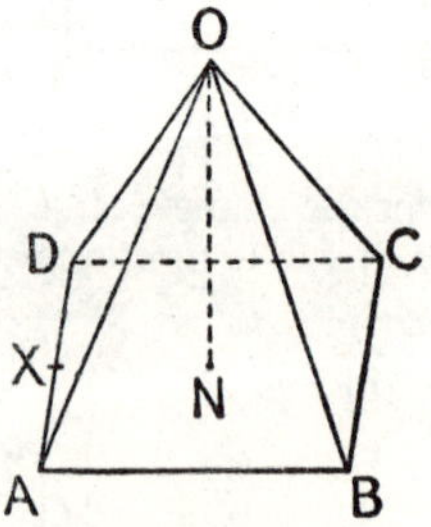

FIG. 264

(i) By symmetry, N is the mid point of the square $ABCD$.

$$AC^2 = AB^2 + BC^2$$
$$= 50.$$

Since $AN = \frac{1}{2}AC$, $AN^2 = \frac{1}{4}AC^2 = 12{\cdot}5$.

From the triangle ANO,

$$NO^2 = AO^2 - AN^2$$
$$= 64 - 12{\cdot}5$$
$$= 51{\cdot}5.$$
$$NO = 7{\cdot}176 \text{ m} = 7{\cdot}18 \text{ m (to 3 sig. fig.)}.$$

(ii) The projection of OA on the base is AN.

Therefore the angle OA makes with the base is $O\hat{A}N$.
From the triangle OAN,

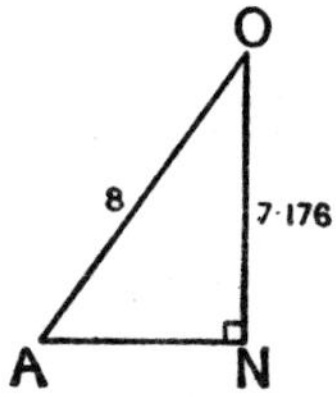

FIG. 265

$$\sin O\hat{A}N = \frac{7{\cdot}176}{8} = 0{\cdot}897.$$

$$\therefore\ O\hat{A}N = 63°\ 46'.$$

(iii) The intersection of the plane OAD with the base is AD.
If X is the mid point of AD, XN and XO are perpendicular to AD, one lying in each plane.

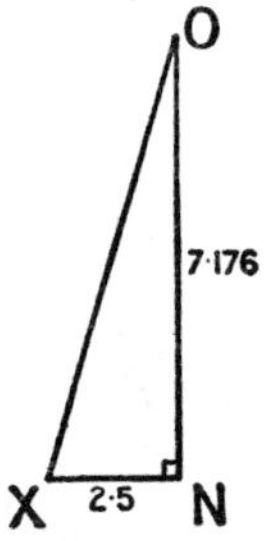

FIG. 266

Therefore the angle between the planes OAD and $ABCD$ is OXN.
From the triangle OXN,

$$\tan O\hat{X}N = \frac{7{\cdot}176}{2{\cdot}5}$$
$$= 2{\cdot}8704.$$
$$\therefore\ O\hat{X}N = 70°\ 48'.$$

Example 3. $ABCD$ is a tetrahedron (the solid formed by joining four points in space). Given that $AB = BC = CA = 4$ m and that $DA = DB = DC = 5$ m, calculate

(i) the height DG of the tetrahedron;
(ii) the angle BD makes with the plane ABC;
(iii) the angle between the planes DAB and ABC.

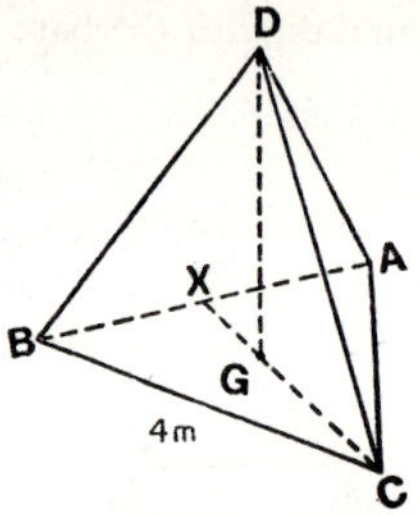

FIG. 267

(i) The perpendicular DG from D to the plane ABC meets ABC at the centre of the equilateral triangle ABC.

If X is the mid point of AB, $X\hat{A}G = 30°$, $AX = 2$ m and

$$\frac{AG}{AX} = \sec 30° = \frac{2}{\sqrt{3}}.$$

$$\therefore\ AG = \frac{4}{\sqrt{3}}\ \text{m}.$$

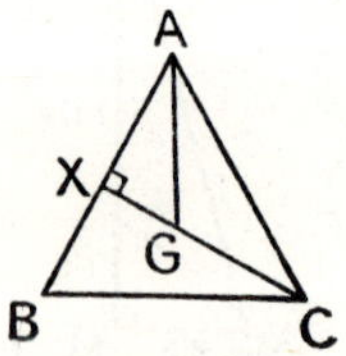

FIG. 268

Also
$$XG = 2\tan 30° = \frac{2}{\sqrt{3}}.$$

From the triangle DAG,

$$\begin{aligned} DG^2 &= AD^2 - AG^2 \\ &= 25 - \tfrac{16}{3} = \tfrac{59}{3} \\ &= 19{\cdot}67, \end{aligned}$$

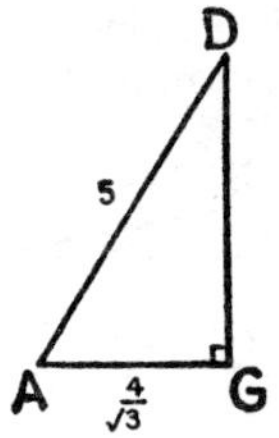

FIG. 269

and so $DG = 4{\cdot}435 = 4{\cdot}44$ m (to 3 sig. fig.).

(ii) The projection of BD on the plane ABC is BG.
The angle required is therefore $D\hat{B}G$.

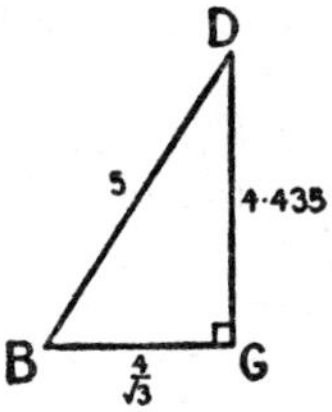

FIG. 270

From the triangle DBG,

$$\sin D\hat{B}G = \frac{4{\cdot}435}{5} = 0{\cdot}887.$$

$$\therefore\ D\hat{B}G = 62^\circ\ 30'.$$

(iii) The planes DAB and ABC intersect in AB. GX and XD are perpendicular to AB, one in each plane, and the angle required is DXG.

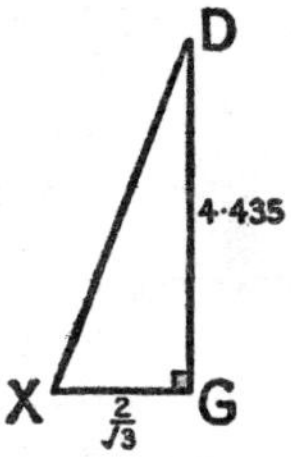

FIG. 271

From the triangle DXG,

$$\tan D\hat{X}G = \frac{4{\cdot}435}{2/\sqrt{3}} = 3{\cdot}841.$$

$$\therefore\ D\hat{X}G = 75^\circ\ 24'.$$

Example 4. *ABCD* is a desk, 1 m by 0·75 m, which is inclined at 30° to the horizontal. Find the inclination of the diagonal *AC* to the horizontal.

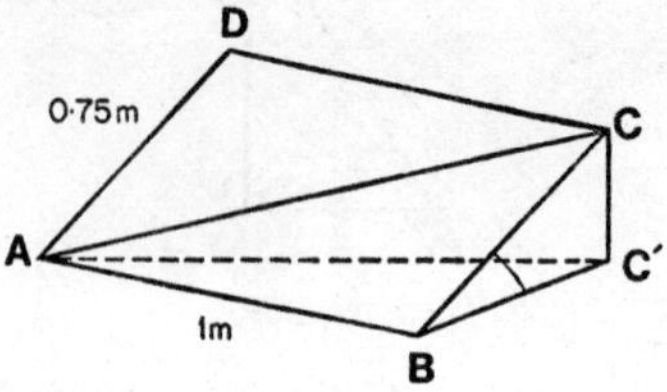

FIG. 272

If C' is the foot of the perpendicular from C to the horizontal plane through AB, the projection of AC on this horizontal plane is AC'.

The angle required is CAC'.

From the triangle CAB,

$$AC^2 = 1^2 + 0{\cdot}75^2 = 1{\cdot}5625$$

$$\therefore AC = 1{\cdot}25 \text{ m.}$$

From the triangle BCC',

$$\frac{CC'}{0{\cdot}75} = \sin 30° = \tfrac{1}{2}$$

$$\therefore CC' = 0{\cdot}375.$$

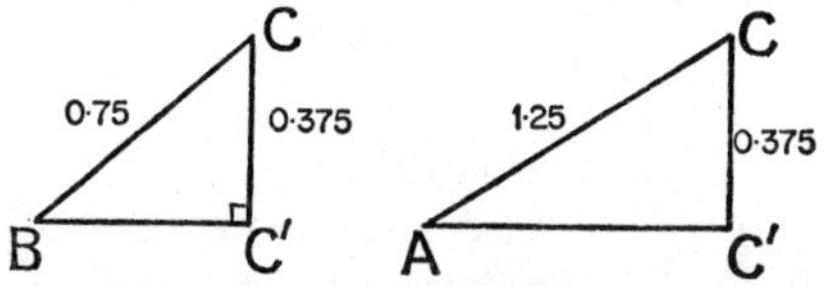

FIG. 273

From the triangle CAC',

$$\sin C\hat{A}C' = \frac{0{\cdot}375}{1{\cdot}25} = 0{\cdot}3.$$

$$\therefore C\hat{A}C' = 17° \, 28'.$$

EXERCISES 111A

The figure shows a box in which $AB = 4$ m, $BC = 3$ m and $CC' = 2$ m. Calculate the following:

1. The angle between the lines AB and AC'.

2. The angle between the lines AC' and AC.

3. The angle between the lines AC' and $A'C$.
4. The angle between the lines AC' and BD'.
5. The angle AC' makes with the plane $ABCD$.

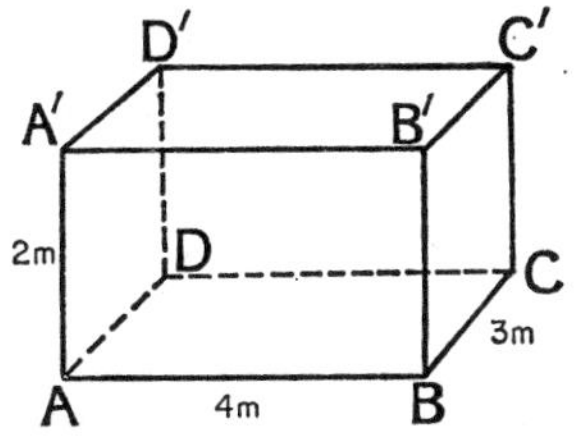

FIG. 274

6. The angle AD' makes with the plane $ABCD$.
7. The angle AB' makes with the plane $ABCD$.
8. The angle between the planes $ABCD$ and $ABC'D'$.
9. The angle between the planes $ADC'B'$ and $ABCD$.
10. The angle between the planes $AD'B'$ and $ABCD$.

EXERCISES 111B

The figure shows a box in which $PQ = 3$ m, $QR = 4$ m and $QQ' = 3$ m. Calculate the following:

1. The angle between the lines PQ' and PS.
2. The angle between the lines PQ' and PQ.
3. The angle between the lines PQ and PS'.

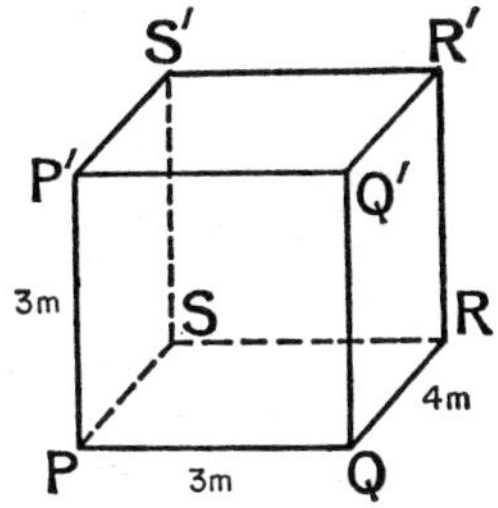

FIG. 275

4. The angle between the lines PQ' and PR'.
5. The angle PQ' makes with the plane $PQRS$.
6. The angle PR' makes with the plane $PQRS$.
7. The angle PS' makes with the plane $PQRS$.

8. The angle between the planes *PQR'S'* and *PQRS*.

9. The angle between the planes *PSR'Q'* and *PQRS*.

10. The angle between the planes *PQ'S'* and *PQRS*.

EXERCISES 112: MISCELLANEOUS

1. The edges of a box are 3 cm, 6 cm and 7 cm. Calculate the angles which a diagonal makes with the faces.

2. The face of a desk is a square and slopes at 30° to the horizontal, Find the angle which a diagonal of the square makes with the horizontal.

3. Fig. 276 shows a pyramid on a square base, of side 8 m. If $OA = OB = OC = OD = 12$ m, find the height *ON* of the pyramid.

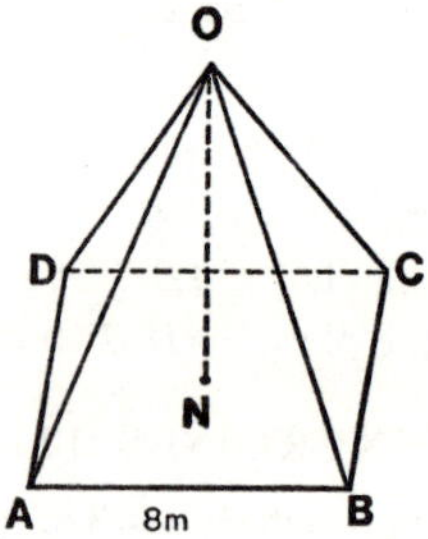

FIG. 276

4. In Fig. 276, find the angle *OA* makes with the plane *ABCD*.

5. In Fig. 276, find the angle between the planes *AOD* and *ABCD*.

6. In Fig. 276, find the angle between the planes *DOA* and *COB*.

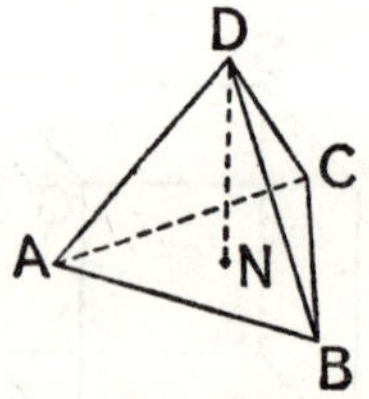

FIG. 277

7. Fig. 277 shows a tetrahedron in which $AB = AC = CB = 4$ m and $DA = DB = DC = 6$ m. Find the height *DN* of the tetrahedron.

8. In Fig. 277, find the angle *DA* makes with the plane *ABC*.

9. In Fig. 277, find the angle between the planes *ADC* and *ABC*.

10. The face of a clock is inclined at 30° to the vertical. If a hand is horizontal at 15.00h, what is the inclination of a hand to the horizontal at 14.00h?

11. In order to climb a hill of gradient 1 in 6, a cyclist rides so that he makes an angle of 45° with the line of greatest slope. What is the gradient of his route?

12. An isosceles triangle *ABC* with $AB = AC$ is placed so that *BC* is horizontal and the plane of the triangle is inclined at 30° to the horizontal. If angle $ABC = 72°$, find the inclination of *AB* to the horizontal.

13. A ring of radius 10 cm is suspended from a point by four equal strings tied symmetrically to the ring so that it hangs horizontally. If the length of each string is 12 cm, find the inclination of a string to the vertical.

14. Fig. 278 shows a pyramid on a rectangular base. If $AB = 2$ m, $BC = 3$ m and $VA = VB = VC = VD = 4$ m, find (i) the height *VN* of the pyramid; (ii) the angle *VA* makes with the plane *ABCD*; (iii) the angle between the planes *VAB* and *ABCD*.

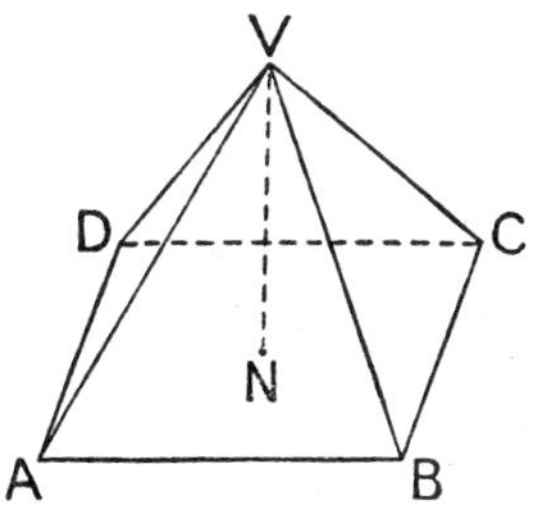

FIG. 278

15. *ABCDO* is a pyramid in which the horizontal base *ABCD* is a square of side 8 cm. If $OA = OB = OC = OD = 12$ cm, find (i) the height *ON* of the pyramid; (ii) the angle *OA* makes with the horizontal; (iii) the angle the plane *OAB* makes with the horizontal; (iv) the angle between *OA* and *OC*; (v) the angle between the planes *OAD* and *OBC*.

16. A tetrahedron *ABCD* has its horizontal base *ABC* an equilateral triangle of side 3 m. If $DA = DB = DC = 6$ m, find (i) the height *DN* of the tetrahedron; (ii) the angle *DA* makes with the horizontal; (iii) the angle between the plane *ADC* and the horizontal; (iv) the angle between the planes *DAB* and *DBC*.

17. From a point *A* due south of a tower, the angle of elevation of the top of the tower is 5° 30′. From a point *B* due east of the tower, the angle of elevation of the top of the tower is 8° 20′. If the distance $AB = 200$ m, find the height of the tower.

18. A hillside is a plane which slopes at an angle α to the horizontal. A track on the hillside makes an angle β with the line of greatest slope. Find the inclination of the track to the horizontal.

19. A ring of radius 8 cm is suspended by 5 strings each of length 12 cm attached symmetrically to the ring, which hangs horizontally. Find (i) the angle between adjacent strings; (ii) the angle which each string makes with the horizontal.

20. A square *ABCD* is rotated through an angle of 30° about the side *AB*. Find the angle between the old and new positions of the diagonal *AC*.

30

PLAN AND ELEVATION

Projection

It is impossible accurately to represent a solid on paper. We can draw what we see but this is merely an impression and cannot have the third dimension of the object. The stereoscopic picture is now familiar to us all and we have all seen and heard of devices to make a picture 'stand out'. An attempt to represent a solid on a plane surface is called a **projection.** All maps and charts are projections of a part of the earth's surface. There are various kinds of projection and the only one we shall consider is called orthogonal projection.

If P is a point in space and N is the foot of the perpendicular from P to a given plane, N is called the projection of P on that plane. The projection of a solid on a plane is the shadow cast by light which is perpendicular to that plane.

For example, the projection of a sphere on any plane is a circle. The projection of a right circular cone with its axis vertical on a vertical plane is a triangle; on a horizontal plane is a circle. Engineers and architects draw projections of an object on a horizontal plane and some vertical planes as the most convenient way of showing the shape of an object. With experience, a draughtsman is able to visualise the shape of an object from these projections.

Plan and elevation

Fig. 279 shows a box open at the top and at the front. If a solid is placed on the floor of this box, the projection of the solid on the four planes of the box (one horizontal and three vertical) are those usually required by an engineer.

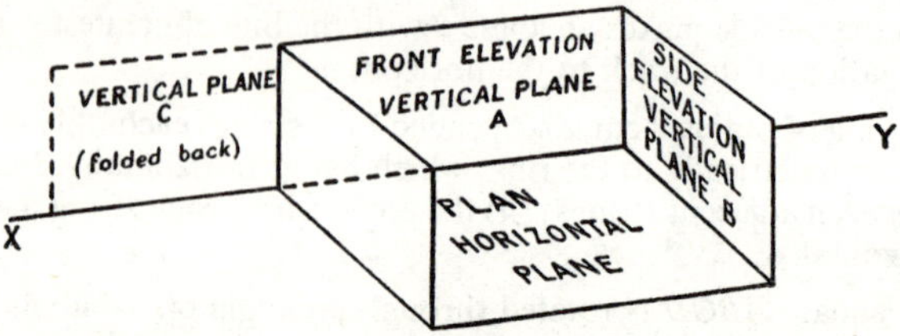

Fig. 279

The projection on the horizontal plane is called the **plan;** the projection on the vertical plane *A* is called the **front elevation;** the projections on the vertical planes *B* and *C* are called the **side elevations.**

Now open the box by swinging the horizontal plane about the line *XY* and folding back the vertical planes *B* and *C* so that all the faces of the box lie in the one plane *A*. The views will now be arranged as in Fig. 280.

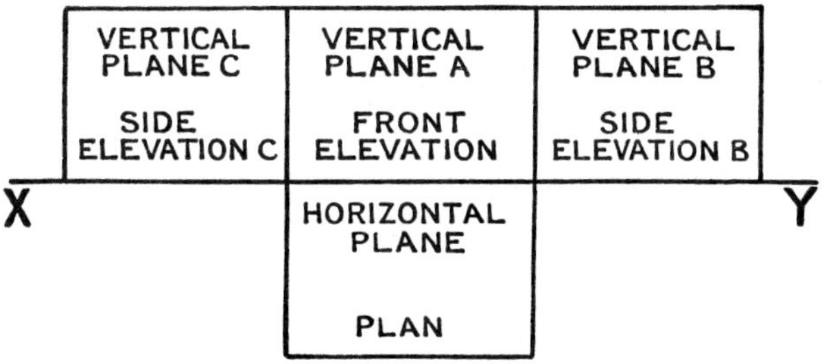

FIG. 280

Notice that each of the side elevations represents the side of the object remote from it. This arrangement of the views is called **'first angle projection'.** There is another method of arranging the views so that each of the side elevations represents the side of the object next to it. This is called **'third angle projection',** but it is not used in this book.

Example 1. Draw the plan and elevation of the shed with a sloping roof and door shown in Fig. 281.

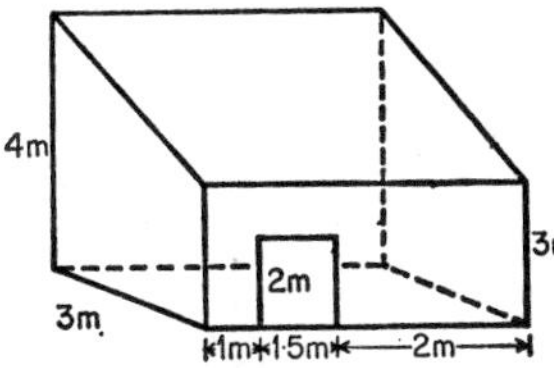

FIG. 281

(N.B. There are conventions about the types of lines used, which you should know and follow.)

1. Use continuous bold lines for visible outlines.
2. Use continuous thin lines for dimension lines and projection lines.
3. Use broken lines for hidden detail.

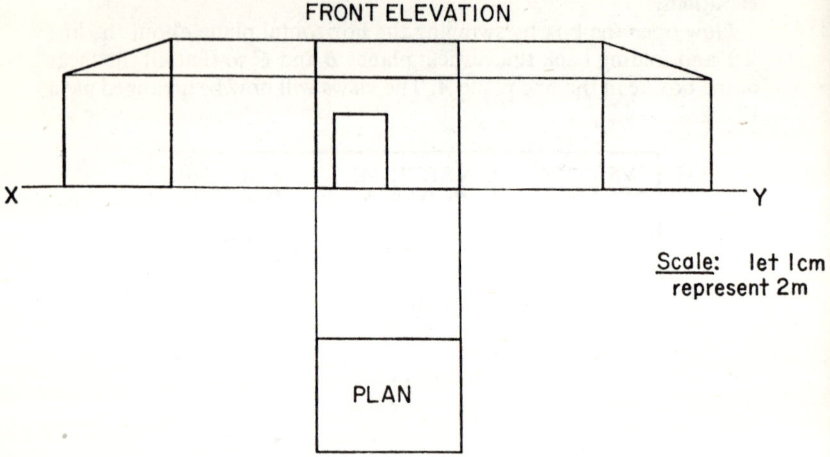

FIG. 282

4. For dimension lines, use thin lines with an arrow at each end, broken to include the figure giving the length.
5. (General instructions.) Drawings should be made on drawing paper and not graph paper, preferably using drawing boards and **T**-squares. The scale should be shown above the drawing.

Example 2. Draw the plan and elevation of the metal stud shown in Fig. 283.

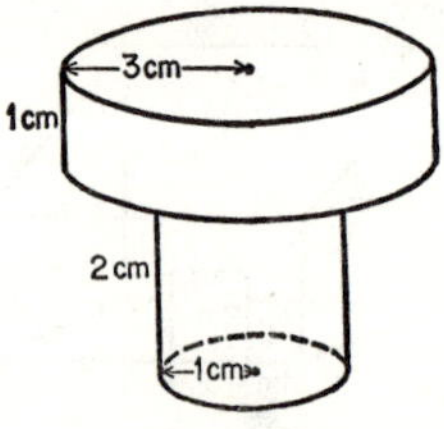

FIG. 283

Notice that here the side elevations and the front elevation are all identical. Also note the dotted circle in the plan which tells us that there is a hidden cylinder under the larger cylinder.

QUARTER SIZE

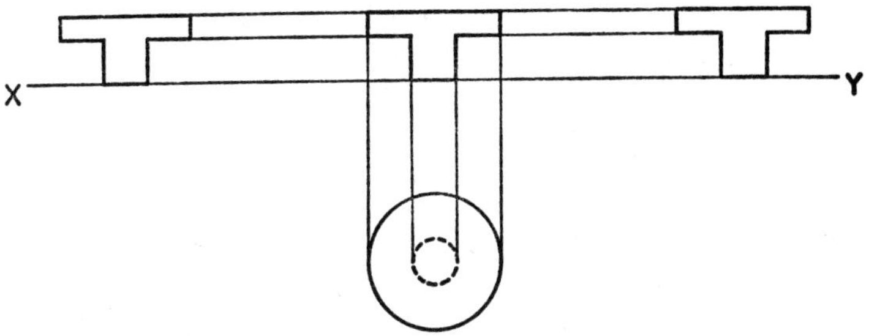

FIG. 284

Example 3. Draw half size the plan, front elevation (view from *A*) and side elevation (view from *B*) of the casting shown in Fig. 285.

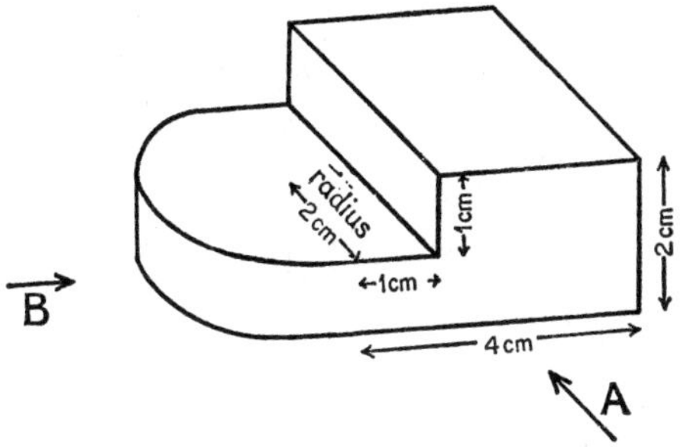

FIG. 285

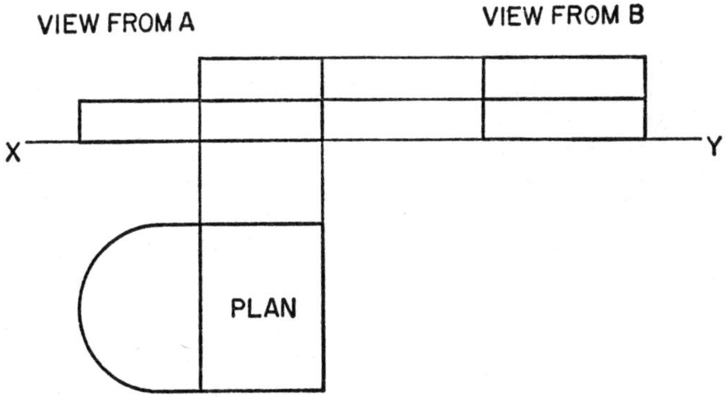

FIG. 286

EXERCISES 113A

Draw plan and elevations for the solids in questions **1** to **10.**

1. A rectangular block, length 4 cm, breadth 3 cm, height 2 cm. The longest edges are parallel to the *XY* line.

2. A cube of side 4 cm, standing symmetrically on one of its edges which is perpendicular to the *XY* line.

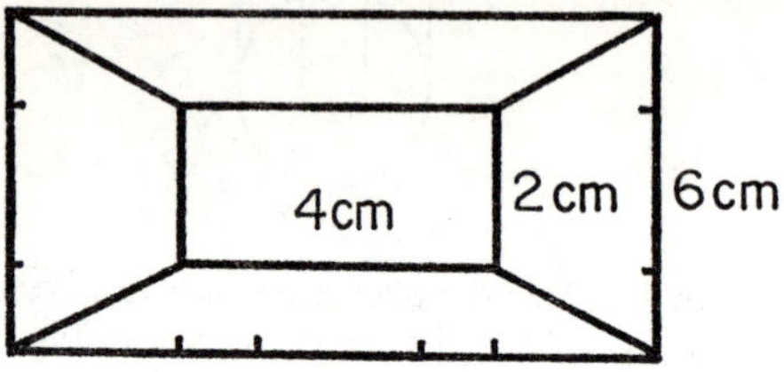

FIG. 287

3. A match-box standing on an end with four edges parallel to the *XY* line. Length = 4 cm, height = 1 cm, breadth = 3 cm.

4. A cylinder of height 8 cm, radius of base 2 cm, standing on the horizontal plane.

5. A pyramid on a square base of side 4 cm with two edges parallel to the *XY* line. The height of the pyramid is 6 cm.

6. A pyramid on a square base of side 4 cm with two edges making an angle of 30° with the *XY* line. The height of the pyramid is 6 cm.

7. A cube of side 4 cm resting on the horizontal plane with two edges making 30° with the *XY* line.

8. A prism of length 4 cm with each end an equilateral triangle of side 3 cm. It is placed so that its long edges are parallel to the *XY* line.

9. The same prism as in question **8** with its long edges perpendicular to the *XY* line.

10. A prism of length 4 cm whose ends are regular hexagons of side 2 cm. The edges of length 4 cm are parallel to the *XY* line.

11. The plan of a brick with sloping faces is shown in Fig. 287. Draw front and side elevations given that the height of the brick is 2 cm.

12. Draw a rough sketch of the solid whose plan and elevation are shown in Fig. 288.

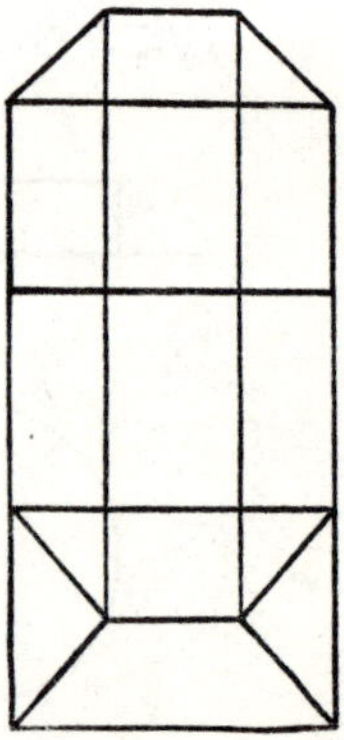

FIG. 288

EXERCISES 113B

Draw plan and elevations for the solids in questions **1** to **10**.

1. A rectangular block, length 6 cm, breadth 4 cm, height 2 cm. The longest edges are perpendicular to the *XY* line.

2. A cube of side 3 cm standing on one of its edges which is perpendicular to the *XY* line.

3. A match-box standing on one of its largest faces with four long edges parallel to the *XY* line.

4. A cylinder of length 6 cm, radius of base 2 cm, standing with its axis parallel to the *XY* line.

5. A pyramid on a square base of side 4 cm with a diagonal perpendicular to the *XY* line. The height of the pyramid is 6 cm.

6. A pyramid on a square base of side 4 cm with two edges making 45° with the *XY* line. The height of the pyramid is 6 cm.

7. A cube of side 4 cm resting on the horizontal plane with two edges making 45° with the *XY* line.

8. A prism of length 4 cm with each end an equilateral triangle of side 2 cm. Its long edges are perpendicular to the *XY* line.

9. The same prism as in question **8** with its long edges parallel to the *XY* line.

10. A prism of length 4 cm whose ends are regular octagons of side 2 cm. The edges of length 4 cm are parallel to the *XY* line.

11. Fig. 289 shows the plan of a roof. The height of the roof is 2 m. Draw front and side elevations.

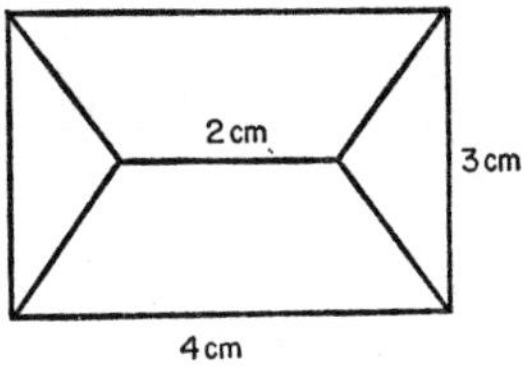

FIG. 289

12. Draw a rough sketch of the solid whose plan and elevation are shown in Fig. 290.

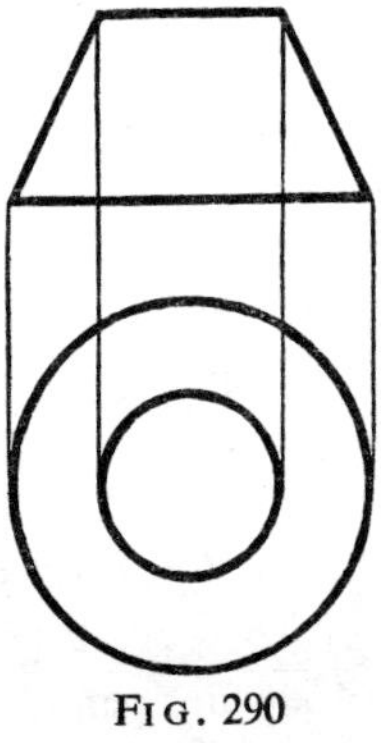

FIG. 290

31

SINE AND COSINE FORMULAE

IF a triangle has its angles given in size, its sides can vary in length but will always be in the same ratio (see similar triangles). We do not know, however, how the ratios of the sides depend on the angles. We do know that if two of the angles are equal, the sides opposite the equal angles are also equal (isosceles triangle). But will the side opposite the 60° angle in a 30°, 60°, 90° triangle be twice as long as the side opposite the 30° angle? The answer to this question is no. Sides are not proportional to the opposite angles but to the sines of the opposite angles and this fact is commonly given in the form of the sine formula which tells us that

$$\frac{a}{\sin A} = \frac{b}{\sin B} = \frac{c}{\sin C}.$$

THE SINE FORMULA

Proof of the sine formula

This is proved for acute and obtuse-angled triangles.

(i) *When the triangle ABC is acute-angled*

Draw AD perpendicular to BC.

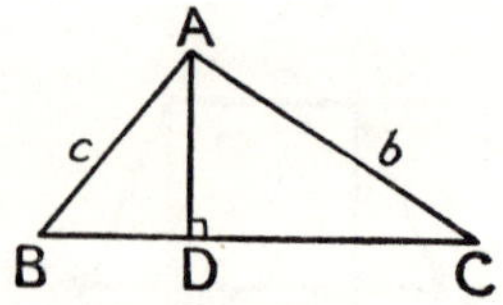

FIG. 291

From the triangle ABD,

$$AD = c \sin B;$$

from the triangle ADC,

$$AD = b \sin C.$$

$$\therefore c \sin B = b \sin C$$

or

$$\frac{b}{\sin B} = \frac{c}{\sin C}.$$

Similarly, by drawing the perpendicular from B to AC,

$$\frac{a}{\sin A} = \frac{c}{\sin C}.$$

$$\therefore \frac{a}{\sin A} = \frac{b}{\sin B} = \frac{c}{\sin C}.$$

(ii) *When the angle C is obtuse*

Draw the perpendicular AD from A to BC produced.
From the triangle ACD,

$$\begin{aligned} AD &= b \sin (180° - C) \\ &= b \sin C. \end{aligned}$$

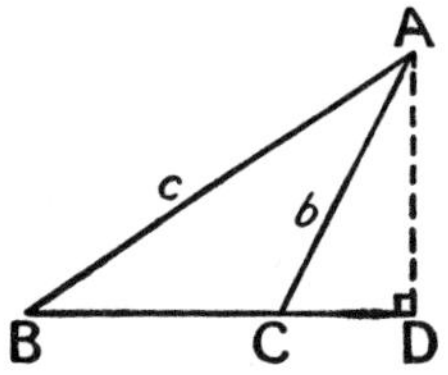

FIG. 292

From the triangle ABD,

$$AD = c \sin B.$$

$$\therefore b \sin C = c \sin B \quad \text{or} \quad \frac{b}{\sin B} = \frac{c}{\sin C}.$$

As before,

$$\frac{a}{\sin A} = \frac{b}{\sin B} = \frac{c}{\sin C}.$$

Never use the sine formula to solve a right-angled triangle; it is not wrong but is unnecessarily long.

Generally do not use the sine formula to solve an isosceles triangle; it is simpler to draw the perpendicular from the vertex to the base.

Given two angles and a side

Given two angles of a triangle and a side, the other sides and angles may be calculated.

Example. In a triangle ABC, $A = 40°$, $B = 52°$ and $a = 30{\cdot}2$ cm. Calculate the other sides and angles.

$$C = 180° - 40° - 52° = 88°.$$

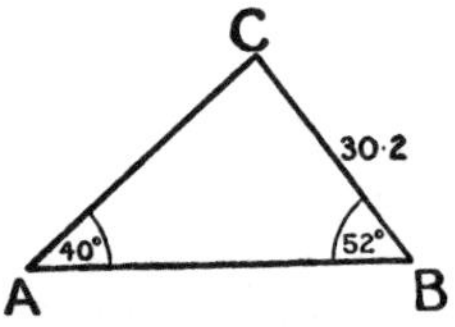

FIG. 293

Using the sine formula,

$$\frac{30{\cdot}2}{\sin 40^\circ} = \frac{b}{\sin 52^\circ} = \frac{c}{\sin 88^\circ}.$$

$$\therefore\ b = \frac{30{\cdot}2 \sin 52^\circ}{\sin 40^\circ} \text{ and } c = \frac{30{\cdot}2 \sin 88^\circ}{\sin 40^\circ}.$$

No.	Log.
30·2	1·4800
sin 52°	$\bar{1}$·8965
	1·3765
sin 40°	$\bar{1}$·8081
37·01	1·5684

No.	Log.
30·2	1·4800
sin 88°	$\bar{1}$·9997
	1·4797
sin 40°	$\bar{1}$·8081
46·94	1·6716

Therefore $b = 37{\cdot}0$ cm and $c = 46{\cdot}9$ cm (to 3 sig. fig.).

The ambiguous case

Suppose that we are given two sides and one angle of a triangle. If the angle is included between the given sides, the shape of the triangle is fixed.

If the angle is not included, there are two possible shapes for the triangle. Suppose that the angle A is given and also the sides c and a. Construct the angle A and mark off AB equal to its given length. With centre B and radius equal to the given value of a draw an arc. This arc will generally cut the third side at two points C_1, C_2, and ABC_1 and ABC_2 are the two triangles satisfying the given conditions.

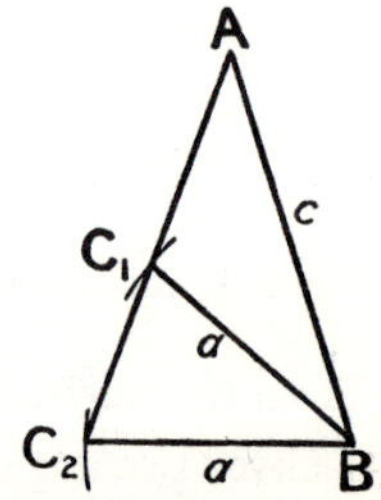

FIG. 294

Since BC_1C_2 is isosceles,

$$\text{angle } BC_1C_2 = \text{angle } BC_2C_1$$

and the angles AC_1B, AC_2B are supplementary.

The ambiguous case arises when, and only when, the arc cuts at two points C_1, C_2 on the same side of A.

For this to occur, the angle A must be acute and a must be smaller than c.

For the arc to cut at all, a must be greater than the perpendicular from B to AC.

$$\therefore\ a > c \sin A.$$

The two cases arise quite naturally in a trigonometrical solution.

Example. Solve the triangle ABC given that $a = 7$, $c = 12$ and $A = 30°$.

Using the sine formula,

$$\frac{7}{\sin 30°} = \frac{12}{\sin C}.$$

$$\therefore \sin C = \frac{12 \sin 30°}{7} = 0{\cdot}8571,$$

and $$C = 58°\ 59' \quad \text{or} \quad 121°\ 1'.$$

(We have found the two supplementary values for the angle C.)

(i) If $C = 58°\ 59'$, $A = 30°$, $B = 180° - 58°\ 59' - 30° = 91°\ 1'$.

Using the sine formula,

$$\frac{7}{\sin 30°} = \frac{b}{\sin 91°\ 1'}$$

and $$b = 14{\cdot}0.$$

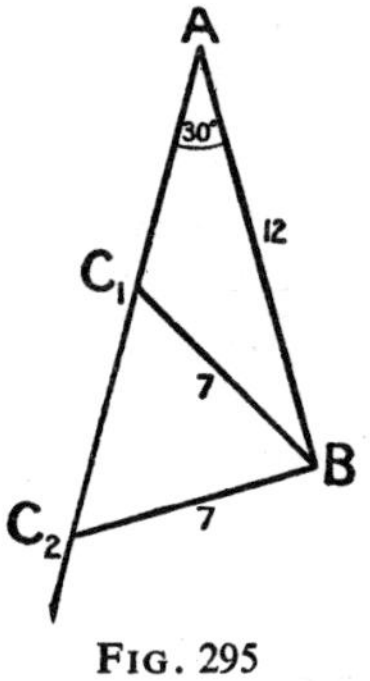

FIG. 295

(ii) If $C = 121°\ 1'$ and $A = 30°$, $B = 180° - 151°\ 1' = 28°\ 59'$.

Using the sine formula,

$$\frac{7}{\sin 30°} = \frac{b}{\sin 28°\ 59'}$$

and $$b = 6{\cdot}8.$$

EXERCISES 114A

Solve the following triangles:

1. $a = 8{\cdot}52$, $B = 28°$, $C = 64°$.
2. $b = 7{\cdot}24$, $B = 86°$, $C = 48°$.
3. $c = 8{\cdot}4$, $B = 112°$, $C = 42°$.

4. $a = 4{\cdot}21$, $B = 62°$, $C = 54°$.
5. $b = 28{\cdot}1$, $A = 81°$, $B = 42° \ 30'$.
6. $A = 42°$, $a = 4{\cdot}2$, $b = 7{\cdot}1$.
7. $A = 38°$, $a = 7{\cdot}1$, $b = 4{\cdot}2$.
8. $A = 80°$, $a = 12{\cdot}3$, $b = 12{\cdot}8$.
9. $A = 26°$, $a = 4{\cdot}3$, $b = 5{\cdot}2$.
10. $A = 51°$, $a = 2{\cdot}7$, $b = 3{\cdot}1$.

EXERCISES 114B

Solve the following triangles:

1. $a = 21{\cdot}7$, $B = 42°$, $C = 51°$.
2. $b = 8{\cdot}34$, $B = 79°$, $C = 24°$.
3. $c = 11{\cdot}1$, $B = 108°$, $C = 25°$.
4. $a = 14{\cdot}8$, $B = 62° \ 30'$, $C = 51°$.
5. $b = 28{\cdot}7$, $A = 80° \ 24'$, $B = 61° \ 27'$.
6. $A = 41° \ 30'$, $a = 4{\cdot}8$, $b = 6{\cdot}0$.
7. $A = 112°$, $a = 7{\cdot}1$, $b = 4{\cdot}2$.
8. $A = 80° \ 27'$, $a = 10{\cdot}8$, $b = 11{\cdot}9$.
9. $A = 22° \ 10'$, $a = 3{\cdot}7$, $b = 4{\cdot}4$.
10. $A = 49°$, $a = 22{\cdot}7$, $b = 31{\cdot}2$.

THE COSINE FORMULA

The cosine formula is used to solve a triangle given either (i) three sides, or (ii) two sides and the included angle.

It tells us that in any triangle ABC,

$$c^2 = a^2 + b^2 - 2ab \cos C.$$

Angle C acute *Angle C obtuse*

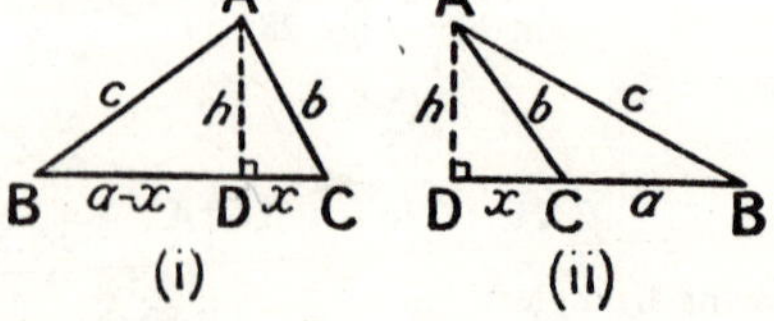

FIG. 296

Draw AD perpendicular to BC.

Draw AD perpendicular to BC produced.

In the triangle ADC,

$$h^2 = b^2 - x^2.$$

In the triangle ADB,

$$h^2 = c^2 - (a - x)^2.$$

$$\therefore b^2 - x^2 = c^2 - (a - x)^2$$

or $$b^2 = c^2 - a^2 + 2ax.$$

From the triangle ACD,

$$\frac{x}{b} = \cos C;$$

substituting,

$$c^2 = a^2 + b^2 - 2ab \cos C.$$

In the triangle ADC,

$$h^2 = b^2 - x^2.$$

In the triangle ADB,

$$h^2 = c^2 - (a + x)^2.$$

$$\therefore b^2 - x^2 = c^2 - (a + x)^2$$

or $$b^2 = c^2 - a^2 - 2ax.$$

From the triangle ACD,

$$\frac{x}{b} = \cos (180° - C) = - \cos C;$$

substituting,

$$c^2 = a^2 + b^2 - 2ab \cos C.$$

The formula $c^2 = a^2 + b^2 - 2ab \cos C$ is therefore true for every triangle ABC whether C is acute or obtuse; but remember that, if C is obtuse, the value of $\cos C$ is negative.

If $C = 90°$, $\cos C = 0$ and the formula becomes $c^2 = a^2 + b^2$ (Pythagoras).

If C is acute, $c^2 < a^2 + b^2$; if C is obtuse, $c^2 > a^2 + b^2$ and we have a simple method of finding whether an angle of a triangle is acute or obtuse.

The cosine formula may be put as $\cos C = \dfrac{a^2 + b^2 - c^2}{2ab}$, which is the form needed for solving a triangle given its sides.

The following results are, of course, also true.

$$b^2 = a^2 + c^2 - 2ac \cos B \quad \text{or} \quad \cos B = \frac{a^2 + c^2 - b^2}{2ac};$$

$$a^2 = b^2 + c^2 - 2bc \cos A \quad \text{or} \quad \cos A = \frac{b^2 + c^2 - a^2}{2bc}.$$

(N.B. Do not use the cosine formula to solve an isosceles triangle.)

Example 1. Given $b = 3$, $c = 4{\cdot}8$ and $A = 120°$, solve the triangle ABC.

$$a^2 = b^2 + c^2 - 2bc \cos A = 9 + 23{\cdot}04 - 28{\cdot}8 \cos 120°.$$

$$\cos 120° = - \cos 60° = -\tfrac{1}{2};$$

$$\therefore a^2 = 32{\cdot}04 + 14{\cdot}4 = 46{\cdot}44 \quad \text{and} \quad a = 6{\cdot}815.$$

Using $$\frac{a}{\sin A} = \frac{b}{\sin B},$$

$$\frac{6{\cdot}815}{\sin 120^\circ} = \frac{3}{\sin B}.$$

$$\therefore \sin B = \frac{3 \sin 120^\circ}{6{\cdot}815} = \frac{3 \sin 60^\circ}{6{\cdot}815}$$

0·4771
$\bar{1}$·9375
0·4146
0·8334
$\bar{1}$·5812

and $B = 22^\circ\ 25'$.

(N.B. The angle B cannot be obtuse because a triangle cannot have two obtuse angles.)

$$\therefore C = 180^\circ - 120^\circ - 22^\circ\ 25' = 37^\circ\ 35'.$$

(N.B. As a check, notice that since c is greater than b, C should be greater than B.)

Example 2. Given $a = 4{\cdot}12$, $b = 6{\cdot}82$, $C = 42^\circ\ 30'$, solve the triangle ABC.

$$c^2 = a^2 + b^2 - 2ab \cos C = (4{\cdot}12)^2 + (6{\cdot}82)^2 - 2(4{\cdot}12)(6{\cdot}82) \cos 42^\circ\ 30'$$

$$= 16{\cdot}97 + 46{\cdot}51 - 41{\cdot}43$$
$$= 22{\cdot}05.$$
$$\therefore c = 4{\cdot}695.$$

0·3010
0·6149
0·8338
$\bar{1}$·8676
1·6173

From the sine formula,

$$\frac{\sin A}{4{\cdot}12} = \frac{\sin 42^\circ\ 30'}{4{\cdot}695}.$$

(N.B. Calculate the angle opposite the smaller of the given sides. This cannot be obtuse.)

$$\therefore \sin A = \frac{4{\cdot}12 \sin 42^\circ\ 30'}{4{\cdot}695}$$

and $A = 36^\circ\ 21'$.

Finally $$B = 180^\circ - 42^\circ\ 30' - 36^\circ\ 21'$$
$$= 101^\circ\ 9'.$$

0·6149
$\bar{1}$·8297
0·4446
0·6717
$\bar{1}$·7729

Example 3. Given $a = 7{\cdot}12$, $b = 6{\cdot}43$, $c = 8{\cdot}27$, find the angles of the triangle ABC.

(N.B. Start by finding the smallest angle which cannot be obtuse; continue with the sine formula and find the smaller of the two remaining angles.)

$$\cos B = \frac{7{\cdot}12^2 + 8{\cdot}27^2 - 6{\cdot}43^2}{2(7{\cdot}12)(8{\cdot}27)}$$
$$= \frac{50{\cdot}69 + 68{\cdot}39 - 41{\cdot}34}{2(7{\cdot}12)(8{\cdot}27)}$$
$$= \frac{77{\cdot}74}{2(7{\cdot}12)(8{\cdot}27)}.$$
$$B = 48° \ 42'.$$

1·8906
0·3010
0·8525
0·9175
$\bar{1}$·8196

From $$\frac{\sin A}{a} = \frac{\sin B}{b},$$
$$\sin A = \frac{7{\cdot}12 \sin 48° \ 42'}{6{\cdot}43}.$$
$$A = 56° \ 18'.$$

0·8525
$\bar{1}$·8758
0·7283
0·8082
$\bar{1}$·9201

Finally $$C = 180° - 48° \ 42' - 56° \ 18'$$
$$= 75° \ 0'.$$

EXERCISES 115A

Solve the following triangles:

1. $a = 3{\cdot}7$, $b = 4{\cdot}2$, $C = 110°$.
2. $a = 8{\cdot}4$, $b = 2{\cdot}6$, $C = 24°$.
3. $b = 21{\cdot}2$, $c = 14{\cdot}3$, $A = 60° \ 22'$.
4. $c = 2{\cdot}81$, $a = 4{\cdot}32$, $B = 95° \ 28'$.
5. $c = 4{\cdot}73$, $a = 14{\cdot}2$, $B = 80°$.
6. $a = 2{\cdot}43$, $b = 7{\cdot}12$, $c = 6{\cdot}43$.
7. $a = 3{\cdot}12$, $b = 4{\cdot}82$, $c = 4{\cdot}82$.
8. $a = 7{\cdot}64$, $b = 6{\cdot}82$, $c = 12{\cdot}3$.
9. $a = 4{\cdot}13$, $b = 18{\cdot}1$, $c = 17{\cdot}6$.
10. $a = 5{\cdot}42$, $b = 11{\cdot}2$, $c = 10{\cdot}9$.

EXERCISES 115B

Solve the following triangles:

1. $a = 4{\cdot}2$, $b = 4{\cdot}8$, $C = 130°$.
2. $a = 11{\cdot}2$, $b = 13{\cdot}4$, $C = 32°$.
3. $b = 20{\cdot}8$, $c = 12{\cdot}6$, $A = 48° \ 15'$.
4. $c = 3{\cdot}21$, $a = 5{\cdot}26$, $B = 96° \ 43'$.
5. $c = 5{\cdot}62$, $a = 15{\cdot}3$, $B = 70°$.

6. $a = 3{\cdot}71$, $b = 8{\cdot}42$, $c = 7{\cdot}15$.

7. $a = 4{\cdot}62$, $b = 7{\cdot}31$, $c = 7{\cdot}31$.

8. $a = 11{\cdot}2$, $b = 12{\cdot}4$, $c = 21{\cdot}6$.

9. $a = 18{\cdot}4$, $b = 22{\cdot}2$, $c = 12{\cdot}7$.

10. $a = 26{\cdot}7$, $b = 33{\cdot}3$, $c = 19{\cdot}4$.

An example illustrating the solution of a problem by means of the sine and cosine formulae is now given.

Example. The angles of elevation of the top Y of a vertical mast from two points A, B on the same level as its foot X are 32° 14′ and 22° 28′ respectively. If the height of the mast is 52 m and the bearings of A and B from X are 270° and 220° respectively, find the distance AB and the bearing of B from A.

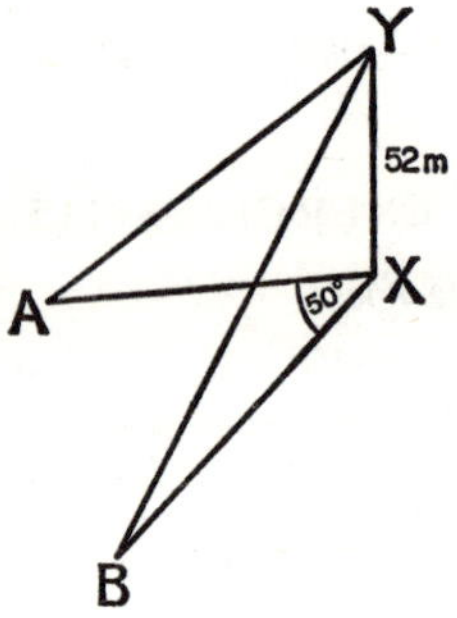

FIG. 297

From the triangle AXY,

$$\frac{AX}{52} = \cot 32° \, 14'.$$

$$\therefore \; AX = 82{\cdot}47.$$

From the triangle BXY,

$$\frac{BX}{52} = \cot 22° \, 28'.$$

$$\therefore \; BX = 125{\cdot}7.$$

But

$$\begin{aligned} AB^2 &= AX^2 + XB^2 - 2AX.XB \cos A\widehat{X}B \\ &= (82{\cdot}47)^2 + (125{\cdot}7)^2 - 2(82{\cdot}47)(125{\cdot}7) \cos 50° \\ &= 6802 + 15{,}800 - 13{,}330 \\ &= 9272. \end{aligned}$$

$$\therefore \; AB = 96{\cdot}29 \quad \text{or} \quad 96{\cdot}3 \text{ m}.$$

0·3010
1·9163
2·0995
$\bar{1}$·8081
4·1249

From

$$\frac{\sin X\hat{B}A}{AX} = \frac{\sin 50°}{96{\cdot}29},$$

$$\sin X\hat{B}A = \frac{82{\cdot}47 \sin 50°}{96{\cdot}29}.$$

$$\therefore\ X\hat{B}A = 41°\ 1'.$$

$$X\hat{A}B = 180° - 50° - 41°\ 1'$$
$$= 88°\ 59'.$$

1·9163
$\bar{1}$·8843
1·8006
1·9836
$\bar{1}$·8170

The bearing of B from A is $90° + 88°\ 59' = 178°\ 59'$.

The area of a triangle

The area of a triangle is equal to half the product of base and altitude.

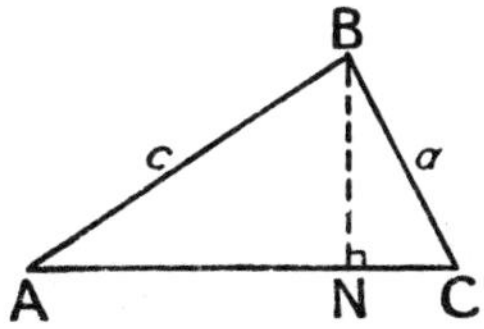

FIG. 298

In Fig. 298, the area,

$$\Delta = \tfrac{1}{2}BN.AC.$$

From the triangle ABN,

$$\frac{BN}{c} = \sin A.$$

$$\therefore\ BN = c \sin A \quad \text{and} \quad \Delta = \tfrac{1}{2}bc \sin A.$$

By symmetry, $\tfrac{1}{2}ac \sin B$ and $\tfrac{1}{2}ab \sin C$ are also equal to Δ.

To find the area of a triangle, therefore, multiply half the product of any two sides by the sine of the included angle. Another formula, not proved here, for the area of a triangle is $\sqrt{s(s-a)(s-b)(s-c)}$, where s is the semi-perimeter and equals $\tfrac{1}{2}(a+b+c)$.

Example. The sides of a triangle are 8·1 m, 6·3 m and 4·8 m. Find its area, and the smallest angle.

$$s = \tfrac{1}{2}(8{\cdot}1 + 6{\cdot}3 + 4{\cdot}8) = 9{\cdot}6.$$

$$\therefore\ \Delta = \sqrt{(9{\cdot}6)(1{\cdot}5)(3{\cdot}3)(4{\cdot}8)}$$
$$= 15{\cdot}10 \text{ m}^2 = 15{\cdot}1 \text{ m}^2 \text{ (to 3 sig. fig.)}.$$

The smallest angle, x, is opposite the smallest side.

$\therefore\ \tfrac{1}{2}(6{\cdot}3)(8{\cdot}1) \sin x = 15{\cdot}1.$

From which $x = 36°\ 18'$.

0·9823
0·1761
0·5185
0·6812
2) 2·3581
1·1791

EXERCISES 116A

Find the areas of the following triangles:

1. $a = 2{\cdot}4$, $b = 3{\cdot}2$, $C = 60°$.

2. $a = 4{\cdot}6$, $b = 7{\cdot}8$, $C = 82°$.

3. $a = 6{\cdot}2$, $c = 4{\cdot}8$, $B = 71°$.

4. $a = 4{\cdot}2$, $c = 7{\cdot}1$, $B = 110°$.

5. $a = 2{\cdot}4$, $b = 3{\cdot}2$, $c = 4{\cdot}1$.

6. $a = 7{\cdot}8$, $b = 9{\cdot}2$, $c = 11{\cdot}3$.

7. $a = 8{\cdot}23$, $b = 9{\cdot}16$, $c = 10{\cdot}24$.

8. $a = 7{\cdot}12$, $b = 11{\cdot}23$, $c = 16{\cdot}41$.

EXERCISES 116B

Find the areas of the following triangles:

1. $a = 2{\cdot}8$, $b = 7{\cdot}1$, $C = 30°$.

2. $a = 4{\cdot}7$, $b = 8{\cdot}2$, $C = 74°$.

3. $a = 6{\cdot}18$, $b = 8{\cdot}2$, $C = 64°$.

4. $a = 8{\cdot}16$, $c = 7{\cdot}24$, $B = 120°$.

5. $a = 2{\cdot}8$, $b = 3{\cdot}1$, $c = 4{\cdot}7$.

6. $a = 7{\cdot}4$, $b = 12{\cdot}2$, $c = 16{\cdot}4$.

7. $a = 8{\cdot}12$, $b = 11{\cdot}4$, $c = 12{\cdot}3$.

8. $a = 7{\cdot}0$, $b = 8{\cdot}0$, $c = 9{\cdot}0$.

EXERCISES 117: MISCELLANEOUS

1. Y is due north of X. The bearings of Z from X and Y are 26° 30′ and 42° 40′ respectively. Given that XYZ are all at the same level and that $XY = 1$ km, find the distance YZ.

2. A ship steams 4 km due north from a point and then 3 km on a bearing of 040°. How far is the ship from the point?

3. The angles of elevation of the top of a tower from two points A, B in line with its foot and on the same level are 27° and 32° respectively. If the distance AB is 21 m, find the height of the tower.

4. The distance between two houses as the crow flies is 500 m. To walk from one to the other it is necessary to go 350 m due north and then 300 m on another road. What is the bearing of the second road?

5. First slip is standing 10 m from the batsman's wicket at an angle of 160° with the pitch. How far is he from the bowler's wicket?

6. The distance from a tee T to the hole H on a golf course is 400 m. A golfer drives 230 m but his shot is 10° off the direct line. How far is his ball from the hole?

7. In the triangle ABC, $b = 3$, $c = 5$ and $A = 120°$. Find a.

8. In the triangle ABC, $b = 3{\cdot}1$, $c = 1{\cdot}4$ and $A = 46°$. Find B.

9. A and B are two observation stations, B being 10 km due west of A. At 09.00h a ship is observed to be due north of A and at a bearing of 064° from B. At 10.00h it is observed to be at a bearing 032° from A and 071° from B. Find the course and speed of the ship.

10. In the triangle ABC, $a = 14{\cdot}6$, $B = 52°\ 10'$ and $C = 77°$. Calculate the perimeter of the triangle.

11. Find the least angle of a triangle whose sides are 6·2 m, 7·3 m and 8·4 m. Find also its area.

12. In the triangle ABC, $A = 50°$, $b = 6$ m and $c = 8$ m. Calculate the angles B and C and the area of the triangle.

13. A road runs east and west. X and Y are two points of the road 150 m apart. The bearings of a point Z from X and Y are 215° and 202° respectively. Calculate the distance YZ.

14. The sides of the triangle ABC are given in metres by $a = 4{\cdot}8$, $b = 7{\cdot}2$ and $c = 9{\cdot}3$. Calculate the angle B and the area of the triangle.

15. A boat travelling in a direction 222° reaches a point P from which two buoys X and Y are seen both due south of P. Y is known to be 200 m due south of X. The boat continues on the same course and reaches a point Q from which the bearing of X is 140° and that of Y is 165°. Calculate the distance PX.

16. Calculate the angle between the diagonals of a parallelogram whose sides are 5·1 and 2·5 cm and contain an angle of 70°.

17. The hands of a clock are 4 cm and 5 cm long. Find the distance between the ends of the hands at 16.00h.

18. Two circles of radii 5 cm and 6 cm have their centres 8 cm apart. Calculate the acute angle between the tangents at one of the two points of intersection of the circles.

19. The sides of a rhombus are each 4·2 cm. One angle of the rhombus is 58°. Calculate the lengths of the diagonals.

20. $ABCD$ is a trapezium with AB, DC parallel. $AB = 2$ cm, $BC = 3$ cm, $CD = 6$ cm and the angle BCD is 120°. Calculate the length of AD.

21. An observer M is 30 m from the base X of a tower XY and on the same level as X. The tower has a vertical mast YZ. If the angles of elevation of Y and Z from X are 40° and 50° respectively, find the height of the mast.

22. The angles of elevation of a balloon from two points A, B which are 0·3 km apart, are 62° and 48° respectively. If the balloon is vertically above the line AB, find its height.

23. A boat steaming due north is 2 km away in a direction 070°. 5 minutes later the bearing of the boat is 040°. Find the speed of the boat.

24. In the triangle ABC, $a = 6$ cm, $b = 7$ cm and $c = 8$ cm. Find the length of the line joining A to the point on BC distant 3 cm from B.

25. In Fig. 299, CT is the tangent at C to the circle and $AB =$ 4 cm. Calculate the length of CT.

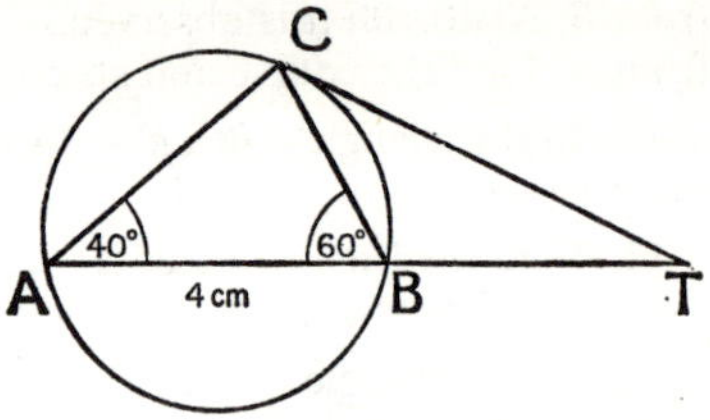

FIG. 299

26. The sines of the angles of a triangle are in the ratios 2 : 3 : 4. Find the ratios of the cosines.

27. A yacht sails 2 km due north and then 3 km on a bearing of 030°. How far is it from the starting point.

28. Observations are taken from two points P and Q which are on the same horizontal ground as the foot F of a vertical flagstaff. If the angle $PFQ = 48°$ and the angles of elevation of the top of the flagstaff from P and Q are 32° and 40° respectively, find PQ given that the flagstaff is 24 m high.

29. The area of an acute-angled triangle is 1·6 cm². If two of the sides are 3·2 and 1·8 cm long respectively, find the angle included between these sides.

30. From a point P the bearings of two landmarks L and M are 308° and 222° respectively. L is 500 m from M on a bearing of 008°. Calculate the distance PL.

31. A vertical tower AB is 40 m high. X and Y are two points on the same level as the foot A of the tower, X being west and Y north-west of the tower. The angles of elevation of the top of the tower from X and Y are 25° and 32° respectively. Find the distance XY.

32. A rhombus has sides of length 6 cm and the length of one of the diagonals is 7 cm. Find the angles of the rhombus.

32

THE CIRCLE AND SPHERE

Length of circular arc

EQUAL arcs of a circle subtend equal angles at its centre. Therefore the length of an arc of a circle is proportional to the angle it subtends at the centre. For example, if one arc of a circle is double another, the angle which the first arc subtends at the centre of the circle is double the angle subtended by the second arc.

The circumference of a circle is $2\pi r$ and the angle the whole

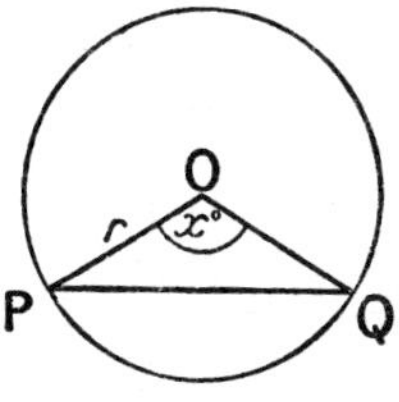

FIG. 300

circumference subtends at the centre is 360°. Therefore, if an arc PQ of a circle of radius r subtends an angle $x°$ at the centre of the circle,

$$\frac{\text{arc } PQ}{2\pi r} = \frac{x}{360},$$

and the length of the arc PQ is $\dfrac{2\pi rx}{360}$ or $\dfrac{\pi rx}{180}$.

Area of circular sector

Similarly the area of the circular sector POQ is proportional to the angle x. The area of the whole circle is πr^2.

$$\therefore \frac{\text{Area of sector } POQ}{\pi r^2} = \frac{x}{360},$$

and the area of the sector is $\dfrac{\pi r^2 x}{360}$.

Area of segment

The chord PQ divides the area of the circle into two parts, called the major segment and the minor segment. The area of the minor segment is equal to (the area of the sector POQ) − (the area of the triangle POQ).

The area of the triangle POQ is $\frac{1}{2}r^2 \sin x$.

$$\therefore \text{the area of the minor segment } POQ = \frac{\pi r^2 x}{360} - \frac{1}{2}r^2 \sin x$$

$$= \frac{1}{2}r^2\left(\frac{\pi x}{180} - \sin x\right).$$

Radian measure

The formulae for length of arc and area of sector may also be expressed in terms of radian measure.

A **radian** is the angle subtended at the centre of a circle by an arc equal in length to its radius. Since the angle at the centre is proportional to the arc on which it stands, an arc of length πr will subtend an angle of π radians (written π^c) at the centre. But this is the angle subtended at the centre by a semi-circle and therefore

$$\pi^c = 180° \quad \text{and} \quad 1^c = 57{\cdot}3° \text{ approximately.}$$

A table is provided in most books of tables to help in converting degrees to radians and vice-versa.

If the angle subtended at the centre of a circle of radius r by an arc is x radians, the length of the arc is rx.

$$\text{In this case, the area of the sector} = \frac{x}{2\pi}\text{(area of circle)}$$

$$= \frac{x}{2\pi}(\pi r^2)$$

$$= \frac{1}{2}xr^2.$$

Example. A chord PQ of a circle of radius 5 cm subtends an angle of 70° at the centre. Find (i) the length of the chord PQ; (ii) the length of the arc PQ; (iii) the area of the sector POQ; (iv) the area of the minor segment cut off by PQ.

Let O be the centre of the circle and ON the perpendicular from O to PQ. Then N is the mid point of the chord PQ and NO bisects the angle POQ.

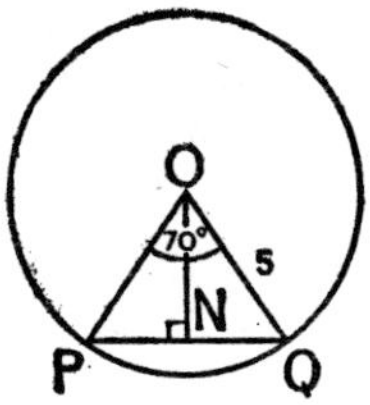

FIG. 301

(i) From the triangle PON,

$$\frac{PN}{5} = \sin 35° = 0{\cdot}5736.$$

$$\therefore PN = 2{\cdot}868$$

and the length of the chord PQ is 5·74 cm.

(ii) $$\frac{\text{The arc } PQ}{2\pi(5)} = \frac{70}{360}.$$

$$\therefore \text{ the length of the arc } PQ = \frac{70\pi}{36} = 6{\cdot}11 \text{ cm.}$$

(iii) $$\frac{\text{The area of the sector } POQ}{\pi(5)^2} = \frac{70}{360}.$$

$$\therefore \text{ the area of the sector} = \frac{7 \times 25\pi}{36}$$

$$= 15{\cdot}28 \text{ or } 15{\cdot}3 \text{ cm}$$

(to 3 sig. fig.).

(iv) $$\text{The area of the triangle } POQ = \tfrac{1}{2}(5)^2 \sin 70°$$
$$= 11{\cdot}74 \text{ or } 11{\cdot}7 \text{ cm}^2$$

$$\therefore \text{ the area of the minor segment} = 15{\cdot}28 - 11{\cdot}74$$
$$= 3{\cdot}54 \text{ cm}^2 \text{ (to 3 sig. fig.).}$$

EXERCISES 118A

1. A chord PQ of a circle of radius 4 cm subtends an angle of 50° at the centre. Find the length of the arc PQ.

2. A chord XY of a circle of radius 6·2 cm subtends an angle of 38° at the centre of the circle. Find the difference in length between the chord and the minor arc XY.

3. A chord PQ of a circle of radius 5·5 cm subtends an angle of 42° at the centre O. Find the area of the sector POQ.

4. A chord AB of a circle of radius 10·4 cm subtends an angle of 35° at the circumference. Find the area of the minor segment cut off by the chord.

5. A chord of a circle of radius 12 cm is distant 5 cm from the centre. Find the length of the major arc cut off by the chord.

6. A chord of a circle of radius 7 cm is 4·8 cm long. Find the length of the minor arc on which it stands.

7. A chord *AB* of a circle, centre *O* and radius 5·6 cm, is 3·0 cm long. Find the ratio of the areas of the major and minor sectors *AOB*.

8. Find the angles subtended at the circumference of a circle of radius 8 cm by a chord 6 cm long.

9. Convert 117° 10′ to radians.

10. The angle subtended at the centre of a circle of radius 5 cm is 2 radians. Find the area of the sector.

EXERCISES 118B

1. A chord *PQ* of a circle of radius 5 cm subtends an angle of 40° at the centre. Find the length of the minor arc *PQ*.

2. A chord *XY* of a circle of radius 6·8 cm subtends an angle of 42° at the centre of the circle. Find the difference in length between the chord *XY* and the minor arc *XY*.

3. A chord *PQ* of a circle of radius 6·2 cm subtends an angle of 52° at the centre *O*. Find the area of the minor sector *POQ*.

4. A chord *AB* of a circle of radius 8·2 cm subtends an angle of 50° at the circumference. Find the area of the minor segment cut off by *AB*.

5. A chord of a circle of radius 18 cm is distant 6 cm from the centre. Find the length of the minor arc cut off by the chord.

6. A chord of a circle of radius 8 cm is 4·2 cm long. Find the length of the minor arc on which it stands.

7. A chord *AB* of a circle, centre *O* and radius 10 cm, is 4 cm long. Find the ratio of the areas of the major and minor sectors *AOB*.

8. Find the angles subtended at the circumference of a circle of radius 4·8 cm by a chord 3·0 cm long.

9. Express 1·42 radians in degrees and minutes.

10. The area of a sector of a circle of radius 4 cm is 20 cm^2. Find the angle of the sector in radians.

Latitude and longitude

In Fig. 302, *N* and *S* represent the North and South poles of the Earth. The line *SN* is called the axis of the Earth and *O* is the centre of the Earth.

The Equator is the line in which the Earth's surface is cut by a plane through the centre perpendicular to *NS*.

A Great Circle is a section of the Earth's surface by any plane through *O*. Its radius is equal to the radius of the Earth. The shortest distance along the Earth's surface between any two places is the minor arc of the Great Circle passing through them.

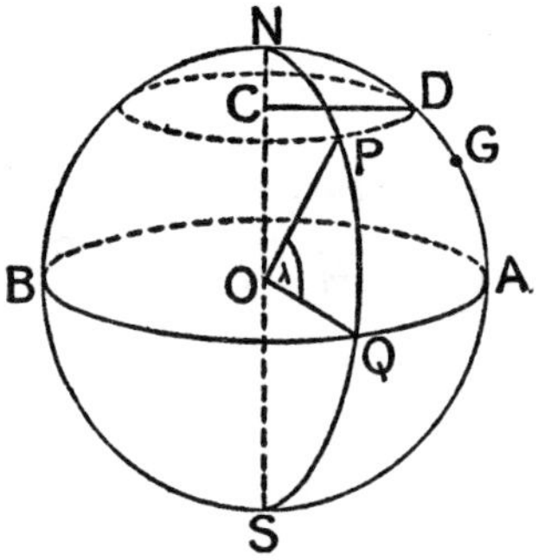

FIG. 302

A Small Circle is any other circle lying on the Earth's surface.

A Meridian of Longitude is a great circle which passes through N. and S.

The Prime Meridian is that meridian which passes through Greenwich.

A Parallel of Latitude is a section of the Earth's surface by a plane parallel to the equator.

Suppose that any meridian of longitude *NPQS* cuts the equator at *Q* and a parallel of latitude at *P*. The angle which *PO* makes with the plane of the equator is called the latitude of *P*. In the figure, it is shown as the angle *POQ* ($\lambda°$).

All places on the same parallel of latitude have the same latitude. The latitude of a place can vary from 90° N. (North Pole) to 90° S. (South Pole).

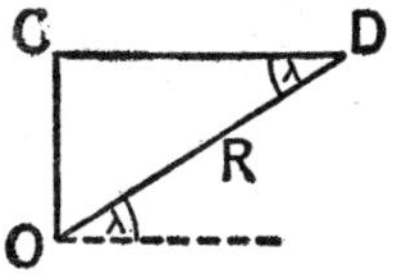

FIG. 303

If *NAS* is the prime meridian, the angle between the planes *NPQS* and *NAS* is equal to the longitude of *P*. It is represented by the angle *PCD* or by the angle *QOA*. All places on the same meridian of longitude have the same longitude. The longitude of a place can vary from 180° E. to 180° W.

Considering the triangle *COD* and calling the radius of the Earth *R*, the radius of the parallel of latitude λ is *CD*.

Since $\dfrac{CD}{R} = \cos\lambda$, the radius of the parallel of latitude λ is $R\cos\lambda$.
If $\theta°$ is the longitude of P, then $PCD = \theta°$. The length of the arc PD is $\dfrac{\theta}{360} \times 2\pi R\cos\lambda$.

The nautical mile

The nautical mile is the length of arc of the meridian which subtends an angle of 1 minute at the centre of the Earth. Taking the radius of the Earth to be 6370 km,

$$1 \text{ nautical mile} = \frac{1}{60 \times 360} \times 2\pi \times 6370$$
$$= 1{\cdot}85 \text{ km}.$$

A knot is a speed of 1 nautical mile per hour.

Local time

Local time at any place P depends on the longitude of P. Two places diametrically opposite on the equator differ in time by 12 hours and in longitude by 180°. The difference in time for 1° longitude is therefore $\dfrac{12 \times 60}{180}$ or 4 minutes.

Example. Two places P, Q both on the parallel of latitude 26° N. differ in longitude by 40°. Find (i) the distance between them along their parallel of latitude; (ii) the shortest distance between them along the Earth's surface.

The radius of the parallel of latitude = 6370 cos 26° km.

(i) The distance between the places along the parallel of latitude

$= \frac{40}{360}$ of the circumference of this circle

$= \frac{40}{360} \times 2\pi \times 6370\cos 26°$

$= 3997$ km $= 4000$ km (to 3 sig. fig.).

(ii) The chord PQ subtends an angle of 40° at the centre of a circle of radius 6370 cos 26°.

$$\therefore \quad \frac{\frac{1}{2}PQ}{6370\cos 26°} = \sin\frac{40°}{2} = \sin 20°$$

and $$\tfrac{1}{2}PQ = 6370\cos 26°\sin 20°.$$

Suppose that PQ subtends an angle of $2x°$ at the centre of the Earth.

$$\text{Then} \qquad \sin x = \frac{\tfrac{1}{2}PQ}{6370} = \cos 26° \sin 20°$$

$$\log \sin x = \bar{1}{\cdot}9537 + \bar{1}{\cdot}5341 = \bar{1}{\cdot}4878$$

$$\text{and } x = 17° \, 54'.$$

The angle subtended by PQ at the centre of the Earth is $2x$ or 35° 48′. The minor arc of this great circle is the shortest distance between P and Q along the Earth's surface.

$$\text{This distance} = \frac{35° \, 48'}{360°} \times 2\pi \times 6370 = \frac{35{\cdot}8 \times 2\pi \times 6370}{360}$$

$$= 3980 \text{ km (to 3 sig. fig.)}.$$

EXERCISES 119A

(Take the radius of the Earth to be 6370 km.)

1. Two places on the Equator differ in longitude by 24°. What is the distance between them?

2. Find the radius of the circle of latitude 60° N.

3. Find the distance along the parallel of latitude between two places on the parallel of latitude 50° N. which differ in longitude by 36°.

4. The Earth rotates on its own axis once in 24 hours. What is the speed of a place whose latitude is 30° N?

5. Find the difference in local time between Paris (48° 50′ N., 2° 20′ E.) and Greenwich.

6. A ship sails 100 km due east. If her longitude changes by 4°, find her latitude.

7. What is the distance over the North Pole of two places both in latitude 60° N., if their longitudes differ by 180°?

8. Two places on the same meridian have latitudes 30° N. and 20° S. Find the distance between them along their meridian.

9. Compare the distances travelled in an hour by two places of latitudes 30° N. and 60° N. respectively.

10. Two places P and Q both in latitude 40° N. differ in longitude by 30°. Find the distance between them measured along the parallel of latitude.

EXERCISES 119B

(Take the radius of the Earth to be 6370 km.)

1. Two places on the Equator differ in longitude by 32°. Find the distance between them.

2. Find the radius of the circle of latitude 30° S.

3. Find the distance along the parallel of latitude between two places on the parallel of latitude 40° N. which differ in longitude by 24°.

4. Find the distance moved in 30 minutes by a place whose latitude is 40° S.

5. Find the difference in local time between two places both in latitude 35° S. if their longitudes differ by 26°.

6. A ship sails 100 km due north. Find the change in her latitude.

7. Find the distance over the South Pole between two places both in latitude 70° S. if their longitudes differ by 180°.

8. Two places on the same meridian have latitudes 40° N. and 50° S. What is their distance apart along their meridian?

9. Compare the distances travelled in an hour by two places of latitudes 30° N. and 20° S. respectively.

10. Two places P and Q both in latitude 60° N. differ in longitude by 28° 20′. Find the distance between them measured along their parallel of latitude.

EXERCISES 120: MISCELLANEOUS

1. The minute hand of a clock is $2\frac{1}{2}$ cm long. Find the distance moved by the tip in 35 minutes.

2. An arc of a circle of radius 5 cm is 4 cm long. Find the length of the chord joining its ends.

3. A piece of wire in the form of an arc of a circle of radius 10 cm and subtending an angle of 50° at the centre is bent into the form of a complete circle. Find its radius.

4. An equilateral triangle is inscribed in a circle of radius 5 cm. Find the area of the minor segment cut off by one of the sides.

5. A piece of wire in the form of a square of side 4 cm is bent into an arc of a circle of radius 10 cm. Find the distance between the ends of the wire.

6. A regular hexagon is inscribed in a circle of radius 5 cm. Find the area of the hexagon.

7. A regular octagon (8-sided figure) is inscribed in a circle of radius 10 cm. Find the area of the octagon.

8. A continuous belt (Fig. 304) passes round two circles of radii 3 m and 5 m whose centres are 10 m apart. Find the length of the belt.

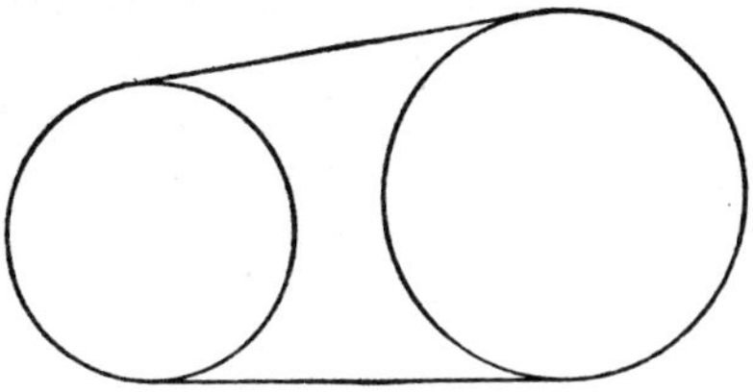

FIG. 304

9. A sector of a circle of angle 40° is bent into the form of a cone. Find the semi-vertical angle of the cone.

10. A cone of semi-vertical angle 30° is bent into the form of a sector of a circle. Find the angle of the sector.

11. If P and Q are two points on the parallel of latitude 60° S. such that the difference in their longitudes is 90°, find the angle subtended by PQ at the centre of the Earth.

12. A sphere centre C is of radius R. Two points P, Q on its surface are such that the angle PCQ is $2\theta°$. Find the length of the chord PQ.

13. Find the distance measured along the surface of the Earth of the North Pole from any place in latitude 60° N.

14. A ship sails 100 km due east and finds that her longitude has altered by 2°. Find her latitude.

15. Find the distance measured along their parallel of latitude between Greenwich (latitude 51° N.) and a place of latitude 51° N. and longitude 90° E.

16. A chord XY of a circle of radius 10 cm subtends an angle of 80° at the centre O. Find (i) the length of the chord XY; (ii) the area of the sector XOY.

17. Two places P and Q both in latitude 40° N. differ in longitude by 15°. Find (i) the distance between P and Q measured along their parallel of latitude; (ii) the length of the straight line joining P to Q.

18. The ropes of a swing are 3·6 m long and the seat when stationary is 60 cm above the ground. If at the highest points of its arc, the seat is 1·8 m above the ground, find the length of arc of the swing.

19. An arc of a circle of radius 5 cm is 4 cm long. What angle does the arc subtend at the centre of the circle?

20. Find the distance travelled in 1 hour due to the rotation of the Earth by a place whose latitude is 48° N.

21. A regular hexagon circumscribes a circle of radius 8 cm. Find the area of the hexagon.

22. What is the area of the minor segment of a circle of radius 4 cm cut off by a chord of length 5 cm?

23. A regular polygon of 8 sides is inscribed in a circle of radius 10 cm. Find the difference in area between the polygon and the circle.

24. A sector of a circle of angle 60° is bent into the form of a cone of vertical angle $\theta°$. Find θ.

25. Find the distance measured along a meridian between the parallel of latitude 30° N. and the equator.

26. Three observation stations X, Y, Z have latitudes and longitudes as shown in the table:

	Latitude	*Longitude*
X	42° 10′ N.	1° W.
Y	42° 10′ N.	1° 30′ W.
Z	42° N.	1° 30′ W.

Find (i) the distance between X, Y measured along their parallel of latitude; (ii) the distance between Y and Z measured along the meridian.

27. Two places both in latitude 35° N. differ in longitude by 60°. Calculate the distance between the two places measured along the parallel of latitude.

28. A ship is in latitude 52° N., longitude 24° W. Find how far the ship is from the North Pole measured along the meridian.

29. A regular octagon is circumscribed about a circle of radius 8 cm. Find the area of the octagon.

30. What is the shortest distance over the Earth's surface between P (32° N.; 8° W.) and Q (40° N.; 172° E.)?

33

COURSE AND TRACK; TRIANGLE OF VELOCITIES

Course

THE direction in which an aircraft is heading is called its course. The course is almost invariably given in the three digit notation (e.g. 075° or 282°).

Track

The direction of the path of an aircraft over the ground is called the track.

The track will be the same as the course only when the wind is blowing directly behind or directly against the aircraft (tail wind or head wind) or when there is no wind at all. Otherwise the wind will blow the aircraft off its course and on to the track.

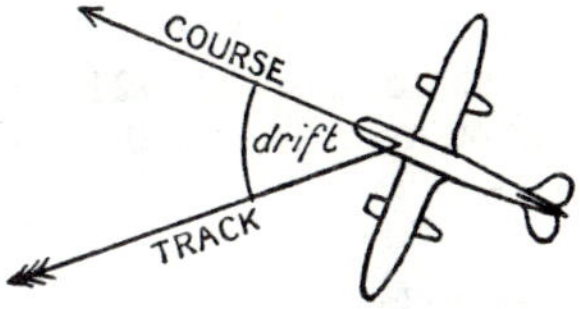

FIG. 305

Drift

The angle from the course to the track is called the drift.

Wind

The direction *from which the wind blows* is called the direction of the wind.

The course will always be indicated by one arrow, the wind by two arrows and the track by three arrows.

(N.B. In any triangle of velocities, the number of arrows clockwise should equal the number of arrows counterclockwise. The number of arrows in each case should be three.)

Air-speed

The air-speed is the speed of the aircraft in still air.

Ground speed

The ground speed is the speed of the aircraft over the ground.

Triangle of velocities

ABC shows a typical triangle of velocities. *AB* represents in magnitude and direction the course and air-speed; *BC* represents in

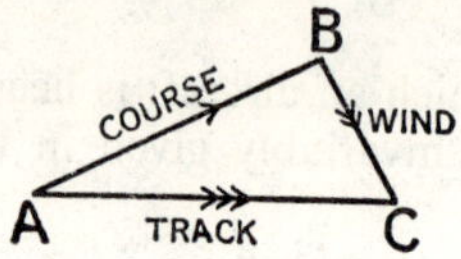

FIG. 306

magnitude and direction the wind velocity; *AC* represents in magnitude and direction the track and ground speed.

To find the track and ground speed

Given the course and air-speed and the wind velocity and direction the track and ground speed may be found either by drawing or by calculation as in the following example.

Example. An aircraft whose air-speed is 220 knots flies on a course of 070°. The wind blows at 40 knots from 320°. Find the track and ground speed.

By drawing

Take 1 cm to represent 40 knots.

Draw *AB* to represent the course and air-speed (070°, $5\frac{1}{2}$ cm).

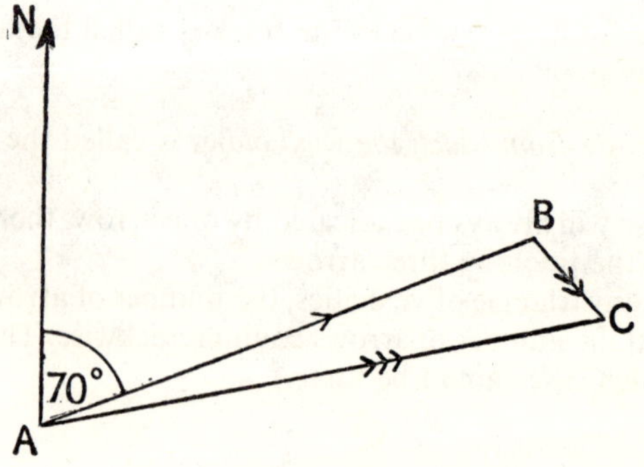

FIG. 307

From B draw BC to represent the wind. Then AC represents the track and ground speed.

By measurement, the track is 079° and the ground speed is 236 knots ($AC = 5{\cdot}9$ cm).

By calculation

First draw a rough sketch of the triangle of velocities.

The angle $ABC = 70° + 40° = 110°$.

Find AC by the cos formula.

$$\begin{aligned} AC^2 &= (220)^2 + (40)^2 - 2(220)40 \cos 110° \\ &= 48{,}400 + 1600 + 2(220)40 \cos 70° \\ &= 48{,}400 + 1600 + 6020 \\ &= 56{,}020. \\ \therefore\ AC &= 236{\cdot}6. \end{aligned}$$

The ground speed is 236·6 knots.

By the sine formula,

$$\frac{\sin B\hat{A}C}{40} = \frac{\sin 110°}{236{\cdot}6}.$$

$$\therefore\ B\hat{A}C = 9°\ 9'.$$

The track is 079° to the nearest degree.

EXERCISES 121A

Find the track and ground speed in each of the following:

1. Course 090°, air-speed 280 knots; wind 004°, 40 knots.

2. Course 175°, air speed 250 knots; wind 080°, 50 knots.

3. Course 282°, air-speed 320 knots; wind 080°, 50 knots.

4. Course 320°, air-speed 320 knots; wind 100°, 40 knots.

5. Course 240°, air-speed 270 knots; wind 340°, 50 knots.

EXERCISES 121B

Find the track and ground speed in each of the following:

1. Course 070°, air-speed 280 knots; wind 310°, 60 knots.

2. Course 180°, air-speed 300 knots; wind 080°, 40 knots.

3. Course 260°, air-speed 350 knots; wind 010°, 50 knots.

4. Course 310°, air-speed 300 knots; wind 024°, 40 knots.

5. Course 124°, air-speed 290 knots; wind 060°, 50 knots.

To find the speed and direction of the wind

Given the course and air-speed and the track and ground speed, the speed and direction of the wind may be found either by drawing or by calculation as in the following example.

Example. The course and air-speed of an aircraft are 070° and 220 knots; its track and ground speed are 082° and 240 knots. Find the speed and direction of the wind.

By drawing

Scale: let 1 cm represent 40 knots.

Draw AB $5\frac{1}{2}$ cm in length to represent the air-speed.

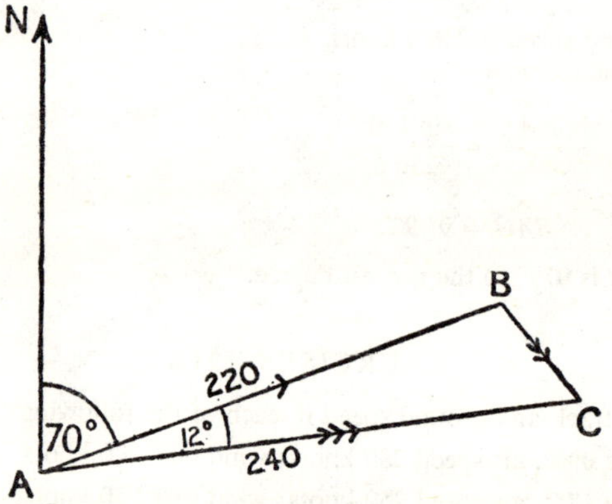

FIG. 308

Draw AC 6 cm in length to represent the ground speed. Then BC represents the wind in magnitude and direction.

By measurement, the wind velocity is 52 knots (1·3 cm) from 324°.

By calculation

First draw a rough sketch of the triangle of velocities.

By the cos formula,

$$\begin{aligned} BC^2 &= (220)^2 + (240)^2 - 2(220)(240)\cos 12^\circ \\ &= 48\,400 + 57\,600 - 103\,300 \\ &= 2700. \\ \therefore\ BC &= 51{\cdot}96. \end{aligned}$$

By the sine formula,

$$\frac{\sin B}{240} = \frac{\sin 12°}{51 \cdot 96}.$$

$$\therefore B = 73° 50' \quad \text{or} \quad 106° 10'.$$

Since $B > C$, $B = 106° 10'$.

The direction from which the wind blows is

$$360° + 70° - 106° 10' = 324° \text{ to the nearest degree.}$$

The wind blows at 52 knots from 324°.

EXERCISES 122A

Find the wind velocity in each of the following:

1. Course 165°, air-speed 280 knots; track 165°, ground speed 260 knots.
2. Course 050°, air-speed 220 knots; track 047°, ground speed 225 knots.
3. Course 170°, air-speed 320 knots; track 180°, ground speed 300 knots.
4. Course 320°, air-speed 300 knots; track 325°, ground speed 280 knots.
5. Course 220°, air-speed 280 knots; track 215°, ground speed 270 knots.

EXERCISES 122B

Find the wind velocity in each of the following:

1. Course 320°, air-speed 300 knots; track 320°, ground speed 330 knots.
2. Course 040°, air-speed 225 knots; track 046°, ground speed 240 knots.
3. Course 165°, air-speed 320 knots; track 168°, ground speed 350 knots.
4. Course 270°, air-speed 290 km/h; track 275°, ground speed 320 km/h.
5. Course 350°, air-speed 250 knots; track 345°, ground speed 260 knots.

To find the course and ground speed

The navigator usually knows his air-speed, the track required and the speed and direction of the wind. From this information he can deduce the course required and his ground speed either by drawing or by calculation as in the following example.

Example. Given that the track required is 040°, the air-speed is 220 km/h and that the wind is blowing from 140° at 40 km/h, find the necessary course and the ground speed.

By drawing

Let 1 cm represent 40 km/h.

Draw BC equal in length to 1 cm to represent the wind.

Draw a line through C to represent the direction of the track.

With centre B and radius $5\frac{1}{2}$ cm, swing an arc to cut the track at A. Then the direction of AB gives the course and AC represents the ground speed.

By measurement, the course is 050° and the ground speed is 224 km/h (5·6 cm).

By calculation

First draw a rough sketch of the velocity triangle.

The angle $ACB = 40° + 40° = 80°$.

By the sine formula,

$$\frac{\sin A}{40} = \frac{\sin 80°}{220}.$$

$$\therefore A = 10° 19'$$

(the obtuse angle is obviously not permissible).

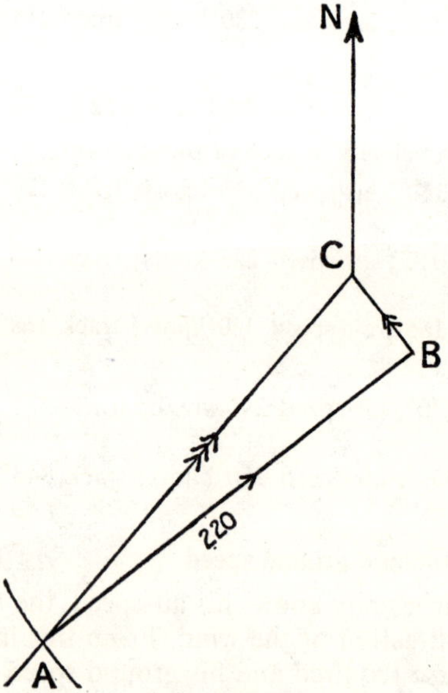

FIG. 309

By subtraction,

$$B = 89° \, 41'.$$

By the sine formula,

$$\frac{AC}{\sin 89° \, 41'} = \frac{220}{\sin 80°}.$$

$$\therefore AC = 223{\cdot}1.$$

The course required is 40° + 10° = 050° to the nearest degree and the ground speed is 223 km/h.

EXERCISES 123A

Find the course and the ground speed from the following:

1. Track 090°, air-speed 300 km/h; wind 40 km/h from 060°.

2. Track 160°, air-speed 280 knots; wind 30 knots from 040°.

3. Track 225°, air-speed 250 knots; wind 50 knots from 110°.

4. Track 320°, air-speed 240 knots; wind 20 knots from 120°.

5. Track 007°, air-speed 220 knots; wind 30 knots from 320°.

EXERCISES 123B

Find the course and the ground speed from the following:

1. Track 080°, air-speed 300 knots; wind 20 knots from 020°.

2. Track 170°, air-speed 280 knots; wind 30 knots from 220°.

3. Track 220°, air-speed 240 knots; wind 40 knots from 160°.

4. Track 260°, air-speed 220 km/h; wind 25 km/h from 008°.

5. Track 320°, air-speed 225 knots; wind 30 knots from 160°.

EXERCISES 124: MISCELLANEOUS

1. An aircraft on a course of 090° whose air-speed is 250 knots experiences a wind of 25 knots from 025°. What are its track and ground speed?

2. An aircraft flying at an air-speed of 260 knots on a course of 290° encounters a wind of 25 knots from 340°. What are its track and ground speed?

3. The navigator of an aircraft flying at an air-speed of 220 knots, on a course of 135°, fixes his position at 0900 hours. A second fix is obtained at 0915 hours. The distance and direction of the second fix from the first are 50 nautical miles and 125°. What is the speed and direction of the wind?

4. In an aircraft flying at an air-speed of 200 knots, it is desired to make good a track of 080°. If the wind is blowing at 40 knots from 300°, what will be the course and the ground speed?

5. An aircraft whose air-speed is 220 knots is required to make good a track of 040°. The wind is 30 knots from 310°. What are the course and ground speed?

6. A navigator notes that his course is 090° and that his air-speed is 275 knots. If the wind is 20 knots from 160°, find the track and ground speed.

7. A navigator steers a course of 050° and the air-speed is 220 knots. After 20 minutes, he notes that he has made good a track of 047° and that the distance travelled is 75 nautical miles. What is the speed and direction of the wind?

8. An aircraft is flown from a place P to another place Q, 400 sea miles due north. If the air-speed is 350 knots and the wind is blowing from the east at 40 knots, find the course the aircraft should steer.

9. The air-speed of an aircraft is 240 knots and the course set is 080°. A wind of 40 knots is blowing from 320°. Find the ground speed of the aircraft and the angle of drift.

10. A navigator flying on a course of 070° at an air-speed of 220 knots makes good a track of 075° with a ground speed of 240 knots. Find the speed and direction of the wind.

SPECIMEN PAPERS

PAPER I

Time—2 hours

SECTION I (44 marks)

Answer all the questions in this section

1. (i) Simplify $\dfrac{7\frac{4}{5}}{1\frac{2}{3} - \frac{4}{5}} - 5\frac{1}{5}$.

(ii) Express 1·0986 (*a*) correct to three decimal places,
(*b*) correct to three significant figures.

(iii) Express 89 g as a fraction of 2 kg.

2. (i) Solve the equation $\dfrac{x}{3} - \dfrac{x-4}{4} = 2$.

(ii) Solve the simultaneous equations $3x - 2y = 5$, $4x - 3y = 7$.

(iii) Express as a single fraction $\dfrac{x}{3} - \dfrac{x-y}{4}$.

3. (i) Construct a parallelogram given that the diagonals of lengths 4·8 cm and 7·2 cm include an angle of 60°.

(ii) Each interior angle of a regular polygon is 5 times each exterior angle. Find the number of sides of the polygon.

4. In a triangle ABC, the angle $A = 40°$ and the angle $B = 70°$. Given that $AB = 6{\cdot}2$ cm, calculate the length of BC.

SECTION II (56 marks)

Answer any four questions in this section

5. A swimming pool is 30 m long and 8 m wide. The water at the shallow end is 1 m deep and at the other end is 3 m deep. Find the number of cubic metres of water in the tank.

If the pool is filled by water flowing at 2 m/sec through a circular pipe of internal radius 4 cm, find the time taken to fill the pool.

[Take π to be 3·142.]

6. Draw the graph of $y = x^2 - 3x$ for values of x between -3 and $+3$. Use your graph to solve the equations $x^2 - 3x = -1$ and $x - 3 = -\dfrac{2}{x}$.

7. Prove that the angle subtended at the centre of a circle by an arc of that circle is double the angle subtended by that arc at any point of the circumference.

A, B, P are three points on the circumference of a circle centre O. The chord AP is produced to Q so that $PQ = PB$. Prove that the angle AOB is four times the angle AQB.

8. (i) Differentiate $3x^2 - \frac{2}{x}$.

(ii) Calculate the area between the curve $y = x^2 - 3x$ and the axis of x.

9. $ABCD$ is a tetrahedron in which $BC = CA = AB = 4$ m and $DA = DB = DC = 5$ m. Calculate (i) the angle which the edge DA makes with the face ABC, (ii) the angle between the faces DAB and ABC.

10. A helicopter wishes to complete a journey of 100 km due north. Its air speed is 80 km/h and the wind is blowing at 30 km/h from the north-east. Find the course set by the helicopter and the time taken to complete the journey.

PAPER II

Time—2 hours

SECTION I (44 marks)

Answer all the questions in this section

1. (i) Divide 9·114 by 4·34 exactly.

(ii) The average weight of 19 boys in a class is 45 kg. A new boy of weight 50 kg joins the class. Find the new average weight of the class.

(iii) The price of an article increases by 8% to £8·10. Find the original price of the article.

2. Factorise (i) $2a^2 - ab - b^2$;

(ii) $(4x - 1)^2 - y^2$;

(iii) $x(x - 1) - 2(x - 1)$.

3. (i) In a triangle ABC, $AB = 4$ cm and $BC = 5$ cm. The length of the perpendicular from C to AB is 2·5 cm. Calculate the length of the perpendicular from A to BC.

(ii) In a triangle XYZ, the internal bisectors of the angles Y and Z meet at I. Given that the angle YIZ is twice the angle YXZ, prove that the angle YXZ is 60°.

4. In the triangle ABC, the angle $A = 120°$ and $AB = 3$ cm, $AC = 7$ cm. Calculate the length of BC.

SECTION II (56 marks)

Answer any four questions in this section

5. A man buys a house for £5000 and estimates that it will cost him £55 a year for repairs. He wishes to let it at a rent which will give him a clear return of 7% on his capital. Find the yearly rent.

The tenant has to pay rates at $92\frac{1}{2}$ new pence in the £. If the rateable value of the house is £58, find the total cost to the tenant per week of rates and rent combined. Give your answer to the nearest new penny.

6. If $x = \dfrac{y-1}{y-3}$, express y in terms of x.

Find the values of x which make x equal to y.

7. Prove that the opposite angles of a cyclic quadrilateral are supplementary.

TP, TQ are tangents from a point T to a circle centre O. Prove that the angle PQT is half the angle POQ.

8. In question 7, if the angle $PTQ = 80°$ and the radius of the circle is 4 cm, calculate the length of TP and the length of the chord PQ.

9. Two places P and Q are on the circle of latitude 50° N. and differ in longitude by 15°. Find the distance between P and Q along their circle of latitude.

[Take the earth to be a sphere of radius 6370 km and π to be 3·142.]

10. A tetrahedron $ABCD$ is such that BCD is horizontal and equilateral. If $BC = CD = BD = 6$ cm and $AB = AC = AD = 8$ cm, draw the plan and elevation on a vertical plane parallel to BC.

PAPER III

Time—2 hours

SECTION I (44 marks)

Answer all the questions in this section

1. (i) Multiply 1·23 by 0·864.

(ii) A man sells a car for £420 at a loss of 30%. What did it cost him?

(iii) A train travels 320 km in 5 hours. How long would it take a train to travel 400 km at the same speed?

2. The amount of money accrued when £P is invested for T years at R% per annum is given in pounds by $A = P + \dfrac{PRT}{100}$.

(i) Express P in terms of A, R and T.

(ii) Find P given that $A = 392$, $R = 4$ and $T = 3$.

3. Construct a triangle ABC of area 5 cm^2 given that $AB = 4$ cm, $BC = 3$ cm. Measure the other side of the triangle in each of the two possible cases.

4. An equilateral triangle is inscribed in a circle of radius 2 cm. Calculate the side of the triangle and its area. Calculate also the area of the minor segment cut off by a side of the triangle.

SECTION II (56 marks)

Answer any four questions in this section

5. A grocer mixes two kinds of tea costing 90 new pence a kg and 80 new pence a kg in the ratio 4 : 3 by weight. At what price must he sell the mixture to gain $16\frac{2}{3}\%$?

If he wants to sell the tea at the same price as before, find in what ratio he should mix the blends in order to gain 20%.

6. A cyclist cycles from Cambridge to Bedford 48 km away at a steady 16 km/h. He leaves Cambridge at 09.00h and is passed by a motorist who leaves Cambridge at 10.00h and travels at a steady 48 km/h. The motorist spends $\frac{1}{2}$ hour in Bedford and then returns to Cambridge at the same speed. Find graphically when and where the cyclist is passed by the motorist on his return journey.

7. James finds that 3 golf balls and 6 tennis balls cost him £1·42½. The cost of 6 golf balls and 3 tennis balls is £1·72½. Find the cost of 6 golf balls and 6 tennis balls.

8. Prove that the acute angle which a chord of a circle makes with the tangent through its point of contact is equal to the angle subtended by the chord in the alternate segment of the circle.

Two circles intersect at A and B. The tangents to the circles at A meet the circles again at P and Q. Given that PBQ is a straight line, prove that the angle PAQ is a right angle.

9. F is the foot of a vertical tower FT which stands on horizontal ground. From two points A and B on the ground, the angles of elevation of the top of the tower are 35° and 44° respectively. If the height of the tower is 80 m and the angle AFB is 60°, find the distance AB.

10. (i) Evaluate $\int_3^4 \left(x + \frac{1}{x^2}\right) dx$.

(ii) If the distance in metres gone by a particle travelling in a straight line in t seconds is given by $s = 3t - t^3$, find the velocity of the particle after $\frac{1}{2}$ sec.

PAPER IV

Time—2 hours

SECTION I (44 marks)

Answer all the questions in this section

1. (i) Given that 1 inch = 2·54 cm, express 16 cm in inches correct to two significant figures.

(ii) I spend $\frac{1}{7}$ of my income on rent and $\frac{1}{4}$ of the remainder on house-keeping expenses. If after paying these expenses, I have £900 left, find my total income.

(iii) Express 4 cm 8 mm as a percentage of 1 metre.

2. (i) What number must be added to $(x^2 - 16x)$ to make the result a perfect square?

(ii) Factorise $x^2 - 16x - 36$.

(iii) A greengrocer buys potatoes at £p per kg and sells them at d new pence per kg. Find his profit per cent in terms of p and d.

3. X and Y are points on the sides AB, AC of a triangle ABC such that XY is parallel to BC. If $AX = 4$ cm, $BX = 2$ cm, write down the values of the ratios (*a*) $XY : BC$; (*b*) $YC : AC$; (*c*) $\triangle AXY : \triangle ABC$.

If the area of the quadrilateral $XYCB$ is 10 cm², find the area of the triangle ABC.

4. Use tables to evaluate correct to three significant figures

$$\text{(i)}\ \sqrt[3]{\frac{18 \cdot 21}{27 \cdot 39}}; \qquad \text{(ii)}\ \sqrt{(14 \cdot 1)^2 + (28 \cdot 3)^2}.$$

SECTION II (56 marks)

Answer any four questions in this section

5. A wire in the shape of a circle of radius 8 cm is bent to form an equilateral triangle. Find the area of the triangle and express the area of the triangle as a percentage of the area of the circle.

[Take π to be 3·142.]

6. (i) Write down the values of $16^{\frac{3}{4}}$ and $\tan^2 60°$.

(ii) If y varies inversely as x^2 and $y = 3$ when $x = 4$, find (*a*) the value of y when $x = 16$, (*b*) the value of x when $y = 12$.

7. A ring of radius 60 cm is suspended horizontally by 4 strings each 1·20 m long and each attached to a nail O. The strings are attached to points P, Q, R, S equally spaced on the ring. Calculate

(i) the angle OP makes with the horizontal;

(ii) the angle between OP and OQ.

8. *ABCD* is a trapezium in which *AB* is parallel to *DC*. The side *DC* is produced to *F* so that $DC = CF$ and *AF* meets *CB* at *X*. If $BX = 2CX$, prove that *ABFD* is a parallelogram. If it is also given that the area of *CXF* is 3 cm², find the area of the quadrilateral *ABCD*.

9. The earth rotates on its axis once in 24 hours. Find the speed of a place *X* on the earth's surface whose latitude is 45° S. due to this rotation. Find also the latitude of a place whose speed is half that of *X*.

[Take the earth to be a sphere of radius 6370 km and π to be 3·142.]

10. A regular tetrahedron *ABCD* has sides of length 8 cm. By making suitable drawings, find the length of the line joining the mid points of *AB* and *CD*.

PAPER V

Time—2 hours

SECTION I (44 marks)

Answer all the questions in this section

1. (i) Find the largest and smallest of the fractions $\frac{2}{7}, \frac{3}{10}, \frac{7}{22}, \frac{9}{28}$ and express the difference between them as a decimal correct to 2 significant figures.

(ii) Find the simple interest on £340 in 2 years at $3\frac{1}{2}\%$ per annum.

2. (i) Factorise $(x^2 - 3x + 2)$ and $(x^2 - 4)$.

(ii) Find the L.C.M. of $(x^2 - 3x + 2)$ and $(x^2 - 4)$.

(iii) Simplify $\dfrac{4}{x^2 - 4} - \dfrac{1}{x^2 - 3x + 2}$.

3. (i) *ABCD* is a quadrilateral in which $AD = BC$, and the diagonal $AC =$ the diagonal *BD*. If the diagonals meet at *X*, prove that $DX = CX$.

(ii) Each interior angle of a regular polygon is 108° larger than each exterior angle. Find the number of sides of the polygon.

4. (i) Find two values of θ, given that $\sin \theta = 0{\cdot}46$.

(ii) Evaluate correct to three significant figures

$$\frac{\tan 53^\circ\ 12' \sin 42^\circ\ 17'}{\cos 28^\circ\ 10'}.$$

SECTION II (56 marks)

Answer any four questions in this section

5. A shopkeeper marks his goods to make 30% profit but allows 5% discount for cash. Find his percentage profit on a cash sale.

If he sells an article for £12·35 cash, find his actual profit.

6. An express train from London to Bournemouth is scheduled to travel the 176 km in a certain time. If the average speed of the train were reduced by 8 km/h, the train would arrive 10 minutes late. Find the scheduled time.

7. $ABCD$ is a square of side 6 cm. The points X, Y, Z lie on AB, BC, CD respectively such that $BX = 3$ cm, $BY = 4$ cm and $CZ = 2$ cm. Calculate the area of the triangle XYZ and the angle ZXY to the nearest half degree.

8. Find the least value of the expression $(2x^2 - 3x)$. Find also the gradients of the curve $y = 2x^2 - 3x$ at the points where it cuts the axis of x and hence draw a rough sketch of the curve.

9. The 3rd, 5th and 8th terms of an arithmetic progression are consecutive terms of a geometric progression. Find the common ratio of the geometric progression and prove that the 5th term of the arithmetic progression is double the 2nd term.

10. Prove that $\sin^2\theta + \cos^2\theta = 1$.

In an acute-angled triangle ABC, $\cos A = \frac{8}{17}$ and $\cos C = \frac{4}{5}$. If N is the foot of the perpendicular from B to AC, calculate the ratio $BN : AC$.

PAPER VI

Time—2 hours

SECTION I (44 marks)

Answer all the questions in this section

1. When the price of coal is £9·75 a tonne, find
(i) the cost of 100 kg;
(ii) the cost of 2 tonnes 500 kg;
(iii) the weight of coal which can be purchased for £117.

2. If a temperature of $C°$ Centigrade is the same as a temperature of $F°$ Fahrenheit, there is a connection of the form $C = aF + b$ between C and F, where a and b are constants. Given that a temperature of 0° *C.* is equivalent to a temperature of 32° *F.* and that 100° *C.* is equivalent to 212° *F.*, find the values of a and b.

Find also the Fahrenheit equivalent of a tem rature of 60° *C.*

3. (i) The angles of a triangle are $x°$, $3x°$, $5x°$. Find x.
(ii) The angles of a quadrilateral are in the ratios 1 : 2 : 3 : 4. Find them.
(iii) The angles of a pentagon are such that four are equal and the fifth is 20° greater than each of the equal angles. Find them.

4. The angles of elevation of the top of a tower from two points A and B, on the same level as its foot and in line with it, are 32° and 44° respectively. If $AB = 50$ m and A and B are on the same side of the tower, find the height of the tower.

SECTION II (56 marks)

Answer any four questions in this section

5. A man estimates that the cost of his holiday in 1967 was made up of 60% hotel bills, 15% travelling expenses and 25% incidentals. In 1968, he knows that hotel costs have risen by $12\frac{1}{2}$% and travelling expenses by 10%, but he hopes to reduce incidental expenses by 5%. Find the percentage increase in the total cost of his holiday.

If his holiday in 1968 actually cost him £9·30 more than in 1967, find the cost of his holiday in 1967.

6. (i) Solve the equation $2x^2 - 3x - 7 = 0$.

(ii) Prove that the product of three consecutive whole numbers added to the middle of the numbers is equal to the cube of the middle number.

7. A boy on the edge of a circular pond of radius 30 m sees a tree which he estimates is diametrically opposite him and 15 m from the edge of the pond. Find the shortest distance the boy must walk to reach the tree.

[Take π to be 3·142.]

8. Prove that parallelograms on the same base and between the same parallels are equal in area.

ABCD is a parallelogram. The side *BC* is produced to *E* so that $BC = CE$. The side *AD* is produced to *F* so that $DF = 2AD$. The point of intersection of *FE* and *DC* is *X*. Prove that the area of the triangle *AXD* is equal to that of the parallelogram *ABCD*.

9. Find the points of intersection of the line $y = 2x$ with the curve $y = x^2 + x$. Find also the area included between the line and the curve.

10. Four balls of radius 2 cm and with centres *A, B, C, D* are placed on a horizontal plane in such a way that *ABCD* is a square of side 4 cm. A fifth ball of radius 2 cm rests on top of the other four and touches each of them. Draw the plan and an elevation on a vertical plane perpendicular to *BD*.

PAPER VII

Time—2 hours

SECTION I (44 marks)

Answer all the questions in this section

1. (i) Given that 1 nautical mile = 1·85 km, express a kilometre as a decimal of a nautical mile, correct to two significant figures.

(ii) Find the cost of 6 dozen eggs at $2\frac{1}{2}$ new pence each.

(iii) The length of John's stride is 75 cm. Find how many strides he takes in walking $\frac{3}{4}$ km.

2. (i) Solve the equation $\frac{1}{x} = \frac{1}{2} + \frac{1}{3}$.

(ii) Simplify $\frac{1}{2x + 2} + \frac{1}{3x + 3}$.

(iii) Solve the equation $x + \frac{1}{x} = \frac{10}{3}$.

3. *ABC* is a triangle inscribed in a circle. The tangents to the circle at *B* and *C* meet in *X*; the tangents at *C* and *A* in *Y* and those at *A* and *B* in *Z*. If the angles of the triangle *XYZ* are 50°, 60°, 70° respectively, find the angles of the triangle *ABC*.

Prove that $CY > BZ$.

4. *PQ* is a chord of a circle of radius 8 cm and centre *O*. If the angle $POQ = 98°$, calculate the difference in length between the arc *PQ* and the chord *PQ*.

[Take π to be 3·142.]

SECTION II (56 marks)

Answer any four questions in this section

5. A man borrows £10 000 at 4% per annum interest. If he repays £2500 at the end of each year, find, to the nearest new penny, how much is still owing after the fourth repayment.

6. Draw the graph of $y = x + \frac{1}{x}$ from $x = 1$ to $x = 5$. From your graph find a solution of each of the following equations.

(i) $x + \frac{1}{x} = 3$; (ii) $x^2 - 4x + 1 = 0$; (iii) $2x^2 - 7x + 2 = 0$.

7. The area between the curve in question 6, the axis of *x* and the ordinates $x = 1$ and $x = 5$ is rotated through 4 right angles about the axis of *x*. Find the volume generated.

8. Mr. French buys 4 tonnes of coal and 5 tonnes of anthracite in a certain year and his fuel bill for that year is £95·50. The following year he buys 1 tonne less of coal but ½ tonne more of anthracite and reduces his fuel bill by £3·75. Assuming there has been no change in the price of coal or anthracite, find the cost of a tonne of anthracite.

9. Two circles of radii 5 cm and 3 cm touch externally at *P*. A common tangent to the circles touches the larger at *S* and the smaller at *T*. The tangent at *P* meets *ST* at *X*. Calculate the lengths of *ST*, *PX* and find the radius of the circle which passes through *X* and the centres of the two circles.

10. A pyramid vertex P has a square base $ABCD$ which is horizontal and of side 4 cm. Given that each slant edge is 6 cm long, draw the elevations on vertical planes parallel to AC and AB. From your elevations, find

(i) the height of the pyramid;

(ii) the angle which a sloping face makes with the base.

PAPER VIII

Time—2 hours

SECTION I (44 marks)

Answer all the questions in this section

1. (i) Find the radius of a circle of circumference 44 cm. [Take π to be $\frac{22}{7}$.]

(ii) Express $2\frac{4}{5}$, $3\frac{1}{8}$ and their product as exact decimals.

(iii) Find the area of the walls of a room 20 m long, 14 m wide and 10 m high.

2. (i) If $y = z + \sqrt{x^2 + y^2}$, express x in terms of the other letters.

(ii) n plates are bought for $(x - 3)$ new pence each and another $2n$ plates for $(x + 1)$ new pence each. Three plates are broken but the rest are sold for $(x + 2)$ new pence each. Find and simplify an expression for the total profit.

3. Find whether the triangles whose sides are (*a*) 4, 5, and 6, (*b*) 3, 4 and 6 are acute or obtuse angled.

(ii) Two fences are 1·8 m and 2·4 m high, and the distance between them is 3 m. A boy 1·5 m tall positions himself so that the tops of the fences are in line. Find the distance of the boy from the nearer fence.

4. (i) If $\tan\theta = \frac{2}{3}\tan 72°$, find a value for θ.

(ii) If $\cos x = \dfrac{p}{q}$, find a value for $\tan x$.

SECTION II (56 marks)

Answer any four questions in this section

5. In the balance sheet of a club, the listed price of furniture is depreciated by 15% each year. If this year the furniture is listed at £578, what was it listed at the year before last?

6. (i) Solve the equation $3x^2 - 5x - 7 = 0$.

(ii) Solve the equation $3^x = 7$.

7. AB is a diameter of a circle centre O. The chord DC of the circle is parallel to AB. Given that the angle $BAC = 25°$, find the angles COD, CAD, ADO, ADC, CBD and ABD.

8. Construct the triangle ABC given that $AB = 3{\cdot}5$ cm, the angle $C = 50°$, the area of the triangle is $5\frac{1}{4}$ cm^2 and that AC is larger than BC.

9. Two places are on the same parallel of latitude 52° 30′ N. and their longitudes differ by 180°. Find the distance between the places
(i) along the great circle over the North Pole;
(ii) along their parallel of latitude.
[Take the earth to be a sphere of radius 6370 km and π to be 3·142.]

10. The air speed of a trainer is 180 km/h. If the wind is blowing from the east at 30 km/h, calculate
(i) the course which the pilot has to set if he wishes to travel due north;
(ii) the ground speed of the trainer when the pilot sets a course due north.

PAPER IX

SECTION I (44 marks)

Answer all the questions in this section

1. (i) Find the exact value of $14{\cdot}7 \times 0{\cdot}0725$.
(ii) Express the speed of an aircraft travelling at 824 km/h as a decimal of the speed of sound (330m/sec). Give your answer to three significant figures.
(iii) Three classes of 18, 20 and 22 pupils sit for an examination. The average marks scored by the three classes are respectively 60, 56 and 50. Find the average mark of all the pupils in the three classes.

2. (i) Find the value of $a^3 - a^2 b - b^3$ when $a = -2$ and $b = -3$.
(ii) Simplify $(x - 1)(x + 3) - (x - 2) - (x^2 - 1)$.
(iii) Solve the equations $\dfrac{x - y}{2} = \dfrac{x + y + 1}{5} = \dfrac{x + y}{4}$.

3. (i) Construct the triangle ABC in which $BC = 4$ cm, the angle $B = 90°$ and the angle $C = 60°$.
(ii) L and M are points on opposite sides of a straight line AB. The distances of L and M from the line are 2·4 cm and 3·6 cm. Find the distance of the middle point of LM from the line.

4. ABC is an equilateral triangle of side 40 m on horizontal ground. AT is a vertical tower. The angle of elevation of the top of the tower T from B is 50°. Given that X is a point on the tower 10 m from the top, calculate
(i) the height of the tower;
(ii) the angle of elevation of X from C.

SECTION II (56 marks)

Answer any four questions in this section

5. An investor buys 400 Distillers 50 new pence shares at £1·60. If the company declares a dividend of 16%, find the net amount received by the investor after he has paid income tax at $42\frac{1}{2}$%. Find also his net percentage return on the cash invested.

6. The ratio of the ages of a man and his wife is 8 : 7. In ten years' time, the ratio of their ages will be 10 : 9. Find their present ages. Find how many years ago the ratio of their ages was 7 : 6.

7. ABC is an acute-angled triangle inscribed in a circle and P, Q, R are the middle points of the minor arcs BC, CA, AB respectively. Prove that AP is perpendicular to QR.

8. $ABCD$ is a quadrilateral in which $AB = 5$ cm, $BC = 3$ cm, $CD = AD = 7$ cm. Given that the angle B of the quadrilateral $= 120°$, find the angle D.

9. A solid $ABCDXY$ has a horizontal rectangular base $ABCD$ in which $AD = 5$ cm and $AB = 6$ cm. The triangular faces ADX and CBY are equilateral triangles and each slopes inwards at an angle of 60° with the base. Draw the plan of the solid and the elevation of a vertical plane parallel to BC.

10. In the solid described in question **9**, calculate
(i) the height of the line XY above the face $ABCD$;
(ii) the length of XY;
(iii) the angle AX makes with the face $ABCD$.

PAPER X

Time—2 hours

SECTION I (44 marks)

Answer all the questions in this section

1. (i) A train travels $37\frac{1}{2}$ km in 50 minutes. Find the average speed in kilometres per hour.
(ii) Express £8·$37\frac{1}{2}$ as a fraction of £15·$12\frac{1}{2}$, in its lowest terms.
(iii) If the simple interest paid on a loan of £320 in $3\frac{1}{2}$ years is £50·40, find the rate per cent per annum.

2. (i) Simplify $\dfrac{1}{(x-1)(x-2)} + \dfrac{1}{(x-2)(x-3)}$.
(ii) Factorise $2x - 3y - 2ax + 3ay$.
(iii) Solve the equation $\dfrac{x}{3} + \dfrac{x-1}{2} = 2$.

3. (i) O is the centre of a circle which passes through three points A, B and D which are in that order on the circle. The parallelogram $ABCD$ is completed. If the angle $BOD = 72°$, calculate the angles of the parallelogram.

(ii) In the triangle XYZ, the angle $Y = 83°$ and the angle $Z = 33°$. The internal bisector of the angle X meets YZ at D. Find which is the larger of XD and DZ.

4. ABC is a triangle in which $AB = 8{\cdot}2$ cm, $AC = 9{\cdot}6$ cm and the angle $A = 42° \, 34'$. Calculate the length of BC and the area of the triangle ABC.

SECTION II (56 marks)

Answer any four questions in this section

5. A cube of side 4 cm is dropped into a cylindrical vessel of radius 3 cm containing water. Find the rise in the water level in the cylinder when

(i) the original depth of water was 5 cm;

(ii) the original depth of water was 1 cm.

[Take π to be $3{\cdot}142$.]

6. Given that H varies directly as C and inversely as the square of R and that $H = 1$ when $C = 8$ and $R = 2$, calculate

(i) the value of C when $H = 2$ and $R = 3$;

(ii) the value of R when $C = 9$ and $H = 2$.

Find also the percentage increase in the value of C when H and R each increases by 2%.

7. Prove the Theorem of Pythagoras.

ABC is a triangle which has a right angle at A. The foot of the perpendicular from A to BC is D. Prove that

$$BC^2 - 2AC^2 = BD^2 - DC^2.$$

8. Three villages P, Q and R are situated so that $PQ = 3$ km, and $QR = 4$ km. The bearing of Q from P is 040° and the bearing of R from Q is 020°. Find the distance PR and the bearing of R from P.

9. (i) Differentiate (*a*) $x^3 - 3x^2 + 2x$; (*b*) $x^3 + \frac{1}{x}$.

(ii) Evaluate (*a*) $\int_1^4 (x^2 + 1)\, dx$; (*b*) $\int_2^3 \left(1 - \frac{1}{x^2}\right) dx$.

10. A cube of side 4 cm has an open top. The cube rests on level ground and a sphere of radius 3 cm rests on the top four edges of the cube. Find the height of the top of the sphere above the ground.

LOGARITHM TABLES

LOGARITHMS

	0	1	2	3	4	5	6	7	8	9	1	2	3	4	5	6	7	8	9
10	0000	0043	0086	0128	0170	0212	0253	0294	0334	0374	4	8	12	17	21	25	29	33	37
11	0414	0453	0492	0531	0569	0607	0645	0682	0719	0755	4	8	11	15	19	23	26	30	34
12	0792	0828	0864	0899	0934	0969	1004	1038	1072	1106	3	7	10	14	17	21	24	28	31
13	1139	1173	1206	1239	1271	1303	1335	1367	1399	1430	3	6	10	13	16	19	23	26	29
14	1461	1492	1523	1553	1584	1614	1644	1673	1703	1732	3	6	9	12	15	18	21	24	27
15	1761	1790	1818	1847	1875	1903	1931	1959	1987	2014	3	6	8	11	14	17	20	22	25
16	2041	2068	2095	2122	2148	2175	2201	2227	2253	2279	3	5	8	11	13	16	18	21	24
17	2304	2330	2355	2380	2405	2430	2455	2480	2504	2529	2	5	7	10	12	15	17	20	22
18	2553	2577	2601	2625	2648	2672	2695	2718	2742	2765	2	5	7	9	12	14	16	19	21
19	2788	2810	2833	2856	2878	2900	2923	2945	2967	2989	2	4	7	9	11	13	16	18	20
20	3010	3032	3054	3075	3096	3118	3139	3160	3181	3201	2	4	6	8	11	13	15	17	19
21	3222	3243	3263	3284	3304	3324	3345	3365	3385	3404	2	4	6	8	10	12	14	16	18
22	3424	3444	3464	3483	3502	3522	3541	3560	3579	3598	2	4	6	8	10	12	14	15	17
23	3617	3636	3655	3674	3692	3711	3729	3747	3766	3784	2	4	6	7	9	11	13	15	17
24	3802	3820	3838	3856	3874	3892	3909	3927	3945	3962	2	4	5	7	9	11	12	14	16
25	3979	3997	4014	4031	4048	4065	4082	4099	4116	4133	2	3	5	7	9	10	12	14	15
26	4150	4166	4183	4200	4216	4232	4249	4265	4281	4298	2	3	5	7	8	10	11	13	15
27	4314	4330	4346	4362	4378	4393	4409	4425	4440	4456	2	3	5	6	8	9	11	13	14
28	4472	4487	4502	4518	4533	4548	4564	4579	4594	4609	2	3	5	6	8	9	11	12	14
29	4624	4639	4654	4669	4683	4698	4713	4728	4742	4757	1	3	4	6	7	9	10	12	13
30	4771	4786	4800	4814	4829	4843	4857	4871	4886	4900	1	3	4	6	7	9	10	11	13
31	4914	4928	4942	4955	4969	4983	4997	5011	5024	5038	1	3	4	6	7	8	10	11	12
32	5051	5065	5079	5092	5105	5119	5132	5145	5159	5172	1	3	4	5	7	8	9	11	12
33	5185	5198	5211	5224	5237	5250	5263	5276	5289	5302	1	3	4	5	6	8	9	10	12
34	5315	5328	5340	5353	5366	5378	5391	5403	5416	5428	1	3	4	5	6	8	9	10	11
35	5441	5453	5465	5478	5490	5502	5514	5527	5539	5551	1	2	4	5	6	7	9	10	11
36	5563	5575	5587	5599	5611	5623	5635	5647	5658	5670	1	2	4	5	6	7	8	10	11
37	5682	5694	5705	5717	5729	5740	5752	5763	5775	5786	1	2	3	5	6	7	8	9	10
38	5798	5809	5821	5832	5843	5855	5866	5877	5888	5899	1	2	3	5	6	7	8	9	10
39	5911	5922	5933	5944	5955	5966	5977	5988	5999	6010	1	2	3	4	5	7	8	9	10
40	6021	6031	6042	6053	6064	6075	6085	6096	6107	6117	1	2	3	4	5	6	8	9	10
41	6128	6138	6149	6160	6170	6180	6191	6201	6212	6222	1	2	3	4	5	6	7	8	9
42	6232	6243	6253	6263	6274	6284	6294	6304	6314	6325	1	2	3	4	5	6	7	8	9
43	6335	6345	6355	6365	6375	6385	6395	6405	6415	6425	1	2	3	4	5	6	7	8	9
44	6435	6444	6454	6464	6474	6484	6493	6503	6513	6522	1	2	3	4	5	6	7	8	9
45	6532	6542	6551	6561	6571	6580	6590	6599	6609	6618	1	2	3	4	5	6	7	8	9
46	6628	6637	6646	6656	6665	6675	6684	6693	6702	6712	1	2	3	4	5	6	7	7	8
47	6721	6730	6739	6749	6758	6767	6776	6785	6794	6803	1	2	3	4	5	5	6	7	8
48	6812	6821	6830	6839	6848	6857	6866	6875	6884	6893	1	2	3	4	4	5	6	7	8
49	6902	6911	6920	6928	6937	6946	6955	6964	6972	6981	1	2	3	4	4	5	6	7	8
50	6990	6998	7007	7016	7024	7033	7042	7050	7059	7067	1	2	3	3	4	5	6	7	8
51	7076	7084	7093	7101	7110	7118	7126	7135	7143	7152	1	2	3	3	4	5	6	7	8
52	7160	7168	7177	7185	7193	7202	7210	7218	7226	7235	1	2	2	3	4	5	6	7	7
53	7243	7251	7259	7267	7275	7284	7292	7300	7308	7316	1	2	2	3	4	5	6	6	7
54	7324	7332	7340	7348	7356	7364	7372	7380	7388	7396	1	2	2	3	4	5	6	6	7
	0	1	2	3	4	5	6	7	8	9	1	2	3	4	5	6	7	8	9

LOGARITHMS

	0	1	2	3	4	5	6	7	8	9	1	2	3	4	5	6	7	8	9
55	7404	7412	7419	7427	7435	7443	7451	7459	7466	7474	1	2	2	3	4	5	5	6	7
56	7482	7490	7497	7505	7513	7520	7528	7536	7543	7551	1	2	2	3	4	5	5	6	7
57	7559	7566	7574	7582	7589	7597	7604	7612	7619	7627	1	2	2	3	4	5	5	6	7
58	7634	7642	7649	7657	7664	7672	7679	7686	7694	7701	1	1	2	3	4	4	5	6	7
59	7709	7716	7723	7731	7738	7745	7752	7760	7767	7774	1	1	2	3	4	4	5	6	7
60	7782	7789	7796	7803	7810	7818	7825	7832	7839	7846	1	1	2	3	4	4	5	6	6
61	7853	7860	7868	7875	7882	7889	7896	7903	7910	7917	1	1	2	3	4	4	5	6	6
62	7924	7931	7938	7945	7952	7959	7966	7973	7980	7987	1	1	2	3	3	4	5	6	6
63	7993	8000	8007	8014	8021	8028	8035	8041	8048	8055	1	1	2	3	3	4	5	5	6
64	8062	8069	8075	8082	8089	8096	8102	8109	8116	8122	1	1	2	3	3	4	5	5	6
65	8129	8136	8142	8149	8156	8162	8169	8176	8182	8189	1	1	2	3	3	4	5	5	6
66	8195	8202	8209	8215	8222	8228	8235	8241	8248	8254	1	1	2	3	3	4	5	5	6
67	8261	8267	8274	8280	8287	8293	8299	8306	8312	8319	1	1	2	3	3	4	5	5	6
68	8325	8331	8338	8344	8351	8357	8363	8370	8376	8382	1	1	2	3	3	4	4	5	6
69	8388	8395	8401	8407	8414	8420	8426	8432	8439	8445	1	1	2	2	3	4	4	5	6
70	8451	8457	8463	8470	8476	8482	8488	8494	8500	8506	1	1	2	2	3	4	4	5	6
71	8513	8519	8525	8531	8537	8543	8549	8555	8561	8567	1	1	2	2	3	4	4	5	5
72	8573	8579	8585	8591	8597	8603	8609	8615	8621	8627	1	1	2	2	3	4	4	5	5
73	8633	8639	8645	8651	8657	8663	8669	8675	8681	8686	1	1	2	2	3	4	4	5	5
74	8692	8698	8704	8710	8716	8722	8727	8733	8739	8745	1	1	2	2	3	4	4	5	5
75	8751	8756	8762	8768	8774	8779	8785	8791	8797	8802	1	1	2	2	3	3	4	5	5
76	8808	8814	8820	8825	8831	8837	8842	8848	8854	8859	1	1	2	2	3	3	4	5	5
77	8865	8871	8876	8882	8887	8893	8899	8904	8910	8915	1	1	2	2	3	3	4	4	5
78	8921	8927	8932	8938	8943	8949	8954	8960	8965	8971	1	1	2	2	3	3	4	4	5
79	8976	8982	8987	8993	8998	9004	9009	9015	9020	9025	1	1	2	2	3	3	4	4	5
80	9031	9036	9042	9047	9053	9058	9063	9069	9074	9079	1	1	2	2	3	3	4	4	5
81	9085	9090	9096	9101	9106	9112	9117	9122	9128	9133	1	1	2	2	3	3	4	4	5
82	9138	9143	9149	9154	9159	9165	9170	9175	9180	9186	1	1	2	2	3	3	4	4	5
83	9191	9196	9201	9206	9212	9217	9222	9227	9232	9238	1	1	2	2	3	3	4	4	5
84	9243	9248	9253	9258	9263	9269	9274	9279	9284	9289	1	1	2	2	3	3	4	4	5
85	9294	9299	9304	9309	9315	9320	9325	9330	9335	9340	1	1	2	2	3	3	4	4	5
86	9345	9350	9355	9360	9365	9370	9375	9380	9385	9390	1	1	2	2	3	3	4	4	5
87	9395	9400	9405	9410	9415	9420	9425	9430	9435	9440	0	1	1	2	2	3	3	4	4
88	9445	9450	9455	9460	9465	9469	9474	9479	9484	9489	0	1	1	2	2	3	3	4	4
89	9494	9499	9504	9509	9513	9518	9523	9528	9533	9538	0	1	1	2	2	3	3	4	4
90	9542	9547	9552	9557	9562	9566	9571	9576	9581	9586	0	1	1	2	2	3	3	4	4
91	9590	9595	9600	9605	9609	9614	9619	9624	9628	9633	0	1	1	2	2	3	3	4	4
92	9638	9643	9647	9652	9657	9661	9666	9671	9675	9680	0	1	1	2	2	3	3	4	4
93	9685	9689	9694	9699	9703	9708	9713	9717	9722	9727	0	1	1	2	2	3	3	4	4
94	9731	9736	9741	9745	9750	9754	9759	9763	9768	9773	0	1	1	2	2	3	3	4	4
95	9777	9782	9786	9791	9795	9800	9805	9809	9814	9818	0	1	1	2	2	3	3	4	4
96	9823	9827	9832	9836	9841	9845	9850	9854	9859	9863	0	1	1	2	2	3	3	4	4
97	9868	9872	9877	9881	9886	9890	9894	9899	9903	9908	0	1	1	2	2	3	3	4	4
98	9912	9917	9921	9926	9930	9934	9939	9943	9948	9952	0	1	1	2	2	3	3	4	4
99	9956	9961	9965	9969	9974	9978	9983	9987	9991	9996	0	1	1	2	2	3	3	3	4
	0	1	2	3	4	5	6	7	8	9	1	2	3	4	5	6	7	8	9

	0	1	2	3	4	5	6	7	8	9	1	2	3	4	5	6	7	8	9
·00	1000	1002	1005	1007	1009	1012	1014	1016	1019	1021	0	0	1	1	1	1	2	2	2
·01	1023	1026	1028	1030	1033	1035	1038	1040	1042	1045	0	0	1	1	1	1	2	2	2
·02	1047	1050	1052	1054	1057	1059	1062	1064	1067	1069	0	0	1	1	1	1	2	2	2
·03	1072	1074	1076	1079	1081	1084	1086	1089	1091	1094	0	0	1	1	1	1	2	2	2
·04	1096	1099	1102	1104	1107	1109	1112	1114	1117	1119	0	1	1	1	1	2	2	2	2
·05	1122	1125	1127	1130	1132	1135	1138	1140	1143	1146	0	1	1	1	1	2	2	2	2
·06	1148	1151	1153	1156	1159	1161	1164	1167	1169	1172	0	1	1	1	1	2	2	2	2
·07	1175	1178	1180	1183	1186	1189	1191	1194	1197	1199	0	1	1	1	1	2	2	2	2
·08	1202	1205	1208	1211	1213	1216	1219	1222	1225	1227	0	1	1	1	1	2	2	2	3
·09	1230	1233	1236	1239	1242	1245	1247	1250	1253	1256	0	1	1	1	1	2	2	2	3
·10	1259	1262	1265	1268	1271	1274	1276	1279	1282	1285	0	1	1	1	1	2	2	2	3
·11	1288	1291	1294	1297	1300	1303	1306	1309	1312	1315	0	1	1	1	2	2	2	2	3
·12	1318	1321	1324	1327	1330	1334	1337	1340	1343	1346	0	1	1	1	2	2	2	2	3
·13	1349	1352	1355	1358	1361	1365	1368	1371	1374	1377	0	1	1	1	2	2	2	3	3
·14	1380	1384	1387	1390	1393	1396	1400	1403	1406	1409	0	1	1	1	2	2	2	3	3
·15	1413	1416	1419	1422	1426	1429	1432	1435	1439	1442	0	1	1	1	2	2	2	3	3
·16	1445	1449	1452	1455	1459	1462	1466	1469	1472	1476	0	1	1	1	2	2	2	3	3
·17	1479	1483	1486	1489	1493	1496	1500	1503	1507	1510	0	1	1	1	2	2	2	3	3
·18	1514	1517	1521	1524	1528	1531	1535	1538	1542	1545	0	1	1	1	2	2	2	3	3
·19	1549	1552	1556	1560	1563	1567	1570	1574	1578	1581	0	1	1	1	2	2	3	3	3
·20	1585	1589	1592	1596	1600	1603	1607	1611	1614	1618	0	1	1	1	2	2	3	3	3
·21	1622	1626	1629	1633	1637	1641	1644	1648	1652	1656	0	1	1	2	2	2	3	3	3
·22	1660	1663	1667	1671	1675	1679	1683	1687	1690	1694	0	1	1	2	2	2	3	3	3
·23	1698	1702	1706	1710	1714	1718	1722	1726	1730	1734	0	1	1	2	2	2	3	3	4
·24	1738	1742	1746	1750	1754	1758	1762	1766	1770	1774	0	1	1	2	2	2	3	3	4
·25	1778	1782	1786	1791	1795	1799	1803	1807	1811	1816	0	1	1	2	2	2	3	3	4
·26	1820	1824	1828	1832	1837	1841	1845	1849	1854	1858	0	1	1	2	2	3	3	3	4
·27	1862	1866	1871	1875	1879	1884	1888	1892	1897	1901	0	1	1	2	2	3	3	3	4
·28	1905	1910	1914	1919	1923	1928	1932	1936	1941	1945	0	1	1	2	2	3	3	4	4
·29	1950	1954	1959	1963	1968	1972	1977	1982	1986	1991	0	1	1	2	2	3	3	4	4
·30	1995	2000	2004	2009	2014	2018	2023	2028	2032	2037	0	1	1	2	2	3	3	4	4
·31	2042	2046	2051	2056	2061	2065	2070	2075	2080	2084	0	1	1	2	2	3	3	4	4
·32	2089	2094	2099	2104	2109	2113	2118	2123	2128	2133	0	1	1	2	2	3	3	4	4
·33	2138	2143	2148	2153	2158	2163	2168	2173	2178	2183	0	1	1	2	2	3	3	4	4
·34	2188	2193	2198	2203	2208	2213	2218	2223	2228	2234	1	1	2	2	3	3	4	4	5
·35	2239	2244	2249	2254	2259	2265	2270	2275	2280	2286	1	1	2	2	3	3	4	4	5
·36	2291	2296	2301	2307	2312	2317	2323	2328	2333	2339	1	1	2	2	3	3	4	4	5
·37	2344	2350	2355	2360	2366	2371	2377	2382	2388	2393	1	1	2	2	3	3	4	4	5
·38	2399	2404	2410	2415	2421	2427	2432	2438	2443	2449	1	1	2	2	3	3	4	4	5
·39	2455	2460	2466	2472	2477	2483	2489	2495	2500	2506	1	1	2	2	3	3	4	5	5
·40	2512	2518	2523	2529	2535	2541	2547	2553	2559	2564	1	1	2	2	3	4	4	5	5
·41	2570	2576	2582	2588	2594	2600	2606	2612	2618	2624	1	1	2	2	3	4	4	5	5
·42	2630	2636	2642	2649	2655	2661	2667	2673	2679	2685	1	1	2	2	3	4	4	5	6
·43	2692	2698	2704	2710	2716	2723	2729	2735	2742	2748	1	1	2	3	3	4	4	5	6
·44	2754	2761	2767	2773	2780	2786	2793	2799	2805	2812	1	1	2	3	3	4	4	5	6
·45	2818	2825	2831	2838	2844	2851	2858	2864	2871	2877	1	1	2	3	3	4	5	5	6
·46	2884	2891	2897	2904	2911	2917	2924	2931	2938	2944	1	1	2	3	3	4	5	5	6
·47	2951	2958	2965	2972	2979	2985	2992	2999	3006	3013	1	1	2	3	3	4	5	5	6
·48	3020	3027	3034	3041	3048	3055	3062	3069	3076	3083	1	1	2	3	4	4	5	6	6
·49	3090	3097	3105	3112	3119	3126	3133	3141	3148	3155	1	1	2	3	4	4	5	6	6
	0	1	2	3	4	5	6	7	8	9	1	2	3	4	5	6	7	8	9

	0	1	2	3	4	5	6	7	8	9	1	2	3	4	5	6	7	8	9
·50	3162	3170	3177	3184	3192	3199	3206	3214	3221	3228	1	1	2	3	4	4	5	6	7
·51	3236	3243	3251	3258	3266	3273	3281	3289	3296	3304	1	2	2	3	4	5	5	6	7
·52	3311	3319	3327	3334	3342	3350	3357	3365	3373	3381	1	2	2	3	4	5	5	6	7
·53	3388	3396	3404	3412	3420	3428	3436	3443	3451	3459	1	2	2	3	4	5	6	6	7
·54	3467	3475	3483	3491	3499	3508	3516	3524	3532	3540	1	2	2	3	4	5	6	6	7
·55	3548	3556	3565	3573	3581	3589	3597	3606	3614	3622	1	2	2	3	4	5	6	7	7
·56	3631	3639	3648	3656	3664	3673	3681	3690	3698	3707	1	2	3	3	4	5	6	7	8
·57	3715	3724	3733	3741	3750	3758	3767	3776	3784	3793	1	2	3	3	4	5	6	7	8
·58	3802	3811	3819	3828	3837	3846	3855	3864	3873	3882	1	2	3	4	4	5	6	7	8
·59	3890	3899	3908	3917	3926	3936	3945	3954	3963	3972	1	2	3	4	5	5	6	7	8
·60	3981	3990	3999	4009	4018	4027	4036	4046	4055	4064	1	2	3	4	5	6	6	7	8
·61	4074	4083	4093	4102	4111	4121	4130	4140	4150	4159	1	2	3	4	5	6	7	8	9
·62	4169	4178	4188	4198	4207	4217	4227	4236	4246	4256	1	2	3	4	5	6	7	8	9
·63	4266	4276	4285	4295	4305	4315	4325	4335	4345	4355	1	2	3	4	5	6	7	8	9
·64	4365	4375	4385	4395	4406	4416	4426	4436	4446	4457	1	2	3	4	5	6	7	8	9
·65	4467	4477	4487	4498	4508	4519	4529	4539	4550	4560	1	2	3	4	5	6	7	8	9
·66	4571	4581	4592	4603	4613	4624	4634	4645	4656	4667	1	2	3	4	5	6	7	9	10
·67	4677	4688	4699	4710	4721	4732	4742	4753	4764	4775	1	2	3	4	5	7	8	9	10
·68	4786	4797	4808	4819	4831	4842	4853	4864	4875	4887	1	2	3	4	6	7	8	9	10
·69	4898	4909	4920	4932	4943	4955	4966	4977	4989	5000	1	2	3	5	6	7	8	9	10
·70	5012	5023	5035	5047	5058	5070	5082	5093	5105	5117	1	2	4	5	6	7	8	9	11
·71	5129	5140	5152	5164	5176	5188	5200	5212	5224	5236	1	2	4	5	6	7	8	10	11
·72	5248	5260	5272	5284	5297	5309	5321	5333	5346	5358	1	2	4	5	6	7	9	10	11
·73	5370	5383	5395	5408	5420	5433	5445	5458	5470	5483	1	3	4	5	6	8	9	10	11
·74	5495	5508	5521	5534	5546	5559	5572	5585	5598	5610	1	3	4	5	6	8	9	10	12
·75	5623	5636	5649	5662	5675	5689	5702	5715	5728	5741	1	3	4	5	7	8	9	10	12
·76	5754	5768	5781	5794	5808	5821	5834	5848	5861	5875	1	3	4	5	7	8	9	11	12
·77	5888	5902	5916	5929	5943	5957	5970	5984	5998	6012	1	3	4	5	7	8	10	11	12
·78	6026	6039	6053	6067	6081	6095	6109	6124	6138	6152	1	3	4	6	7	8	10	11	13
·79	6166	6180	6194	6209	6223	6237	6252	6266	6281	6295	1	3	4	6	7	9	10	11	13
·80	6310	6324	6339	6353	6368	6383	6397	6412	6427	6442	1	3	4	6	7	9	10	12	13
·81	6457	6471	6486	6501	6516	6531	6546	6561	6577	6592	2	3	5	6	8	9	11	12	14
·82	6607	6622	6637	6653	6668	6683	6699	6714	6730	6745	2	3	5	6	8	9	11	12	14
·83	6761	6776	6792	6808	6823	6839	6855	6871	6887	6902	2	3	5	6	8	9	11	13	14
·84	6918	6934	6950	6966	6982	6998	7015	7031	7047	7063	2	3	5	6	8	10	11	13	15
·85	7079	7096	7112	7129	7145	7161	7178	7194	7211	7228	2	3	5	7	8	10	12	13	15
·86	7244	7261	7278	7295	7311	7328	7345	7362	7379	7396	2	3	5	7	8	10	12	13	15
·87	7413	7430	7447	7464	7482	7499	7516	7534	7551	7568	2	3	5	7	9	10	12	14	16
·88	7586	7603	7621	7638	7656	7674	7691	7709	7727	7745	2	4	5	7	9	11	12	14	16
·89	7762	7780	7798	7816	7834	7852	7870	7889	7907	7925	2	4	5	7	9	11	13	14	16
·90	7943	7962	7980	7998	8017	8035	8054	8072	8091	8110	2	4	6	7	9	11	13	15	17
·91	8128	8147	8166	8185	8204	8222	8241	8260	8279	8299	2	4	6	8	9	11	13	15	17
·92	8318	8337	8356	8375	8395	8414	8433	8453	8472	8492	2	4	6	8	10	12	14	15	17
·93	8511	8531	8551	8570	8590	8610	8630	8650	8670	8690	2	4	6	8	10	12	14	16	18
·94	8710	8730	8750	8770	8790	8810	8831	8851	8872	8892	2	4	6	8	10	12	14	16	18
·95	8913	8933	8954	8974	8995	9016	9036	9057	9078	9099	2	4	6	8	10	12	15	17	19
·96	9120	9141	9162	9183	9204	9226	9247	9268	9290	9311	2	4	6	8	11	13	15	17	19
·97	9333	9354	9376	9397	9419	9441	9462	9484	9506	9528	2	4	7	9	11	13	15	17	20
·98	9550	9572	9594	9616	9638	9661	9683	9705	9727	9750	2	4	7	9	11	13	16	18	20
·99	9772	9795	9817	9840	9863	9886	9908	9931	9954	9977	2	5	7	9	11	14	16	18	20
	0	1	2	3	4	5	6	7	8	9	1	2	3	4	5	6	7	8	9

NATURAL SINES (left-hand column and top)

Differences (ADD)

	0′	6′	12′	18′	24′	30′	36′	42′	48′	54′	—	1′	2′	3′	4′	5′	
0°	·0000	0017	0035	0052	0070	0087	0105	0122	0140	0157	·0175	3	6	9	12	15	89°
1	·0175	0192	0209	0227	0244	0262	0279	0297	0314	0332	·0349	3	6	9	12	15	88
2	·0349	0366	0384	0401	0419	0436	0454	0471	0488	0506	·0523	3	6	9	12	15	87
3	·0523	0541	0558	0576	0593	0610	0628	0645	0663	0680	·0698	3	6	9	12	15	86
4	·0698	0715	0732	0750	0767	0785	0802	0819	0837	0854	·0872	3	6	9	12	14	85
5	·0872	0889	0906	0924	0941	0958	0976	0993	1011	1028	·1045	3	6	9	12	14	84
6	·1045	1063	1080	1097	1115	1132	1149	1167	1184	1201	·1219	3	6	9	12	14	83
7	·1219	1236	1253	1271	1288	1305	1323	1340	1357	1374	·1392	3	6	9	12	14	82
8	·1392	1409	1426	1444	1461	1478	1495	1513	1530	1547	·1564	3	6	9	12	14	81
9	·1564	1582	1599	1616	1633	1650	1668	1685	1702	1719	·1736	3	6	9	11	14	80
10	·1736	1754	1771	1788	1805	1822	1840	1857	1874	1891	·1908	3	6	9	11	14	79
11	·1908	1925	1942	1959	1977	1994	2011	2028	2045	2062	·2079	3	6	9	11	14	78
12	·2079	2096	2113	2130	2147	2164	2181	2198	2215	2233	·2250	3	6	9	11	14	77
13	·2250	2267	2284	2300	2317	2334	2351	2368	2385	2402	·2419	3	6	8	11	14	76
14	·2419	2436	2453	2470	2487	2504	2521	2538	2554	2571	·2588	3	6	8	11	14	75
15	·2588	2605	2622	2639	2656	2672	2689	2706	2723	2740	·2756	3	6	8	11	14	74
16	·2756	2773	2790	2807	2823	2840	2857	2874	2890	2907	·2924	3	6	8	11	14	73
17	·2924	2940	2957	2974	2990	3007	3024	3040	3057	3074	·3090	3	6	8	11	14	72
18	·3090	3107	3123	3140	3156	3173	3190	3206	3223	3239	·3256	3	6	8	11	14	71
19	·3256	3272	3289	3305	3322	3338	3355	3371	3387	3404	·3420	3	5	8	11	14	70
20	·3420	3437	3453	3469	3486	3502	3518	3535	3551	3567	·3584	3	5	8	11	14	69
21	·3584	3600	3616	3633	3649	3665	3681	3697	3714	3730	·3746	3	5	8	11	14	68
22	·3746	3762	3778	3795	3811	3827	3843	3859	3875	3891	·3907	3	5	8	11	13	67
23	·3907	3923	3939	3955	3971	3987	4003	4019	4035	4051	·4067	3	5	8	11	13	66
24	·4067	4083	4099	4115	4131	4147	4163	4179	4195	4210	·4226	3	5	8	11	13	65
25	·4226	4242	4258	4274	4289	4305	4321	4337	4352	4368	·4384	3	5	8	11	13	64
26	·4384	4399	4415	4431	4446	4462	4478	4493	4509	4524	·4540	3	5	8	10	13	63
27	·4540	4555	4571	4586	4602	4617	4633	4648	4664	4679	·4695	3	5	8	10	13	62
28	·4695	4710	4726	4741	4756	4772	4787	4802	4818	4833	·4848	3	5	8	10	13	61
29	·4848	4863	4879	4894	4909	4924	4939	4955	4970	4985	·5000	3	5	8	10	13	60
30	·5000	5015	5030	5045	5060	5075	5090	5105	5120	5135	·5150	3	5	8	10	13	59
31	·5150	5165	5180	5195	5210	5225	5240	5255	5270	5284	·5299	2	5	7	10	12	58
32	·5299	5314	5329	5344	5358	5373	5388	5402	5417	5432	·5446	2	5	7	10	12	57
33	·5446	5461	5476	5490	5505	5519	5534	5548	5563	5577	·5592	2	5	7	10	12	56
34	·5592	5606	5621	5635	5650	5664	5678	5693	5707	5721	·5736	2	5	7	10	12	55
35	·5736	5750	5764	5779	5793	5807	5821	5835	5850	5864	·5878	2	5	7	9	12	54
36	·5878	5892	5906	5920	5934	5948	5962	5976	5990	6004	·6018	2	5	7	9	12	53
37	·6018	6032	6046	6060	6074	6088	6101	6115	6129	6143	·6157	2	5	7	9	12	52
38	·6157	6170	6184	6198	6211	6225	6239	6252	6266	6280	·6293	2	5	7	9	11	51
39	·6293	6307	6320	6334	6347	6361	6374	6388	6401	6414	·6428	2	4	7	9	11	50
40	·6428	6441	6455	6468	6481	6494	6508	6521	6534	6547	·6561	2	4	7	9	11	49
41	·6561	6574	6587	6600	6613	6626	6639	6652	6665	6678	·6691	2	4	7	9	11	48
42	·6691	6704	6717	6730	6743	6756	6769	6782	6794	6807	·6820	2	4	6	9	11	47
43	·6820	6833	6845	6858	6871	6884	6896	6909	6921	6934	·6947	2	4	6	8	11	46
44	·6947	6959	6972	6984	6997	7009	7022	7034	7046	7059	·7071	2	4	6	8	10	45
	—	54′	48′	42′	36′	30′	24′	18′	12′	6′	0′	1′	2′	3′	4′	5′	

Differences (SUBTRACT)

NATURAL COSINES (right-hand column and bottom)

NATURAL SINES (left-hand column and top)

Differences (ADD)

	0′	6′	12′	18′	24′	30′	36′	42′	48′	54′	—	1′	2′	3′	4′	5′	
45°	·7071	7083	7096	7108	7120	7133	7145	7157	7169	7181	·7193	2	4	6	8	10	44°
46	·7193	7206	7218	7230	7242	7254	7266	7278	7290	7302	·7314	2	4	6	8	10	43
47	·7314	7325	7337	7349	7361	7373	7385	7396	7408	7420	·7431	2	4	6	8	10	42
48	·7431	7443	7455	7466	7478	7490	7501	7513	7524	7536	·7547	2	4	6	8	10	41
49	·7547	7559	7570	7581	7593	7604	7615	7627	7638	7649	·7660	2	4	6	8	9	40
50	·7660	7672	7683	7694	7705	7716	7727	7738	7749	7760	·7771	2	4	6	7	9	39
51	·7771	7782	7793	7804	7815	7826	7837	7848	7859	7869	·7880	2	4	5	7	9	38
52	·7880	7891	7902	7912	7923	7934	7944	7955	7965	7976	·7986	2	4	5	7	9	37
53	·7986	7997	8007	8018	8028	8039	8049	8059	8070	8080	·8090	2	3	5	7	9	36
54	·8090	8100	8111	8121	8131	8141	8151	8161	8171	8181	·8192	2	3	5	7	8	35
55	·8192	8202	8211	8221	8231	8241	8251	8261	8271	8281	·8290	2	3	5	7	8	34
56	·8290	8300	8310	8320	8329	8339	8348	8358	8368	8377	·8387	2	3	5	6	8	33
57	·8387	8396	8406	8415	8425	8434	8443	8453	8462	8471	·8480	2	3	5	6	8	32
58	·8480	8490	8499	8508	8517	8526	8536	8545	8554	8563	·8572	2	3	5	6	8	31
59	·8572	8581	8590	8599	8607	8616	8625	8634	8643	8652	·8660	1	3	4	6	7	30
60	·8660	8669	8678	8686	8695	8704	8712	8721	8729	8738	·8746	1	3	4	6	7	29
61	·8746	8755	8763	8771	8780	8788	8796	8805	8813	8821	·8829	1	3	4	6	7	28
62	·8829	8838	8846	8854	8862	8870	8878	8886	8894	8902	·8910	1	3	4	5	7	27
63	·8910	8918	8926	8934	8942	8949	8957	8965	8973	8980	·8988	1	3	4	5	6	26
64	·8988	8996	9003	9011	9018	9026	9033	9041	9048	9056	·9063	1	3	4	5	6	25
65	·9063	9070	9078	9085	9092	9100	9107	9114	9121	9128	·9135	1	2	4	5	6	24
66	·9135	9143	9150	9157	9164	9171	9178	9184	9191	9198	·9205	1	2	3	5	6	23
67	·9205	9212	9219	9225	9232	9239	9245	9252	9259	9265	·9272	1	2	3	4	6	22
68	·9272	9278	9285	9291	9298	9304	9311	9317	9323	9330	·9336	1	2	3	4	5	21
69	·9336	9342	9348	9354	9361	9367	9373	9379	9385	9391	·9397	1	2	3	4	5	20
70	·9397	9403	9409	9415	9421	9426	9432	9438	9444	9449	·9455	1	2	3	4	5	19
71	·9455	9461	9466	9472	9478	9483	9489	9494	9500	9505	·9511	1	2	3	4	5	18°
72	·9511	9516	9521	9527	9532	9537	9542	9548	9553	9558	·9563	1	2	3	4	4	17
73	·9563	9568	9573	9578	9583	9588	9593	9598	9603	9608	·9613	1	2	2	3	4	16
74	·9613	9617	9622	9627	9632	9636	9641	9646	9650	9655	·9659	1	2	2	3	4	15
75	·9659	9664	9668	9673	9677	9681	9686	9690	9694	9699	·9703	1	1	2	3	4	14
76	·9703	9707	9711	9715	9720	9724	9728	9732	9736	9740	·9744	1	1	2	3	3	13
77	·9744	9748	9751	9755	9759	9763	9767	9770	9774	9778	·9781	1	1	2	3	3	12
78	·9781	9785	9789	9792	9796	9799	9803	9806	9810	9813	·9816	1	1	2	2	3	11
79	·9816	9820	9823	9826	9829	9833	9836	9839	9842	9845	·9848	1	1	2	2	3	10
80	·9848	9851	9854	9857	9860	9863	9866	9869	9871	9874	·9877	0	1	1	2	2	9
81	·9877	9880	9882	9885	9888	9890	9893	9895	9898	9900	·9903	0	1	1	2	2	8
82	·9903	9905	9907	9910	9912	9914	9917	9919	9921	9923	·9925	0	1	1	2	2	7
83	·9925	9928	9930	9932	9934	9936	9938	9940	9942	9943	·9945	0	1	1	1	2	6
84	·9945	9947	9949	9951	9952	9954	9956	9957	9959	9960	·9962	0	1	1	1	1	5
85	·9962	9963	9965	9966	9968	9969	9971	9972	9973	9974	·9976	0	0	1	1	1	4
86	·9976	9977	9978	9979	9980	9981	9982	9983	9984	9985	·9986	0	0	1	1	1	3
87	·9986	9987	9988	9989	9990	9990	9991	9992	9993	9993	·9994						2
88	·9994	9995	9995	9996	9996	9997	9997	9997	9998	9998	·9998						1
89	·9998	9999	9999	9999	9999	1·000	1·000	1·000	1·000	1·000	1·0000						0
	—	54′	48′	42′	36′	30′	24′	18′	12′	6′	0′	1′	2′	3′	4′	5′	

The bold type indicates that the integer changes.

Differences (SUBTRACT)

NATURAL COSINES (right-hand column and bottom)

NATURAL TANGENTS (left-hand column and top)

Differences (ADD)

	0′	6′	12′	18′	24′	30′	36′	42′	48′	54′	—	1′	2′	3′	4′	5′	
0°	0·0000	0017	0035	0052	0070	0087	0105	0122	0140	0157	0·0175	3	6	9	12	15	89°
1	0·0175	0192	0209	0227	0244	0262	0279	0297	0314	0332	0·0349	3	6	9	12	15	88
2	0·0349	0367	0384	0402	0419	0437	0454	0472	0489	0507	0·0524	3	6	9	12	15	87
3	0·0524	0542	0559	0577	0594	0612	0629	0647	0664	0682	0·0699	3	6	9	12	15	86
4	0·0699	0717	0734	0752	0769	0787	0805	0822	0840	0857	0·0875	3	6	9	12	15	85
5	0·0875	0892	0910	0928	0945	0963	0981	0998	1016	1033	0·1051	3	6	9	12	15	84
6	0·1051	1069	1086	1104	1122	1139	1157	1175	1192	1210	0·1228	3	6	9	12	15	83
7	0·1228	1246	1263	1281	1299	1317	1334	1352	1370	1388	0·1405	3	6	9	12	15	82
8	0·1405	1423	1441	1459	1477	1495	1512	1530	1548	1566	0·1584	3	6	9	12	15	81
9	0·1584	1602	1620	1638	1655	1673	1691	1709	1727	1745	0·1763	3	6	9	12	15	80
10	0·1763	1781	1799	1817	1835	1853	1871	1890	1908	1926	0·1944	3	6	9	12	15	79
11	0·1944	1962	1980	1998	2016	2035	2053	2071	2089	2107	0·2126	3	6	9	12	15	78
12	0·2126	2144	2162	2180	2199	2217	2235	2254	2272	2290	0·2309	3	6	9	12	15	77
13	0·2309	2327	2345	2364	2382	2401	2419	2438	2456	2475	0·2493	3	6	9	12	15	76
14	0·2493	2512	2530	2549	2568	2586	2605	2623	2642	2661	0·2679	3	6	9	12	16	75
15	0·2679	2698	2717	2736	2754	2773	2792	2811	2830	2849	0·2867	3	6	9	13	16	74
16	0·2867	2886	2905	2924	2943	2962	2981	3000	3019	3038	0·3057	3	6	9	13	16	73
17	0·3057	3076	3096	3115	3134	3153	3172	3191	3211	3230	0·3249	3	6	10	13	16	72
18	0·3249	3269	3288	3307	3327	3346	3365	3385	3404	3424	0·3443	3	6	10	13	16	71
19	0·3443	3463	3482	3502	3522	3541	3561	3581	3600	3620	0·3640	3	7	10	13	16	70
20	0·3640	3659	3679	3699	3719	3739	3759	3779	3799	3819	0·3839	3	7	10	13	17	69
21	0·3839	3859	3879	3899	3919	3939	3959	3979	4000	4020	0·4040	3	7	10	13	17	68
22	0·4040	4061	4081	4101	4122	4142	4163	4183	4204	4224	0·4245	3	7	10	14	17	67
23	0·4245	4265	4286	4307	4327	4348	4369	4390	4411	4431	0·4452	3	7	10	14	17	66
24	0·4452	4473	4494	4515	4536	4557	4578	4599	4621	4642	0·4663	4	7	11	14	18	65
25	0·4663	4684	4706	4727	4748	4770	4791	4813	4834	4856	0·4877	4	7	11	14	18	64
26	0·4877	4899	4921	4942	4964	4986	5008	5029	5051	5073	0·5095	4	7	11	15	18	63
27	0·5095	5117	5139	5161	5184	5206	5228	5250	5272	5295	0·5317	4	7	11	15	18	62
28	0·5317	5340	5362	5384	5407	5430	5452	5475	5498	5520	0·5543	4	8	11	15	19	61
29	0·5543	5566	5589	5612	5635	5658	5681	5704	5727	5750	0·5774	4	8	12	15	19	60
30	0·5774	5797	5820	5844	5867	5890	5914	5938	5961	5985	0·6009	4	8	12	16	20	59
31	0·6009	6032	6056	6080	6104	6128	6152	6176	6200	6224	0·6249	4	8	12	16	20	58
32	0·6249	6273	6297	6322	6346	6371	6395	6420	6445	6469	0·6494	4	8	12	16	20	57
33	0·6494	6519	6544	6569	6594	6619	6644	6669	6694	6720	0·6745	4	8	13	17	21	56
34	0·6745	6771	6796	6822	6847	6873	6899	6924	6950	6976	0·7002	4	9	13	17	21	55
35	0·7002	7028	7054	7080	7107	7133	7159	7186	7212	7239	0·7265	4	9	13	18	22	54
36	0·7265	7292	7319	7346	7373	7400	7427	7454	7481	7508	0·7536	5	9	14	18	23	53
37	0·7536	7563	7590	7618	7646	7673	7701	7729	7757	7785	0·7813	5	9	14	18	23	52
38	0·7813	7841	7869	7898	7926	7954	7983	8012	8040	8069	0·8098	5	9	14	19	24	51
39	0·8098	8127	8156	8185	8214	8243	8273	8302	8332	8361	0·8391	5	10	15	20	24	50
40	0·8391	8421	8451	8481	8511	8541	8571	8601	8632	8662	0·8693	5	10	15	20	25	49
41	0·8693	8724	8754	8785	8816	8847	8878	8910	8941	8972	0·9004	5	10	16	21	26	48
42	0·9004	9036	9067	9099	9131	9163	9195	9228	9260	9293	0·9325	5	11	16	21	27	47
43	0·9325	9358	9391	9424	9457	9490	9523	9556	9590	9623	0·9657	6	11	17	22	28	46
44	0·9657	9691	9725	9759	9793	9827	9861	9896	9930	9965	1·0000	6	11	17	23	29	45
	—	54′	48′	42′	36′	30′	24′	18′	12′	6′	0′	1′	2′	3′	4′	5′	

The bold type indicates that the integer changes.

Differences (SUBTRACT)

NATURAL COTANGENTS (right-hand column and bottom)

NATURAL TANGENTS (left-hand column and top)

	0′	6′	12′	18′	24′	30′	36′	42′	48′	54′	—	1′	2′	3′	4′	5′	
												Differences (ADD)					
45°	1·0000	0035	0070	0105	0141	0176	0212	0247	0283	0319	1·0355	6	12	18	24	30	**44°**
46	1·0355	0392	0428	0464	0501	0538	0575	0612	0649	0686	1·0724	6	12	18	25	31	**43**
47	1·0724	0761	0799	0837	0875	0913	0951	0990	1028	1067	1·1106	6	13	19	25	32	**42**
48	1·1106	1145	1184	1224	1263	1303	1343	1383	1423	1463	1·1504	7	13	20	26	33	**41**
49	1·1504	1544	1585	1626	1667	1708	1750	1792	1833	1875	1·1918	7	14	21	28	34	**40**
50	1·1918	1960	2002	2045	2088	2131	2174	2218	2261	2305	1·2349	7	14	22	29	36	**39**
51	1·2349	2393	2437	2482	2527	2572	2617	2662	2708	2753	1·2799	8	15	23	30	38	**38**
52	1·2799	2846	2892	2938	2985	3032	3079	3127	3175	3222	1·3270	8	16	24	31	39	**37**
53	1·3270	3319	3367	3416	3465	3514	3564	3613	3663	3713	1·3764	8	16	25	33	41	**36**
54	1·3764	3814	3865	3916	3968	4019	4071	4124	4176	4229	1·4281	9	17	26	34	43	**35**
55	1·4281	4335	4388	4442	4496	4550	4605	4659	4715	4770	1·4826	9	18	27	36	45	**34**
56	1·4826	4882	4938	4994	5051	5108	5166	5224	5282	5340	1·5399	10	19	29	38	48	**33**
57	1·5399	5458	5517	5577	5637	5697	5757	5818	5880	5941	1·6003	10	20	30	40	50	**32**
58	1·6003	6066	6128	6191	6255	6319	6383	6447	6512	6577	1·6643	11	21	32	43	53	**31**
59	1·6643	6709	6775	6842	6909	6977	7045	7113	7182	7251	1·7321	11	23	34	45	56	**30**
60	1·7321	7391	7461	7532	7603	7675	7747	7820	7893	7966	1·8040	12	24	36	48	60	**29**
61	1·8040	8115	8190	8265	8341	8418	8495	8572	8650	8728	1·8807	13	26	38	51	64	**28**
62	1·8807	8887	8967	9047	9128	9210	9292	9375	9458	9542	1·9626	14	27	41	55	68	**27**
63	1·9626	9711	9797	9883	9970	**0057**	**0145**	**0233**	**0323**	**0413**	2·0503	15	29	44	58	73	**26**
64	2·0503	0594	0686	0778	0872	0965	1060	1155	1251	1348	2·1445	16	31	47	63	78	**25**
65	2·1445	1543	1642	1742	1842	1943	2045	2148	2251	2355	2·2460	17	34	51	68	85	**24**
66	2·2460	2566	2673	2781	2889	2998	3109	3220	3332	3445	2·3559	18	37	55	73	91	**23**
67	2·3559	3673	3789	3906	4023	4142	4262	4383	4504	4627	2·4751	20	40	60	79	99	**22**
68	2·4751	4876	5002	5129	5257	5386	5517	5649	5782	5916	2·6051	22	43	65	87	108	**21**
69	2·6051	6187	6325	6464	6605	6746	6889	7034	7179	7326	2·7475	24	47	71	95	119	**20**
70	2·7475	7625	7776	7929	8083	8239	8397	8556	8716	8878	2·9042	26	52	78	104	130	**19**
71	2·9042	9208	9375	9544	9714	9887	**0061**	**0237**	**0415**	**0595**	3·0777	29	58	87	116	144	**18**
72	3·0777	0961	1146	1334	1524	1716	1910	2106	2305	2506	3·2709	32	64	97	129	161	**17**
73	3·2709	2914	3122	3332	3544	3759	3977	4197	4420	4646	3·4874	36	72	108	144	180	**16**
74	3·4874	5105	5339	5576	5816	6059	6305	6554	6806	7062	3·7321	41	81	122	163	203	**15**
75	3·7321	7583	7848	8118	8391	8667	8947	9232	9520	9812	4·0108	46	93	139	186	232	**14**
76	4·0108	0408	0713	1022	1335	1653	1976	2303	2635	2972	4·3315	53	107	160	214	267	**13**
77	4·3315	3662	4015	4373	4737	5107	5483	5864	6252	6646	4·7046	62	124	186	248	310	**12**
78	4·7046	7453	7867	8288	8716	9152	9594	**0045**	**0504**	**0970**	**5·1466**	73	146	220	293	366	**11**
79	5·1446	1929	2422	2924	3435	3955	4486	5026	5578	6140	5·671	87	175	263	350	438	**10**
80	5·671	5·730	5·789	5·850	5·912	5·976	6·041	6·107	6·174	6·243	6·314						**9**
81	6·314	6·386	6·460	6·535	6·612	6·691	6·772	6·855	6·940	7·026	7·115						**8**
82	7·115	7·207	7·300	7·396	7·495	7·596	7·700	7·806	7·916	8·028	8·144						**7**
83	8·144	8·264	8·386	8·513	8·643	8·777	8·915	9·058	9·205	9·357	9·514						**6**
84	9·514	9·677	9·845	10·02	10·20	10·39	10·58	10·78	10·99	11·20	11·43	UNTRUSTWORTHY					**5**
85	11·43	11·66	11·91	12·16	12·43	12·71	13·00	13·30	13·62	13·95	14·30						**4**
86	14·30	14·67	15·06	15·46	15·89	16·35	16·83	17·34	17·89	18·46	19·08						**3**
87	19·08	19·74	20·45	21·20	22·02	22·90	23·86	24·90	26·03	27·27	28·64						**2**
88	28·64	30·14	31·82	33·69	35·80	38·19	40·92	44·07	47·74	52·08	57·29						**1**
89	57·29	63·66	71·62	81·85	95·49	114·6	143·2	191·0	286·5	573·0	∞						**0**
	—	54′	48′	42′	36′	30′	24′	18′	12′	6′	0′	1′	2′	3′	4′	5′	
												Differences (SUBTRACT)					

The bold type indicates that the integer changes.

NATURAL COTANGENTS (right-hand column and bottom)

LOG SINES (left-hand column and top)

Differences (ADD)

	0′	6′	12′	18′	24′	30′	36′	42′	48′	54′	—	1′	2′	3′	4′	5′	
0°	−∞	$\bar{3}$·242	5429	7190	8439	9408	0200	0870	1450	1961	$\bar{2}$·2419						89°
1	$\bar{2}$·2419	2832	3210	3558	3880	4179	4459	4723	4971	5206	$\bar{2}$·5428	UNTRUSTWORTHY					88
2	$\bar{2}$·5428	5640	5842	6035	6220	6397	6567	6731	6889	7041	$\bar{2}$·7188						87
3	$\bar{2}$·7188	7330	7468	7602	7731	7857	7979	8098	8213	8326	$\bar{2}$·8436	21	41	62	83	103	86
4	$\bar{2}$·8436	8543	8647	8749	8849	8946	9042	9135	9226	9315	$\bar{2}$·9403	16	32	48	64	80	85
5	$\bar{2}$·9403	9489	9573	9655	9736	9816	9894	9970	0046	0120	$\bar{1}$·0192	13	26	39	52	66	84
6	$\bar{1}$·0192	0264	0334	0403	0472	0539	0605	0670	0734	0797	$\bar{1}$·0859	11	22	33	44	55	83
7	$\bar{1}$·0859	0920	0981	1040	1099	1157	1214	1271	1326	1381	$\bar{1}$·1436	10	19	29	38	48	82
8	$\bar{1}$·1436	1489	1542	1594	1646	1697	1747	1797	1847	1895	$\bar{1}$·1943	8	17	25	34	43	81
9	$\bar{1}$·1943	1991	2038	2085	2131	2176	2221	2266	2310	2353	$\bar{1}$·2397	8	15	23	30	38	80
10	$\bar{1}$·2397	2439	2482	2524	2565	2606	2647	2687	2727	2767	$\bar{1}$·2806	7	14	20	27	34	79
11	$\bar{1}$·2806	2845	2883	2921	2959	2997	3034	3070	3107	3143	$\bar{1}$·3179	6	12	19	25	31	78
12	$\bar{1}$·3179	3214	3250	3284	3319	3353	3387	3421	3455	3488	$\bar{1}$·3521	6	11	17	23	28	77
13	$\bar{1}$·3521	3554	3586	3618	3650	3682	3713	3745	3775	3806	$\bar{1}$·3837	5	11	16	21	26	76
14	$\bar{1}$·3837	3867	3897	3927	3957	3986	4015	4044	4073	4102	$\bar{1}$·4130	5	10	15	20	24	75
15	$\bar{1}$·4130	4158	4186	4214	4242	4269	4296	4323	4350	4377	$\bar{1}$·4403	5	9	14	18	23	74
16	$\bar{1}$·4403	4430	4456	4482	4508	4533	4559	4584	4609	4634	$\bar{1}$·4659	4	9	13	17	21	73
17	$\bar{1}$·4659	4684	4709	4733	4757	4781	4805	4829	4853	4876	$\bar{1}$·4900	4	8	12	16	20	72
18	$\bar{1}$·4900	4923	4946	4969	4992	5015	5037	5060	5082	5104	$\bar{1}$·5126	4	8	11	15	19	71
19	$\bar{1}$·5126	5148	5170	5192	5213	5235	5256	5278	5299	5320	$\bar{1}$·5341	4	7	11	14	18	70
20	$\bar{1}$·5341	5361	5382	5402	5423	5443	5463	5484	5504	5523	$\bar{1}$·5543	3	7	10	14	17	69
21	$\bar{1}$·5543	5563	5583	5602	5621	5641	5660	5679	5698	5717	$\bar{1}$·5736	3	6	10	13	16	68
22	$\bar{1}$·5736	5754	5773	5792	5810	5828	5847	5865	5883	5901	$\bar{1}$·5919	3	6	9	12	15	67
23	$\bar{1}$·5919	5937	5954	5972	5990	6007	6024	6042	6059	6076	$\bar{1}$·6093	3	6	9	12	15	66
24	$\bar{1}$·6093	6110	6127	6144	6161	6177	6194	6210	6227	6243	$\bar{1}$·6259	3	6	8	11	14	65
25	$\bar{1}$·6259	6276	6292	6308	6324	6340	6356	6371	6387	6403	$\bar{1}$·6418	3	5	8	11	13	64
26	$\bar{1}$·6418	6434	6449	6465	6480	6495	6510	6526	6541	6556	$\bar{1}$·6570	3	5	8	10	13	63
27	$\bar{1}$·6570	6585	6600	6615	6629	6644	6659	6673	6687	6702	$\bar{1}$·6716	2	5	7	10	12	62
28	$\bar{1}$·6716	6730	6744	6759	6773	6787	6801	6814	6828	6842	$\bar{1}$·6856	2	5	7	9	12	61
29	$\bar{1}$·6856	6869	6883	6896	6910	6923	6937	6950	6963	6977	$\bar{1}$·6990	2	4	7	9	11	60
30	$\bar{1}$·6990	7003	7016	7029	7042	7055	7068	7080	7093	7106	$\bar{1}$·7118	2	4	6	9	11	59
31	$\bar{1}$·7118	7131	7144	7156	7168	7181	7193	7205	7218	7230	$\bar{1}$·7242	2	4	6	8	10	58
32	$\bar{1}$·7242	7254	7266	7278	7290	7302	7314	7326	7338	7349	$\bar{1}$·7361	2	4	6	8	10	57
33	$\bar{1}$·7361	7373	7384	7396	7407	7419	7430	7442	7453	7464	$\bar{1}$·7476	2	4	6	8	10	56
34	$\bar{1}$·7476	7487	7498	7509	7520	7531	7542	7553	7564	7575	$\bar{1}$·7586	2	4	6	7	9	55
35	$\bar{1}$·7586	7597	7607	7618	7629	7640	7650	7661	7671	7682	$\bar{1}$·7692	2	4	5	7	9	54
36	$\bar{1}$·7692	7703	7713	7723	7734	7744	7754	7764	7774	7785	$\bar{1}$·7795	2	3	5	7	9	53
37	$\bar{1}$·7795	7805	7815	7825	7835	7844	7854	7864	7874	7884	$\bar{1}$·7893	2	3	5	7	8	52
38	$\bar{1}$·7893	7903	7913	7922	7932	7941	7951	7960	7970	7979	$\bar{1}$·7989	2	3	5	6	8	51
39	$\bar{1}$·7989	7998	8007	8017	8026	8035	8044	8053	8063	8072	$\bar{1}$·8081	2	3	5	6	8	50
40	$\bar{1}$·8081	8090	8099	8108	8117	8125	8134	8143	8152	8161	$\bar{1}$·8169	1	3	4	6	7	49
41	$\bar{1}$·8169	8178	8187	8195	8204	8213	8221	8230	8238	8247	$\bar{1}$·8255	1	3	4	6	7	48
42	$\bar{1}$·8255	8264	8272	8280	8289	8297	8305	8313	8322	8330	$\bar{1}$·8338	1	3	4	6	7	47
43	$\bar{1}$·8338	8346	8354	8362	8370	8378	8386	8394	8402	8410	$\bar{1}$·8418	1	3	4	5	7	46
44	$\bar{1}$·8418	8426	8433	8441	8449	8457	8464	8472	8480	8487	$\bar{1}$·8495	1	3	4	5	6	45
	—	54′	48′	42′	36′	30′	24′	18′	12′	6′	0′	1′	2′	3′	4′	5′	

The bold type indicates that the integer changes.

Differences (SUBTRACT)

LOG COSINES (right-hand column and bottom)

LOG SINES (left-hand column and top)

Differences (ADD)

	0′	6′	12′	18′	24′	30′	36′	42′	48′	54′	—	1′	2′	3′	4′	5′	
45°	1̄·8495	8502	8510	8517	8525	8532	8540	8547	8555	8562	1̄·8569	1	2	4	5	6	44°
46	1̄·8569	8577	8584	8591	8598	8606	8613	8620	8627	8634	1̄·8641	1	2	4	5	6	43
47	1̄·8641	8648	8655	8662	8669	8676	8683	8690	8697	8704	1̄·8711	1	2	3	5	6	42
48	1̄·8711	8718	8724	8731	8738	8745	8751	8758	8765	8771	1̄·8778	1	2	3	4	6	41
49	1̄·8778	8784	8791	8797	8804	8810	8817	8823	8830	8836	1̄·8843	1	2	3	4	5	40
50	1̄·8843	8849	8855	8862	8868	8874	8880	8887	8893	8899	1̄·8905	1	2	3	4	5	39
51	1̄·8905	8911	8917	8923	8929	8935	8941	8947	8953	8959	1̄·8965	1	2	3	4	5	38
52	1̄·8965	8971	8977	8983	8989	8995	9000	9006	9012	9018	1̄·9023	1	2	3	4	5	37
53	1̄·9023	9029	9035	9041	9046	9052	9057	9063	9069	9074	1̄·9080	1	2	3	4	5	36
54	1̄·9080	9085	9091	9096	9101	9107	9112	9118	9123	9128	1̄·9134	1	2	3	4	5	35
55	1̄·9134	9139	9144	9149	9155	9160	9165	9170	9175	9181	1̄·9186	1	2	3	3	4	34
56	1̄·9186	9191	9196	9201	9206	9211	9216	9221	9226	9231	1̄·9236	1	2	3	3	4	33
57	1̄·9236	9241	9246	9251	9255	9260	9265	9270	9275	9279	1̄·9284	1	2	2	3	4	32
58	1̄·9284	9289	9294	9298	9303	9308	9312	9317	9322	9326	1̄·9331	1	2	2	3	4	31
59	1̄·9331	9335	9340	9344	9349	9353	9358	9362	9367	9371	1̄·9375	1	1	2	3	4	30
60	1̄·9375	9380	9384	9388	9393	9397	9401	9406	9410	9414	1̄·9418	1	1	2	3	4	29
61	1̄·9418	9422	9427	9431	9435	9439	9443	9447	9451	9455	1̄·9459	1	1	2	3	3	28
62	1̄·9459	9463	9467	9471	9475	9479	9483	9487	9491	9495	1̄·9499	1	1	2	3	3	27
63	1̄·9499	9503	9506	9510	9514	9518	9522	9525	9529	9533	1̄·9537	1	1	2	3	3	26
64	1̄·9537	9540	9544	9548	9551	9555	9558	9562	9566	9569	1̄·9573	1	1	2	2	3	25
65	1̄·9573	9576	9580	9583	9587	9590	9594	9597	9601	9604	1̄·9607	1	1	2	2	3	24
66	1̄·9607	9611	9614	9617	9621	9624	9627	9631	9634	9637	1̄·9640	1	1	2	2	3	23
67	1̄·9640	9643	9647	9650	9653	9656	9659	9662	9666	9669	1̄·9672	1	1	2	2	3	22
68	1̄·9672	9675	9678	9681	9684	9687	9690	9693	9696	9699	1̄·9702	0	1	1	2	2	21
69	1̄·9702	9704	9707	9710	9713	9716	9719	9722	9724	9727	1̄·9730	0	1	1	2	2	20
70	1̄·9730	9733	9735	9738	9741	9743	9746	9749	9751	9754	1̄·9757	0	1	1	2	2	19
71	1̄·9757	9759	9762	9764	9767	9770	9772	9775	9777	9780	1̄·9782	0	1	1	2	2	18
72	1̄·9782	9785	9787	9789	9792	9794	9797	9799	9801	9804	1̄·9806	0	1	1	2	2	17
73	1̄·9806	9808	9811	9813	9815	9817	9820	9822	9824	9826	1̄·9828	0	1	1	1	2	16
74	1̄·9828	9831	9833	9835	9837	9839	9841	9843	9845	9847	1̄·9849	0	1	1	1	2	15
75	1̄·9849	9851	9853	9855	9857	9859	9861	9863	9865	9867	1̄·9869	0	1	1	1	2	14
76	1̄·9869	9871	9873	9875	9876	9878	9880	9882	9884	9885	1̄·9887	0	1	1	1	2	13
77	1̄·9887	9889	9891	9892	9894	9896	9897	9899	9901	9902	1̄·9904	0	1	1	1	1	12
78	1̄·9904	9906	9907	9909	9910	9912	9913	9915	9916	9918	1̄·9919	0	1	1	1	1	11
79	1̄·9919	9921	9922	9924	9925	9927	9928	9929	9931	9932	1̄·9934	0	0	1	1	1	10
80	1̄·9934	9935	9936	9937	9939	9940	9941	9943	9944	9945	1̄·9946	0	0	1	1	1	9
81	1̄·9946	9947	9949	9950	9951	9952	9953	9954	9955	9956	1̄·9958	0	0	1	1	1	8
82	1̄·9958	9959	9960	9961	9962	9963	9964	9965	9966	9967	1̄·9968	0	0	0	1	1	7
83	1̄·9968	9968	9969	9970	9971	9972	9973	9974	9975	9975	1̄·9976	0	0	0	1	1	6
84	1̄·9976	9977	9978	9978	9979	9980	9981	9981	9982	9983	1̄·9983						5
85	1̄·9983	9984	9985	9985	9986	9987	9987	9988	9988	9989	1̄·9989						4
86	1̄·9989	9990	9990	9991	9991	9992	9992	9993	9993	9994	1̄·9994						3
87	1̄·9994	9994	9995	9995	9996	9996	9996	9996	9997	9997	1̄·9997						2
88	1̄·9997	9998	9998	9998	9998	9999	9999	9999	9999	9999	1̄·9999						1
89	1̄·9999	9999	0000	0000	0000	0000	0000	0000	0000	0000	0·0000						0
	—	54′	48′	42′	36′	30′	24′	18′	12′	6′	0′	1′	2′	3′	4′	5′	

The bold type indicates that the integer changes.

Differences (SUBTRACT)

LOG COSINES (right-hand column and bottom)

LOG TANGENTS (left-hand column and top)

Differences (ADD)

	0′	6′	12′	18′	24′	30′	36′	42′	48′	54′	—	1′	2′	3′	4′	5′	
0°	−∞	$\bar{3}$·2419	$\bar{3}$·5429	$\bar{3}$·7190	$\bar{3}$·8439	$\bar{3}$·9409	$\bar{2}$·0200	$\bar{2}$·0870	$\bar{2}$·1450	$\bar{2}$·1962	$\bar{2}$·2419						**89°**
1	$\bar{2}$·2419	2833	3211	3559	3881	4181	4461	4725	4973	5208	$\bar{2}$·5431						**88**
2	$\bar{2}$·5431	5643	5845	6038	6223	6401	6571	6736	6894	7046	$\bar{2}$·7194						**87**
3	$\bar{2}$·7194	7337	7475	7609	7739	7865	7988	8107	8223	8336	$\bar{2}$·8446	20	41	62	83	104	**86**
4	$\bar{2}$·8446	8554	8659	8762	8862	8960	9056	9150	9241	9331	$\bar{2}$·9420	16	32	48	65	81	**85**
5	$\bar{2}$·9420	9506	9591	9674	9756	9836	9915	9992	**0068**	**0143**	$\bar{1}$·0216	13	26	40	53	66	**84**
6	$\bar{1}$·0216	0289	0360	0430	0499	0567	0633	0699	0764	0828	$\bar{1}$·0891	11	22	34	45	56	**83**
7	$\bar{1}$·0891	0954	1015	1076	1135	1194	1252	1310	1367	1423	$\bar{1}$·1478	10	20	29	39	49	**82**
8	$\bar{1}$·1478	1533	1587	1640	1693	1745	1797	1848	1898	1948	$\bar{1}$·1997	9	17	26	35	43	**81**
9	$\bar{1}$·1997	2046	2094	2142	2189	2236	2282	2328	2374	2419	$\bar{1}$·2463	8	16	23	31	39	**80**
10	$\bar{1}$·2463	2507	2551	2594	2637	2680	2722	2764	2805	2846	$\bar{1}$·2887	7	14	21	28	35	**79**
11	$\bar{1}$·2887	2927	2967	3006	3046	3085	3123	3162	3200	3237	$\bar{1}$·3275	6	13	19	26	32	**78**
12	$\bar{1}$·3275	3312	3349	3385	3422	3458	3493	3529	3564	3599	$\bar{1}$·3634	6	12	18	24	30	**77**
13	$\bar{1}$·3634	3668	3702	3736	3770	3804	3837	3870	3903	3935	$\bar{1}$·3968	6	11	17	22	28	**76**
14	$\bar{1}$·3968	4000	4032	4064	4095	4127	4158	4189	4220	4250	$\bar{1}$·4281	5	10	16	21	26	**75**
15	$\bar{1}$·4281	4311	4341	4371	4400	4430	4459	4488	4517	4546	$\bar{1}$·4575	5	10	15	20	25	**74**
16	$\bar{1}$·4575	4603	4632	4660	4688	4716	4744	4771	4799	4826	$\bar{1}$·4853	5	9	14	19	23	**73**
17	$\bar{1}$·4853	4880	4907	4934	4961	4987	5014	5040	5066	5092	$\bar{1}$·5118	4	9	13	18	22	**72**
18	$\bar{1}$·5118	5143	5169	5195	5220	5245	5270	5295	5320	5345	$\bar{1}$·5370	4	8	13	17	21	**71**
19	$\bar{1}$·5370	5394	5419	5443	5467	5491	5516	5539	5563	5587	$\bar{1}$·5611	4	8	12	16	20	**70**
20	$\bar{1}$·5611	5634	5658	5681	5704	5727	5750	5773	5796	5819	$\bar{1}$·5842	4	8	12	15	19	**69**
21	$\bar{1}$·5842	5864	5887	5909	5932	5954	5976	5998	6020	6042	$\bar{1}$·6064	4	7	11	15	19	**68**
22	$\bar{1}$·6064	6086	6108	6129	6151	6172	6194	6215	6236	6257	$\bar{1}$·6279	4	7	11	14	18	**67**
23	$\bar{1}$·6279	6300	6321	6341	6362	6383	6404	6424	6445	6465	$\bar{1}$·6486	3	7	10	14	17	**66**
24	$\bar{1}$·6486	6506	6527	6547	6567	6587	6607	6627	6647	6667	$\bar{1}$·6687	3	7	10	13	17	**65**
25	$\bar{1}$·6687	6706	6726	6746	6765	6785	6804	6824	6843	6863	$\bar{1}$·6882	3	7	10	13	16	**64**
26	$\bar{1}$·6882	6901	6920	6939	6958	6977	6996	7015	7034	7053	$\bar{1}$·7072	3	6	9	13	16	**63**
27	$\bar{1}$·7072	7090	7109	7128	7146	7165	7183	7202	7220	7238	$\bar{1}$·7257	3	6	9	12	15	**62**
28	$\bar{1}$·7257	7275	7293	7311	7330	7348	7366	7384	7402	7420	$\bar{1}$·7438	3	6	9	12	15	**61**
29	$\bar{1}$·7438	7455	7473	7491	7509	7526	7544	7562	7579	7597	$\bar{1}$·7614	3	6	9	12	15	**60**
30	$\bar{1}$·7614	7632	7649	7667	7684	7701	7719	7736	7753	7771	$\bar{1}$·7788	3	6	9	12	14	**59**
31	$\bar{1}$·7788	7805	7822	7839	7856	7873	7890	7907	7924	7941	$\bar{1}$·7958	3	6	9	11	14	**58**
32	$\bar{1}$·7958	7975	7992	8008	8025	8042	8059	8075	8092	8109	$\bar{1}$·8125	3	6	8	11	14	**57**
33	$\bar{1}$·8125	8142	8158	8175	8191	8208	8224	8241	8257	8274	$\bar{1}$·8290	3	5	8	11	14	**56**
34	$\bar{1}$·8290	8306	8323	8339	8355	8371	8388	8404	8420	8436	$\bar{1}$·8452	3	5	8	11	14	**55**
35	$\bar{1}$·8452	8468	8484	8501	8517	8533	8549	8565	8581	8597	$\bar{1}$·8613	3	5	8	11	13	**54**
36	$\bar{1}$·8613	8629	8644	8660	8676	8692	8708	8724	8740	8755	$\bar{1}$·8771	3	5	8	11	13	**53**
37	$\bar{1}$·8771	8787	8803	8818	8834	8850	8865	8881	8897	8912	$\bar{1}$·8928	3	5	8	10	13	**52**
38	$\bar{1}$·8928	8944	8959	8975	8990	9006	9022	9037	9053	9068	$\bar{1}$·9084	3	5	8	10	13	**51**
39	$\bar{1}$·9084	9099	9115	9130	9146	9161	9176	9192	9207	9223	$\bar{1}$·9238	3	5	8	10	13	**50**
40	$\bar{1}$·9238	9254	9269	9284	9300	9315	9330	9346	9361	9376	$\bar{1}$·9392	3	5	8	10	13	**49**
41	$\bar{1}$·9392	9407	9422	9438	9453	9468	9483	9499	9514	9529	$\bar{1}$·9544	3	5	8	10	13	**48**
42	$\bar{1}$·9544	9560	9575	9590	9605	9621	9636	9651	9666	9681	$\bar{1}$·9697	3	5	8	10	13	**47**
43	$\bar{1}$·9697	9712	9727	9742	9757	9772	9788	9803	9818	9833	$\bar{1}$·9848	3	5	8	10	13	**46**
44	$\bar{1}$·9848	9864	9879	9894	9909	9924	9939	9955	9970	9985	0·0000	3	5	8	10	13	**45**
	—	54′	48′	42′	36′	30′	24′	18′	12′	6′	0′	1′	2′	3′	4′	5′	

The bold type indicates that the integer changes.

Differences (SUBTRACT)

LOG COTANGENTS (right-hand column and bottom)

WEIGHTS AND MEASURES

LENGTH

British

12 inches (in.)	=1 foot (ft.).
3 feet	=1 yard (yd.).
22 yards	=1 chain (ch.).
10 chains	=1 furlong (fur.).
8 furlongs	=1 mile (mi.).

220 yards	=1 furlong.
1760 yards	=1 mile.

100 links	=1 chain.
$5\frac{1}{2}$ yards	=1 pole (p.), rod, perch.
40 poles	=1 furlong.
4 inches	=1 hand.
6 feet	=1 fathom.
600 feet	=1 cable.

1 knot = 1 nautical mile per hour.
= about 6080 feet per hour.

Metric

10 *milli*metres (mm.)	=1 *centi*metre (cm.).
10 centimetres	=1 *deci*metre (dm.).
10 decimetres	=1 metre (m.).
10 metres	=1 *deka*metre (Dm.).
10 dekametres	=1 *hecto*metre (Hm.).
10 hectometres	=1 *kilo*metre (Km., km.).

Approximate equivalents

1 inch	= 2·540 cm.
1 yard	= 0·9144 m.
1 mile	= 1·6093 Km.
1 metre	= 39·37 in.
	= 1·0936 yd.
1 Km.	= 0·6214 mi.
	= about $\frac{5}{8}$ mi.

AREA

144 (or 12^2) sq. inches	=1 sq. foot.
9 (or 3^2) sq. ft.	=1 sq. yard.
484 (or 22^2) sq. yd.	=1 sq. chain.
10 sq. ch.	=1 acre (ac.)
640 acres	=1 sq. mile.

$30\frac{1}{4}$ (or $5\frac{1}{2} \times 5\frac{1}{2}$) sq. yd.	=1 sq. pole (p.).
40 sq. poles	=1 rood (r.).
4 roods	=1 acre.
4840 sq. yards	=1 acre.
10,000 (or 100^2) sq. links	=1 sq. chain.

100 (or 10^2) sq. mm.	=1 sq. cm.
100 (or 10^2) sq. cm.	=1 sq. dm.
100 (or 10^2) sq. dm.	=1 sq. m.

and so on.

1 are (a.) = 1 sq. dekametre.
100 centiares (ca.) = 1 are.
100 ares = 1 hectare (Ha.).

Approximate equivalents

1 sq. in.	= 6·4516 sq. cm.
1 sq. cm.	= 0·15500 sq. in.
1 acre	= 0·4047 Ha.
1 are	= 119·6 sq. yd.
1 hectare	= 2·471 ac. (about $2\frac{1}{2}$ ac.).

LOG TANGENTS (left-hand column and top)

Differences (ADD)

	0′	6′	12′	18′	24′	30′	36′	42′	48′	54′	—	1′	2′	3′	4′	5′	
45°	0·0000	0015	0030	0045	0061	0076	0091	0106	0121	0136	0·0152	3	5	8	10	13	44°
46	0·0152	0167	0182	0197	0212	0228	0243	0258	0273	0288	0·0303	3	5	8	10	13	43
47	0·0303	0319	0334	0349	0364	0379	0395	0410	0425	0440	0·0456	3	5	8	10	13	42
48	0·0456	0471	0486	0501	0517	0532	0547	0562	0578	0593	0·0608	3	5	8	10	13	41
49	0·0608	0624	0639	0654	0670	0685	0700	0716	0731	0746	0·0762	3	5	8	10	13	40
50	0·0762	0777	0793	0808	0824	0839	0854	0870	0885	0901	0·0916	3	5	8	10	13	39
51	0·0916	0932	0947	0963	0978	0994	1010	1025	1041	1056	0·1072	3	5	8	10	13	38
52	0·1072	1088	1103	1119	1135	1150	1166	1182	1197	1213	0·1229	3	5	8	10	13	37
53	0·1229	1245	1260	1276	1292	1308	1324	1340	1356	1371	0·1387	3	5	8	11	13	36
54	0·1387	1403	1419	1435	1451	1467	1483	1499	1516	1532	0·1548	3	5	8	11	13	35
55	0·1548	1564	1580	1596	1612	1629	1645	1661	1677	1694	0·1710	3	5	8	11	14	34
56	0·1710	1726	1743	1759	1776	1792	1809	1825	1842	1858	0·1875	3	5	8	11	14	33
57	0·1875	1891	1908	1925	1941	1958	1975	1992	2008	2025	0·2042	3	6	8	11	14	32
58	0·2042	2059	2076	2093	2110	2127	2144	2161	2178	2195	0·2212	3	6	9	11	14	31
59	0·2212	2229	2247	2264	2281	2299	2316	2333	2351	2368	0·2386	3	6	9	12	14	30
60	0·2386	2403	2421	2438	2456	2474	2491	2509	2527	2545	0·2562	3	6	9	12	15	29
61	0·2562	2580	2598	2616	2634	2652	2670	2689	2707	2725	0·2743	3	6	9	12	15	28
62	0·2743	2762	2780	2798	2817	2835	2854	2872	2891	2910	0·2928	3	6	9	12	15	27
63	0·2928	2947	2966	2985	3004	3023	3042	3061	3080	3099	0·3118	3	6	9	13	16	26
64	0·3118	3137	3157	3176	3196	3215	3235	3254	3274	3294	0·3313	3	7	10	13	16	25
65	0·3313	3333	3353	3373	3393	3413	3433	3453	3473	3494	0·3514	3	7	10	13	17	24
66	0·3514	3535	3555	3576	3596	3617	3638	3659	3679	3700	0·3721	3	7	10	14	17	23
67	0·3721	3743	3764	3785	3806	3828	3849	3871	3892	3914	0·3936	4	7	11	14	18	22
68	0·3936	3958	3980	4002	4024	4046	4068	4091	4113	4136	0·4158	4	7	11	15	19	21
69	0·4158	4181	4204	4227	4250	4273	4296	4319	4342	4366	0·4389	4	8	12	15	19	20
70	0·4389	4413	4437	4461	4484	4509	4533	4557	4581	4606	0·4630	4	8	12	16	20	19
71	0·4630	4655	4680	4705	4730	4755	4780	4805	4831	4857	0·4882	4	8	13	17	21	18
72	0·4882	4908	4934	4960	4986	5013	5039	5066	5093	5120	0·5147	4	9	13	18	22	17
73	0·5147	5174	5201	5229	5256	5284	5312	5340	5368	5397	0·5425	5	9	14	19	23	16
74	0·5425	5454	5483	5512	5541	5570	5600	5629	5659	5689	0·5719	5	10	15	20	25	15
75	0·5719	5750	5780	5811	5842	5873	5905	5936	5968	6000	0·6032	5	10	16	21	26	14
76	0·6032	6065	6097	6130	6163	6196	6230	6264	6298	6332	0·6366	6	11	17	22	28	13
77	0·6366	6401	6436	6471	6507	6542	6578	6615	6651	6688	0·6725	6	12	18	24	30	12
78	0·6725	6763	6800	6838	6877	6915	6954	6994	7033	7073	0·7113	6	13	19	26	32	11
79	0·7113	7154	7195	7236	7278	7320	7363	7406	7449	7493	0·7537	7	14	21	28	35	10
80	0·7537	7581	7626	7672	7718	7764	7811	7858	7906	7954	0·8003	8	16	23	31	39	9
81	0·8003	8052	8102	8152	8203	8255	8307	8360	8413	8467	0·8522	9	17	26	35	43	8
82	0·8522	8577	8633	8690	8748	8806	8865	8924	8985	9046	0·9109	10	20	29	39	49	7
83	0·9109	9172	9236	9301	9367	9433	9501	9570	9640	9711	0·9784	11	22	34	45	56	6
84	0·9784	9857	9932	**0008**	**0085**	**0164**	**0244**	**0326**	**0409**	**0494**	1·0580	13	26	40	53	66	5
85	1·0580	0669	0759	0850	0944	1040	1138	1238	1341	1446	1·1554	16	32	48	65	81	4
86	1·1554	1664	1777	1893	2012	2135	2261	2391	2525	2663	1·2806	20	41	62	83	104	3
87	1·2806	2954	3106	3264	3429	3599	3777	3962	4155	4357	1·4569						2
88	1·4569	4792	5027	5275	5539	5819	6119	6441	6789	7167	1·7581	UNTRUST-					1
89	1·7581	1·8038	1·8550	1·9130	1·9800	2·0591	2·1561	2·2810	2·4571	2·7581	∞	WORTHY					0
	—	54′	48′	42′	36′	30′	24′	18′	12′	6′	0′	1′	2′	3′	4′	5′	

Differences (SUBTRACT)

The bold type indicates that the integer changes.

LOG COTANGENTS (right-hand column and bottom)

INDEX

ANSWERS

ANSWERS TO ARITHMETIC SECTION

EXERCISES 1A (p. 8)

1. 23·2. **2.** 0·465. **3.** 27·6. **4.** 260. **5.** 445.
6. 4430. **7.** 0·845. **8.** 42·1. **9.** 0·0222. **10.** 0·0627.

EXERCISES 1B (p. 8)

1. 9·14. **2.** 175. **3.** 0·223. **4.** 0·00168. **5.** 1·41.
6. 0·000115. **7.** 0·296. **8.** 2·30. **9.** 3·07. **10.** 318.

EXERCISES 2A (p. 10)

1. 1·3806. **2.** $\bar{3}$·3436. **3.** $\bar{4}$·2863. **4.** $\bar{1}$·4403. **5.** $\bar{3}$·7037.
6. 5·35. **7.** 0·424. **8.** 0·375. **9.** 0·299. **10.** 0·0168.

EXERCISES 2B (p. 10)

1. 0·3885. **2.** $\bar{4}$·1537. **3.** $\bar{1}$·1333. **4.** $\bar{3}$·8111. **5.** $\bar{1}$·4722.
6. 3·18. **7.** 0·918. **8.** 0·832. **9.** 0·574. **10.** 2·09.

EXERCISES 3 (p. 12)

1. 0·0780. **2.** 2·58. **3.** 48·7. **4.** 4990 cm^3. **5.** 0·223.
6. 0·945. **7.** 1·70. **8.** 153. **9.** 1·21. **10.** 7·90.
11. 0·748. **12.** 52·5. **13.** 0·00835. **14.** 123. **15.** 1·11.
16. 0·878. **17.** 0·656. **18.** 21·8. **19.** 0·919. **20.** 1190.
21. 0·876. **22.** 29·7. **23.** 13·7. **24.** 14·2. **25.** 0·859.
26. 1·22. **27.** 0·703. **28.** 0·0518. **29.** 0·165. **30.** 0·00102.

EXERCISES 4A (p. 18)

1. 11·6 cm^2. **2.** $4\frac{8}{13}$ cm. **3.** 7·2 cm. **4.** 180 cm^2.
5. 4·5 cm. **6.** 62 cm^3. **7.** 20 m^3. **8.** 0·9.
9. 4000 kg. **10.** 100.

EXERCISES 4B (p. 18)

1. 42·4 cm^2. **2.** 6 cm. **3.** 13 cm. **4.** 49·1 cm^3.
5. 4 m. **6.** 100 m^3. **7.** 156 cm^3. **8.** 108 m.
9. 600 m^3. **10.** 1000 kg.

EXERCISES 5A (p. 23)

1. 4·46 cm. **2.** 3·66 cm. **3.** 1·99 cm. **4.** 106 g.
5. 4330 cm^3. **6.** 377 cm^2. **7.** 5·82 cm. **8.** 283 cm^2.
9. 11·3. **10.** 96·8 cm^3. **11.** 12 cm. **12.** 110 cm^3.

EXERCISES 5B (p. 24)

1. 154 cm. **2.** 405 m^2. **3.** 3140. **4.** 9·08 cm^3.
5. 302 cm^2. **6.** 2·93 cm. **7.** 4·67 cm. **8.** 9·65.
9. 264 cm^3. **10.** 2980 cm^3. **11.** 28 cm. **12.** 7 cm.

EXERCISES 6 (p. 26)

1. $\frac{2}{3}$ cm. **2.** 2730 m^2. **3.** 900. **4.** 0·0015 cm.
5. $\frac{4}{27}$ cm. **6.** 11·3 cm^2. **8.** 2·59. **9.** 100.
10. 1920 g. **11.** 16·7 m/sec; 2 min. **12.** 1040 m^3.
13. 99·3 cm^2. **14.** 1670. **15.** 720 m^3; 384 m^2.
16. 16 cm. **17.** 2·19 m. **18.** 16·7 cm. **19.** 16·4 cm^2.
20. 123. **21.** 0·87 cm. **22.** 6360. **23.** $4\frac{1}{2}$ cm^3.
24. 2·02 cm. **25.** 2·88 cm. **26.** 19·5 m^3; 52·8 m^2.
27. 7·68. **28.** $\sqrt{\frac{9}{4\sqrt{3}}}$. **29.** 5·54 m; 12·8 m^3.
30. 7·14 m; 57·1 m^3.

EXERCISES 7A (p. 29)

1. $\frac{4}{150}$. **2.** $\frac{3}{10}$. **3.** $\frac{1}{3}$. **4.** $\frac{1}{3}$. **5.** $\frac{1}{24}$.
6. $\frac{1}{8}$. **7.** 40. **8.** $\frac{1}{10}$. **9.** $\frac{7}{1000}$. **10.** $\frac{1}{100}$.

EXERCISES 7B (p. 30)

1. $\frac{3}{8}$. **2.** $\frac{3}{7}$. **3.** $\frac{5}{48}$. **4.** $\frac{10}{9}$. **5.** $\frac{250}{21}$.
6. $\frac{5}{7}$. **7.** $\frac{500}{41}$. **8.** $\frac{1}{50}$. **9.** $\frac{7}{50}$. **10.** $\frac{75}{2}$.

EXERCISES 8A (p. 31)

1. 8 cm, 14 cm, 16 cm. **2.** 9 cm, 21 cm, 30 cm.
3. £2, £3. **4.** £70, £105, £175. **5.** 54, 36, 24.
6. 20. **7.** £80, £40, £20. **8.** £4, £3, £1·50.
9. 8 : 12 : 21. **10.** 50, 25, 50.

EXERCISES 8B (p. 31)

1. 54, 72, 120. **2.** £750, £500, £250. **3.** £3·75, £4, £4·25.
4. 9 cm, 12 cm, 15 cm. **5.** 21. **6.** 21. **7.** £9, £12.
8. £5, £2·50. **9.** £15, £10. **10.** 21 : 14 : 24.

EXERCISES 9A (p. 32)

1. 35·4. **2.** 3·47. **3.** $47\frac{1}{2}$. **4.** 74. **5.** $4\frac{3}{8}$.
6. $4\frac{2}{5}$. **7.** 38. **8.** 36. **9.** $37\frac{1}{2}$. **10.** £4·$27\frac{1}{2}$.

EXERCISES 9B (p. 33)

1. 1·19. **2.** 45·6. **3.** 5·21. **4.** $17\frac{1}{2}$. **5.** $91\frac{1}{2}$.
6. 70·4. **7.** 21. **8.** 4·2. **9.** £2·$12\frac{1}{2}$. **10.** 8·82.

EXERCISES 10A (p. 34)

1. 20. **2.** 25. **3.** £0·60. **4.** £5·62$\frac{1}{2}$. **5.** £54.
6. $\frac{1}{2}$. **7.** £10. **8.** 12. **9.** £5. **10.** $9\frac{1}{11}$.

EXERCISES 10B (p. 35)

1. 20. **2.** £32. **3.** $37\frac{1}{2}$. **4.** $38\frac{8}{9}$. **5.** £25.
6. $16\frac{2}{3}$. **7.** £3. **8.** £11·25. **9.** $6\frac{1}{4}$% fall. **10.** 188.

EXERCISES 11 (p. 38)

1. £24. **2.** £750, £1500, £3000. **3.** 264.
4. 16. **5.** $9\frac{1}{3}$. **6.** 8·16. **7.** 12·5. **8.** 800.
9. £5·75. **10.** £75. **11.** £5·50. **12.** $66\frac{2}{3}$.
13. £80. **14.** $9\frac{1}{11}$. **15.** £2000. **16.** 78·5. **17.** 100.
18. $8\frac{1}{3}$, £37·40. **19.** 200. **20.** 50. **21.** 6.
22. 51·2. **23.** £11, 229. **24.** £550, $28\frac{4}{7}$. **25.** £3. **26.** £2·70.
27. £50. **28.** 92·7. **29.** 46·1. **30.** 80%, $23\frac{1}{2}$ new pence.
31. 16. **32.** 57·9. **33.** 25; 25. **34.** $43\frac{3}{4}$. **35.** $33\frac{1}{3}$.

EXERCISES 12A (p. 43)

1. £136. **2.** £18·15. **3.** $3\frac{1}{2}$. **4.** $2\frac{1}{2}$. **5.** 5 years.
6. $2\frac{1}{2}$ years. **7.** £1640. **8.** £200. **9.** £500. **10.** £505.

EXERCISES 12B (p. 43)

1. £80·80. **2.** £22. **3.** $2\frac{1}{2}$. **4.** $3\frac{1}{2}$.
5. 4 years. **6.** $2\frac{1}{2}$ years. **7.** £848. **8.** £750.
9. £97·60. **10.** £500.

EXERCISES 13A (p. 45)

1. £24·97. **2.** £45·18. **3.** £9·45.
4. £46·26. **5.** £27·82.

EXERCISES 13B (p. 46)

1. £43·10. **2.** £17·05. **3.** £24·05.
4. £22·41. **5.** £37·87.

EXERCISES 14 (p.47)

1. £2759·50. **2.** £545. **3.** £219.
4. £1169·86. **5.** 3·1%. **6.** 14·2 years. **7.** 4·7.
8. 4th. **9.** £5065. **10.** 120 days. **11.** £215·04.
12. £170·30. **13.** £188·38. **14.** £165, £222. **15.** 8 years.
16. £45·98. **17.** £34·30. **18.** 15 years. **19.** 49,719.
20. £65. **21.** £3870·68. **22.** £700. **23.** £34·20.

24. £3193. **25.** 16·4. **26.** £98·70.
27. 78%, £3120. **28.** $\frac{£y^4}{x^3}$. **29.** £0·07½.
30. £108. **31.** £318·36. **32.** £726.
33. £36. **34.** 10 years. **35.** £268.

EXERCISES 15A (p. 51)

1. £46·44. **2.** £71·76. **3.** 75 new pence. **4.** 3·5 new pence. **5.** £52.

EXERCISES 15B (p. 51)

1. £88·36. **2.** £59·07. **3.** 77 new pence.
4. £480 000. **5.** £72.

EXERCISES 16A (p. 52)

1. £57·40. **2.** £840. **3.** £387·50. **4.** £208. **5.** £1000.

EXERCISES 16B (p. 52)

1. £46·80. **2.** £507. **3.** £223·12½. **4.** £480. **5.** £116.

EXERCISES 17A (p. 54)

1. £97·50. **2.** £40. **3.** £350. **4.** £145, £11.
5. £1300. **6.** £532·40, £14·96. **7.** £52·50.
8. £20. **9.** £1050. **10.** 5000.

EXERCISES 17B (p. 55)

1. £90. **2.** £24. **3.** £555. **4.** 107. **5.** £270.
6. 160. **7.** £40. **8.** £18. **9.** £1·50. **10.** £4.

EXERCISES 18A (p. 56)

1. $4\frac{4}{9}$. **2.** $6\frac{2}{13}$. **3.** $7\frac{1}{2}$. **4.** $5\frac{5}{11}$. **5.** $5\frac{5}{17}$.

EXERCISES 18B (p. 56)

1. $4\frac{2}{3}$. **2.** $6\frac{2}{5}$. **3.** 5. **4.** $4\frac{16}{21}$. **5.** 8.

EXERCISES 19 (p. 57)

1. £134. **2.** £9·17. **3.** £79. **4.** £113·40.
5. £190. **6.** Flat by £29. **7.** $7\frac{11}{27}$. **8.** 13.20.
9. £1. **10.** £500, £12·50. **11.** 1·4%. **12.** Gain $33\frac{1}{3}$%.
13. $28\frac{29}{32}$. **14.** £222·30. **15.** £1400. **16.** Increase £90.
17. £110. **18.** £117·32½. **19.** £44. **20.** $4\frac{1}{2}$%.
21. 4·28%. **22.** £500. **23.** £750. **24.** £1170.
25. £800. **26.** £800. **27.** $77\frac{7}{9}$. **28.** £22.
29. £245, £9·45. **30.** £32·08.

ANSWERS TO ALGEBRA AND CALCULUS SECTION

EXERCISES 20A (p. 66)

1. $(x+2)(x+3)$. **2.** $(x-10)(x+2)$. **3.** $(x-3)(x+2)$.
4. $(x-2)(x-3)$. **5.** $(x-5)(x-3)$. **6.** $(x-6)(x+2)$.
7. $(x+9)(x+2)$. **8.** $(x^2+6)(x^2+4)$. **9.** $(x+y)(x+3y)$.
10. $(x^2-5y)(x^2+y)$. **11.** $(x+1)(2x-3)$. **12.** $(2x+3y)(x-2y)$.
13. $(3x+2)(x-3)$. **14.** $(5x+2y)(x+3y)$. **15.** $(3x-2)(2x-5)$.
16. $(3+x)(2-x)$. **17.** $(3-2x)(4+3x)$. **18.** $(2x+5)(x+3)$.
19. $(2x+5)(x-3)$. **20.** $(4x+5)(3x-2)$.

EXERCISES 20B (p. 66)

1. $(x+4)(x+2)$. **2.** $(t-9)(t+2)$. **3.** $(u-6)(u+1)$.
4. $(v+5)(v+2)$. **5.** $(y-6)(y+4)$. **6.** $(x-11y)(x+y)$.
7. $(x+8y)(x+2y)$. **8.** $(x^2+4)(x^2+1)$. **9.** $(x+5y)(x+y)$.
10. $(z^2-4x)(z^2+2x)$. **11.** $(2p-7)(p+1)$. **12.** $(3a+2b)(2a+5b)$.
13. $(3l-4m)(2l-3m)$. **14.** $(7x+2)(x-3)$. **15.** $(4x^2+1)(3x^2+2)$.
16. $(4+x)(3-x)$. **17.** $(3-2x)(1+x)$. **18.** $(4y+1)(3y+2)$.
19. $(5+2x)(3-x)$. **20.** $(5+4x)(2-3x)$.

EXERCISES 21A (p. 67)

1. $(x+4)(x-4)$. **2.** $(p+3q)(p-3q)$. **3.** $(5x-y)(5x+y)$.
4. $(5a+4b)(5a-4b)$. **5.** $(a+2b-2c)(a-2b+2c)$.
6. $(3a+2b-2c)(3a-2b+2c)$. **7.** $(5a-5b+c)(5a-5b-c)$.
8. $(a-b+c-d)(a-b-c+d)$.
9. $(2a-2b+c-d)(2a-2b-c+d)$. **10.** $(1+3x)(1-3x)$.
11. $(2+5a)(2-5a)$. **12.** $(1+a-b)(1-a+b)$.
13. $(1+3a-3b)(1-3a+3b)$. **14.** $(4+a-b)(4-a+b)$.
15. $(5+4a-4b)(5-4a+4b)$. **16.** $(6+z)(6-z)$.
17. $3(6+z)(6-z)$. **18.** $(z^2+1)(z+1)(z-1)$.
19. $(x^2+4)(x+2)(x-2)$.
20. $(2a-2b+5c-5d)(2a-2b-5c+5d)$.

EXERCISES 21B (p. 68)

1. $(x+7)(x-7)$. **2.** $(a+8b)(a-8b)$. **3.** $(5p+8q)(5p-8q)$.
4. $(p+3q^2)(p-3q^2)$. **5.** $(1+7x)(1-7x)$.
6. $(3a-3b+c)(3a-3b-c)$.
7. $(a-b+3c-3d)(a-b-3c+3d)$. **8.** $(7+2x)(7-2x)$.
9. $(p+7r-7s)(p-7r+7s)$. **10.** $(3+a-b)(3-a+b)$.
11. $(1+4x^2)(1+2x)(1-2x)$. **12.** $7(1+3x)(1-3x)$.
13. $(4p+7q)(4p-7q)$. **14.** $(6+5z)(6-5z)$.
15. $(4+7a-7b)(4-7a+7b)$. **16.** $(x^4+4)(x^2+2)(x^2-2)$.
17. $(5a-5b+7c-7d)(5a-5b-7c+7d)$. **18.** $(a+9b^2)(a-9b^2)$.
19. $(2a-b+9c-3d)(2a-b-9c+3d)$.
20. $(12a+8b+5p+10q)(12a+8b-5p-10q)$.

EXERCISES 22A (p. 69)

1. $(x+y)(h+m+n)$. **2.** $(x+q)(p-6)$. **3.** $(x+y)(1-a)$.
4. $(x-q)(c-d)$. **5.** $(a-x)(b-y)$. **6.** $(a-1)^2(a+1)$.
7. $(a+b+c)(h+p)$. **8.** $(2a-b)(x+1)$. **9.** $(2a-b)(x-1)$.
10. $(a+b)(x+y)(x-y)$. **11.** $(b+c)(a-b-c)$.
12. $(a-3)(b-2c)$. **13.** $(x+y)(x-y-6)$.
14. $(x-y)(x+y-6)$. **15.** $(x+y)(x-y-1)$.
16. $(x-y)(x+y-1)$. **17.** $(x-4)(x-y)$. **18.** $(x+5)(x-y)$.
19. $(a+b)(c+d+1)$. **20.** $(a+b)(c+d-1)$.

EXERCISES 22B (p. 69)

1. $(a+b)(p-2q)$. **2.** $(a-b)(p-2q)$.
3. $(x+y)(a+b-2)$. **4.** $(x+y)(a+b-x-y)$.
5. $(a+1)(a^2+1)$. **6.** $(1+c)(3ab+2c)$.
7. $(p-q)(p+q+4)$. **8.** $(p-q)(p+q-5)$.
9. $(h+k)(h-k-6)$. **10.** $(a+2b)(a-2b-c)$.
11. $(a-3b)(a+3b-x)$. **12.** $(a+b)(a^2+a+1)$.
13. $(x-1)(2-x)$. **14.** $(h-k)(a-b)$.
15. $(h-k)(ah+ak+b)$. **16.** $(y-1)(x-1)$.
17. $(a-b)(a+c)$. **18.** $(a-b)(a-c)$.
19. $(x-2b)(x-c)$. **20.** $(z-2a)(z+b)$.

EXERCISES 23A (p. 70)

1. $(2a+b)(4a^2-2ab+b^2)$. **2.** $(z+1)(z^2-z+1)$.
3. $(z^2+1)(z^4-z^2+1)$. **4.** $(z+1)(z-1)(z^4+z^2+1)$.
5. $(a-bc)(a^2+abc+b^2c^2)$. **6.** $(a-3bc)(a^2+3abc+9b^2c^2)$.
7. $(4h-k)(16h^2+4hk+k^2)$. **8.** $(4h+3)(16h^2-12h+9)$.
9. $(a-2)(a^2+2a+4)$. **10.** $(2-3b)(4+6b+9b^2)$.

EXERCISES 23B (p. 70)

1. $(3a+b)(9a^2-3ab+b^2)$. **2.** $(z+2)(z^2-2z+4)$.
3. $(z^2+2)(z^4-2z^2+4)$. **4.** $(z^2-2)(z^4+2z^2+4)$.
5. $(h-2mn)(h^2+2mnh+4m^2n^2)$.
6. $(1-3bc)(1+3bc+9b^2c^2)$. **7.** $(4-h)(16+4h+h^2)$.
8. $(4h-3)(16h^2+12h+9)$. **9.** $(5a-1)(25a^2+5a+1)$.
10. $(2-5x)(4+10x+25x^2)$.

EXERCISES 24A (p. 70)

1. $(a+1)(a+1-x)$. **2.** $(x+3)(x+1+a)$.
3. $(x+y+z)(x+y-z)$. **4.** $(2z+2x+1)(2z-2x-1)$
5. $(z+2)(z+1+a)$. **6.** $(x+1)(a-x-3)$.
7. $(x+p+y)(x+p-y)$. **8.** $(4x+1)(x+1-y)$.
9. $(1+a-b)(1-a+b)$. **10.** $(x+5)(x+2+y)$.

EXERCISES 24B (p. 71)

1. $(a + 2)(a + 3 + x)$. **2.** $(x + 1)(x + 2 + a)$.
3. $(x + 2 + z)(x + 2 - z)$. **4.** $(z + x + 3)(z - x - 3)$.
5. $(p - 6)(p + 1 + q)$. **6.** $(y + 1)(a - y - 1)$.
7. $(x + 3p + 3y)(x + 3p - 3y)$. **8.** $(2x + 1)(x + 1 + y)$.
9. $(4 + a + b)(4 - a - b)$. **10.** $(x + 4)(x + 3 + y)$.

EXERCISES 25 (p. 71)

1. $(y - 7)(y + 6)$. **2.** 199. **3.** 9180.
4. $(2a - 3b)(a - 6b)$. **5.** 9. **6.** 81.
7. 9. **8.** 4. **9.** $(x + 3)(a - y)$.
10. $(x + 1)(ax + a + 1)$. **11.** $(1 + 3p + q)(1 - 3p - q)$.
12. $(x + 1)(x - 3)$. **13.** $(x + 1)(y + 1)(x - 1)(1 - y)$.
14. $(x - y)(x + y + 1)(x^2 + y^2 + x + y + 2)$. **15.** $(y - 8)(x + 5)$.
16. $x + 2$. **17.** $\dfrac{1}{x + 1}$. **18.** $\left(3a - \dfrac{1}{a}\right)^2$.
19. $(R - r)(R - 3r)$. **20.** $a(b - 2)(b^2 + 2b + 4)$.
21. $x(y + 4)(y^2 - 4y + 16)$.
22. $(1 - 5ab)(1 + 5ab + 25a^2b^2)$.
23. $(3 + 2abc)(9 - 6abc + 4a^2b^2c^2)$.
24. $(a - b + x - y - z)(a - b - x + y + z)$.
25. $(4c + a - b - d)(4c - a + b + d)$.
26. $(3a - 3b + 7c - 7d)(3a - 3b - 7c + 7d)$.
27. $(a + 7)(a + 2 - x)$. **28.** $x(x + 2)(x + 3)(x + 7)$.
29. $3(a + 1)(a + 3)(a^2 + 2a + 3)$. **30.** $a(b^2 + b + 1)$.
31. $x - 3$. **32.** $(a - x)(a + x - 1)$.
33. $(a^2 + b^2)(x^2 + y^2)$. **34.** $(lx + my)(lx + my - 3)$.
35. $4\pi r(3R^2 + 3Rr + r^2)$. **36.** $(x + 5)(x^2 + 4)$.
37. $\frac{1}{2}mu(2v + 3u)$. **38.** 2.
39. $(x - 1)(x - 2)(x - 3)$. **40.** $(x + 1)(x - 1)(x + 4)$.

EXERCISES 26A (p. 74)

1. $\frac{6}{5}$.	**2.** 1.	**3.** 4.	**4.** 1.	**5.** 4.
6. 12.	**7.** 2.	**8.** $\frac{12}{13}$.	**9.** 5.	**10.** -2.
11. 4.	**12.** -15.	**13.** $-\frac{7}{9}$.	**14.** $-\frac{61}{62}$.	**15.** -7.
16. 2.	**17.** $-\frac{1}{3}$.	**18.** 3.	**19.** 0.	**20.** $\frac{1}{4}$.

EXERCISES 26B (p. 75)

1. $\frac{8}{3}$.	**2.** 2.	**3.** $\frac{17}{4}$.	**4.** 1.	**5.** -3.
6. 40.	**7.** 3.	**8.** $\frac{60}{47}$.	**9.** -13.	**10.** $\frac{17}{5}$.
11. $-\frac{6}{7}$.	**12.** -6.	**13.** $\frac{8}{7}$.	**14.** $-\frac{97}{87}$.	**15.** $-\frac{5}{3}$.
16. 7.	**17.** $-\frac{1}{5}$.	**18.** -2.	**19.** No solution.	**20.** $-\frac{6}{25}$.

EXERCISES 27A (p. 78)

1. 6, 2. **2.** $2\frac{1}{2}$, 2. **3.** $2\frac{1}{2}$, 1. **4.** 2, 1. **5.** 1, 1.
6. 2, 1. **7.** 2, 3. **8.** $\frac{3}{5}$, $-\frac{1}{5}$. **9.** 1, 1. **10.** 2, 1.
11. $\frac{16}{7}$, $-\frac{2}{7}$. **12.** 2, 3. **13.** 2, 3. **14.** 13. **15.** $\frac{8}{3}$, $-\frac{17}{3}$.
16. 36. **17.** $\frac{1}{2}$, 1. **18.** 5, 18. **19.** ± 1, ± 4. **20.** 12.

EXERCISES 27B (p. 79)

1. 4, 2. **2.** $\frac{5}{3}$, 3. **3.** 1, 1. **4.** 2, 4. **5.** 1, 1.
6. 2, 1. **7.** 3, 2. **8.** $-\frac{3}{5}$, $-\frac{4}{5}$. **9.** 1, 1. **10.** 3, 2.
11. $\frac{1}{3}$, $-\frac{2}{9}$. **12.** 3, 4. **13.** 4, 2. **14.** $-3\frac{1}{2}$. **15.** 2, 5.
16. 32. **17.** $\frac{19}{14}$, -19. **18.** 4, -5. **19.** ± 2, ± 3. **20.** 11.

EXERCISES 28A (p. 80)

1. 1, 3. **2.** 3, 2. **3.** 6, -1. **4.** -5, -2. **5.** 5, -2.
6. 6, -2. **7.** 4, -2. **8.** 9, 1. **9.** 9, -2. **10.** 2, $\frac{1}{2}$.
11. $\frac{1}{2}$, $\frac{1}{3}$. **12.** $\frac{1}{2}$, $\frac{2}{3}$. **13.** $-\frac{2}{3}$, -4. **14.** 2, $-2\frac{1}{2}$. **15.** 3, -6.
16. 2, $-\frac{3}{2}$. **17.** 4, $-\frac{5}{9}$. **18.** 5, -1. **19.** 5, $-\frac{1}{2}$. **20.** 5, $-\frac{1}{2}$.

EXERCISES 28B (p. 81)

1. 7, -1. **2.** 8, -2. **3.** 2, 12. **4.** 7, -3. **5.** 5, -4.
6. -9, -2. **7.** -3, -6. **8.** -4. **9.** 3, $\frac{1}{2}$. **10.** $\frac{2}{3}$, $-\frac{1}{2}$.
11. $\frac{4}{3}$, $\frac{3}{2}$. **12.** 5, $-\frac{2}{3}$. **13.** 7, $\frac{5}{2}$. **14.** 2, $-\frac{7}{2}$. **15.** 2, -3.
16. 1, $-\frac{18}{7}$. **17.** 3, $-\frac{1}{2}$. **18.** $-2\frac{1}{2}$. **19.** 2, $-\frac{2}{3}$. **20.** 2, $-\frac{2}{3}$.

EXERCISES 29A (p. 83)

1. 2·77, − 1·27. **2.** 0·77, − 0·43. **3.** 4·70, − 1·70.
4. 1·29, 0·31. **5.** 0·81, − 0·53. **6.** − 1·43, − 0·23.
7. − 1, 0·75. **8.** − 1·27, − 0·39. **9.** − 3·37, 2·37.
10. 2·62, 0·38. **11.** 3·87, 0·13. **12.** ± 1·58.
13. − 3·09, 2·09. **14.** 0·77, − 7·77. **15.** − 5·83, − 0·17.
16. − 2·30, 1·30. **17.** 1·62, − 0·62. **18.** − 0·38, − 2·62.
19. 0·86, − 0·19. **20.** 0, − 2.

EXERCISES 29B (p. 84)

1. 3·83, − 1·83. **2.** 1·85, − 0·18. **3.** 2·30, − 1·30.
4. − 0·69, 0·29. **5.** 0·77, − 0·43. **6.** 1·30, − 0·88.
7. − 2·28, − 0·22. **8.** − 1·40, 0·90. **9.** 1·79, − 2·79.
10. 4·79, 0·21. **11.** 5·92, 0·85. **12.** 0·58, − 2·58.
13. 1·41, − 3·91. **14.** 6·16, − 0·16. **15.** 2·39, − 1·89.
16. − 3·62, 2·62. **17.** 0·41, − 4·07. **18.** 3·79, − 0·79.
19. − 3·62, − 1·38. **20.** − 3·55, 1·88.

EXERCISES 30A (p. 85)

1. $\dfrac{d-b}{a-c}$. **2.** $\dfrac{ab}{b-a}$. **3.** $a+b$. **4.** $\dfrac{bc}{b+c-a}$.

5. $\dfrac{ab}{2b-a}$. **6.** $\dfrac{bl-am}{m-l}$. **7.** $-a-b$. **8.** $\dfrac{ap}{q-p}$.

9. $\dfrac{ab}{c(a+b)}$. **10.** $\sqrt{b^2+a^2}$. **11.** $\dfrac{A-2\pi r^2}{2\pi r}$. **12.** $\dfrac{A-\pi t^2}{2\pi t}$.

13. $\dfrac{fv}{v-f}$. **14.** $\dfrac{T^2 g}{4\pi^2}$. **15.** $\dfrac{A-\pi r^2}{\pi r}$. **16.** $\dfrac{2(s-ut)}{t^2}$.

17. $\sqrt{v^2-2fs}$. **18.** $\sqrt{r^2-(y-b)^2}+a$.

19. $\dfrac{bx^2-a}{x^2-1}$. **20.** $\dfrac{2(S-an)}{n(n-1)}$.

EXERCISES 30B (p. 86)

1. $\dfrac{2b-a}{a-b}$. **2.** $\dfrac{a}{a-1}$. **3.** $\dfrac{a}{1-b}$. **4.** $\dfrac{cd}{c+d}$.

5. $\dfrac{2ab-bc-ac}{a+b-2c}$. **6.** $\dfrac{c-d}{ad-cb}$. **7.** $a+b$.

8. $\dfrac{bp-aq}{q-p}$. **9.** $\dfrac{bc+ca+b^2}{b+c}$. **10.** $\sqrt{b^2-y^2}$.

11. $\dfrac{S}{n}-\dfrac{1}{2}(n-1)d$. **12.** $-\dfrac{ax^2+c}{x}$. **13.** $\dfrac{100I}{PT}$.

14. $100\left(\dfrac{A}{P}-1\right)$. **15.** $P-\dfrac{550H}{v}$. **16.** $\dfrac{v^2-u^2}{2s}$.

17. $\dfrac{uv}{u+v}$. **18.** $\dfrac{a}{b}\sqrt{b^2-y^2}$. **19.** $\dfrac{s}{t}-\frac{1}{2}ft$. **20.** $\dfrac{v^2-u^2}{2f}$.

EXERCISES 31A (p. 88)

1. 2, 3 or 3, 2. **2.** 3, 1 or $-\frac{2}{3}$, $\frac{25}{3}$. **3.** $\frac{1}{2}$, $\frac{1}{3}$.
4. 1, 1. **5.** 2, 1 or $-\frac{1}{2}$, $-\frac{1}{2}$.

EXERCISES 31B (p. 88)

1. 3, 4 or 4, 3. **2.** 1, 2 or $\frac{3}{2}$, $\frac{1}{2}$. **3.** 1, $\frac{1}{2}$.
4. ± 2, ± 3. **5.** $\frac{4}{3}$, $\frac{5}{3}$.

EXERCISES 32 (p. 88)

1. 1·2, − 3·5. **2.** $\dfrac{rS}{2}-\pi r^3$. **3.** $a \pm b$. **4.** − 3.

5. 3. **6.** $\sqrt{R^2-\dfrac{W}{q\pi}}$. **7.** 2, $-\frac{2}{7}$.

8. $\sqrt{P^2-(z+H)^2}$. **9.** 6, $7\frac{1}{2}$. **10.** − 1, 10.

11. $-\frac{5y}{3}$ or $-8y$.
12. $\frac{1}{24}, \frac{13}{30}$.
13. $2\frac{1}{4}, -\frac{3}{4}$.
14. ± 1.
15. $-1\frac{1}{2}$.
16. 1·17, − 0·95.
17. $a, 2 - a$.
18. 2·4.
19. $\frac{gtd}{gt^2 - d}$.
20. $\frac{3Q(Z+1)}{2(1-Z)}$.
21. $-6r$ or $\frac{6r}{5}$.
22. $\frac{1}{3}, \frac{2}{3}$.
23. q, p.
24. $\frac{1}{5}, \frac{12}{5}$.
25. 1·93, 0·40.
26. $\frac{x-c}{2c+3x}$.
27. $3, \frac{19}{8}$.
28. $\frac{x^2 - x + 7}{3(5-x)}$.
29. $-2b \pm 3c$.
30. 0·58, − 0·41.
31. $\frac{mc - bn}{am - bl}, \frac{an - lc}{am - bl}$.
32. $3, -\frac{1}{3}$.
33. $\pm 4, \pm 6$.
34. 3, 2.
35. $1, \frac{1}{2}$ or $\frac{5}{11}, -\frac{7}{22}$.
36. a, b.

EXERCISES 33A (p. 91)

1. $(x-1)(x+1)(x-2)$.
2. $6(x-1)(x+1)$.
3. $(x-a)(x+a)(x-b)$.
4. $(x-a)^2(x+a)$.
5. $(x^2+a^2)(x+a)(x-a)$.
6. $y(y-1)(y-2)$.
7. $z(z-1)^2$.
8. $z(z-1)(z+1)$.
9. $3(t-1)(t+1)$.
10. $(p-1)(p-2)(p-3)$.

EXERCISES 33B (p. 91)

1. $(x-1)(x-2)(x+2)$.
2. $6(x+1)^2$.
3. $(x+a)(x-a)(x-1)$.
4. $x(x-a)^2$.
5. $(x^2+1)(x+1)^2$.
6. $y(y-1)(y+1)$.
7. $3y(y-1)(y+1)$.
8. $z(z-1)(z+1)$.
9. $6(a-b)(a+b)$.
10. $(x-1)(x+1)(x-2)(x+2)$.

EXERCISES 34A (p. 93)

1. $\frac{17}{12x}$.
2. $\frac{2x}{(x+1)(x-1)}$.
3. $\frac{2x}{(2-x)(4-x)}$.
4. $\frac{x}{12}$.
5. $\frac{(x+1)^2}{x(x+2)}$.
6. $\frac{x+3}{12x}$.
7. $\frac{3-x}{2(x+1)(x-1)}$.
8. $\frac{1}{(a-c)(c-b)}$.
9. $\frac{x+4}{x(x+1)(x+2)}$.
10. $\frac{3}{x(x+2)}$.

EXERCISES 34B (p. 93)

1. $\frac{1}{6x}$.
2. $\frac{x+6}{4(x+2)}$.
3. $\frac{x+3}{(x-3)(1-x)}$.
4. $\frac{11x-19}{12}$.

5. $\dfrac{2(x+1)}{x(x+2)(x+3)}$. 6. $\dfrac{2(x+1)}{3x}$. 7. $\dfrac{11-4x}{(x+2)(x-2)}$.

8. 0. 9. $\dfrac{3-x}{x(x-1)(x+1)}$. 10. $\dfrac{3}{x(x-2)}$.

EXERCISES 35A (p. 95)

1. $(500 - pP - qQ)$. 2. 49 p new pence. 3. $\sqrt{\dfrac{V}{\pi h}}$ cm.

4. $\pi y(y + 2x)$. 5. $2\pi r(r + h)$. 6. $\dfrac{xy}{100}$.

7. $2z(x + y)$ m^2. 8. $4x$ minutes past noon; $4y$ minutes to noon.

9. $\dfrac{xm + 12y}{x + 1}$. 10. $\left(\dfrac{P - Q}{P}\right)100$.

11. $\dfrac{(pP + qQ)(100 + z)}{1000\,(p + q)}$ new pence. 12. $\dfrac{hk}{x^2}$.

13. $\left(\dfrac{x}{u} + \dfrac{y}{v}\right)$ hours; $\dfrac{(x + y)uv}{xv + yu}$ km/h. 14. $(2pr + \pi r^2)$ m^2. 15. $\dfrac{xs}{100g}$.

EXERCISES 35B (p. 95)

1. $z(x - 2z)(y - 2z)$ cm^3. 2. $\dfrac{xyz}{n}$. 3. $(xg + yh)$ g.

4. $\dfrac{1000c}{1000x + y}$. 5. $\dfrac{3x}{2v}$ hours; $\frac{4}{3}v$ km/h.

6. $2r(p + q) - xy - 2cd$. 7. $x(50 + w)$ new pence.

8. $(3x + 2y)$ new pence. 9. $\dfrac{xp + yq}{x + y}$. 10. $\dfrac{px - qy + rz}{p - q + z}$.

11. $\dfrac{19x}{12V}$ hours. 12. $\left(Aa + 7Ab + \dfrac{Ca}{2} + \dfrac{7Cb}{2}\right)$ new pence.

13. $3x + 5y - 3p - 5q$. 14. $\dfrac{pqs}{xyz}$. 15. $\sqrt{\dfrac{xy - A}{\pi}}$ m.

EXERCISES 37A (p. 99)

1. 10. 2. -20. 3. $(x + 1)(x - 1)(x - 4)$. 4. -6, 11.
5. 3. 6. -1, 1. 7. $(x - 3y)(x + y)(x + 2y)$.
8. $(x - 1)(x + 3)(x - 2)$. 9. 1, 2. 10. $k = 7$; $(x + 1)(x + 3)$.

EXERCISES 37B (p. 100)

1. 28. **2.** 16. **3.** $(x - 1)(x + 2)(x + 3)$.
4. 0. **5.** 2, − 1. **6.** 7, 14.
7. $(x + y)(x + 2y)(x + 3y)$. **8.** $(x - 1)(x + 3)(x + 4)$.
9. − 1, − 2. **10.** $k = 1$; $(x + 2)(x + 3)$.

EXERCISES 38 (p. 100)

1. $(2p + q)$ m. **2.** $\frac{1}{2(x^2 - 1)}$. **4.** − 8.

5. 1, − 4. **6.** 28. **7.** $\frac{1}{1000}\pi x^2 y$. **8.** $\frac{2y^2 - x^2}{xy}$.

9. $\frac{101n}{x + y}$. **10.** 4. **11.** 0. **12.** $21\frac{1}{4}$.

13. $\frac{pq(x + y)}{qx + py}$ km/h. **14.** $\frac{mx}{m + n}$, $\frac{nx}{x + n}$. **15.** 5, 8.

17. $x(a^2 + x^2)(a^2 - x^2)$. **18.** $\frac{1}{abc}$. **19.** $\frac{x^2 + 2x + 4}{2x}$.

20. $\frac{11 + 17x}{12(x^2 - 1)}$. **22.** 3, 4, 5. **24.** $\frac{3\sqrt{3A}}{\pi}$.

26. $k = -5$; 2, − 3. **27.** $\frac{25Ex + 3My}{300(E + M)}$. **28.** $\frac{xp - yq}{x + y}$.

30. $\frac{x - y}{xy(x + y)}$. **31.** $\frac{2}{(x + 2)(x + 6)}$. **33.** $\frac{2}{(1 + x)(1 - x)}$.

34. $\frac{2x^2 - 2x + 1}{x - 2}$, $\frac{y^2 + 2y + 2}{y - 2}$. **35.** $\frac{3y^2}{y^2 + y + 1}$. **36.** $\frac{2t^2}{1 - t}$.

37. $\frac{ab}{4a^2 - 25b^2}$. **38.** $\frac{7}{8}$. **39.** 3, 12.

40. $(2x - 1)(3x - 1)(x - 1)$. **41.** $(x + 2)(3x + 1)(2x + 1)$.

EXERCISES 39A (p. 104)

1. 16. **2.** 24. **3.** 7 km. **4.** 40 and 80.
5. $\frac{51}{68}$. **6.** 36. **7.** $10y + x$.
8. 48 km. **9.** 220. **10.** £1600.

EXERCISES 39B (p. 105)

1. 160 km. **2.** 40. **3.** £1400. **4.** 37. **5.** 2 km.
6. 400. **7.** 300. **8.** 336 km. **9.** 8. **10.** 26 and 27.

EXERCISES 40A (p. 107)

1. 100, 2. **2.** 400. **3.** 2000, 3000.
4. 8p. **5.** 39. **6.** 1 new penny. **7.** £7.
8. 30 new pence. **9.** 3 km. **10.** 16, 30.

EXERCISES 40B (p. 108)

1. 8p. **2.** 300. **3.** 3, 4. **4.** 16p.
5. 78. **6.** 40. **7.** 600.
8. $12\frac{1}{2}$ new pence. **9.** 4 km. **10.** 45, 60.

EXERCISES 41A (p. 110)

1. 6. **2.** 12 m. **3.** 12, 5. **4.** 32 km/h.
5. 11. **6.** 40. **7.** 1 km/h.
8. 18 m. **9.** 12 cm., 13 cm. **10.** 20.

EXERCISES 41B (p. 111)

1. 4. **2.** 26 m. **3.** 30, 40. **4.** 50 km/h. **5.** 21.
6. 10p. **7.** 6 km/h. **8.** 20 m. **9.** 14, 20. **10.** 4.

EXERCISES 42 (p. 111)

1. 280. **2.** £800. **3.** 2 km. **4.** $3\frac{1}{2}$ new pence.
5. $2\frac{1}{2}$ km. **6.** 1 h 12 min. **7.** 440. **8.** 12.
9. 12. **10.** 12. **11.** 18. **12.** 48 km.
13. 6 km. **14.** 60 km. **15.** 18 cm^3. **16.** 75 new pence.
17. £6. **18.** 20 km. **19.** 25, 77. **20.** 973.
21. 30 km/h. **22.** 20. **23.** £600. **24.** $1\frac{1}{2}$ new pence.
25. 10. **26.** 20 m. **27.** 300. **28.** 5.
29. 20 days. **30.** 32. **31.** 6 m. **32.** 5 hours.
33. $\frac{13}{17}$. **34.** 6 km/h, 5 km/h. **35.** 3.

EXERCISES 46A (p. 122)

1. 160 km. **2.** 11.32h. **3.** 13.44h. **5.** 105 km.

EXERCISES 46B (p. 123)

1. 17.00h. **2.** 120 km. **3.** 3200 km. **4.** $58\frac{1}{2}$ km. **5.** 200 km.

EXERCISES 47 (p. 123)

1. 3, − 0·8. **2.** $1\frac{1}{2}$ cm. **3.** 12·8 km/h, 16 km/h. **4.** 11·02.
5. (i) 1; (ii) 2.4; − 0.4. **6.** 1·6, − 0·6. **9.** $\frac{1}{2}$, − 2.
10. 10 km from start. **11.** 3. **13.** 122·5 m; 10 sec.
14. $A = 0, B = -1; \pm 2$. **15.** 11·16. **16.** 5·4, 2·6.
17. $A = -1, B = 8$. **21.** 12 km. **22.** 2·6, 0·4.
23. 1·40. **24.** 2·2. **27.** 36 cm. **28.** 18.

EXERCISES 48A (p. 128)

1. $\frac{1}{27}$.	**2.** 4.	**3.** $\frac{1}{4}$.	**4.** 8.	**5.** $\frac{1}{8}$.
6. 8.	**7.** $\frac{1}{3}$.	**8.** $\frac{1}{1000}$.	**9.** 4.	**10.** $\frac{13}{12}$.

EXERCISES 48B (p. 128)

1. $\frac{1}{8}$.	**2.** 2.	**3.** $\frac{1}{2}$.	**4.** $\frac{1}{5}$.	**5.** $\frac{1}{25}$.
6. $\frac{1}{27}$.	**7.** $\frac{1}{16}$.	**8.** $\frac{1}{64}$.	**9.** $\frac{8}{3}$.	**10.** $\frac{5}{4}$.

EXERCISES 49A (p. 129)

1. 4.	**2.** 4.	**3.** $\frac{3}{2}$.	**4.** 3.	**5.** $\frac{1}{2}$.
6. $\frac{3}{2}$.	**7.** $\frac{1}{2}$.	**8.** $\frac{1}{3}$.	**9.** $\frac{5}{2}$.	**10.** $\frac{5}{6}$.
11. 2.	**12.** 3.	**13.** 1.	**14.** 2.	**15.** 0.
16. 100.	**17.** $\frac{1}{100}$.	**18.** 27.	**19.** 2.	**20.** 2.

EXERCISES 49B (p. 129)

1. $\frac{1}{2}$.	**2.** 3.	**3.** -1.	**4.** -2.	**5.** $\frac{5}{2}$.
6. $\frac{3}{2}$.	**7.** $\frac{3}{2}$.	**8.** $\frac{1}{3}$.	**9.** $\frac{2}{3}$.	**10.** $\frac{1}{2}$.
11. 0.	**12.** 5.	**13.** 4.	**14.** -3.	**15.** $-\frac{1}{2}$.
16. 10,000.	**17.** $\frac{1}{10}$.	**18.** 16.	**19.** 3.	**20.** 64.

EXERCISES 50A (p. 131)

1. 2.	**2.** 1.	**3.** 1.	**4.** 4.	**5.** 4.
6. 2.	**7.** 3.	**8.** 3.	**9.** $\frac{1}{2}$.	**10.** $2\frac{1}{2}$.

EXERCISES 50B (p. 131)

1. 2.	**2.** 3.	**3.** 1.	**4.** 3.	**5.** 2.
6. 1.	**7.** 3.	**8.** $\frac{1}{2}$.	**9.** $\frac{2}{3}$.	**10.** 2.

EXERCISES 51 (p. 133)

1. 2·302. **2.** $\frac{100}{x^2}$. **3.** $\frac{6^3}{x^2}$. **4.** $\frac{x^2}{4}$. **5.** $\frac{10}{x}$.

6. (i) $\frac{x^3}{3}$, (ii) $\frac{1}{4}$, (iii) $8x^{-12}$. **7.** $100x^{\frac{3}{4}}$.

8. (i) $\frac{1}{9}$; (ii) 4; (iii) $\frac{3}{2}$. **9.** 1·892. **10.** 1·531. **11.** 1·062.
12. -3. **13.** 0·179. **14.** 32. **15.** 1.
16. 0·3010, 0·7782. **17.** $a^{-\frac{1}{6}}$. **18.** 0 or 1·585. **19.** 2.
20. 2. **21.** 1. **22.** 2·52. **23.** -3. **24.** 8·63.
25. 0, 0·631. **26.** 0, 1. **27.** 2^{6x+1}. **28.** 243.

29. $\frac{10}{y^2}$. **30.** $\frac{z^4}{y^2}$. **31.** (i) 3, (ii) $\frac{3}{2}$, (iii) 6.

32. $\frac{3}{2}p^4$. **33.** $24z^4y^2$. **34.** 1·255. **35.** $2\frac{1}{3}$.

EXERCISES 52A (p. 136)

5. 48. **6.** 18. **8.** 64 kg. **9.** 1·73 : 1. **10.** 30 km.

EXERCISES 52B (p. 137)

3. $\frac{1}{3}$. **4.** $\frac{1}{2}$. **5.** 84. **6.** 20.
8. 21. **9.** 54 kg. **10.** 8 : 1.

EXERCISES 54 (p. 142)

1. $1\frac{1}{4}$. **2.** 225 kg. **3.** 2. **4.** £65.
5. 40 000. **6.** 280 hours. **7.** $7\frac{1}{2}$ new pence. **9.** 35 km/h.
10. directly. **11.** $4\sqrt{6}$ m/sec. **12.** $7\frac{1}{9}$. **13.** doubled.
14. 1152 calories. **15.** 1 : 3. **16.** £$3(y - x)$.
17. 19 kg. **18.** 126 kg. **19.** 100.
21. 40 km/h. **22.** 12 newtons. **23.** 8 : 1. **24.** 400 : 1.

EXERCISES 55A (p. 146)

1. 81. **2.** -109. **3.** 22. **4.** 21. **5.** 8, 13.
6. 2, 9. **7.** 348. **8.** $236\frac{1}{4}$. **9.** $5n - 1$. **10.** $13 - 3m$.

EXERCISES 55B (p. 147)

1. -47. **2.** 99. **3.** 100. **4.** No. **5.** 15. **6.** 6.
7. 2500. **8.** $\frac{3n(n+1)}{2}$. **9.** $\frac{61-n}{10}$. **10.** $2n$.

EXERCISES 56A (p. 149)

1. $2(7)^{39}$. **2.** $\frac{1}{2^{12}}$. **3.** 9. **4.** 18. **5.** 36. **6.** 10, 20.
7. $2^{22} - 4$. **8.** $\frac{3^{17}+1}{4(3^{14})}$. **9.** $6(3)^{n-1}$. **10.** $5(-\frac{1}{2})^{n-1}$.

EXERCISES 56B (p. 149)

1. $5(3)^{23}$. **2.** $-\frac{1}{3^{16}}$. **3.** 22. **4.** No.
5. 70. **6.** 21, 63. **7.** $3(2^{18} - 1)$.
8. $\frac{1-3^{2n}}{2}$. **9.** $\frac{9}{2^{31}}$. **10.** $2^{n-1}xy^{n-1}$.

EXERCISES 57 (p. 150)

1. $\frac{n(n+1)}{2}$; 32. **2.** 780. **3.** £276. **4.** 19.
5. £7970. **6.** 19 years. **7.** 32, 44 etc.
8. 45, 135, 405. **9.** 9. **10.** $-\frac{1}{2}$, 7; $\frac{8}{9}$, $\frac{81}{84}$; 465.

11. $54, \frac{3^5}{2}$. **12.** 4, 6, 8. **13.** $2, 3^n - 1$. **14.** 3.

17. $\frac{x(r-q)+y(p-r)}{p-q}$. **18.** 12th; $82\frac{1}{2}$. **19.** 1683.

20. 1368. **21.** $a\frac{\left(\frac{b}{a}\right)^{\frac{n}{n-1}}-1}{\left(\frac{b}{a}\right)^{\frac{1}{n-1}}-1}$.

22. 3675. **23.** 30. **24.** $\frac{n^2-n+2}{2}$; $\frac{n}{2}(n^2+1)$.

25. $x - \frac{y}{3}, x + \frac{y}{3}$. **26.** 210 log 2. **27.** 66 660. **28.** $1\frac{1}{2}$.

29. 3, 27. **30.** 13.

EXERCISES 58A (p. 156)

1. 6. **2.** 3. **3.** 3. **4.** 5.
5. 8. **6.** 3. **7.** 7. **8.** $4x$.
9. $6x + 1$. **10.** $8x - 1$.

EXERCISES 58B (p. 156)

1. 8. **2.** 7. **3.** 1. **4.** 6
5. 12. **6.** 7. **7.** 4. **8.** $6x$.
9. $4x + 1$. **10.** $12x - 2$.

EXERCISES 59A (p. 158)

1. $8x - 6$. **2.** $3x$. **3.** $3 - 2x$. **4.** $2x + \frac{3}{4}$.
5. $-6 - 4x$. **6.** $8x - 4$. **7.** $2x - 3$. **8.** $4x + 11$.
9. $12x - 1$. **10.** $8x + 3$.

EXERCISES 59B (p. 158)

1. $4x - 8$. **2.** x. **3.** $2 - 2x$. **4.** $2x + \frac{2}{3}$.
5. $-4 - 6x$. **6.** $6x + 3$. **7.** $2x$. **8.** $4x - 11$.
9. $12x + 1$. **10.** $2x$.

EXERCISES 60 (p. 162)

1. $9x^2$. **2.** $\frac{2}{x^3}$. **3.** $2x - \frac{2}{x^3}$.

4. $1 + 4x + 9x^2$. **5.** $3x^2 + 4x + 1$. **6.** $\frac{1}{2\sqrt{x}} - \frac{1}{2x^{\frac{3}{2}}}$.

7. $\frac{1}{2\sqrt{x}} + 1$. **8.** $1 - \frac{1}{x^2}$. **9.** $\frac{1}{x^2}$.

10. $-\frac{1}{x^2} - \frac{2}{x^3}$.
11. $3x^2 + 2x$.
12. $7 + 6x - 12x^2$.
13. $-\frac{1}{x^2} + \frac{2}{x^3}$.
14. $-\frac{1}{2x^{\frac{3}{2}}} + 1$.
15. $1 - \frac{1}{x^2}$.
16. $3y^2 - 1$.
17. $6t + 3t^2$.
18. $2z + 3$.
19. $3 - 2v + 21v^2$.
20. $3t^2 - 3$.
21. $6 + 4x + 9x^2$.
22. $-\frac{2}{x^3} - \frac{2}{x^2}$.
23. $1 + \frac{1}{2x^{\frac{3}{2}}}$.
24. $\frac{5}{2}x^{\frac{3}{2}}$.
25. $1 + 12x + 21x^2$.
26. $3x^2 + 2x + 1$.
27. $1 - \frac{1}{x^2}$.
28. $7x^6$.
29. $-\frac{7}{x^8}$.
30. $7x^6 - \frac{7}{x^8}$.
31. 4.
32. 13.
33. 1, 0.
34. -1.
35. $-\frac{1}{x^2}$.
36. $3t^2 - 12t + 4$.
37. $(-1, 0)$.
38. $-\frac{8}{x^3}$.
39. -1.
40. $2x$; $2\sqrt{y}$.
41. $1 + \frac{1}{z^2}$.
43. $-2\frac{1}{2}$.
44. $\frac{1}{1 + 2t}$.
45. $(0, 0)$ and $(\frac{2}{3}, -\frac{4}{27})$.

EXERCISES 61A (p. 169)

1. -9.
2. 2.
3. -4.
4. ± 2.
5. $-\frac{1}{4}$.
6. ± 2.
7. 144.
8. 9 m^2.
9. 12π cm^2.
10. 10, 10.

EXERCISES 61B (p. 169)

1. -16.
2. 5.
3. -5.
4. ± 16.
5. $-\frac{1}{4}$.
6. ± 4.
7. k^2.
8. k^2 m^2.
9. 24π cm^2.
10. k, k.

EXERCISES 62A (p. 171)

2. 45 m/sec; 24 m/sec^2.
3. 16 m/sec^2.
4. $3 + 2n$, 2.
5. 5 m/sec^2; $\frac{1}{2}$.

EXERCISES 62B (p. 172)

2. 26 m/sec; 18 m/sec^2.
3. 29 m/sec^2.
4. $4 + 4n$, 4.
5. 2 m/sec^2; 2.

EXERCISES 63A (p. 173)

1. $1 \cdot 2$ cm^2/sec.
2. $2 \cdot 7$ cm^3/sec.
3. 3 cm^3/sec.
4. $3 \cdot 2\pi$ cm^2/sec.
5. $7 \cdot 2\pi$ cm^3/sec.

EXERCISES 63B (p. 173)

1. $1 \cdot 2$ cm^2/sec.
2. $2 \cdot 4$ cm^3/sec.
3. $2\frac{1}{4}$ cm^3/sec.
4. $6 \cdot 4\pi$ cm^2/sec.
5. $6 \cdot 4\pi$ cm^3/sec.

EXERCISES 64 (p. 174)

1. 7; (2, 1), $(\frac{2}{3}, \frac{59}{27})$.
2. $94 \cdot 7$ m^2.
3. $312 \cdot 5$ cm^2.
4. 1, min; $1\frac{4}{27}$, max.
5. $\frac{1024}{27}$ cm^3.
7. 0, max; -1, min.
8. 6 m/sec^2; 3 sec.
9. 108 m^2.
10. 1, max; 0, min.
11. $\frac{8}{\pi}$.
12. $7 \cdot 2\pi$ cm^2/sec.
13. $\frac{1}{200\pi}$ cm/sec.
14. $\frac{1}{2}$.
15. 80, max; -28 min.
16. $-\frac{28}{v^{2.4}}$.
17. 0, -2 m/sec^2.
18. (1, 2) and (2, 2).
19. -1, 2, 0.
20. 1 or $-\frac{1}{3}$.

EXERCISES 65A (p. 177)

1. $\frac{x^4}{4}$.
2. $\frac{x^4}{4} + \frac{2x^3}{3}$.
3. $\frac{x^3}{3} + 6x$.
4. $-\frac{1}{x}$.
5. $a\frac{x^3}{3} + b\frac{x^2}{2} + cx$.
6. $\frac{x^3}{3} - \frac{3x^2}{2} + 2x$.
7. $-\frac{1}{2x^2}$.
8. $\frac{x^6}{6}$.
9. $y = 2x + x^2 - \frac{x^3}{3} - \frac{5}{3}$.
10. $y = 3x^2 - 2x + 2$.

EXERCISES 65B (p. 178)

1. $\frac{2}{3}x^{\frac{3}{2}}$.
2. $\frac{x^3}{3} + \frac{3x^2}{2} + 4x$.
3. $\frac{x^3}{3} - 2x^2$.
4. $-\frac{1}{2x^2} - \frac{1}{x}$.
5. $-\frac{a}{x} + bx$.
6. $\frac{x^3}{3} + \frac{x^2}{2}$.

7. $\frac{x^4}{4} + \frac{2x^3}{3}$.

8. $\frac{x^3}{3} - \frac{1}{x}$.

9. $y = 3 + x + x^2 - x^3$.

10. $y = \frac{x^3}{3} + x + 1$.

EXERCISES 66A (p. 179)

1. $s = \frac{3t^2}{2} + t$.
2. $\frac{t^3}{3} + 2$.
3. $\frac{t^3}{6} + 4t$.
4. $\frac{t^3}{3} + \frac{t^2}{2} + t$.
5. $\frac{t^3}{3} + \frac{t^2}{2} + 3\frac{1}{6}$.
6. 39·2 m/sec.
7. 37·4 m/sec.
8. 78·4 m.
9. 35·6 m.
10. 1 sec.

EXERCISES 66B (p. 179)

1. $\frac{t^3}{3} + t$.
2. $\frac{t^2}{2} + t + 4$.
3. $\frac{t^4}{12} + 2t$.
4. $\frac{2t^3}{3} + \frac{3t^2}{2} + t$.
5. $\frac{t^3}{3} - \frac{t^2}{2} + \frac{7}{3}$.
6. 29·4 m/sec.
7. 27·6 m/sec.
8. 19·6 m.
9. 102·4 m.
10. 19·6 m.

EXERCISES 67A (p. 184)

1. $12\frac{2}{3}$.
2. $\frac{1}{6}$.
3. $5\frac{1}{3}$.
4. $\frac{3}{4}$.
5. $6\frac{1}{3}$.
6. $\frac{4}{3}$.
7. 96 m.
8. 150 m.

EXERCISES 67B (p. 184)

1. $16\frac{2}{3}$.
2. $1\frac{1}{3}$.
3. $17\frac{1}{3}$.
4. $3\frac{3}{4}$.
5. 28.
6. $\frac{2}{3}$.
7. 114 m.
8. 84 m.

EXERCISES 68A (p. 188)

1. $\frac{15\pi}{2}$.
2. $\frac{16\pi}{5}$.
3. $\frac{\pi}{2}$.
4. $\frac{53\pi}{15}$.
5. $\frac{448\pi}{3}$.

EXERCISES 68B (p. 188)

1. 40π.
2. $\frac{128\pi}{5}$.
3. $\frac{2\pi}{3}$.
4. $\frac{5}{24}\pi r^3$.
5. $\frac{7}{3}\pi a^3$.

EXERCISES 69 (p. 188)

1. $4\frac{5}{6}$.
2. 29 m.
3. $\frac{\pi}{4}$.
4. $26\frac{2}{3}$ m.
5. $5\frac{1}{3}$.
6. $\frac{9\pi}{2}$.
7. $\frac{x^3}{3} + \frac{x^4}{2} + \frac{x^5}{5}$.
8. 14 m/sec.

9. $\frac{1}{54}$. **10.** $\frac{32}{3}$. **11.** $\frac{5}{3} + 2x - \dfrac{x^3}{3}$. **12.** $\frac{625}{12}$.

13. $\dfrac{16\pi}{15}$. **16.** 11 m/sec²; $20\frac{1}{6}$ m. **17.** 24π.

18. $\frac{28}{3}$. **19.** $\frac{27}{4}$. **20.** $3x^3 + 3x^2 + x$.

21. $15\frac{1}{2}$ m/sec. **22.** $y = \frac{1}{4} + x^3 - \dfrac{x^4}{4}$.

23. $\frac{4}{3}\pi ab^2$. **24.** $y = 4 - 3x^2$.

25. $\frac{2}{3} + \dfrac{3x^2}{2} - \dfrac{x^3}{3}$. **26.** $8\frac{5}{6}$. **27.** $\frac{4}{3}$. **28.** $7\frac{1}{2}$.

ANSWERS TO GEOMETRY SECTION

EXERCISES 70A (p. 201)

1. $11\frac{1}{4}°$. **2.** $6x + y = 360°$. **3.** 140°, 140°, 40°.
4. $y = x + z$. **6.** $p + q + r = 360°$. **8.** 150°.
9. $y + x = 180°$.

EXERCISES 70B (p. 203)

1. 10°. **2.** $y + 5x = 360°$. **3.** 130°, 50°, 130°.
5. $x + y + z = 360°$. **6.** 120°. **7.** 60°.
8. $x + y + z = 180°$. **10.** $p + q + r = 720°$.

EXERCISES 71A (p. 208)

1. 30. **2.** 100°. **3.** Yes, No, Yes.
4. Yes, Yes, No. **5.** 80. **6.** 156°. **7.** 120°, 135°.
8. 84. **9.** 95. **10.** 130°.

EXERCISES 71B (p. 209)

1. 20. **2.** 95°. **3.** Yes, No, Yes.
4. Yes, Yes, No. **5.** 48. **6.** $157\frac{1}{2}°$. **7.** 125°, 145°.
8. 36. **9.** 120°, 140°. **10.** 60°.

EXERCISES 72 (p. 209)

1. 70°. **2.** $(360 - x - y - z)°$. **3.** $(190 - 5x)°$.
4. 15. **5.** 66. **6.** 140°. **7.** $p + q + r$.
9. 20°. **10.** 100°, 30°. **11.** 70°. **12.** 70°.
13. $a + b - y$. **14.** 70°. **15.** 80. **16.** 40.

EXERCISES 74A (p. 218)

1. 65°, 100°, 80°. **2.** 36°. **4.** 50°. **6.** 15°.
8. 30°. **9.** $3x$.

EXERCISES 74B (p. 219)

1. 55°, 80°, 40°. **2.** 30°. **5.** 30°. **6.** 40°.
7. 44°.

EXERCISES 75A (p. 222)

1. No. **2.** $BC < CA < CD$. **3.** $BC > CA > CD$.
10. CX.

EXERCISES 75B (p. 223)

1. Yes. **2.** $CD > AC > BC$. **3.** $AB > AC > CD$.

EXERCISES 76 (p. 225)

1. 150°. **3.** 99°. **5.** 9°. **8.** $22\frac{1}{2}$°.
9. 18. **16.** $AI > BI > CI$. **18.** 9.

EXERCISES 77A (p. 230)

1. 62°, 118°, 118°. **2.** 40°, 140.°

EXERCISES 77B (p. 231)

1. 57°, 123°, 123°. **2.** 56°, 124°.

EXERCISES 78A (p. 233)

1. 5. **2.** 8. **6.** 3.

EXERCISES 78B (p. 234)

1. 2. **2.** $1\frac{1}{4}$. **5.** 3.

EXERCISES 79A (p. 240)

1. (i) 8 cm². (ii) 4 cm. (iii) $1\frac{1}{2}$.
2. (i) 12 cm². (ii) 4 cm. (iii) 3. **3.** 24 cm².

EXERCISES 79B (p. 241)

1. (i) 12 cm². (ii) 3 cm. (iii) 2·4.
2. (i) 10 cm². (ii) 3 cm. (iii) 3 cm. **3.** 5 cm.

EXERCISES 80 (p. 242)

6. $2\frac{1}{4}$ cm. **9.** 2 : 1; 1 : 3; 4 : 1. **16.** 4 : 3; 4 : 3; 4 : 3. **18.** 8 : 9.

EXERCISES 81A (p. 247)

1. $3\frac{1}{3}$, 6, 6. **2.** 4 cm. **3.** 9·6 cm. **4.** 10 cm.
5. 3 : 7. **7.** $\frac{2}{3}$, $\frac{2}{3}$, $\frac{4}{9}$.

EXERCISES 81B (p. 248)

1. $1\frac{5}{7}$, 8, $\frac{1}{20}$. **2.** 4·2 cm. **3.** 8·8 cm. **4.** 6·6 cm.
5. 5 : 7. **7.** $\frac{3}{4}$, $\frac{3}{4}$, $\frac{9}{16}$. **8.** $\frac{2}{7}$.

EXERCISES 82A (p. 250)

1. 4·2 cm. **2.** 10 cm. **4.** 16·8 cm. **5.** 3 : 7.

EXERCISES 82B (p. 251)

1. $2\frac{6}{7}$ cm. **2.** 15 cm. **4.** $11\frac{1}{4}$ cm. **5.** 3 : 1. **6.** $1\frac{7}{8}$ cm.

EXERCISES 83A (p. 256)

1. 13 cm. **2.** 10 cm. **3.** 5 cm. **4.** 12 cm. **5.** Yes. **10.** $2\frac{1}{7}$ cm.

EXERCISES 83B (p. 256)

1. 12 cm. **3.** $1\frac{12}{13}$, $11\frac{1}{13}$ cm. **4.** No. **7.** 10·3 cm. **10.** $\sqrt{98}$ cm.

EXERCISES 84A (p. 258)

2. $2\frac{2}{3}$ cm, $2\frac{1}{3}$ cm, 9 : 1. **9.** 9 : 4, 1 : 1.

EXERCISES 84B (p. 259)

1. 4 : 25. **2.** $4\frac{2}{3}$ cm, 4 cm, 9 : 4. **3.** 3 cm, 1 : 3. **4.** $1\frac{7}{8}$ cm. **5.** 3 m.
6. $\frac{4}{45}$. **9.** 5 : 6.

EXERCISES 85 (p. 260)

3. $2\sqrt{7}$, $\frac{3}{2}\sqrt{7}$ cm. **4.** $\sqrt{x^2 + y^2 - xy}$.

EXERCISES 87A (p. 271)

1. Yes. **2.** $5\frac{3}{8}$ cm. **3.** $1\frac{15}{16}$ cm. **4.** $2\frac{3}{14}$ cm. **5.** $\sqrt{20{\cdot}5}$ cm.
6. $\sqrt{80{\cdot}5}$ cm. **7.** $\sqrt{91{\cdot}75}$ cm.

EXERCISES 87B (p. 271)

1. No. **2.** $2\frac{1}{3}$ cm. **3.** $\frac{1}{2}$ cm. **4.** $\frac{4}{5}$ cm. **5.** $\frac{1}{2}\sqrt{97}$ cm.
6. $\sqrt{37}$ cm. **7.** $\frac{1}{2}\sqrt{265}$ cm.

EXERCISES 88 (p. 271)

4. 3 cm. **16.** 7 cm. **17.** $\sqrt{57}$ cm.

EXERCISES 89A (p. 275)

1. 8 cm. **2.** 5 cm. **3.** $7\frac{1}{24}$ cm. **4.** 1 cm.
5. $2\sqrt{x^2 - y^2}$ cm. **8.** $\dfrac{3\sqrt{3}r^2}{4}$. **9.** $\dfrac{4\sqrt{3}}{3}$ cm.

EXERCISES 89B (p. 276)

1. 24 cm. **2.** 3 cm. **3.** $3\frac{1}{8}$ cm. **4.** 17 cm.
5. $\sqrt{y^2 + \frac{1}{4}x^2}$ cm. **8.** $\dfrac{x}{\sqrt{2}}$ cm. **9.** $\dfrac{x}{\sqrt{3}}$ cm.

EXERCISES 90A (p. 280)

1. 15°. **3.** 45°, 60°, 75°. **5.** 55°, 75°, 105°, 125°.

EXERCISES 90B (p. 280)

1. 18°. **2.** $x + 2y = 180°$. **3.** 45°, 60°, 75°.
5. 45°, 85°, 95°, 135°. **6.** $x + y + z = 180°$. **7.** 70°.

EXERCISES 91 (p.281)

1. $8\frac{1}{2}$ cm. **7.** $2\sqrt{62}$ cm. **8.** $2\sqrt{3}$ cm. **13.** 2 cm.

EXERCISES 92A (p. 287)

3. 55°, 60°, 65°. **5.** 60°. **6.** 11°. **7.** 24°.
8. 42°. **9.** 22°. **10.** 96°.

EXERCISES 92B (p. 287)

3. 66°, 63°, 51°. **5.** $\frac{x + y}{2}$. **6.** $x + \frac{1}{2}y - 90°$. **7.** $y - \frac{x}{2}$.
8. $90° - 2x$. **9.** $x - 90°$. **10.** $360° - 2x - 4y$ or $(2x + 4y)$.

EXERCISES 93A (p. 290)

1. 12 cm. **2.** $9\frac{3}{13}$ cm. **4.** 12 cm. **5.** 12 cm. **6.** 5 cm.

EXERCISES 93B (p. 290)

1. 3 cm. **2.** 4·8 cm. **4.** $\sqrt{4Rr}$.
5. $\sqrt{d^2 - (R - r)^2}$. **6.** $\sqrt{d^2 - (R + r)^2}$. **9.** 5 cm, 4 cm, 1 cm.

EXERCISES 94A (p. 293)

1. 14 cm. **2.** 6 cm. **3.** 2 cm. **4.** 12·5 cm. **5.** 16 cm. **6.** 4 cm.

EXERCISES 94B (p. 293)

1. 8 cm. **2.** 2 cm. **3.** 12 cm. **4.** 8 cm. **5.** 4 cm. **6.** 4 cm.

EXERCISES 95 (p. 294)

21. 8 cm, 12 cm. **23.** $6\frac{1}{2}$ cm.

ANSWERS TO TRIGONOMETRY SECTION

EXERCISES 97A (p. 319)

1. $\frac{3}{5}, \frac{3}{5}, \frac{3}{4}, \frac{3}{4}, \frac{5}{4}, \frac{5}{4}$. **2.** $\frac{5}{12}, \frac{12}{13}, \frac{12}{5}, \frac{13}{12}$. **3.** $\frac{4}{5}, \frac{7}{4}$.
4. $\frac{3}{5}, \frac{3}{5}$. **5.** $\frac{1}{2}, \sqrt{3}$.

EXERCISES 97B (p. 321)

1. $\frac{8}{17}$, $\frac{8}{17}$, $\frac{8}{15}$, $\frac{8}{15}$. 2. $\frac{3}{5}$, $\frac{4}{5}$. 3. $\frac{5}{13}$, $\frac{12}{7}$.

4. $\frac{8}{5}$, $\frac{8}{5}$. 5. 1, $\frac{1}{\sqrt{2}}$.

EXERCISES 98A (p. 322)

1. ·3420, ·3420, 1·1918, 0·2345, 2·002, 4·0121, 3·0031, 3·9969, ·4107, ·8456.
2. 30°, 60°, 39° 50′, 38°, 60°, 26° 34′, 19° 28′, 48° 11′, 45°, 63° 26′.

EXERCISES 98B (p. 323)

1. ·4226, 1·4945, 0·3249, 0·9286, 0·306, 4·975, 4·0029, 4·0031, 2·6640, 1·1547.
2. 60°, 30°, 71° 34′, 30°, 60°, 24° 29′, 11° 32′, 53° 8′, 18° 26′, 45°.

EXERCISES 99A (p. 324)

1. 0·8. 2. $\frac{13}{5}$. 3. $\frac{8}{17}$. 4. $\frac{20}{21}$. 5. $\frac{\sqrt{m^2 + n^2}}{m}$.

EXERCISES 99B (p. 324)

1. 0·6. 2. $\frac{12}{5}$. 3. $\frac{8}{15}$. 4. $\frac{29}{21}$. 5. $\frac{q}{\sqrt{p^2 - q^2}}$.

EXERCISES 100A (p. 328)

1. 1. 2. 1. 3. 1. 4. 4. 5. 1. 6. 1. 7. 1. 8. $\frac{4}{3}$. 9. $\frac{1}{2}$. 10. $\frac{1}{3}$.

EXERCISES 100B (p. 329)

1. 1. 2. 1. 3. 1. 4. $1\frac{3}{4}$. 5. 1. 6. 1. 7. 1. 8. 4. 9. $\frac{3}{4}$. 10. $\frac{3}{4}$.

EXERCISES 101 (p. 329)

3. 2. 4. $\frac{3}{5}$. 5. $\frac{4}{5}$, $\frac{4}{5}$, $\frac{5}{3}$, $\frac{5}{3}$. 6. 1, 1, 1.

7. $\frac{p}{\sqrt{q^2 - p^2}}$. 8. $\frac{8}{17}$, $\frac{15}{17}$, 1. 9. 66, 72, 39.

10. $\frac{\sqrt{b^2 - \frac{1}{4}a^2}}{b}$, $\frac{\sqrt{4b^2 - a^2}}{a}$.

11. $\frac{h}{c}$, $\frac{\sqrt{c^2 - h^2}}{h}$, $\frac{a}{\sqrt{a^2 - h^2}}$.

12. (i), (iv), (v). 14. $\frac{1}{7}$. 15. $\sqrt{2} - 1$.

16. $\frac{\sqrt{3}}{2 + \sqrt{3}}$, $2 - \sqrt{3}$. 18. $\frac{2}{\sqrt{5}}$, $\frac{1}{2}$.

19. $\dfrac{\sqrt{b^2 - a^2}}{b}$. **20.** $\dfrac{m}{l}$. **21.** 1, 1. **22.** 38° 47′.
23. 15°. **24.** 34° 50′. **25.** 2.

EXERCISES 102A (p. 333)

1. 14·3 cm, 4·42 cm. **2.** 4·15 cm, 2·21 cm. **3.** 23·5 cm, 22·0 cm.
4. 10·5 m, 5·73 m. **5.** 13·0 cm, 26·1 cm.

EXERCISES 102B (p. 333)

1. 44·6 cm, 41·3 cm. **2.** 75·7 cm, 72·0 cm. **3.** 6·01 cm, 15·3 cm.
4. 4·73 m, 4·01 m. **5.** 6·88 cm, 10·2 cm.

EXERCISES 103A (p. 334)

1. 44° 25′, 45° 35′. **2.** 36° 52′, 53° 8′. **3.** 70° 17′, 19° 43′.
4. 64° 18′, 25° 42′. **5.** 29° 38′, 60° 22′.

EXERCISES 103B (p. 334)

1. 41° 49′, 48° 11′. **2.** 62° 15′, 27° 45′. **3.** 68° 4′, 21° 56′.
4. 28° 26′, 61° 34′. **5.** 80° 26′, 9° 34′.

EXERCISES 104A (p. 342)

1. 69° 52′. **2.** 8·32 cm. **3.** 6·12 cm. **4.** 24° 14′.
5. 9·3 m. **6.** 376 m. **7.** 8°. **8.** $n = 4{\cdot}13$.
9. 36·7 m. **10.** 75 m. **11.** 153° 26′.
12. 4·36 km, 036° 35′.

EXERCISES 104B (p. 342)

1. 73° 58′. **2.** 10·5 cm. **3.** 4·06 cm. **4.** 56° 19′.
5. 22·4 m. **6.** 308 m. **7.** 9°. **8.** 3·4.
9. 69·1 m. **10.** 30·8 m. **11.** 207°. **12.** 319° 8′.

EXERCISES 105 (p. 343)

1. 12·3 m. **2.** 2·56 cm. **3.** 53° 8′. **4.** 41° 11′.
5. 11 cm. **6.** 11 cm. **7.** 8° 8′. **8.** 8·66 cm.
9. 555 m. **10.** 73° 44′. **11.** 10·2 m. **12.** 14° 53′.
13. 0·37 km. **14.** 41° 24′. **15.** 38° 56′. **16.** 32° 48′.
17. 34·6 m. **18.** 20° 22′. **19.** 073° 19′. **20.** 5·35 m.
21. 51·9 m. **22.** 119° 29′. **23.** 18° 26′.
24. 4·1 cm, 5·6 cm. **25.** 52·6 cm². **26.** 18·1 m, 18′. **27.** 19·3 cm.
28. 25° 45′, 11·5 cm. **29.** $4\sqrt{5}$, 96° 22′, 83° 38′.
30. $\frac{2328}{625}$. **31.** 28° 54′. **32.** 60°, 46° 6′. **33.** 108 m.
34. 8·85 m. **35.** 79·2 m, 15·3 m. **36.** 056° 6′.
37. 27·9 cm, 14·7 cm, 45·3 cm.
38. 4·19 cm, 3·68 cm, 138°, 49° 31′, 130° 29′.
39. 56° 52′, 13·1 m.
40. 18·9 m.

EXERCISES 106A (p. 350)

1. −ve. **2.** +ve. **3.** −ve. **4.** −ve. **5.** −ve. **6.** −ve. **7.** −ve.
8. −ve. **9.** −ve. **10.** −ve.

EXERCISES 106B (p. 350)

1. +ve. **2.** −ve. **3.** −ve. **4.** −ve. **5.** +ve. **6.** −ve. **7.** +ve.
8. +ve. **9.** −ve. **10.** −ve.

EXERCISES 107A (p. 352)

1. − 0·1736.	**2.** + 0·9397.	**3.** − 1·732.	**4.** − 0·9848.
5. − 0·3420.	**6.** 0·5774.	**7.** 5·671.	**8.** − 5·671.
9. − 0·9397.	**10.** + 0·5.	**11.** − 2·0.	**12.** 1·5557.
13. − 1·732.	**14.** − 2·9238.	**15.** − 1·1547.	**16.** 1·1918.
17. − 1·0154.	**18.** 3·8637.	**19.** − 0·4663.	**20.** − 0·3420.
21. − 0·6428.	**22.** 2·0.	**23.** − 1·0154.	**24.** − 11·43.

EXERCISES 107B (p. 352)

1. − 0·3420.	**2.** 0·866.	**3.** − 1·1918.	**4.** − 0·9397.
5. − 0·6428.	**6.** 0·8391.	**7.** − 2·7475.	**8.** 0.
9. − 0·866.	**10.** 0·6428.	**11.** − 1·5557.	**12.** 2·0.
13. − 2·7475.	**14.** − 2·0.	**15.** − 1·3054.	**16.** 0·8391.
17. − 1·0642.	**18.** 2·0.	**19.** − 0·8391.	**20.** − 5·671.
21. − 0·9848.	**22.** − 1·0154.	**23.** − 1·0154.	**24.** 2·7475.

EXERCISES 108A (p. 353)

1. $-\sin x$.	**2.** $-\sin x$.	**3.** $\cot x$.	**4.** $-\cot x$.
5. $\sec x$.	**6.** $\operatorname{cosec} x$.	**7.** $-\operatorname{cosec} x$.	**8.** $-\cot x$.
9. $-\tan x$.	**10.** $-\sec 2x$.		

EXERCISES 108B (p. 353)

1. $-\cos x$.	**2.** $\cos x$.	**3.** $-\sin x$.	**4.** $-\tan x$.
5. $-\sin x$.	**6.** $-\sec x$.	**7.** $-\sec x$.	**8.** $-\cot x$.
9. $\sec x$.	**10.** $\cot 2x$.		

EXERCISES 109 (p. 355)

3. 20.	**4.** 20.	**5.** 113° 35′, 246° 25′.
6. 203° 35′, 336° 25′.	**7.** $30 < x < 150$.	**8.** $60 < x < 300$.
9. 44° 25′, 135° 35′.	**10.** 126° 52′, 233° 8′.	**11.** 63° 26′, 243° 26′.
12. 154° 32′, 334° 32′.	**13.** 158° 12′, 338° 12′.	**14.** 120°, 240°.

15. $\sec x$.	**16.** $-\operatorname{cosec} x$.	**17.** $\sec x$.	**18.** $-\cos x$.
19. $-\tan x$.	**20.** $-\tan x$.	**21.** 126° 52′.	**22.** 233° 8′.
23. 306° 52′.	**24.** 126° 52′.	**25.** 306° 52′.	**26.** 233° 8′.

27. $\sin A$, $-\cos A$, $-\tan A$, $\cos \frac{A}{2}$, $\cos 2A$.

28. $180° < \theta < 225°$ or $315° < \theta < 360°$.
29. 197° 28′, 342° 32′; 101° 32′, 258° 28′; 50° 12′, 230° 12′.

30. $-\frac{1}{4}\sqrt{7}$. **31.** $-\dfrac{\sqrt{q^2-p^2}}{q}$.

32. 1, − 1, 1. **33.** ± 0·1415, ± 0·9899.

34. $\pm\frac{1}{2}\left(t-\dfrac{1}{t}\right)$.

35. 1. **36.** 1. **37.** 1.

EXERCISES 111A (p. 370)

1. 42° 4′. **2.** 21° 48′. **3.** 43° 36′. **4.** 84° 4′. **5.** 21° 48′.
6. 33° 42′. **7.** 26° 34′. **8.** 33° 42′. **9.** 26° 34′. **10.** 39° 48′.

EXERCISES 111B (p. 371)

1. 90°. **2.** 45°. **3.** 90°. **4.** 43° 18′. **5.** 45°.
6. 30° 58′. **7.** 36° 52′. **8.** 36° 52′. **9.** 45°. **10.** 51° 20′.

EXERCISES 112 (p. 372)

1. 46° 12′, 38° 13′, 18°.
2. 20° 42′. **3.** 10·6 m. **4.** 61° 53′.
5. 69° 18′. **6.** 41° 24′. **7.** 5·54 m.
8. 67° 22′. **9.** 78° 13′. **10.** 25° 40′.
11. 1 in 8·5. **12.** 28° 24′. **13.** 56° 26′.
14. 3·57 m; 63° 12′; 67° 13′.
15. 10·58 cm; 61° 53′, 69° 18′, 56° 14′, 41° 24′.
16. 5·75 m; 73° 13′, 81° 12′, 62° 10′. **17.** 16 m.
18. $\sin^{-1}(\sin\alpha\cos\beta)$. **19.** 46° 9′, 48° 11′. **20.** 20° 42′.

EXERCISES 114A (p. 383)

1. $b = 4{\cdot}00$, $c = 7{\cdot}66$, $A = 88°$. **2.** $A = 46°$, $a = 5{\cdot}22$, $c = 5{\cdot}39$.
3. $b = 11{\cdot}6$, $A = 26°$, $a = 5{\cdot}5$. **4.** $b = 4{\cdot}13$, $c = 3{\cdot}79$, $A = 64°$.
5. $C = 56°\ 30'$, $a = 41{\cdot}1$, $c = 34{\cdot}7$.
6. Impossible.
7. $c = 9{\cdot}92$, $C = 120°\ 39'$, $B = 21°\ 21'$.
8. Impossible.
9. $B = 32°$, $C = 122°$, $c = 8{\cdot}32$ or $B = 148°$, $C = 6°$, $c = 1{\cdot}03$.
10. $B = 63°\ 9'$, $C = 65°\ 51'$, $c = 3{\cdot}17$ or $B = 116°\ 51'$, $C = 12°\ 9'$, $c = 0{\cdot}73$.

EXERCISES 114B (p. 384)

1. $b = 14{\cdot}5$, $c = 16{\cdot}9$, $A = 87°$. **2.** $A = 77°$, $c = 3{\cdot}46$, $a = 8{\cdot}28$.
3. $A = 47°$, $a = 19{\cdot}2$, $b = 25{\cdot}0$.
4. $A = 66°\ 30'$, $b = 14{\cdot}3$, $c = 12{\cdot}5$.
5. $a = 32{\cdot}2$, $c = 20{\cdot}2$, $C = 38°\ 9'$.

6. $B = 55^\circ\ 56'$, $C = 82^\circ\ 34'$, $c = 7·18$ or $B = 124^\circ\ 4'$, $C = 14^\circ\ 26'$, $c = 1·81$.
7. $B = 33^\circ\ 15'$, $C = 34^\circ\ 45'$, $c = 4·37$.
8. Impossible.
9. $B = 26^\circ\ 39'$, $C = 131^\circ\ 6'$, $c = 7·39$ or $B = 153^\circ\ 21'$, $C = 4^\circ\ 23'$, $c = 0·78$.
10. Impossible.

EXERCISES 115A (p. 387)

1. $c = 6·48$, $A = 32^\circ\ 28'$, $B = 37^\circ\ 32'$.
2. $c = 6·12$, $B = 9^\circ\ 57'$, $A = 146^\circ\ 3'$.
3. $a = 18·8$, $C = 41^\circ\ 21'$, $B = 78^\circ\ 17'$.
4. $b = 5·37$, $C = 31^\circ\ 22'$, $A = 53^\circ\ 10'$.
5. $b = 14·16$, $C = 19^\circ\ 13'$, $A = 80^\circ\ 47'$.
6. $A = 19^\circ\ 50'$, $B = 96^\circ\ 20'$, $C = 63^\circ\ 50'$.
7. $A = 37^\circ\ 46'$, $B = 71^\circ\ 7'$, $C = 71^\circ\ 7'$.
8. $A = 33^\circ\ 48'$, $B = 29^\circ\ 45'$, $C = 116^\circ\ 27'$.
9. $A = 13^\circ\ 10'$, $B = 90^\circ\ 20'$, $C = 76^\circ\ 30'$.
10. $A = 28^\circ\ 23'$, $B = 78^\circ\ 52'$, $C = 72^\circ\ 45'$.

EXERCISES 115B (p. 387)

1. $c = 8·16$, $A = 23^\circ\ 13'$, $B = 26^\circ\ 47'$.
2. $c = 7·11$, $A = 56^\circ\ 38'$, $B = 91^\circ\ 22'$.
3. $C = 37^\circ\ 8'$, $B = 94^\circ\ 37'$, $a = 15·6$.
4. $b = 6·47$, $A = 53^\circ\ 50'$, $C = 29^\circ\ 27'$.
5. $C = 21^\circ\ 32'$, $A = 88^\circ\ 28'$, $b = 14·4$.
6. $B = 96^\circ\ 30'$, $A = 26^\circ$, $C = 57^\circ\ 30'$.
7. $B = C = 71^\circ\ 35'$, $A = 36^\circ\ 50'$.
8. $A = 22^\circ\ 24'$, $C = 132^\circ\ 26'$, $B = 25^\circ\ 10'$.
9. $A = 56^\circ$, $B = 89^\circ\ 6'$, $C = 34^\circ\ 54'$.
10. $A = 53^\circ\ 18'$, $B = 91^\circ\ 4'$, $C = 35^\circ\ 38'$.

EXERCISES 116A (p. 390)

1. 3·32. **2.** 17·8. **3.** 14·1. **4.** 14·0. **5.** 3·84.
6. 35·6. **7.** 35·8. **8.** 32·6.

EXERCISES 116B (p. 390)

1. 4·97. **2.** 18·5. **3.** 22·8. **4.** 25·6. **5.** 4·18.
6. 42·1. **7.** 44·9. **8.** 26·8.

EXERCISES 117 (p. 390)

5·89 or

1. 1·61 km. **2.** 6·59 km. **3.** 57·9 m. **4.** 079° 43'.
5. 31·6 m. **6.** 178 m. **7.** 7.
8. 108° 40'. **9** 2·78 km/h; 100° 9'.

10. 47·8. **11.** 45° 40′; 21·9 m^2.
12. 47° 58′, 82° 2′; 18·4 m^2. **13.** 546 m.
14. 49° 45′; 17 m^2. **15.** 181 m. **16.** 50° 33′.
17. 7·8 cm. **18.** 87° 8′. **19.** 4·07, 7·34. **20.** 6·08.
21. 10·6 m. **22.** 0·81 km. **23.** 18·7 km/h. **24.** 6·89 cm.
25. 6·61 cm. **26.** 14 : 11 : − 4. **27.** 4·84 km. **28.** 28·7 m.
29. 33° 45′. **30.** 280 m. **31.** 60·8 m.
32. 71° 22′, 108° 38′.

EXERCISES 118A (p. 395)

1. 3·49 cm. **2.** 0·075 cm. **3.** 11·1 cm^2. **4.** 15·3 cm^2.
5. 48 cm. **6.** 4·9 cm. **7.** 10·6 : 1.
8. 22° 1′, 157° 59′. **9.** 2·04. **10.** 25 cm^2.

EXERCISES 118B (p. 396)

1. 3·49 cm. **2.** 0·11 cm. **3.** 17·5 cm^2. **4.** 25·6 cm^2.
5. 44·3 cm. **6.** 4·27 cm. **7.** 14·7 : 1.
8. 18° 12′, 161° 48′. **9.** 81° 22′. **10.** 2·5.

EXERCISES 119A (p. 399)

1. 2670 km. **2.** 3190 km. **3.** 2570 km. **4.** 1440 km/h.
5. $9\frac{1}{3}$ min. **6.** 77°. **7.** 6680 km. **8.** 5570 km.
9. 1·732 : 1. **10.** 2560 km.

EXERCISES 119B (p. 400)

1. 3560 km. **2.** 5520 km. **3.** 2040 km. **4.** 639 km.
5. 1 hr. 44 min. **6.** 54′. **7.** 4440 km. **8.** 10 010 km.
9. 1·085 : 1. **10.** 1580 km.

EXERCISES 120 (p. 400)

1. 9·16 cm. **2.** 3·89 cm. **3.** 1·4 cm. **4.** 15·4 cm^2.
5. 14·3 cm. **6.** 65 cm^2. **7.** 283 cm^2. **8.** 45·5 m.
9. 6° 22′. **10.** 180°. **11.** 41° 24′. **12.** $2R \sin \theta$.
13. 3330 km. **14.** 63° 17′. **15.** 6300 km.
16. 12·9 cm, 69·8cm^2. **17.** 1278 km, 1274 km.
18. 6·1 m. **19.** 45° 50′. **20.** 1120 km. **21.** 222 cm^2.
22. 3 cm^2. **23.** 31·4 cm^2. **24.** 19° 12′. **25.** 3330 km.
26. 41·2 km, 18·5 km. **27.** 5470 km. **28.** 4230 km.
29. 112 cm^2. **30.** 12 000 km.

EXERCISES 121A (p. 405)

1. 098°, 280 knots. **2.** 186°, 260 knots. **3.** 278°, 367 knots.
4. 316°, 351 knots. **5.** 230°, 280 knots.

EXERCISES 121B (p. 405)

1. 079°, 318 knots. **2.** 187°, 310 knots. **3.** 253°, 370 knots.
4. 302°, 290 knots. **5.** 134°, 270 knots.

EXERCISES 122A (p. 407)

1. 165°, 20 knots. **2.** 162°, 14 knots. **3.** 107°, 60 knots.
4. 270°, 32 knots. **5.** 283°, 24 knots.

EXERCISES 122B (p. 407)

1. 140°, 30 knots. **2.** 280°, 30 knots. **3.** 016°, 30 knots.
4. 135°, 40 km/h. **5.** 100°, 25 knots.

EXERCISES 123A (p. 409)

1. 086°, 260 km/h. **2.** 154°, 290 knots. **3.** 215°, 266 knots.
4. 322°, 259 knots. **5.** 001°, 200 knots.

EXERCISES 123B (p. 409)

1. 077°, 287 knots. **2.** 175°, 260 knots. **3.** 212°, 219 knots.
4. 266°, 227 km/h. **5.** 317°, 253 knots.

EXERCISES 124 (p. 409)

1. 096°, 240 knots. **2.** 286°, 245 knots. **3.** 191°, 40 knots.
4. 073°, 228 knots **5.** 032°, 218 knots. **6.** 086°, 268 knots.
7. 165°, 13 knots. **8.** 007°. **9.** 262 knots, 008°.
10. 302°, 30 knots.

ANSWERS TO SPECIMEN PAPERS

PAPER I

1. (i) $3\frac{4}{5}$; (ii) 1·099, 1·10; (iii) $\frac{89}{2000}$

2. (i) 12; (ii) $x = 1$, $y = -1$; (iii) $\dfrac{x + 3y}{12}$.

3. (ii) 12. **4.** 4·24 cm. **5.** 480; 8h 50 min.

6. 0·38, 2·6 and 1, 2. **8.** $6x + \dfrac{2}{x^2}$, $4\frac{1}{2}$.

9. (i) 62° 29′; (ii) 75° 24′. **10.** 015° 23′, 1 hour 47 min.

PAPER II

1. (i) 2·1; (ii) $45\frac{1}{4}$ kg; (iii) £7·50.
2. (i) $(2a + b)(a - b)$; (ii) $(4x - 1 - y)(4x - 1 + y)$; (iii) $(x - 1)(x - 2)$.
3. (i) 2 cm. **4.** 8·89 cm. **5.** £405, £8·82.

3. 65°, 60°, 55°. **4.** 1·61 cm. **5.** £1082·43.
6. (i) 2·62; (ii) 3·73; (iii) 3·19. **7.** 157·5.
8. £11·50. **9.** $\sqrt{60}$, $\sqrt{15}$, 4. **10.** 5·3 cm, 69° 20′.

PAPER VIII

1. (i) 7 cm; (ii) 2·8, 3·125 8·75; (iii) 680 m².
2. (i) $\sqrt{z^2 - 2yz}$; (ii) $(7n - 3x - 6)$ new pence.
3. (i) Acute, obtuse; (ii) 1·5 m. **4.** (i) 64° 1′; (ii) $\dfrac{\sqrt{q^2 - p^2}}{p}$.
5. £800. **6.** (i) 2·57, − 0·91; (ii) 1·77.
7. 80°, 40°, 65°, 115°, 40°, 25°.
9. (i) 8340 km; (ii) 12 200 km.
10. (i) 009° 30′; (ii) 182·5 km/h.

PAPER IX

1. (i) 1·06575; (ii) 0·694; (iii) 55.
2. (i) 31; (ii) x; (iii) $x = 3$, $y = 1$.
3. (ii) 0·6 cm. **4.** 47·7 m, 43° 17′.
5. £18·40, 2·875%. **6.** 40 and 35; 5 years.
8. 60°. **10.** $3\frac{3}{4}$ cm; 1·67 cm; 48° 35′.

PAPER X

1. (i) 45 km/h; (ii) $\frac{67}{121}$; (iii) $4\frac{1}{2}$%.
2. (i) $\dfrac{2}{(y-1)(y-3)}$; (ii) $(2x - 3y)(1 - a)$; (iii) 3.
3. (i) 36° and 144°; (ii) XD. **4.** 6·59 cm; 26·6 cm².
5. (i) 2·26 cm; (ii) 1·30 cm. **6.** (i) 36; (ii) $1\frac{1}{2}$; 6·1%.
8. 6·90 km; 028° 33′.
9. (i) (*a*) $3x^2 - 6x + 2$; (*b*) $3x^2 - \dfrac{1}{x^2}$; (ii) (*a*) 24; (*b*) $\frac{5}{6}$.
10. 9·24 cm.

6. $y = \dfrac{3x - 1}{x - 1}$; 3·73 or 0·27.
8. 4·77 cm, 6·13 cm. **9.** 1070 km.

PAPER III

1. (i) 1·06272; (ii) £600, (iii) $6\frac{1}{4}$ hours.
2. (i) $\dfrac{100A}{100 + RT}$; (ii) 350. **4.** 3·46 cm, 5·20 cm^2, 2·46 cm^2.
5. £1; 1 : 2. **6.** 11.37$\frac{1}{2}$h; 6 km from Bedford.
7. £2·10. **9.** 102 m. **10.** (i) $3\frac{7}{12}$; (ii) $2\frac{1}{4}$ m/sec.

PAPER IV

1. (i) 6·3 in.; (ii) £1400; (iii) 4·8.
2. (i) 64; (ii) $(x - 18)(x + 2)$; (iii) $\dfrac{d - 100p}{p}$.
3. (*a*) $\frac{2}{3}$; (*b*) $\frac{1}{3}$; (*c*) $\frac{4}{9}$; 18 cm^2.
4. (i) 0·873; (ii) 31·6. **5.** 122 cm^2; 60·5.
6. (i) 8, 3; (ii) $\frac{3}{16}$, 2. **7.** (i) 60°; (ii) 41° 24′.
8. 27 cm^2. **9.** 1180 km/h. **10.** 5·7 cm.

PAPER V

1. (i) $\frac{2}{7}$, $\frac{9}{28}$; 0·036; (ii) £23·80.
2. (i) $(x - 1)(x - 2)$, $(x + 2)(x - 2)$; (ii) $(x - 1)(x - 2)(x + 2)$; (iii) $\dfrac{3}{(x + 2)(x - 1)}$.
3. (ii) 10. **4.** (i) 27° 23′ and 152° 37′; (ii) 1·02.
5. $23\frac{1}{2}$; £2·35. **6.** 1 hour 50 minutes.
7. 7 cm^2; 27° 30′. **8.** $-\frac{9}{8}$; ± 3. **9.** $1\frac{1}{2}$.
10. 15 : 28.

PAPER VI

1. (i) £0·97$\frac{1}{2}$; (ii) £24·37$\frac{1}{2}$; (iii) 12 tonnes.
2. $\frac{5}{9}$, $-\frac{160}{9}$; 140°.
3. (i) 20; (ii) 36°, 72°, 108°, 144°; (iii) 104°, 124°.
4. 88·5 m. **5.** $7\frac{3}{4}$%; £120. **6.** (i) 2·77, $-$ 1·27.
7. 103 m. **9.** (0, 0) and (1, 2); $\frac{1}{6}$.

PAPER VII

1. (i) 0·54; (ii) £1·80; (iii) 1000.
2. (i) $1\frac{1}{5}$; (ii) $\dfrac{5}{6x + 3}$; (iii) 3 or $\frac{1}{3}$.